MAN AND HIS GODS

BOOKS BY HOMER W. SMITH

KAMONGO

END OF ILLUSION

MAN AND HIS GODS

HOMER W. SMITH

MAN
AND HIS
GODS

FOREWORD BY ALBERT EINSTEIN

 Little, Brown and Company · *Boston* · 1952

The lines from *Gilgamesh: Epic of Old Babylonia* by William Ellery Leonard
(Copyright 1934 by William Ellery Leonard) are used by permission of The Viking
Press, Inc., New York.

*Published simultaneously
in Canada by McClelland and Stewart Limited*

PRINTED IN THE UNITED STATES OF AMERICA
BY THE HADDON CRAFTSMEN, SCRANTON, PA.

To Margaret

At every crossway on the road that leads to the future, each progressive spirit is opposed by a thousand men appointed to guard the past. Let us have no fear lest the fair towers of former days be sufficiently defended. The least that the most timid among us can do is not to add to the immense dead weight which nature drags along.

Let us not say to ourselves that the best truth always lies in moderation, in the decent average. This would perhaps be so if the majority of men did not think on a much lower plane than is needful. That is why it behooves others to think and hope on a higher plane than seems reasonable. The average, the decent moderation of today, will be the least human of things tomorrow. At the time of the Spanish Inquisition, the opinion of good sense and of the good medium was certainly that people ought not to burn too large a number of heretics; extreme and unreasonable opinion obviously demanded that they should burn none at all.

Let us think of the great invisible ship that carries our human destinies upon eternity. Like the vessels of our confined oceans, she has her sails and her ballast. The fear that she may pitch or roll on leaving the roadstead is no reason for increasing the weight of the ballast by stowing the fair white sails in the depths of the hold. They were not woven to molder side by side with cobblestones in the dark. Ballast exists everywhere; all the pebbles of the harbor, all the sand of the beach, will serve for that. But sails are rare and precious things; their place is not in the murk of the well, but amid the light of the tall masts, where they will collect the winds of space.

— MAETERLINCK: *Our Social Duty*.

Contents

FOREWORD

~~~~~~

Foreword

PROFESSOR Smith has kindly submitted his book to me before publication. After reading it thoroughly and with intense interest I am glad to
comply with his request to give him my impression.

The work is a broadly conceived attempt to portray man's fear-induced
animistic and mythic ideas with all their far-flung transformations and
interrelations. It relates the impact of these phantasmagorias on human
destiny and the causal relationships by which they have become crystallized into organized religion.

This is a biologist speaking, whose scientific training has disciplined
him in a grim objectivity rarely found in the pure historian. This objectivity has not, however, hindered him from emphasizing the boundless
suffering which, in its end results, this mythic thought has brought upon
man.

Professor Smith envisages as a redeeming force, training in objective
observation of all that is available for immediate perception and in the
interpretation of facts without preconceived ideas. In his view, only if
every individual strives for truth can humanity attain a happier future;
the atavisms in each of us that stand in the way of a friendlier destiny can
only thus be rendered ineffective.

His historical picture closes with the end of the nineteenth century, and
with good reason. By that time it seemed that the influence of these mythic,
authoritatively anchored forces which can be denoted as religious, had been
reduced to a tolerable level in spite of all the persisting inertia and hypocrisy.

Even then, a new branch of mythic thought had already grown strong,
one not religious in nature but no less perilous to mankind — exaggerated

nationalism. Half a century has shown that this new adversary is so strong that it places in question man's very survival. It is too early for the present-day historian to write about this problem, but it is to be hoped that one will survive who can undertake the task at a later date.

ALBERT EINSTEIN

MAN AND HIS GODS

Prologue

WHEN in 1863 Thomas Huxley coined the phrase 'Man's Place in Nature,' it was to name a short collection of his essays applying to man Darwin's theory of evolution. *The Origin of Species* had been published only four years before, and the thesis that man was literally a part of nature, rather than an earthy vessel charged with some sublimer stuff, was so novel and so offensive to current metaphysics that it needed the most vigorous defense. Half the civilized world was rudely shocked, the other half skeptically amused.

Nearly a century has passed since the *Origin* shattered the complacency of the Victorian world and initiated what may be called the Darwinian revolution, an upheaval of man's ideas comparable to and probably exceeding in significance the revolution that issued from Copernicus's demonstration that the earth moves around the sun. The theory of evolution was but one of many factors contributing to the destruction of the ancient beliefs; it only toppled over what had already been weakened by centuries of decay, rendered suspect by the assaults of many intellectual disciplines; but it marked the beginning of the end of the era of faith.

It was said by one horrified reviewer of Darwin's book that if his views held, then humanity 'would suffer a damage that might brutalize it, and sink the human race into a lower grade of degradation than any into which it has fallen since its written records tell us of its history!' (Like many of his Victorian contemporaries, the writer knew little of human history.) No one can deny that since the *Origin* was published man has given a good exhibition of his lowly nature. Darwin's book can explain man's bestial propensities, but it is scarcely responsible for them. Yet in truth much that hitherto served to hold civilization together, to give life meaning and direction, to keep courage in men's hearts, has fallen away because of it. It was inevitable that men should live differently because the book had been written.

Now that the *Origin* has begun to do its work man stands among the ruins left from some five millenniums of civilization, surrounded by shattered hopes and burned-out creeds where once were impregnable faith and assured belief, asking himself again, What is his place in nature? Why should he live? And how? This question has from time immemorial played a dominant role in his thoughts. Repeatedly he has reshaped the answer, and always the answer has reshaped the pattern of his life, socially, economically and politically, and frequently set the limits to his physical and intellectual freedom.

All students of history must at times have felt despairingly that this history has been inevitable, that it could not have happened otherwise. If this be true, then of course the history that is to come cannot be modified. Historians may debate the relative importance of ideas as against other factors in the shaping of this history: but any application of the principle of determinism implies that history would have been different had the determinants been different — among other things had man's ideas been different. The Scholastics condemned reason and examination as fallible and feeble tools, and fallible and feeble they seem to be as opposed to the dead weight of vulgar belief that stands against them as a mountain stands against the wind and rain: yet perspective reveals that mountains do wear away, and the student who scans the past in its entirety takes heart in the conviction that man's future history will be changed by ideas more even than has the past.

This volume closes with the end of the nineteenth century. It is difficult to appraise one's contemporaries; they are too much a beam in the eye. If an appraisal were rashly to be ventured, it might incline towards an unwarranted pessimism: despite a clearer vision in some quarters of the meaning of liberty and responsibility, and despite some notable progress in natural philosophy, the first half of our century seems, with respect to ideas, to have regressed a little into the penumbra of intellectual eclipse. Historians of the future may look back upon the nineteenth century as we look back upon the early days of Greece, seeing it as a brilliant period for the human intellect but with promises unfulfilled, aborted because that intellect was too immature for its promises to complete gestation. Perhaps this pessimism is also a beam in the eye, so this book closes with the end of the century in which Darwin lived. It begins, fragmentally and imperfectly, at the beginning, in so far as the beginning can be perceived.

ii

The basic fact of the past, and of the future, is that man and the anthropoid apes together constitute a natural biological group, known as the superfamily Hominoidea. They possess in common hundreds of anatomical characters that demonstrate their kinship and that set them off from their nearest relatives, the lower Old World apes, as well as from all other mammals.

The men who inhabit the world today all belong to a single species, *Homo sapiens,* as demonstrated by their anatomical relationships and by the fact that they can interbreed, but they are divided by most authorities into a few geographical varieties or races, the Australoids, Bushmen and Hottentots, Pygmies, Negroids, Mongoloids, and Europeans. Also a member of this species was neolithic man (New Stone Age), whose remains are scarcely distinguishable from modern races, and who appeared in Europe, Asia and Egypt at the close of the Pleistocene Period or shortly after the beginning of what the geologist calls Recent Time (15,000 years). Neolithic man appeared after the greatest severity of the last glacial age had passed, probably at a date not earlier than 13,000 B.C. With the increasing opportunities for migration that followed the last retreat of the ice his divergent descendants invaded each other's territory and, during the course of historic times, produced the complex mixture that forms the modern European population.

Back of the Neolithic Age stretches the long interval of the Paleolithic, or Old Stone Age, which is anthropologically parallel to the geologic Pleistocene Period, nearly 1,000,000 years in length. It was during this long interval that man developed from a fumbling apelike creature into a skilled worker of fine tools. The three latest of the paleolithic forms — Cro-Magnon man (*Homo sapiens fossilis*), Neanderthal man (*Homo neanderthalensis*) and Heidelberg man (*Homo heidelbergensis*) — are so distinctly human that they are included with recent man in the single modern genus Homo.

Heidelberg man, whose remains date from about the middle of the Paleolithic, is poorly known, but roughly contemporary with him are forms so different from modern man that new genera have been erected by some authorities to include Piltdown man (*Eoanthropus dawsonii*), Peking man (*Sinanthropus pekinensis*) and the Java ape-man (*Pithecanthropus erectus*), forms evolved early in the Pleistocene Period, the last two perhaps at its beginning.

It required close to 1,000,000 years to transmute the dawn man, *Eoanthropus,* into neolithic man, while 40,000 years have given no detectable evidence of the evolution of the latter, for the significant differences between the pure Mediterranean, Alpine and Nordic types of modern Europe are much less than the differences between Cro-Magnon and neolithic man, if indeed these represent different species. In the long view of evolution *Homo sapiens* is simply a survival from the Neolithic Age.

The basal criterion of a true species is its inability to breed with another species. The common root of the anthropoid apes and man is found in the middle Miocene; if the human stock ceased to interbreed with the anthropoid stock at about this time, an interval of 10,000,000 years would have elapsed before the appearance of the hominid stock at the close of the Pliocene. Assuming a generation every 12 years, 800,000 generations of men-no-longer-apes would have existed before they acquired the rudimentary capacity of speech or the facility to chip flint instruments. Calculated in the same manner, *Homo sapiens* (including neolithic man) has inhabited the earth for not over 1500 generations (18,000 years), a mere fraction of the time required to transmute the ancestral ape into early man. Lengthening the cycle of a generation to 20 years, the whole history of civilization comprises scarcely more than 300 generations. The rapid development in technical and intellectual activity in this period cannot be interpreted as evidence of acceleration in man's evolution: civilization is nothing more than the accumulation of experience and knowledge; it reflects nothing other than the use to which man has put his brain, which is probably not superior, and quite possibly inferior, to the brain of Cro-Magnon.

iii

When we speak of the Age of Man we usually think of the period in which man has been a tool maker and has known the use of fire, though we may justifiably expand this term to include the entire period when manlike creatures, whether or not possessing tools or even rudimentary speech, can clearly be distinguished as having deviated from anthropoid evolution. In this broader sense, the Age of Man reaches back of *Pithecanthropus, Eoanthropus* and *Sinanthropus,* who were distinctly more human than apelike; they might have been the progenitors of modern men while it is inconceivable that they could have been the progenitors of modern apes.

One important feature of ape-to-man evolution was a retardation of the rate of development, a delay in the reaching of individual maturity. The gross anatomical differences between man and the great apes are more quantitative than qualitative, and appear to be attributable in part to the fact that both prenatal and postnatal development in man are considerably retarded. An adult man much more closely resembles an infant gorilla than he does the adult of that species; in fact, it is not inaccurate to say that *Homo sapiens* represents an anthropoid whose development in certain respects has not only been greatly slowed but arrested at an early stage. The most important consequences of this retardation are that the time during which the cranium remains plastic and the brain has an opportunity to enlarge is greatly prolonged; and that the young are cared for over a longer period, during which time they remain amenable to education and enjoy an opportunity for the transmission of cultural experience from one generation to another.

It may be that early man made many things with his hands which, because of their destructible nature, have not survived, but it is doubtful if he did anything that required a higher type of cerebration than does the preparation of fine flint instruments. The anthropologist Leakey had to spend several years in experimentation before he could chip a flint ax equal in workmanship to the average ax turned out by the men of the late Paleolithic. He found that success depended on a knowledge of the cleavage planes in the lump of flint, on the ability to strike a blow of just the right force and direction at the proper point, and on the exercise of considerable skill in the selection of the striking tools. It would seem that by random pounding a man might quickly learn the relative hardness of various objects and thus come to choose flint in preference to softer materials for his weapon, but it is inconceivable that without instruction he could in the space of a single lifetime discover how to chip a flint equal to even the poorer neolithic scrapers. Actually, the development of the art of flint chipping required close to a million years — and this in spite of the fact that no animal is more curious, more impelled to feel things, handle them, bite them, tear them to pieces, pound them, to experiment with them in every conceivable way, than are young apes and children. Curiosity and manual restlessness have been the chief forces that have impelled man's exploration of the world and ultimately enabled him to win what control he has of it, but it is appalling to observe how long he took to come into his own.

I

The Talisman

THE last of the Pleistocene ice had scarcely withdrawn from the Pyrenees and Caucasus before neolithic man followed the line of melting snow to the north. Along the ever-greening banks of the turbulent rivers he lived by hunting the reindeer, the woolly rhinoceros and mammoth, the wild horse and bear, while in the coastal regions he fished among the ice floes or speared walruses and seals. From the eighth millennium before the Christian Era, Europe from England to the Urals was forested with pines, oaks and hazels, and supplied an adequate if chilly habitat for advanced peoples who chipped excellent flints, clothed themselves in sewn skins, shaped and baked a coarse pottery, and built dog sleds with wooden shoes. But the rigors of the seasonal climate and the necessity of ever moving onwards in search of game did not encourage communal life, and until after the beginning of the Christian Era the hunters of the north continued to shelter themselves in caves or thickets, or at best to erect crude huts of saplings founded on a circle of stones and roofed with thatch or skins.

In the south, however, in China, India, Mesopotamia, the Mediterranean basin and Africa, the amelioration of climate which accompanied the Pluvial Period created more favorable living conditions. About the fifth millennium B.C., several branches of the human stock, long experienced in the making of fine weapons and in hunting game, simultaneously developed a communal life based on agriculture. This art has arisen independently many times, in Egypt, Asia Minor, several places in central Asia, in northern India, central and southern China, perhaps in Abyssinia, and in North and South America, but in no instance is it clear how the start was made. Because of the minuteness of the seed and the long period of quiescence which usually intervenes between fruition and germination, the relation of seed to plant is by no means obvious, and indeed is unrecognized by many living peoples. Grant Allen suggested that agriculture was discovered in connection with the interment of the dead, the grave being the one piece of ground which primitive man had occasion to harrow and weed, to fertilize with bone and flesh, and, most importantly, to enrich with funerary deposits of grain and fruit, and thereby to plant with seed. One may take it that a people who covered their dead with earth and fortified the departed with gifts of grain and water would soon be reaping crops.

There were three regions in which circumstances particularly favored the development of agriculture: the valley of the Indus, the common valley of the Tigris and Euphrates, and the valley and delta of the Nile. Authorities do not agree as to which of these localities should have priority, and it is not with the intent of assigning it greater antiquity that Egyptian culture is given precedence here, but because the records of the Nile are better preserved and because Egyptian culture more than Indian or Mesopotamian, predominantly shaped the subsequent beliefs of the Western World.

Both by its character and its role in history, the Nile is unique among rivers; it has shaped man's ideas to a greater extent than any other purely terrestrial phenomenon. The rise and fall of its waters have been as a pulse to quicken his mental development, even while they sustained his life from season to season. Its delta, which Herodotus called 'the river's gift to man,' might have been specially designed to cradle his infant arts.

In the late Pleistocene the Mediterranean reached to the foot of the eminence on which stand the pyramids of Cairo, forming a gulf which stretched between the hills of Libya on the west and those of Arabia on the east. In the last 50,000, or perhaps 20,000 years, the river has built out a delta of rich alluvium so black that the Egyptians called their country 'the Black Land.' This delta, historically called Lower Egypt, is a flat plain a hundred miles in length covered with water-loving plants and rushes and transected by innumerable marshy channels and rich lagoons. South of the delta, the river narrows between the Libyan and Arabian hills, and at Cairo begins the true valley of the Nile, and Egypt proper. Beyond Cairo and as far south as Thebes the river bed has cut deep into soft limestone, lying in places a thousand feet below the plateau of the desert. Though this valley sometimes reaches a width of a hundred miles, it averages scarcely over ten. Beyond Thebes the limestone gives way to red and yellow sandstone, the erosion of which has supplied the Libyan Desert with its shifting sands, and here Egypt is nothing but a gorge between two towering escarpments of naked rock rarely more than two miles apart, while occasionally the desert sand flows down the lateral canyons to the water's edge. At places the water has worn entirely through the sandstone to the underlying crystalline rocks, the outcroppings of which form numerous islands and churning, unnavigable rapids. It was chiefly the barrier to navigation presented by these cataracts that set the southern limit to the Egyptians' world.

For sixteen hundred miles — all the river that was available to the ancient Egyptians — the stream winds a sinuous course through barren desert without receiving a single tributary on either side. Throughout this length it rises and falls in an annual and apparently causeless flood, the recession of which leaves the valley transformed from a serpentine black mud flat into a bright green garden. The enigma of this annual flood remained unexplained until nineteenth-century explorers penetrated to the heart of Africa. They found that the first tributary to the river is the White Nile which drains the central plateau of equatorial Africa, wherein lie the great buffer lakes of Victoria, Albert and Edward; downstream are added the Sobat, Blue Nile and Atbara, draining the mountains of Abyssinia. Abyssinia has no great lakes to act as reservoirs and the rain which falls unfailingly from June to August drains rapidly off the mountains and throws the middle and lower Nile into a flood which ranges in height from fifty feet at the First Cataract to twenty-five in the delta. The waters begin to rise at Memphis about June 21 and to recede at the end of September. Were this flood to fail, the entire population of the Nile Valley would die of starvation within a year. For the inhabitants of the valley the first rise of the water is the chief event of the calendar; the time of its appearance has been recorded for well over five thousand years.

ii

In paleolithic times most of the Sahara Desert was a park land or savanna and enjoyed an abundant rainfall. While Neanderthal was pursuing the woolly rhinoceros and mammoth in France and England, a more generalized type of man was chipping flint hand axes in Algeria for the pursuit of bears, jackals, cave hyenas, lions, Barbary sheep and deer; rock engravings now located in the almost inaccessible heart of the desert where not a tree or beast is to be found show bulls, oryx, sheep and dogs. With the close of the Pluvial Period North Africa began to suffer a slow process of desiccation, and as the savannas shrank to mere oases, animals and men were forced to compete for the dwindling supplies of water and to enter into that symbiotic relationship called domestication. From earliest times hunters from the plateaus on either side had visited the valley, leaving their implements on its terraced walls; now under the pressure of spreading desiccation this influx of nomads was greatly accelerated and some of the visitors lingered long enough at particular sites to be called permanent inhabitants. The earliest of these settlers, the Tasians of Deir Tasa, made fine flint axes sharpened with a ground edge to cut timber where now no timber grows; they made rough earthenware pots which they decorated with incised lines, probably in imitation of basketry, and which they baked over a smoking fire; they apparently wove linen of a sort, and may have cultivated the ground; they painted their eyes and faces with ocher and malachite, and decorated themselves with perforated shells from the Red Sea, and with cylindrical beads of bones and ivory — all evidences of a concern with magic.

Close by in the Fayum a related people had domesticated swine, cattle, sheep and goats, learned to hunt with bows and arrows, to fish with hooks and harpoons, and to cultivate emmer wheat and barley identical with modern species. At Merimde, in the delta, a third culture had added miniature celts or stone axes to their art; these were pierced for suspension on necklaces and unquestionably served as amulets. No graves have been found at Fayum, but the peoples of Tasa and Merimde buried their dead, though apparently without grave offerings. These sites were abandoned, at a rough guess, by 10,000 B.C.

A later and more advanced people at Badari, above Assiut, gave their cattle and sheep ceremonial burial, and placed their human dead in graves lined with matting, the body generally facing west and sometimes accompanied by female figurines carved from ivory or molded in clay. They used malachite as a cosmetic, and had discovered, probably by accidentally dropping this substance into the fire, how to make copper beads. Their pottery, shaped without a wheel, achieved a delicacy and simple perfection never exceeded at the height of Egyptian civilization, the vases and bowls being of extreme thinness and decorated with an exquisite ripple effect, and fired to produce a brown or red body with blackened interior and rim. They used the boomerang and wore necklaces of copper tubes and glazed quartz, bracelets and rings of ivory, and pottery nose plugs. Their concern with magic had increased to the point where amulets were now made in the shape of the antelope and hippopotamus. The Badarians may be dated at about 5000 B.C., and are considered to be the physical and cultural ancestors of the so-called 'predynastic' Egyptians.

The earliest of these people, the Amratians, were presumably identical with the true Egyptians. They appear to have lived in autonomous villages, each village having its revered animal deity which was identified by a replica or clan ensign. From these villages there grew the nomes or political units of dynastic Egypt, and from the local totems, the gods of the dynastic pantheon. The Amratians possessed slaves and personal property, but there is no sign of kings or powerful overlords. They chipped copper as they would chip stone, but they did not hammer or melt it. They traded with far distant countries, as is attested by gold from Nubia, obsidian from western Asia, cedar from Byblos, marble from Paros and emery from Naxos. The art of making pottery had degenerated, but they rode the river in serviceable boats made of bundles of papyrus lashed together and propelled by as many as eight pairs of oars and perhaps a sail. Unlike the Egyptians of a later day, they did not slaughter the wives, servants and cattle of a dead man to supply him with company in the other world, but they buried with him substitute statuettes, the forerunners of the *ushabti* figures of Egyptian times. Only occasionally did an Amratian man take his dog, for which apparently no substitute of clay would do, with him into the other world, but he had in the grave a liberal provision of food, weapons, ornaments and malachite. The funerary vases and slate palettes were decorated with vivid scenes forecasting the tomb decorations of later kings, and the amulets now included diverse animals, birds, and fishes, as well as human figurines.

Elsewhere other cultures, similar in fundamentals but diversified in details, were developing in more or less isolated areas. The Gerzean culture of Upper Egypt ultimately dominated the Badarian and introduced as amulets, perhaps as images of totems already deified, the falcon, symbol of the god Ra, and the cow, symbol of the goddess Hathor. The Gerzeans broke the funerary ornaments, vases and implements in order to 'kill' them too. The corpse was placed in a wooden coffin or laid upon a bier of twigs, and before the close of the period rich men were having their graves lined with mud bricks. In one notable tomb the walls had been plastered with mortar and decorated with a painting depicting scenes of the chase, combats between men and ships, and great magical dances: here, certainly, was the tomb of an 'overlord' who was on the way to becoming a king.

iii

When the dynastic period opened, Egypt was probably much as it is today, a vast sandy desert in which the valley was the only habitable portion and the river the only route of travel. By contrast with the barren mountains on the east or the sterile dunes on the west the green valley must have seemed like paradise. The quiet lagoons, walled in by papyrus reeds, were covered with white, pink and blue lotus blossoms and edged with delicate aquatic plants. As soon as the flood subsided the valley became carpeted with grasses and reeds, and ferns filled out the shady recesses. Flowers blossomed in profusion: roses, jasmine, narcissi, lilies, oleanders, the Egyptian privet (said to be the flower of paradise because the dye henna, made from its stalks and leaves, was red, the life-giving color). Palms and trees afforded food and shade: dates and doms, figs, apricots, prickly pears, grapes, pomegranates and bananas (called the fruit of paradise because it is always ripe), locusts, mimosas, ash, mulberries, tamarisks, olives and sycamores.

There were many birds; fish were abundant and grew to gigantic size. In the desert there were no animals more dangerous than the hyena, fox, gazelle, ostrich and rabbit, and the large animals of the swamps: the hippopotamus, crocodile, ox, boar, lion and wildcat were not prone to invade the cultivated land. The one animal the Egyptians had cause to fear was the snake — much of the Egyptian magic was concerned with antidoting snake bite, and one of the special favors of Thoth was protection against this injury.

If the periodicity of the Nile afforded the Egyptian a few months of luxury, it was also a test of his ingenuity and providence. During low Nile the valley passed into estivation, the fields became parched, the marshes shrank into pools of mud, the trees and bushes became sterile, and the hungry carnivores concentrated along the shrunken watercourse, fighting for survival. The transience of nature's beneficence stimulated thrift and promoted study of the storage of fruit and seeds, and supplied the optimal circumstances for the discovery of agriculture. The food gatherer was forced to muster all his intelligence, courage and foresight and become a farmer.

However the neolithic Egyptian obtained his first clue to agriculture, he advanced steadily. He learned to make holes in the earth with a pointed stick, then to furrow it in continuous rows that grew longer as he trained himself, and then his oxen, to pull a plow. As many a Nile fellah does today, he covered the seed by driving his sheep back and forth across the fields. He learned to construct large containers of clay in which to store the grain. He learned to barter, and of necessity to measure, count and keep tallies, to map his fields, and to estimate their area and appraise their value. He could not move about freely, even if inclined to do so, for the valley itself was densely populated and there were only desert and mountains on either side. Moreover, the vats and granaries in which he stored his supplies of fruit and seed were too large to be dragged from place to place; and since these valuable stores were safe only in the citadel of a permanent abode, he had to join with his fellows in defending them against lazy neighbors or robbers. The periodic flooding of the Nile Valley, more than any other circumstance on earth, promoted the development of a culture based upon conservative economics and produced the type of man who lived by an artificial harvest, stored his food, his oxen and his plow in a permanent home of his own; and who was forced by his dependence on his fellow men to participate in a community prepared to defend itself with military vigor. It was from these primitive farmers that there came the patience and the manual skill, the intelligence, the creative imagination and artistic taste, the indomitable courage, cheerful optimism and kindly humor that in a relatively short period were to achieve the first great civilization on earth.

In studying the fragmentary list of Egyptian kings available to him, Manetho, a historian-priest of Sebennytus writing in the third century B.C., noted that they could be grouped on the basis of blood descent or other close relationship into a number of royal lines, and accordingly he broke up the list into 'dynasties,' a method of subdivision which modern historians retain. The period from the Ist to the end of the VIth Dynasty (3400–2475 B.C.) is commonly known as the Old Kingdom. During this period, when the seat of government was at Memphis, Egyptian culture made its most fundamental advances.

With the XIth Dynasty (2160 B.C.) of Thebes began the Middle Kingdom, and with the XVIIIth Dynasty, the most spectacular period of Egyptian history. Military successes carried the power of the Pharaoh far into Asia Minor, so that the period is appropriately known as the New Empire or New Kingdom. This empire was allowed to fall to pieces by the fanatical priest-king Amenhotep III (Akhnaton) about 1350 B.C., and in spite of partial reorganization under the Ramessids in the (?)XXth Dynasty, the political power of Egypt was ended. In the XXIst Dynasty (945 B.C.) the government passed into the hands of the priests of Amen and all development ceased. In the XXVIth Dynasty (525 B.C.) Egypt, now a weak sacerdotal state, was occupied by the Persian Cambyses, losing an independence which it never again achieved until recent times (1922).

iv

The earliest Egyptians, perhaps no more but certainly no less than any other primitive people, were intensely occupied with the supernatural. During the long ages in which they had lived a hand-to-mouth existence, gathering food where they could and chipping away at flints as necessity demanded, they had doubtless endured vague and generally fearsome relations with the spirits of trees and animals and of their disembodied ancestors, but they had lacked both the opportunity and the stimulus to develop an integrated theology. Then it was that the River Nile watered the humanly innate desire for an everlasting happy life and caused that desire to blossom and to bear an unbelievably strange fruit. Nearly every one of the rudiments of civilization — writing, carpentry, stonemasonry, sculpture, painting, dancing, a stable government with taxes and tax collectors, temples with priests and services and capital trusts intended to function in perpetuity — all these were most favorably fostered, if indeed they were not directly engendered, by the Egyptians' efforts to gain immortality by magic means.

The Egyptians viewed the magic inherent in things and words as an effective force which could be transferred from one amulet to another, from one sacred image to another, or from one man to another. The gods had used magic to create the world, and the magicians used it to control both the world and the gods.

Judging from the literature of the dynastic period, blood sacrifice of human beings never played a major role in Egyptian magic. Circumcision had early been elevated to an apparently universal custom, and with the increased emphasis attached to this single ritual and the routine sacrifice of animals in the temples there was perhaps less need for repeated human bleedings. Nevertheless, the people of the Nile continued in the magic use of red. They tinctured their nails with henna extracted from the privet, and continuously applied red ocher in the form of carmine paste to the face and body. They used their leisure to polish red cornelian into beads, replicas of sacred animals, and a variety of amulets. To obtain this precious stone they maintained for centuries mines in the mountains bordering the Red Sea. The only other stone they valued as highly was malachite, which they mined at great trouble and military cost in the distant Sinai Peninsula. They early learned from the river valley that green is the color of rejuvenated life, and they ground the malachite with resin, forming an adhesive mixture which was applied in crescents above and below the eyes to give health and protection against evil powers. Palettes for grinding this cosmetic are among the commonest objects found in predynastic graves, and it was the continuous use of this mineral that ultimately led to the discovery that in a charcoal fire it was transformed into copper. White was the color of ritual cleanness and it was affected in matters of dress by all the people who could afford it. White linen was obligatory for the priests, who had to change their garments and wash their hands every time they entered the sacred precincts of the temple.

Next in order of popularity as a magic agent was the cowrie shell. This object has ever had a strange fascination for the primitive mind; some aspect of it — the pink luster of its interior, the mottled brown or black and white markings on its convoluted surface — has exerted an irresistible appeal the world over and in all ages. The Egyptians treasured it as a talisman of good fortune, and particularly of fertility, and in a few instances the shell was used as intertribal currency. They reproduced amulets of it in wood, clay, or precious stones; such amulets, together with real cowrie shells, were deposited at the sacred tombs of Osiris at Abydos and elsewhere literally by the millions. The king's umbilical cord — his twin spirit — was treasured in predynastic times, and on gala occasions brought forth from its shrine and carried through the streets, gaily decorated with ribbons. It has been suggested that this custom was the origin of the standard, or flag, which ultimately came to serve as a substitute for the precious twin in promoting success in warfare by its supernatural power.

Nor did the practitioners of magic deviate significantly from the worldwide custom of murder by image. Out of nail parings, hair, a drop of saliva, of other fragments of the body, the sorcerers compounded figurines of wax or clay which they pierced with needles, burned or buried alive, in order to bring illness or death to those they hated. Relying upon such paraphernalia, which they preserved in mysterious chests, and upon verbal execrations, they harassed men with apparitions and terrifying voices, plagued them with spectral diseases, caused women to be the victims of infatuations, to forsake those they had loved and to love those they had previously detested, while they as obligingly protected others against these very evils. Their exploits became legendary wonders. In the presence of the Pharaoh Khufu (Kheops), one magician decapitated a goose, a snake and a bull, and then at his command each head moved back and rejoined its body. Another wonder-worker parted wide the waters of a deep lake that he might walk on dry ground to recover a lost jewel; another stopped the sun in its course, another rent the earth, another correctly prophesied the future; another read the contents of an unopened roll of papyrus —

nothing was impossible to these servants of the supernatural, and on occasion the more courageous sorcerer-priests threatened to pull down the very pillars that supported the heavens and to destroy the gods themselves if their commands were not obeyed immediately.

The most potent supernatural instrument of the magicians was the written word. If we accept the view that writing began as pictographic representation, which in turn arose from magic signs associated with the hunt, then paleolithic man must be credited with the discovery of its first principles, perhaps as far back as 30,000 B.C. He drew pictures of food and animals, the latter sometimes with extraordinary skill, on the walls of his caves and on his weapons, apparently with the belief that the graphic representation of an object could magically give him control over it. When he made replicas of the cowrie shell he was obviously multiplying his magic capital; and since a good picture is scarcely less a 'representation' than is a wooden or clay replica, once having discovered the art of making images that 'spoke silently to the eyes,' it was but a short step to the rapid inflation of all magic wealth. The Egyptians had brought the art of 'representation' to the stage of crude pictographic writing early in predynastic times. Though it does not date the origin of continuous hieroglyphic writing, the oldest example of the kind is an ebony label found in the tomb of Aha Menes, the third king of the Ist Dynasty. Shortly thereafter the hieroglyphic script appeared in a highly developed form. The scribes by whose genius the art was transmitted and perfected were no doubt deemed to possess a superhuman talent, and to the end of their history the inhabitants of the Nile Valley never abandoned the conviction that written symbols possessed unlimited magic power, that an incantation inscribed upon a bit of papyrus, an amulet or a slab of stone could move all things in earth or heaven to a chosen end.

The early hieroglyphic was a mixture of pictorial representation of fractional parts of animals or objects, with a few conventional ideographs to indicate abstractions. Some objects, such as the crescent moon, a lion, a man, a fish, were represented literally, while abstractions were represented by symbols, as a feather was used to indicate truth or justice. These pictographs and symbols were gradually compounded both phonetically and ideologically to express ideas of all kinds, until a single noun or verb came to have a little of everything in it — a few pictures, several syllabics, some phonetic letters and an ideograph or two.

Since the hieroglyphic system required long years of study and a sustained effort of memory for its mastery, probably very few Egyptians, apart from the professional scribes, ever possessed a working knowledge of it. With the development of speedier cursive scripts the ability to read the hieroglyphic dwindled, and after the Roman Empire it remained a forgotten tongue until Thomas Young in 1818 gave to nine characters complete or partial values which are still accepted. Four years later Champollion, in consequence of his studies of the Rosetta stone and of an obelisk from the Island of Philae, was able to give a complete system of decipherment and was the first European to understand an Egyptian inscription.

The untrained eye sees in the ancient hieroglyphic writing chiefly a mysterious and teasing beauty which obscures its primal significance. For it has been questioned whether writing, instead of having been a benefit to the Egyptians, did not rather injure them. Nilotic legend had it that the god Thoth had invented writing and given it to men, and that when Thoth revealed his clever discovery to King Thamos, the monarch immediately raised an objection against it. Children and young people, he said, who had hitherto been forced to apply themselves diligently to learn and retain whatever was taught them, would cease entirely to apply themselves now that they possessed a means of storing up knowledge without trouble. The wise king failed to see the real danger in the 'ingenious art of painting words and of speaking to the eyes' — that it was destined to be the most powerful tool with which to propitiate, and even to command, the gods.

v

By virtue of the diversified political units which went into its imperial make-up, Egypt was destined to a polytheism of the most complex kind. In the late predynastic period, the country had been divided into forty-two districts or nomes, each more or less independent of and antagonistic toward its neighbors. These nomes had, in addition to their household and tribal deities, their chief political divinities, probably resident in an image which was guarded in a shrine and carried to the battlefield when its votaries wanted its help in achieving victory. With the unification of Lower and Upper Egypt few of these local divinities were abandoned, the majority being absorbed into the common pantheon together with the legends concerning them. An Egyptian never doubted that his neighbor's gods were just as real, if less powerful, than his own, and consequently theology grew by syncretism and competition until it became a phantasmagoria of shadowy forms, endlessly substituting or exchanging roles in the drama of creation. As a city or nome advanced in prestige its priests, anxious to enhance the power of their deity, claimed for him the attributes and prerogatives of his competitors. Many deities were singly or collectively worshiped from one end of the valley to the other and all principalities agreed in proclaiming their sovereign power; but when the people began to particularize their attributes and forms, and the relations that subsisted between them, unanimity was at an end.

Even the symbolic identification of the gods was fluent in the extreme. The most distinguished deity of the Nile, the sun god, appeared in a variety of guises. In human form he was called Atum and wore upon his head the double crown of Egypt. He was also identified with the sacred scarab or dung beetle, Khepra. This beetle rolls dung into a ball which it then pushes to a cavity in the earth. After laying its eggs in the dung ball the beetle closes the mouth of the cavity with sand and proceeds to roll another ball in order to lay more eggs. The Egyptians supposed that the young beetles came out of the dung, self-created, and they saw in the dung beetle a mystical symbol of the sun god who daily rolled the ball of the sun across the sky. They reasoned that the solar ball was rolled by a great sky beetle, the self-created Khepra, who was not only immanent in all beetles but who daily created the universe. More widely, however, the sun god was conceived as a newborn child at dawn, when he was called Horus-of-the-East, as Ra, a hero in the prime of life at noon, and as Temu, an old man tottering with feeble steps at sunset. As Ra he sailed across the sky, the 'Field of Rushes,' in a splendid bark called the 'Boat of Millions of Years' accompanied by the gods of his train, and at night he returned to the east by way of the underworld, or variously by the western arc of the celestial river. Ra was usually depicted as a falcon, or a disk with falcon's wings. Ra was the ruler of the heavens, the celestial counterpart of Pharaoh, who lived upon Truth and judged the dead. By the IVth Dynasty he was the official god of the king, and although he was later displaced in the hearts of the people by the grain god, Osiris, the solar theology long continued to hold the royal affection.

Subordinate to Ra, though probably of greater age, was Ptah, the craftsman god of Memphis, patron of the arts and of wisdom, and famed for his miraculous cures and divinations. Possibly a deified ancestor who on earth had been a skillful worker in metals and stones, he was represented as a bearded mummy. He was early conceived as an intangible being who was self-created, self-subsisting, eternal. He had created all things — earth, animals and men, even the other gods — merely by 'thinking' them into existence. The god Horus was said to be Ptah's heart or mind, and the god Thoth was his 'word' which gave expression or existence to his creative thoughts. This ethereal concept of deity was at its zenith at the very beginning of recorded Egyptian history; under the influence of the solar theology, and later of Osiris, it was permanently replaced by grossly material beliefs. Although Ptah remained the Cause of Causes throughout the dominance of the Memphite kings, he never appealed to the masses — he was too vague, abstract and incomprehensible for the common run of men.

Thoth, who was represented as an ibis-headed man or a dog-headed baboon, was, as Ptah's 'spoken word,' the orderer of the cosmos, the personification of wisdom, the inventor of language, letters and numbers, astronomy, architecture, medicine, indeed of all knowledge. It was he who set the stars in their courses, instituted temple worship and devised the incantations by which the magicians controlled both the natural and the supernatural world. Like Ptah, Thoth was a great healer and in his dual capacity as the 'wise one' and the inventor of writing he was the divinity of magic. He was the god who knew all the mighty 'words of power,' the prayers, the ceremonies, the formulas for all occasions, using them in the 'correct voice' and with the proper gestures. He even knew the secret names of the deities and hence could command the supreme beings to his will. In power as a sorcerer he was exceeded by none, and rivaled only by the clever Isis, who had come into her command of magic by stealing the 'secret name' of Ra.

Osiris was originally a local divinity of Mendes in the delta, whose power spread after the close of the Old Kingdom until he became the most popular god in Egypt; his success in unseating Ra, Ptah and other gods was attributable in part to the fact that he was par excellence god of the dead, the 'dead god' who assured his followers of eternal life. He was also identified with grain and (among other gods) with the River Nile. Like Ptah, Osiris was represented as a mummy.

Isis, Osiris's beloved wife and sister, was the divinity of the fertile black soil of the river valley, and the goddess of love and of maternity. Osiris and Isis had two brothers, Set and Horus the Elder, and a sister, Nephthys. Set was the 'Lord of Slaughter,' the 'Warrior of Egypt,' the great hunter, and also the ruler of northern Egypt and of the deserts. Horus was originally worshiped as the hawk, but later he was identified with the sky, of which Ra, the sun, was but the right eye and Thoth, the moon, the left. Another Horus, 'Horus the Child' or 'Horus the Younger,' was the posthumous child of Osiris and Isis, and was usually considered to be the reincarnation of Osiris. He was early drawn as a young boy standing between Isis and Nephthys, or as a child seated on a lotus flower, but after the XXVIth Dynasty he was widely depicted as a nursing infant in his mother's lap.

Among other deities who grew to national importance were Hathor, Apis, Anubis and Atum. Hathor was the goddess of the sky, the 'Mistress of Heaven,' the female counterpart of Ra, the goddess of love, the sponsor of joy and music, and the patroness of childbirth. She was represented as a cow, her sacred animal, or as a cow with a human body and bearing a globe, the solar disk, between her horns. Apis was a god of Memphis who was worshiped in the form of a bull and conceived variously to be the incarnation of Osiris, the 'son of Ptah,' or the 'living replica of Ptah.' In the Ptolemaic Period (305–30 B.C.) he was fused with Osiris to form Serapis. Anubis, the jackal, was the guardian of the dead, the guide who led the departed to the judgment hall of Osiris. Though not of great power, he was nonetheless of considerable personal importance to every man. Atum did not come into importance until the period of the Empire. Originally the sun god of Heliopolis, he was fused with Ra to form Atum-Ra, whose priests during the ascendancy of the Theban dynasties gained control of Egypt and established the sacerdotal state.

The Egyptians delighted in gods who were at one moment material animals or objects, and at another, shadowy beings 'mysterious of shape' and 'multiple of faces.' They never visualized their deities as truly anthropomorphic beings, and with a few exceptions, never depicted them with human forms, but as animal or half-animal creatures suggestive of another world. Although their religious beliefs had advanced to the point where the gods were highly personalized, they adhered stubbornly to the conviction that their deities were incarnate in certain animals, and they held these animals sacred and on occasion paid them the same homage as they paid the gods themselves. The lion and the hawk were sacred to Horus, the bull to Ptah and Apis, the cobra (uraeus) to Ra, the ram to both Ra and Osiris, the pig and the hunting dog (saluki) to Set, the dog-headed ape and the ibis to Thoth, the swallow to Isis, the scarab to Khepra, the jackal to Anubis, and in the late Graeco-Roman period deities had become incarnate in the hippopotamus, stag, hedgehog, mouse, crocodile, turtle, vulture, cat, scorpion and frog. Animal representation never offered difficulty to the Egyptian imagination. Of course not every jackal was actually Anubis, the solicitous guide to the nether world, for that deity was above and more enduring than all jackals; yet any jackal slinking through the shadows was touched by divinity, for it was thus that Anubis elected to reveal himself to the eyes of man.

Except for Aapep, a serpent who fought Ra each morning to prevent the rising of the sun, the gods were on the whole impartial or indifferent to good and evil. Misfortunes were generally ascribed to the machinations of sorcerers or to dismal demons who populated the nether world, but the latter were largely the product of individual imagination and, not being officially recognized by the priests, failed to supply a systematic demonology.

Set was an evil god, rather than a god of evil. In earliest times he had been credited with the murder of Osiris, and he forever typified the less admirable human traits. He was a prime liar and a breeder of mischief, and was forever destroying or attempting to destroy the good works of Osiris. The legends of the 'Contendings between Set and Osiris' comprise both the coarsest chapter in Egyptian literature and one of the best portraits ever drawn of a really debased, perfidious villain. But Set was never honored by being made commander in chief of the mischievous sprites and tormenting demons; he was only the bad boy of the celestial family. His uncommendable ways were less evil because they were so entirely human. He long remained the respected god of war, and during the XIIIth to XVIIth Dynasties he was perhaps the national god of the delta. Then in the XIXth Dynasty for reasons unknown, but probably related to national politics, he fell into such opprobrium that his name was stricken from all the monuments. It was only after this defilement that the nicknames the 'Evil One' and 'Stinking Face' were applied to him. Despite every opportunity the notion of truly supernatural Evil never became canonical in Nilotic belief.

When the shaman first emerges in the historic period he appears as the guardian of the sacred temple and the mediator between men and gods. It was his duty in the early morning to break the clay seal which protected the sacred room wherein the god was housed and to attend the deity with the necessary ritual — washing, anointing and filling the chamber with the perfume of incense. He greeted the worshipers, led them in chanting hymns, in bowing in adoration and in making sacrifices and libations; he alone interpreted the sacred books and spoke for the divinity. One of his most important duties was to mediate between the king and god in divination. In accordance with the wishes of the king he laid before the image a petition usually beginning: 'O God of Goodness, my Lord,' or 'Lord, may we lay before thee a serious affair?' and then stating the case. The reply often came in sealed writing, but in certain instances the statue of the divinity revealed its answer directly; if it remained motionless, the request was refused or the answer was no; but if the deity acquiesced, it made some movement of the head or arms, spoke out directly

to the priest or king, or wrote its answer on the temple wall. The bull of
Apis, sumptuously maintained in a temple of Memphis, gave oracles by
refusing or accepting the food offered by the petitioner. At other times
the suppliant whispered his request into the bull's ear and drew his answer from the first words he heard after he left its presence. Another
mode of obtaining divine advice was by incubation. The king or the priest,
after rendering his petition in a prayer, slept in the temple and during the
night the answer was revealed in a dream, or delivered in the first words
heard after the sleeper left the temple in the morning.

These guardians of the temple were probably the first astronomers. To
know just when the Nile was going to overflow was of the utmost importance. To come into possession of this knowledge the dweller in the
delta had but to watch the stars, for Sothis (Sirius), the Dog Star, rose
above the horizon just before dawn on the day when the normal flood
began. River and star were but different manifestations of Osiris, and by
discovering this uniformity in nature the priest could tell ignorant human
beings when the god was going to manifest himself. And who was more
likely to note the passing months and years than the temple attendant who
perforce must procure for the god (and for himself) meal after meal from
a people who were prone to be forgetful? The man who first discovered
the Sothis-Nilotic cycle was doubtless a tongue-in-the-cheek shaman who
took advantage of his discovery to impress everyone with his esoteric
power. He had in his possession knowledge never before available to any
human being, for he could tell the people when to prepare the ground
and plant the seed, when the flood would begin and when it would sub-
side. He could measure the annual circle of the winds, the reproduction of
animals, the bleeding of women, the germination of the seed, the birth of
men. Because he knew so much it appeared that he knew everything, and
he quickly convinced the Egyptians that it was his rites and ministrations
that, by appealing to the gods, sustained these rhythms. It was his sacred
attentions that brought Sothis into the morning sky, caused Isis to drop
a tear into the celestial river, stirred the Nile into its flood and revivified
the barren earth. He alone could mediate between men and gods because
he alone knew the histories and the wishes of the supernal beings.

One of the products of his ministrations was the invention of the calendar. Primitively the Egyptians had marked time by the simple twenty-
eight-day cycle of the moon. Then the discovery that the heliacal rising of
Sothis coincided with the annual flood laid the basis for an arbitrary year
of twelve months, each consisting of thirty days, with five extra or inter-
calary days added to keep the calendar in step with the seasons. This

Sothic year, which was inaccurate by only one quarter of a day, appears from reliable calculations to have been inaugurated on July 19 of a year falling within the interval 4356 B.C. and 4380 B.C. — a thousand years before the union of Lower and Upper Egypt and longer before the oldest surviving written record.

vi

The vagueness, multiplicity and mutability that characterized the Egyptian pantheon characterized the Egyptian's notions of himself. In addition to the body, or *khat,* a man possessed a *ren,* a *khaibut,* an *ab,* an *aakhu,* a *ka,* and a *ba.* The *ren* was his name, the *khaibut* his shadow, the *ab* his heart. These words, however, had unusual meanings, for both a man's name and his shadow enjoyed to a certain degree an independent existence of their own, while a man's name not only possessed magic power but was vulnerable in that the owner could be injured by magic operations upon it. If he had a secret name, it must on no condition be discovered or he would be left helpless against the incantations of all who knew it. His shadow could leave his body, as indeed it did every night, and journey elsewhere. The heart was deemed to be the seat of intelligence or wisdom, as well as of conscience, and it was responsible for a man's actions. The *aakhu* was perhaps a primordial life spirit akin to the spirit of the living grain. *Ka* has been translated as person, personality, self, individual, genius, image, semblance, ghost, and even by that jack-of-all-meanings, spirit, but perhaps its context is most nearly paralleled by the notion of an immaterial 'double' comparable to the 'twin spirit' of the afterbirth; it came into existence at birth, and looked precisely like its living double, attended him as a presiding genius throughout life, and passed ahead of him at death into his tomb. The *ba,* on the other hand, came into existence only at or after death; it may perhaps be translated as the spectral, reassembled, resurrected man, formed when his *ren, khaibut, ab, aakhu* and *ka* rejoined his *khat,* or body.

The *ka,* or double, continued after death to perform all the functions of human life, sharing the same joys and sorrows as the living, delighting in the same amusements, requiring the same nourishment, suffering the same risks, even that of death. It continued to exist rather from an instinctive horror of annihilation than from any joy of life. At night hunger, thirst, loneliness and misery might drive it from the tomb to prowl about fields and villages, greedily devouring whatever food might have been discarded.

It did not permit its family to forget it, but entered their houses and their bodies, struck them with disease or madness and, if ravenous, even sucked their blood. The only effectual means of preventing these visitations was for the living to keep the *ka* well supplied with provisions in the tomb.

If a man were to be fully 'resurrected' and to enjoy the hereafter, it was necessary for the *ka* and all other parts to be reunited with the physical body; separated from this body they remained lost, helpless, spectral fragments of a man. In conceiving that the afterlife required the preservation of the body for their reattachment, the Egyptians were almost unique and this notion constitutes the primary motivating factor in the development of their civilization.

Buried in the hot, dry sand of Egypt the body failed to decompose; the skin changed rapidly into a tough, blackish parchment which wrinkled and shrank to the bones as the flesh became desiccated; the tough skin and ligaments held the skeleton together and gave to the corpse an almost miraculous integrity. One may imagine that the early Egyptians assumed that the desiccated corpse was not really, not completely dead, but rather living in some state of suspended animation analogous to that which gripped the land, the trees and even some of the fish during low Nile. All that was required was to bring the proper magic to bear upon it at the proper time and place and it would be reanimated, even as the Nile Valley was reanimated annually by the priest's incantation and the river's flood. The first and essential step was to preserve the body until the time of its revitalization.

Though the process of mummification was begun in the Old Kingdom, it did not reach a high degree of elaboration for a thousand years. At first it was only the king who was mummified, because only he was entitled to immortality; later the privilege was extended until it was available to all who could afford it. According to later descriptions of the process in Greek literature, the time required for embalming varied from forty to one hundred and twenty days.

The embalmers belonged to hereditary profession and developed the practice both as a religious ritual and an art. In some localities the body was preserved by treatment with oil of cedar, myrrh, cinnamon and other drugs and spices, in others it was steeped in bitumen or, more rarely, placed in honey which preserved it almost unchanged, or in natron, a natural mixture of salt and soda, which simply pickled it. Bitumen penetrated the bones so completely that the arms and legs broke like brittle glass, and burned so freely, giving out great heat, that at one time such mummies were used for fuel by the modern natives of western Thebes.

In the more elaborate process of mummification the viscera were mummified separately and placed in four so-called canopic jars, each of which
was dedicated to a son of Horus. The preservation of the viscera was
essential because the welfare of the body in the nether world depended
absolutely upon its having every part complete.

A green scarab, symbol of the god Khepra and inscribed with a magic
spell conveying resurrection and eternal life, was placed in the body
where the heart had been. After the body had been treated with preserva-
tives it was covered with sweet-smelling unguent and bandaged with strips
of linen many yards long. These bandages were gaudily colored or inscribed with many spells and incantations, the names of gods and other
words of power; each bandage had a special name and magic purpose.
When completely bandaged the body was sewn into a saffron-colored
sheet held in position by wide strips of brownish linen. A handsomely
painted wooden covering, which had a human face and was closely shaped
to fit the mummy, covered the bandaged body; the mummy and cover
were then placed in an inner coffin or linen-plaster cartonnage case with a
molded face, and this in turn was placed in a heavy outer coffin, the lid
of which was sealed with dowels and liquid plaster. The inner and outer
coffins, as well as the mummy cover, were decorated with scenes of gods
and goddesses, and with events from the life of the deceased, and inscribed with as many spells and words of power, prayers, and praises as
could be crowded on. The finer mummies were literary and religious, as
well as mortuary, masterpieces. Thus were the dead assured of resurrection, a favorable trial before Osiris, and a safe and happy future life.

The Egyptians buried their corpses with considerable care. When a
grave dug in the sand proved to be inadequate protection against the
depredation of animals, it was excavated in solid rock, in an area set aside
for the use of the whole community. The body was placed in the bottom
of the rock pit, the top of which was closed by a roof of poles and brush-
wood overlaid with sand so that it resembled the desert landscape. Later
a wood lining was given to the pit, and a wooden coffin stood free in the
center. It has been suggested that the first carpentering done by the
ancient Egyptians was the making of these coffins for the preservation
of the dead.

By the Ist Dynasty (3400 B.C.) bricks had been invented and were
used to raise the walls of the pit above the level of the ground and to
make a closed roof, so that the burial place became a sealed mausoleum
of brickwork, the mastaba, reproducing the house of the living. By the
IIIrd Dynasty great blocks of sandstone were quarried from the cliffs of

the valley, and the pyramidal tomb, built with brick or stones set back at regular intervals in the manner of steps, had been introduced. The IVth Dynasty (*ca.* 2900 B.C.) saw the culmination of this type of tomb in the smooth Pyramids at Cairo, which represent, if not the most prolonged, certainly the most intense physical effort ever expended by man in the cutting and transportation of rock. The stonework in the Pyramid of Khufu (Kheops) is done with a skill and accuracy scarcely exceeded in later times. Some of its 2,300,000 limestone blocks average 2½ tons apiece, and not a few weigh 50 tons, the whole weighing 5,570,000 tons. Facing stones were transported great distances from the quarries, ferried across the Nile and elevated to considerable heights. They are trimmed with an average error of only one part in 16,000 of lineal and one in 17,000 of angular measure, and it is the more remarkable that they were apparently quarried and trimmed with only stone tools. Built into the massive pile of masonry are secret passages leading to the burial chamber at its heart, as well as narrow ventilating shafts which pass from the burial chamber to the exterior and which supplied the workmen with air until the sarcophagus was in place and the entrance sealed. The burial chamber is ingeniously designed to resist the tremendous weight of material which presses down upon it, and although an earthquake has shaken the structure, not one of the stones which encase the chamber has moved perceptibly since it was fixed in place.

Herodotus, when he was traveling in Egypt, was told that 100,000 men worked ten years in building the roads over which the stones in the tomb of Khufu were brought from the quarries, and twenty years in erecting the pyramid itself; but it is possible that work was carried on during only a few months of the year when men could be spared from the soil. In Herodotus's time there was an inscription upon the pyramid which related, according to his interpreter, that 1600 talents of silver had been expended just for radishes, onions and garlic for the workmen. The interpreter can never be refuted, for the outer covering of the pyramid was subsequently torn away by the Mohammedans to build the mosques of Cairo; but according to Egyptologists, Herodotus was told a typical dragoman's tale. If Khufu put any inscription upon his tomb, it had to do with the gods and immortality and not with vegetables.

The data quoted by Herodotus cannot be given any historical value, but the cost in labor was certainly tremendous and both Khufu and Khafra, who built the second pyramid at Gizeh, of which the Sphinx was part of the chapel, can be credited with having erected the most colossal works ever put together by forthright handicraft. Both Pharaohs were afterwards accused of merciless cruelties in these works, but some historians have dismissed this as a late fable. Egyptian literature reveals no evidence of slave labor on such a scale. On the contrary it suggests that it was the organized ability and co-operation of thousands upon thousands of people which built the pyramids, a people willing and skilled and proud to participate in so magnificent a task. Apparently the workers were employed only during the flood when work upon the land had to cease, so that the ventures had something of the nature of unemployment relief projects. That the people felt no animosity against these kings is further attested by the fact that the service of Khufu's temple was maintained with few interruptions from the IVth to the XXVIth Dynasty, a period of more than 2000 years.

Though the building of pyramids continued from the beginning of the IVth to the end of the XIVth Dynasty, a period of 1400 years, the Pyramid Age proper ends with the five pyramids at Sakkara, in the ancient cemetery of Memphis, which were erected by Unas, the last king of the Vth, and Teta, Pepi I, Merenra and Pepi II, the first four kings of the VIth Dynasty (2625–2475 B.C.). After the VIth Dynasty the sepulchers were of more modest size, but in later times, and especially in the period of the empire, tombs just as magnificent in many ways as those of the Pyramid Age were carved out of the sandstone cliffs which formed the walls of the river valley at Thebes. Some of these cliff tombs were veritable subterranean palaces cut from the solid rock.

vii

Our knowledge of the beliefs of the Old Kingdom comes largely from the Sakkara pyramids of the Vth and VIth dynasties, which are unique among the tombs of the Pyramid Age in that their chambers and corridors are covered with hieroglyphics deeply incised in the stone and inlaid with green paste. The Sakkara texts are, with the possible exception of the so-called Memphite drama, the oldest literary records extant. At the time when these pyramids were built the worship of Ra was reserved for the king, who was destined in the natural course of events to become a god. It was axiomatic throughout Egyptian history that the Pharaoh was in essence a supernatural being, the physical embodiment of Ra. It is possible that at an intermediate period in the development of the kingship, the king or overlord had been put to death in the prime of life in order to transfer his still virile power to his successor, but by the dynastic period the actual sacrifice of the king had been replaced by a ceremonial sacrifice, the Sed festival, a mock death which is possibly depicted in low relief on the great mace head of the Pharaoh Narmer of the 1st Dynasty. In later times, when the Pharaoh was conceived as Osiris, the periodic Sed festival served to dramatize his death and resurrection, and to confirm or renew his divine power by identifying him with this god.

It had been the tradition, long before the worship of Osiris became widespread, for the Pharaoh to trace his ancestry direct to Ra, and it was to keep the solar blood uncontaminated that the king usually married his sister, or in some instances his daughter or another divine relation. Though incest was forbidden to ordinary men, the union of the king and his sister was considered to be the highest and most divine form of love, and the terms 'brother' and 'sister' were used poetically in the sense of lover and mistress. When an invader of mundane antecedents gained the throne it was always discovered by the priests that he was descended from the solar god by a hitherto unsuspected genealogy, or that he had been conceived by Ra, who had descended to earth secretly and begotten him by a mortal mother in order to rejuvenate the race. In fact, Ra consorted with Egyptian women of low and high rank whenever it was necessary to elevate vulgar blood to a royal position, and from the XVIIIth Dynasty on it was dogmatically held that the god Amen was the father of every Pharaoh, and that he took on the outward appearance of the royal consort in order to visit the queen.

Being of supernatural birth and closest to the gods in life, it was natural that the king should join the gods on his demise. Alive, the king was the state, the source of all its power and greatness; translated to the hereafter he was the sun and vital force upon which men were wholly dependent for prosperity; should he die, famine and destruction would come. With the royal wish for immortality the people of Egypt were always in accord, at least in principle. And in the Pyramid Texts all the magic power of words is concentrated on the effor to insure the royal ka of a safe journey to the solar heaven.

The sun god's realm lay in the sky to the east, and to reach it the king had to be ferried across a great lake in a reed bark which was poled by a mysterious and taciturn boatman. Alternatively, he could fly to the solar kingdom as on the wings of a falcon, or ascend a ladder let down from the sun's rays. Whatever the route, the journey was most hazardous and uncertain. The boatman on the lake might refuse to take the passenger, the falcon's wings might fail, the sun's ladder might not appear; or, upon the king's arrival at the far shore, the gates to the beyond might not be open.

The Pyramid Texts guarantee that the deceased will encounter none of these difficulties. The boatman is cajoled with flattery or emphatically commanded into obedience; the king's ability to fly is praised again and again until there can be no doubt about the worthiness of his wings; the sun's ladder is safely lowered by a detailed description of the event; the doors are declared open with such powerful spells that no doors could possibly resist. The sun god himself is threatened with destruction if the king is not promptly admitted at the gates of the sky.

The sun god, and almost synonymously, the dead king, is depicted in the Pyramid Texts as the most glorious being imaginable. He is conceived as a falcon flying across the sky, or as a great hunter drifting across the heavens, the 'Field of Rushes,' in a bark made of reeds. It is said of him that he is 'a stallion of a man . . . he carries off women from their husbands to the place he willeth whensoever he hath a mind to do so . . . he hath had union with Nuiut . . . he hath smelled the odor of Isis . . . he hath had union with a maiden . . . she hath given food to him and hath served him as a wife on this day.' Then without a sense of contradiction he becomes an imperishable star, or fowls in the Field of Rushes, or he takes command of the solar bark itself; he punishes the wicked by throwing them into a deep pit filled with fire where they are instantly destroyed; he consumes the magnificent offerings which are carried by his people to the chapel of his tomb; he is surrounded by sky goddesses and enjoys celestial fruits; he hunts down men and other gods with lassos and devours them, eating especially the heart for the wisdom which it contains, the entrails for their magic power, the lungs and legs and thighs. He eats the Red, he swallows the Green, until he is nourished on 'satisfied organs' and is himself 'satisfied.' He draws sustenance from the Tree of Life which grows in the Isles of the Blest in the midst of the Field of Offerings, in search of which he sets out in the glorious company of the morning star. He serves Ra joyously, and yet he himself plays the part of Ra and it is in the role of this deity that he receives the gifts tendered to the temple and acquires godlike control of the fortunes of men. It is not surprising to find that he was born of Isis and conceived by Ra, that he came forth before the earth came forth, before men were born, before death came forth, and that he was present at the birth of the gods themselves.

This eschatological conglomeration was partly attributable to the naïveté of the Pyramid Age and partly to the circumstance that the Pyramid Texts are a mixture of many faiths, primitive ancient star worship, the abstract cult of Ptah, the solar splendor of Ra and the newly rising cult of Osiris, all competing with one another for dominance in theology. The one common feature is the reliance upon the magic power of the written declaration: whatever is proclaimed often and emphatically enough is thereby brought about. Even death itself is thus abolished: the devotees of the solar faith refused to mention it by name except in application to a foe; they referred to it only by denial, or they called it a 'landing,' a 'mooring' or just 'not living.'

viii

The supreme celestial being, as much as the earthly one, required for his continued existence food and drink, sacrifices, servants, fields, cattle, all the appurtenances of royalty. Consequently as each monarch ascended to the throne he began to amass a fortune and to erect and equip a tomb appropriate to his future magnificence. He laid aside stores of riches with which to purchase the sustenance necessary for his maintenance in perpetuity; this wealth he turned over to trusted nobles and friends, appointing them and their descendants executors of his tomb forever. He built vast coffers to store the grain from his own lands, levied taxes upon his subjects, established a treasury, and sent out tax collectors who scoured the land searching out any man who failed to pay the levy. When this was not enough, he drafted men into an army with which he sought to confiscate riches and slave labor in foreign lands. He created a 'kingdom' and commandeered its wealth and power to the end of assuring himself eternal glory.

In the Old Kingdom the king took with him into the other world his wives or concubines and an adequate company of nobles, couriers and slaves. Zer of the Ist Dynasty was content with the immolation of no less than 334 persons, of whom 70 were from the royal harem, these sacrifices being buried in graves regularly arranged around his own tomb. Zet, Semti and Enezib, also of the Ist Dynasty, took 174, 137 and 64 persons, respectively, with them to the beyond, and on a varying scale the custom lasted into the Middle Kingdom, when Hepzefa of Siut was buried with 300 Ethiopians and Mentuhotep with his six princesses. In addition to the human sacrifices were large numbers of food animals, one king being buried with 1000 oxen to insure him against a depleted larder.

To protect the king against possible mishaps there were included in his tomb amulets of the cow of Hathor, the vulture of Isis, the hawk of Horus, the backbone of Osiris, the genital organs of Isis, the Heart, which was the source of all life and thought, the Papyrus Column, which bestowed strength and vigor, and the Life amulet, an elongate cross surmounted by a circle. Above all these providers of well-being was the scarab, the sacred beetle of Khepra, the god who created the world afresh each morning. At first the Egyptians used the scarab amulet merely to endow themselves with the power, health and strength of the great sky beetle. Then they associated the sun's cycle with life and death; if the sun could rise again, so might a man, provided he possessed a scarab on his mummy. So with the dead they buried scarab amulets of wood, stone, ivory, glazed faïence, amethyst, cornelian, lapis lazuli and other semiprecious stones, on which were engraved the name of the deceased, the names of great kings (themselves magic words of power) or a recitation of great events. So popular did the amulet ultimately become that it was adopted by the living as a personal seal or for adornment, and finally scarabs were manufactured in untold quantities and sold as souvenirs or mementos to tourists, so that after the opening of the New Kingdom they literally served the same purpose as modern postcards, and had an equal value.

As king followed king into the other world in ever more glorious tombs and with ever more glorious equipment, the tomb became the receptacle for the finest Egyptian art. Upon its walls the painter inscribed in colored scenes the exploits of the deceased and extolled his virtues in beautifully executed hieroglyphs. The sculptor plucked from the groves and marshes the palm frond, the papyrus leaf and the lotus flower, and captured birds and animals to reproduce them in the stately colonnades and friezes. The dead king was furnished jewels, rings, armlets, anklets of silver and gold, necklaces of cornelian, jasper, mother-of-pearl, lapis lazuli, amethyst, sardonyx, onyx, agate or garnet, as well as furniture elaborately decorated with painted carving, jewels and gold. The tomb supplies of food and drink were placed in jars and vases made of granite, diorite, basalt, porphyry, gilded wood, glass, bronze, gold and alabaster; in form and execution many of these vessels achieved perfection.

The Egyptians suffered from irritation of the eyes caused by the glare of the sun on the river, particularly at flood time, so they supplied the king with kohl and other salves to protect his eyes. It was the custom for guests at a feast to sit with a contrivance on the head to hold a scented unguent which, being slowly melted by the heat of the body, ran down the hair and spread over the arms and shoulders, and cones of such unguents were included in the tombs, along with mirrors, tweezers, skin scrapers, hairpins, pumice stone to soften the skin, scented oils, pastes, pomades, red lip salve, and henna to stain the nails. Some of the tombs of the IInd Dynasty even contained privies for the royal *ka*.

By the time of the Middle Kingdom it had become the custom to substitute for actual sacrifices painted stone or wooden images of animals and slaves of various kinds, farmers, brewers, butchers, bakers and musicians. It was believed that at the appropriate 'word of power' from the dead all these figures would become vitalized. At first these images were life-sized, but as the hereafter was democratized between the VIth and XIth Dynasties they became smaller and cheaper, until even the poorest man could afford to buy himself a few servants. These statuettes, or *ushabti* (respondent) figures, were buried in such numbers that it has been said the census of the other world was multiplied tenfold, and the museums of this world overpopulated by them. The practice of the burial of statuettes was ultimately extended to foods, furniture, and the like, and finally there was substituted merely a 'tablet of offerings' on which were engraved the images of the things offered, such as fowl, fruits, haunches of beef, bread, and so on. The gods were enjoined by an incantation upon the 'tablet of offerings' to supply the deceased with all those articles that were engraved thereon, those 'things which chanted declamation makes real.'

Buried in an everlasting tomb with every conceivable accessory, protected by every imaginable amulet, the dead king was still not completely safe; for the very hieroglyphic writing on the walls spelling out the magic texts contained miniature figures of men, animals and reptiles which might themselves come to life and torment him. Consequently it became the practice to deprive these figured beings of their legs or bodies, to chop them in half, or even to replace them with impotent substitutes, these measures of safety in no way impairing the magic power of the incantation.

ix

The Pyramid Age had within itself the germs of its own destruction. Priests and high officials, finding great wealth placed within their hands for the maintenance of the service of the dead, could after a few generations be held to no accounting and inevitably appropriated it for their own ends. Soon many of them were living as kinglets. The country was ridden by excessive taxation and the brutal tax collectors were the most feared and the most hated of public officials. Corruption spread and by 2500 B.C. the centralized government began to collapse and the country became divided into loosely affiliated feudal states which, though nominally forming a nation, periodically fell apart into warring factions. In the VIIth Dynasty there were seventy kings in as many days; the VIIIth Dynasty, although it lasted a hundred years, produced no ruler strong enough to hold the land together, and it was divided and redivided among petty barons whose rule was little better than a state of anarchy.

With the collapse of the monarchy, princelets and petty officials, and finally even serfs and slaves down to the humblest fellahs, conceived that they too could aspire to immortality. Under priestly influence the worship of the dead and of the gods acquired new fervor and developed into cults of national proportions; the temple rituals were elevated into national ceremonies, the sacred days into national holidays. The Book of the Dead was written upon inexpensive strips of papyrus and the necessary spells for assuring a man a happy afterlife were purchased by the yard.

With the democratization of the hereafter the solar faith gave way to the Osirian theology, which had long been in competition with it. As the bright visions of the sun god's realm had moved the rulers of the Old Kingdom to the heroic efforts of the Pyramid Age, so in the Middle and New Kingdoms the legends of Osiris and Isis were to shape the lives of ordinary men.

Against the royal glory of the solar hereafter, as described in the earlier of the Sakkara pyramids, Osiris was mentioned only as the ruler of *Tuat,* the realm of the dead, the *truly* dead, from which the king had happily escaped to become one with Ra. By implication *Tuat* was the dark, cold, cheerless emptiness of the abandoned grave to which the lowly people were predestined, a nether world beyond the edge of the desert and inhabited by disembodied *bas* and other miserable specters. Before the last of the Sakkara pyramids had been built the *Tuat* had been transferred to the sky and illumined by Solar splendor, to the confusion of Ra and the Solar priests.

It is related in a papyrus of the XXVIth Dynasty that Osiris, Horus the Elder, Set, Isis and Nephthys were the children of Keb, the earth, and Nut, the sky. Osiris and his sister Isis embraced within their mother's womb, and Isis brought forth a son called Horus (the Younger); Set and Nephthys also embraced before birth and Nephthys brought forth a son called Anubis.

A later record of the legend, though perhaps an earlier variant, is given in Plutarch's *De Iside et Osiride.* Here it is told that the goddess Nut coupled with Keb by stealth, and was discovered by Ra, who straightway declared a curse upon her that she should not be delivered of a child in any month of any year. Thoth, who also was in love with Nut and was moreover indebted played at dice with the moon and won from that deity a seventy-second part of every day; having compounded five whole days out of these parts he added them to the Sothic year of three hundred and sixty days, thus bringing the lunar and solar year in harmony. These five extra days were untouched by the sun god's curse, and Nut was therefore permitted to have five children, Osiris, Isis, Set, Nephthys and Horus the Elder. Again it is said that Osiris and Isis fell in love with each other and copulated in the womb of Nut. This brother and sister marriage was taken in the case of Osiris and Isis to represent the union of the Nile and the fertile land, a marriage which was repeated annually when the river rose and the earth came forth green and fruitful from its embraces. This yearly union of Osiris and Isis was at once an epitome of human desire and satisfaction, and the very source of bread, fruit, fish — of all the products of the valley of the Nile.

If the river rose on the appointed day, it was due to no mechanical function of a being to whom the consequences of his acts were a matter of indifference — the god was acting with purpose and deliberation, and out of his affection for man. As though to present a visible and indubitable sign of this affection, he bore on his tides the cardinal emblems which all men understood. The rising flood sweeps before it the stagnant growths of the vast Sudan and is so richly colored when it reaches the delta as to be called Green Nile. After a few days this color gives way to gray or blue, and then at the height of the flood, when the turbulent stream is tearing down the sandstone banks of Upper Egypt, to a dark red, occasionally so intense as to look like freshly shed blood. Green Nile, the color of resurrection; Red Nile, the color of life; could a god give clearer evidences of himself? With no sense of contradiction, Osiris was also the living spirit of the grain and seed that, dying yearly, were revitalized by the annual flood. As the god of grain and crops, he passed into the bodies of all who consumed the fruits of the earth. The spirit of the Nile and the spirit of the grain were one, for did not the river impart to the quiescent seed the very essence of life?

The spirit of the forbidding desert that borders both sides of the Nile was Osiris's brother, Set, who was cruel and treacherous, always waiting to shrivel the harvest with his burning breath or to smother the river and the Black Land under drifting sand. Evil was apparently innate in Set — in one account it was related that he tore his mother's womb at birth and made his way into the world through her side.

At first Osiris and Set had each kept to his own half of the world. Then Set, ever jealous of his brother, married his sister Nephthys in order that he might be inferior to Osiris in nothing. Nephthys had no children by Set, for the sterile desert brought barrenness to all it touched, and she sought fertilization from another source. It was rumored that she had made Osiris drunk, drawn him to her arms without his knowledge and borne him a son. The child of this furtive union was the jackal, Anubis, who prowled along the edges of the desert, and who stood as sponsor for the dead in the Judgment Hall. This irregular invasion of the domain of Set by Osiris was the beginning of open strife between the brothers, one all goodness and life, laboring to produce abundance; the other, evil and death, striving only to destroy. Set was also jealous because Osiris was beloved by all mankind; for these reasons, and perhaps because he was dissatisfied with Nephthys and wanted Isis, whose reputation as a devoted wife and able manager filled the country, he devised a plan to destroy his brother. Osiris had been in Asia, teaching men the arts and agriculture, and when he returned Set took the occasion to put his brother out of the way. He gave a banquet in Osiris's honor to which he invited seventy-two of his conspirators. Having secretly taken the measurements of Osiris's body, he prepared a richly adorned chest which he brought in at the feast. When all rejoiced at the sight of its beauty, Set promised to give it to the one whom it would exactly fit. All tried it, but it fitted none, until at last Osiris got into it and lay down. Quickly Set and his conspirators closed the cover, nailed it firmly shut, soldered it together with melted lead and threw it into the Nile, which carried it out to sea.

In the oldest record, the Memphite Drama, Osiris is said to have drowned in his 'new water' (the inundation), while the Pyramid Texts simply relate that Set murdered him at Nedyt, which may have been an ancient name for Byblos. The gods friendly to Osiris, fearing that they would suffer harm, hid themselves in the bodies of animals to escape the malignity of the new king. The grief-stricken Isis cut her hair, put on mourning robes and fled to the delta in search of the body of her lord. In the Pyramid Texts it is said that she found it there, and the spirit of Osiris visited her secretly so that she bore a son Horus, whom she hid in a basket of rushes.

In the later legend Isis had to engage in a long search in which she was accompanied by Nephthys, both being in the form of birds, and the lamentations of the two sisters were the most sacred expression of sorrow known to the Egyptians. It was told that the waves had washed the chest ashore off the coast of Byblos and a tamarisk had there grown up so quickly that it had quite enclosed it. The king of that country, having admired the tree, had caused it to be cut down and placed as a pillar beneath his house. Isis entered the service of the king as a nurse and drew the chest out from the pillar; then she took it to Egypt, where she hid it in the Nile while she rejoined her son Horus.

Set, while hunting by moonlight, discovered the chest and opened it, and, recognizing Osiris, cut the corpse into fourteen pieces, which he scattered widely. Once more Isis had to set forth on a woeful pilgrimage to recover the body of her lord. She found all the parts except the phallus, which had been devoured by the great Nile catfish, and buried them where they were found. Ever after men revered each of these spots as the grave of their benefactor: Busiris, where his backbone was buried; Abydos, where his head rested in a small chest; Athribis, which was honored with his heart. Some of the divine parts were miraculously multiplied, for Memphis as well as Abydos claimed to be the repository of his head, and the number of his legs would have sufficed for several ordinary mortals. Isis made a magic model of the lost phallus and ever after the Egyptians celebrated the feast of Pamylia in its honor.

When Horus had grown to be a man, he left his hiding place in the rushes to avenge the death of his father. He encountered Set and they had a terrible fight; one of Horus's eyes was torn out and Set was emasculated, but at last Set was vanquished and he acknowledged Horus as the new monarch of the earth. Thoth, the god of wisdom, replaced the eye of Horus and restored sight to it by spitting upon it.

Then Horus set about reassembling the fragments of his father's body, which Isis had buried. When these were complete, he prepared, under the direction of Anubis, the inventor of the art of embalming, a mummy which was so skillfully made that it would last forever; but rather than being a warm, breathing body, spontaneous in movement and capable of thought and speech, Osiris was an immobile, cold, blackish mass, adequate only to assure the continuity of the *ka*. This body's inertness condemned it to vegetate in the darkness of the tomb without pleasure and almost without consciousness of its existence. So Thoth, Isis, Horus and Anubis applied themselves to giving it life again. Thoth, the inventor of magic words and writing, showed how to inscribe the protective bandages with the proper figures and formulas; how to decorate the body with amulets of special efficacy for its different parts; how to draw on the boards of the coffin and the walls of the sepulchral chamber scenes depicting Osiris's glorious adventures, both in this world and in the life which they sought for him in the hereafter; and how to open the mouth, the eyes, the ears, and to loosen the arms and legs, to restore breath to the throat and movement to the heart by magic rituals. With Thoth's assistance the severed phallus was joined to Osiris's body and empowered to perform its natural function. As the last step in the resurrection, Horus gave his eye to Osiris to eat, whereupon Osiris was restored to life, and became a god.

No sooner was Osiris resurrected than Set proceeded to prefer charges against him, charging that Horus was not the son of Osiris but a bastard whom Isis had conceived after the death of her husband. To settle the matter for all time the two brothers were called before the Ennead, the tribunal of nine gods at Heliopolis. Thoth, acting as Osiris's advocate, completely cleared both father and son. The gods decided that Osiris was 'justified' and made him king of the nether world. Thereafter the word 'justified' was applied to the dead to mean innocent, triumphant, assured of immortality, and the resurrected dead were called 'justified of Osiris.'

To the masses of the Pyramid Age the glory of the solar realm, the magic power of precious stones and gold and amulets, and the wondrous litanies of the priests were but matters of reputation; while the humanity and death of Osiris, the treachery of Set, the passion of Isis and Nephthys, the filial devotion of Horus, the trial before the tribunal of gods — all these were comprehensible to the humblest people, who sensed themselves to be closely akin in both substance and destiny to the grain that withered and died and was trod into the fields, only to come to life again. It was Osiris, the living spirit of the grain, who died in the falling seed and was revitalized by Isis; who was killed by Set and preserved to eternal happiness by the filial love of Horus. If the love of Isis, the sacrifice of Horus, the wisdom of Anubis and Thoth could give life to Osiris, could they not do the same for them?

So the worship of Osiris spread among the people and, coming into conflict with the solar theology, invaded the latter to such an extent that in the last of the five reigns in which the Sakkara pyramids were built it is as Osiris himself, the 'resurrected,' that the king climbs up the sun's ladder or is ferried in the sun god's bark. By the end of the Middle Kingdom (1580 B.C.) the hereafter had become thoroughly democratized and the great sun god Ra had been retired to an ancestral role and forced to illumine the Osirian nether world. It was related that as Ra became old, his bones changed to silver, his flesh to gold, his hair to lapis lazuli, and in this time of decrepitude Isis, who was wiser than all the gods except Ra himself, had deposed him by stealing his secret name. Ra had mounted Hathor, the Cow of Heaven, who rose and stretched out across the earth so that her belly formed the sky, supporting herself on her four legs as on so many pillars. Thereafter the sun god busied himself organizing and ruling the new world which he found upon her back, the Field of Rushes, and Osiris was left all-powerful in the nether world.

x

The regal splendor of the sun god's realm was not imitated in the Land of the Dead over which Osiris ruled. The *Tuat,* or nether world, was not actually subterranean, but lay far to the west, beyond the 'Mountain of the Sunset.' It was a fellah's paradise where the wheat grew to three cubits' height and there was never any hunger. The happy inhabitants could go fishing or fowling among the reeds or, if they were so inclined, lounge in the shade of the trees that were perpetually green, or retire into their painted pavilions to tell amusing tales and to play at draughts. Their lives were, however, not entirely free of care. The walls of the kingdom had to be defended against the partisans of Set, the canals and dykes had to be maintained, the ground had to be tilled and grain had to be sowed, reaped and garnered. It was to perform such burdens in the solar realm that servants of all kinds had once been sacrificed at the tombs of kings and princes, and now that *Tuat* was available to the poor they entered it well equipped with *ushabti* figures, statuettes of farmers, soldiers, bakers and the like in wood, clay, faïence or other inexpensive materials. It was only necessary to arouse these miniature servants by the proper incantation and they would come to life and take up a man's responsibilities.

The kings of the Ist Dynasty had ruled from This, a city near Abydos, and were buried there. About 2000 B.C. the name of one of these kings, Zer, began to be read, or misread, as Khenti, and thence to be identified with Khenti-amenti, an ancient god of Abydos who was now himself identified as Osiris under another name. Thus Zer's tomb by accident became the burial place of the murdered god, and by the XVIIIth Dynasty it was revered as a holy sepulcher, the most sacred spot in Egypt. The greatest of all blessings was to be buried there; if this were impossible, those who could afford it arranged to have their mortal remains conveyed to Abydos for a few days before interment in their native soil, or had false tombs erected for them near the sepulcher of the god.

There was held at intervals at Abydos a festival called the Sed, a passion play which began with Osiris's life as a king, depicted his death, the finding of his body and its entombment, the grief of the burial, the fight between Set and Horus, and finally the raising of the dead king to be a god. In this ceremony the living king was identified as the reborn Osiris. This festival so held the affection of the people that they prayed that after death they might be allowed to participate in its celebration, and its dramatic representation of the life, death and resurrection of the god was duplicated on a smaller scale in other cities throughout the land.

In later, and probably in earlier times, there were closely interwoven in the Osirian faith the three chief historical threads of magic: agrarian fruition, human fertility and personal resurrection. Images of Osiris planted with grain were watered by the priests and, at the time of plowing and sowing of the land, were buried in the fields with elaborate funeral rites and mimic grief. The sprouting seed, representing the body of the dismembered god, was a magic device to promote abundant crops. Similar grain images of Osiris were buried with the mummy, the quickening of the seed serving to quicken the resurrection of the dead.

In the temple at Philae there reposed a statue of the god which indicated in the plainest way that even in death his generative power was not extinct, but only suspended, ready to prove the source of life and fertility when the opportunity should offer. Priapic images of the god, each about a cubit in height and with a phallus almost as large as the rest of the figure and worked by strings, were on festival occasions carried through the streets behind a flute player and followed by women singing the god's praises. The force of these national ceremonies, which moved the people to mass hysteria, coupled with the doctrine that every commoner might, like the king, be resurrected and join the gods, did much to spread the Osirian faith and its doctrine of a judgment.

The journey to the Osirian realm was a long and difficult one through unknown desert mountains and beset with every conceivable danger. It had been to guide the dead and to protect them from misadventure on this journey that Thoth had produced what is known as the 'Book of the Dead,' a term ignorantly applied to the mysterious rolls of papyrus invariably found in coffins of the New Kingdom. When in time the inscriptions on the papyri were translated, they were found to be a collection of magic incantations intended to protect the deceased on his journey to the nether world, and to revitalize his mummy; and the correct reading of the hieroglyphic title proved to be 'Coming Forth into the Day.' The Book of the Dead remained in use from 3000 B.C., or perhaps earlier, until long after the beginning of the Christian Era, and though many additions were made from period to period, nothing that aided a man's chances of safety in the other world seems ever to have been rejected.

The opening chapter of the Book of the Dead in all the great papyri begins with a laudatory incantation to Ra, the sun god, and is followed by another to Osiris. There then follow spells to protect the *ba* on his journey to the nether world, to enable him to avoid the great crocodile, the serpent, the lynx, the beetle, and the terrible snake goddesses, spells to protect him from being decapitated, and to keep him from dying a second time. To aid him in finding his way he was supplied with a map, and since in the nether world he might find himself forced to walk upside down, he was given a spell for 'not walking head downward.' Important were the spells to 'open the mouth of the deceased,' and to enable him to breathe and think and drink and eat, and equally important was the spell which gave him control over his 'heart' so that it would not belie his testimony and bear witness against him in the final judgment. There were spells enabling him to gain access to the solar bark of Ra; to assume at will the form of the divine hawk, Khepra, or the light god, the son of Ra, or the earth serpent, or the crocodile; to enable him to obtain a boat in which to sail the Field of Rushes, or a ladder by which to ascend to the solar kingdom; or to enable him to build a house and to supply it with servants, to plant trees and dig a garden pool. There was included a spell for 'becoming a magician' so that the *ba* could himself take care of any unforeseen difficulties or dangers; and another spell protected him from having this magic power taken away from him by other magicians who might be his enemies. As if this were not enough, a spell was included which contained words of such power that should the deceased fail to be 'justified' he could cast the sun god himself down into the Nile. A *ba* armed with an adequate recension of the Book of the Dead was prepared to face the hereafter with perfect confidence.

In the Old Kingdom the incantations of the Book of the Dead were confined to the pyramids in which the kings were buried, but beginning with the VIth and continuing to the XIth Dynasty they were written upon the boards of the coffins of commoners, frequently with great haste and carelessness. Sometimes the same text was copied several times in the same coffin, the coffin makers striving simply to cover the boards with inscriptions as rapidly and thoroughly as possible. With the opening of the New Kingdom the texts came to be written on long rolls of papyrus, partly because they were now too numerous to be placed on the coffin boards, and partly because they had to be inexpensive in order to meet the great demand.

If the *ba* followed the prescriptions of the Book of the Dead to the letter, he reached his goal without fail. On leaving the tomb he turned his back on the valley and, magic staff in hand, climbed over the hills which bounded it on the west and plunged boldly into the desert, then across the land of the sacred sycamores and a terrible country infested with many dangers, until step by step he ascended the mountains which surround the world and came to a great river across which he was carried by a ferryman. On the further shore he was met by the gods and goddesses of the court of Osiris, who acted as a guard of honor to convey him into the Judgment Hall.

At the further end of this hall, which was lit only by a mysterious twilight, sat Osiris swathed in the white bandaging of the mummy case, wearing a necklace of red stones, his green face surmounted by a tall white diadem bearing the 'feathers of truth.' Behind him stood Isis and Nephthys, and around the walls were arranged the forty-two gods who had died and been restored to life like their lord, all clothed in mummy wrappings, waiting silently until they should be addressed. The *ba* advanced humbly to the foot of the throne carrying in its outstretched hands the image of its heart, the organ of its conscience or intelligence, or its eyes, the organs of its sins and virtues. In the middle of the hall stood a Great Balance, manipulated by Thoth, one pan of which was weighted by a feather representing 'law' or 'truth.' Anubis, the jackal, led the *ba* up to the balance and placed its heart upon the other pan. In the exquisite Theban papyrus which depicts the weighing of the heart of Ani, Thoth manipulated the balance and mercifully bore upon the side of truth in order that the judgment might be favorably inclined. The dog-headed ape announced the result, which Thoth recorded with a palette of reed. The assembled gods pronounced the verdict: the defendant either was, or was not, justified. He whose heart was light in the balance was instantly destroyed by a monster with the head of a crocodile, the forequarters of a lion and the hindquarters of a hippopotamus. That an adverse verdict might be rendered against the dead was clearly recognized in principle, but as clearly deemed to be inconceivable in fact.

Osiris, the mummy, watches over the proceedings without a word. He is at once spectator, auditor and arbiter of the judgment. Above all he is the king who was betrayed, killed, mourned and buried; who was resurrected by love and filial devotion; who was tried before the gods and, because he was justified, admitted unto godhood. He is silently eloquent of man's rebellion against death, and of his theory that by amulets and incantations he can avoid personal annihilation and achieve a blessed immortality.

xi

With so much emphasis in the Pyramid Texts and the Book of the Dead on the magical means of reaching the hereafter, it must not be overlooked that the last act in the Osirian drama, the weighing of the 'heart' in the scales of Thoth, is after all an appraisal of a man's character, and it is interesting to note what deeds are deemed to counterbalance the symbolic feather. Information on this point comes from the Book of the Dead itself, from the one hundred and twenty-fifth chapter, called the Negative Confession. This chapter opens with a hymn of adoration to Osiris which, in some recensions, is followed by a preliminary and apparently archaic list of denials; then, in the form of an address to the gods of the nether world, is given the Negative Confession proper. The list of offenses given in different papyri vary, no doubt because these lists were drawn up by the scribes without the restraint or guidance of canonical literature, but all copies are alike in principle. Omitting the salutations, the declaration of innocence in the late papyrus of Nebseni (*ca.* 1600 B.C.) may be taken for examination. The transgressions number forty-two, one for each god in the Judgment Hall, each of whom had authority to punish a particular offense:

(1) I have not done iniquity.
(2) I have not committed robbery with violence.
(3) I have done violence to no man.
(4) I have not committed theft.
(5) I have not slain man or woman.
(6) I have not made light the bushel.
(7) I have not acted deceitfully.
(8) I have not purloined the things which belonged to the god.
(9) I have not uttered falsehood.
(10) I have not carried away food.
(11) I have not uttered evil words.
(12) I have attacked no man.
(13) I have not killed the beasts which are the property of the gods.
(14) I have not eaten my heart (i.e., done anything to my regret).
(15) I have not laid waste ploughed land.
(16) I have never pried into matters.
(17) I have not set my mouth in motion against any man.
(18) I have not given way to anger concerning myself without cause.
(19) I have not defiled the wife of a man.
(20) I have not committed transgression against any party.
(21) I have not struck fear into any man.
(22) I have not violated sacred times and seasons.
(23) I have not been a man of anger.
(24) I have not made myself deaf to words of right and truth.
(25) I have not stirred up strife.
(26) I have made no man to weep.
(27) I have not committed acts of impurity or sodomy.
(28) I have not eaten my heart.

(29) I have abused no man.
(30) I have not acted with violence.
(31) I have not judged hastily.
(32) I have not taken vengeance upon the god.
(33) I have not multiplied my speech overmuch.
(34) I have not acted with deceit, or worked wickedness.
(35) I have not cursed the king.
(36) I have not fouled water.
(37) I have not made haughty my voice.
(38) I have not cursed the god.
(39) I have not behaved with insolence.
(40) I have not sought for distinctions.
(41) I have not increased my wealth except with such things as are my own possessions.
(42) I have not thought scorn of the god who is in my city.

It is evident that the compiler had difficulty in finding as many transgressions as there were gods, the traditional number of which was probably derived from the number of nomes in predynastic Egypt, and consequently he had to resort to repetition. Violence is denied three times and deceit twice, while other denials are ambiguous and verge on duplication.

Nothing comparable to the one hundred and twenty-fifth chapter is known before the XVIIIth Dynasty (*ca.* 1500 B.C.), and on internal evidence this is taken to be later in origin than the introductory declaration of innocence. In the presumably older list, transgressions against the gods and the persons of others occupy the most prominent position, while in the Confession the most numerous transgressions are those of character and disposition. Were still earlier lists available, one might confidently expect to find an increased number devoted to primitive taboos against the supernatural.

The Negative Confession, in keeping with the rest of the Book of the Dead, is purely a magic ritual; by forestalling each god with an emphatic denial, the adverse decision of that deity is automatically averted. Since there were but forty-two gods, forty-two denials were all that were required to assure the suppliant of justification. Hence the list cannot be taken to represent a summary of contemporary ethics. There is abundant literary evidence that many personal and social virtues were highly esteemed which are not here enumerated: charity, hospitality, modesty, justice and incorruptibility, the obligations of marriage, filial duty, and respect for old age; nor is it to be argued that the Egyptians did not conceive these to be important in the Judgment. The chief value of the document consists in its forthright exhibition of the belief that morality has a supernatural virtue.

The use of morality to obtain celestial bliss is so removed from the ordinary, primitive methods of purification that the two were separated, it may be supposed, by a long period of development, a period falling within the late predynastic period and the Old Kingdom. The only literary material which may be assigned an older date than the Pyramid Texts is the so-called Memphite Drama, which dates from the Ist Dynasty and is the oldest written record of human thought. This document is written on a black basalt slab which was found in the ruins of the Temple of Ptah at Memphis. Long displaced from its honored position as a sacred stele, a modern Egyptian farmer had used it for a nether millstone and for years on end had ground his grain upon its inscribed surface. The stone itself dates only from the eighth century B.C., the period of the renaissance when the Egyptians were again turning in great reverence to the study of all the writings of the past. It was prepared by the Ethiopian Pharaoh Shabaka, who had found in the Temple of Ptah an ancient papyrus so eaten by worms that it was scarcely legible, and the Pharaoh, wishing to preserve 'the words of the ancestors,' had had them copied on to the stone so that they were 'more beautiful than before.' Internal evidence has satisfied all authorities that the archetype from which the copy was made must have been written at the opening of the dynastic period, or about 3400 B.C. The modern miller had drilled a hole in the center of the stone and cut channels which radiated to the edge like the spokes of a wheel; this mutilation, combined with the merciless grinding of the upper stone, has left only the first and last third of its precious text intact. What remains is a drama or miracle play such as the Egyptians loved, wherein Ptah of Memphis creates the world and its moral order. It is related that through his heart Horus came to Ptah, through his tongue Thoth came to Ptah, and the heart and tongue of Ptah brought forth all the other members of the Divine Company, which were as his teeth and lips. Through these in turn Ptah 'created the sight of the eyes, the hearing of the ears, the breathing of nose, that they may transmit to the heart [understanding],' and by pronouncing the names of things he brought into existence 'all gods, all men, all cattle, all reptiles, all living, while he thinks and while he commands everything that he desires.'

That Ptah, the spirit 'self-created, self-existent and living for eternity,' was a judge before whom the dead king must appear is clear from the surviving traces of his cult in the Pyramid Texts. Nothing remains in the Memphite Drama to reveal the specific nature of his favors, but here it is explicitly stated on what grounds these favors will be granted. The hieroglyphic inscription says frankly that 'As for him who does what is loved and him who does what is hated, life is given to the peaceful [literally, the one bearing peace] and death is given to the criminal [literally, the one bearing guilt].'

The Egyptians of the age of Ptah were not given to abstractions, and there is no mention here of 'good' and 'evil,' only 'he who does what is loved' and 'he who does what is hated.' 'What is loved' and 'what is hated' may be taken to refer to both men and gods, since the kingdom of earth and the kingdom of the hereafter were organized along entirely parallel lines. Man had been striving to do 'what is loved' by the spirits of trees, rivers and animals as long as he had been a thinking creature, for the simple reason that this precept had proved to be most successful in his relations with other men. The Egyptians were undoubtedly the first to elevate the precept into a broad principle of morality. They had a word for it, *maat*, which is usually translated as 'law,' but to which must also be given the meanings 'correct,' 'justice,' 'truth' and 'righteousness.' These several meanings can only be distinguished by the context as, for example, when correct and truth are meant in a factual or mathematical sense, when justice is meant in the legal sense, and when righteousness is meant in the moral sense. It is improbable that the Egyptians made any sustained effort to distinguish these several meanings, since with them the law of the land was the 'word' of the god-king, and mathematical truth was the 'foresight' or 'word' of Thoth, which itself comprised all 'truth' from astronomy to magic; while both were as incontrovertibly 'right' as the movements of the sun or river. Such distinction as was made, and this was chiefly in context, was in the use of the word *maat* in its special relation to morality.

Maat does not occur in the Memphite Drama but the omission may be accidental, for the concept of doing 'that which is loved' is the cardinal principle of Memphite morality and is identical with the usage of the word in subsequent centuries. By the Vth Dynasty *maat* was in common use and even appeared in the royal name of the first king of that dynasty, Userkaf, who called himself the 'Doer of Maat.' Shortly afterwards the principle of *maat* appears in the Osirian pantheon personified as a goddess of the same name. The symbol of this goddess, Maat, was a woman's head surmounted by a feather, though frequently the feather alone was used, as in the pan of the balance of Thoth or in the crown of Osiris. Accepting the usual interpretation of the word, one may for the Egyptians of the late Pyramid Age discount all other meanings and translate the name of this goddess as 'Righteousness.'

After the Memphite Drama, the oldest Egyptian treatise dealing with human conduct consists of a collection of maxims or proverbs called the Instruction of Ptahhotep. The existing papyrus, which is incomplete, dates from the Middle Kingdom, by which time the collection of maxims had come to serve as a model for the instruction of school children in wise conduct and good manners, as well as in rhetoric and the appropriate expression of ideas. Though the text had no doubt been re-edited, the attribution of the original authorship of the greater part of the work to one Ptahhotep who was vizier under King Issy about 2675 B.C. is generally accepted. The author, striving to attain a style characterized by subtlety and freshness of expression, frequently couched his thoughts in similes and metaphors which, though intelligible to the ancient Egyptians, are all but incomprehensible to modern readers. Enough of his meaning is clear, however, to reveal his wide experience with men and insight into character. According to tradition, Ptahhotep retired at 110 years of age after having served several kings. In his later life he had probably been richly rewarded by his monarchs and had spent much of his time in contemplation and in reducing his beliefs to writing. His 'wisdom' was unquestionably venerable even when he undertook its literary reduction. No doubt he had at hand many ancient manuscripts from which he selected such ideas as he esteemed, turning them into new phrases and metaphors, and instilling into them some of his own experience and profundity.

'Sire, my Lord,' he says in presenting the work to his monarch, 'when age is at the point and decrepitude has arrived, debility comes and a second infancy, upon which misery falls heavily every day: the eyes become smaller, the ears narrower, strength is worn out while the heart continues to beat; the mouth is silent and speaks no more; the heart becomes darkened and no longer remembers yesterday; the bones become painful, everything which was good becomes bad, taste vanishes entirely; old age renders a man miserable in every respect, for his nostrils close up, and he breathes no longer, whether he rises up or sits down. If the humble servant who is in thy presence receives an order to enter on a discourse befitting an old man, then I will tell thee the language of those who know the history of the past, of those who had heard the gods; for if thou conductest thyself like them, discontent shall disappear from among men, and the two lands [Upper and Lower Egypt] shall work for thee.' Thus did old age offer its one lingering bit of usefulness, wisdom, to the present and the future, such wisdom of men and gods as should drive discontent and strife from out the land.

Less than half of Ptahhotep's admonitions deal with administrative and official duties, most of them being concerned with personal conduct. They inculcate gentleness, moderation and discretion, and are concerned with the relationship of husband to wife, son to father, servant to king, the dangers of another's harem and of strange women, and even with deportment at the table. Knowledge, he observes, is indispensable for getting on in the world, and he recommends the careful observation of men as well as the study of the priceless works of the past. As for advice to others, he says, 'Let thy mind be deep and thy speech scanty . . . be silent, for it [silence] is better than *teftef* flowers. Speak thou when thou knowest that thou solvest difficulties. It is a craftsman who speaks in council and speech is more difficult than any craft. . . . Worthy speech is more hidden than greenstone, being found even among slavewomen at the millstone.'

Although Ptahhotep could doubtless recall nearly a century of Egypt's greatness, and there was available to him in written history or in legend a past that stretched away in the dimness of many centuries, he could not discern that the impressive national order of the Pyramid Age had come into existence out of the chaos of many warring forces. On the contrary it seemed to him that things had been going in the reverse direction, that 'in the beginning' there had been harmony, peace and plenitude, a 'Golden Age' which had been ended by the death of Osiris, by the strife between Set and Horus, by the rebellion of men against Ra. The mighty world state of which he was Grand Vizier was now held together only by certain modes of conduct, and in his inverted mirage of history he conceived that these modes of conduct had descended as moral mandates from the far-off time 'before death came forth.' Whatever was good must be a survival of the Golden Age, and whatever was effective must be an expression of the gods. Though he instructed youth to give attention to the temple, to make sacrifices to the gods, to observe the details of ritual, he conceived these to be formalities of minor import. His cardinal precept he might have taken from the Memphite text itself: 'Great is righteousness; its dispensation endures, nor has it been overthrown since the time of its maker; for punishment is inflicted on the transgressor of its laws. . . . Although misfortune may carry away wealth . . . the power of righteousness is that it endures.'

Thus it might seem to one who lived in the Pyramid Age and had seen glorious kings pass on to immortality in the sun god's realm. The magnificent services, the expensive sacrifices, the songs, the dramas which were enacted in the temples of these tombs, all proclaimed that 'righteousness endures.' If we may believe the eulogies which the Egyptians who followed Ptahhotep inscribed upon their tombs, it was an age, and perhaps the first age, in human history when men were consciously striving to attain righteousness. One man says that no one who had worked upon his tomb was dissatisfied with the pay; another that he had made no man weep; a third that he had fed the hungry, clothed the naked, fed the wolves of the mountains and the fowl of the sky; that he was beloved of his father, praised by his mother, excellent in character to his brother and amiable to his sister. Such were the declarations inscribed on every grave for the reason, as the explorer Karkhuf (2600 B.C.) frankly admitted on his tomb, that 'I desired that it might be well with me in the great God's presence.' In broad perspective all this moral 'cleanness' is akin to the more primitive modes of purification, as is more frankly revealed in the self-eulogy of the scribe Nu, who says, 'I am pure. I am pure. I am pure. I have washed my front parts with the water of libations, I have cleansed my hinder parts with drugs which make wholly clean, and my inward parts have been washed in the liquor of *maat*. There is no single member of mine which lacketh righteousness.'

It would be inconsonant with every fact to impute to the people of the Old Kingdom any notions of good and evil more abstract than the words of the Memphite text: '. . . life is given to the peaceful and death is given to the criminal.' Impelled by the wish to go on living forever, the Egyptians had utilized to the utmost red and green pigments, cowrie shells and symbolic amulets; they had bent their every talent for carpentry, stonemasonry, architecture, sculpture, painting, the preservation of the body, to the service of the dead; and from the invention of writing to its fullest development this art was chiefly concerned with 'words of power.' When the priestly author of the Memphite text, and after him, Ptahhotep, attributed a magic power to those forms of conduct which, in the experience of the Old Kingdom, made for peace between man and man, or between man and his Pharaoh, and held that such conduct also made for peace between man and gods, it was but the addition of a new talisman. It appeared that righteousness might be a more powerful talisman simply because it was a new one, as the magic word had taken precedence over mummification, and mummification over simple burial, and burial over red and green pigments. That it failed to displace completely the more primitive methods of purification and to become the sole means of attaining eternal bliss was simply because there was no dramatic legend or rationalized theory of good and evil to give it force.

xii

The Old Kingdom had been a period of almost uninterrupted political, social and artistic development. Its achievements, with justice, truth and righteousness, had been epitomized in the goddess Maat. It must have seemed to Ptahhotep, living at the peak of the Pyramid Age, that this sublime order of things would go on forever. He could not know that the day was just ahead when architecture and craftsmanship and engineering, all the ordered magnificence of the Old Kingdom, would fall into utter decay, while sages and social prophets would seek for *maat* in vain.

Within a few centuries of Ptahhotep's time the temple services had been abandoned and the buildings themselves entirely covered with blown sand. A Heliopolitan priest of the XIIth Dynasty, Khekkeperri-soneb, contemplating the misery that descended upon Egypt during the Feudal Period, wrote: 'Maat is cast out, iniquity is in the midst of the council hall. The plans of the gods are violated, their dispositions are disregarded. The land is in distress, mourning is in every place, towns and districts are in lamentation. All men alike are under wrongs; as for respect, an end is made of it. . . . When I would speak thereof, my limbs are heavy laden. . . . I am meditating on what has happened. Calamities come to pass today, tomorrow afflictions are not past. . . . Nobody is free from evil; all men alike do it. . . . The poor man has no strength to save himself from him that is stronger than he.'

The Feudal Period was the first great age of disillusionment, one that in after centuries the Egyptians were to remember as the bitterest time in their history. Yet the abandoned offering tables, the silence and desolation of the great tombs which stretched for sixty miles along the river did not stir in their minds any skepticism of the efficacy of massive masonry or of pigments, amulets, incantations and righteousness to purchase immortality. Rather in their disillusionment they banked more and more on the life to come, and attributed the catastrophe that had descended upon Egypt to the evil of men's ways. The scribe Ipuwer, harkening back to the Golden Age when the sun god was Pharaoh, says, 'Would that he had discerned their character in the first generation. Then he would have smitten evil. He would have stretched forth his arm against it. He would have smitten the seed thereof and their inheritance.'

About 2400 B.C., Khati II, a king of the IXth Dynasty, emulating the example of Ptahhotep of 500 years before, endeavored to put upon papyrus the wisdom of his years. In a manuscript called the 'Instruction addressed to Merikere,' who was presumably the king's son, the Pharaoh gives his advice on the nature of profitable conduct, and in doing so unwittingly records the changing complexion of Egyptian culture. A man should do *maat,* he says, that he may be established here, but the fortunes of this world, good or bad, are fleeting and unimportant. The son is admonished to think of the next world and the judges before whom even he, a king, will have to sit:

> The court of judges who judge the unworthy, thou knowest that they are not lenient on that day of judging the wretched, in the hour of executing the writ. . . . Set not thy mind on the length of days, for they [the judges] view a lifetime as an hour. A man surviveth after death and his deeds are placed beside him like mountains. For it is eternity, abiding yonder, and a fool is he who disregards it. As for him who reacheth it without having committed iniquity, he shall abide there like a god, striding on like the lords of eternity. . . . Adorn thy dwelling of the West [the tomb] and embellish thy seat in the necropolis, as one who hath been upright, as one who hath done righteousness. . . . Make enduring monuments for the gods, for it maketh live the name of the maker thereof. Let a man do what is profitable to his soul, the monthly purification, taking the white sandals and visiting the temple, unveiling the mysteries, entering the holy-of-holies, and eating bread in the temple. . . . Make enduring monuments according to thy fortune, for a single day is wont to yield eternity, and an hour may be enduring for the future. The gods know of the one who does any service for them. . . . More acceptable is the virtue of the upright man than the ox of him that doeth iniquity. . . . [Nevertheless] offer to gods that they may do the like for thee, with offerings for replenishing the offering table and with inscription, for that is what perpetuates thy name. The gods take knowledge of him that offers to them.

Khati lived in one of the most critical periods in Egyptian history, a turning point after which the skepticism of the Feudal Age was replaced by veneration for the past. As the Old Kingdom grew misty through the thickening years, it seemed that the peace, honesty, justice and prosperity that had marked that Golden Age were attributable to the wisdom of its great men, a wisdom embodied in the writings of Ptahhotep and other ancient sages. So from the ancient manuscripts Khati fashioned shackles for all men to come: 'Maat,' he says to his son, 'comes to thee well brewed, after the manner of the ancestors. Imitate thy fathers, for their words abide in writing. Read that thou mayest imitate their knowledge. Thus shall you too become wise and virtuous.'

Even as he admonished his son to imitate the ancestors, Khati's eyes must have rested upon one of the countless tombs lining the banks of the Nile for miles, wherein those ancestors had sought eternal life. A thousand years had gone by since the first *mastaba* had been built, two centuries had elapsed since the priests had abandoned the last temple to the care of the jackal who now alone inhabited its shadows. The abandoned offering tables, the prostrate columns and fallen architraves must have stirred in his mind a sincere doubt of the efficacy of amulets, tomb offerings, incantations and the like, as of the sheer force of massive masonry, to purchase immortality, but confidence in the talismanic power of righteousness remained unshaken:

'More acceptable is the virtue of the upright man than the ox of him that doeth iniquity. One generation passeth on to another among men, and the gods, who know character, have hidden themselves. . . . They confound by what is seen of the eyes. . . . Well bestead are men, the flocks of god [the Sun god, Ra]; for he made heaven and earth according to their desire, he quenched their thirst for water, he made the air that their nostrils might live. They are his likeness which came forth from his limbs. He rises in the sky according to their desire, he made for them plants and the animals, fowl and fish, to nourish them. He slew his enemies, he chastised his children, because of their plots in making rebellion. He made the light according to their desire, that he might sail the sky to see them. He raised a protection around them; when they weep he heareth. He made for them rulers in the egg [rulers predestined before birth] to support the back of the feeble.' Thus Khati, reacting to the pessimism of the Feudal Period, laid the foundations of the theory of a righteous universe. If righteousness is that which is loved by the gods, then the gods must themselves be righteous, and the cosmos must be such a gift from the gods to men as a righteous man would make to his beloved brother.

This remarkable document may fairly be said to mark the climax of Egyptian thought. The ancient manifold of physical and verbal magic, of amulets and incantations and sacerdotal formulas, ultimately engulfed Nilotic culture and smothered it entirely, but the maxim of the Memphite text, the wisdom of Ptahhotep and the reflections of Khati were destined to escape into new channels. A universe created for the special benefit of man, a resurrection and a blessed immortality, the notion of righteousness as the most powerful talisman, were to shape the subsequent culture of the Occident.

xiii

The political disorganization that existed during the invasion of the country by the Hyksos (1800–1580 B.C.) was brought to an end by Aahmes I, founder of the great XVIIIth Dynasty. Under Aahmes and his successors, Amenhotep I, Thothmes I, Thothmes II, Queen Hatshepsut and, greatest of all, Thothmes III, Egypt became an empire that in power and geographical extent, in wealth and art and brilliance, was the greatest the world had seen, or was to see for another millennium. Conquests in Syria and Mesopotamia directed to the Nile a steady flow of gold, silver, jewels, precious woods, perfumes, metals, slaves and other riches until Egypt grew rich beyond her dreams. A considerable fraction of this wealth was given to the god Amen of Thebes, whose priests appropriated to their deity many of the legends and all the important attributes of the ancient sun god, and began calling him Amen-Ra.

The powerful military forces set up by Thothmes III served his son, Amenhotep II, so well during his twenty-seven years of rule that he scarcely perceived the growing danger of Hatti, the country north of Mitanni, from which a rude barbarian people, the Hittites from the highlands of Anatolia, were casting jealous eyes upon Egypt's Asiatic outposts, and he died in peace and was buried in the Valley of the Kings in a rock-hewn tomb whose roof of blue was spangled with golden stars.

Under the next king, Thothmes IV, the Hittite danger became more evident, and the Pharaoh decided that it would be the course of wisdom to protect Egypt by a closer alliance with the buffer state of Mitanni. In due course, the Mitannian princess went to Egypt to become Thothmes's secondary wife, Mutamuya. It may be that Mutamuya carried with her the seed of the monotheism that was soon to destroy the great military empire of the Nile.

This marriage was apparently the first instance of a Pharaoh's wedding the daughter of a foreign sovereign. The great Thothmes III, one imagines, would have foreseen and done something to prevent the coming storm; but his grandson, Thothmes IV, was neither a fighter nor a prophet, and it probably seemed to him that a diplomatic marriage would serve well enough to keep the barbarians off Egypt's soil. Thothmes reigned but a few more years and was succeeded by Mutamuya's son, who was the third Pharaoh to take the name of the Theban god.

So resplendent now was Egypt's glory that Amenhotep III has been called the Golden Emperor. He was chiefly interested in hunting boars and lions, in building magnificent buildings and in surrounding himself with splendor. Like his father he went in for marital innovations: while still in his early teens he took as his great royal wife an Egyptian woman, Tiy, who was not of solar birth, a marriage that was against the long-established tradition of the Pharaohs; and for a second wife, ten years later, he followed the precedent of his father and chose the Mitannian princess, Gilukhipa, no doubt intending thereby to further strengthen Egypt's Asiatic affiliations. Confident that this bond would ward off the Hittites, he gave no more attention to his borders.

Amenhotep III apparently favored his divine namesake, for on a stele which was to become notable in history chiefly because a later Pharaoh, Merenptah, appropriated it and on it engraved the first mention of the Israelites, the king declared his piety towards Amen-Ra in generous terms. But what is more significant, Amenhotep elevated a strange god, Aten, to royal favor. One of the king's many architectural efforts was a new palace on the western bank of the Nile at Thebes, and on the royal grounds he constructed a great artificial lake, and on the lake he placed a barge named 'Aten-gleams' — the name Aten being that of an unimportant god of Thebes of whom almost no one had heard, but who in the very near future was to bring about a theological revolution. It would seem that Aten was favored by his wife, Queen Tiy, and the barge was so named to humor her, there being no evidence that the king himself was an Aten worshiper.

In the reign of Amenhotep III, Egypt reached the peak of her wealth and glory. From Nubia and the Sudan, from Cyprus, Sinai, Palestine and all of Syria, riches had been pouring into her coffers for nearly a century. Merchants and couriers laden with wealth traveled between the Nile and the Euphrates or Orontes with a degree of safety that has perhaps not been equaled since. Chiefs speaking a dozen tongues wrote to the king on baked clay tablets in the cuneiform script of the East, pledging their undying allegiance. It was an age characterized by copious international correspondence, and the scribes filed countless letters from Babylon, Hatti and Carchemish in the House of Rolls at Thebes, with admirable care for their preservation but deplorable negligence of their contents. If an occasional prudent governor sounded an alarming note about a rebellion of Armorites on the Phoenician coast, about marauding bands of Khabiri (Hebrews) in Palestine, or about the perfidy of men who, even as they wrote servile letters to the king, were conniving in rebellion with the Hittites, he was probably reprimanded for disturbing his majesty with unpleasant things. One quick stroke of the sword and the Armorites would no doubt have fallen to their knees, the Khabiri and the Hittites would have retired respectfully. But the Golden Emperor was not the striking kind; he had, as Baikie put it, but one prayer: "Lord, grant peace in our time," and he died in the midst of pomp and magnificence, leaving the crisis to his son, Amenhotep IV.

xiv

Of Amenhotep IV it can be said that he involves more mystery and has evoked more heated controversy than any other individual in ancient history. He ascended to the throne of the greatest empire on earth at an age probably no greater than fourteen, a physiologically abnormal child who was more at home with the women of the harem than with men. To Queen Tiy, who was a strong-willed and independent woman, a weakling son must have been more a source of chagrin than pleasure and it is quite likely that she early abandoned him to the other women of the harem. In this strange coterie there were possibly his grandmother, Mutamuya, and his elder stepmother, Gilukhipa, both of whom may have survived long enough to influence him, as well as the youngest stepmother, Tadukhipa, whom he himself later married. Was it only because of the long-established custom by which a Pharaoh inherited his father's harem that Tadukhipa became his wife? Or did a bond of affection, fostered by the relatively slight difference in their years, develop between them while they were together in the harem? In accordance with tradition, for his royal wife and queen he chose his sister Nerfertiti ('The Beautiful One has come'), but this fact, combined with the accidental preservation of two magnificently sculptured busts which well prove the merit of her name, seems to have promoted this beautiful woman to an overexalted role. Behind the formal life in which Nerfertiti is the dominant figure lies the unfathomable but not insignificant mystery of one, two or perhaps three Oriental women who might shield and form the character of a misfit, royal waif.

The first inscription of Amenhotep's reign characterized him as High Priest of Aten, and shortly afterwards he erected a temple to this god at Karnak. Karnak was a stronghold of Amen-Ra, and it must have offended the wealthy followers of that god to have the king erect a temple to this upstart deity. Perhaps Queen Tiy wanted to see her god publicly honored among the many gods of the ancient pantheon, but certainly she was not solely responsible for Amenhotep's new affection. Somewhere he was picking up new ideas.

One possibility is that the new theology which the king was advancing stemmed from the priests of Ra. Back in the time when Amenhotep's great-great-grandfather, Thothmes III, had been expanding the boundaries of empire, theological ideas had been expanding in a parallel manner. The gods of the Nile, arising as local deities, had until that time retained their provincial interests and the widest extension of their domain had never reached beyond the valley and the delta. Gradually as the military power of the Pharaoh spread eastward into new lands, the power of the Egyptian deities followed in its train and Amen-Ra was spoken of as a 'lord of the whole world,' as 'seeing the whole earth.' His priests boldly asserted that he shone on Babylon, Carchemish and Thebes alike, and that all men, of every nation, were equally dependent on him. This came close to truth, for Amen-Ra had been enriched by a succession of great Pharaohs who never forgot to dedicate a portion of their spoil to the deity to whom they owed their victories; the god controlled a very substantial fraction of all the arable land in Egypt; his coffers were full of gold, silver and precious stones, and he owned vast herds of cattle and commanded a huge staff of officials and slaves who cared for his temples and his lands. The High Priest of Amen-Ra at Karnak was virtually director of the priesthoods of all the Egyptian gods. Indeed, Amen-Ra was worshiped in Canaan as the equal of Baal and Ashtoreth, and possessed temples there as well as in Syria and Palestine. This rapid gain in power of Amen-Ra, whom the priests of Ra considered to be an interloper, had caused them deepest concern. They had every reason to be jealous of him, and it was very much to their interests to break his power, if not by a return to the old ritual, then by the substitution of a new one closely affiliated with the ancient solar tradition. So it may have been secretly in the temples of Ra that the new Aten was conceived.

Or it may have been secretly in the harem that Mutamuya, Gilukhipa or his stepmother-wife, Tadukhipa, infected Amenhotep with Oriental abstractions foreign to the Nile.

Whatever his origin, the new god emerged in glory when Amenhotep, after a few years on the throne, suddenly set about establishing a theology of his own. The god Aten had originally represented merely the physical sun, but now Amenhotep stripped that body of all the gross theological conceptions which had been linked with it ever since the Pyramid Age and endowed it with new esoteric meaning. The ancient symbols of Ra — the pyramid, the falcon, the lion and cat — he replaced by a simple circle representing the sun's disk from which diverging beams radiated downward, each ray ending in a human hand. Presumably this symbol was conceived to indicate the new sun god's power to reach out and touch with his beams every aspect of life, every man, every country in the world; perhaps the king thought that such a symbol would appeal as strongly to the people of the Sudan and Syria as to the dwellers along the Nile for whom alone such archaic figures as the pyramid or falcon had any meaning. To revise the sun god's name and symbol was not enough: the king insisted upon the abandonment of all the magic rituals and temple sacrifices to which Egyptians of every creed were long accustomed; and when the priests of Amen-Ra, Osiris and other gods, and even the people themselves, proved obdurate, he forcibly closed the temples of the other gods, punished the priests and confiscated their property and revenue, and forbade the people to worship any deity but Aten. In the sixth year of his reign he changed his own name Amenhotep, 'Beloved of Amen,' to Akhnaten, 'It is well with Aten,' while he suffixed to Nerfertiti's name, Neferneferuaten, 'Beautiful are the Beauties of Aten.' He had the plural word 'gods' erased from all the monuments and obliterated the hated name of Amen wherever it might appear. He even insulted the memory of his father and robbed the Golden Emperor of his hope for immortality by hammering out the name of Amenhotep III on that king's tomb.

Finding Thebes, the stronghold of Amen-Ra, encumbered with too many temples and polytheistic traditions, he abandoned the capital outright and built himself a new city at a site, now called Tell el-Amarna, which he named Akhetaten, 'Aten is satisfied.' He was at this time probably not ever twenty-one years old. Here he repaired with his wife and daughters, his court and priests, and tried to build a new life that should be unprofaned.

Something of the nature of Akhnaten's dream is revealed in his sacred title, Ankh-em-Maat, 'Living in Truth.' One aspect of the new scheme of things can be learned from the art of the period, for here as in theology he broke completely with the past. 'Living in Truth' apparently meant for Akhnaten the acceptance of reality with no conventional gloss. What was, was right; its propriety was evident by its very existence. He had his family depicted in scenes that lacked the conventional reserve of Pharaonic decoration. In one scene the royal couple are shown sitting side by side, their arms lovingly twined round one another, while two daughters play the role of fan bearers and another sits informally at her parents' feet. In another, in which the king and queen are driving in a chariot, the queen has turned around to kiss her husband. The public display of affection between the king and queen was below the dignity of a Pharaoh, and it was unprecedented for them to be formally portrayed in the kissing act.

In a dinner scene the king is gnawing on a great bone with obvious pleasure, while Nerfertiti grasps a whole roast duck in her right hand; the king and queen and the queen mother are drinking wine out of generous cups as one young princess leans against her mother and another slyly helps herself from a cake plate. A statuette of the king shows him kissing a small daughter who sits upon his knee. It is almost as though the artists had received a royal command to exhibit the intense affection that existed between the king and his family. The more one considers all the circumstances, the more one suspects the emphasis.

If his portraits are to be trusted, Akhnaten was himself deformed — his head was oversize, his buttocks enlarged and his breasts well developed. But on the principle that what was, was right, the king had himself depicted with no sparing of these abnormalities. It is probable that the effort at truthful representation overshot itself and that in later portraits the king's unusual figure was grossly exaggerated, for in some instances even the indubitably beautiful queen and her children were depicted as monstrosities. Perhaps what was 'true' for the Pharaoh must by convention be 'true' for his family and everyone else.

Meanwhile, Akhnaten's governors were writing letter after letter warning him of the troubled condition of the east. It had been twenty years since Amenhotep III had made his single expedition into Syria, and the provinces had grown indifferent to Thebes; everywhere they were restive and in some places the local officials openly refused to send the usual tribute to the west. The Amorites were conniving with the Hittites in an anti-Egyptian movement. The Canaanites were becoming insubordinate, while Khabiri tribes were invading Palestine. Governors of the Asiatic provinces were reiterating their dire plight in every message. The emissary in Byblos warned the king that "the whole land is going to ruin"; that of Tunip cried, "Your city weeps, and her tears are running, and there is no help for us. For twenty years we have been sending to our Lord, the King, the King of Egypt; but there has not come to us a word from our Lord, not one"; while the emissary in Beth-Ninurta (which was later called Jerusalem) warned that "If there are no troops this year, let the King send an officer to fetch me and my brothers, that we may die with my Lord, the King." There are reasons to think that some of these messages never reached Akhnaten but were intercepted by the interpreters in Egypt who either wanted to spare themselves trouble or who were actually conniving with Syrian traitors. Be that as it may, Akhnaten continued to rely for protection on the kinship of himself and his wives with the king of Mitanni, any fear of invasion that he may have had being quieted by the repeated assurances of that potentate's friendship and power. He carefully filed his emissaries' messages in his new House of the Rolls at Tell el-Amarna, and devoted himself with increased fervor to the worship of Beauty and Truth. He succeeded in converting his official retinue to the new cult by lavishing favors upon them, and apparently he erected temples in several Syrian cities, as well as in Nubia, Hermonthis, Memphis and Thebes. Artists and musicians were encouraged to prepare magnificent murals or to devise new dances, and poets were called upon to write majestic hymns and prayers, all extolling Aten's beneficence and grandeur.

The only certain information on Akhnaten's doctrines is that obtained from fragments of these hymns and prayers as they were inscribed in the tombs which the king built for himself, his family and his courtiers at Tell el-Amarna. It is a meager source, for in the reaction that followed the king's death almost everything pertaining to Aten was destroyed. The surviving fragments have been made to do excessive duty in interpreting Aten's nature, but there are certain points which stand out beyond argument.

Atenism was a solar doctrine transformed by the substitution of abstractions and universals for gross details and local human myths. Aten was the single divine being who had created all things. Beautiful, glittering, high over every land, his rays touched the earth at every point and shone in the face of men, although his footsteps, his way of going, remained unseen. His works were manifold, even if hidden from the eyes of men. He sent winter to bring coolness, lest men might taste too much of his power; he sent rain as waves upon the mountains to water their fields; he created the germ in woman, the seed in man, and nursed the son in the womb. The fledgling in the egg chirped because he gave it breath and brought it forth at term. When he rose in the east, darkness was driven away, men stood upon their feet, raised their arms in adoration and set about their work. The cattle in their pastures, the trees and plants, the birds fluttering in the marshes, the antelopes that danced upon their feet, every creature that flew or walked lived because he shone upon them. Aten was god not merely of the Nile valley, but of all the world. In far-off Babylonia, Syria and Kush, as in the land of Egypt, he set every man of every color in his place, supplied his necessities and reckoned his days.

It is generally agreed that Akhnaten was the first to achieve the idea of monotheism. As the end product of a solar doctrine which had been undergoing rapid transformation in parallel with the expanding empire, its universalism probably had its origin in the military consolidation of Egypt and the Asiatic provinces. Where Aten differed from Ra was in his jealousy of other gods, his abhorrence of sacred images of any kind, and in forthright condemnation of all other forms of worship. Akhnaten's doctrine is distinctively monotheistic chiefly because of this unprecedented eruption of iconoclasm and intolerance. Further differences between Aten and the old solar beliefs are to be found in the abstract nature and affective attributes of the godhead: Ra of the Pyramid Age had pursued a carnal life in the solar heavens, drinking wine, stealing women, killing other gods and eating their vitals in order to obtain the Red and Green; and he had in time grown senile and had been forced to abdicate by Isis's theft of his magic power. Not even Amen, god of wind, had escaped anthropomorphic materialization and had perforce been identified with Ra in order to justify his claims. But abruptly in Akhnaten's hands the carnal aspects of the deity disappear entirely; Aten possesses only the intangible, immaterial qualities of light, heat or radiance: he has not even an image apart from the disk with radiating arms of light. If not truly an abstract deity, he is at least extraordinarily dematerialized. At the same time he apparently drops magical devices of every kind. There is an altar on which incense is burned and offerings are placed, but there are no amulets or words of power except as talismanic potency is transferred to the almost personal hymns of praise and prayers. Paradoxically, as the deity loses human outlines he acquires in increased degree the human traits of love and beneficence. Akhnaten, as it were, destroyed the ancient carnal gods in order to sublime from their remains a divine attar of affection.

Perhaps it was because he was so moved by emotional exuberance, so engrossed with love of nature and concerned with beauty, that there is in Akhnaten's hymns and prayers, at least so far as they have been preserved at Amarna, little emphasis on righteousness. The king explicitly identifies himself with *maat* in his royal name and in several utterances, but translators here interpret this word as 'truth.' If Aten was at all concerned with human behavior it was with its affective rather than its moral pattern. His chief priest, Akhnaten, was so suffused with this affection that the sordid necessities of living in this world and the best methods of winning to an eternal blessedness in the next were forgotten as completely as black shadows were dispelled by Aten's brilliant light. The Judgment was forgotten, magical amulets and incantations were cast aside, the coffin tests were replaced by hymns of praise, and the heart scarab no longer bore a spell to avert an unfavorable decision before the tribunal of the gods, but a simple prayer in the name of Aten for a long life and a happy one.

Akhnaten has received more than his share of extravagant praise and blame. There can be no doubt that he was natural and spontaneous, with little respect for the ancient conventions and traditions of his time; history records no individual before him, and few after him, so capable of throwing tradition bodily overboard. That he was a poet, a dreamer, an idealist possessed with an illusion of the sweet reasonableness of creation, is evident. What manner of man he was otherwise remains something of a mystery. Breasted calls him a 'god-intoxicated man,' 'the first Individual in history,' 'a lovely idealist . . . ecstatic in his sense of the beauty of the eternal and universal light.' Budge uses the adjectives 'clever, unusually precocious, fearless, courageous and obstinate,' and speaks of his 'religious madness.' 'Satisfied with his religion and happy in his domestic circle he passed several years in playing the priest and directing the choral services in his temple, and the religious dances, and the acrobatic performances in which his followers delighted.' Shorter speaks of him as an 'unbalanced genius,' one who 'possessed the mind and outlook of a fanatic.' Elliott Smith examined a mummy which was believed to have been the king's — the point has never been settled — and concluded that he suffered from an endocrine disease some of the characteristics of which are infantilism, feminization of the body and character, and not infrequently profound mental disbalance. But the mummy is claimed by later authorities not to be that of Akhnaten, and much better evidence, which possibly will never be forthcoming, would be required to appraise accurately the make-up of this exotic king.

What can be accepted is that Akhnaten's esoteric doctrines proved to be wholly abominable to the Egyptians. His richly endowed priests, drawn from the previously obscure Aten cult or from his own court, were a source of jealousy to the deposed priests of Amen whom he had treated as criminals. The common run of men mistrusted a deity who loved their enemies as much as themselves. Long familiar with the picture of Ra riding across the sky in his magnificent bark, and with the resurrection of Osiris in the growing grain, they failed utterly to comprehend the movements of the sun and the prosperity of the crops in terms of the beneficence of an almost immaterial being. They could not understand why the sacred holiday feasts, the stirring dramas of the temples, the daily rituals and customs that were the very heart of communal life should suddenly become iniquities. The mourners who left their dead in the cemeteries of the plateau were denied the comfort of Osiris; they could not even place in the coffin a few spells to help the dead on his journey to the nether world, for the scribes had been forbidden to copy the Book of the Dead. The shepherd who protected his flocks by leaving a small offering for the goddess of the tree or spring, the fisherman who threw overboard a handful of his catch to appease the crocodile, the mother who used a spell to cure her sick babe, were commanded to put aside these well tried customs in which they had every confidence and to place their trust in a new god who was a total stranger. It was as though the people had been ordered to throw themselves from the highest cliffs of the valley in the faith that Aten's rays would carry them safely to the earth.

In the meantime, first the Amorites and then the Hittites gained control of Syria, and Egyptian authority in the north came to a quick and humiliating end. In the south, city after city was captured, sacked and burned by the Canaanites and Khabiri, until the collapse of the Asiatic provinces was revealed for the major disaster that it really was. Faced with the dismemberment of the empire, the nobles of Akhnaten's court deserted him and filtered back to Thebes. Surrounded only by a few friends, the king died in 1358 B.C., knowing no doubt that he had failed not only in what he most wanted to achieve, the establishment of his god of love, but also in the responsibilities of a Pharaoh.

Immediately after Akhnaten's death the discontent and bitterness which he had excited set into a violent reaction. He was succeeded by his son-in-law, who died within two years; and then the double crown went to Tutankhaten, the husband of Ankhsenamen, Akhnaten's third daughter, who was probably not over twelve years old, and possibly no more than nine, at his succession. Putty in the hands of the priests of Amen-Ra, Tutankhaten (Beautiful-is-the-Life-of-Aten) quickly changed his name back to Tutankhamen (Beautiful-is-the-Life-of-Amen) and permitted the deposed deity to pay Aten back in kind: Amen-Ra's temples were rebuilt and their wealth returned, and Aten's wealth was confiscated.

In subsequent years the bitterness engendered by Akhnaten's persecution of the priests of Amen-Ra and Osiris, by his loss of Syria, and by his esoteric doctrines generally, became so great that all inscriptions referring either to his god or himself were utterly destroyed, thus damning him to annihilation beyond the tomb as well as in this world. The city which he had built at Tell el-Amarna was abandoned and soon fell into decay. Covered by mud and sand it remained lost from history for thirty-two centuries, until an old woman was found one day in Cairo peddling at a shilling the basketful some cuneiform tablets which she had found in the desert — the relics of the 'House of the Rolls' where Akhnaten had filed his records of state and those of his father, the Golden Emperor. History has a queer way of serving its disciples, for much of the invaluable literature of the New Empire, correspondence touching every corner and every affair of the civilized world of the 14th century B.C., was sold to tourists and lost before its value was recognized, while the tomb of Akhnaten's son-in-law, Tutankhamen — a 'tenth-rate Pharaoh of a decadent Egypt' — simply because in the reaction which followed Aten's fall it had been carefully hidden beneath the sand, was destined to remain intact for the modern tomb robbers who have deciphered Egypt's history. Tutankhamen was a mere child at his death and by no means a rich Pharaoh, yet the gold and jewels and exquisite art which his tomb contained have provided the most complete and magnificent example yet known of the splendor of a Pharaoh's grave.

Though later kings were momentarily to recapture the country beyond the Isthmus, Egypt's frontiers were broken and she remained henceforth in almost unceasing conflict with the armies of Hatti, Assyria and Babylonia. The priests of Amen, restoring themselves to power under Tutankhamen, soon elevated the office of high priest to a place inferior only to that of the king, and by 100 B.C. the chief priest had become the king. From this time on, with few interruptions, Egypt remained a theocracy. Amenism became the state church, the high priest became the head of both state and church, and the fortunes of the nation were decided by the temple oracles. In the restoration of 700 B.C. the people of the Nile momentarily became conscious of their great past and scribes sought out the ancient papyri and carefully copied them. But in this process of conserving and exalting the sacred words of the ancestors, who three millenniums before had laid the foundations of civilization, they only sank deeper and deeper into fetish worship, into the innumerable rituals and incantations of a sacerdotal state, until they seemed to Herodotus to be 'the most religious people in the world.'

I I

The Great Mother

FROM remote antiquity the Egyptians knew well enough that they could not indicate upon their maps the actual location of mountains which upheld the sky. They maintained the cosmological fiction because it was elastic, the invisible pillars of heaven being easily pushed farther afield as knowledge of new lands was brought home by venturesome wanderers. Yet it was with a certain justice that the men of the Old Kingdom considered their country to be the center of the world, themselves to be the only civilized beings, for at the farthest limits of their travels they found only barbarians to whom the finer arts of agriculture, masonry, sculpture, painting and the like were quite unknown. The Egyptians, moreover, were never great explorers, their expeditions being confined to the upper reaches of the Nile or the Red Sea coast, or at the farthest venturing across the Isthmus of Suez into the Sinai Peninsula. Consequently even the country of Syria which lay immediately beyond the wedge of Sinai remained for them an almost unknown land until the period of the New Empire when Thothmes brought its western edge under the double crown.

Yet even while the Pharaohs were building the great pyramids, neolithic culture was crystallizing into a civilization of sorts far to the east of Syria, in the valley of the Tigris and Euphrates. Like that of Egypt, the civilization of Mesopotamia had its origin in the rich alluvium of a river valley which was flooded yearly, but unlike the Nile, the Tigris and Euphrates held no mystery in their pulsation. Arising in the snow-covered mountains of Armenia, these rivers ran a relatively short course to the Persian Gulf and were accessible to navigation from beginning to end, so that the peoples who inhabited their banks were enabled to observe the inevitable sequence of rain and flood.

The climate of Mesopotamia has changed so much that it is difficult to believe that the country was once the paradigm of the Garden of Eden.

Where as late as the time of Herodotus there stood the great cities of Ur, Sumer and Babylon, there remain now but hummocks of earth scarcely distinguishable from the surrounding desert of sterile, ever shifting sand, about the most intolerable sites for human habitation of any place on earth. In the hot season the temperature reaches 137° in the shade, while dust storms, so dense that they may completely hide the sun, envelop the country for six weeks on end. As in all desert countries, winter is equally extreme. This change in climate is attributable in part to desiccation of the land. At an early date the Euphratean peoples had learned to restrain the river between high artificial banks and to divert its water through a network of irrigation canals; then, around 300 B.C., the river burst its man-made banks and cut a new channel for itself; when the artificial water supply which had maintained a grassy cover failed, the soil dried out and blew away until there was left only desert sand. With no evaporation from soil or verdure to cool the air in summer, and no blanket of humidity to preserve the sun's heat in winter, the temperature now ranges between extremes which are suggestive of the atmosphereless moon.

Yet in the days of Abraham, Sumer was one vast granary and Ur and Babylon were competing for the domination of a great and wealthy empire. The countryside was dotted with prosperous hamlets, villages and farms, and rich with crops of vegetables, wheat, barley, sesame and fruits. Along the irrigated land the grass reached a height of fifteen feet, while on the surrounding prairie flowers grew in such luxuriance that in the lush season one who walked among them was dusted with their multicolored pollen. Moist hollows held the date palm which, as in Egypt, proved to be the most valuable of trees, for from its fruit the people manufactured bread, wine, vinegar and cakes, the wood being turned into numerous utensils and the stones used for charcoal fires or given as fattening food to cattle, pigs and sheep. The Mesopotamians tended the date with loving care and early discovered how to fertilize the female flowers by shaking over them the flowers of the male palm. The fig, apple, almond, apricot and olive, plane trees, cypresses, tamarisks, acacias and of course the grape vine made up a great orchard that stretched from the Armenian mountains down to the Persian Gulf. Fish and birds were abundant; the dog, ass, sheep and ox were domesticated before historic times, and the lion, elephant, panther, deer, wild ass and boar were indigenous inhabitants.

Stone was rare in Mesopotamia and was not used except as decoration or for statuary. The principal element of construction was brick, prepared by mixing the clay of the marshes with straw or reeds and drying the square or oblong packet in the sun. Artificial firing was sometimes used, but even at their best these bricks softened in the rain and ultimately consolidated into a compact mass, which explains why the ancient houses constructed of them are today but mounds of earth irregularly eroded by rain and covered with windblown sand. Everywhere the excavator finds a story of alternate building and dissolution; generation after generation built upon the decomposed and leveled residue of their predecessors' houses until the last abode stands many feet above the natural land. Even the citizens of the twentieth century B.C. walked over the homes and tombs of forgotten dead.

The Mesopotamian city possessed an almost appealing ugliness: its brick buildings, huddled close together, were all alike, their flat roofs relieved only by stepped battlements in the angles of the streets — if the narrow passageways between the houses could be so dignified, for they were rarely straight for a distance of more than half-a-dozen houses and they so interlaced with each other that they resembled a tangled spider web. They were either dusty or muddy and invariably littered with refuse left to be cleaned away by flocks of ravens or by wandering goats or dogs. Though the dull brickwork was occasionally ornamented by an inlay of red, black or yellow terra cotta cones arranged in geometric patterns, or by awnings of colored matting or woven rugs stretched above the roofs, on the whole the city was a vast conglomerate of angular lights and shadows monotonously repeated in every view.

The outstanding building in the city was the temple or *ziggurat* (high place), a great tower of solid brickwork built in three or more stages with sloping sides and reinforced by buttresses that gave it the appearance of a stepped pyramid. Stairways led to the top of each stage, where were planted flowers and trees, and finally to the uppermost cubicle wherein the god was housed. In the surrounding court were temples and shrines to minor gods, kitchens and living quarters for the attendants, counting rooms and warehouses, all the accessories of a rich and busy temple. The lower courses of the *ziggurat* and of the court walls were faced with vertical stripes of black and white bricks; the great gates were of boxwood overlaid with bronze, with hinges of silver and door posts of gold; the temple and frequently the smaller shrines were paneled inside with cedarwood, their ceilings painted blue and set with golden stars and crescent moons, their floors covered with matting and rugs; and along the walls were arranged statues of minor gods carved in diorite or alabaster and crowned with gold. The walls of the sanctuary were sheathed with thin gold cut into a pattern of overlapping scales and set with lapis lazuli and agate and turquoise-blue paste. One of the most important rooms high up in the *ziggurat* was the dark bed chamber to which the priestess went by night to become the bride of the god, and by this mystic marriage to renew the fertility of the soil and the strength of the king's arms.

The essence of worship was sacrifice, since that which was sacrificed was shared between the god, his priests who performed the sacrifice and the worshiper who supplied it. The god demanded the first fruits, the best of that which by his favor had been bestowed on man, and so to him the farmer brought his cattle and barley, the peasant his jars of milk and cheese, the merchant his wool and linen, incense, spices, copper and gold, and porters staggered through the temple gates bent under massive blocks of diorite to be carved into a divine image, or of hard wood for the furnishing of a new temple. Crowds milled about the attendants who counted and weighed or otherwise appraised the ever flowing stream of gifts while they kept careful tallies and wrote out duplicate receipts on damp tablets of clay, one for the donor and one to be filed in the temple archives. Among the chattels brought to the *ziggurat* the most notable were the male and female slaves who were sold to the highest bidder, or contributed to the god himself: for the god controlled vast gardens and farms which had to be worked, innumerable industries where were manufactured utensils, jewelry, cotton or linen goods, as well as great mines and trade routes; and in addition he required for the services of the temple troops of laborers, eunuchs, women singers and sacred courtesans. The practice of slavery, never more widespread in history than here, constituted the primary basis of economics, and laws designed to protect both slave and master were among the earliest to be formulated in the East. Indeed, such laws were an outstanding feature in the famous code which Hammurabi engraved upon the diorite shaft that he set up in the temple of the great god Marduk in Babylon, and, even more than the laws of Egypt, supplied the principles of equity to the Mediterranean world.

So important was the holy traffic of the temple that at the opening of Mesopotamian history the priests virtually controlled the country. They acted as intermediaries in all business transactions, they lent grain and precious metals at high rates of interest, they dictated the laws of marriage, slavery and real estate, and otherwise by their sacred trusteeship invaded all economic life. It was the essential tragedy of the Land of the Two Rivers, the prototype of the Garden of Eden, that it never gained freedom from the dominance of the priestly mind.

ii

At Kish, Ur, Susa and Tell al-Ubaïd, excavations have penetrated through the stratified debris of the ancient cultures to find at the lowermost level pottery and other artifacts belonging to the first inhabitants who occupied these sites for any period of time. Any reading of the stratigraphic record must allow considerable latitude for error, for the discoveries at various sites are not as yet satisfactorily collated, nor are authorities agreed on dates, but a free reconstruction indicates that about 5000 B.C. there were settled along the Euphrates one or more types of neolithic people who made a good pottery not greatly different from the almost contemporary Badarian and Tasian cultures of Egypt. At this time another neolithic people, the proto-Elamites from the Iranian plateau, were spreading southward and westward to establish colonies at Susa, Eridu, Ur, Tell al-Ubaïd and other sites along the two rivers. A third group, the Sumerians, were invading the country from the Persian Gulf and bringing with them pictographic writing and the arts of making bricks and of building cities on mounds raised some feet above the water level.

Then, about 4200 B.C., came the great flood which echoes in Babylonian and Semitic lore. Floods were not uncommon in the lowlands of Mesopotamia where the rivers rise rapidly as spring melts the ice and snow in the northern mountains, but this one laid down a six- to ten-foot layer of clay and mud at Kish and Tell al-Ubaïd, indicating that water had covered the lowlands to a depth of perhaps twenty feet. The severity of this particular flood implies exceptionally heavy spring rains combined with the sudden melting of northern snow fields left from the Gschnitz glaciation of some ten centuries before. The reed huts of the earlier inhabitants were washed away and perhaps most of the people were drowned; only the Sumerians who took refuge in their unique, elevated brick cities escaped wholesale destruction.

Perhaps at the time of their immigration by way of the Persian Gulf, and certainly by a short time afterwards, the Sumerians had developed pictographic writing, invented the chariot which was pulled by oxen, and learned the use of bronze. Excavations in the royal cemetery at Ur indicate that by 3100 B.C. they were organized into distinctive classes of slaves, shepherds, agriculturists, craftsmen and merchants, priests, soldiers and government officials. Gold was brought from many lands, silver from Persia, bronze from Oman, lapis lazuli from the Pamirs, amazonite from southern India, conch shells from the Persian Gulf; calcite for vases, diorite for cups, cornelian for beads, malachite for eye paint — all came from far-away lands and meant trade, discipline, order and the exchange of ideas.

Mesopotamia was hopelessly exposed to aggression from every side, but apart from the danger of foreign invasion no city ever let down its guard against its nearest neighbor. After the Flood the Sumerians gained control of the country and founded the Ist Dynasty of Erech, but they were displaced shortly by the rise of Ur to military power, and for the next millennium the country was engaged in a tug of war between competing city states. About 2500 B.C. the Sumerian and Semitic peoples were consolidated around the city of Akkad under the leadership of Sargon to form the first mighty eastern empire, the Kingdom of Sumer and Akkad. As in the case of Horus, it was afterwards related that Sargon had been born in concealment and set adrift in a basket of bulrushes on the waters of the Euphrates; he had been rescued by Akki, the husbandman, who brought him up as his own son until, when he had reached the age of manhood, the goddess Ishtar fell in love with him; then, his true origin becoming known, the crown was placed upon his head and he entered on a career of foreign conquest.

The empire founded by Sargon was disrupted in a few years (2370 B.C.) by the invasion of the Guti, and in succeeding centuries underwent a series of vicissitudes. In the meantime Babylon, midway between Sumer and Ur, had so grown in strength that its Amorite king, Hammurabi (1940 B.C.), was able to consolidate the land into an empire that greatly exceeded Sargon's in extent and embraced most of western Asia. Yet like all its predecessors, Hammurabi's empire was short-lived, and about 1780 B.C. it fell before the Hittites and the Kassites, the latter bringing with them a strange 'animal of the mountains,' the domesticated horse. Not until 800 B.C. was reconsolidation possible; then the city-state of Assur expelled the invaders permanently and, by probably the cruelest warfare in history, united the country of the Two Rivers with all of Syria and Palestine into the second great empire of the East, Assyria.

While the geography of Mesopotamia tended to produce perpetual war, its physical features were responsible for the fact that, apart from fighting, the people were preoccupied with trade. Since there was no flint for the making of fine tools, no stone and practically no timber, there was no massive architecture and relatively little art. Apart from farming and brickmaking the chief outlet for endeavor was in commerce, and from first to last the Sumerians, Babylonians and Assyrians were travelers, bankers and keepers of accounts. Yet since wealth and good business, like good crops, were favors of the gods, the oldest monumental buildings were temples to the deities, and the oldest written records were the ledgers of sacred scribes. But nothing could be more typical of Mesopotamian culture than the facts that amulets were transformed by the Semites of prehistoric times into magic 'seals' wherewith a man could consecrate or put his taboo upon whatever other men might covet, and that writing was first developed not to record the worship of divinities or the exploits of kings but for the practical device of keeping accounts.

Because of the difficulty of drawing accurate pictograms on clay tablets the Sumerian writing rapidly degenerated into conventional cuneiform symbols which were made with the beveled tip of a reed, the bricks and prisms of fine clay on which these symbols were commonly inscribed being rendered hard and durable by baking. If desired, privacy was obtained by covering the inscribed tablet with another layer of clay on which was inscribed the name and address of the recipient, after which the tablet was given a second baking.

iii

No contemporary literature is available to reveal the details of life or the beliefs of the Sumerians of the time of Ur. The extant records go back scarcely beyond 2000 B.C., and for knowledge of the people of ancient Akkad and Babylon, history is chiefly indebted to the Assyrian king, Ashurbanipal, who ruled from Nineveh about the middle of the seventh century B.C. Ashurbanipal, though ferociously cruel to his enemies, as were all Mesopotamian kings, was a savant, an educated man, a patron of learning and a lover of books; in fact, among the spoils of war he treasured most highly those written works of his enemies which dealt with their history and their gods.

He sent his scribes into all the ancient seats of learning, Akkad, Assur, Babylon, Nippur, Ur, to make copies of the books that were preserved in these places, and these copies he installed in his own palace, or in the nearby temple of Nebo. These books consisted of tablets of the finest homogeneous clay which lent itself admirably to the cuneiform script, and they were written with rare mistakes in a uniform, almost perfect hand. It is possible that the king inscribed and baked many of them himself. The decipherment of the ancient Sumerian literature presented innumerable difficulties, even in Ashurbanipal's time, and to facilitate translation it was necessary to draw up bilingual texts consisting of the signs in one column and, in adjacent columns, the names given to these signs, the phonetic spelling, and the Sumerian or Assyrian equivalents, often with a gloss to complete the explanation.

Perhaps it was the deflection of Ashurbanipal's energy from political and military strategy to scholarly matters that accounted for his difficulties in affairs of state; he let a treacherous brother weaken the solidarity of his empire by fomenting rebellion in Babylon, he failed to hold Egypt in subjugation, and he permitted the Scythians, or Medes, as the Greeks called them, to grow to dangerous power in the East. When he died, the Assyrian empire was drained of its resources and military strength, and only a few years passed before its complete collapse. In 612 B.C. the Scythians occupied Nineveh, and a few decades later the Persians under Cyrus tore down the walls and leveled the buildings with military thoroughness. But they neglected Ashurbanipal's library as of no significance and it lay buried under the fallen bricks. The wind blew a shroud of sand over the ruins until the whole of Nineveh was to all outward appearances but an outcropping of desert rock. When, in 1845, archaeologists began excavating a mud pile representing the remains of an unidentified city, they found there the remnants of this great king's books.

It was unfortunate that the fire-stained, broken contents of Ashurbanipal's library, which represented thousands of volumes, suffered more injury from careless packing when first discovered than they had suffered from the hands of the Medes and Babylonians. The strangely marked bits of clay were thought to be merely decorated pottery, the significance of the inscriptions being then unknown; they were dumped into baskets, with great breakage, and sent down the river on rafts to be shipped to England on a passing man-of-war. But from such fragments as were saved, and from others collected from the ruins of the temple of Nebo and totaling nearly 30,000, there comes most of what knowledge is available about the ancient cities of the Fertile Crescent.

Long before Hammurabi codified the laws of Mesopotamia, the people had read into the constellations the personalities of many deities. The gods of Ur and Babylon, of the Sumerians and Semites, had been mingled together in inextricable confusion as new deities had risen to power by virtue of the military prowess of one or another of the great cities of the empire, but out of the diverse elements there had been forged a major pantheon. Shamash was originally the sun, Sin the moon, and Ishtar both the evening star which precedes the appearance of the moon and the morning star which heralds the approaching sun, and in the beginning Ea had charged Sin, Shamash and Ishtar with the ruling of the sky, apportioning the day and the night between them. Marduk was originally the local god of Babylon, but when that city came to the front politically under Hammurabi, he advanced in prestige until to all purposes he usurped the divine leadership. His chief feast fell at the time of the spring equinox and became for every Babylonian a general New Year period of rejoicing. He was probably first conceived as embodied in the spring sun which brought new life and light, more primitively perhaps as a god of vegetation. With his rise to supremacy there was coupled to his name the Semitic word Ba'al, meaning lord or master, so that he came to be called Bel-Marduk.

Of special interest among the books in Ashurbanipal's library are those recounting the history of Bel-Marduk, and known as the *Seven Tablets of Creation,* or the *Fight between Bel-Marduk and the Dragon, Tiamat.* Though it is probable that none of these was actually inscribed before Ashurbanipal's time, the legend they record can be traced by other fragments as far back as 2000 B.C., and that it was in existence in the time of Sargon (2500 B.C.) is indicated by fragmentary evidence. In addition to the Nineveh records, Berossus, a priest of Marduk, wrote a history of Babylon in Greek in 280 B.C., and fragments of this history preserved in the works of later Greek writers afford a confirmation of the cuneiform texts.

In the beginning, according to the *Seven Tablets of Creation,* there were only Tiamat (primordial substance) and Apsu (matter), the mother and father of all things. These beings engendered Mummu (confusion, chaos), with whom they were mingled together in a single, formless mass. After countless eons of quiescence, one might say of divine peace, there were evolved from this admixture a number of gods and a number of grotesque demons. After further eons the gods and demons, by their ceaseless movement, clamor and song, troubled the peace of Tiamat: 'Indeed they upset Tiamat's belly by song in the midst of the divine abode.' Apsu was troubled, too, and when he could not diminish their brawl he summoned Mummu and together they went to Tiamat to complain. 'They lay down [on a couch] facing Tiamat. They took counsel together about the gods [their children]. Apsu took up his word and said, To Tiamat, the holy one, he made mention of a matter, [saying] Their way has been vexatious to me. By day I find no peace, by night I have no rest. Verily, I will make an end of them, I will have their way scattered. Let there be silence established; lo, then we shall rest.'

Thus spoke Apsu, wishing to destroy the gods who annoyed him by bringing 'order' into the formless world. Tiamat was outraged at Apsu for proposing such a thing, and recommended kindness. Mummu encouraged his father, however, and offered to destroy the gods for him. So they plotted, but the rumor of the plot escaped and the gods took secret counsel to defend themselves. Ea, 'the prudent god, the exalted one,' by sympathetic magic induced Apsu to go to sleep, and slew him, and in a mad whirl of battle Mummu's manly parts were cut off, his joints were loosened, his 'light' was removed and misery was made his lot. Then the gods returned to the begetting of their kind and to their noisy ways. Tiamat, angered by Apsu's death, now turned upon the gods herself. She spewed out a mass of demons to aid her, among which were the constellations, the Viper, the Snake, the Lakhamu, the Whirlwind, the Dog, and Scorpion-man, the mighty Stormwind, the Fish-man and the Capricorn, and these she put under the direction of Kingu, her second husband, to whom she also gave the Tablet of Destinies, fastening it upon his breast, saying, "As for thee, thy command shall not fall empty, what goeth forth from thy mouth shall be established." The gods, alarmed by the frightful mobilization of Tiamat's forces, held counsel again, thinking in their fright, "Nowhere is there a god who will attack Tiamat. He would not escape from Tiamat's presence with his life." However, such a courageous one was found in the god Marduk; but Marduk astutely demanded before going into battle that he be exalted: "If I am to be your avenger to slay Tiamat, and bestow life on you, Summon a meeting, proclaim and magnify my position, Sit yet down together in friendly fashion in Upshuk-kinaku, Let me determine destinies by the opening of my mouth even as ye do. Whatsoever I bring to pass let it remain unaltered. That which my mouth uttereth shall neither fail nor be brought to nought." When the gods agreed to this request, Marduk, having first tested his newly acquired divinity by making a cloak to disappear and reappear, and thereby knowing himself to be King of the Gods, took for his arms the winds and the lightning and met Tiamat in a mighty conflict in which he slew her and scattered her allies.

The death of Tiamat, primordial substance and the mother of the gods, occurred when she opened her mouth to its greatest extent, for then Marduk made the four winds of the heavens and the seven winds of the typhoon to enter her so that her lips could not close, and the raging winds filled her belly and gripped her heart. He then shot an arrow into her, cleaving her bowels, piercing her heart, destroying her life. The gods were of course greatly pleased with Marduk's success, as indeed was Marduk himself. He thereupon devised a cunning plan to dispose of Tiamat once and for all. He slit her 'open like a shellfish into two pieces. The one half he raised up and made the heavens as a shade therewith; He pulled the bolt, he posted a guard, He ordered them not to let her water escape.'

Then he assigned gods to inhabit the holy places — that is, he set in heaven the sun and moon and the constellations, and gave them the laws which they were never to transgress. From the other half of Tiamat's body Marduk created the earth. The portion of the tablet which may have contained the details of this event is most unfortunately missing.

The gods who had fought at Tiamat's side, Marduk chastized. Kingu, 'who led the rebellion against the gods, he crushed utterly, and took from him the precious Tablet of Destinies which never should have been his in the first place, and sealed it upon his own breast.' Then he fettered this rebellious deity and confined him in a 'dark place.'

It was not long before the gods complained of boredom, their existence being dull because they lacked worshipers to make them offerings. So Marduk devised another 'cunning plan': "I will create the Man. The service of the gods shall be established, and they shall be at rest." Marduk's plan was to create man out of the blood of a god and the bone of earth, and at Ea's suggestion, and 'for the consolation of the gods,' Kingu, the rebellious god, was sacrificed. Kingu was bound, his blood was let, and from it Ea 'fashioned mankind for the service of the gods, and set the gods free.' Everyone was so pleased with the final arrangement that Marduk was chosen and empowered as their leader, not only decreeing the fates of men from the Tablet of Destinies which he wore upon his breast, but also ordering the affairs of the heavens. Men, grateful to Marduk, their hero and creator, built for him a temple at a site which Marduk himself picked out on the banks of the Euphrates; and they called the temple Ba-Bel — the 'Gate of God.'

iv

Among the elements in the *Seven Tablets of Creation* which are notable for their historical precedent are the notion of chaos or confusion as a primeval state, the general story of creation which, authorities agree, furnished the pattern for the later Hebrew version, and the rebellious god who was punished and locked up in a dark place. Of chief significance, however, for Mesopotamia itself was the Tablet of Destinies which Marduk carried upon his breast.

The people of the Two Rivers accepted the principle of causality in its most elementary form. When two events had been noticed to happen one after the other, they assumed that the first was the cause of the second; if a plague followed the eclipse of the sun on a particular day, it was expected that a recurrence of the eclipse on the same day would be followed by a recurrence of the plague. Since so many phenomena followed the recurring cycle of the stars, they logically read celestial causes behind all terrestrial events. They conceived that the gods assembled every morning to deliberate on the affairs of the day, when Ea submitted to them the fates which were about to be fulfilled; after these had been approved, a record was made of them on Marduk's Tablet of Destinies.

It is not clear why the gods left any escape from the fate inscribed on Marduk's tablet, but escape there was, by means of divination. In Egypt divination had been a matter of obtaining celestial advice, and even on occasion required some celestial cogitation; but along the Tigris and Euphrates the day's agenda was not subject to amendment, and the sole hope of the victims of the divine decisions was to discover these decisions in advance; accordingly as they were favorable or unfavorable, the victim could move to or from the trap.

The belief in divination served to give direction to Mesopotamian culture as belief in a future life had given direction to the culture of the Nile, the force of the custom being such as to give the priesthood complete domination of the country for over thirty centuries. The king, as high priest of the state, took the responsibility for divination in national affairs, while the daily needs of the people were met by the vast staff of temple priests. The gods revealed their plans to the seers in dreams, or inspired them to speak, or caused the statues in the temples to give answers, or signaled their assent or dissent from stones, trees, springs and weapons. Prophetic significance was attached to the behavior of drops of oil on water, the actions of dogs, horses, birds, fish and serpents, the burning of fire or the rising of smoke, and one of the most popular means of reading the dispositions of the divinities was in the observation of the entrails, and especially the livers, of sacrificial animals. The liver was supposed to be the seat of life, and the interpretation of slight variations in its conformation and markings constituted a specialty, inscribed clay models of sheep livers being used to educate novices in the art. All dreams were charged with prophecy, and there were special divinities of dreams to whom prayers were addressed for favorable visitations; since revelation could best be obtained in sacred places, it was the custom for applicants to incubate, or sleep in the temple, after offering the appropriate sacrifice. Incubation was also practiced to cure disease, and was so systematized that the priests not only prescribed stimulants to induce the desired therapeutic ecstasies but, failing to cure the sick man, would sleep for him on the incubation floor.

A notable feature of the Mesopotamian pantheon was its general viciousness. On occasion Marduk's tablet might decree good health and fortune for a man, but the general lot seems to have been an almost continuous state of misery, as though the gods were chronically choleric. No venture could succeed unless the relevant god was in the proper mood. Particular hours, days, weeks and months were dedicated to the making of bricks, the planting of seed, the reaping of grain or the making of wine; to do any of these tasks at the wrong time would be disastrous. Every seventh day was sacred to the moon god, Sin, an evil day on which a man dare not eat cooked flesh, change his garment, offer sacrifices, ride in a chariot, give an oracle, speak a malediction or begin anything new lest the venture be attended by dire misfortune.

No country ever seems to have suffered more from the malignancy of the supernatural. Written texts preserve the names of several thousand gods on whose whims human affairs depended, and the number of lesser spirits, demons, goblins, imps, ghouls, good and evil genii must have been uncountable. These baleful beings, usually grouped in bands of seven, lurked in graves, in shadows, in mountains, in dens in the earth, behind rocks and trees and hedges, in the storehouse, the oven, the door, even in the libation vase. 'They are wicked, they are wicked,' was the universal opinion. Such was the trepidation of the people that scarcely a day passed without their repairing to the temple to fortify themselves against the attacks of demons by sacrifice, purification with sacred water or oil, fumigation in the smoke of torches or aromatic censers, by burning a waxen image of the demon, or by confession. The last was carried to the point where the people confessed categorically and in an all-inclusive manner, in order to avoid the possibility of failing to confess and therefore being punished for some forgotten or unconsciously committed transgression.

Yet in spite of daily ablutions and purifications, in spite of frequent sacrifices and repeated consultation with the oracles, in spite of the fact that the people lived in a constant state of penitence, the malignant beings kept the upper hand. Misfortune continued to be a part of life, and death continued to be its end.

It was perhaps because the moist soil of Mesopotamia promoted the rapid decomposition of the corpse that the people never made any effort at mummification, and when they rendered the traditional services to the departed, they never posited that the afterlife was dependent upon the preservation of the body. Up to the time of Sargon, the dead, at least in the city of Ur, had been buried in cemeteries in which the graves were arranged regularly and one above another. With the body there were usually interred a few clay vessels for food and drink; in the case of wealthy persons the funerary equipment might be of copper or stone and include a modest quantity of jewelry. The pit tombs of the kings of the Ist Dynasty of Kish were almost as richly equipped as the royal tombs of Egypt; they contained chariots drawn by asses, wagons with oxen, and personal accessories, jewelry and the like frequently made of gold and lapis lazuli. With the bones of these great chiefs were the bones of servants, men-at-arms, charioteers and harpists who had been despatched to join the king. These tombs were dug as pits, sometimes to a depth of twenty feet, through layers of broken pottery, bricks and rubbish which had been accumulating through the centuries, and yet failed to reach the bottom of this debris, showing the long period during which the site had been occupied.

The life which the dead led in the spirit world was definitely worse than that which the living led in this one, and the people resigned themselves to face it as a dreadful but necessary end. The land of the dead, Aralû, was under the domination of the angry goddess Allat, who was full of grim menace and easily provoked to violence, and her husband, Nergal, god of fever and plague. Allat's realm was situated in the western part of the earth and was surrounded by seven walls. Here newcomers were passed through a sort of judgment in which their fate was determined by the lavishness of the offerings and sacrifices which they had made in life. Those who were wanting were consumed by leprosy to the end of time, while those who met the demands of Allat were permitted to drag out a miserable existence in gloom, eating the dust of the earth, suffering from the pangs of thirst and hunger, shivering with cold and constantly plagued by the demons of darkness. Domestic affection, friendships, all memories were effaced, nothing remaining but an inexpressible regret at having been exiled from the world and an excruciating desire to reach the light once more.

v

The Mesopotamian peoples forever cherished the legend that somewhere in the far corners of the earth there grew a magic fruit which would save a man from the twilight realm of Allat, and their greatest legend was the epic tale of Gilgamesh and his search for the Tree of Life. This tale occupied twelve tablets in the royal library at Nineveh, and aroused considerable interest when it was discovered that the eleventh tablet contained, as a legend within the legend, the story of the Great Flood, the ark and the destruction of men, and recounted how the Babylonian Noah, Uta-

Napishtim, was saved by the gods for immortality. Confirmatory fragments of the tale have been discovered at Ashur, Boghaz-Keui and
elsewhere in Asia Minor, on tablets of much older date than those in
Ashurbanipal's library, and seals of princes who reigned before 2500 B.C.
are engraved with episodes in which the hero and his great chief friend
Engidu are struggling with various monsters.

Gilgamesh, a man of remarkable physique and heroic character, had, according to the legend, so captivated the youth of his time by his prodigious
feats of strength and his unexcelled beauty that the elders of the city complained to Ishtar of the state of neglect to which the younger generation
had relegated them. 'He has no longer a rival in their hearts, but thy subjects are led to battle and Gilgamesh does not send one child back to his
father. Night and day they cry after him: "It is he, the shepherd of Erech,
the well-protected, he is its shepherd and master, he the powerful, the perfect and the wise."' Even the women did not escape: 'He leaves not a
single virgin to her mother, a single daughter to a warrior, a single wife
to her master.' Ishtar and the gods hearkened to the prayer of the men
of Erech and commanded the goddess Aruru to create a rival to Gilgamesh. Aruru washed her hands, took a bit of clay, cast it upon the earth
and kneaded it into a male creature who was called Engidu. Engidu's
whole body was covered with hair and his tresses were as long as those of
a woman; he was different in every way from the people of the country,
and lived in the forest eating herbs like the gazelle, drinking with the wild
cattle and roaming with the beasts of the field. Mighty in stature, invin-
cible in strength, omniscient of the past and the future, he obtained complete mastery of all the creatures of the forest and would undoubtedly
have triumphed over Gilgamesh had not the god Shamash devised a plan
to convert these two mighty warriors from enemies into lifelong friends.
So terrible was Engidu that no mere mortal could approach him, but
Shamash thought that where the strongest of men might fail by employing force, a woman might succeed by the attractions of pleasure. So
Shamash sent a hunter to the temple of Ishtar, there to choose from among
the priestesses the most beautiful. This the hunter did, and he proceeded
with the priestess to the water hole in the mountains where Engidu drank
with the animals and sported with the beasts of the water.

> The hunter went yonder and got him a priestess.
> They made themselves ready, went forth straight on.
> On the third day they came to their goal:
> The hunter and the priestess sat themselves down.

One day, a second day, they sat by the watering-place.
The wild beasts come along and drink at the watering-place.
Glad is the throng of the flood.
So too comes he, Engidu . . .
With the gazelles he eats the plants,
With the beasts he drinks at the watering-place,
His heart is happy with the throng of the flood.
Then the priestess saw him, the great strong one,
The wild fellow, the man of the steppes:
"There he is, woman!
Loosen thy buckle,
Unveil thy delight,
That he may take his fill of thee!
Hang not back, take up his lust!
When he sees thee, he will draw near.
Open thy robe that he rest upon thee!
Arouse in him rapture, the work of woman.
Then will he become a stranger to his wild beasts,
Who on his own steppes grew up with him.
His bosom will press against thee."
Then the priestess loosened her buckle,
Unveiled her delight,
For him to take his fill of her.
She hung not back, she took up his lust,
She opened her robe that he rest upon her.
She aroused in him rapture, the work of woman.
His bosom pressed against her.
Engidu forgot where he was born.
For six days and seven nights
Was Engidu given over to love with the priestess.
When he had sated himself with the fill of her,
He raised up his face to his wild ones:
At sight of Engidu, the gazelles flee away,
The wild of the fields shrink back before him.
Then Engidu marveled,
His body stood as in a spell,
His knees quivered, because his wild ran off . . .
The speed of his onset is not what it was.
He hearkens and opens his ear:
He turns about and sits down at the feet of the priestess.
He looks the priestess in the face,
And to what the priestess now speaks
His ears give heed.

The woman of Ishtar painted for him a bright picture of Erech and of the pleasant rewards that would come to him as a friend of Gilgamesh. "Thou who are superb, Engidu, as a god, why dost thou live among the beasts of the field? Come, I will conduct thee to Erech, the well-protected, to the glorious house, the dwelling of Anu and Ishtar, to the place where is Gilgamesh whose strength is supreme and who, like Urus, excels the heroes in strength." He hung upon her words and was pleased with the anticipation of having a friend. He said, "Let us go, priestess; lead me to the glorious and holy abode of Anu and Ishtar, to the place where is Gilgamesh whose strength is supreme and who, like Urus, prevails over the heroes by his strength. I will fight with him and manifest to him my power; I will send forth a panther against Erech and he must struggle with it."

So Engidu and the priestess proceeded to Erech, where Shamash tried to persuade him not to return to his mountain home. Not only would the priestess belong to him forever, but Gilgamesh would endow him with a great bed cunningly wrought, and give him a place beside him where the princes of the earth should kiss his feet; and Gilgamesh also sent on offer of entertainment, saying, however, that he would expect the customary present from a stranger and would exercise his privilege over the woman who accompanied him.

The first meeting of Gilgamesh and Engidu took place when the former came in the night to claim his right to the priestess, and Engidu violently resisted him, the two heroes fighting like bulls until Engidu was finally worsted. But the result of this combat was that the two became fast friends.

So Gilgamesh and Engidu went on various glorious exploits, one of which was the rescue of Ishtar herself, who was held captive in a cedar forest in the mountains of the east by a fearful ogre called Humbaba. After a fierce conflict, Gilgamesh and Engidu succeeded in slaying Humbaba, whereupon Ishtar offered her love to Gilgamesh.

Gilgamesh is washing himself and dressing in splendid attire, putting on his white garments, adorning himself with the royal insignia and binding on his diadem, when Ishtar sees him and is consumed by the mortal passion. 'To the love of Gilgamesh she raised her eyes, the mighty Ishtar, and she said, "Come, Gilgamesh, be my husband now. Thy love, give it to me as a gift to me and thou shalt be my spouse and I shall be thy wife. I will place thee in a chariot of lapis and gold, with golden wheels and mountings of onyx: thou shalt be drawn in it by great lions, and thou shalt enter our house with the odorous incense of cedarwood. When thou shalt have entered our house, all the country by the sea shall embrace thy feet, kings shall bow down before thee, the nobles and the great ones, the gifts of the mountains and of the plains they will bring to thee as tribute. Thy oxen shall prosper, thy sheep shall be doubly fruitful, thy mules shall spontaneously come under the yoke, thy chariot horse shall be strong and shall gallop, thy bull under the yoke shall have no rival." '

Gilgamesh is not tempted by the goddess and he repels her with abuse and contempt and insolently inquires what had become of her other mortal husbands. To be loved by the goddess Ishtar is no blessing: her love is a ruin that gives no shelter, a door that lets in the storm, a crazy building, a pitfall, defiling pitch, a leaky vessel, a crumbling stone, a worthless charm, an ill-fitting shoe. "Who was there with thy lord that had an advantage thereby?" he asks her:

> I will unfold the tale of thy lovers. Tammuz, the spouse of thy youth, thou hast condemned him to weep from year to year. Alla, the spotted sparrow hawk, thou lovedest him, afterward thou didst strike him and break his wing: he continues in the wood and cries: "Oh my wings." Thou didst afterwards love a lion of mature strength, and then didst cause him to be rent by blows seven at a time, thou lovedest also a stallion, magnificent in battle; thou didst devote him to death by the golden whip: thou didst compel him to gallop for ten leagues, thou didst devote him to exhaustion and thirst, thou didst devote to tears his mother Silili. Thou didst also love the shepherd Tabulu, who lavished incessantly upon thee the smoke of sacrifices, and daily slaughtered goats to thee; thou didst strike him and turn him into a leopard; his own servants went in pursuit of him and his dogs followed his trail. Thou didst love Ishullanu, thy father's gardener, who ceaselessly brought thee presents of fruit and decorated every day thy table. Thou raisedest thine eyes to him, thou seizedest him: "My Ishullanu, we shall eat melons, then shalt thou stretch forth thy hand and remove that which separates us." Ishullanu said to thee: "I, what dost thou require from me? Oh, my mother, prepare no food for me. I myself will not eat: anything I should eat would be for me a misfortune and a curse and my body would be stricken by a mortal coldness." Then thou didst hear him and didst transform him into a dwarf, thou didst set him up in the middle of a couch; he could not rise up, he could not get down from where he was. Thou lovest me now. Afterwards thou wilt strike me as thou didst these.

Ishtar was filled with rage and went up to heaven and complained to Anu, her father, "My father, Gilgamesh has despised me. Gilgamesh has enumerated my unfaithfulnesses, my unfaithfulnesses and my ignominies."

Anu replied in effect that it was her own fault. "Canst thou not remain quiet now that Gilgamesh has enumerated to thee thy unfaithfulnesses, thy unfaithfulnesses and thy ignominies?" But the angry Ishtar would not allow the outrage to go unpunished and she made Anu create a heavenly bull to destroy Gilgamesh, threatening that otherwise she would destroy every living thing in the entire universe by suspending the impulses of desire and the effect of love. So Anu created a bull, the terrible Urus, which thereupon attacked the city of Erech. The bull destroyed three hundred men before Gilgamesh and his great friend Engidu could slay it. Ishtar was now more angry than ever and cursed Gilgamesh. When Engidu heard Ishtar's maledictions he tore out the bull's phallus and threw it in the face of the goddess, saying, "Could I but get at thee, I would serve thee like him; I would hang his entrails about thee." Then Ishtar gathered together all her priestesses, her female votaries, her frenzied women, and together they intoned a dirge, a lamentation over the phallus.

Gilgamesh prepared from the bull's horns vessels to hold unguent for the gods and, after dedicating them in the temple, he and Engidu washed their hands in the Euphrates and took their way back to the city where the people thronged around to admire them. As Gilgamesh looked upon the women of Erech, who joined in the celebration, he asked, "Who is splendid among men, who is glorious among heroes?" To which the answer was, "Gilgamesh is splendid among men. Gilgamesh is glorious among heroes."

The beginning of the seventh tablet is badly damaged, and in the opening lines Engidu lies dying of some unexplained disease, cursing the tree from whose wood the door of his death-chamber has been fashioned:

> Had I known, thou door,
> That this would come to pass,
> And that beauty would bring this disaster,
> I had lifted the axe
> And shattered thee all! . . .

He curses Ishtar:

> Be the streets thy dwelling,
> In the shadow of the wall shalt thou house.
> Be thy feet ever weary,
> May the outcast and the despoiled
> Smite thee on the cheeks . . .
> Because thou didst lure me away from my fields.

He recounts to Gilgamesh a vision of the land of death to which he is departing:

> To a way whose road turneth not,
> To the house whose inhabitants do without light,
> Where dust is their nourishment and clay their food.
> They are as birds clothed with wings,
> They see not the light,
> They dwell in the darkness. . . .

For twelve days Engidu lies stricken, with Gilgamesh by his side seeing what it is to die, learning now to fear death. His heart is filled with grief, he buries his friend and sets out across the steppes dreading the time when he must follow him to the land of darkness. He sets out in search of the Tree of Life, for only thus can he avoid the fate of his beloved friend. No man had ever been successful in this quest, for the Tree of Life grew in a remote and terrible country, the road to which was hard and beset by many dangers, but spurred on by his fervent desire he finally makes his way to the land of his ancestor, Uta-Napishtim, who had become immortal. The various adventures that beset the hero, the dangers that he overcame, the manner in which he obtained the magic plant — which was called 'when-old-the-man-becomes-young-again' — only to lose it to a serpent while he was bathing in a pool, cannot be recounted here, but it may be noted that it was when he asked Uta-Napishtim for immortality that the latter, explaining how he himself had come by eternal life, related the story of the Flood and of the great ark which he had built and into which he had taken all the animals.

Into the tale of Gilgamesh the people of Mesopotamia had woven threads of their history, their encounters with lions and other ferocious animals, and much of their cosmology; yet these, like the affection of the brave Gilgamesh for his great chief friend Engidu, his seduction by Ishtar, the woman whom all men loved and no man could trust, and the curse she laid upon him when he spurned her, are but embroidery on the epic theme of man's search for immortality.

vi

Although Ishtar plays a major role in the drama of Gilgamesh, her importance would be misjudged were this legend alone considered. She was, in fact, the principal goddess of Mesopotamia and, next to Marduk, perhaps the most popular deity in the Babylonian pantheon.

Ishtar, so it was related in Nineveh and Babylon, had chosen **Tammuz,** 'son of light' (Dumuzi in Sumerian), to be the lover of her youth, having become entranced with him while watching him shepherding his flocks under the great tree of Eridu, which covers the whole earth with its shade. Then Tammuz was mortally wounded by a wild boar and was cast into the kingdom of Allat. One means remained by which he might be restored to the light of day: his wounds must be washed in the waters of the fountain of youth, which flowed in the land of death, and Ishtar resolved to go in quest of this marvelous spring. The undertaking was fraught with danger, for no one might travel into Aralû without having previously gone through the terrors of death. She arrived at the dark country which is surrounded by seven high walls and approached by seven gates, each guarded by a pitiless warden.

At the first gate she knocked, demanding to be let through, threatening otherwise to tear down the walls, to excite the dead so that they would eat the living. When Allat heard that Ishtar was demanding admission, she gave orders to have the gates opened, but only providing the goddess of love should be treated according to the ancient laws. Mortals enter the world naked and naked they must leave it: and since Ishtar had decided to share their lot she must divest herself of her garments. As she passes through the first gate the guardian removes from her head the great crown. When she asks, "Why, guardian, dost thou remove the great crown from my head?" the reply is "Enter, my lady. Such is the law of Allat." At the second gate the guardian takes the rings from her ears, and so on from gate to gate. Now her necklace with its attached amulets, now the tunic which covers her bosom, now her enameled girdle, her bracelets and the rings on her ankles, until at the seventh gate she is divested of her last covering.

At length she arrives in the presence of Allat and she throws herself upon the goddess of death in order to wrest from her by force the life of her beloved Tammuz. But Allat overcomes her and has her bound and given over to the torments of the other world. In the meantime the world of the living is wearing mourning on account of Ishtar's death. In the absence of the goddess of love the rites of love are no longer performed, the passions of animals and men are suspended, the race is about to become extinct, the earth is a desert and the gods are left without votaries or offerings. The gods are very much concerned, but they know they cannot get Ishtar back without effecting the resurrection of Tammuz. Ea, the supreme god, he who alone can modify the laws imposed upon creation, at length decides that an exception to the law of death will have to be made.

So he creates a messenger whom he sends to Allat commanding the release of Ishtar and her lover. Allat is outraged at this invasion of her rights but she can do nought but obey the orders of the supreme divinity.

And thus it was that Ishtar and her lover returned to earth. Thereafter the fate of Tammuz was in her hands. Every year she must bathe him in pure water, clothe him in a robe of mourning and play to him sad airs upon a flute, while her priestesses intoned their doleful chants and tore their breasts in sorrow: only thus, as long as she celebrated in his behalf the prescribed ceremonies, would his heart take fresh life and his youth flourish once more between springtime and springtime.

Some historians believe that the original of Ishtar was the Semitic goddess Ashtar or Astarte. It is generally accepted that the Semites, before their specialization from other Arabian peoples, possessed a matriarchal society made up of the mothers and their brothers and children who inhabited a particular oasis in the Arabian desert. The fathers were men of other tribes, dwelling in other oases, who contracted only temporary unions with the women of neighboring clans. Descent was traced through the mother, who was not only the head of the clan but its leader in battle, and all masculine authority, such as it was, was vested in the brother or the maternal uncle of the matriarch. In such a society the chief deity would of course be a counterpart of the matriarch, and if male divinities existed they must have been conceived as divine uncles rather than as divine fathers, since fatherhood was biologically unrecognized.

Other historians see in Ishtar a Euphratean deity who absorbed the Semitic Astarte. The priority of either goddess is, however, obviously suspect when one recalls the neolithic images of pregnant women with full breasts and enlarged or steatopygous buttocks that are found all the way up the peninsula of Italy, around the Adriatic and down into Greece, across Phoenicia, Syria and Palestine, along the Nile and down both the Tigris and Euphrates to the Persian Gulf. It must be accepted that these neolithic figurines bespeak beliefs which foreshadowed all the Great Mother cults of protohistoric time.

Ishtar's nature was a confusing mixture of antitheses. As a cruel goddess of war she was identified with the morning star; robed in flames, armed with bow, two quivers and a sword, she gave oracular direction and success in arms to a long line of mighty kings from Sargon down to Ashurbanipal. As the sympathetic mother of mankind she listened to the supplications of the diseased, the unhappy, all who were struck by misfortune. As a giver of earthly blessings she was mistress of the magic arts and counteracted the wiles of demons. As goddess of love she was identified with the evening star and was, like Isis, the spirit of fertility in man and beasts and of the green things of the earth. Green was her special color, and the *ashera* or post, a conventional symbol of the living tree, was sacred to her. The dove, probably because of its erotic temperament, was her sacred bird. The fact that she had first loved Tammuz, as Gilgamesh recounted, then a bird, a lion, a stallion, a shepherd, a gardener and finally himself indicated how impartially she distributed her favors.

Ishtar's descent into Aralû presents a parallel instance to the death and resurrection of Osiris, where a legendary drama acquired magic power: on the principle of sympathetic magic, that a desired effect can be obtained by imitating it, the resurrection of Tammuz through Ishtar's grief was dramatically represented annually in order to insure the success of the crops and the fertility of the people. Each year during the winter rains the earth was thrilled by the god and was fructified by him, pouring forth its abundance of flowers and fruits; each year in the summer heat the god died, and the earth was plunged into grief and barrenness, only to be made joyous again by his resurrection. Each year men and women had to grieve with Ishtar over the death of Tammuz and celebrate the god's return, in order to win anew her favor and her benefits.

Ishtar's temple in Babylon was maintained by women to whom the rigid constraints of the harem and the veil had no appeal, or those who were forced, either by divorce or the denial of their husbands, to walk the streets. It was reported by Herodotus that every woman born in the country had once during her lifetime to enter the enclosure of the temple and wait there upon a stranger. The wealthy made their way to the temple in closed chariots followed by a considerable train of slaves:

> The greater number seat themselves on the sacred pavement, with a cord twisted about their heads — and there is always a great crowd there coming and going; the women being divided by ropes into long lanes, down which strangers pass to make their choice. A woman who has once taken her place here cannot return home until a stranger has thrown into her lap a silver coin, and has led her away beyond the limits of the sacred enclosure. As he throws the money he pronounces these words, "May the goddess Mylitta [Mulitta, 'she who causes to bear'] make thee happy!". . . The silver coin may be of any value, but none may refuse it, that is forbidden by the law, for, once thrown, it is sacred. The woman follows the first man who throws her the money, and repels no one. When once she has accompanied him, and has thus satisfied the goddess, she returns to her home, and from thenceforth, however large the sum

offered to her, she will yield to no one. The women who are tall or beautiful soon return to their homes, but those who are ugly remain a long
time before they are able to comply with the law; some of them are
obliged to wait three or four years within the enclosure.

With the exception of Isis, Ishtar was worshiped for as many centuries as
any deity conceived by mankind, her votaries repairing to her temples with
not only oriental casualness but a feeling of sanctity and righteousness.
They could only serve her truly who shared her pains and pleasures: the
women wept each year with Ishtar over the fatal wound of Tammuz; to
serve at least once in her temple was a religious duty; the self-mutilated
eunuchs and the boys and men who dressed themselves as women and
gave themselves to womanly pursuits had about them an aura of sanctity;
the men who sought the embraces of her priestesses simultaneously experienced communion with the Fruitful Goddess, the Divine Mother. In later
days a newly developing asceticism led men to condemn her worship as an
evil thing, but they continued by fasting or self-torture, dancing, singing,
bloody sacrifices and other orgies to provoke a perverted ecstasy in order
to establish communion with the deity.

In Gilgamesh's recital of her 'unfaithfulnesses and ignominies,' Ishtar is
pictured as maltreating every lover. Perhaps this fickleness is but an echo
of duplicity on the part of the ancient Semitic matriarchs whom men loved
at the risk of life, or of the tragedy in which her first lover, Tammuz, died;
or perhaps it is an epitome of her dual aspect as goddess of both love and
war. Whatever the reason for her antithetic composition, when the people
of the East depicted the Mother of All Living as full of contradictions,
made her at once cold and passionate, chaste and lascivious, faithful and
treacherous, kind and cruel, they achieved notable success in the deification
of creation.

I I I

The Heaven Is My Throne and the Earth My Footstool

BETWEEN Egypt and Mesopotamia lay the heterogeneous country of Syria, a buffer land never completely subjugated by either power. Its mountains, rivers and deserts were so disposed as to militate against political consolidation, and its many tribes, the Canaanites, Amorites, Aramaeans, Midianites, Hivites, Jebusites, Ammonites, Ishmaelites, Edomites, Moabites and others whose names are long forgotten, were incapable of uniting for long even against a foreign invader. Only the Philistines, who occupied the coastland from Jaffa southward, were permanently federated and even among them each city-state had its own ruler. No corner of the world has been the scene of more sanguinary engagements, or witnessed century after century so many armies crossing and recrossing its borders. Sargon had nibbled at it in building his Sumerian empire; Babylon and Assur had repeatedly sent armies westward in the endeavor to subjugate its fortified cities; the Mitannians and the even more powerful Hittites had stormed it repeatedly from the north; while Thothmes III had garrisoned it with Egyptian troops in order to assure a westerly flow of tribute. For the Syrians warfare was the common state of existence and they resolutely refused to be pacified.

The Bedouins of Syria belonged to that language group which modern scholars call Semites (sons of Shem), a term designating both recent or ancient peoples whose languages are closely related, as closely, for example, as are French, Italian, Spanish and Portuguese. The various Semitic peoples, however, are not necessarily related by blood for they include the Akkadians, Assyrians, Amorites, Canaanites, Aramaeans, Phoenicians, Carthaginians, Israelites, Ammonites, Moabites, Edomites, Nabateans, Southern Arabs, Sabaeans and Abyssinians. The most widely accepted theory is that the original Semitic stock arose in Arabia, whence it radiated into Africa, Syria, Mesopotamia and northern lands.

In Syria the Bedouins were mostly nomadic shepherds, perpetually quarreling with each other for rights to the most fertile wadies and the permanent springs, and Egyptian and Mesopotamian records reveal that they were given to harassing the important trade routes between the Nile and the Euphrates. In the time of Rim-Sin, a king of Larsa who was overthrown by Hammurabi (1910 B.C.), a people known to the Sumerians as the Habiru were living in southern Mesopotamia; they were not Sumerians, but Aramaean (Syrian) nomads who came in from the desert to enroll as mercenaries with the Sumerians. The philological equivalence of the words Habiru and Hebrew are accepted by all authorities.

In their later traditions the Hebrews described themselves as of twelve tribes descended from Abraham of Ur, these tribes having been united by Moses after an exodus from Egypt, and welded together by Saul and David into the ephemeral nation of Israel. Woolley accepts the tradition of Abraham as essentially historical, except that the Hebrew patriarch is not to be interpreted as one man but as a composite of several generations of a family whose home was in Ur during the reign of Rim-Sin (1970–1940 B.C.); possibly it was when Hammurabi gained control of the city that a general migration of the Habiru into northern Syria occurred, certain of the tribes subsequently migrating into Palestine in the fifteenth and fourteenth centuries.

The next certain evidence of the Hebrews is from the Nile, though this evidence is not consonant with the traditional sojourn of Joseph in that land and the exodus under Moses. When or why any of Abraham's descendants entered Egypt is unknown. They may have been among the Semitic mercenaries or servants who accompanied the Hyksos when this hated people first brought ruin upon Egypt; certainly during the rule of the Shepherd Kings (1800–1580 B.C.) the attraction which the Nile valley had for foreigners was considerably increased: immigrants were welcomed and the royal palace was open to foreign counsellors and favorites, while Semitic dancing girls and concubines were highly esteemed. Throughout this period and later, famine, war in Syria and expansion of the Mesopotamian cities all conspired to drive westward not only isolated individuals but whole families and tribes, and it may have been that before the founding of the New Kingdom one or more Semitic groups, closely related by blood, were established in Egypt. So many Syrians were taken back to Egypt by Thothmes III and other conquerors of the XVIIIth Dynasty, many of them women who became wives or concubines of officers and nobles, that the physiognomy along the Nile developed a definite Egypto-Syrian cast.

Again it is recorded in the Tell el-Amarna letters of Akhnaten's time that Syria and Palestine were being periodically disturbed by people called the Habiri, a term which is also to be equated with the Hebrews. In the cuneiform idiom they are referred to as 'cut-throats' or 'brigands,' and in view of their half predatory, half nomadic life and mercenary habits it is probable that there were as many fighting with as against Egyptian troops. In the century following Akhnaten's death, the Egyptians were forced on several occasions to make sorties into Palestine in order to force the Hittites northwards, and perhaps some Hebrews returned with the army as mercenaries, while it is equally possible that some were carried back as captives. Seti I and Rameses II both brought back a spoil of slaves after punishing the Syrians, and finally about 1220 B.C., Merneptah, Rameses's successor, had to 'pacify' the land once more. On the back of a large stele which this Pharaoh appropriated from the temple of Amenhotep III at Thebes, and which is now called the 'Israel stele' because it is the first monument in which this word is used, he recorded a hymn of victory which reads in part:

> The kings are overthrown, saying 'Salam'!
> Not one holds up his head among the nine nations of the bow.
> Wasted is Tehenu,
> The Hittite Land is pacified,
> Plundered is the Canaan, with every evil,
> Carried off is Askalon,
> Seized upon is Gezer,
> Yenoam is made as a thing not existing.
> Israel is desolated, her seed is not,
> Palestine has become a [defenseless] widow for Egypt.
> All lands are united, they are pacified;
> Every one that is turbulent is bound by King Merneptah.

Merneptah's monument proves that by 1220 B.C. one or more of the Habiri tribes having the name Isra-el (ruled by God) had achieved sufficient political and military unity in Canaan to be ranked with the inhabitants of the cities of Tehena, Askalon, Gezer and Yenoam. Thus the Hebrews were established in Canaan and Palestine certainly as early as the reign of Rameses II (1292–1225 B.C.), the traditional Pharaoh of the exodus, and they had probably been established there for close on to two centuries. These appear to have been the Leah tribes who called their deity

Yahweh, while one or more of the Rachel tribes, living in Egypt, knew him as Elohim, at least until the name Yahweh was traditionally revealed to them on the occasion of the exodus.

ii

It is pertinent to interpolate here a brief summary of the political history of the Hebrews and of their sacred work, the Old Testament.

In the period between 1090 and 1000 B.C., while Egypt was too feeble to remonstrate and the Assyrians and Hittites were occupied with each other, one or more Habiri tribes under the leadership of Saul and David gained domination over Palestine and formed the monarchy of Israel. (The oldest epigraphic evidence of Hebrew culture, a short Hebrew inscription at Byblos, dates from this or the previous century.) Then, under David's son Solomon, a cruel, vainglorious despot with a burning ambition to live like the king of Assyria, the monarchy became weakened and, in consequence of his tyranny and oppression, it divided on his death into two independent kingdoms, one in the north consisting of ten tribes, centering about Samaria and still carrying the name of Israel, and a second in the south, consisting of two tribes, centering about Jerusalem and known as Judah. For some centuries these two kingdoms remained in intermittent conflict with the Philistines, Amalekites, Moabites and Ammonites, while they struggled with variable success to maintain an independent existence between Assyria and Egypt. In 722 B.C. Samaria was sacked by the Assyrians and 27,000 of the inhabitants of Israel were carried away as prisoners. Their identity was lost among the Assyrians, all that remained of them being the legend of the lost Ten Tribes. Though this was the end of the Kingdom of Israel, the term Israel has come to be applied to the smaller and more robust sister state, Judah, and generically to all the descendants of its inhabitants.

Shortly after 600 B.C., when the center of power in the East shifted from Assur to Babylon, the Babylonians found in the small Israelite kingdom a troublesome neighbor who was aiding their enemies of the Nile. They twice invaded Jerusalem and severely punished the people. On the second occasion the walls of the city were wholly demolished, the important buildings leveled and a large number of the prominent inhabitants were removed to Babylon. This captivity, or Exile, lasted until 538 B.C., when the Persians under Cyrus conquered Babylon, at which time many of the captives returned to Jerusalem as Persian subjects.

An independent national existence was never again achieved, but the Hebrews dreamed always of what might have been, or what might still be; and these dreams, coupled with an unquenchable desire for national unity and independence, impelled the development of their religious literature. At the close of the Babylonian captivity the Hebrews possessed a considerable body of folklore, legends, genealogies and fragments of history, which the priests now arranged into a composite work (practically represented in the first five books of the Old Testament, the Pentateuch), and finally edited about the time of Ezra (*ca.* 400 B.C.). Any appraisal of the Old Testament must recognize that the history of Israel from the earliest days to the Babylonian captivity had been transmitted largely by oral tradition. At this period history was never written as such and, judging from all parallels in Mesopotamia and Syria, the most in the way of pre-exilic written sources which the scribes had available to them was a miscellany of king lists, genealogical tables, tribal laws and moral anecdotes. Even these written records had of necessity been copied and recopied many times, in which process the legends and even the presumptively historical facts had been re-edited and given new meanings as the viewpoint of the scribes changed with the passing centuries. Moreover, the priestly writers had a completely nonhistorical bias; they were so zealously intent on pleading a special cause — Yahwism in all its aspects — that they remained unaware of or quite indifferent to a vast array of contradictions and incompatibilities in the finished work. From the time of the Reformation it was believed by Christians that this literature was divinely inspired and literally true to the letter of the word, and only in the nineteenth century did scholars come to see it in its proper historical light: on critical analysis the Biblical books in many instances were found to have historical value, but the very sanctity that produced them and led to their preservation proved to be the chief reason for questioning their historicity at every point.

The Pentateuch is now recognized to stem from three more or less independent sources, the Yahwistic and Elohist versions which were probably not committed to writing before 750 B.C., and the Priests' Code which was composed as an amplification of Deuteronomy shortly after the return from Babylon (*ca.* 535-469 B.C.). The Pentateuch (plus Chronicles and Kings) was probably arranged in its present order before 300 B.C., though a standard Hebrew text (the Masoretic text) was not finally established until the second century of the Christian Era. This text, of which no copy is extant, in turn supplied the model from which the Torah and Old Testament were derived. The Hebrew text was originally written in consonants only, the vowels being supplied by the reader; then at some time between the sixth and eighth centuries of the Christian Era a system of vowel points was invented and applied to the ancient text, and such was the subsequent force of this innovation that after its widespread adoption all the manuscripts which had not been so re-edited were destroyed or allowed to perish. Consequently no copy of the Hebrew text of any part of the Old Testament is known that can be dated with any certainty earlier than the tenth century. A copy of the Prophetic Books preserved at Leningrad, bearing the date A.D. 916, has long been accepted as the oldest surviving, primary Hebrew record. (Scrolls bearing much of Isaiah and fragments of Genesis, Deuteronomy and the Apocrypha, preserved in jars and found by Arabs near the Dead Sea in 1947, are believed by Professor Sukenik of Hebrew University to antedate the Christian Era. Some scholars place their date in the sixth century B.C., but others suspect them to be forgeries and in any case do not date them earlier than the Middle Ages.)

For earlier redactions of the Old Testament scholars must rely on Greek, Latin, Syriac and other translations which differ markedly among themselves in consequence of their checkered history. Until the third century of the Christian Era writing was confined to papyrus rolls, a number of such rolls being required to contain all the books of the Old Testament, and since these rolls were circulated separately and separately translated by scribes who frequently had more zeal than skill, the various rolls probably differed on one point or another in almost every paragraph. In the third century the papyrus codex, or book of papyrus leaves, was introduced, and in the fourth century the vellum codex, and then the various texts began to be gathered into simple volumes. Editors and redactors selected from the diverse translations available to them on papyrus those texts which seemed to be most suitable, this work of selection going on in several independent centers, such as Alexandria, Greece, Constantinople and Rome, until there were produced a number of stem texts which differed considerably from each other.

The first translation of the Old Testament from Hebrew into Greek had been the Septuagint, which had been prepared from various Hebrew papyri by a number of translators (traditionally seventy) in the third century B.C.; this originally included only the Pentateuch, but other books were added by the first century B.C. and in the first century after Christ the collection was accepted by the Jews of the Dispersion as Holy Scripture and passed on as such to the Christian Church. In both Hebrew and Christian hands, however, the papyri underwent independent changes until in the fourth century Jerome collected numerous Hebrew manuscripts, edited them and translated them into Latin to produce the Vulgate text. For textual purposes this possesses but little value, since Jerome presupposed a Hebrew original practically identical with the stereotyped Masoretic text, and made his selections accordingly. It is this Vulgate which is still used by the Catholic Church, but the oldest extant fragments date from the sixth to the ninth century and these have now been shown to differ markedly from the stem texts on which Jerome's compilation was based. In view of Jerome's limited sources, his edition must itself have differed considerably from the older Hebrew manuscripts.

In the preparation of the standard English Bible (King James Version, 1611), the translators unfortunately relied chiefly upon a Greek text which had been collected and edited by Erasmus in 1516, who had in turn used the few Greek manuscripts that were available in Basle. In the light of recent examination Erasmus's sources appear to have stemmed largely from what scholars call the Byzantine text, one which had been gradually assembled at Constantinople between the fourth and eighth centuries and which differs substantially from other texts that by their concordance appear to approach more closely to the original Hebrew manuscripts.

The oldest extensive manuscript of the Septuagint in any language consists of 235 leaves of the Greek Codex Sinaiticus which dates from the fourth century, discovered by Tischendorf in the monastery of St. Catherine at Mount Sinai in 1844 and 1859. The Codex Vaticanus, also in Greek, which has been preserved in the Vatican Library since 1481, is a nearly complete copy of the Old and New Testaments and is also dated as fourth century. Next in age is the Greek Codex Alexandrinus, also a nearly complete copy of the Old and New Testaments dating from the fifth century, which was preserved at Constantinople until 1627 when it was presented to Charles I. The Chester Beatty Papyri are remnants of twelve manuscripts allegedly found by natives buried in one or more jars in a Coptic graveyard in Egypt; they comprise two substantial portions of Genesis, small fragments of Isaiah, Jeremiah, Ezekiel, Daniel, Esther and Ecclesiasticus from the third and fourth centuries, and a portion of Numbers and Deuteronomy which is said to be not later than the first half of the second century. A fragment of Deuteronomy is contained on a few bits of papyrus which were used in making a mummy cartonnage case found in Egypt; these date from the middle of the second century B.C. and are by some three centuries the earliest manuscript of any portion of the Bible yet discovered, with the possible exception of the Hebrew fragments mentioned above.

In view of the fact that the oldest manuscripts, incomplete as they are, represent the nth edition in the process of copying and recopying, editing and re-editing which has gone on for centuries it is not surprising that all extant copies differ markedly from each other and from the King James Version. The Revised Version of 1881 incorporates the results of much recent research on the ancient manuscripts but can scarcely be considered either final or identical with any ancient copy, and the choice between the King James Version and the Revised Version is largely a matter of literary taste.

iii

The traditions of the Israelites, as set forth in the Pentateuch (and excluding numerous contradictory details) relate that in a time of famine the sons of Jacob, a descendant of Abraham, had migrated into Egypt where their brother, Joseph, was prime minister; there they had been welcomed and given land in the province of Goshen, and had resided until forced into slavery by a hostile Pharaoh. Under the leadership of Moses, and after numerous dramatic episodes in which Moses's god had 'hardened the heart' of the Pharaoh to prevent the Israelites from leaving (and which afforded the god an opportunity to exhibit his supernatural powers) they had escaped from Egypt to wander in the 'wilderness' for forty years, until at last they had reached the promised land of Canaan.

Whether any such mass exodus of Hebrews out of Egypt ever actually occurred is undetermined. Those historians who answer affirmatively place it at about 1450 B.C., a date which is obtained from internal evidence in the Pentateuch, and from the fact that the Habiri, as demonstrated by the Tell el-Amarna letters, were creating trouble in Palestine by 1370 B.C. and were well established there certainly before the time of the Merneptah stele (1220 B.C.). Recent excavations at Jericho show that the walls of this town were leveled by an earthquake between 1413 and 1300 B.C., which is consonant with the Hebraic dates and traditions. In this view the 'Rameses' of the oppression is either a synonym for 'Pharaoh' or some unknown Egyptian ruler of that name, for no Rameses is recorded in Egyptian history until a much later time.

Whatever the date of the traditional migration, and assuming it to have a historic basis, it is obviously impossible to accept the Exodus account that there went out of Egypt 'about six hundred thousand on foot that were men, beside children. And a mixed multitude went up also with them; and flocks, and herds, even very much cattle.' Apart from the 'mixed multitude,' this would mean a million and a half men, women and children, and an equal number of cattle and sheep, and any such mass movement would certainly have resounded loudly in Egyptian or Syrian history, while any such number of persons and animals would certainly have died of starvation within a short time in the deserts and mountains of Sinai. It is more likely that the legend of the exodus is a garbled and fanciful account of the flight from Egypt to Palestine of a relatively few members of the Rachel tribe under the leadership of a patriarch who fled the country because he had come afoul of the Egyptian law; or perhaps it only reflects the continuous infiltration of Hebrews into and out of Egypt over the period between the Hyksos invasion (1800 B.C.) and the reign of Merneptah (1200 B.C.), and their gradual rise to power in Palestine. Later, when they were politically established in that country, their Egyptian experiences and the adventures which they had had at one point or another in their travels were developed into a tale of epic proportions.

Moses was, by tradition, learned in the wisdom of the Egyptians, and Egyptian influence in early Israelite thought is evident in many places. Though the name Moses was related by Sayce to the Assyrian word *masu,* meaning hero or leader, other Egyptologists have emphasized its affinity to the Egyptian word *mose,* meaning son, while Yahuda equates it with the Egyptian *mu-sheh,* meaning 'child of the Nile.' Like Horus, beloved god of Egypt, and also like Sargon, founder of the kingdom of Sumer, Moses had been born in secret and hidden in a basket among the bulrushes. A malicious god, Set, sought to destroy Horus; a malicious Pharaoh sought to destroy Moses. Buto, the goddess of the north, found and reared Horus while his mother visited him secretly; a Pharaoh's daughter found and reared Moses, his mother being employed as his nurse. When Horus grew to manhood he slew Set, who had wronged his father; when Moses grew to manhood he slew an Egyptian who was wronging a Hebrew. To escape punishment, Moses fled from Egypt to the land of Midian, where he lived with Jethro, the ministrant of the god Yahweh who appears at this stage to have been the local deity of a sacred volcanic mountain; and, on the occasion of the burning bush, Moses's great mission to deliver the Israelites from bondage was revealed to him by Jethro's god who proved to be the hitherto unrecognized god of Moses's ancestor, Abraham. The god first told Moses his 'secret name,' thus imparting to him such magic power that in Egypt Moses would have been stronger than the god himself. Then the god expounded a guileful plan to coerce the Pharaoh into letting the Israelites leave Egypt and to persuade them to follow Moses.

The plan involved various 'wonders' or magical operations in the form of typical Egyptian plagues. In an incident involving the god, Moses and his wife, it was revealed that the bloodletting rite of circumcision, which was indubitably in vogue in Egypt in earliest dynastic times, was to be substituted for human sacrifice. Moses carried a magic staff which was also a serpent, and he revered the healing power of the shining brazen image of the serpent divinity, Uraeus, the symbol of the Egyptian king. On the sacred mountain he acquired a highly sacred stone from the god, which was forever after surrounded by Egyptian mystery and preserved in a chest or 'ark' comparable to the sacred chests used by Egyptian priests.

Such Nilotic elements are those which one would expect to find among Semites who had lived in Egypt at any period from the Hyksos invasion to the time of Rameses. The ancient literature of that country, such as the writings of Ptahhotep, was probably not readily available to any except the priests who because of its sacred nature kept it closely guarded either in the House of Rolls or in the temples; certainly if any of the more abstract 'wisdom' of the Nile was carried away by Moses and his companions, it was lost in the wilderness or in Canaan where they finally settled down.

The Israelites of Syria at the time of Rameses and Merneptah lived as they had lived for a thousand years, pasturing their flocks on the thin herbage in the valleys, moving onward from well to well whenever the supply of fodder was exhausted, and coming into the cities only when forced to do so by the onset of winter or the assault of enemies. They reverenced as abodes of supernatural beings the springs upon which they and their flocks were so dependent, or any tree that was of excessive size or grew miraculously in a desert cleft. As late as the Hellenistic period it was accepted that trees had perception, passion and reason, and in earlier days men sensed in these mysterious organisms potent beings who exerted a profound influence upon human fate. Such were the 'terabinths of soothsayers,' the 'palm tree of Deborah,' or the unusual tamarisk or pomegranate at Gibeah where Saul abode. Tree worship was interwoven in the cult of Ishtar, and in the absence of a tree the nomads erected near a sacred spring or artificial altar a bare pole, or *asherah,* to represent the god. Like the peoples of Ur and Babylon, the nomads revered sacred images, or *ephods,* which the soothsayer consulted, or before which he cast lots to divine the future, and *teraphim,* images of venerated ancestors; the latter were preserved in each household with reverential care, attended with ritual and sacrifice by the family or tribal patriarch, and were consulted in all grave crises. Such were the images which Rachel stole from her father, which Micah consulted, and the worship of which Hosea and Zechariah condemned with vehemence.

The Israelites had their animal gods, the sacred serpent, a brazen image of which Moses brought out of Egypt, and the golden calf, which was probably the counterpart of the highly revered Hathor, Mother Goddess of the Nile. Deified animal ancestors were possibly represented in certain tribal names such as Simeon (hyena), Caleb (dog), Hamor (ass), Rachel (ewe) and Tesh (wild cow), and the worship of these totems may have furnished the original taboos against eating the flesh of particular species, though the majority of such taboos as they appeared in later Judaism were outgrowths of priestly legalism.

Although every field, vineyard, well and spring had its divine possessor and protector, the Israelites turned whenever possible to mountains as the abode of divine beings. They designated such gods generically by the Syriac name of Baalim, the 'lords' of such-and-such places, the Baal of Lebanon, of Mount Hermon or Mount Peor. The evidence of the Pentateuch reveals an early and impressive experience with some mountain, probably a volcano, in which lived a deity whose name, too terrible to be pronounced, was, in keeping with the custom of omitting vowels, spelled YHWH and was probably pronounced Yahweh. (The Tetragrammaton was incorrectly translated in fourteenth century manuscripts as Jehovah, a word formed by combining YHWH with the vowels of *adhonay,* or Lord, on the erroneous assumption that the synonymy in Hebraic usage afforded a key to the pronunciation of the Tetragrammaton. Actually, *adhonay* was substituted merely to avoid saying the holy name.) In many places in Syria there are evidences of recent volcanic activity, and there is much to favor the view that Yahweh was originally the spirit of an active crater. He appears repeatedly in images that could only arise from an intimate experience with such a peak, as in the pillar of cloud by day and the pillar of fire by night that guided the Israelites, in the thunders and lightnings and the thick cloud and the voice of a trumpet exceeding loud that accompanied the appearance of the god upon the mountain when 'the smoke thereof ascended as the smoke of a furnace, and the whole mount quaked greatly.' Centuries later it echoes in the prophet Isaiah's words: 'Behold the name of Yahweh cometh from afar, his anger burneth, and violently the smoke riseth on high: his lips are full of indignation, and his tongue is a devouring fire.'

Although the Israelites always spoke of Yahweh as coming from Sinai, Jethro's mountain, where Yahweh revealed himself to Moses, was not in the Sinai peninsula but in the land of the Midianites which lay to the east of the Gulf of Akaba in Arabia proper; the erroneous association of Yahweh with Sinai stems from the subsequent encampment of the Israelites near the foot of the mountain of the Law during the exodus. This mountain of the Law may or may not have been Mount Sinai: the Pentateuchal writers sometimes called it Sinai, and sometimes Horeb. Traditionally it was such a mountain that over a million people could encamp at its base for some time with pasture and drink for their cattle; it rose from the wilderness so sharply that its base could be fenced in, yet it was easily ascended and its peak could be seen by a great multitude below. It is impossible to fit Sinai or any other existing mountain into this description, but it was probably Mount Sinai that supplied many of the legends of the exodus and some of the attributes of the deity who sponsored this migration.

Among the Bedouins Mount Sinai was sacred to the moon god, Sin, from whom it derived its name. Sin, by nature of his nocturnal light, was the favored god of nomadic peoples, their guide and protector at night when they must do most of their wandering in a hot country. He was conceived to be the father of the gods, their chief and leader, and the god of wisdom. His symbol was a conical stone surmounted by a gilded crescent, and his service even down to late times involved human sacrifice. Sin was worshiped at Mount Sinai well into the Christian Era, and the rocky caves which abound in its jagged walls and deeply cut valleys had harbored his priests a thousand years before the Exodus. The ruins of temples at Serabit reveal altars for incense and sacrifice, tanks for ablutions, stone pillars suggesting phallic beliefs and a vast accumulation of ashes from burnt offerings. When the Israelites left their 'mountain of the Law' they carried with them Sin's commandments to make an altar to burn incense upon, this altar to have 'horns' for a ceremonial blood offering, lavers for the hands and feet, a tabernacle in which to worship the god and the ritual of burnt offerings. Every seventh day, the unlucky day of the moon god throughout the East, had become a sabbath or sacred day. To argue that the Israelites acquired these practices, which were ancient and widespread throughout Arabia and Syria, solely from the cult of a single mountain, Sinai or any other, would of course be forced; the point is that in their own tradition Sinai was the place upon which Yahweh descended with fire and smoke and earthquake to instruct Moses about the Sabbath, the making of an altar of unhewn stone with horns, the rituals of the blood offering and the burnt offering, the feast of the harvest and first fruits, the sacrifices of the first-born, all the sacred Law that was the foundation of

Israel, and much of this 'law' was pre-existent in the moon god's cult.

Yet as Jeremiah later said, 'For according to the number of thy cities were thy gods, O Judah, and according to the number of the streets of Jerusalem have ye set up altars to that shameful thing, even altars to burn incense to Baal.' Yahweh, slowly taking shape in a welter of polytheism, took one or another attribute from various of Israel's early gods. Above all else, he was a god of generation. The Israelites never doubted that with his help they would some day outnumber their enemies, for the god had appeared to Abraham and promised to make him 'a father of many nations'; and later, when Abraham complained 'To me thou hast given no seed,' the god 'brought him forth abroad, and said, Look now toward heaven, and tell the stars, if thou be able to number them: and he said unto him, So shall thy seed be.' Repeatedly the god promises fruitfulness: 'I will multiply thee exceedingly'; 'thou shalt be a father of many nations'; 'And I will make thee exceeding fruitful, and I will make nations of thee, and kings shall come out of thee'; 'for a father of many nations have I made thee'; of Sarah he said, 'she shall be a mother of nations; kings of people shall be of her'; of Ishmael, 'I have blessed him and will make him fruitful, and will multiply him exceedingly; twelve princes shall he beget, and I will make him a great nation.' To the agricultural Egyptians, who needed food and not numbers, Osiris was above all the personification of the fertility of the soil and seed, and the power of resurrection; but the shepherd-warrior peoples living in sparsely populated Palestine were not interested in agriculture and they had no notion whatever of a happy afterlife. What they wanted chiefly was to resist their foes by force of arms, to which end they had to multiply their numbers as rapidly as possible. So the god promised them, 'I will multiply thy seed as the stars of the heaven, and as the sand which is upon the seashore; and thy seed shall possess the gate of his enemies.'

From this and other evidence, many students have identified Yahweh as a phallic stone such as was revered by neolithic man and by more recent peoples. It is not to be denied that phallic symbolism has been attributed to megalithic monuments, amulets, signs, incantations and literary allusions, in which the *suggestio concupiscentiae* is purely fortuitous. The Semitic *asherim,* or sacred poles, have been so identified, but the evidence is unconvincing and it is more likely that as substitutes for a sacred tree they were erected indifferently in the worship of any deity. Although Kennett thought that Yahweh was a golden serpent brought perhaps from Egypt and preserved in the ark until its loss or destruction, possibly as late as the reformation in the days of Hezekiah, and Barton that he was a sacred meteorite, the belief that he was a phallic deity has much more support in evidence.

The Semites were among the most assiduous of stone worshipers in the ancient world. From the fact that sacred stones were usually erected on or near the summit of a hill, they came to refer to any megalithic monument as a 'high place.' A particular stone which was the abode of deity was called Beth-el, the 'house of god,' though this term was also applied to sacred springs and other sacred localities. Among a circle of stones, the Beth-el is usually identifiable by its superior size, its unique position, or by the fact that it has been worn smooth by being repeatedly anointed. The conical menhir, called a *massebah* (to set up), was especially revered, and so numerous were they with the accompanying *asherim* it could be said that they might be found 'on every high hill, and under every green tree.' A cup was frequently hollowed out in the altar stone to receive the libation of wine or oil, or the blood of human or animal sacrifice, and in some instances channels were dug in the altar to drain the blood into a neighboring subterranean grotto. On the altar an entire animal might be consumed by fire, to ascend as a sweet-smelling savor to the god whose blessing the worshipers acquired by partaking of the sacred flesh or anointing themselves with its blood. Seers incubated near the altar to obtain oracular information, and the recurring seasons as well as occasions of victory were celebrated there with music, dancing and wine; men sacrificed their blood and gave themselves up to an orgy of ecstasy in which they were visited by oracular visions, while women received the fertility of the god.

It was in keeping with what was apparently a neolithic tradition that the sacred stones were never cut with the chisel, for fear of disturbing the embodied spirit; and thus it was that Yahweh said unto Moses, 'And if thou wilt make me an altar of stone, thou shalt not build it of hewn stone: for if thou lift up thy tool upon it, thou hast polluted it,' and it was such an unhewn stone that Jacob took for a pillow and afterwards consecrated by pouring oil upon it, or that he set up for a covenant pillar with Laban, or on the altar at Shilan, or on the grave of Rachel, or at Luz where his god appeared to him; and such was the great stone which Joshua set up 'under an oak, that was by the sanctuary of Yahweh.' The prophet Isaiah contemptuously says to the recalcitrant polytheist: 'Among the smooth stones of the stream is thy portion; they, they are thy lot: Even to them hast thou poured a drink offering, thou hast offered a meat offering.' The stone of Bethel was apparently a menhir, the cairn of Mizpeh a sepulchral monument; Joshua's Gilgal was twelve standing stones; and it was at

these sacred places that Samuel judged Israel. He 'took a stone and set it
between Mizpeh and Shen,' and its name, Eben-ezer, meant the stone of
help, and he directed Saul to go to the stone circle of Gilgal, adding, 'I
will come down unto thee, to offer burnt offerings, and to sacrifice sacrifices of peace offerings.' There also it was that 'they made Saul king before
Yahweh in Gilgal; and there they sacrificed sacrifices of peace offerings
before Yahweh.'

One of the most interesting of the high places which have been found
in Palestine is that at Gezer, where the Canaanites worshiped. It contained
ten monoliths or upright pillars, varying from five to nearly eleven feet in
height, one of which was the sacred stone, as the smooth spots on it show.
It is a kind of stone not found near Gezer and was apparently brought
from Jerusalem. Mesha, king of Moab, related that he dragged the altar
stones of his enemies away from their original locations and erected them
to his own god, Chemosh, and it is possible that the Gezer stone was thus
carried away from Jerusalem as the booty of war, and the other stones
erected to do it honor. Judging from the scarabs found at Gezer, this high
place was in use in 2000 B.C., and it continued to be a place of worship
down to the time when the Jews were carried off to Babylon. Among the
fragments of pottery is a brazen serpent, suggesting that live sacred snakes
may have been kept in the temple, and it may have been here that Hezekiah broke the images, cut down the sacred trees and destroyed 'the brazen
serpent that Moses had made' and to which the children of Israel were
burning incense. Beneath this high place is a cemetery of newborn infants,
some of the bodies displaying marks of fire, and most of them enclosed
in large jars into which they had often been put head first. That the children were live sacrifices is probable from the fact that throughout the traditions of the East dead bodies were unclean and would never be brought
near a sanctuary. That the cult of the Mother Goddess had intermingled
with stone worship at Gezer is shown by the fact that a great many
plaques bearing the figure of Ishtar (whom the Israelites called Ashtoreth)
were found in the ruins. The great high place at Petra, one among twenty
in this locality, is conjectured by Robinson, its discoverer, to have been the
central sanctuary of the Edomites, and it may mark the spot where religious rites were celebrated by the sons of Esau. Other high places have
been discovered at Migiddo, Tell es-Safi, Tell Ta'annek and elsewhere.

Under the command of his god, Abraham went to the land of Moriah
to offer his only son Isaac as a burnt offering upon a mountain to which
the god directed him; it was on this mountain, just outside Jerusalem,
that Solomon built his Temple. The mountain is surmounted by a great

rock surface which is now enclosed in the Mosque of Omar; the Moham-medans still regard it as a sacred rock, and on it can still be traced the blood channels which were probably carved there by Solomon or someone before his time.

It has been propounded that the Semites in pre-Israelite days had passed through a phase of matriarchal culture in which descent was traced through the women, who not only ruled the clan but led its members on to the battlefield. In such a culture it is the Mother Goddess who is chiefly revered, as in the case of Ishtar and Astarte; and, as in these cults, the creatress of flocks and the divinity of maternity would be likely to esteem an enduring symbol of generation. The dominant role of phallism in the worship of the Syrian Astarte would establish the presupposition of phal-lic worship among the Israelites: before the Beth-el of Yahweh, erected near the sacred spring, victims could be slain and offerings of blood and oil could be rubbed or poured upon the god without contaminating the sacred waters.

Ancient phallic stones are still standing in western Syria, but in Pales-tine such monuments are rare because after the captivity the Israelites, having learned the folly of 'idolatry,' looked down upon stone worship with contempt and zealously eradicated all these 'idols.' They failed, how-ever, to expunge from their sacred literature an abundance of phallic-megalithic metaphors. Moses says of his god, 'He is the rock,' David sings, 'exalted be the god of the rock of my salvation,' and throughout the Psalms the identification occurs repeatedly: 'Thou art my rock and my fortress'; 'Who is God save Yahweh, and who is a rock save our God?'; 'Lead me to the rock that is higher than I'; 'Yahweh is my defense, and my God is the rock of my refuge'; 'O come, let us sing to Yahweh: let us make a joyful noise to the rock of our salvation.' Samuel says, 'There is none holy as Yahweh: for there is none beside thee: neither is there any rock like our God,' and joins with the Psalmist in declaring, 'The God of my rock; in him will I trust: he is my shield, and the horn of my sal-vation, my high tower, and my refuge, my saviour.' The Deuteronomist inquires, 'Where are their gods, their rock in whom they trusted, which did eat the fat of their sacrifices, and drank the wine of their offerings?' The priestly author of this book, which was 'found' in the Temple about 621 B.C., naïvely reveals the nature of his god in a passage which later edi-tors failed to purify: 'They sacrificed unto devils, not to Yahweh; to gods whom they knew not, to new gods that came newly up, whom your fathers feared not. Of the rock that begat thee thou art unmindful, and hast forgotten Yahweh that formed thee.'

The postexilic scribes undoubtedly removed many allusions to phallic worship, or blunted them to make them appear merely figurative, but as a figurative expression the 'rock' of salvation, power, refuge and judgment associated with a god of procreation is too frequent and too artificial to be fortuitous. That the rock was not figurative but literal is shown by the fact that Yahweh was concrete and tangible. The most sacred object in Israel was the chest called the 'ark,' which was carried about by the people from place to place and taken into battle, as the Egyptians carried the king's umbilical cord or other fetishes onto the battlefield to give them victory. It is made clear by repeated statement that the Israelites believed that their success in arms depended upon the strength of their god, whose presence coincided with the presence of this ark; were they to admit permanent defeat, it would prove that the god of their enemies was stronger than their own. Indeed, it was Yahweh himself who was in the ark, for when David took the ark to Jerusalem, it was carried on a new cart and the people 'played before Yahweh on all manner of instruments,' and David himself 'danced before Yahweh with all his might.' It was stored in a tent until Solomon built a great temple for it, 'the house of Yahweh,' and then it was brought into the holy of holies, 'into the oracle of the house, to the most holy place, even under the wings of the cherubim,' or, as a later gloss has it, it was enshrined 'between the thighs of the building.' The postexilic assertion that 'There was nothing in the ark save the two tables of stone, which Moses put there at Horeb, when Yahweh made a covenant with the children of Israel, when they came out of the land of Egypt,' is at once an admission that the ark's contents were rock and a denial of its true function. The denial has little weight inasmuch as the decalogue which, according to the postexilic writers, was inscribed on the two tablets incorporates the advanced morality of Amos, Hosea, Jeremiah and other prophets, and differs in all but three commandments from the decalogue as it existed before the Exile, and which, according to Kennett, read as follows:

> (i) I am Yahweh thy god, thou shalt worship no other god. (ii) The feast of unleavened cakes thou shalt keep; seven days thou shalt eat unleavened cakes. (iii) All that openeth the womb is mine; and all thy cattle that is male, the firstlings of ox and sheep. (iv) My sabbaths shalt thou keep; six days shalt thou work, but on the seventh day thou shalt rest. (v) The feast of weeks thou shalt celebrate, even the first-fruits of wheat harvest. (vi) The feast of ingathering thou shalt celebrate at the end of the year. (vii) Thou shalt not sacrifice my sacrificial blood upon leavened bread. (viii) The fat of my feast shalt not remain all night

until the morning. (ix) The fruit of the first-fruits of thy ground thou
shalt bring into the house of Yahweh thy god. (x) Thou shalt not seethe
a kid in its mother's milk.

The view that what the ark originally contained was a phallic stone,
perhaps with, perhaps without some 'words of power' inscribed upon it,
is therefore highly probable. In its travels it had acquired the name of
Jethro's volcanic god YHWH, a secret name of such magic power in the
Egyptian manner that the true pronunciation was transmitted only to
qualified disciples. He who pronounced the Tetragrammaton profanely
was threatened with dire punishment. For this reason the writers of the
Old Testament commonly substituted the Syriac word, Adonai, meaning
'my Lord.' The deity had assimilated many of the attributes of the moon
god of Sinai, as well as those of the family and tribal images, the teraphim.
It was a jealous rock which would allow no other sacred rocks to remain
undemolished within its tribal boundaries, for when the Philistines recognized and captured the ark at Ebenezer it plagued them even as Yahweh
had plagued the Egyptians, until their own sacred stone, Dagon, fell down
and broke in its presence. They were glad to be rid of the Israelite deity.
It was so powerful that when the men of Bethshemesh ventured to open
the ark to look upon it, the sacred presence smote them down, 'fifty thousand and threescore and ten men,' so that they sent a messenger to the
inhabitants of Kirjathjearim begging them to take the deity away.

If Yahweh rejoiced in human sacrifices he was no different from any
other Syrian god. That the practice of sacrificing a human victim to supply
a foundation deity for important buildings, widespread in later times, was
observed in Syria is indicated by the fact that at Megiddo the skeleton of
a fifteen-year-old girl was found built into a wall, and when Hiel, the
Bethelite, built Jericho, 'he laid the foundation thereof in Abiram his first-
born, and set up the gates thereof in his youngest son Segub, according to
the word of Yahweh.' When delivering the Israelites from Egypt, Yahweh
himself had heartlessly killed the first-born in every Egyptian home, 'from
the firstborn of Pharaoh that sat on his throne unto the firstborn of the
captive that was in the dungeon; and all the firstborn of cattle'; and in payment for delivering his people, he demanded that 'thou shalt set apart
unto Yahweh all that openeth the matrix, and every firstling that cometh
of a beast which thou hast; the males shall be Yahweh's and every firstling
of an ass thou shalt redeem with a lamb; and if thou wilt not redeem it,
then thou shalt break his neck: and all the firstborn of man among thy
children shalt thou redeem.'

That the tribe of Israel at the time of the Exodus had generally adopted circumcision as a substitute for this redemption is indicated by Yahweh's covenant with Moses, but the old ritual was not abandoned completely. Human sacrifice had been generously tempered by the substitution of animals, particularly the ram; it was only because Abraham dutifully 'bound Isaac his son and laid him on the altar upon the wood' that Yahweh stayed the father's hand. But Yahweh was not always content with the blood of circumcision or the first-born of animals, and in crises he demanded the more potent sacrifice. Jephthah offered up his daughter as a thank offering for victory; Samuel hewed Agag to pieces before the face of Yahweh; and David sought to pacify Yahweh by a sacrifice of seven of the sons of Saul.

During the early history of Israel many Semitic peoples worshiped a god called Moloch (the king) and, buried in prohibitions against the practice of child sacrifice, are numerous evidences that Moloch was identified by the Israelites as Yahweh himself. The custom of burning children long persisted at Jerusalem, the sacrifice being made at a place situated in the valley of Hinnom, just outside the walls of the city, which bore the name of Tophet. Evidence of a later date indicates that the children were rolled from the hands of a bronze image of the god into a pit of fire. In this custom the kings of Judah and its neighbors sometimes set an example, for Ahaz and Manasseh both caused their children to be sacrificed in this manner, and when the king of Moab was besieged by the Israelites and hard beset, he offered his eldest son, who should have reigned in his stead, for a burnt offering 'on the wall.' Philo of Byblos, in his work on the Jews, relates: 'It was an ancient custom in a crisis of great danger that the ruler of a city or nation should give his beloved son to die for the whole people, as a ransom offered to the avenging demons; and the children thus offered were slain with mystic rites. So Cronus, whom the Phoenicians call Israel, being the king of the land and having an only-begotten son called Jeoud, dressed him in royal robes and sacrificed him upon an altar in a time of war, when the country was in great danger from the enemy.'

At a later time the moralists found in child sacrifice one of the reasons for Israel's misfortunes. Jeremiah repeatedly bemoans the fact that the people of Jerusalem had 'built the high places of Tophet, which is in the valley of the son of Hinnom, to burn their sons and their daughters in the fire,' and the same lament is uttered by Ezekiel. It is inferred that there were several Tophets. Traditionally, under the rule of Josiah the Tophet of Hinnom was destroyed and the people commanded that 'no man might make his son or his daughter to pass through the fire to Moloch,' but Kennett believes that the reference is unreliable and that sacrifice may have continued there until the sixth century B.C., and in outlying districts of

Palestine, Ammon, Moab or Edom, down to the second century B.C. However, Jerome reported in the fourth century of the Christian Era that Tophet was then a pleasant and shady spot watered by the rills of Siloam and laid out in delightful gardens.

The horror of Tophet may not have been as great as it would seem, for when the Israelites watched their children pass into the fire they were moved by a sense of heroic duty. They would have been ashamed to offer to their god only the paltry things that money could buy. The supreme sacrifice appropriate to the god who had delivered them from bondage in Egypt and on whom they staked their all, was that which they loved most, and they were not a people to falter.

Kennett has suggested that the sacrifice of the first-born may have been based on the circumstance that in Israel as among Semites elsewhere the *kedheshim* or sacred men acted as the surrogates of the deity in stimulating the generative powers of nature, and since the first-born had been fathered by the deity, it was rightfully his. A potent factor in favoring the burnt sacrifice was no doubt the primitive attitude towards the magic power of blood, as revealed by Yahweh's injunction to Moses to forbear from eating blood and to avoid coming in contact with it: 'For the life of all flesh is the blood thereof.' Everything that blood had touched was unclean and had to be ritually purified. It is also possible that the burnt sacrifice goes back to the volcanic origin of Yaweh, or to the cult of the moon god at Sinai.

As time went on Yahweh disposed of competing gods by the simple expedient of absorbing them. Unlike other deities of the ancient world he was a very jealous god, and the first commandment given to Moses enjoined the Israelites from worshiping any other. Consequently when the tribes were united under David, when Jerusalem was made the capital of Israel and when Yahweh was at last enshrined by Solomon in the holy of holies of the national Temple, the religion of Israel was both monotheistic and purified of idolatry to the extent of having no graven image except the mysterious presence in the ark; nevertheless, Yahweh was still the ethnic god of one small tribe and his presence did not extend beyond the ark that had been his original abode. It required the physical destruction of this embodiment, in the calamity that was to come upon Jerusalem in the sixth century, to effect his liberation and transformation into an omnipresent, etherealized deity.

iv

Enough has been written on the subject of Hebrew morality to fill a large library, but the ancient Egyptian scribe who, thinking of the sun god's celestial realm, wrote at a date prior to 3000 B.C.: 'Life is given to him who does what is loved, and death is given to him who does what is hated,' anticipated most of what there was to say. The Memphite maxim is fundamental to all morality, and to the understanding of the beliefs of Israel.

It is obvious that the moral features of any religion must not be judged by the particular character of its precepts, for to do so is to assume unwarrantedly that moral canons have their genesis in some frame that has absolute and universal, rather than relative and local, co-ordinates. To the Israelites, willful contact with blood, or with anything that had been rendered 'unclean' by blood, was immoral because it was forbidden by divine command; whereas the sacrifice of the first-born child in the fire of Tophet was an act of the highest moral order, because the deity esteemed it. Judgments cannot be rendered in terms of right or wrong, good or bad, material or spiritual, for these are but categories into which conduct is arbitrarily classified by the local moral code, and the highest authority which any moral code has is the approval of the people who make it. It follows that the only sense in which any religion can be said to be 'moral' is in respect to the extent to which it impresses some mode of conduct, regardless of its particular nature, upon its adherents.

Using the word in the above sense, Yahwism in its final form was extremely moral, its restrictive character being its dominant feature. To the Hebrews of the newborn nation of Saul and David religion was patriotism, tribal solidarity and military victory. Above all else they desired to achieve national greatness. They were perpetually in conflict with the tribes about them, and in cycles which varied inversely with the national safety they manifested decreased or increased religious fervor. When not oppressed by fear of invasion the people became indifferent to their ethnic god and turned to the worship of Astarte or other deities revered by neighboring tribes; the strongest single factor leading them away from the Mosaic code was the peacetime marriage with non-Israelite women. Then in another crisis the prophets would search out the transgressors and exhort them to cast aside their gentile wives and to repent of all their other ssions, and in these prophetic exhortations the 'commandments' of y became multiplied many fold. If the survival of Yahwism over other cults was in great part owing to the life-and-death struggles which Israel fought with the Philistines and other enemies, these same struggles, combined with the mystery and adaptability of the deity, slowly shaped the vast complex of the Hebraic moral code.

Prophecy among the Israelites was a characteristic form of divination partaking of the nature of both an exalted profession and a religious frenzy. The prophets foretold the future by casting arrows or lots, by dreams, or by incubation on a high place; they ranged from magicians to kings, from worldly individuals who participated in the life of the community to austere mountain recluses; their notions ranged from the most primitive magic to the most unselfish conceptions of society. Most of their revelations were characterized by orgiastic attacks in which they poured out intense patriotism combined with zealous devotion to the current doctrines of Yahweh, and as Israel's self-consciousness developed they became the interpreters of Yahweh's will, the voice of the people's conscience and the arbiters of national politics. Their true merit is difficult to evaluate, for without exception their words have been reworked by later writers prone to interpolate into their frenzied outpourings the advanced principles of later generations and intent upon demonstrating that these principles stemmed from Yahweh through his chosen mouthpieces, just as the earlier exegetes made it appear that the deity revealed himself to Moses on the occasion of the burning bush and entrusted him with the Law among the fires and vapors of Sinai's summit.

The one certain thing about prophecy is that it shaped Israel's laws. Since the people never conceived that a blight of crops, a plague, a famine or defeat in arms could be the result of aught but Yahweh's wrath, prophetic vision discovered in every adversity a new iniquity of the people and set against it an appropriate prohibition. The ceremonial code thus evolved under the accumulating visions of the seers became ever more restrictive, until it culminated in the book of Deuteronomy. The nucleus of this work, of which the present text is a postexilic elaboration, was 'found' in the Temple about 621 B.C., even as one tradition had it that the original recension of the Book of the Dead had been 'found' in a temple over 2000 years earlier. This was a most critical period in Israel's history. 'A very forward generation' had provoked Yahweh's wrath: Judah had suffered under Assyrian tyranny for a hundred years and saw no hope for the amelioration of her woes, and the people were steeped in gloom. One day King Josiah, who was but eighteen years old, sent a servant to Hilkiah, the high priest, with an order covering the payment of workmen who were repairing the Temple, and the servant came hurrying back with astounding news: Hilkiah had found a book in the house of Yahweh, the very Book of the Law as written down by Moses. Josiah had the book brought and read to him and, very much alarmed, immediately consulted the prophetess Huldah, who pronounced it to be in truth the Law of Moses. Whereupon the King summoned the inhabitants of Jerusalem and read in their ears all the words of the discovered covenant.

If the people did not obey these laws, so Hilkiah's book threatened, Yahweh would direct more misfortunes against Israel than he had ever let loose upon the hated Egyptians: a multitude of blights would strike the fields, the stores, the kine, all that men owned and everything they set their hands to do; the people would suffer with the botch of Egypt, and with the emerods, and with the scab and itch; madness and blindness, consumption, fever, inflammation and extreme burning would beset them; blotches that could not be healed would appear from the soles of the feet to the top of the head, and men would be struck down by sword, by blasting and by mildew; heaven would turn to brass and earth to iron, rain would turn to dust and cover the fields, wives would be unfaithful, sons and daughters would be given into slavery — so on and on through every imaginable misfortune until the people of Israel had been scattered from one end of the earth unto the other. On the other hand, blessings of every sort were promised the people if they hearkened to the voice of Yahweh — the voice of Yahweh being purportedly here set forth in the form of the Law as it had been originally imparted to Moses.

The Deuteronomic code may have been written some fifteen to twenty-five years before it was 'discovered,' that is, during the reign of Josiah's grandfather Manasseh, for that king had favored the worship of the 'host of heaven' and had set up altars to strange gods in Jerusalem itself. It is equally possible that the work was a pious fraud perpetrated by Hilkiah and his priests with the idea of forcing it, as indeed they succeeded in doing, upon the young king and the people by sheer terrorism. It contained many of the ethics which had been at least nominally esteemed in Egypt and Babylonia for centuries, with such innovations as had been made by the prophets: it condemned child sacrifice, adultery, fornication, incest, sodomy and rape, dishonest weights and other unfair practices; it prescribed consideration for the poor, the widowed, the fatherless and the priest, and the free release of debtors and slaves every seven years. Its ethics were, however, subordinate to its chief intent of furthering the exclusive and ritualistic worship of Yahweh. It reaffirmed burnt offerings, sacrifices, tithes, heave offerings, free-will offerings, the firstlings of herds and flocks, the use of unleavened bread, the observance of the Sabbath and of the feasts of the Passover and of the Tabernacles and the Weeks, while it reiterated the prohibitions against eating the flesh of any beast that did not both cleave the hoof and chew the cud, or any flesh not drained of blood, against wearing woolen and linen garments at the same time, and against seething a kid in its mother's milk. It prohibited the eating of any flesh that dieth of itself, but sanctioned the giving of this flesh to a stranger or its sale to an alien. It forbade usury among the Hebrews but approved it between Hebrews and outsiders. It prescribed that one who used divination, or was an observer of times, or an enchanter, or a witch, or a charmer, or a consulter of familiar spirits, or a wizard, or a necromancer, as well as a stubborn and rebellious son or a maiden falsely pretending to virginity, should be stoned to death. It commanded that the people immediately destroy all high places and idols, *asherim* and stone pillars, and expel the sacred men and women from the temples, and all altars and images of other gods were to be burned in the fire. Any man of Israel who had gone out to worship another god should be killed and his cattle with him, and his city should be burned. Idolators should be stoned to death, and any stranger within the city who worshiped another god, and any prophet who invited men to worship other gods, even a brother or sister or son or daughter or wife or friend who did this, should be stoned outside the city gates until they died.

So terrible were the curses threatened by the Deuteronomist if the Israelites did not return to Yahweh as their only god that King Josiah and the people of Jerusalem were frightened into the quickest reform in history. When the king and his people entered the Temple and 'made a covenant before Yahweh, to walk after Yahweh, and to keep his commandments and his testimonies and his statutes with all their heart and all their soul, to perform the words of this covenant that were written in this book,' the gates of the most enduring walls ever to imprison men — the Hebraic Law — shut silently behind them.

v

What magic was to Egyptian culture, prophecy was to Hebraic culture — both its genesis and its ruin. Frazer has said: 'Prophecy of the Hebrew type has not been limited to Israel; it is indeed a phenomenon of almost world-wide occurrence; in many lands and in many ages the wild, whirling words of frenzied men and women have been accepted as the utterances of an indwelling deity. What does distinguish Hebrew prophecy from all others is that the genius of a few members of the profession wrested this vulgar but powerful instrument from baser uses, and by wielding it in the interests of a high morality rendered a service of incalculable value to humanity. That is indeed the glory of Israel.' This evaluation, however, requires not only the separation of prophetic gold from dross, but it fails to take cognizance of the heritage which was bequeathed to Israel by Egypt. Recent appraisals of Nilotic literature reveal that much that had previously been conceived to be the peculiar genius of Israel was long antedated by, if not derived from, the culture of the Nile. Social consciousness and a humane ethical code, for example, were abundantly contained in the maxims of Ptahhotep, whose 'wisdom,' if Breasted's dating is accepted, was formulated in writing nearly two thousand years before the Kingdom of Israel was founded. Although Ptahhotep did not neglect the services of the gods, propitiation of the deity certainly looms no larger in his thoughts than in those of Amos, Hosea or Samuel; and, with whatever reservations the talismanic power of righteousness is accepted, both the Egyptian and the Hebrew moralists subsumed within the term all the social virtues which they esteemed. 'Great is righteousness'; wrote the Grand Vizier, 'its dispensation endures, nor has it been overthrown since the time of its maker [the sun god, Ra]: for punishment is inflicted on the transgressor of its laws. . . . Although misfortune may carry away wealth, the power of righteousness is that it endures. . . . Make righteousness to flourish and thy children shall live. . . . Established is the man whose standard is righteousness, who walketh according to its ways.' Twenty centuries elapse before the prophet Amos turns in fiery denunciation of his fellow men: 'But seek not Beth-el, nor enter into Gilgal, and pass not to Beer-sheba: for Gilgal shall surely go into captivity, and Beth-el shall come to nought. . . . I hate, I despise our feast days, and I will not smell in your solemn assemblies. Though ye offer me burnt offerings and your meat offerings, I will not accept them: neither will I regard the peace offerings of your fat beasts. Take thou away from me the noise of thy songs; for I will not hear the melody of thy viols. But let judgment run down as waters, and righteousness as a mighty stream.'

Perhaps it had been in the 'words of the ancestors' which he bade his son read that Khati had found an echo of Ptahhotep; 'more acceptable is the virtue of the upright man than the ox of him that doeth iniquity. . . . Set not thy mind on the length of days, for they [the judges] view a lifetime as an hour. A man surviveth after death and his deeds are placed beside him like mountains. . . . The gods, who know character, have hidden themselves, they confound by what is seen of the eyes.' Seventeen centuries later Samuel echoes, 'Behold, to obey is better than sacrifice, and to hearken than the fat of rams.' True, Samuel was thinking of the tribulations of Israel, and gave no thought to the possibilities that 'a man surviveth after death,' but he was equally unaware that 'the gods have hidden themselves.' Nearly a hundred generations of Egyptians had looked forward to the Osirian Judgment before the author of the Book of Proverbs observed that 'Yahweh weigheth the hearts,' and, echoing Samuel, 'To do justice and judgment is more acceptable to Yahweh than sacrifice.'

When and to what extent Egyptian literature became available to the Hebrews is not known. The possibility that the fugitives of the Exodus carried it away with them may be dismissed completely in favor of the supposition that Egyptian literary works were available to them in the prophetic period. Egyptian influence is evident in the royal tombs and burial customs at Byblos as early as 2000 B.C., and in subsequent centuries Egyptian troops carried into Syria Egyptian gods, and Egyptian priests served these gods in Egyptian temples. Transfusion of ideas probably occurred until Hebrew thought had developed so far in its own direction that it had become exclusive. It would be beyond the range of probability that the Hebrews could forever remain ignorant of all except the most primitive Egyptian notions.

The question of a possible relation between Hebrew monotheism and that of Akhnaten has been left open or answered negatively by most historians. In the violent reaction which followed that king's death (1362 B.C.), nearly all visible evidences of his doctrines had been obliterated; if any Semites in either Egypt or Syria had been favorably inclined to Akhnaten's deity, there seems to have been no lasting impression of details for there is but a single parallel between the one-god-Aten and the Yahweh of the Pentateuch. This is the similarity between the fragments of the Aten hymns preserved at Tell el-Amarna and Psalm 104. Breasted has contrasted them verse by verse and metaphor by metaphor, and the parallelism is too close for accident. These verses are, however, such as would be useful to any god — Ra, Amen-Ra, Aten or Yahweh — and do not imply that Palestine was indebted to Egypt for the monotheistic doctrine. Though the doctrine of monotheism was not actualized in the body of the Old Testament until long after the Exile, and perhaps as late as 300 B.C., the first exposition of the monotheistic principle in Hebrew literature was traditionally attributed to Amos, who preached at Bethel shortly after 700 B.C.; at a minimum, therefore, five centuries intervened between the two ideas. It was as a special product of their tribal jealousy and ambition, and independently of any precedent, that the Israelites developed their own particular type of monotheism, an exclusive rather than inclusive type, as is indicated by the first commandment: 'Thou shalt have no other gods before me.'

The two chief Egyptian features emerging in the voice of Yahweh's prophets are a deity who has dominion of all the earth, and the doctrine of the talismanic power of righteousness. It was Amos who asserted that Yahweh demanded not sacrifices but righteous conduct and it was Amos who first presented to the God of Israel the dominion of the universe: 'Seek him that maketh the seven stars and Orion, and turneth the shadow of death into the morning, and maketh the day dark with night: that calleth for the waters of the sea, and poureth them out upon the face of the earth: Yahweh is his name . . . he that formeth the mountains, and createth the wind, and declareth unto man what is his thought . . . Are ye not as children of the Ethiopians unto me, O children of Israel? saith Yahweh. Have not I brought up Israel out of the land of Egypt? and the Philistines from Caphtor, and the Syrians from Kir?' These two ideas — the idea of the One God and the idea of the supernatural power of right-eousness — are the most highly esteemed elements in the Old Testament, yet they go back to the Middle Kingdom and to the sun god Ra, and in the time of Amos could no doubt have been found in literature in any part of the Mediterranean world.

vi

The quick reform effected by King Josiah under the threats of the Deuteronomist did not save Jerusalem. Egypt, recovering from the blows of Ashurbanipal, had thrown off the Assyrian yoke and was preparing to cross Palestine in order to strike against the northern Assyrian provinces. The Scythians were moving into the country around Samaria, intent upon stealing this northern fragment of the original kingdom of Saul and David away from Assyria; and on the Euphrates, an upstart prince, Nabopolassar, had got the upper hand in Babylon and was about to carve out a kingdom for himself. A spirit of conflict was everywhere in the air and, sensing the coming danger, the little state of Judah banked everything upon her god.

Josiah brought forth from the Temple 'the vessels that were made for the Baal, and for the grove [Ashera], and for all the host of heaven: and he burned them without Jerusalem in the fields of Kidron.' He abolished all the shrines and priesthoods of other gods, even the temples said to have been built by Solomon for Chemosh, Milcom and Ashtoreth; he prohibited the worship of Yahweh in all high places other than in the one holy of holies, the Temple of Jerusalem. At last Judah was purified of polytheism and all idolatrous usages, and had put its sole trust in the god of Abraham.

But it was too late. The Egyptians marching against Assyria invaded Palestine and Josiah, siding with Assyria, was slain and Judah captured. Within the space of three years Judah found herself the helpless vassal of a broken Egypt, the nominal ally of a defeated Assyria, and the enemy of the ascendant power of Babylon. Jeremiah implored the Hebrews to throw in their lot with the new Babylonian kingdom, but they continued to maintain subversive relations with Egypt until in 596 B.C. Nebuchadrezzar was forced to punish them. He laid siege to Jerusalem and took as prisoners many of its inhabitants. Still the people, always looking to Egypt for help, plotted rebellion under Zedekiah; a second time Nebuchadrezzar was forced to proceed against Jerusalem and now convinced of the infidelity of its people he determined to destroy the city. After a siege of some months his soldiers were able to carry out his commands. The walls were leveled, the Temple was burned, all that was worth destroying was utterly demolished; the high priest and other leaders were put to death, and a large number of the important inhabitants were again carried off to Babylon (586 B.C.). As the prophets had so long foretold, Jerusalem had fallen and the Temple had been destroyed.

If the prophets had failed to save Jerusalem, Amos, Isaiah, Jeremiah and the Deuteronomist had saved Yahweh from destruction. It has been the otherwise invariable sequence of history that every intensely national religion has been extinguished with the nation's overthrow: but all that was required for Yahweh to survive the fall of Judah was complete etherealization, separation from the wells and springs, the altars and temples, that were forever fastened to the land. This had been half effected by Josiah's concentration of all worship in the Temple of Jerusalem, the holy of holies which had been built by David, who had himself housed Yahweh 'between the thighs of the building.' And the transmutation was completed by the Babylonian troops.

'What, in this disaster, became of the Yahweh himself?' asks Allen. How fared the ark, the Rock of Israel, in the general destruction? The Hebrew annalist, he notes, though plaintively enumerating every pot and shovel and vessel destroyed by the Babylonians, never so much as mentions the most precious item of all, the ark of the god. Perhaps the historian shrank from relating the final disgrace of his country's deity; perhaps a sense of reverence prevented him from recording it; perhaps he knew nothing of what had finally been done with the cherished stone around which Israel had hoped to build a nation. Perhaps, indeed, the ark had long since disappeared from the Temple and the priests had never let the people know it. Its fate is hidden in impenetrable mystery. If the Yahweh of Saul and David and Solomon was still sheltered in the Temple, the ruthless troops of Nebuchadrezzar probably broke it into pieces and left it lying among the other stones. In any case, the physical presence in the ark, and the ark itself, are revered no more. The Israelites were left with a god who had no well, no spring, no tree, no graven image, no temple, no home anywhere on earth — and therefore no boundaries. Unseen, and having no altar before which he must be worshiped, he was omnipresent and could be worshiped anywhere.

'The heaven is my throne, and the earth is my footstool: where is the house that ye build unto me?'

vii

The city to which Nebuchadrezzar carried off the captives from Jerusalem was one of the wonders of the Orient. The grandeur that was Babylon is now wholly dust, but fancy may reconstruct it as it was when the captives from Jerusalem first passed its gates. Where remain only disintegrated piles of clay, colorful temples and palaces take shape; pomp and magnificence again parade through streets whose only vestiges are buried rubble.

There had been nothing in Jerusalem to compare with Babylon, and it is scant wonder that to the Jews it seemed a 'city of gold' and the 'glory of the Kingdoms.' None of them had ever seen so fine a palace or city walls so thick, or dreamed of anything so grand, so tall, so rich with golden images and vessels and turquoise tiles as Ba-Bel, the temple of the celestial Bel-Marduk. One imagines that the Babylonians tried to explain to these people from Palestine, who had revered a god shut up in a box, about the stars and how these stars were gods who controlled the destinies of men, the Jews listening to these tales with only half an ear, not being much better disposed toward the gods of Babylon than toward its king and army. Nevertheless certain episodes lingered in their memories. The story of the Great Flood, as it was related by Uta-Napishtim to Gilgamesh, they used with changes in names and localities as the foundation for an epic of their own. On the legend of how the great Bel-Marduk had cut Tiamat in half they patterned their own story of creation, relating that the god had made the earth and the firmament by dividing the primeval waters into the waters that were above and the waters that were beneath the firmament (the Hebrew word for 'the deep,' *tehōm,* being derived from Tiamat); how he had put the heavenly bodies in their places to mark the day from the night, and how he had created man and commanded him to exalt his name in the sanctuary. It was difficult for them to picture Yahweh in the heavens, so they transferred him to Gilgamesh's land of Eden, the most fertile country in the world according to the Babylonians, one great garden of trees and flowers and fruits. The traders from Persia knew of such a marvelously fertile land: it was on a mountain which they called *Pairidaeza* or Paradise, and it was here that there grew the Tree of Everlasting Life.

It had been in Eden that Engidu had been created out of clay by Aruru, and had lost immortality by reason of the woman whom Shamash had sent to seduce him. Perhaps they confused Engidu, the man who slept and ate with the animals, with Etana who, wishing to procure from Ishtar a drug to alleviate the birth pangs of his wife, had presumed to gain to heaven by soaring aloft on the wings of an eagle, but having reached the place where there was no living thing to be seen and from which the earth appeared no more than a garden plot, the great sea no more than a puddle of water, was overcome with fear and fell and was dashed to pieces on the ground. They may have confused Engidu with the first man, Adapa, or Adamu, as the Babylonians sometimes called him. Or they may have chiefly remembered Gilgamesh himself, who undertook his epic journey to find the Tree of Knowledge, or the Tree of Life — for knowledge and wisdom were equivalent to magic, which was the key to eternal life — only to have a serpent steal it away from him.

Not that these tales were wholly new: some had been old when Abraham abandoned Ur for Haran and with slight changes they were circulating throughout Canaan at the time of Saul and David, as is demonstrated by the fact that two of the Tell el-Amarna letters contain them as school exercises; again when Ahaz erected an altar in Jerusalem patterned after the Assyrian altar at Damascus, and when Manasseh permitted altars to the host of heaven to be set up in Yahweh's temple, Babylonian literature must have entered with her gods. Now in the retelling, however, these tales acquired new meaning and became adapted to the God of Israel. It was related that the first man, Adam, had been created of clay, and had been immortal until a wise serpent had said that one who ate of the Tree of Knowledge should be as a god — deceitfully failing to mention that to retain this high estate the eating of the fruit must be continued. Adam had eaten of the Tree and had been punished for presumption and driven out of Eden; and because they hated Ishtar, and because they were afraid of blood and of the chronic uncleanness that was attached to woman, they laid the blame of the debacle on Adam's mate.

Not the least of the captives' troubles in Babylon was the multiplicity of languages confronting them, for they despised all peoples who spoke a foreign tongue and deemed their own to be Yahweh's dialect. After the Exile, and after Babylon had been destroyed by Cyrus, they spun the legend of the men who presumed to build a tower whose top should reach to heaven; and Yahweh, seeing this presumption and fearing that 'now nothing will be restrained from them, which they have imagined to do,' destroyed the tower, confounded language until men no longer understood each other and scattered them over the face of the earth.

Of those Jews who were carried into captivity, some, convinced that the destruction of Jerusalem proved the impotence of Yahweh and the superior might of Marduk and his court, abandoned the God of Israel; while others, perhaps only a minority, looking with disdain upon the grandeur of Babylon and holding that everything pertaining to the city was unclean, drew themselves apart to dream of Palestine. In retrospect the rolling hills of that country seemed to have been eternally green and fruitful, the cities ineffably lovely, the warriors and prophets of the past loomed as supermen. To assuage the sickness in their hearts they related tales of the glories of old Israel and of Moses, David and Solomon, tales that the scribes patched into the tattered rolls of parchment which had been secretly saved in the destruction of the city and carried to Babylon under the tunics of the devout. As they wept by the waters of Babylon they conceived and began to cherish a new idea; shifting from the view that the calamities of Israel were Yahweh's punishment for her iniquities, the prophets began to say that she had a secret mission: the Israelites were Yahweh's chosen people by whom he intended in his own time to conquer the world, not with chariots and battering rams, but with righteousness. In this new role of Yahweh's 'suffering servant,' Israel was serving a great end; she suffered, was despised, rejected, chastened and afflicted that others might be blessed: 'I will also give thee for a light to the Gentiles, that thou mayest be my salvation unto the end of the earth.'

For forty years the faithful Jews were kept in captivity, listening to the ancient tales of Sumer and Akkad and of Babylon, all the while thoroughly hating their captors. Cherishing the new prophetic doctrine of the coming Kingdom of the Lord, dreaming of the day when those who were now laughed at and spat upon would be the mightiest conquerors of all and wicked Babylon would be destroyed and punished for its iniquities, they drew around themselves tightly and ever more tightly the innumerable rituals that isolated them from strangers. They remained a people apart, moved by a zeal which persecution and ridicule only fired to greater intensity.

Then a new power appeared in the person of Cyrus. The Persian general probably had not the slightest interest in the Jews, but they had every reason to look upon him as Yahweh's messenger. In 539 B.C. he destroyed Babylon, an event which could only be interpreted as Yahweh's retribution upon that wicked city; and, tolerant towards subject races and their religions, within a year he permitted and probably aided those Jews who wished to do so to return to Jerusalem.

At this point the thread of Judaic history is broken. The Jews who had remained in Palestine during the captivity and those who remained in Babylonia after the return are henceforth dropped from the record. How many Jews went into captivity or how many returned is undetermined; the figure of 4600 cited by Jeremiah is perhaps closer to the truth than the 10,000 'men of valour,' 7000 'men of might' and 1000 'craftsmen and smiths' recorded in II Kings. In any case it is the returning exiles who in tradition are made to appear as the founders of the new Israel, as it had been the exiles entering Canaan from Egypt who had been made to appear as the founders of the old.

Against almost overwhelming difficulties the walls of the city were rebuilt (444 B.C.) and a golden crown was made ready for the coronation of the king whom Yahweh was to send. When after long years of waiting the king did not appear and instead political jealousies among the leaders and recurrent warfare with the Edomites, Philistines and Samaritans kept Jerusalem in a perpetual state of chaos and poverty, the high hopes of Israel slowly turned to bitterness. Once more prophetic vision, fired in the cause of nationalism, attributed the postponement of Israel's glory to Yahweh's wrath. Once more the seers exhorted the people to righteousness and under Ezra and Nehemiah ritual purity was re-emphasized and the Deuteronomic code extended, compounded and further multiplied. The Sabbath, once a festival, was made a holy day given over entirely to Yahweh's worship; the world was divided into the holy and the profane; men were divided into clean and unclean, Jews and goyim, and the Jews were required to put aside their gentile wives. Israel became a 'holy congregation' ruled by a high priest, its only intellectual forum, the synagogue.

Slowly through the years the scribes edited the Pentateuch and gradually added the other books of the Old Testament, and in this rewriting they wove the past and present into such a tangled skein that it is impossible to tell with certainty where the new begins and the old leaves off. And as the scribes wrote they built around Israel a wall stronger than any brick — a wall destined to preserve her against disintegration or any change whatever: the Holy Law which, so the priests insisted, Yahweh had given directly into Moses's hands on Sinai's clouded summits.

viii

In the fourth century there came the Greeks, in the second century the Syrians, in the first century the Romans; but against all foreigners the pious Jews kept alive the faith in Israel as the 'chosen people.' Each national crisis seemed only to bring the coming of the king a little nearer. The tide of Greek culture spread by Alexander exposed the Jews to rationalism and diluted their language with new words and ideas, but it left untouched the fundamental Judaic faith. Antiochus looted the Temple, expelled the priests and forbade the Jews to observe the Sabbath, to practice the rite of circumcision and to worship Yahweh in any manner, but he only stirred them to such a war for religious freedom that a tiny band of priests and peons, fighting with little more than their bare fists, defeated four successive Syrian armies and at last drove the invaders out of the country.

When Rome pushed its frontiers eastward Pompey discovered that the Jews would not fight on the Sabbath unless attacked, so he kept guard for six days and took advantage of the seventh to push his siege works against their fortifications. It was on a Sabbath that he took Jerusalem and, with the aid of other Jews, slaughtered 12,000 who remained at worship in the Temple in the face of death. In theory the Roman state was a stable empire; actually it was an almost perpetual state of war, and when the Jews were not quarreling among themselves, they were the deserving, or more rarely the undeserving, victims of these imperial conflicts. No program of co-operation, no martial threat could repress their ambition for national freedom, and rebellion was always in the air. Throughout the time when Palestine was a Roman province it had to be garrisoned with Roman soldiers to keep the Jews and Samaritans from war, or within Jewry itself, to keep the Sadducees, Pharisees and Zealots from cutting each others' throats over the interpretation of the Law. But Roman domination could not prevent the Jews from dreaming their dreams of the coming Kingdom of Yahweh: in the apocalyptic gospels mystical visions and tortuous calculations proved that all the predictions of the prophets had come true, or were about to come true: the world was soon to be destroyed in a great holocaust, and a messiah, one anointed by Yahweh, would descend from heaven and pass judgment on Israel's enemies. 'Repent ye,' the apocalyptic writers cried, 'for the Kingdom of Heaven is at hand!' 'Repent ye' meant for all practical purposes closer adherence to the Law and greater hatred of the Romans and all gentiles.

In A.D. 67, Nero was forced to send Vespasian into Galilee to quell a rebellion over seventeen talents which had been unlawfully appropriated from the treasury of the Temple. Vespasian advanced to the walls of Jerusalem to find three rival factions warring within the city for the control of the Temple. He isolated Jerusalem and left the inhabitants to starve while he subjugated the surrounding country. By 70 Nero had died and Vespasian had been proclaimed emperor, so he delegated Titus to take the city. Only when Titus's troops had moved up to the walls did the inhabitants leave off murdering each other to join hands in self-defense, yet two factions began to fight for possession of the town's granary and, after repeated raids and massacres, succeeded in burning it. Meanwhile the Romans went at the walls with battering rams; the first wall fell in fifteen days, the second in another nine, but still the Jews would not surrender. They huddled in the upper city, dying of starvation, murdering each other for scraps of meat, or risking crucifixion by stealing out at night to pick a few herbs in the fields between the Roman camps. Undermining the Roman mounds so that the battering rams fell down, they flung themselves at the enemy with such clawing and slashing of their nails that the Roman soldiers had to retreat. So Titus built a high wall of earth around the city and sat down to wait. Hard Roman that he was, and used to war, he begged them to surrender in order to stop the horror, but they only scraped together the debris of the city and with it refortified the inner wall. The air reeked with the stench of dead bodies and men fought for the privilege of eating straw, leather or offal. What Titus asked was that they give the city over to Rome; they replied that the city belonged to Yahweh and was not theirs to give. In the end, when they were starved to the point where resistance was impossible, the Romans came in, slaying until their arms were tired. When the destruction was over there was scarcely a stone in place or a piece of wood unburnt, and for the second time Jerusalem was a mass of ruins. The Law required that Yahweh be worshiped and that sacrifices be made only in the one Temple of the holy city: when in the year 70 the Temple was destroyed and Jerusalem as a holy city ceased to be, there remained of Israel only the Law to bind together its scattered people.

I V

The Resurrected God and the Clever Ghost

SHE whom the Babylonians called Ishtar, the Semites generally knew as Ashtoreth, the Phrygians as Cybele, the Persians as Anaitis, while after her the Greeks patterned Astarte, Demeter and Aphrodite, and the Romans, Venus. As the goddess of passion and fecundity descending to the underworld to rescue her lover, she reappeared in the legends of Ariadne, Cytherea, Urania, Genetyllis, Caelestis, Nymphia and Diana; in one guise or another she epitomized the impulse of desire and love, the spirit of germination and fruition, the very vitality of the earth, throughout the length and breadth of the Mediterranean world.

Every city in Asia Minor had its temple for the goddess, the most famous perhaps being the one at Byblos in Phoenicia, a holy place to which the devout made pilgrimages from all parts of the country. The local tradition related a drama similar to that of Ishtar: One morning Astarte caught sight of Adonis (Adon, 'my lord') and became entranced by him, but the happiness of the lovers lasted only a short while before Adonis was killed by a wild boar. The goddess mourned over her lover's body and buried it and, ransomed by her tears, Adonis was resurrected, his love no whit less passionate than before. Again the legend bespoke the earth thrilled by the first breath of spring and abandoning herself to his caresses, being fructified by him and pouring forth the abundance of her flowers and fruits. Then summer kills the spring, the flowers die and the grain withers as Astarte withdraws into her grief, and life would cease should Adonis fail to be revivified.

The precise spot on Mt. Lebanon where Astarte first caught sight of Adonis, unveiled herself before him, and buried his mutilated body is known. In the woods that hide the base of a great amphitheater of red and barren cliffs lies a lake, the outlet of which is a river that in ancient days was called the Adon, and near the lake stood the temple of the god. The temple cloisters were centered on a spacious court in which stood the obelisk of stone, the holy image of the goddess; in one direction its porticoes looked out upon the lofty cliffs, in the other, upon the dark gorge that winds between the buttresses of the mountains to the near-by sea.

At the summer solstice, the season when the wild boar ripped open the divine hunter, it was the custom for the priests to prepare a small wooden image and to hide it in one of a number of terra-cotta jars in which were planted freshly sprouted seeds. These 'gardens of Adoni' were hidden in the caves and wild thickets, set out in the temple and at the door of every house, and left until the tender plants had withered. Then for several days troops of women and girls, their heads disheveled or shorn, their raiment torn, their faces scratched by their nails, their breasts and arms scarified with knives, searched for their idol over hill and dale, crying in despair, "Oh Adoni, Oh Adoni, what has become of thy beauty?" Having found the image they brought it to the feet of the goddess, washed it while displaying its wounds, anointed it with sweet-smelling unguents, wrapped it in a shroud and buried it with solemn mourning in the god's tomb.

The dreary summer passed and with the first days of September the autumnal rains, washing the earth from the cliffs, turned the river into a red flood that formed a crimson fringe along the edges of the sea; then, too, the scarlet anemone (*naaman,* 'darling'), stained with the god's blood, blossomed in the woods. Adonis had come back to life, and those who had lately mourned his death now joined with Astarte in expressions of delight. In the temple the god was declared resurrected and ascended unto heaven in the presence, if not before the eyes, of the multitude.

Here as elsewhere in the East, Astarte's temples were maintained by women dedicated to the goddess, and by male attendants many of whom had castrated themselves in a wild theandric ceremony. Neither the men nor women *hierodouloi* lost caste in Astarte's service; their vocation was regarded as revealing uncommon virtue, and rewarded with mixed wonder, piety and reverence. As far back as the days of Hammurabi the women of Ishtar had been protected by law and even given privileges to which ordinary women could not lay claim, and in instances the sacred service was undertaken by one or more daughters of the king. At Byblos, as in Babylonia, all wives and virgins not connected with the temple placed themselves once at least at the disposal of the strangers who gathered to celebrate the resurrection of the god, the coin which they received becoming the property of the temple. This custom, it has been suggested, stemmed from the *jus prima noctis:* originally the bride had been given the first night to the priest who, acting as the surrogate of the god, gave assurance of fertility, and in time the consecrating act came to be left to divine chance in the form of the stranger. In later days the surrender of the person could be redeemed by cutting off the hair, which was sheared presumably on or after the wedding night.

Astarte's temple at Hierapolis in Lebanon acquired a world-wide reputation and people from all over Arabia and Phoenicia thronged to its annual festival. At the height of the celebration the men who intended to enter the services of the goddess, stimulated to a frenzy by wild music, cast off their clothes and emasculated themselves with sacred swords, while ascetics won sanctity and lasting renown by ascending tall pillars on the summits of which they maintained vigils of a week. The shrine of Astarte and Adonis and its sacred obelisk in the Cyprian city of Paphos appear on coins of Imperial Rome unchanged in design from representations on the royal graves at Mycenae, which date from a thousand years earlier.

At Ephesus, home of the Amazons, the goddess of fertility was depicted as Artemis, a many-breasted female swathed below the waist in grave-clothes; in other copies her animal essence was revealed by a variety of creatures — lions, rams, goats, stags, bees, bulls, or snakes — half emerging from her body, while her vegetable essence was indicated by wreaths of blossoms, necklaces of acorns or sheaves of grain and fruit around her neck and waist. In her orgies men dressed in the skins and skulls of goats and other animals, and calling themselves Satyrs, frolicked in imitation of Dionysus. The Artemision, where stood her sacred tree, altar and wooden image, was, according to Greek reports, several times rebuilt and on the last occasion was restored by common contributions of Croesus and other kings of Asia, but required one hundred and twenty years for its completion. The term *parthenos* was commonly applied to Artemis, but this meant 'unmarried' and not 'virginal,' as it is modernly translated. The chaste goddess whose chief delight was to follow the hunt is a product of the aesthetic Hellenic impulse which glossed over the primal characters of the ancient deities: the pristine Artemis was concerned with the loss of virginity and not its preservation, for from this loss there sprang the ripening corn, the sprouting meadow, the fertility of man.

The Phrygian Cybele, the 'Mother of the Gods,' had for a lover Attis, who was destined to become almost as famous as Dionysus. According to one legend, Attis was beloved by the hermaphroditic monster Agdistis, who had been deprived of male organs by the gods; about to wed the king's daughter, Attis was struck with madness by the jealous Agdistis, emasculated himself, and died from loss of blood, but Zeus kept the body undecayed, allowing the hair to grow and the little finger to move, until he was rescued by Cybele. In another legend Cybele was the carnal lover of Attis, and when her father the king discovered her fault and killed her lover she roamed the earth in wild grief. Or again, the Great Mother was inspired with chaste love for Attis, which he pledged himself to reciprocate; on his proving unfaithful she slew the nymph of his affection, whereupon in madness he mutilated himself as a penalty.

In 206 B.C. the sacred stone which embodied Cybele at Pessinus was taken to Rome, by command of the Sibylline Books, to reinforce the arms of that city against Hannibal. Thereafter her priests became a familiar sight in the capital city; clad in female garb, wearing their hair long and fragrant with ointment, they moved through the streets to the accompaniment of flutes, cymbals, tambourines and castanets, while the people showered the image of the goddess with roses. In the spring a freshly cut pine tree was brought to the sanctuary, its trunk swathed like a corpse and decked with violets (which were said to have sprung from the blood of Attis as anemones had sprung from the blood of Adonis), and an effigy was tied to the middle of the stem in dramatization of the god's death. On the next day the chief ceremony seems to have been the blowing of trumpets, but the third day was devoted to animal sacrifices and to the emasculation of the novices who were being inducted into the priesthood. While the high priest and the lesser clergy worked themselves into a mad frenzy with wild music, gashing their bodies and spattering the altar and sacred tree with flowing blood, the novices, wrought up to the highest pitch of excitement by self-scourging and laceration, castrated themselves and dashed the severed organs against the image of the goddess. Later the instruments of fertility were reverently wrapped up and buried in the earth. The blood sacrifice, the self-mutilation, the burial of the phalli, all aided to recall the dead Attis to life, while a sacramental meal of flesh and blood effected a mystic union between the god and his worshipers. On the fourth day the divine resurrection was celebrated with a ceremonial purification of the image and other sacred objects, and on the last day the people gave themselves over to a licentious carnival called the Hilaria.

Elsewhere in Greece the Mother Goddess was known as Aphrodite. Aphrodite found Adonis as a comely youth and hid him in a chest which she put in charge of Persephone, queen of the nether world. When Persephone opened the chest and beheld the beauty of the child she refused to give him back to Aphrodite, though the goddess herself descended to the nether world to ransom him. The dispute between the goddesses of love and death was finally settled by Zeus, who decreed that Adonis should abide with Persephone in the underworld for half the year, and with Aphrodite in the upper world for the other half. Her festivals, or Aphrodisia, centered in Cythera, Crete and Cyprus, but at the peak of Hellenic influence were celebrated in all the great cities from Egypt to the Black Sea. At the climax of the festival the image of the dead god was exposed and, after the performance of certain rites, was restored to life. Those who desired to be initiated received on entering the temple a phallus and a lump of salt, and gave a piece of money (recalling Ishtar's coin) to the temple treasury. In some instances her cult emphasized chastity and austerity, but this appears to have been exceptional, for her hetaerae were familiar throughout the Hellenic period and it was the custom for public spirited citizens to consecrate one or more slave women to the temple. One day of the festival was given up to the hetaerae and another to respectable women.

At Argos the chief festival of Aphrodite was called Hysteria (womb) and swine were sacrificed to her, the pig and boar being sacred to Adonis as they were to Attis; while at the Feast of Wantonness, women dressed as men and men as women, the men even wearing veils. Plato divided the goddess into two principles: Aphrodite Pandemos, who personified the sensual love of the body, and Ourania Aphrodite, who personified the intellectual love of the mind. This distinction, however, was never recognized by her votaries or by the state.

The most popular transformations of Astarte and Adonis were in the Eleusinian and Orphic Mysteries. The former revolved about Demeter and her daughter Persephone. In its earlier form, the legend appears to have related that one day Persephone was gathering flowers in a meadow when Hades, ruler of the world below, abducted her. Demeter, refusing to be consoled, withdrew her blessing and the earth would have become unfruitful, the human race would have perished, but for the interference of Zeus, who ruled that Persephone should be restored for eight months of every year to her mother. In later time Adonis appears in the drama as Dionysus or Bacchus, at once the lover and the only-begotten son of Demeter, and in this incestuous role usurped the leading part. Although Dionysus-Bacchus was apparently never worshiped in a temple, the Mysteries henceforth became less an agricultural rite than a medium for communion with the god and a preparation for the afterlife by a mystic initiation.

All that is known of the Eleusinian initiation is that within the temple there was enacted on the central stage a mystery play based on the abduction of Persephone and the birth, death and revival of Dionysus-Bacchus, the Eleuthereos or 'Liberator,' and that at one part of the ceremony something was shown to the novice, something was said to him and something was tasted by him. According to the gentile Hippolytus, one of the 'things seen' was 'that great and marvelous mystery of perfect revelation, a cut cornstalk'; while others averred that the 'things tasted' included a barley drink, while in the 'things said,' the audience gazed up to heaven and cried aloud, "Rain!" and gazed down upon the earth and cried, "Conceive!" These opinions to the contrary, the oath of secrecy was so well preserved that the Mysteries of Eleusis are as obscure today as in the millennium of their popularity.

Similar to the Eleusinian Mysteries and having many adherents in Crete and western Hellas, was the cult of Dionysus as developed in the Orphic Mysteries. The Orphists, like the Eleusinians, hid the forms and teaching of their worship so well that all appraisals are largely guesswork. Euripides described the worship of Dionysus, before it had been tempered by Greek aestheticism, as given over to a wild ecstasy in which men wandered in the mountains, tore live animals to pieces in order to devour their raw flesh and indulged in sexual irregularities. These practices were apparently in abeyance in Plato's time, for he speaks of the Orphic teachers more moderately as 'quacks and soothsayers, who flock to the rich man's doors, and try to persuade him that they have a power at their command, which they procure from heaven, and which enables them by sacrifices and incantation performed amid feasting and indulgence, to make amends for any crime committed by the individual himself, or by his ancestors . . . and they produce a host of books, written by Musaeus and Orpheus, which form their ritual. . . . Their Mysteries deliver us from the torments of the other world, while the neglect of them is punished by an awful doom.'

Dionysus was represented as a youth of soft, nearly feminine form, as a bearded and draped man, or as an infant. As a god of fertility he was represented as a phallus, and as a god of trees his image was an upright post draped in a mantle and adorned with a bearded mask. He was also represented as a bull, and a live bull or calf was probably the principal sacrifice which was torn to pieces and eaten by his devotees in the belief that they were killing the god, eating his flesh and drinking his blood. As at Eleusis, the sacred men and women of his temple re-enacted his death and resurrection as part of the mysteries of initiation.

The Orphic teachers propounded a doctrine of reincarnation and assumed that man's body held imprisoned in the impure flesh a divine spark which could by sacraments, abstinences and other purifications be elevated ultimately to a divine estate. They were preoccupied with the after-life and were possibly the first to formulate the notion of a purgatory which was a posthumous punishment and purification for the Dionysian realm. Through the Orphic Mysteries Dionysus brought the sacrament to Greece; the lyric incantations designed for his worship produced the first metric prose, and in the mimetic performance of the god's birth, death and resurrection was born Greek Tragedy.

The doctrine of an afterlife, which the Orphic cults held in common with the worshipers of Demeter and Bacchus at Eleusis, gave them a strong appeal among the masses. Quite probably under the influence of Osiris and of Egyptian notions of the nether world, it became the custom to bury with the body Dionysiac hymns which, as incantations, served to guard the deceased in the underworld and to afford him instructions as to the route to Hades's realm, and on how to address the servants of Per-sephone. As Osiris had died and been resurrected, so Dionysus died, and as the dead Egyptian was identified with Osiris by magic declaration, so the worshiper of Dionysus immitted the spirit of the god by partaking of his live flesh and blood.

Last to be introduced from the Orient into the Mediterranean world was the cult of Mithra, the Persian sun god. This was distinguished by a certain novelty in its doctrines, or at least by sharp differences between these doctrines and those of the Mesopotamian-Phoenician gods. Mith-raism was a degenerate form of Zoroastrianism, the national religion of the Persian-Iranian people, this in turn having stemmed from the more primi-tive Mazdaism the literature of which had been developed in the second millennium B.C. before the separation of the Persians and Hindus from a common stock.

According to the Mazdean legends, there were in the beginning two primeval spirits, Ormazd (Ahura-Mazdah), the personification of light and good, and his twin brother, Ahriman, the personification of darkness and evil. These two brothers were pitted against each other in perpetual warfare. To aid him, Ormazd had created the male principle, Mithra, out of whose light and heat were compounded the sun and moon, and the female principle, Anahita, or moisture, rain and water; these in turn brought forth the seven 'holy immortal ones': Justice or Truth, Right Order, Obedience, Prosperity, Piety or Wisdom, Health and Immortality, all of whom had the nature of angels. These angels were aided by a host of sub-angelic beings of a generally good character. Ahriman, in oppo-sition, created a legion of evil powers, or daēvas (whence demon and devil) who manifested themselves in disease and death, filth, chaos, in everything antagonistic to Ormazd. Since all that was, all that could be, was a manifestation of the struggle of Ormazd and Ahriman for supremacy, the world of substance, thought and action was sharply divided between the opposition of good and evil: light, heat, fire, moisture, rain and wind were powers of good, while darkness, drought and storm were powers of evil. All wishes, all experience, all knowledge, were either good or evil; there was no intermediate ground, no attribute, value or quality of indeterminate or indifferent character. In every action man was free to choose on which side he would fight: if he chose to fight with Ahriman, so let it be; if he chose to fight with Ormazd, then his duty lay in speaking the truth and combating falsehood by obeying the commands of law and the True Order, by tending his cattle and fields and resisting the lawless, predatory nomads, by carrying on war against devil worshipers, and by keeping the pure creations, earth, water and especially fire, free from all pollution. The places of worship of Ormazd were simple circles of stones in the center of which burned the sacred fire, which was revered as the god himself. His votaries had neither temples nor statues, holding it to be unworthy of the deity to be symbolized by any finite form. Inscriptions at Boghaz-keui reveal that Mazdaism was known west of the Euphrates in the fourteenth century B.C. Yet in later times it was asserted that the founder of the cult had been one Zoroaster (Zarathustra) who apparently lived in the seventh century B.C. Whether real or legendary, Zoroaster only identifies an effort at reform, and after the sixth century B.C. abstract Persian thought ran riot and produced a weird mixture of degenerate ritual and vague immaterialities now headed by the sun god, Mithra.

Legend had it that Mithra had been born of a rock, the miraculous birth having been seen by certain shepherds who brought gifts and adored him. The outstanding event in his career had been his destruction of a sacred bull created by Ormazd; the blood of the animal gave origin to the life of the earth, while its soul rose to the celestial spheres to become, under the name of Silvanus, the guardian of herds. Then Ahriman tried to destroy the world, first by drought, then by flood, then by fire; the drought Mithra defeated by discharging an arrow against a rock and miraculously drawing water from it, the flood by aiding one man to escape with his cattle in an ark, while from the fire only the creatures of Ormazd survived. Then Mithra ascended to heaven where he served as a mediator between Ormazd and the world.

Mithra was figured carrying the two keys of the firmament, one to the entrance and one to the exit of the heavens. Each day of the week was marked by the adoration of a special planet, the sun being the most sacred, and Sunday was called the Lord's day, after one of Mithra's titles. His birthday was at the winter solstice, his triumph and ascension at the spring equinox. On the latter occasion an image was buried in a rocky tomb and withdrawn as reliving, in much the manner of the Attis-Adonis-Dionysus rites. In Mithraic doctrine, life was conceived to be a spark of divine fire which had descended from the highest heaven to acquire a gross and corrupted envelope of flesh and to engage in a continual struggle with the powers of evil.

Though Mithra was manifest in the sun, and a deity both of light and of vegetable and animal increase, the Mithraeum was usually a natural cave or, in its absence, an artificial subterranean crypt at one end of which was placed a relief showing the god killing a bull. Here neophytes, sworn to secrecy, were initiated into the Mithraic Mysteries, of which there were seven degrees, one involving a communion of bread and wine, another a purification of the hands and tongue with honey, the third a simulated death and resurrection, and in a fourth the subject was marked on the forehead with a symbolic sign. Mystic rituals such as the repetition of sacred formulas, the chanting of music, and purification by baptism, by the ringing of bells, by the sacred fire of the temple candles and by flagellation, served to induce in the initiate a state of ecstatic exaltation. The highest degree was held by the priests who were addressed as 'Pater,' a name later corrupted to 'papa' and then to 'pope.'

The chief rite of initiation for those who could afford it was the baptism by the blood of the bull, or the *taurobolium,* which some believe to have been adapted from the rites of Attis and Cybele. In this ceremony the novice descended into a pit the top of which was covered with a grating; then a bull was brought over the grating and slaughtered by having its throat cut, its hot, steaming blood pouring down upon the subject beneath, who drenched his face and body in it and was thereby cleansed of his transgressions, 'born again for eternity.' After this rebirth, the initiate was clothed in white and fed for some time on milk like a newborn babe.

The advance of Mithraism was attributable in part to the aid which it gave its votaries in finding their way in the spirit world — a feature which it shared with the Eleusinian and Orphic mysteries. Apart from legend, so similar were the major doctrines and practices that Anahita was in many places identified with Cybele or Astarte, and Mithra with Attis. Mithraism had a single advantage over its competitors: within its democratic ranks a poor man might advance by title and degree of initiation in the esteem of his fellows and even reach a vastly superior position. Its outstanding disadvantage lay in the fact that it excluded women from its privileges, whereas women had always played a major role in the other mysteries.

Mithraism was prevalent in Greece in early days, but never gained wide popularity until the later Hellenic age. It had its greatest success in Rome, to which city it was carried, according to Plutarch, in 67 B.C. by captive Cilician pirates; after remaining dormant there for some time, it began to spread among the slaves, the army and the mercantile families, many of whom were of Asiatic origin or had Asiatic contacts, and ultimately became popular with the governors, military commanders and other members of the ruling classes, until under Aurelian (270–275) it was made the official or state religion. Following the army and the trade routes, it spread to the Upper Danube, into Gaul and as far north as Britain. During the second and third centuries it was one of the most popular cults in the West, at least in Rome itself and most of Italy, and bade fair to become a world religion.

ii

From the sixth century B.C. to the third century of the Christian Era resurrected gods in one guise or another were worshiped throughout western Asia, northern Africa, Europe as far west as Spain and as far north as the Baltic. Three common features were important in all these cults: the ecstatic experience in which communion was established with the deity, a sacramental meal to aid or symbolize this communion, and a drama to mimic the divine death and resurrection.

As the Greeks used the term, *ekstasis* was a verbal noun derived from *existemi,* meaning 'to put a person out' (of his senses). Originally *ekstasis* meant insanity or bewilderment, but in late Greek it came to be used to describe the withdrawal of the spirit from the body, escape from one's own nature. Ecstasy might take the orgiastic form in which an outburst of mental activity led to prophesying or inchoate speech accompanied by a display of physical force, or it might appear as a paralytic trance in which the subject was inert and sensible only to his own hallucinations. Though either state might occur spontaneously, the orgy was customarily induced by a stimulus such as spiritous liquors or various drugs, or by wild music, dancing, whirling, flagellation, self-laceration or the sight of blood; the paralytic trance was aided by intense concentration on some part of the body, such as the navel or the tip of the nose, or on some external object heavily charged with mystic implications. It was well demonstrated in medieval and later times that either the excitatory or paralytic ecstasy can in rare instances so occlude sensation that the most brutal mortal injuries, such as those sustained in crucifixion, burning or evisceration, are borne consciously, yet without pain.

Ecstasy in various degrees of intensity had long been used as a magic tool to promote the growth of vegetation, to bring down rain or to raise a wind, but it was also esteemed for its own sake, as a novel and more intense mood of life. By virtue of its contagious nature the orgiastic ecstasy was apt to be more prevalent in the ancient cults than the paralytic trance, which requires for its induction quiet and concentration as well as a special, personal propensity. It was universally accepted that during either the orgiastic or paralytic trance the subject achieved contact and communion with the god, and experienced a rapture that would avail him until death.

Through the Dionysiac cults the sacramental meal was introduced to Greece as an ecstatic instrument; no doubt in earlier periods the participants literally did tear a living animal to pieces and devour the warm flesh and blood, until through the development of the drama and substitution by legend the sacrament was tempered into a symbolic meal. In this tempering, however, it lost little of its ecstatic force: whether a man partook of the blood of the god, the bread of the god, or the wine of the god, he was made 'full of the god,' for the divine body was in all these substances.

Although the dead god theme in apparently every case — Osiris, Tammuz, Adonis, Dionysus and Mithra — had its origin in the cycle of growth and decay attending the natural seasons, it was the invariable history of the theme that it became identified as a symbolic expiatory sacrifice — the dying god became a scapegoat for man's transgressions. Proportionately as legend and growing doctrine made it possible for the teachers to emphasize the sense of mystical uncleanness, the function of the supernatural drama was shifted from the productiveness of nature to personal salvation, and sacrifice was made the instrument of future blessedness. There is every reason to believe that in the transitional stages separating primitive agrarian magic from the classical mysteries, the symbolic death of the god had been represented by the real immolation of a human being. These transitional stages are almost wholly lost in illiterate prehistory, but some information on them is discoverable in legends and in the conservative habits of remote communities where ancient customs persisted into the historic period.

It has been noted that human sacrifice was rare in Egypt, and it is more surprising, in view of their ferocious cruelty to prisoners of war, that the Babylonians and Assyrians were also relatively innocent in this respect. It was from the western Semites that human sacrifice entered European culture. The sacrifice of the first-born among the Canaanites and its persistence in Israel and the sacrifice of adults in times of national crises have been noted previously. Phoenicia and Carthage, according to Greek historians, both offered children to Cronos, a not improbable charge in view of the well attested service of Moloch. The burning of children to Moloch (or Cronos) clearly had an expiatory function; it was prompted by the conviction that the anger of the god had been incurred and thus imperiled the well-being of the community, and that the life of one or more of its members must be surrendered in expiation of the guilt. The question of how the sacrifice purified the community of blame must remain beyond examination when dealing with an age lacking a contemporary literature, but in any case no single formula is adequate to cover the varying circumstances. The only safe generalization is that it has ever been held that the individual is inferior to the community and, as against the community, has no rights: 'It is expedient for us, that one man should die for the people, and that the whole nation perish not.'

Puzzling as human sacrifice is to the naïve view, it has never deeply puzzled the anthropologist. It is an act so unified with the culture of the people who practice it that it presents nothing horrible or even extraordinary. It is believed that human sacrifice reached its most elaborate development with the Aztecs. One Spanish historian estimated that the number of victims sacrificed to the god Xipa annually exceeded the number who died a natural death in the entire country of Mexico. Cortez reported 136,000 skulls in the great temple, and Prescott estimated that the yearly toll throughout the Empire exceeded 20,000, and perhaps totaled 50,000 victims. The record appears to have been reached at the dedication of the new temple of Hiutzilopochtli in 1486, when there were slain 70,000 prisoners of war who had been held in reserve for this occasion over a period of years.

This wholesale slaughter was not the madness of a demented people, but the logical application of a faith. The Aztecs gave to their gods whatever they themselves valued: food, clothing, flowers, jewelry, incense, the first fruits of the harvest, of hunting and fishing and of the handicrafts. Animal sacrifices were made on a tremendous scale, but the most acceptable, the indispensable offering, was human blood. The frequent bleedings and mutilations to which the people and the priests subjected themselves served, by the magic power of blood, to keep the gods young and vigorous and to assure their favorable disposition. Small quantities of blood were, however, a cheap price to pay for the continued welfare of the nation, and it was only by occasional human sacrifice on a large scale that these lesser donations could be made effective. Hence war to maintain an adequate supply of victims was to the Aztecs a religious duty. They wanted living prisoners and, not understanding mortal combat, fell an easy prey to the Spaniards who fought to kill.

In cultures lacking a theology adequate to support the immolation of a human victim, animal sacrifice is of course the rule, the custom being sustained by a strong web of tradition and ceremonial ritual. However, many historians are convinced that human sacrifice is the more primitive, the ritual perhaps demanding a 'willing' human victim, secured by the bribe of a period of royal ease and license; as 'willing' victims became hard to procure, one 'bought with a price' was substituted, representing a victim duly paid for by the community, or alternatively a condemned criminal was used. Except among a few isolated tribes the animal substitute has been the general rule throughout the last three or four millenniums. Yet Robertson, adding together the figures of anthropologists, remarks that the number of human beings sacrificed in late prehistoric and historic times must be reckoned in thousands of millions, all of them immolated to the gods in behalf of the welfare of the community.

The persistence of the practice among peoples of primitive culture in Africa and India and, until recent date, in northern Europe, suggests that it may once have been the custom in certain countries of the ancient world to sacrifice the king in times of national emergency, in anticipation of his natural death, or even periodically. It required only the co-identification of king and god, and the attribution to the god of responsibility for the revitalization of nature, to set the stage for a periodic ceremony to renew the crops. Yet strangely enough, Egypt, where the Pharaoh was the god and the god was personally responsible for the crops, was at least two millenniums ahead of the rest of the ancient world in abandoning king sacrifice. Whatever may have been the original custom, after the opening of the dynastic period a purely dramatic symbolization in the form of the great Sed festival, which was celebrated at Abydos every thirty years over a period of many centuries, sufficed both to identify the Pharaoh with Osiris and to renew the godhead.

The gods were, strictly speaking, never immortal. As Ra grew old his bones turned to silver, his flesh to gold and his azure locks to lapis lazuli. Osiris, Tammuz, Adonis, Attis and their counterparts had all died a violent death and been resurrected. Zeus was buried in Crete, Apollo and Dionysus at Delphi, Cronos in Sicily, and the graves of Hermes, Aphrodite and Ares could be seen in Cyprus and Thrace. In Babylonia the deities attained immortality by eating the Tree of Wisdom or the Plant of Everlastingness, while the gods of Greece were kept young by divine ambrosia and nectar. Each of these aging gods was, moreover, not so much an individual as a personal continuum repeatedly refreshed by the advent of a new king who had been fathered by the god: the manner in which Queen Hatshepsut and King Amenhotep III publicized their parentage left no doubt about the literal interpretation of the divine impregnation. Syrian potentates identified themselves with Adonis or Dionysus, while there can be no question that the king or high priest in the service of Ishtar and Astarte played the part of a divine bridegroom in the annual festivals, and the children born of temple unions must have enjoyed some measure of divinity. Astarte's temple must have been well stocked with semi-divine princes and princesses any one of whom might succeed the god or goddess in the temple, and from this raw material the godhead might be renewed whenever an inadequacy of the divinity was manifest.

Whatever royal sacrifice was observed around the Mediterranean in ancient times, it had been mitigated by substitution before the historic period. Of the substitutive sacrifice, the best known and probably the oldest example is the Perso-Babylonian festival of the Sacaea which, according to Berossus, was celebrated annually at Babylon. Here a prisoner who had been condemned to death replaced the king, and for his brief term of royal office bore the name of Zoganes (perhaps *sagan,* 'substitute' or 'deputy'). He was dressed in the king's robes, seated on the king's throne, allowed to issue whatever commands he pleased, to eat, drink and enjoy himself and to lie with the king's concubines. During the five days of the festival, masters and servants changed places, the servants giving orders and the masters obeying them. At the end of the five days the victim was stripped of his royal robes and scourged, and then either hanged or impaled.

The records of propitiatory sacrifice in Asia Minor are abundant and unimpeachable. Strabo recounts that in his time (*ca.* 63 B.C.–21 A.D.) the Albanians maintained a number of *hierodouloi* and when one of these became divinely possessed he was seized, bound with sacred fetters and maintained sumptuously for a year, at the end of which time he was anointed with ointments and slain by piercing through the side with a sacred lance. Eusebius reports the annual sacrifice to Zeus in the same manner in the Cyprian city of Salamis, a custom which persisted until the time of Hadrian (*ca.* 125 A.D.), and Quintus Curtius attests the annual sacrifice of a boy to Cronos at the Phoenician city of Tyre. Curtius is also authority for the statement that the Carthaginians maintained the custom of an annual sacrifice to Moloch until the destruction of the city in 146 B.C., Pliny asserting that the victim was sacrificed to Hercules.

Several Greek and Latin writers attest the Carthaginian sacrifice of children to Moloch. As related by Diodorus, it appears that when the Carthaginians were defeated by Agathocles they ascribed their disaster to Moloch's wrath, for whereas in former times they had been wont to sacrifice to him their own offspring, they had latterly fallen into the habit of buying children or rearing them to be victims. So, to appease the angry god, two hundred children of the noblest families were picked out for sacrifice and the tale of victims was swelled by not less than three hundred more who volunteered to die for the fatherland. One by one they were placed on the sloping hands of the brazen image from which they were rolled into the pit of fire, while all the place in front of the image was filled with a tumultuous music of fife and drum to drown their shrieks. Childless people among the Carthaginians bought children from poor parents and slaughtered them, says Plutarch, as if they were lambs or chickens, and a mother had to stand by and see it done without a tear or a groan, for if she wept or moaned she lost all the credit, and the child was sacrificed none the less. Infants were thus publicly sacrificed by the Carthaginians down to the Proconsulate of Tiberius (12 B.C.), who remonstrated by crucifying the priests on the trees beside their temples. According to Tertullian, whose testimony is prejudiced, however, the practice went on secretly as late as A.D. 200.

The Greek literati disdained human sacrifice and even as early as the Homeric poems, when Achilles slew twelve Trojans on Patroclus's pyre to supply the latter with thralls, it was said that 'evil was the deed which he contrived'; yet long afterwards Greek writers were moved in the interest of historic accuracy to record that it was frequently resorted to in time of stress. Pausanias and Porphyry attest that a human sacrifice was offered to Zeus at Mt. Lycaeus in time of drought, the custom extending down to the second century after Christ, and the latter author records that every year at Rhodes, at the festival of Cronos, a criminal kept back for this purpose was led outside the gates of the city and put to death after being given wine to stupefy him; in the Rhodian myth the sacrificial victim had originally been the only-begotten son of the god, who had sacrificed him after dressing him in royal robes. A similar annual sacrifice was observed at Salamis in Cyprus, in honor of Aglauros, the daughter of Cecrops, and at the temple of Apollo in Leucas a criminal was thrown over the cliff into the sea every year as a scapegoat; only here the severity of his fall was mitigated by attaching live birds and feathers to his body, and men waited in small boats to rescue him and carry him beyond the boundaries. Porphyry refers to additional instances of human sacrifice among the Greeks at Rhodes, Chios, Tenedos, Salamis, Crete, Athens and Sparta, and the flagellation of Spartan boys at the altar of Artemis Orthea is declared by Pausanias to have been instituted by Lycurgus in place of the older custom of killing a man who was selected by lot. Bordering between history and legend are the reports that Themistocles sacrificed three Persian captives to Dionysus before the battle of Salamis, and that Epimenides the Cretan in the course of his purification of Athens sacrificed one or more youths. Several authorities state that at one time outcasts were maintained by the Athenians at public expense and in moderate luxury, so that if calamity such as plague, drought or famine befell the city, two of these victims could be sacrificed as scapegoats, one for the men and one for the women. Whether these are identifiable with two victims allegedly proposed for sacrifice in the summer festival of the Thargelia is uncertain. More certainly legendary is the narrowly averted immolation of Iphigenia to Artemis, in order to raise wind for the Greek fleet becalmed at Aulis, and of Polyxena whose death at the tomb of Achilles was urged by Neoptolemus to get the fleet home from Troy.

That many victims were criminals or social outcasts did not matter: a man's fitness to serve as a gift to the god was not dependent on his moral qualities or social rank, and it was the absence of such discrimination that made possible the animal substitute. Greek legends abound in instances where, by a ruse or revelation, the human victim was spared and an animal accepted in his place, as a goat or bull was substituted for a human victim in the rites of Dionysus. Such a legend is that of the Minotaur, the monster with the body of a man and the head of a bull which King Minos of Crete had shut in the labyrinth. To avenge the death of his son, who had been killed by the Athenians, Minos demanded that seven Athenian youths and seven maidens should be sent every ninth years to be devoured by the Minotaur. When the third sacrifice came around Theseus volunteered to go. With the help of Minos's daughter, Ariadne, with whom he fell in love, Theseus slew the Minotaur.

The Minotaur has been interpreted as a sun god (Moloch or Cronos), and the union of Pasiphaë and the bull which produced it as recounting the mythical marriage of the sun and the moon which was acted as a solemn rite by the king and queen of Crete, who wore the masks of a bull and cow respectively, while the tribute of seven youths and seven maidens from Athens served to renew the sun god's power. The legend relates that the victims were shut up in the labyrinth to be devoured by the Minotaur, but it is more likely that they were originally roasted alive in a bronze image of a bull. The heroic Theseus, who killed the Minotaur, and Ariadne, who aided her lover by giving him a thread with which to find his way out of the labyrinth, reveal the mitigation of the sacrifice before advancing culture. The legend of the Minotaur leads to Dionysus, for it was on the way home that Ariadne was slain by Artemis, and it was Dionysus who found her and, enchanted by her beauty, awakened her and made her his wife.

In the Roman period the frequency of human sacrifice diminishes. Several laws, one passed under Tiberius in 97 B.C. prohibiting the killing of adults or children to sanctify an oath, to divine the future or for other magic purposes, afford indirect evidence that these practices were not uncommon though probably limited to the more backward classes. Tiberius also forbade the immolation of human beings in the worship of Saturn in Africa, as well as the sacrifices of the Druids; the Cyprian cult of Jupiter was similarly censored in the time of Hadrian. The Romans looked upon the custom as barbaric and forbade its private practice, but, like the Greeks, resorted to it in public emergency. Pacuvius served as a voluntary sacrifice for the well-being of Augustus, Curtius threw himself in full armor into the chasm which had opened in the ground of the Forum, in order to close the abyss, and two Romans pledged themselves to die in order that Caligula might recover from illlness. In 46 B.C. Caesar caused two soldiers to be sacrificed to Mars as a penalty for mutiny, in the belief that the god who had been angered by the mutiny would be pacified by the oblation. Pompeius threw several men into the sea, probably as an offering to Poseidon, and on the Ides of March in 41 B.C., the enlightened Octavian is reported to have sacrificed three hundred men at the altar of the *Divus Julius,* his intention being to placate the *manes* of the murdered dictator. Even if the custom was not generally approved, faith in its efficacy did not fail and in the second century the Emperor Commodus sacrificed a man to Mithra, probably on an occasion when there was a dearth of corn.

It was the custom in imperial Rome to hold each year a winter revel which was called the Saturnalia. This festival was supposed to commemorate the merry reign of Saturn, the god of sowing and of husbandry, who had long ago lived on earth as a righteous and beneficent king. In Saturn's time, so it was said, the earth brought forth abundantly, no sound of war or discord troubled it, no baleful love of lucre worked like poison in the blood of the industrious and contented peasantry, slavery and private property were alike unknown, all men had all things in common. At last the good king died and with him vanished the Golden Age. Men cherishing his memory reared shrines in his honor and named hills and holy places after him and, on this annual occasion, indulged in feasting and revelry and the many pursuits of pleasure in a carnival that lasted for seven days. This carnival was similar to the Sacaea in that the distinction between the free and the servant classes was temporarily abolished. The slave might rail at his master, intoxicate himself like his betters and sit down at the table with them, and not a word of reproof could be administered for conduct which at any other season would have been punishable by imprisonment or death. Masters changed places with their slaves and waited on them at table, and not until the serf had done eating and drinking was the board cleared and dinner set for the master himself.

Presiding over the Saturnalia was a mock king whose every order had to be obeyed. From fragmentary evidence it appears that even in the time of the empire this mock king may have served as a human sacrifice. A Greek manuscript dating from the fourth century A.D., written by a Christian and recounting the history of the martyrs, relates that at this time it was the custom of the Roman soldiers at a certain station to celebrate the Saturnalia in the following manner: thirty days before the festival they chose by lot from among themselves a young and handsome man who was then clothed in royal attire to resemble Saturn. Attended by a multitude of soldiers, he went about in public with full license to indulge his passions and to taste every pleasure. This short but merry reign was ended when the thirty days were up and the festival of Saturn had come, for then he had to cut his own throat on the altar of the god whom he impersonated. In A.D. 303, the lot fell upon a Christian soldier, Dasius, who refused to play the part of the heathen god and soil his last days by debauchery. The threats and arguments of his commanding officer failing to shake his determination, he was beheaded, as the Christian martyrologist faithfully records, at Durostorum, by the soldier John, on Friday, the twentieth day of November, being the twenty-fourth day of the moon, at the fourth hour. What is apparently the sarcophagus of this mock Saturn, now St. Dasius, was discovered in the cathedral of Ancona in 1906. That a Christian historian should invent such a tale in connection with the canonization of a revered saint is highly improbable, and his account suggests that well into the Christian era a mock king's death might be no imitative drama.

iii

In sharp contrast to the gods of the mysteries and the resurrection cults were the Olympians of Greek poetry, standing revealed in the compilations of Homer and Hesiod as immortal men and women of superhuman substance and power: Zeus, Hera, Hades, Poseidon, Demeter, Hestia and their kin had so outgrown the aboriginal forces of nature that they could faithfully mirror the wars, intrigues and amours of men in the manner of characters in an heroic tale. They lived in a royal palace above all other immortals, attended by Hebe, the cupbearer, Themis, in charge of food, Hephaistos, the smith and mason, Athena, supervisor of the domestic arts, and Hermes, the messenger. They quarreled over the best sacrifices, they roared with laughter when Hephaistos surprised his wife Aphrodite and Ares in a love tryst and, excepting Hera, his wife, they ever looked with envy on Zeus's prowess as a lover. By the period of the *Iliad* that same artistic genius which sought perfection in sculpture, rhyme and poetry had so completely humanized the inhabitants of Olympus that their vulgar origin from the thunderstorm, mountains, springs and trees had been all but forgotten. For certain types of minds they represented the only true gods, so that Aristophanes the scoffer could say of the barbarians, 'They worship Sun and Moon, we worship real gods such as Apollo and Hermes.'

Aristophanes's 'real gods' were but little concerned with human morals, or human affairs in any way. It was only when a sailor facing shipwreck sacrificed a juicy cock to Poseidon that the god of waters gave him any personal attention; only when all the Hellenic states united to wage war against the Persians was Zeus Hellenios stirred to active aid in their defense; and only after the development of communal life when homicide became a civil crime did the chthonian Zeus demand appeasement for the shedding of kindred blood. The gods of Olympus were too busy with their own affairs to bother with common mortals except in response to very special petitions or in emergencies. In the respect that the relationship between man and gods had no moral fiber, the Olympian pantheon stood in sharp contrast to Judaism and, in only slightly lesser degree, to the popular mysteries. In part this fact is attributable to the circumstance that down to the fourth century Greek philosophy developed among a leisured class which lived on slave labor, among men who were accustomed to the unemotional discussion of the world and its nature. They had little interest in social justice because they fully enjoyed what they conceived to be social justice. Hebrew prophecy, on the other hand, born of the misfortunes of

Israel, voiced the hopes and miseries of a frustrated people. For the philosophers, a god who was involved in all the petty affairs of men could not
be Zeus; for the prophets, a Yahweh who failed to be thus involved could
not be God.

It has been said that the Greeks attained their distinctive influence
in the world because they — or rather the Ionians — liberated thought
from the bondage of religious ritual: it serves as accurately to say it
was because they had no moral gods to bind their thoughts with divine
imperatives. It is a corollary of this fact that the Greeks in general had no
systematically developed beliefs in regard to the hereafter. No doubt a
variety of notions about the spirit existed throughout the Greek states
between the time of the Homeric poems (1000 B.C.) and the opening of
the Christian Era, but with few exceptions these notions appear to have
had this much in common: the dead had no solid substance to be grasped
or touched — that was why they were called 'shades' or 'images' — and
they were deaf and dumb and impotent to act, for how could a shade,
which was a mere fragment of a man, his 'last breath' which he gave up
when he expired, hear without ears, talk without tongue, or act without
bones and muscles? Even if the shade survived in or near the grave for a
short period before its final dissolution, it had no consciousness of the
affairs of this world and no intercourse with other shades, for it had no
capacity to think. The early Greeks were no more astute than other peoples
in their anatomical speculation, and variously identified the organ of
thought and feeling as the midriff, heart or brain, but they were consistent
in holding to the simple view that the dissolution of the body put an end
to all bodily operations, that since death destroyed the body it destroyed
the Self.

As a special gift the dead might be allowed to retain their consciousness,
as when Persephone granted Tiresias a mind, 'even though he was dead,'
or when Menelaus and the heroes of Thebes and Troy were allotted life
in the Islands of the Blest, while it was a miracle when Pelops and Gany-
mede were carried off bodily to Olympus. Phlegyas burned the temple of
Apollo (though with some justification considering that god's behavior
toward his daughter Coronis!); Ixion suffered from an unfortunate amour
with Juno, and Tityus from an indiscreet love of Latona; Tantalus stole
the gods' favorite food, or according to some, their favorite dog; Salmoneus
imitated their lightning, and Sisyphus insulted Pluto and prattled an erotic
indiscretion of Zeus: these were accordingly preserved in order to be punished in the other world. Ordinary mortals anticipated no such offenses,
and hence no such punishments. Every page of Greek literature bears the

names of divine beings, yet the whole is impressively silent on the fortunes of the common dead. The tragic dramatists, Aeschylus, Sophocles and Euripides — the first two exponents of the highest contemporary religious thought, the last, its critic — describe the gods in great detail both as observers and participants in relation to the human pageant, but if they venture to suggest that the personal drama extends beyond the grave it is in very tentative terms; their most penetrating analysis of ethics reveals no suggestion of postmortal reward or punishment. For Sophocles the Eleusinian mystic alone finds happiness in Erebos, and only because the Orphic doctrine propounded that a divine spark is entrapped within the flesh is it distinguished from the background of general disbelief in survival after death. It was specifically to this Orphic cult that Pythagoras and his doctrines of the transmigration of the soul belong, while Pindar's 'three trials' and ultimate heroic reincarnation of the departed stem from Pythagoras and thus the Orphic cult.

Pluto was by nature a resident of the earth, as Poseidon was a resident of the sea, and when a man went below the ground he entered the subterranean god's domain just as he passed under the three-pronged scepter of the god of waters when he left the land. The chthonian Zeus was spoken of as 'the host of all those whose work is done,' those who had entered the earth: but neither Pluto nor subterranean Zeus plagued men with demonic torments or filled them with morbid anxiety about their destiny after death. The only satisfactory epitaph of Hellas was, 'Earth to earth and air to air.' The expression 'shades of the departed' meant no more than the ineffable fragments of rapidly decomposing personality which clung close to the graves except, perhaps, at the feast of the Anthesteria, when the houses were smeared with pitch or sulphur and the shades were allowed to revisit their former homes for a single night, after which they were summarily dismissed with, "Out, shades, the Anthesteria is over!"

With no divine morality and no hopes and fears projected into the hereafter to bind their thoughts with *a priori* conceptions of first causes and ultimate destinies, the early Ionians were free to take creation as the Here and Now, and open to any reasonable interpretation. Slavery had not yet developed to the point where the ruling class regarded the arts and crafts, all technical labor, with contempt, and wisdom was not only fruitful but among all ways of life held the promise of better things. The rich legacies of empirical observation acquired from Egypt and Mesopotamia invited a new interpretation free of the coarse mythology with which they had been encumbered, and free also of the necessity of sustaining the vested interests of the priest and king. Thus was born, in the Ionian city of

Miletus, the first attempt to arrive at a purely naturalistic interpretation of the cosmos. Thales (?640–550 B.C.), a student of Egyptian and Babylonian astronomy, and himself the inventor of much of the geometry of lines later accredited to Euclid, could propound that the sun and moon were not gods but fiery bodies; he could conceive that behind the multiplicity of phenomena there was one universal and material element, water, from which all things, whatever their diversity, were produced by metamorphosis; and he could accurately predict the solar eclipse of May 28, 585 B.C., and by so doing excite in the Hellenes a lasting curiosity in the art of calculation and a fearsome respect for numbers.

With Thales there began a school of thinkers who were known as the *physiologoi* (*phusis,* 'nature,' *logia,* 'knowledge'). In familiar terms these men would be called physicists, or more broadly, physicalists, that is, votaries of *phusis,* or nature. Thales's young companion, Anaximander (611–547 B.C.), also an astronomer and geometrician, conceived the One, the universal substance, to be an endless and unlimited mass subject neither to old age nor decay, but perpetually yielding water, earth, mist and fire by transmutation. Life, he said, had been formed in the sea and driven out onto the land by the subsidence of the water, and had undergone a progressive evolution under the opposing stresses of unity and opposites. Anaximenes (*ca.* 526 B.C.), friend of Anaximander, held that air was the primeval substance: it condensed into wind, cloud, water, land and stone, the three forms of matter, gas, liquid and solid, being progressive stages in this condensation. Earthquakes he believed were caused by the solidification of an originally fluid earth; life and soul were one, an animating and expansive force present in everything and identifiable with a special form of movement in the universal substance.

Thales had recognized the phenomena of 'change' in the metamorphosis of water into diverse things; Anaximander spoke of 'change' in two directions, growth and decay; and Anaximenes coined the terms 'condensation' and 'rarefaction' to designate directions of 'change' in his primordial air. Then Heraclitus (540–475 B.C.) abandoned the eternal, material atoms of his predecessors and substituted 'change' itself as the fundamental reality. 'Being,' he said in effect, is but a convenient literary antithesis to 'not-being'; reality is an intermediate state between being and not-being, it is the 'process' itself of becoming or of ceasing to be. In this view, substance is but the pattern of change or transformation. Heraclitus was famous for his aphorism, 'A man cannot step into the *same* stream twice'; the discovery that the stream is never twice the same is now less startling than it was in Heraclitus's time, and the paraphrase, 'The *same* man cannot step twice into any stream,' more effectively conveys the problem which he posed for the atomists, in that it questioned the substantive qualities and the continuous existence of man himself.

To describe the ordered nature of the cosmos, the force that kept the stars in their courses and that maintained harmony of motion in waves and winds and regularity in all things, Heraclitus used the term *logos*. For this word there is no satisfactory equivalent in any other language, the best approximation being perhaps the idea of 'human reason' or, from another point of view, the physical idea of 'natural law.' Greek writers spoke of the *logos* as the 'essential reason' of the universe, as though within Heraclitus's 'motion' there was concealed an inherent tendency to plan and the knowledge wherewith to carry this plan into execution. At a later time the Stoics actually deified the *logos,* but as Heraclitus used the word he apparently meant something that was not above the cosmos but an essential part of it; it was merely the 'law' which 'change' or 'motion' was unto itself.

The idea of causality was contained implicitly in the *logos* of Heraclitus as well as in the primordial substances of Thales and his friends, but it was first explicitly worded by Leucippus of Miletus (ca. 450 B.C.), who is credited with the assertion that nothing happens without a cause, but everything with a cause or of 'necessity,' necessity meaning in accordance with the thing's being, or with its nature.

The man who, however, explicitly if quite unintentionally framed the doctrine of causality in terms of 'law' was he who above all the *physiologoi* was held in highest honor, Democritus of Thrace (b. 470 B.C.). Recasting the theories of the Ionians, Democritus first distinguished between a substance and its qualities: whereas, according to convention, there appeared to be black and white, sweet and bitter, hot and cold, which could be added and subtracted, in truth there are only atoms, eternal, invisible and so small they cannot be divided, immersed in an infinite void or vacuum. Democritus postulated a large but undetermined number of atoms differing in nature and size; by differences in composition, position and arrangement these give rise to the compounds and the multitude of qualities which are to be perceived by sense. Color and taste and heat and cold and the other obvious features that impress the senses do not exist of themselves, but are derivatives of relation. As atoms are eternal, so is motion, which has its origin in preceding motion, and so on ad infinitum. Democritus substituted for the previous ideas of a shaping spirit and for the *logos* of Heraclitus the idea of fixed and necessary modes of motion, or laws, and he said that he would prefer to find the explanation for one natural phenomenon to being king of the Persians. He conceived the cosmos to be an ordered system wherein worlds are born, grow, decay and perish; at every moment planets arise, collide and die; there is no preordained plan, only an infinitely complex, mutable congeries of atoms joining and separating, each in its lawful manner. Life is maintained by the inhalation of fresh atoms to replace those lost by exhalation, and when respiration, and consequently the supply of atoms, ceases, the result is death. A soul pervades the body of both man and animals, and receives sensations by contact, by emanations or by images. This soul, which is responsible for perception, consists merely of a different kind of atom, round, smooth and specially mobile, and closely resembling the fire atoms floating in the air. The soul atoms everywhere penetrate the body: in the head they are responsible for reason, in the heart for anger, and in the liver for desire, and when the body perishes, the soul atoms, like all the other atoms in it, are again dispersed. In this atomic scheme man's ego is but a fleeting pattern. 'All human affairs,' Democritus is alleged to have said, 'are worthy only of laughter.'

In all the speculations of the *physiologoi,* the gods were dismissed as no more than barbaric superstitions, or at best literary and poetic images. The first principles of Thales and the other atomists, and even of the dynamist, Heraclitus, excluded the interference of capricious deities from earth, sea, stars and life, and if the term 'god' was used it was in a secular sense, the god having been reduced to atomic dimensions, to 'the dull catalog of common things.' The *physiologoi* were, therefore, branded as atheists. After teaching in Athens for thirty years, Anaxagoras was arrested in 434 B.C. on a charge of denying the godhead of the sun and moon, and it required the eloquence of Pericles to secure his life, though even the great civic leader could not save him from banishment. In 411 B.C. Protagoras was convicted of atheism for teaching that 'man is the measure of all things.' Protagoras meant that 'reality' is a matter of interpretation rather than a thing in itself; there is no 'divine truth' above and beyond man's own powers of perception and judgment and all laws, physical, economic and social, are valid only as agreeable conventions. Every individual is, as it were, his own measuring rule. It is probable that Democritus escaped condemnation only because he kept away from Athens, the deistic center of Greek culture.

The outstanding victim of Athenian condemnation, however, was Socrates, who was executed in 399 B.C. because he had been adjudged guilty, 'firstly, of denying the gods recognized by the state and introducing new divinities, and secondly, of corrupting the young.'

The charge is in no way ambiguous, yet the expression 'and introducing new divinities' leaves much to be desired since the father of philosophy is not usually accredited by historians with advocating a new worship of any kind. Voltaire made up a story about two Athenians who were discussing Socrates when one remarked, "That is the atheist who says there is only one god." It is, however, clear that the 'new divinities' did not refer to philosophic monotheism. Xenophon explains the expression as referring to Socrates's claim that from time to time he received a 'divine sign,' an inner voice which forewarned him of disadvantageous consequences of contemplated acts; though Socrates frequently mentioned this 'voice,' his attitude toward it was one of humorous half-belief and it is unlikely that there was any antipathy to him on account of it, or if there were, that the pretension to the possession of a personal oracle would have been so described. Nor is it likely that the charge applied to his dissent from conventional religious customs, for this was covered in the first clause, and it is unlikely that the Athenian court on this important occasion would have been guilty of tautology. The 'new divinities' which Socrates introduced must be sought in some explicit teaching which was offensive to current views.

When, in 423 B.C., Aristophanes presented his comedy, *The Clouds,* he made Socrates and his friend Chaerophon the butt of his satire by portraying them as 'wise souls' running a 'thought factory.' The play took its name from the chorus which was composed of cloud goddesses, in parody of the materialists' theory that air, water, clouds and gods are much the same thing, and the reactionary Aristophanes was out to attack this materialism and the underlying spirit of skepticism by focusing the offensive views in Socrates. In the comedy, the cloud goddesses are of course not goddesses at all, since the gods are no longer 'current coin' with the materialists. An oath is taken, not on Zeus or Apollo, but on the new quasi-divinities, Air, Chaos and Respiration. The materialists had contended that justice is not an irrevocable, divine decree, but a debatable proposition to be decided in every case by argument. In which view, it seemed to Aristophanes, a man could by the astute use of words justify any form of conduct, and he maliciously paraphrases the proposition by saying that in the 'thought factory' they teach two logics, a Worse and a Better, a man by the former being enabled to evade even the payment of a just debt.

The 'thought factory' of Socrates is located next door to the house of one Strepsiades, whose money had been seized by a galloping consumption — to wit, a son, Pheidippides, whose fondness for the horses and other expensive pleasures has brought his father to the verge of bankruptcy. Strepsiades, hearing how in the thought factory they dispense a Worse and Better logic, and how by the Worse logic a man may prevail even though his case is a dishonest one, tries to persuade his son to study under Socrates in order that he may learn how he can outwit his creditors.

> That is the thought factory of wise souls.
> There dwell the men who teach — aye, who persuade us,
> That Heaven is one vast fire extinguisher
> Placed round about us, and that we're the cinders.
> Aye, and they'll teach (only they'll want some money),
> How one may speak and conquer, right or wrong.

Pheidippides, however, has no desire to be educated in logic either Worse or Better, so to avoid bankruptcy Strepsiades is forced to go to the thought factory himself. He is admitted by a student, and finds other students wandering about, looking at the ground. Strepsiades thinks they may be looking for truffles, but no, his student guide says, they're diving into the deepest secrets of nature.

STREPS.   Then why's their rump turned up towards the sky?
STUDENT   It's taking private lessons on the stars.

The guide is showing Strepsiades about the factory and explaining everything, when Socrates makes his stage entrance by being lowered from the ceiling in a basket.

STREPS.   Hallo! Who's that? that fellow in the basket?
STUDENT   That's HE.
STREPS.   Who's HE?
STUDENT   Socrates.
STREPS.   Socrates!
           You sir, call out to him as loud as you can.
STUDENT   Call him yourself: I have not leisure now.

The guide, thinking of some neglected task, hurries away and leaves Strepsiades staring up at the basket.

STREPS.   Socrates! Socrates! Sweet Socrates!
SOCRATES   Mortal! Why call'st thou me?
STREPS.   O, first of all, please tell me what you are doing.
SOCRATES   I walk on air, and contemplate the Sun.
STREPS.   O then from a basket you contemn the gods,
           And not from the earth, at any rate?

SOCRATES   Most true,
        I could not have searched out celestial matters
        Without suspending judgment, and infusing
        My subtle spirit with the kindred air.
        If from the ground I were to seek these things,
        I could not find: so surely doth the earth
        Draw to herself the essence of our thought.
        The same too is the case with water cress.

The last line served merely to give the stupid Strepsiades something he could understand, for the rest was intended to be above his comprehension. It was not, however, above the comprehension of the audience, which saw not only through Strepsiades's simplicity but through the double meaning which had been packed into every line.

The business of hanging Socrates up in a basket and talking about 'suspended judgment' was perhaps a brazen pun. But the suspension immediately acquires a second meaning when Socrates, looking down upon the foolish Strepsiades, says "*Mortal!* Why call'st thou *me?*" It would seem that into that one line and gesture Aristophanes crowded a 'new divinity' — in the form of Socrates himself. In this bit of dramaturgy is perhaps the clue to the middle phrase of the atheistic charge.

There is nothing in Plato's dialogues (to which one must turn for nearly all extant information on Socrates) to indicate that the philosopher ever advocated his own apotheosis. However, there can be discovered in the dialogues a hint of what Aristophanes and his audience were laughing at. Quite in contrast to previous literature, there appears full-fledged in the *Apology* and the *Republic* the idea of the 'immortal soul,' practically in that form which it has ever since preserved. Twice in the *Apology* Socrates is made to assert that his mission is to get men 'to care for their soul' and to make it as good as they can; and, in the *Republic,* Socrates's companions are described as startled when they hear that the master believes the individual soul to be immortal. The convictions expressed in the dialogues are frequently Plato's rather than Socrates's, but since the soul later became the central theme in Plato's system it is all the more improbable that the pupil would attribute so startling a conception to his master unless Socrates had in truth invented it.

Cicero and Augustine believed that Pherecydes of Syros (sixth century B.C.) had been the first to teach the immortality of the soul, but Pherecydes's soul was no other than the Orphic divine spark, and had nothing to do with running the living body. On the evidence of Plato's references and of Aristophanes's comedy, Burnet has argued that Socrates was the first to formulate the immortal soul which possesses consciousness, which is the seat of knowledge and error, and which is responsible for a man's thoughts and actions. The forerunner of this notion cannot be found in either Egyptian eschatology or the demoniac specters of Babylonia, nor was there any precedent in current Greek belief. The Athenian ghosts, if not actually engendered by death's disintegration, were at best fragments comparable to the half disintegrated body, seeking to escape the grave and find some haven where they themselves might for a short while avoid decomposition. They possessed but a small number of those features recognized in the current anatomy of character and personality, and it would be ludicrous to charge a live man with being inhabited and controlled by such a fragmentary specter. The Socratic soul, if it may be so designated, was a new spiritual entity which, far from being fragmentary and inferior in power to the animal body, was by virtue of its prerogative of domination entitled to a definitely superior status. Yet here the break with precedent was not so complete as when, in the single word 'immortal,' this invisible inhabitant was equipped to endure indefinitely by being cut away not only from respiration and nutrition, but also from the otherwise universal phenomenon of corruption.

It cannot be supposed that this new conception of incorruptibility was an eschatological tour de force. There was available in the doctrines of the *physiologoi* the idea of the transmutation of primordial substance; the exact nature of this world-stuff could be left to the atomists, but however it was conceived, it was agreed that it was *indestructible* and had existed *for all time*. For motive power there were variously the *nous* or shaping spirit predicated by Anaxagoras, the *logos* or reason of Heraclitus, or the self-contained 'law' of Democritus — again the exact description was of less importance than was the fact that each of these 'operators' was an essentially secular agent characterized by *rationality,* that is, an impulse to form and organize and execute in an orderly manner. It but required that the vulgar spectral fragments of the grave be summed together and endowed with the indestructibility of the physicalists' world-stuff and the rationality of their world force, in order to have an immortal soul that by the attributes of indestructibility, rationality and personality partook of the essence of divinity.

Of all Greek thinkers, Socrates might be expected to apply to his physical body Heraclitus's dictum, 'All things change.' Yet he was in no position to resolve the first illusion of integrated animal consciousness, the illusion of a persistent personal identity, and when he spoke of personal immortality he must have entertained the notion of personal unchangeableness. To the man who steps into a stream, it is only the *stream* that changes.

Moreover, Socrates had good reason to defend a doctrine of personal immortality. He lived in what has been called the First Age of Freedom, an age when Athens was being torn between the newly born democratic spirit and the highhanded conservatism of the landed oligarchs. The democrats claimed in effect that every citizen of the state was his own agent and on a parity with every other, while against them the oligarchs claimed that social differences and privileges were foreordained by nature, and hence some individuals counted and some did not. Socrates had started life as a sculptor of the lower class and, what is quite possible, a slave. In middle life good fortune attended him and he associated himself with the oligarchs, even to the point of becoming a close friend of his playwright-critic, Aristophanes; but when *The Clouds* was written Socrates was a poor man and a democrat, and what more natural than to resolve the conflict between the individualism of the democratic spirit and the political and economic stratification of the oligarchic state by proposing that every citizen in this state had his counterpart in the realm of the unseen world, an eternal and yet willful, spiritual entity of aristocratic lineage?

To the aristocratic audiences who laughed uproariously at *The Clouds,* the expression 'wise souls' could mean only 'clever ghosts,' a countersense the absurdity of which was exaggerated by the notion of their running a 'thought factory.' As though ghosts could think! The Athenians of the day were afraid of Socrates the philosopher, and it was escape from fear through laughter when Aristophanes burlesqued him as a new and ridiculously impossible personal divinity descending from heaven in a basket. Yet that basket seems to have contained immortality for every serf and slave whom the aristocrats despised.

iv

'I thank God,' said Plato, 'that I was born Greek and not barbarian, freeman and not slave, man and not woman; but above all, that I was born in the age of Socrates.' If Winspear's socio-economic analysis is accepted, this innocent sounding sentence is the keynote to Plato's philosophy, which was a long continued effort to defend and rationalize the oligarchic state and its social inequalities.

Greek culture had long been undergoing a change in fundamental structure. In the early days the land bordering the Aegean had been held more or less collectively by the tribe and men had tilled it or grazed their cattle upon it as a tribal privilege. Then across the period spanned by the Homeric poems the growth of city-states had led to intense economic competition, to trans-Aegean maritime adventure, and to the growth of trade; and trade had produced wealth which sought safety by reinvestment in the land until private property had become a social distinction and the foundation of landed aristocracy, so that there were now the landed and landless, in addition to the freeman and the slave. Monogamy had become exalted as feminine constancy — so necessary to the preservation of hereditary titles — had become more valuable, and those families which inherited their lands spoke of themselves as having had 'good' fathers. Slavery, having arisen in the forced labor of captives of war, had grown to such proportions that members of the same tribe, even of the same family, might fall into servitude to their own kin. Society had placed its sanction on the right of private property, and was prepared to protect it against fraud and theft and violence, and against the protest of the poor and dispossessed. Where the Egyptians spoke of *maat* as truth, righteousness or justice, the Greeks spoke of *diké,* a word which once had meant merely 'custom,' and then the natural manner or fashion of things: it was the *diké* of wind to blow, of birds to fly, of water to be wet, it is the *diké* of the cosmos that 'we' should own the land and have all the privileges and that 'you' should be a slave and laborer. Inevitably *diké* became Dike, the goddess, representing an eternal and divine principle of verity, the maiden daughter of Zeus. Needless to say, Dike was born an aristocrat.

As Athens became the center of the Aegean commercial empire she removed offensive city-states from competition by absorbing them into her 'alliance,' whereby the 'allies' paid heavy tribute to a few Athenian aristocrats who, by Dike's authority, enjoyed a virtual monopoly of political and social privilege. In Aristotle's words, 'the constitution was in all respects an oligarchy, and the poor were enslaved to the rich, they and their wives and children. . . . All land was in the hands of a few men. If anyone failed to pay his dues, he and his children could be delivered into slavery. And all loans were made on the security of the person up to the time of Solon. He was the first "champion of the people." '

Dike may have been born an aristocrat, but after the coup of Clisthenes, which enabled the democrats to capture the power in the Senate, the assembly and the popular jury courts, the democrats began to claim that they had truth and justice on their side. Then in 480 B.C. the vulgar mercantile interests under Themistocles, with the aid of the Spartan army, successfully resisted a Persian offensive and the democrats began to dream

of empire: the proletariat and those who were paid for service on jury or
senate, the sailors of the fleet (that 'sea-going mob,' the oligarchs called
them), the shipowners and traders, the moneylenders, wheat speculators
and all others who stood to profit from the adventure began to demand
overseas expansion and increased profits. Under Pericles this dream of
empire was well on its way to realization when it precipitated the long
and bitter Peloponnesian war (431–400 B.C.) between Athens and Sparta,
which ended with the defeat of the Athenian fleet and army, and the liberation of her 'allies' from a hated economic subjugation.

Following the defeat of the Athenian navy at Aegospotami, a small
group of extreme conservatives, led by the 'Thirty,' seized the power in
Athens in defiance of the constitution and, with the support of the detested
Spartan army, held control for about eight months. In the ensuing bitter
conflict between oligarchs and democrats treachery and treason were suspected everywhere and no man knew whom he might trust; and the
Thirty, in order to make certain of their position, indulged in the unprecedented retaliatory measure of having fifteen hundred citizens, outstanding
for their democratic fervor, put to death.

Socrates, now grown comparatively rich and influential, having abandoned his first wife, Xantippe — she of the shrewish and scolding tongue
— had married into a proud and patrician family and had become scarcely
more than a puppet and apologist for the aristocrats. When the democrats
regained control he was looked upon as a traitor, if not principally responsible through his skeptical and materialistic teachings for the excesses
of his friends, and haled to trial. From a philosophic nuisance he had become a political menace. Actually, the court had no desire to put him to
death and only wanted him to leave Athens, since he was too intelligent
and dangerous a citizen for a democracy to have around. But when he
refused to offer any defense for himself, when he even refused to compromise and, as an alternative, suggested that he be entertaind for life free
of charge in the Prytaneum, he drew down upon himself the ire of the
jurors and a verdict of guilty. The trial ending at the Delian festival, thirty
days had to elapse before he could drink the hemlock, and during this time
he held long conversations with his friends, whose offers of escape he
stubbornly refused on the grounds that the state, like the citizen, must do
its 'duty.' The death scene, familiar from Plato's description, closed with
the suddenly recollected thought: "Crito, I owe a cock to Asklepius; will
you remember to pay the debt?" Seventy years old, he had so long beheld
the foibles and foolishness of men that perhaps he felt indebted to the god
of healing for permitting him now to escape from life.

Plato was twenty-eight when Socrates died and the bitterness against democracy which his teacher's death engendered never left him. Unlike his master, he was an aristocrat by birth; his family had ever kept to itself within its inherited lands and privileges, aloof from any taint of democratic connection or liberal thought. Following Socrates's condemnation by the democrats Athens was not the safest place for one of his closest friends, who was also a hotheaded, blue-blooded enemy of the people, and Plato decided to travel. He spent some years in southern Italy, Sicily and Egypt, and in Syracuse became embroiled in an effort to reform the government of that city and got himself kidnaped and sold into slavery, from which he was ransomed by a friend. Returning at last to Athens he founded in the gymnasium of Academus the school henceforth known as the Academy, where he began to elaborate 'philosophy' into an overwhelming antidemocratic argument, by taking the argument from earth to heaven.

Socrates had said that his mission was not to teach any positive doctrine but to convict men of ignorance mistaking itself for knowledge; his method had been to place himself at the standpoint of ignorance and to invite others to join him there, in order that, proving all things, he and they might hold fast to that which is good. Plato's method was to argue from the 'best opinion' of Socrates to 'absolute knowledge' by way of an infallible 'autonomy of the intellect'—the offshoot of Socrates's 'clever ghost.' He proceeded thus to construct a system, loose and rambling though it may be, which embraced the cosmos, its origin, its structure and its moral code. Plato began by thinking in terms of aristocratic superlatives, and the superlative became the essence of all this thought. The burning aspiration to find an aristocratic, enduring kind of 'truth' led him to create it for himself.

Admittedly the Athenian democracy was a parody on 'democratic' government. Of 400,000 inhabitants, 250,000 were slaves without any political rights, and of the rest only a few politicians took any interest in the affairs of state. Political opinions were shaped by passionate orators who 'went ringing on in long harangues, like brazen pots which, when struck, continue to sound till a hand is put upon them.' Wisdom was conceived to issue from mere numbers, and the high court, or Dikastra, which consisted of more than a thousand members in order to make bribery expensive, was selected by alphabetical lot. Socrates had had no sympathy with this ignorant rule by the mob and especially with the policy of electing the governing body by lot, and perhaps it was the denial of the intrinsic value of this form of election which was indicated by the charge, 'denying the gods recognized by the state.' 'Corrupting the young' is taken to mean that he had taught some of the younger oligarchs their contempt for democracy. The same charges could of course have been leveled against Plato, but the fire of revolution had now died out and he was permitted to pursue philosophy in peace, devoting himself to the theoretic task of finding the way whereby the wisest and the best men might be discovered and then enabled and persuaded to rule, so that all things between man and man, or between man and state, would be in fact as they should be in theory.

As his ultimate end, Plato sought to define *maat,* or *diké,* or as the modern tongue would have it, justice: for if there is such a thing as justice it must be a principle that can permeate and rule not only all of politics, but all of life. Men have ever observed that discord, chaos, accident, characterize all things, and they have ever sought some principle of permanence, some all-pervading law, that will give meaning to the transitory and evanescent, something that will explain or disentangle the confused web of discord that is their lives. 'What is justice?' had been the earliest philosophical question ever asked by the Greek. For the Greeks the discords of life were largely subsumed within the discords of government, and Heraclitus had replied, 'We must know that war is common to all and strife is justice.' This might do for a vulgar, materialistic atomist, but would it serve the ends of the state, of man nobly conceived, of the cosmos in the whole?

With regard to justice in the matter of government, Plato had seen enough in Athens to realize that both the aristocratic pattern based on birth and the oligarchic pattern based on wealth are charged with evil; both must ultimately lead to revolution, which in turn leads to democracy, and democracy, if anything, is the worst of the three. Its chief allure, the equal right of all to hold office, is its weakest point. Plato could not imagine anyone so stupid as to wish to turn government over to mob rule. When a man is ill he calls a physician well certified in respect to his impartiality, honesty and competence, or if he so much as wishes his shoes mended, he goes to an expert; but in democracy it is presumed that any man is competent to administer the complex affairs of a city or state who can get votes by his good looks, by playing on the gullibility of the mob, by high-sounding oratory, empty promises, bribery, false alarms, or the strategy of political organizations. Democracy is a tyranny of unscrupulous politicians who keep themselves in power by telling the ignorant masses what to think. Plato conceived that there were divinely selected men within the state to whom wisdom and truth came naturally and, were the opportunity given them to do so, they could be prepared by proper training to make good leaders. Only such natural born philosopher-kings would be fit to guide a nation. 'Until philosophers are kings, or the kings and princes of this world have the spirit and power of philosophy, and wisdom and political leadership meet in the same man . . . cities will never cease from ill, nor the human race.'

The question may be raised whether wisdom and truth are in the aristocratic manner innate in some men and not in others, or whether in the democratic manner they emerge only from the 'common deed of man.' To Plato, the question could only be answered in one way: the propensity to seek wisdom and truth are inborn characters. He believed that the existing inequalities of society and the prerogatives of the aristocratic few rested on an unchallengeable, natural basis. It was the truth of Dike, it was 'justice.' Democracy implied not only *change* in personality and privilege, but the very *rightness* of this change as a natural process. The Democrats talked about the equality of all men, and about an equity in the courts which took account of contingency, of accident, in opposition to the aristocratic principle of justice which was eternal and took no account of any man or any circumstance. Democracy elevated upstart merchants, sailors and other lowborn radicals within the state and set their rights and authority on a parity with its own. Carried to its logical conclusion this democratic process would be identical with anarchy since every man would be a law unto himself: an unthinkable condition because this is the very denial of law, order, harmony, of the absolute and unchangeable, of justice itself. And to deny the absolute and unchangeable is to deny the possibility of knowledge and even of truth, for it is only the unchanging that can be either knowable or true: if a thing is changing in all its parts it can in no wise be known and must remain unknown even while changing, and any assumed knowledge of it is false, and if it is always changing it cannot exist, and therefore it cannot be true.

This argument was not original with Plato, but had been used effectively by the Pythagoreans, particularly against the contention of Heraclitus that 'being' is 'process.' Pythagoreanism like Platonism was an apology for aristocratic rule and landed conservatism, launched against the Ionian atomists whose iconoclastic attitudes in the sixth century B.C. had worked as a ferment for unrest and change. Pythagoras by tradition was a mathematician, and is supposed to have contributed with Thales much that appears in the first six books of Euclid. Mathematics had ever been a medium for establishing communion with the gods; the mathematician-priests of Egypt and Babylonia were in their time the chief spokesmen of the divinities, and that Aristotle (who incidentally was the first to use this fateful word) should call the mystical Pythagoras a 'theologian' shows that the Greek heavens were no exception.

Against the 'formless,' the 'limitless' primordium of the atomists, Pythagoras set the importance of 'limits': the 'limitless' by itself was as nothing, but once limited it yielded the point, twice limited the line, thrice limited the plane, and four times limited the solid. Since all created things must be limited, creation consisted of 'limits' — that is, of numbers which are the very essence of limits. Lack of order was synonymous with non-existence since it was indescribable and hence unknowable; only the strictly ordered approached absolute existence; the abstractly mathematical, because it was most perfectly ordered, was the very essence of being. Thus numbers themselves were the primordia of all things: the active or male principle was the number one; the passive or female principle was the number two; marriage or the union of the dual forces was the number three; and so on until one number explained a horse, another a man, a third justice — which some Pythagoreans held to be four, the square of the first even number, while others held it to be nine, the square of the first odd number. The master is said to have agreed to accept the gods individually when he had found the mathematical equations appropriate to them.

Having exalted abstract numbers to an existence above the transient flux of the material world, the Pythagoreans, with a strong ascetic bias, sought to establish all social sanctions in mathematical harmonies and proportions, and, like the Athenians, attempted to impose this 'truth' upon their neighbors by fire, knife and other forcible means in the conviction that it was their duty to 'free' their fellow men from 'injustice' and 'falsehood' by converting them to their own point of view, or at least by forcing them into the Pythagorean union represented by Croton, Sybaris, Catana, Rhegium and other towns of Sicily and southern Italy. If the people of Croton believed that to be conquered and told how to order their lives according to the supernal mystical numbers was a loss of freedom it was only because they were abysmally ignorant.

The *physiologoi* had asserted that what truly exists is matter, which contains within itself all the laws necessary to its existence and operation, and that all else is but the expression of the capacity of material, indestructible atoms to undergo change and movement. In this view, what was, was just: ugliness and beauty, order and disorder, good and evil, were all equally just, because all equally lawful. Even the death of Socrates was just, for justice was the intrinsic law of hemlock-the-poison, of Socrates-the-man, of the tribunal which tried him and of the popular support which gave this tribunal its power.

Before he began to develop a philosophy of his own Plato was a Pythagorean. At the conclusion of his labors at the Academy he had woven together the Pythagorean belief in the primacy of numbers and the doctrine of the changeless, the static and unalterable, to form his philosophic system. This philosophy is nowhere simply or consistently set forth but deviously expounded throughout the *Dialogues*. It is not dispassionately rational but infused with the mystic glow of a religious convert, or rather of a religious discoverer, for he was enthralled by the 'wise soul'—the god-in-man in the person of Socrates. With the aid of this 'clever ghost' he developed his dualistic antithesis of 'soul' and 'body,' and by this antithesis ultimately explained away the whole of observable nature as a mirage of error.

In Platonic philosophy it is the 'wise soul' which perceives. However, untutored by Plato, it perceives erroneously. Things as they appear to the uninstructed soul are in greater or lesser degree misleading, illusory, chimerical: at one extreme is mere appearance, which is identical with complete ignorance; at the other extreme is knowledge, which is to be equated with pure truth or reality; and in between is opinion, which is a varying mixture of ignorance and truth. Since that which is wholly false and illusory cannot exist, ignorance is non-being; while knowledge is identical with being, since that which is true must also be real. Since what is true must always be true, truth is absolute—changeless and eternal—and is indeed the only reality.

Socrates had emphasized that we are acquainted on the one hand with particular objects and, on the other, with certain features common to many objects of a similar kind, these common features being more 'universal' and therefore more enduring than the particular objects which share them. There are, for example, many individual circles, as opposed to the 'circularity' which is possessed by all such figures. A particular circle is drawn by hand and proves to be slightly eccentric, so it is erased and another circle is drawn, and another, and another, and so on through a thousand circles—no one of them is ever perfect, no one of them is indestructible or will last forever, no one of them accurately represents all possible circles. But the archetype of the perfect circle was there before the hand attempted the first circle and will survive after the last circle has been erased. No particular circle can ever attain such indestructibility or immortality or such perfection as the universal circle of which it is only an approximate model or copy. Extending the argument, all objects of what-

ever kind approach in greater or lesser degree some perfect form, all behavior approaches some perfect law; particular men come and go, as do
particular cities or particular laws, but 'man' and 'city' and 'law' endure
through all generations and even through all the forms of thinking.

To indicate the difference between individual things and characters common to many things Socrates had used the terms 'particulars' and 'universals.' One knows where to find particulars but in what part of the
cosmos do these universals have their being? It becomes immediately apparent that they belong to the realm of thought, since they consist of conceptual relations: the universal circle is something which is 'conceived' to
exist apart from all particular circles, and no one has actually *seen* it,
though he may have seen many particular circles that approach it closely.
It is, moreover, equally apparent that the *universal* does not exist in any
individual man's concepts, for individual men live and die, but the *universal* circle exists forever; it exists, so Plato thought, apart from any man's
thinking, and thus it may be called an 'absolute.' Being absolute, it is
perfect and eternal. It must therefore exist in some universal mind, which
can only be the mind of God (Zeus).

When Plato sought to define universals, in contradistinction to particulars, language difficulties presented themselves. The term 'concept,' derived
from the past participle of 'conceive,' and signifying 'to take to oneself'
(in this sense abstracting or removing from several objects some common
relation having no existence apart from the mind of the observer), not
being available to him, he turned back to Pythagoreanism to find a suitable word. In Homeric Greek the word ἰδεῖν, meaning 'to see,' had come
to mean the 'looks' or 'outward appearance' of a thing, and thence its true
structure or essential nature, and the Pythagoreans had used ἰδεῖν to
describe their geometric figures, the pyramid, cube, and so on, as the
ultimate elements of reality; Democritus had called his atoms ἰδέαι, and
in the language contemporary with Plato, Empedocles's four elements
were described by the same term. Thus the word already meant ultimate
realities, and Plato naturally incorporated it into his philosophy in this
pristine sense, his only contribution being to insist upon the incorporeal
and absolute nature of the ἰδέα to which every particular or object is an
approximation. The Platonic Idea (we may capitalize the word to preserve its philosophic connotation) is not perceived by sense directly, but
is only to be discovered by knowledge; furthermore it is not a *thought*
but an *object* of thought.

In brief, the 'particulars' of the everyday world, particular men, or cities,
or laws, particular circles, apples or billy goats, are but imperfect images

of the perfect and eternal Ideas in the divine mind, but a shadow show, a mere hallucination. That other world, the divine mind wherein endure forever the unchangeable absolutes of which the stars and earth and all vegetable and animal kinds, all circles and cubes and polyhedrons, all laws and principles, all billy goats, are but representatives — that is in truth the real world. Man fails to perceive this truth immediately, so Plato thought, because he and his perception are particularistic and imperfect; only as he searches for and discovers the universals which exist apart from and outlast all particular objects, as numbers exist apart from and outlast all numbered things, does he discover himself to be in error.

As in its beginnings, so to its ultimate application, Plato's philosophy was concerned with politics and social sanctions, and in his masterpiece, the *Republic,* he constructed a perfect state which would bring about the perfect life and function as an organ of justice, even as the wise soul is an organ of justice in the individual body. Again he follows the Pythagorean system in developing a special ruling and possessing class, believing, aristocratically if excusably, that intelligence is a fixed and static character transmitted within a given class. Women are to be allowed to breed from their twentieth to their fortieth, men from their thirtieth to their fiftieth years, warriors being given the greatest sexual freedom so that the most children would be born of their stock. Although intercourse is to be free beyond these age limits, abortion or infanticide is to be used to prevent the offspring from growing up. In all cases in which children are permitted to survive they are to be taken from their elders, since paternal influence is usually reactionary and adverse. The family is to be abolished and infants are to be raised in a public crèche and later educated by the state and then assigned to the various tasks for which they are best fitted; those of aristocratic birth are to be given further training in preparation for becoming rulers. Those who fail to qualify are to be made auxiliaries of government, officers and clerks, while those who succeed will continue into the higher studies of the philosophy of the state. They will be taught to think clearly and critically, to understand human nature and the means and ends of government, and will at last be thrown upon the world to prove their mettle by competing with men of business, with hardheaded individuals of experience and cunning, to the end that they shall learn what cannot be learned from the printed page. Out of this last elimination there will emerge men, perhaps fifty years of age, scarred by experience, sobered and self-reliant, free of vanities and illusions who shall become the 'guards' or rulers of the state.

Since men are by nature acquisitive, jealous, combative, erotic and generally not to be trusted, how can they be expected to enter into such a scheme of things? How can those who fail to qualify be reconciled to a subordinate place? Will not jealousies and disappointments be the seed of discontent and of ultimate revolution? Plato foresaw this difficulty and devised an answer. He believed that a state could not be strong and unified unless it believed in a god. A mere 'cosmic force,' a 'first cause' that was not a personal deity, could not inspire hope or devotion, offer comfort to the distressed or courage to the downtrodden, or restrain greed and passion. The social force of a belief in a god is enhanced when it is joined with a belief in personal immortality. Granted that such beliefs cannot be demonstrated, and may be false, they will, he argued, do no harm and may do immeasurable good. So he suggested that the children of the state be taught to believe in an afterlife and in a just and punishing god merely as a political expediency. It could be pointed out to them that the god had made men differently, some of gold, some of silver, some of brass and some of iron; the oracle of the god could constantly proclaim that when a man of iron tried to be a man of gold and to rule the state, he would be destroyed. By this and similar strategems the populace could be kept subservient to the guards, who could presumably change the strategems from time to time as the need arose.

Justice, to the discovery of which Socrates and so many other Greek thinkers had devoted themselves, turned out in Plato's *Republic* to consist of the freezing for all time of aristocratic privilege: 'Each man shall confine himself to one pursuit in the city, the pursuit for which his nature is most *naturally* [aristocratically] adapted. And to do one's task and not to meddle in many is justice, which can then be defined as one man, one task for which he is naturally fitted.' The Democrats, who with sound logic might have defended their idea as an ἰδέα in the mind of Zeus, an ultimate reality worth aiming for, stood convicted of a vulgar and unphilosophic error, since that which is in a state of flux cannot be identified with the divine.

It is difficult to believe that Socrates would have approved founding the education of the young and the entire system of government upon a colossal program of deceit. When he could have saved himself by accepting banishment and compromising his conviction of the right of every man to think and speak, he chose to stand his ground and tell his judges that if he died Athens would lose more than he would. It can not be said, however, that Plato was inconsistent or dishonest. Greek talent was for the most part artistic. The aim of the Greek artist was that the end product should be beautiful: nothing else mattered, and if beauty was lacking there was nothing to compensate. In attaining this end the Greek artistic impulse was wholly consistent and honest. Plato was an artist and a plutocrat, and the artistic impulse and the plutocratic bias shaped his philosophy. With typical artistic disregard of all values other than the aesthetic, he did not hesitate to deceive the citizens of his Republic in order to achieve what seemed to him a perfect system of plutocratic government. And he as unhesitatingly pronounced the apparently substantial world to be a mirage in order to have as the ultimate basis of creation a series of forms and principles which to him savored of plutocratic perfection. Those who lie gladly to others lie easily to themselves, and the 'greatest philosopher of all times' may fairly be charged with self-deception.

v

Plato's 'noble lies' were, however, not long in being challenged. It is related that one day when he was lecturing in the Academy, there was only one pupil present — Aristotle (384–322 B.C.) — and he was asleep. And this pupil, despite his lifelong admiration for Plato, came ultimately to deny the validity of the theory of Ideas at its very roots. Son of the physician to Amyntas II, King of Macedon, and himself experienced in the odor of disease, suffering and death, Aristotle esteemed ugly brute facts as highly as Plato esteemed the artistic conception of perfection. At the close of his life he left behind him such an encyclopedia of ugly facts that one of the chief intellectual tasks of the Middle Ages was the recovery of as much of his works as could be gleaned from imperfect and incomplete Latin abstracts; later medieval writers thought that the New Age had actually begun when the first full text of his books was brought to the West from Constantinople fifteen hundred years after they had been written. At the age of forty-one he had been employed by King Philip of Macedon to act as tutor to Alexander, his passionate and epileptic son. Though Alexander gained little from his teacher, Aristotle gained much from his pupil, for five years later when Philip had united the Greek states by conquest and then had died under an assassin's hand, Alexander conquered the world and endowed Aristotle with unprecedented wealth. Alexander's hunters, gamekeepers, gardeners and fishermen supplied him with all the zoological and botanical material he desired, and it is alleged that at one time he had a thousand men collecting for him flora and fauna throughout Greece and Asia. The school, or Lyceum, which he founded in Athens did not follow the tradition of Plato's Academy, which had been devoted to mathematics and politics, but had for its chief interest the examination and description of the world, the 'apparent' world of the sense, not the 'real' world of Ideas.

On the question of Plato's immutable Ideas, Aristotle conceived that the Socratic term 'universal' merely indicated certain features which are common to a large number of individuals, such common features, for example, as might be discovered in the groups: animals, men, dogs, feet. These universals he considered to be predicates (that which we say of something) and not objective realities; they exist merely as mental images and figures of speech. What exists in reality is a world of substantial things. Socrates is a man and an animal (of which we say) tall, white, a husband, in the market, yesterday, sitting, talking, listening (all predicates). There are no universal forms, no supernatural Ideas, no man-in-general or animals-in-general, but only particular animals and plants, particular substances, water, wood, earth, moon, sun, stars. Each body or substance is what it is because its matter is conjoined with an 'essence,' that which gives the body or substance its specific quality. Natural bodies and substances are corruptible, but essences are eternal since they can always be found in some individual body or substance somewhere.

Man is composed of matter and essence, or soul. It is his soul which imbues him with growth, sensation, appetite, locomotion and reason. Plants have a nutritive soul, animals a nutritive, sensitive, appetitive and locomotive soul, but only man has reason or intellect. Intellect alone is immortal, it is alone divine, requiring no bodily organ for its activity, manifestation or existence. In possessing intellect man is therefore a third kind of substance; he is like natural substance in bodily matter, and therefore corruptible, like supernatural substance in reason or intellect, and therefore immortal. God only contemplates, man contemplates, seeks happiness and operates as an efficient cause on other natural things.

When Aristotle and Plato diverged on the issue of atoms *versus* universals, in effect they divided the world of Greek thinkers, and of all subsequent thinkers, between them. As Coleridge has said, 'Every man is born either a Platonist or an Aristotelian.' The generalization reflects the fact that men are forced for the purposes of living to elect one or the other interpretation: they must either be Aristotelians and put their faith in natural things, or Platonists and put their faith in supernatural absolutes. Stubbornness goes to such lengths that the advocates of both schools lay claim to the name of 'Realists' — though the Aristotelians, wishing to preserve meaning in language, prefer to call the Platonists 'Idealists.'

Though for Plato God represented the universal mind, he was in no sense a monotheist. He contemplated no revolution in Greek polytheism apart from the expurgation from the stories of the gods of the coarser elements of conflict, vengeance and sexuality. Nor did he desire to abolish sacrifice or idolatry. He ranged the Olympian deities somewhere below the supreme god, Zeus, and above the planets and the sun, but he did not believe that the gods could be immortal since they had been born, and whatever was born must die.

For Aristotle, on the other hand, a god was a mere logical necessity, a rhetorical period rounding out his thought. Behind all motion he deduced that there must be a Prime Mover who is himself Unmoved, and so he conceived of God as supernatural substance apart from natural substances, an impersonal force, with no desire, no will, no purpose. He is the essence of knowing, of reason, of intellect, but he is so perfect that he lacks nothing. His only occupation is to contemplate the essence of all things; and since he himself is the essence of contemplation he can only contemplate himself.

In 323 B.C. Alexander died and the Macedonian party was overthrown; Athenian independence was proclaimed and Athens went wild with patriotic joy. A priest made the charge that Aristotle had taught that prayer and sacrifice were of no avail, and Aristotle fled the city, saying that he would not give his beloved Athens a chance to sin twice against philosophy. He died at Chalcis within a year, bequeathing to a storm-tossed world his encyclopedic works, and a refutation of Platonic doctrine which was to be ignored for sixteen centuries.

Greek science, marking the first great intellectual age, did not truly spend itself until a Christian bishop burned the hated pagan library at Alexandria, the last great storehouse of the treasures of antiquity, more than seven centuries after Plato's death; but the chain of circumstances that led to that combustion can be traced back, however circuitously, to the Academy as surely as though Plato himself had set the flame. The Ionian *physiologoi* had started the world on an orderly, naturalistic interpretation of the cosmos; they had begun the discovery of the uniformity of nature and the analysis of cause and effect in materialistic terms; in mathematics, astronomy, physics and medicine they had achieved more in a few centuries than can be credited to all previous history. By the fourth century or shortly afterwards Alcmaeon and Erasistratus in physiology, Pythagoras in acoustics, Empedocles and Anaxagoras in physics, Strato in pneumatics, had laid the foundations of the experimental method. Except for the catastrophe that overcame it, Ionian science had within its grasp a control of natural affairs and human affairs such as the world was not to dream of again for many centuries. Except for that catastrophe, Ionian science might have speeded the development of the natural and social sciences by this interval.

Except for Plato — who disdained any investigation of nature in favor of his hypostasized ideas, who conceived man as an immortal soul temporarily inhabiting an inconsequential house of clay, who dismissed the world of material *realia* for a world of dreams, who did not believe in the gods himself but who recommended imprisonment for the skeptic who out of religious disquietude questioned their authority, and death for the atheist who denied their very existence (except for the Plato who made of all philosophy a living lie). In the *Phaedo* Plato makes Socrates say, "If we are ever to know anything absolutely, we must be free from the body and behold the actual realities with the eye of the soul alone. . . . While we live we shall be nearest to knowledge when we avoid, so far as possible, intercourse and communion with the body, except what is absolutely necessary, and are not infected by its nature, but keep ourselves free from it until God himself sets us free." This was the element of Academic philosophy that by way of Neoplatonism was transmitted to the early Christian church. It might appropriately have been intoned as a dirge over all intellectual effort by Bishop Theophilus when, at the order of the Christian emperor Theodosius, he sent his incendiaries to fire the Alexandrian library.

The intellect was henceforth divorced from the brute facts of life, and for the Roman Empire all problems were to be resolved largely by the antithesis of masters and slaves. The examination of nature, impossible for the slaves, became for the masters a questionably respectable diversion, since the slaves were expected to do the work of controlling nature and if any deficiency were discovered the number of slaves could be increased. Augustine in the fourth century accepted slavery as God's will and attempted to rationalize it, as it was axiomatically accepted by Philo in the first century B.C. and by Aristotle and Plato in the fourth. This progressive development of slavery was in part responsible for the death of Greek science, as for the ultimate decay of the Empire, but it was Plato and the corpus of his philosophy that gave slavery its philosophic warrant, even as they shut the prison door upon the best of the Greek intellect.

In the nine centuries through which the Academy endured untutored Greeks, like their equally untutored Roman neighbors, continued to bemoan their miserable lot in life and to remain fearful of death, even as they continued to make oblations and sacrifices in the temples and to observe the festivals of the dying and resurrected gods, no more sincerely hopeful of a decent way of living or of personal immortality than they had been when Aristophanes lowered Socrates, the clever and incorruptible ghost, from heaven by a rope and basket.

V

'New Wine Is Not Poured
into Old Wineskins'

WHEN a child was born in the ancient village of Rome three men came at night and struck the house with a hatchet, a mortar and a besom, and therewith three gods came into existence who belonged to that child alone. Another deity sprang up when the infant uttered its first cry, and yet another when the *bulla,* a sort of protective amulet equivalent to a lucky name, was hung around its neck. When the child took its first step, when it was purified and adopted into the family, when it was named, when it came of age, when it first undertook a domestic art or craft, when it married — at each new undertaking, whether on the farm, in the shop or in the pursuit of a profession, a new spiritual entity or *numina* came into being to serve the occasion, until finally the *genius,* the familiar spirit of the grown man, took charge.

Individual *penates* guaranteed the traditional family rights over its stores of grain and food; an individual *lar* guarded the boundaries of the domicile, but every street and crossroad also had a *lar* — there were a thousand in the city, said Ovid, each represented by an altar. These *numina* scarcely existed apart from the person, object, place or occasion which they apotheosized, and, like their wild congeners which inhabited the trees, springs, woods, rivers and fields, they acquired being and were annihilated with their worldly counterparts.

It has been said of Rome that she won all of the gods of all the world to her dominion — it was easy for the Romans to take unto themselves the multitudinous gods of their empire because they already had an infinity of their own. The great *dei* of the city-state had begun as *numina:* Jupiter, god of the sky and stars; Janus, god of the doorway and city gate; Mars god of war and of herds and crops; and Vesta, goddess of the home and hearth. Under the Etruscan kings anthropomorphic deities were imported in the persons of Diana, Jupiter, Juno and Minerva, and that impersonal voice which was to play such an important part in Roman history, the Sibylline Oracle. This last consisted of three books of Greek hexameter verse, the legend being that nine volumes had been offered in sale by a Sibyl, or prophetess, to Tarquin the Proud; when he refused them, she burned three and offered him the remaining six at the same price; when he again refused them, she burned three more and offered him the remaining three still at the same price. Tarquin bought them and thereafter they came to be consulted by the politician-priests on all questions of importance concerning both religious practice and governmental policy.

In 493 B.C. the Greek triad, Demeter, Dionysus and Persephone, came to Rome under the name of Ceres, Liber and Libera, and within fifty years Apollo and Asklepios followed them under their own names, while Aphrodite came as Venus, Hermes as Mercurius, Herakles as Hercules, Poseidon as Neptunus, and Artemis was assimilated to Diana. In 218 B.C. the Carthaginian general Hannibal invaded Italy and, in spite of repeated supplications and sacrifices to all the *numina* and *dei* known to the inhabitants, Roman arms wavered on the verge of defeat for twelve years; when survival seemed impossible the Sibylline Books were consulted and the oracle advised that Hannibal would be repelled if the sacred stone which embodied Cybele and which reposed in her temple in Phrygia were brought to Rome. So the King of Pergamus, to whom the temple and stone belonged, consenting, Cybele came to Rome in 206 with elaborate ceremony. Although the Great Mother did everything that was anticipated in the way of expelling Hannibal, her worship was at first restricted to the Phrygian priests who had accompanied her, her orgiastic rites being considered too dangerous for the Romans, but in 191 B.C. her image was transferred to a new temple on the Palatine hill and opened to the populace. With Cybele came Attis, and in a few years Dionysus followed with his orgies and mysteries.

Then, from the war with Hannibal to the founding of the Empire (218–31 B.C.), Hellenism spread its rationalistic exercises westward to throw Latin theology into a state of flux and to bring into the minds of a critical few a sense of detachment from the gods. When the Greek historian, Polybius, considered the problems presented by sociology in the second century B.C., he concluded that the Romans were in the main extraordinarily honest only because they feared the gods — his own countrymen, he admitted regretfully:

. . . if entrusted with a single talent, though protected by ten checking-clerks, as many seals and twice as many witnesses, yet cannot be induced to keep faith. However, the Romans have managed to forge the main bond of social order out of something which the rest of the world exe-crates: I mean, out of Superstition. In dramatizing their superstition theatrically and introducing it into private as well as public life, the Romans have gone to the most extreme lengths conceivable; and to many observers this will appear extraordinary. In my opinion, however, the Romans have done it with an eye to the masses. If it were possible to have an electorate that was composed exclusively of sages, this chicanery might perhaps be unnecessary; but, as a matter of fact, the masses are always unstable and always full of lawless passions, irrational temper and violent rage; and so there is nothing for it but to control them by 'the fear of the unknown' and play-acting of that sort.

Strabo, writing nearly a century later, was even more blunt: 'A rabble of women and promiscuous vulgarians cannot be induced to answer to the call of Philosophic Reason if you are wanting to lead them to piety and holiness and faith. In dealing with people of that sort, you cannot do without superstition; and superstition, in its turn, has to be fed with fairy tales and hocus-pocus.' Cicero's assertion, relative to the mysteries, that 'when we call the corn Ceres and the wine Bacchus we use a common figure of speech; but do you imagine that any one is so insane as to believe that the thing he feeds upon is a god?' was largely rhetorical since the bulk of the Roman populace was prepared to believe in any and every transmutation.

There were many Romans who held that if the Roman empire was founded on piety, piety was in turn founded upon deception. Not that pious deception was considered to be politically unsound so long as the populace, like Plato's ideal citizens, were so unintelligent as not to discover it. The Roman historian Varro conceived that there were three varieties of religion: mythical, or that which was of literary interest only; physical, and on this, the less said in public the better; and civil, in which it was to the best interest of the state to deceive the people. Diodorus admitted with approval that 'the myths which are told of the affairs in Hades, though pure invention at bottom, contribute to make men pious and upright,' while Livy asserted that Numa had 'put the fear of the gods' upon the people 'as the most effective thing for an ignorant and rough multitude.' Lucretius, the last exponent of Ionian science, denied the government of the world by capricious gods and condemned the whole apparatus of popu-lar faith, its prayers, vows, offerings and divinations, as false and evil. He denied the immortality of the soul, for the soul, he argued, is as much a part of the body as the hand or foot, and forms with it one whole, so constituted that neither can exist without the other. He refused the argument of expediency, however, for to him the people seemed driven by the unreasonable fear of death and degraded by idle and even dangerous superstitions. Against the vision of Agamemnon's cruel sacrifice of Iphigenia to Artemis he declared vehemently, 'How many evils has religion caused!'

Such skepticism, however, made its way only at the literate level, and there but insecurely. It seems clear enough that the ruling class fostered religion as an instrument of civil policy and mental oppression, and that Lucretius's *De Rerum Natura,* the most passionate and justly the most famous rationalistic document of ancient times, was an effort to free men from the loathly *religio,* sponsored, however hypocritically, by Pindar, Plato, Aristotle, Polybius, Varro and Cicero, into which the Graeco-Roman world had sunk. But Lucretius's efforts went in vain. The mythological *Aeneid* continued to be taught in all the schools of the Empire, while the *De Rerum Natura* was condemned, and Seneca, in the first century of the Christian Era, was forced to the apologetic 'the whole base throng of gods assembled by a superstition coeval with time we must worship, without forgetting that we do so to set an example, not because they exist.'

In the two republican centuries that produced the memorable Latin literature, although many people of wealth and culture had deserted the temples and allowed them to fall into desuetude, the masses clung steadfastly to the conviction that the gods lived and gave or withheld prosperity, that personal favor was to be obtained by means of religious mystery and ritual, that corn and wine were the very body and blood of the god. The dead lived in the bowels of the earth from which they emerged at appointed times to receive libations of wine, milk, honey and oil, or the blood of sacrificial victims offered at the grave, but they had neither sense nor volition, and nothing to fear or to hope for in the afterworld; trouble and worry were over, pain was forgotten, there was no punishment or retribution by offended deities, only peace and comfort in a dreamlike state which, though never interfering with this life, was never entirely out of contact with it. The Romans called the dead *di manes* (the good), rarely using the term in the singular. Father and grandfather and great-grandfather — the dead were numbered beyond counting, beyond memory, beyond all imagination. They were important collectively but not individually. Their generic fate was one of generic semibeing. Only the gods enjoyed a truly supernatural, personal existence.

When Gaius Octavianus, in 31 B.C., brought to an end the civil war that had followed on the death of Julius Caesar, and, by capturing Alexandria, spread the power of Rome across the sea, he was hailed as the savior of the republic and given the title of Augustus — the 'Majestic.' The empire of which he was now the head held forth such promise of peace and order as had not been known in Rome for years — such indeed as had never been known to encompass the entire civilized world. Augustus, perhaps sharing in some measure Virgil's dream of a new Golden Age like unto that of the days of Saturn, perhaps himself a trifle pious in the sentimental manner of men who have suddenly and unaccountably achieved great things, decided to bring to his task of reconstruction the tool of civil piety. He restored the temples of Venus, Apollo, Mars and Vesta, encouraged the sacrificial priesthoods, and reinstituted all the ancient festivals. Among the cults which offered promise of renascence was the Brethren of Civales, a brotherhood whose chief duty it had been to lead a solemn procession round the crops in May and so insure the blessing of the gods on the most important source of human sustenance. It had also been the duty of the Brethren to assist the members of the reigning house in matters of personal worship, a duty which they continued to discharge on behalf of Gaius Octavianus, until shortly all notable events in the life of the emperor and even of his family — births, marriages, journeys and safe return, the assumption of secular and priestly offices — had become occasions for the Brethren to offer vows, prayers or thanksgivings at the temples and altars throughout the city. It was not long before the figure of the *genius Augustus* appeared between those of the *lares* at the meetings of the streets, inculcating the idea that the emperor stood to the public religion of the city as the *paterfamilias* stood to the private religion of the home.

The fate of the *genius Augustus* was forecast in the scheme of things. The tendency to deify important men had long been evident in the divine honors paid to Faminius, Lucullus, Sulla, Marcellus, Scipio Africanus and Julius Caesar, the last probably having accepted divine honors during his life. On Julius's death the senate had decreed that he should be treated as a god, the title *divus* (divine) having been conferred on him by law in 44 B.C., and the worship of the *divus* Julius was already established as a national cult when the image of the *genius Augustus* appeared among those of the other gods. Rome was now a dominion that included nearly all the world, a new *imperium* which centered in the person of Augustus; logically there should be one among all her gods who favored no one creed or color but who stood as the spiritual counterpart of the majestic emperor. In the multitudinous pantheon there was no single deity who could claim this dominant position, since jealousies between the priesthoods effectively obstructed the claims of any, such as Jupiter or Apollo, who might by tradition have been fitted to occupy the spiritual throne. So the Roman Senate solved the dilemma by elevating the *genius Augustus,* even while the emperor was still alive, to the supreme head of the pantheon.

This move had the enthusiastic approval of the people and it was not long before the birthplace of the *divus Augustus* was set apart as a sacred spot and stories of his miraculous birth and of the portents which accompanied it began to circulate, and on his death it was testified that certain people had seen him ascend to heaven. A new order of priests and a new series of rites were created to propitiate the *Divus* and it soon became a crime to profess reluctance to worship him. There was, indeed, little resistance to the new god, the provinces if anything being more enthusiastic in instituting the new worship than were the inhabitants of Italy; to them Caesar was a friend who had brought confidence and stability out of endless civil conflicts, and the cities of the east vied with each other for the honor of erecting a temple to the *Divus* at their own expense, and were frequently refused permission because it was deemed that they could not afford a building worthy of the divine majesty.

An inscription dating from about 9 B.C. and celebrating the divine birthday reads:

> This day has given earth an entirely new aspect. The world would have gone to destruction had there not streamed forth from him who is now born a common blessing. Rightly does he judge who recognizes in this birthday the beginning of life and of all the powers of life: now is that ended when men pitied themselves for being born. . . . The providence which rules over all has filled this man with such gifts for the salvation of the world as designate him the Savior for us and for the coming generations: of wars he will make an end, and establish all things worthily. By his appearing are the hopes of our forefathers fulfilled: not only has he surpassed the good deeds of men of earlier time, but it is impossible that one greater than he can ever appear. The birthday of God has brought to the world glad tidings that are bound up in him. From his birthday a new era begins.

Thus did Augustus even while living join the Olympian immortals.

ii

Although the worship of the *Divus* constituted the official state religion, it remained but one among a dozen cults which in tradition and current approbation were esteemed as equally true and valid. In view of the heterogeneity of the imperial population a completely tolerant polytheism was a political necessity as well as a political expedient. The populace of Rome itself was scarcely Roman save in the upper strata, the mass being comprised of soldiers, slaves, traders and craftsmen drawn from all parts of the world. The city was but a sample of the Empire, a great sprawling hegemony loosely held together by warring dictators and governed by ambition and perfidy, obsequiousness and corruption, brutality and force — the very antithesis of the 'new era' promised by the panegyrist.

Indicative of the temper of the times were the gladiatorial games in which the spectacle of bloodshed and death afforded the main amusement to both the upper and lower classes. Introduced to Rome about 264 B.C. as religious ceremonies at the tombs of the great and intended as human sacrifices to appease the *manes* of the dead, they came to be used to instill courage into soldiers before their departure for war, and subsequently as mere political and public displays. Caesar and Pompey greatly multiplied them, each seeking to ingratiate himself with the people, and Pompey introduced combat between men and animals while Caesar held a mortuary game at the tomb of his daughter. Although Augustus ordered that not more than 120 men should fight on a single occasion, it appears that 10,000 gladiators may have fought in his reign. In addition to their mortuary function, gladiatorial combats were held by officials on coming into office, by conquerors to secure popularity, on every occasion of public rejoicing and by rich tradesmen desirous of acquiring a social position. The purveyance of gladiators became an important profession and great arenas, of which the Colosseum is the most imposing, were erected to accommodate the crowds.

The desire for novelty impelled the invention of every refinement of cruelty. When the single combat became insipid, the victims were multiplied until hundreds of animals died in a single day — five thousand were used at the dedication of the Colosseum by Titus — and under Trajan the games continued for 123 successive days. Lions, tigers, elephants, rhinoceros, hippopotamuses, giraffes, bulls, stags and even crocodiles and snakes were employed for variation. Men, proud of their prowess and anxious for the rich awards to the victors, fought pain-tortured animals or other men to the wild acclaim of the crowds, and criminals were thrown to the beasts with no defense. Women trembled with passion during the fight and noble ladies craved the victor's love, while the tranquil courage with which the gladiators died was celebrated in poetry, art and philosophy. That life should be so cheap, that the bloody slaughter of animals and men and women in the arena should be a spectacle of which the populace never tired, was symptomatically rather than causally related to the social pattern.

'I am entering upon the history of a period,' writes Tacitus of the first part of the first century, 'rich in disasters, gloomy with wars, rent with seditions, nay, savage in its very hours of peace. Four Emperors perished by the sword; there were three civil wars; there were more with foreigners — and some had both characters at once. . . . Rome was wasted by fires, its oldest temples burnt, the very Capitol set in flames by Roman hands. There was defilement of sacred rites; adulteries in high places; the sea was crowded with exiles; island rocks drenched with murder. Yet wilder was the frenzy in Rome; nobility, wealth, the refusal of office, its acceptance — everything was a crime, and virtue the surest ruin. Nor were the rewards of informers less odious than their deeds; one found his spoils in a priesthood or behind a consulate; another in a provincial governorship; another behind the throne, and all was one delirium of hate and terror; slaves were bribed to betray their masters, freedmen their patrons. He who had no foe was destroyed by his friend.'

It was this to which the empire of Augustus, and Virgil's dream of a new Golden Age, had come within the space of half a century, an economically bankrupt empire of masters and slaves. The masters erected marble temples in their gardens, offered the accustomed prayers and sacrifices and saw that the priests were well fed, without, however, forgetting for a moment that their lives depended upon their bodyguards, as the integrity of the empire depended from day to day upon the armed legions which were as much in evidence in Rome as in Gaul and Syria. The slaves, and those partway between slavery and freedom, possessed no property whatever and few civil rights, their lives being valued scarcely more than the cattle of the fields. They milled about the cities with forlorn, unhappy restlessness, the soldier thinking that he might be dead tomorrow, the slave that he might be sold to a crueler master, the freedman that he might be back in servitude. It was common talk that something was soon to happen — matters would be different when Dionysus, or Apollo, or Mithra, came again next year; the Jews talked of a messiah whom they expected to establish a new kingdom; Virgil had written that one day there would be born a child who would 'rule with his father's virtues the world at peace.'

With no outlet for ambition or physical action, no power to break the fetters of unending servitude, the only avenue for hope lay in those mystical and ecstatic experiences which were the presentiments of heaven. Men vacillated between temples of Apollo and Serapis, between mysteries of Mithra and Isis, discoursing on Hades and righteousness and holiness, and seeking in ritual or abstinence or self-mortification an escape from the common lot of misery. Diffusion of Greek ideas had made the old faiths inadequate without displacing them from popular affection; what was needed was a faith that would compound the new abstractions — incorruptible, invisible, perfect, infinite, matter, spirit — with the ancient rituals, one that would also elevate the soldier, slave and pauper from their lowly rank. Above all, it must be a faith that would give meaning to the restlessness and apprehension that everywhere led men to anticipate a catastrophic and perhaps world-wide change.

When the new faith did appear, its novelty was most evident in its declaration that the end of the world, a terrible holocaust which was to be a Day of Judgment and the beginning of the Kingdom of God, was expected next week, or the week thereafter. Originating from one or more Jewish cults which had rebelled against the Law, its sectaries were preaching a Messiah and proselytizing gentiles who had no Jewish blood.

Schisms among the Jews were by no means new. From the days when Hosea, condemning the young married women who sacrificed at the sanctuaries of the sacred trees, had declared that 'Israel slideth back as a backsliding heifer,' the inspired mission of the prophets had been the protection of the faithful from false gods and wicked practices; but as the Wall of Law had grown more stringent by expansion of the priestly code, liberal-minded Jews had in increasing numbers been forced to abandon their fathers' god. Judaism had always been handicapped by the fact that it had only philosophic attraction for those who were not of Jewish birth. Yahweh had little emotional appeal; he was so terrible a moral censor that he could not behold iniquity, so righteous that he could not condone frivolity; he was the very symbol of the imprisoning maze of Judaic purity. He was too awful to be easily loved and, since the exile, so impersonal and ethereal that only the introspective Jewish mind, tutored since birth in the traditions of Israel, could entertain for him a heartfelt affection. Above all, he was the ethnic god of the Jews and his converts were required not only to exchange their beliefs but to forego their racial traditions, their family ties, their daily habits, in order to be acceptable within his fold. The pagans had long laughed at the Jews for their meticulous observance of the Law, and at the Law itself — all this business of circumcision, of Sabbath-keeping, of tithes and temple rituals, of the washing of pots and pans and knives, of blood and butter taboos, was to them an incomprehensible fussiness which meant nothing and achieved nothing, a pathetic comedy of exaggerated holiness. Such Jews as wandered far from the Holy City and rubbed shoulders constantly with the pagans could not themselves keep within the Law and perforce had to abandon it; and it was inevitable that as they acquired knowledge of the human, genial qualities of the gentile gods and of their ceremonies and mystery plays, certain of them should hybridize with gentile faiths.

The Messiah, the central spiritual figure in the doctrines of this new faith, was an orthodox if complex product of pure Jewish speculation. The Old Testament prophets had spoken of the coming of the Kingdom of Yahweh, meaning that on the Day of the Lord all existing governments would be destroyed and Yahweh would appear in person as the supreme ruler of the earth. Joel made it clear that the day on which Yahweh came would be a day of judgment when the unrighteous, or gentiles, would be annihilated. Quite unrelated to this expected military triumph of Israel's god, the messianic doctrine arose about the middle of the second century B.C., engendered independently within the apocalyptic literature. At this period the practice of prophecy had come to be viewed with something more than grave suspicion, Zechariah going so far as to class prophets with idols and unclean spirits, and to enjoin the father and mother of a would-be prophet to slay him out of hand as a liar and imposter. Accordingly, when a man felt himself bursting with prophecy, he was forced to write his cerebrations upon a weather-stained papyrus and to unload them on his neighbors as the work of some ancient sage who had been long dead and could not refute the compliment. Such literature is called pseudepigraphic or apocryphal (written under a false name), and since its purpose was to reveal the future, apocalyptic (to uncover or reveal).

In the stress of the Maccabean war (*ca.* 164 B.C.) one of the fanatic members of the mob of bandits who called themselves Maccabees forged such a prophecy under the name of an ancient sage, Daniel, who traditionally had lived in the period of the captivity. It was made to appear that the Babylonian Daniel had foreseen events up to the date of writing and, in weird oriental symbolism, it was revealed how four empires were to succeed one another, first Babylon, represented by a lion, then Media, represented by a bear, followed by Persia, represented by a leopard, and

Macedonia, represented by a monster which for lack of known equivalent must remain unnamed. In olden days Jeremiah had prophesied that after seventy years Israel would be restored to the blessings of the Kingdom of the Lord under the dynasty of the family of David; now, according to pseudo-Daniel's calculation, 483 years had actually passed since Jeremiah's prediction, and he concluded that what Jeremiah had really meant was that seventy *weeks* of years (490) would pass before all would be fulfilled. Sixty-nine of these weeks having gone by, pseudo-Daniel believed that the Kingdom of the Lord would come when the last week of years had passed. Having used the symbolism of the four beasts to represent the four kingdoms of the earth which had come and the last of which was about to pass, pseudo-Daniel chose to symbolize the coming Kingdom of the Lord by an angelic creature 'like unto a son of man,' who would descend from the clouds, rather than rise out of the troubled deep. The expression was a familiar Semitic one commonly used in a generic sense, as one would speak of a 'son of Greece,' or a 'son of Adam,' and served in pseudo-Daniel's hands merely to give human form to the symbol which stood for the fifth and last kingdom now to come, in contrast to the animals which had previously been used.

At some time between 95 and 64 B.C., the writer or writers of the apocalyptic Book of Enoch (a patriarch who had been carried alive to heaven in the days before the Flood) converted pseudo-Daniel's literary expression into '*the* Son of Man,' a supernatural being who had been created by the deity before the sun or stars. On the last day of the present and dreaded epoch in pseudo-Enoch's view, the dead would arise from their graves, the fallen angels would be ejected from hell, all sinners would be destroyed and the rebellious angels would be confined forever; there would be a new heaven and earth, and a general judgment would be held by this divine being, 'the Son of Man,' after he had taken his place on the throne. Here pseudo-Daniel's literary symbol is apotheosized into a supernatural vicegerent, and, by a quotation from Isaiah, is identified with that prophet's Servant of Yahweh, whom the Lord had 'anointed to preach good tidings unto the meek . . . to bind up the broken-hearted.' An anointed one in Hebrew is *Mashiah,* an epithet applied to a priest or king who had been sanctified by the rubbing on of oil, while in Greek the word for one who had been anointed is *christos;* hence, on the identification in the Book of Enoch, the apotheosized symbol came to be spoken of as the Messiah or Christos.

By the time of II Esdras (*ca.* A.D. 69–96), a new empire had in fact appeared in the form of Rome; the writer of II Esdras, slightly rearranging the prophecy, identified the new world dominion with pseudo-Daniel's fourth beast, and anticipated its quick destruction: 'The time is fulfilled! The Kingdom of God is at hand!' 'The Age is hastening fast to its end!' The world would end with the Emperor Domitian, who was to die by the sword, and then would come 'the Messiah whom the Most High hath kept unto the end of the days, who is sprung from the Seed of David.' From the midst of the sea there was to arise a being in the likeness of a man who was to fly over the clouds of heaven and alight on Mt. Sinai; Zion was to be encompassed by an innumerable host gathered from the four winds of heaven; the whole host would be annihilated by the fiery breath of the Heavenly Man who came in the clouds of heaven, after which the Lost Tribes of Israel would cross the Euphrates and muster in Jerusalem under his rule. The Messiah would reign for 400 years, after which he would die, and then, following seven days of primeval silence, there would be a general resurrection and a judgment, and the righteous would enter into paradise, while the gentiles would pass into Gehenna.

In the Apocalypse of John (*ca.* A.D. 65), which was later received into the New Testament as the Revelation of John, the world is pictured as oppressed by the empire of Rome, when wars, famines, plagues, earthquakes and other calamities fall upon the unfortunate earth; in the midst of meteorological terrors Judaism gives birth to the Messiah who appears on Mt. Sinai in the form of a sacrificial Lamb, and is caught up to the throne of Yahweh after the gentiles gather against him and are destroyed; Satan is chained for a thousand years and there is a 'first resurrection' of the martyrs; the Messiah reigns for a millennium, after which Satan is released for a time and brings out the gentiles from the remote corners of the world; then there is a general and final resurrection of the dead and a last judgment; a new heaven and a new earth are created, a new Jerusalem comes down from heaven and the faithful enter into eternal felicity. Up to this date, the only hint of humanity in the Messiah or Heavenly Man is his identification as 'a son of David,' this expression meaning probably no more than that the coming prince was, of course, to be King of Israel.

The messianic notion is wholly lacking from the four books of the Maccabees, Tobit, Judith, Ecclesiasticus, the Wisdom of Solomon, the Books of Jubilees and the pre-Christian editions of the Sybilline Oracles; hence it represented a fairly circumscribed development within the faith. When, after the middle of the first century the spread of the messianic doctrine was abruptly accelerated by a strong impulse to proselytism, it was as a schism which was vigorously opposed by the orthodox Jewish church.

The chief exponent of the new movement was a Syrian Jew from Tarsus, named Paul, who was possessed of 'a thorn in the flesh, a messenger of Satan,' which has been interpreted as epilepsy. As described in the Acts of Paul and Theda he was 'of a low stature, bald on the head, crooked thighs; handsome legs, hollow-eyed; had a crooked nose; full of grace.' This was apparently spiritual grace, for Paul was always acutely conscious of his physical infirmities. Argumentative and even querulous, he was given to alternating fits of violent rage and severe depression, and in his seizures he emitted inarticulate sounds, i.e., spoke 'in an unknown tongue . . . unto God.' In such moments he experienced ecstatic visions which he prized above all waking realities. According to his own account he had persecuted the followers of the Messiah until one day, on the road to Damascus, he had fallen to earth and had been caught up into the third heaven and heard words which it was not lawful for a man to utter; thereupon he repented of his persecution, and became convinced that he had been personally charged to spread the faith, and to warn people of the coming Doomsday. Impelled by the fear that the last trump would sound before he had fulfilled his mission, he traveled about the empire propounding that the Messiah, whom he called Jesus, had *already* come, had suffered a sacrificial death by crucifixion and had ascended unto heaven. He proclaimed that the Day of Judgment would be next week, or the week after, and that those who wished to be saved should repent and be baptized and protect themselves by participation in a eucharistic meal.

By the end of the first century the Pauline movement had acquired a considerable body of legend which centered on Paul's crucified Messiah, a Jew who was sometimes called Jesus and sometimes Christ. The Greek name Jesus has been equated with the Hebraic Joshua (Yahweh saves), a name which had been possessed by a stormy Old Testament character who had performed some considerable miracles, and which, for this reason if for no other, had the veneration of the Jews. The Syrian form of Jesus, *Yeschu,* comes near to the Hebrew *Yischak,* or Isaac, the only son of Abraham, who was spared from sacrifice by the substitution of a ram, while the Greek word *christos,* from which the members of the cult came to be called *christiani,* had the same import of sanctity by unction for the pagans as for the Hebrews, and was, moreover, very similar to *chresto,* meaning 'good, excellent, gracious.' By these multiple meanings the name appealed to Jew, Syrian and Greek alike.

References in the Talmudic writings do not date before the destruction of the Temple and in any case convey little historical information since they are highly derogatory and admittedly prejudiced. The works of Seneca, Petronius, Pliny the Elder, Juvenal, Martial, Quintilian, Epictetus, Plutarch, Appian and Philo, written in the first century, make no mention of the origin or progress of the sect. Two references occur in the *Antquities* of Josephus (93–94), one a eulogy of Jesus which represents, according to all authorities, a late Christian interpolation, and a second specifying James as the 'brother of Jesus called the Messiah.' This writer, probably for political reasons, does not mention the Christian movement in his comprehensive *History of the Jewish War* (75–79). Clement, a Christian leader of Rome, cited a Pauline epistle and mentioned Paul by name in a document which is variously dated from 95 to 150, and from the time of the Ignatian epistles, which were written sometime between 117 and 150, references to both Paul and Jesus became more frequent. Pliny the Younger, writing to Trajan about the year 111, referred at some length to the new movement in Bithynia and let it appear that it was of at least twenty years' standing in that province, and Suetonius, writing between 117 and 138, records that Claudius (41–54) had 'banished from Rome all the Jews who were continually making disturbances at the instigation of one Chrestos,' and that Nero (54–68) had 'likewise inflicted punishment on the Christians, a sect of men who held a new and maleficent superstition.'

The first explicit statement concerning Jesus's biography in secular literature occurs in the *Annals* of Tacitus, written within a few years to either side of 117. Here, in connection with the burning of Rome under Nero, it is said: 'In order, if possible, to remove the imputation [that Rome had been set on fire by his orders] he [Nero] determined to transfer the guilt to others. For this purpose he punished, with exquisite torture, a race of men detested for their evil practices, by vulgar apellation commonly called *Chrestiani*. The name was derived from *Christus*, who in the reign of Tiberius, suffered under Pontius Pilate, the procurator of Judaea.' Some historians have debated whether this passage is wholly authentic, or contains Christian interpolations, but the answer is relatively unimportant since at this late date Tacitus probably could have obtained the all-important name of Pontius Pilate from Christian tradition.

In the canonical and apocryphal (false, obscure in origin and unapproved) literature of the sect not one line was written by anyone who could credibly claim to have seen Jesus in the flesh. The oldest documents are ostensibly the Epistles of Paul, the earliest of which, I Thessalonians, appears to date from about 51. Paul himself never saw Jesus except as an apparition who appeared to him in a seizure, and he was in any case less interested in a human Jesus than in his (Paul's) new doctrine of redemption; his Jesus is a mystical being possessing no human history, nothing in the way of worldly biography but death and resurrection. In the matter of interpolation the Pauline epistles are not above suspicion, but excluding two questioned passages that refer to the Lord's Supper and to 'the Twelve,' these letters tell only of a cult in which the crucified Jesus figures as the supreme purificatory sacrifice. Though information on the matter may have been current, they contain no reference to Jesus's birth, to his miracles or to his ethical teachings, even though the teachings are subsequently made to appear as the *raison d'être* for the movement, while the miracles are advanced as proof of Jesus's divinity. All that can be recovered from Paul, the source closest to the namesake of Christianity in time, is that Jesus had quit the right hand of God and come to earth in order to serve as a supreme sacrifice for all men, that he had been crucified and had ascended again unto heaven and that redemption from sin could be gained by Jew and Greek regardless of circumcision, through the rite of baptism. If Paul knew more than this, he was not interested in the information and his accounts offer no confirmation of the elaborate details which are recorded in the later gospel narratives.

Of these, the first surviving account is the Gospel of Mark, at the earliest composed just before the destruction of the Temple (*ca.* 66–68). This was obviously a redaction of earlier manuscripts, and itself, perhaps with another manuscript, is supposed to have served as the basis for the compilation of the Gospels of Luke, Matthew and John. The conventionally accepted dates for these are 80 to 95, 100 and 110, respectively, though some critics would place the writing of all four gospels as late as 135 to 142.

Apart from the codices already mentioned in connection with the Old Testament, the oldest surviving manuscripts of the New Testament are represented by the Chester Beatty papyri, which contain fragments of Matthew, Mark, Luke, John and Acts, as well as imperfect leaves of a codex of the Pauline epistles, including portions of Romans, Philippians, Colossians and I Thessalonians, and about one third of Revelation. These are believed to date back to the middle of the third century, or perhaps as early as 200.

Counting these and all later manuscripts of the New Testament, numbering some 4,000 fragments, it has been estimated that the surviving copies present upwards of 150,000 discrepancies; most of these are of course trivial, but not a few are of considerable use to critics in tracing the early history of Christian beliefs before the text became more or less fixed. These differences arose in part from the fact that from the year 65 or thereabouts Christian teachers carried about with them a miscellany of epistles and other documents which were read aloud in the temples in the Jewish manner, and which replaced the fluid oral tradition of the so-called Apostolic Age. These documents consisted of papyrus rolls which were copied as needed, and as their number grew and the differences between them increased, they came not only to reflect but to engender schisms in belief. Of separate gospels, or writings purporting to describe the words and acts of Jesus, there existed in the second century more than fifty which are now known by name, though less than one tenth of them have survived. The four finally incorporated in the New Testament were the result of ecclesiastic selection in the second century, but several additional centuries elapsed before these were safe, not only from copyists' errors and presumed corrections in the text, but from less conscientious interpolations and deletions which were intended to give point to obscure passages or to remove others which proved offensive to the changing creed. Old Testament manuscript discrepancies are almost wholly of the accidental sort which occur unavoidably in copying and translation. New Testament discrepancies, however, are all too frequently intentional and were obviously made by persons who had new matter to insert and felt themselves free to take any liberties they chose. Comparisons of stem texts indicate that most of these interpolations were made in the second and third centuries. A single stem, the Byzantine, an elective compilation of various current manuscripts and itself circulating in several forms, served as the root for most of the Greek texts, as well as the Slavonic, Gothic, Latin Vulgate (383) and Syriac (411). Because of continued interpolation, the accepted text of the New Testament cannot be said to date earlier than the year 350.

Almost from the moment of its inception the Christian movement began to break up into sects over circumcision, marriage, taboos and contentious items in the creed, and with each schism it tended to lose its Jewish character by taking to itself pagan practices and beliefs. Its final pattern was determined not so much by the mystical doctrines which Paul bequeathed it as by the legends, dogma and organization which it acquired in the first three or four centuries of its development. It grew by absorbing competing theological ideas.

Toynbee lists eighty-seven correspondences between the story of Jesus's life and the stories of certain Hellenic 'saviors,' using this term in the human rather than the god-incarnate sense. Similarly there are a large number of common characters, scenes with common senses, common visual correspondences, common properties, and common but more or less unique expressions. In all cases the pagan stories are older, but only rarely would it seem that they directly influenced the Jesus story; rather both the pagan literature and the Christian legend obtained their patterns from the common stream of tradition. Notable among ancient tales as supplying the stuff for hero legends is that of Herakles, the peasant demigod who attained in late Hellenic time an idealized form and heroic stature. Herakles had a royal lineage, but a flaw in his genealogy; he miraculously escaped from a mortal danger in infancy; he was tempted in the wilderness; his career was an ordeal; his work obtained extraordinary publicity; he was commissioned by God to exercise a beneficent royal authority over all mankind; he suffered spiritual agony in the face of supreme challenge; he resigned himself to the will of his heavenly father and was sacrificed; after his death he came to receive religious worship; his mortal remains miraculously disappeared; he descended into hell; he appeared to the women of the entourage; and finally he ascended to heaven in a cloud. It was at Tarsus, the boyhood home of Paul, that Herakles-Sandan died a cruel death in an annual festival in order to enjoy a glorious resurrection.

This process of syncretic growth got the Christians into difficulties in connection with Jesus's paternity. In the ultimately accepted gospels Jesus was said to have been born of a virgin. This story did not become current until the later documents were forming, for Paul, the greatest authority on Jesus, said that he was born 'of the seed of David according to the flesh,' and in an early secular manuscript in the Vatican library, and again in the Sinaitic Codex, it is said that 'Jacob begat Joseph, and Joseph begat Jesus'—that is, Joseph was forthrightly accepted as Jesus's physical father. The first reference to the virginity of Mary outside the New Testament is in the Ignatian espistles (?117–150), and one of the reasons given by critical students for accepting Mark as the earliest gospel is that its author knew nothing of either the birth or childhood of Jesus—Mark's Jesus comes to earth full-formed to begin his ministry under John the Baptist.

The doctrine of the virgin birth was thoroughly familiar to the pagans. A supernatural origin had been ascribed to Egyptian Pharaohs centuries before, and Attis-Adonis had been born of the virgin Myrrha. In the disguise of a serpent the god Aesculapius had fathered Aratus of Sicyon, Apollo had fathered Julius Caesar and Augustus, and other gods had fathered Aristomenes, Alexander the Great, Cyrus, the elder Scipio, Mithra, Hermes, Perseus and Buddha. Juno, the wife of Jupiter, was supposed to become a virgin again each year, and as a virgin was said by the Romans to have born Cybele, Demeter, Leo, and Vulcan.

That Apollo had fathered Plato was solemnly attested by Plato's own nephew, Speusippus, and accepted by Aristotle's pupil, Klearchus, as well as by the historians Anaxilides and Diogenes Laertus. Plato was born of Amphictione when Ariston had been barred from having sexual relations with her until she should have given birth to the child begotten by Apollo. Similarly, before Mary's marriage to Joseph is consummated she becomes with child, and Joseph proposes to put her away when the angel appears to him in a dream and reveals what has come to pass. In obedience to this revelation Joseph 'did as the angel of the Lord had bidden him, and took unto him his wife: and knew her not till she had brought forth her first born son' — the exact instructions that are given to Plato's father. The parallel with the birth of Herakles is even more detailed: Amphitryon, the husband of Herakles's mother Alcmena, refrains, like Joseph and Ariston, from having sexual intercourse with his newly wedded wife until she has conceived and born a child whose paternity is divine. Before the birth of the divine child Alcmena and Amphitryon journey from Mycenae to Thebes, Mary and Joseph from Nazareth to Bethlehem, so that the child has a birth place which is not his parents' home.

The second century Christian apologist, Justin Martyr, writing a dialogue in which he engages with a Jew called Tryphon in defense of Christianity, is twitted by Tryphon, apropos of Jesus's birth, with having picked up a pagan tale comparable to that of Danaë, the daughter of the King of Argos. This king, having been warned by an oracle that Danaë would bear a son by whom he would be slain, confined his daughter in a brazen tower but Zeus descended to her through the windows as a 'shower of gold' (sunlight) and she gave birth to Perseus. To Tryphon's accusation, Justin Martyr replied, 'Why are we Christians alone of men hated for Christ's name, when we do but relate of him stories similar to what the Greeks relate of Hermes and Perseus? . . . What we teach, we learned from Christ and the prophets who preceded him, and it is a true lore and more ancient than that of all other writers that ever existed; but we claim acceptance, not because our stories are identical with those of others, but because they are true.' Then he resorts to what was with him a favorite and unanswerable argument, that Satan had anticipated Christianity and imitated it in advance in the pagan cults: 'When I am told that Perseus was born of a virgin, I realize that here again is a case in which the serpent and deceiver has imitated our religion.'

The casual acceptance of the doctrine of the virgin birth among the pagans did not arise so much from a desire to absolve the mother from carnal intercourse, for this was not generally considered to be debasing, as from the wish to establish divine parenthood. The masses, even though fully cognizant of the physical basis of paternity, were far from believing intercourse to be necessary: they accepted that conception could follow the eating of certain nuts and fruits, the application of certain charms, or even more casual stimuli.

The Gospel of Luke was written, as is stated in its preamble, in order that one Theophilus, to whom it is dedicated, might 'know the certainty of those things, wherein thou hast been instructed.' To the end of making the virgin birth more 'certain' to Theophilus, the divine impregnation of Mary is rehearsed by a similar divine impregnation of her cousin, Elisabeth, the wife of Zacharias, and Zacharias is struck dumb for nine months because of his refusal to believe in the miracle. Presumably this was to be a warning to Theophilus.

In view of its general acceptance among the pagans, the plausibility of divine impregnation stood the Christians in good stead, inasmuch as many of the sect were strongly ascetic and rejected marriage as debasing and in any case unnecessary since the end of the world was at hand. When, after the repeated failure of the Day of Judgment to appear, the church was finally forced to place its sanction on the married state, the virginity of Mary was held as a divine antithesis against the carnal though necessary evil of connubial intercourse.

The Holy Ghost, as the divine power which impregnated Mary was subsequently designated, was depicted as taking the form of the amorous dove, sacred to Ishtar and Astarte, or of rays of light such as Zeus assumed when he visited Danaë and Herodotus said had fallen upon the sacred cow that afterwards gave birth to Apis. In medieval hymns Mary is described as conceiving 'through the ears,' echoing both the Egyptian belief that some animals are thus fertilized and the rabbinic theory, which received support from Tertullian, Origen and other churchmen, that it was through the ears that women were assailed by both good and evil angels. The spirits had a peculiar attachment for women with beautiful hair, and it was to protect them that Paul ordered women to keep their heads covered when in holy places. The lily was soon associated with pictures of the Virgin, the notion being prevalent that women by eating it became pregnant without the touch of man, and hence the flower became the symbol of purity.

The virgin birth was one of many details in which the writers of the gospels sought to demonstrate the fulfillment of Old Testament prophecy: it is specifically of the prophecy in Isaiah vii.14 that Matthew, after relating the appearance of the angel before Joseph, says (i.22), 'Now all this was done, that it might be fulfilled which was spoken of the Lord by the prophet, saying, Behold, a virgin shall be with child, and shall bring forth a son . . .' A prophecy in Micah (v.1) required the Messiah to be born in Bethlehem and not in Joseph's town of Nazareth, as the primitive tradition recorded in Mark assumes him to have been, and to reconcile this contradiction, Luke (ii.1–39) fabricated the story that the Roman emperor, for the purposes of a census, required every man and woman in the world to return by a specified date to the city of his or her birth; in the confusion of this mass exodus Joseph and the pregnant Mary traveled eighty miles over mountainous country to stage a timely arrival in Bethlehem. The census of Quirinus, governor of Syria, was in A.D. 6, yet Jesus was born before the death of Herod, which was in either 4 or 3 B.C., and, if the authority of Tertullian can be opposed to that of Luke, the birth was not in the census of Quirinus but the census of Saturninus, which was in 7 B.C. Matthew's solution of the problem is that after Jesus's birth his parents fled to Nazareth to escape the wrath of Herod (ii.19–23). To fulfill the messianic doctrine Jesus was given a royal descent from David, but to please the antiroyalist Samaritans he was made to repudiate this descent, and the recorded genealogy contains many irreconcilable contradictions.

In the canonical gospels Jesus was said to have been born in a stable, but in apocryphal writings the birthplace, as in the case of Mithra, was given as a cave, and in Mithraic monuments shepherds are shown tendering the infant offerings of first fruits. A particular cave at Bethlehem was long shown by Christians as the one in which Jesus had been born, and Jerome complained that in his day the pagans celebrated the worship of Adonis at that very place. A star, strongly suggestive of Ishtar, marked the evening of the birth, as a star had marked the birth of Mithra, and as other astronomical portents had marked the births of various gods and emperors; it was wise men, or *magi,* who followed it and carried gifts to the newborn infant, as three *magi* accompanied Tiridates to pay obeisance to the Emperor Nero. When Herod has all the innocents of Bethlehem and the surrounding district massacred, he is but imitating the effort of the Egyptian Pharaoh to kill the infant Moses, of Nimrod of Jewish legend trying to kill the infant Abraham, of Joab trying to kill the infant Hadad, and of the Roman senate, as in Suetonius's account, trying to kill the infant Augustus.

As in the legends of the birth, so in the morality of the gospels, there were few precepts which were not paralleled in the literature of other Mediterranean peoples. The Sermon on the Mount, the accepted repository of Christian teaching and piety, was a compilation from Psalms, Isaiah, Ecclesiasticus, the Secrets of Enoch, the Shemone Lesreh (a book of Hebrew prayers) and other sources. That it was compiled late is indicated by references to persecutions and false prophets, and by the mention of gentiles as opposed to Christians, usages which would have been meaningless in Jesus's time when no organized Christian bodies as yet existed. Its cardinal moral principle was but a positive rewording of the advice of the Pharisee, Hillel (40 B.C.), who, when asked by a proselyte to instruct him in the Jewish religion in the time during which he could stand on one foot, replied, "Do not unto others what is hateful to thyself; this is the whole of the Torah, all the rest is commentary."

The truly novel features in Jesus's morality were, first, 'love Jesus,' second, 'save yourself,' and third, 'love poverty of spirit and poverty of person,' — all three themes springing from the apocalyptic expectation that this world's affairs were to be liquidated by an impending catastrophe, and that a new and blessed condition was to be imposed by divine fiat: 'this generation shall not pass away, till all be fulfilled.'

> For I am come to set a man at variance against his father, and the daughter against her mother, and the daughter in law against her mother in law. And a man's foes shall be they of his own household. He that loveth father or mother more than me is not worthy of me: and he that loveth son or daughter more than me is not worthy of me.

> There is no man that hath left house, or parents, or brethren, or wife, or children, for the kingdom of God's sake, Who shall not receive manifold more in this present time, and in the world to come life everlasting.

> If any man come to me, and hate not his father, and mother, and wife, and children, and brethren, and sisters, yea, and his own life also, he cannot be my disciple.

Jesus preaches brotherly love and forgiveness, yet he strictly prohibits his disciples from going to the Samaritans and gentiles, and, apparently referring to the dissemination of the faith, says, "Give not that which is holy unto the dogs, neither cast ye your pearls before swine." He pleads for love to enemies, yet bitterly denounces the Pharisees as hypocrites, serpents, offspring of vipers, and condemns unbelievers to hell where there is everlasting torment. He preaches honesty, yet he instructs his apostles to be as 'wise as serpents and harmless as doves.' He concentrates malice and childishly offended dignity in his threat that 'whosoever shall deny me before men, him will I also deny before my Father which is in heaven.' He preaches peace, but warns his disciples: 'Think not that I am come to send peace on the earth: I came not to send peace, but a sword.' To please the ascetics he is born in a stable and made poor and homeless, to please the worldly he grows up to dine with the sinners and publicans. He insists upon strict observance of the jot and tittle of the Mosaic law, yet he recommends its suppression and fails to keep it himself. He vacillates between mysticism, legalism and simple good works as a means to salvation. He exorcises devils out of one man only to drive them into an innocent man's swine so that the helpless animals rush away to self-destruction. The morality of Jesus is an eclectic system drawn from the multiple morality of the Roman Empire, constrained to a monotheistic pattern and fired to urgent fervor by the impending advent of doomsday.

The trial, crucifixion and resurrection with which the gospels end, although not directly borrowed from pagan custom as were so much of the legend and ethical instruction of the cult, represent an agglutination of familiar dramatic details around Jesus's death which, however considered historically, must be viewed as an expiatory sacrifice. For centuries the peoples of the Mediterranean had annually observed the death and resurrection of their gods. The Osirian drama so beloved by the Egyptians dated back certainly twenty-five, and perhaps thirty-five, centuries. Tammuz too had died a violent death, to be brought to life with the sprouting of the grain. So had Adonis been buried in a rocky tomb, mourned, and declared resurrected and ascended unto heaven. So had Herakles died and been resurrected at Paul's home. Until the pagan cults were forcibly repressed in the fourth century of the Christian period, the death and revival of Osiris, Dionysus, Persephone, Aphrodite, Eurydice, Attis and Mithra were familiar throughout most of the Roman Empire, while other rites, such as those of the Saturnalia, presented the death of the mock king who was sacrificed as a scapegoat for the people.

The passion of Jesus had been foreshadowed in the description of the 'man of sorrows,' which was to be found in Isaiah (i.3), and which was probably written in the sixth century B.C. by the unknown Babylonian prophet called Deutero-Isaiah in an attempt to depict Israel as the suffering servant of Yahweh: 'He is despised and rejected of men; a man of sorrows, and acquainted with grief: and we hid as it were our faces from him; he was despised, and we esteemed him not. Surely he hath borne our griefs, and carried our sorrows: yet we did esteem him stricken, smitten of God, and afflicted. But he was wounded for our transgressions, he was bruised for our iniquities: the chastisement of our peace was upon him; and with his stripes we are healed. All we like sheep have gone astray; we have turned every one to his own way; and the Lord hath laid on him the iniquity of us all.' This poetic epitome of the captive Jews needed only a personal victim and slight modification of its dramaturgy to epitomize the god-king sacrifice prevalent on the Mediterranean shores.

In the account as ultimately formalized in the gospels, Jesus has reached the prime of life wherein beauty and maturity are combined; to fulfill a prophecy in Zechariah he comes to Jerusalem for the climax of the drama wherein a mock king is sacrificed, entering the city acclaimed by the people who cut branches from the trees and strew them in his path. Again in accordance with a prophecy of Zechariah (and not of Jeremiah as Matthew erroneously says) — 'a goodly price that I was priced at of them. And I took the thirty pieces of silver, and cast them to the potter — he is duly purchased by thirty pieces of silver to absolve the murderers from guilt. The mob demands his death and he is charged and tried with no one willing to speak in his defense; he is subjected to degradation, reviled and spat upon, bound with cords, carried before Pilate and accused by false witnesses; when Pilate asks him, "Art thou King of the Jews?" he admits the title by implication. Though Pilate is not convinced that he is worthy of death, the governor (who must be exonerated) yields to the multitude and, washing his hands of all guilt, turns him over to the soldiers, whereupon he is cruelly scourged that his tears may flow. Then he is dressed in royal purple, given a reed scepter in his right hand and crowned with thorns to increase his ignominy while the people mock him. He is offered the anodyne of aromatic vinegar, which he declines, and then he is sacrificed in the Roman fashion of crucifixion (though actually the Romans nailed malefactors to an upright pole with the hands above the head, the crucifix with the arms outstretched not appearing in Christian art until the seventh century). To fulfill the prophecy of Psalm xxii, the soldiers cast lots for his garments. His side is pierced so that from the wound may flow the blood without which the sacrifice would be meaningless. When he is dead his body is taken down and, according to John's account, anointed with a hundred-pound weight of myrrh and aloes and wrapped in linen swathes and buried royally in a great rock tomb which had never before been used — all of which contrasts sharply with the usual fate of ordinary criminals whose bodies were thrown into a common pit. The death is marked by an eclipse, as was alleged to have been the case with Julius Caesar, Augustus and Drusus, although no eclipse is recorded by historians, and if, as it was related, the crucifixion occurred at the Jewish

Passover, the moon was full and a solar eclipse was impossible. On the third day the women came to mourn him, and found an empty tomb. That three days was the period in which revitalization was traditionally believed to be possible is attested by several sources, among them the answer made by Martha when Jesus raised Lazarus from the dead; it had, moreover, been the prophecy of Hosea that 'After two days will he revive us: in the third day will he raise us up.' After the resurrection, Jesus is seen in visions by his followers, and then he ascends to heaven to sit at the right hand of God.

iii

When, at the close of the eighteenth century, Gibbon wrote his history of the Roman empire, he was constrained by popular prejudice in favor of the faith to take Christianity as a going affair, without attempting any inquiry into its origins. It was as radical a task as he could undertake to endeavor to show that the spread of the creed throughout the empire in the first four centuries of its history had been a consequence of natural rather than supernatural forces. In no small measure because of his labors the historians who followed him were under less restraint, but until the middle of the nineteenth century it was still generally held by Christians that the Testaments were 'inspired' and literally true to the letter of the word. But as a result of the accumulated force of a hundred years of textual and archaeological studies, by the last half of the century faith in the miraculous element was generally abandoned, so that of the gospel stories there remained with the appearance of historical certitude only the belief that about the beginning of the Christian Era a Jewish teacher by the name of Jesus was baptized by John and, when the latter was imprisoned, took up preaching, his message being that the Kingdom of God was near at hand and that the Jews — not the gentiles, for that was Paul's distinctive contribution — could be saved by repentance and baptism. He came into conflict with Jewish or Roman law and was crucified, and was possibly mocked by the Roman soldiers. Through certain of his apostles his message was conveyed to the visionary Paul, who discovered in the crucifixion a piacular sacrifice for the redemption of all mankind.

However, in the nineteenth century, it became increasingly clear that none of the teachings could with absolute certainty be ascribed to a real Jesus, and fewer still of the biographical details. The deletion of unacceptable supernatural features from the gospels had reduced the core of acceptable tradition concerning Jesus's life to almost negligible proportions. The first systematic analysis in English of the gospels as historical documents was C. C. Hennell's *An Inquiry Concerning the Origin of Christianity* (1838). It was, however, the scholarly work of David Strauss (1808–1874), notably his *Leben Jesu* (1835), which dealt the literal interpretation of the gospels its severest blow. These documents, in Strauss's view, should not be looked upon as historic accounts but as expressing ideas by means of images and symbols, or, as Strauss said, by myths. In emphasizing the purely ideological character of the Gospel of John and the literary nature of the Jesus therein described, he cast suspicion on the other three gospels. Strauss was an acknowledged biblical scholar and exegete, and his work marks on the one hand the definitive beginning of modern criticism of the New Testament, while on the other it portends, without itself initiating, the attack upon the historicity of the Jesus of Mark, Matthew and Luke.

Strauss paved the way for Bruno Bauer, a German theologian and historian, who in a number of volumes published between 1840 and 1874 and dealing with the synoptic gospels and Pauline epistles arrived at the conviction that Jesus was a literary invention of the author of Mark, who had in his gospel epitomized, as it were, the newly born Christianity. By the end of the century the ferment of skepticism had penetrated further into the liberal interpretation, and in the first three decades of the present century numerous writers abandoned historicity entirely in favor of one or another legendary interpretation, or had retreated to what has been called the 'minimalist position' because they accept that an authentic character (who was possibly named Jesus) played a role in the initiation of the Christian movement, though little or nothing reliable can be asserted about his life or death. Renan's highly popular *Vie de Jésus* (1863) was an intuitional romance, written after this biblical scholar had come to realize that any historical approach to the man Jesus was impossible, and after Renan it was recognized that all efforts to reconstruct a 'life' must belong strictly to the romantic field.

The conjecture that Jesus may have been the victim of a ritual murder at an annual celebration of the rite of the mock king was considered by Frazer, and the modern historian Toynbee notes that the suggestion is not impugned, but is rather fortified, by the fact that Jesus was condemned to death on religious and political grounds and therefore may have been given to the mob by Pilate as a substitute. The name of Barabbas, whom Pilate offered as an alternative to Jesus, is particularly significant in this connection. Frazer believed that Barabbas (son of the father) was not a personal name but a title applied to the condemned criminal selected to play the role of the 'Son of the Father' in the mock king sacrifice. According to Philo, Carabas, which is neither a Greek nor Hebrew nor Aramaic word and which Frazer believed to be a corruption of Barabbas, was the name of a harmless lunatic who was paraded in contempt of Agrippa, as mock king in Alexandria in the year 38. Reinach pointed out that in the Armenian, Syriac and some of the cursive Greek versions of the scene before Pilate 'Jesus Barabbas' appears instead of 'Barabbas', which reading, if not a corruption, implies that Jesus was condemned to be put to death as 'the Barabbas' without any question of substitution for another prisoner. Critics have been strongly adverse to the theory of an authentic mock king sacrifice on the grounds of the improbability that such a sacrifice among Jews or others would be permitted by the Roman government at this late date. It seems to be historically certain, however, that Dasius was beheaded for refusing to play the fatal role of the mock king in a Roman garrison on a remote frontier of Empire at the much later date of 303. Alternatively, Toynbee leans to the view that the mock king ritual may have been superimposed upon Jesus's death by the Roman soldiers as a burlesque; but as between this possibility and the possibilities that, at one extreme, Jesus was literally the victim of a ritual murder or, at the other extreme, that the ritual attached itself as myth to some ordinary Roman crucifixion, he states, 'the problem is not a simple one; and in the present state of our knowledge it would be rash to attempt to decide between the several alternative possible solutions of it . . . we may be content with a general conclusion . . . [that] ritual, as well as myth, is in all probability one of the common sources from which identical elements have flowed, along separate channels of "folk-memory," into the story of Jesus on the one hand and the stories of our pagan historical heroes on the other.'

Notable among the proponents of a purely legendary origin are Robertson and Couchoud, who have dealt, respectively, with the mythological elements in the 'Life' and the history of the development of the gospel texts themselves. In Robertson's view, the gospel story of the Last Supper, Passion, Betrayal, Trial, Crucifixion and Resurrection was originally a transcript of a mystery drama of a kind that had long been familiar to the Egyptians, the Greeks and the Greek-speaking peoples of Asia Minor, a drama symbolizing the primitive rite of human sacrifice and resembling the mock king sacrifice of Attis and other Mediterranean gods. In its oldest and least sophisticated form, as discoverable in Mark, there is simply a presentation of certain events which are huddled one upon another as must

be the case in any sequence intended to be enacted: the scene shifts rapidly
from the Last Supper to the Mount of Olives, thence to Gethsemane;
Jesus prays while all his disciples sleep and no one (except, of course, the
audience) is present to hear his words; Judas enters and identifies him to
the soldiers, and Jesus is taken to the house of the high priest where he is
examined in the middle of the night. False witnesses are procured, Jesus
is questioned, buffeted and presumably led away; and Peter, remaining on
the scene, denies his lord and is convicted of treason by the crowing of the
cock. Morning comes, and Jesus is led before Pilate, condemned and crucified. Perhaps in an epilogue the women came and discovered the empty
sepulcher, and Jesus reappeared and addressed them briefly. Apart from
the resurrection, the entire drama transpires in the twenty-four hours
classically prescribed for dramatic action, with only such dialogue as is
absolutely necessary; there is no description, no analysis, no finespun interpretation as would be expected in a narrative. Constructed for dramatic
presentation only, the original script, as indeed the ultimate presentation
in the gospels, contained little beyond the lines which actors must read
or speak upon the stage.

Complementing Robertson's view of the unhistorical character of Jesus
are the studies of Couchoud who has attempted to reconstruct the development of the messianic doctrine from its inception in Daniel and Enoch to
its final product in the Gospel of Luke. The Book of Enoch and its doctrine of the advent of the Heavenly Man, whom it erroneously identified
with Isaiah's 'anointed one,' or *christos,* must have been well known,
Couchoud argues, in the early part of the first century, and it is presumed
that John the Baptist was one of those who esteemed its prophetic verity.
John, fearlessly facing the prohibition against prophecy, declared 'Repent
ye: for the kingdom of heaven is at hand. . . . And now also the ax is
laid unto the root of the trees,' and in the living waters which flowed down
Jordan he baptized repentant believers by completely immersing them,
thus permitting them to await without apprehension the coming Judgment. Those who were baptized were set aside from all mankind, fasting
and praying while waiting for the Day; holding themselves elect in divine
grace, they kept aloof from Pharisee and Sadducee and disdained the
fiddling rites prescribed by the ancient Law.

The doctrine of a universal cataclysm and the expectation of the coming
of the Heavenly Man continued to spread. In the Book of Enoch the Son
of Man had been given a secret name by God when the deity had called
him from his eternal dwelling place to send him on his mission; pseudo-
Enoch had not revealed this secret name, but a careful scrutiny of the

scriptures succeeded in bringing it to light: it was Joshua, which means 'Yahweh saves.' Hence Joshua in Hebrew, Iesous in Greek, Jesus in Latin, became the personal name of the Heavenly Man, the *christos,* who was to be the supernatural judge and princely vicegerent in the coming Kingdom of God. In this name the *Christiani* could drive away demons, trample on serpents and scorpions and heal the sick, and even unbelievers were known to use it for purposes of exorcism with success.

When Barnabas brought to Antioch the little but fiery and proud Paul who had but recently been 'converted,' there came into the movement a new driving force. It was Paul who added the cross to the messianic doctrine, getting the idea from a passage in Psalms which describes the sufferings of a sick man who thought himself a prey to demon tortures: 'They pierced my hands and my feet,' and 'They part my garments among them, and cast lots upon my vesture.' These expressions conjured up in Paul's mind the Roman method of execution by 'hanging a man to a tree,' and the disposal of the garments of the victim; they gave new meaning to the hitherto vague description of Isaiah's 'man of sorrows.' So Paul preached that the 'Messiah' had already suffered death in the familiar Roman manner. Here he met with vigorous opposition: crucifixion was not a form of sacrifice, for which purpose it would be ineffective since no blood was spilled; on the contrary it was the most humiliating death penalty, and it was condemned by the Deuteronomist who had said that he 'that is hanged [upon a tree] is accursed of God.' Paul replied in effect that not only the words of the Deuteronomist but all the Mosaic Law had been blotted out by the sacrificial crucifixion of the anointed one: he forged from the accursed crucifixion a new and powerful weapon against the orthodox Hebrews who scoffed at his messianic belief and who would preserve the Law at all costs. And to the gentiles who scorned a god who had died in this humiliating manner, he replied that he himself was a 'crucified,' he had a 'thorn in the flesh,' he died daily to bring them the divine message; how much greater then was the crucifixion of the Heavenly Man himself? Projecting his tortured life onto the divine plane, Paul gloried in the death not as a mortal but as a supernal agony; as the mystic rite of baptism united the believer with the *Christos,* so the crucifixion of the *Christos,* who was identical with God, was a mystic source of salvation compared with which the sacrifice of an individual was nothing.

Then, in the Apocalypse of John (*ca.* A.D. 65), Paul's atoning sacrifice was developed into a pageant of glory patterned after the Attisian Mysteries wherein the god dies to ascend from death as a piacular sacrifice.

John rudely drops Paul's crucifixion out of the picture as a clumsy device; to him the Heavenly Man is a god-hero of a divine epic; he is yet to come and he has as yet nothing to do with the earth or with its history. When he appears he will last a thousand years and will leap down from heaven on a snowy horse and draped in a cloak red with dripping blood. As with Paul, so with John, God and Jesus are one person, grammatically and otherwise, but apart from this point the beliefs of the two writers are incompatible.

As the *ekklesia* continued to exchange letters communicating the latest revelations, or a new liturgic prayer, an ambitious author could gain attention merely by prefacing an epistle with a few suggestive lines giving it the pretense of having been written by one of the early apostles. Thus according to the needs of the moment there appeared an 'epistle of James,' three of 'John,' two of 'Peter,' one of 'Jude,' and several of 'Paul,' to mention only those which are generally accepted. Ultimately the question of which of these numerous documents were to be accepted and which rejected became a trying issue, and it was in such a crisis that the faith encountered its first major division of belief over the teachings of Marcion, a shipmaster of Pontus, who held firmly to Paul's mystical crucifixion. It was Marcion, obversely through the resistance aroused by his beliefs, who was destined to forge the major elements of the Christian creed.

Marcion had sought out all that remained of the Pauline epistles, edited them with such interpolations and emendations as he thought needful, and presented them in a compact work, the *Apostolikon*, which was distributed to all the churches. He probably also wrote a life of Paul, and he certainly prepared a gospel which is now lost, but which has been almost completely reconstructed from quotations in Tertullian, Epiphanius, Irenaeus, Hippolytus, Clement, Origen and other early writers. Strongly anti-Jewish, he differed from the Roman churchmen in holding that Christianity was a new religion which had been revealed all at once to Paul; the crucified Christ had nothing in common with the Jewish messiah, and the Father of Christ was a good God, a God of love, who had nought to do with the sanguinary, wrathful and jealous Yahweh of the Jews. Marcion cast aside the Old Testament as an uninspired and superstitious Jewish document and would have relegated Yahweh to the subordinate position of a demiurge.

The most novel feature of Marcion's teaching was contained in the opening sentence of his gospel: 'Now, in the fifteenth year of Tiberius Caesar, Pontius Pilate being governor of Judaea, Jesus, the Son of God, came down from heaven and appeared at Capernaum, a town in Galilee.'

Here, for the first time, is recorded a specific date for Jesus's appearance on earth, but Marcion's Jesus was not truly of the flesh, but a spiritual apparition who appeared suddenly as an adult and had only the semblance of a man.

The belief that Jesus had actually (or seemingly) appeared on earth, at a relatively recent time, and had actually (or seemingly) been crucified, was possibly one which was prevalent in the Asiatic provinces where Marcion lived. The Roman Christians, to judge from the writings of Hermas, apparently never entertained such a notion. However Marcion had come upon the idea, the reference to the erection of Paul's Cross on earth in the historic time of Pilate strongly fortified the whole Christian argument. All the churches were prepared to accept without debate Marcion's introductory assertion concerning the historicity of Jesus's crucifixion and its date; otherwise, they rejected his beliefs and revised his gospel according to their local preferences, the product which received favor in Rome appearing about 135 under the name of Mark. Mark still has the adult Jesus appear suddenly on earth at the beginning of his ministry, but he no longer functions in a purely mystical manner as does Marcion's Jesus: he uses his spittle to cure a blind man, puts his fingers into ear holes, touches tongues, lays on hands, looks up to heaven, heaves, sighs and utters abracadabra in the manner of all professional exorcists.

In Asia Minor about 140, a Christian scribe, who was a converted rabbi, and wrote under the name of a legendary 'Matthew,' noted how much of Marsion's gospel had been omitted from Mark's account, and disliking Marcion's anti-Yahwism, rearranged the material in such a manner as to controvert Marcion and yet make Jesus a Jew. He set out to show that Jesus *was* the Messiah, the Prince of Yahweh who had been promised by the prophets of Israel, and to accomplish this he pieced together a pseudobiographical story in which every syllable of prophecy in the Old Testament was fulfilled in Jesus's life, inventing to this end Jesus's miracles, his intentional obscurity, the obtuseness of his hearers, his employment of parables, his entry into Jerusalem, his betrayal, desertion and arrest, even the use made of the price of his betrayal. One obstacle only presented difficulty: the Messiah must, in accordance with the Old Testament, be a son of David, but he must also be divine in order to conform with the Pauline doctrine. In no way daunted, Matthew began his gospel with a human genealogy which ended: 'And Jacob begat Joseph the husband of Mary, of whom was born Jesus, who is called Christ . . . Now the birth of Jesus was on this wise: When as his mother Mary was espoused to Joseph, before they came together, she was found with child of the Holy Ghost.' Thus, by genealogy and immaculate conception was the messianic identity of Jesus proved.

At Ephesus in Grecian Asia, a second recension of the Markian document appeared under the name of John, being completed before 145. In this, the confused notions of the prophet of that name who had written the incomprehensible apocalypse called Revelation were preserved by making Jesus the embodiment in the flesh of the Word of God, thus satisfying the oriental adoration of the mystic Word.

When, in the reign of the Emperor Antonius Pius, the Roman church cut away from Judaism completely and set out for itself, it was prepared to take the Old Testament with it, contrary to Marcion whom it had condemned chiefly because he denied the flesh-and-blood nature of Jesus. The new literature was reconciled with the old scriptures by maintaining that God had first made a covenant with one people, the Jews, and now he would make a covenant with another people, the Christians; there were then to be two Covenants, an Old and a New, or as the Latin had it, two Testaments. An official selection of literature, however, was now imperative in order both to codify belief and to bring to the notice of the rulers, the literati and sympathizers generally the story of the new faith. The most convincing approach and the only one which would refute Marcion's apparitional Jesus would be to treat him, as Matthew had done, as a historic person fulfilling the messianic prophecies, instead of as a spirit who had put on the semblance of flesh; while the best political maneuver would be to endow the messianic man with all the magic powers attributed to him by Mark, the speaker for the powerful Roman church. Indeed, it appears to have been a Roman in the person of Clement, who was then a sort of general church secretary, who compiled a biography for distribution to all the churches which included a new and 'orderly' gospel of his own. This was concluded about the year 142 and either at this time or later was attributed pseudepigraphically to the Luke who in tradition had been Paul's comrade. Thus by virtue of Luke's name and Clement's finely spun detail, the Roman gospel acquired authoritative force.

In brief, in Couchoud's view, sectarian Jews took the messianic Heavenly Man from Enoch and endowed him with the attributes both of an uncreated god and of a man of flesh who suffered a piacular death. It was Paul who first conceived the death to be as a crucifixion; it was Marcion who first treated the crucifixion as a historic event and, possibly following a popular pagan notion, set the date as under Pontius Pilate; it was the Syrian author of Matthew, anxious to combat the 'apparitional'

Jesus and the anti-Jewish prejudices espoused by Marcion, who gave Jesus a Jewish human mother and identified him with the Messiah of Israel; while it was the Ephesian author of John who made him the embodiment in the flesh of the Word of God. It remained only for Clement, the Roman author of Luke, to write a pseudo biography of a human Jesus divinely born in Nazareth as a subject of Augustus and numbered in the census of Quirinus.

When Plutarch, the pagan apologist, was called upon to consider the theory that Osiris had been a general or other famous personage around whom there had grown a great mass of legends, he replied that to accept this explanation 'would be to shake and loosen a worship and faith which have been firmly settled in nearly all mankind from their infancy. It would be to open a wide door to atheism to enter in at, and to encourage the attempts of those who would humanize the divine nature.' It is in a similar vein that a recent critic of those who would question the historicity of Jesus has replied, 'The strongest and most irrefragable evidence of all is provided by the existence and history of the Christian Church. If the "Christ-Myth" theory is true, and if Jesus never lived, the whole civilized world has for close upon two thousand years lain under the spell of a lie, and the greatest power for good that the world has ever known originated in a delusion.'

The historicity of Osiris is no longer for anyone a vital question. In proportion as critical examination of the evidence for the historicity of Jesus reduces this evidence to a smaller and less certain residue, so in the nature of the problem and in the progress of world thought does the importance of the question itself recede toward the dimensions of academic interest. A proponent of historicity has remarked of the radical critics that it is the most difficult task in the world to prove to nonsense that it is nonsense. But that is a dangerous rapier since it is pointed at both ends and Christian theology now stands revealed as having been excessively vulnerable for nineteen centuries. The ultimate answer to the question of historicity will be found not in sentiment or prejudice, or on the apologetic grounds which Plutarch states, but through the careful and dispassionate evaluation of the social and ideological forces of the first century, as opposed to the obscurely complex biblical texts. The answer will continue to be sought by all historians, Christian and otherwise, who are anxious to guard against an error that would be contrary to the first principles of their task.

iv

In so far as Christianity originated as a movement to temper Judaic legalism, it proved ineffective against the immutability of the parent faith. He who was 'unto Jews a stumblingblock and unto the Greeks foolishness,' had come and gone, and Israel, far from having profited by his advent, was wholly destroyed (or so it seemed after the Romans had demolished Jerusalem). The new religion had quietly borrowed from Judaism the history and morality of the Old Testament and many of the precepts of the Mishna; it had appropriated Yahweh, altering him from a god of righteousness and of the Jews to a god of goodness who was equally a god of gentiles; and it had seen the messianic hope fulfilled. The Jews, however, were not disposed, either by the vicissitudes of their national history or by their immediate circumstances, to permit Yahweh to indulge in sentimental goodness or to love the gentiles, and because he failed to make of them 'a great nation,' they rejected Jesus as the true Messiah. The orthodox looked upon the cult as another 'backsliding,' another 'whoring after new gods,' and the Judaism which had engendered it denied it utterly.

Because they were scoffed at by the Jews, the Christians made it appear that it had been the Jews and Herod Antipas, the Jewish tetrarch, who had tried Jesus and condemned him, and who had urged Pilate, the Roman governor of Judea, to crucify him, Pilate carefully washing his hands of the whole affair. From the Gospel of Mark, through Matthew, John and Luke, into that called of Peter, a veritable crescendo of animus is spun against Herod and the Jewish mob. In the so-called Gospel of Peter, written about A.D. 150, it is related, 'But of the Jews not one washed his hands, neither Herod nor any one of his judges. And as they would not wash themselves, Pilate stood up. And then Herod the king bade the Lord to be brought along, and said to them: "Whatsoever I have ordered you to do, that do unto him."' The Christians dared not lay the blame for Jesus's death on a powerful Roman official and they cleared the Roman governor completely. But they ran no risk in heaping contumely on the scattered and powerless people who had disowned them.

v

Between its inception and its final establishment the syncretic growth of Christianity was so much in evidence that its sponsors were frequently hard pressed to explain the parallels between its doctrines and rituals and those of the pagans, especially the Mithraists. The Mithraic priests baptized that god's devotees with holy water, signed them on their foreheads, transferred the holy spirit to them by the 'laying on of hands' and exorcised devils by holding two or more fingers directed towards the suppliant. The apocalyptic phrase about garments 'washed in the blood of the Lamb' conjoins the Mithraic *taurobolium* and the Passover sacrifice, while the abstinence of Lent was paralleled by periods of forbearance in all the purificatory cults. The candle, the smoke of incense, the amulet and the chanted incantation served to purify and protect the Christians as effectively as they served the Mithraists, or indeed, as they served the ancient Egyptians, Babylonians and most of the peoples of the Mediterranean world. These similarities, according to Justin Martyr and Tertullian, were due to the wicked devil anticipating and imitating Christianity, and the same argument was used by Fermicus to explain the parallel between the crucified Jesus and the Attisian image of a young man fastened to a tree.

The cross, the pine tree of Adonis and the *crux ansata* of the Egyptians were carved upon the grave to ward off evil demons and the manual sign was freely used to protect the living against misfortune and disease. Tertullian reports that, 'At every step, at ever movement, at every coming in and going out, in putting on our clothes and our shoes, in the bath, at table in the evening, lying down or sitting, whatever attitude we assume, we mark our foreheads with a little sign of the cross.' Shortly images of the cross were working miracles and in later centuries people went to the length of marking cattle with it to protect them from disease.

The Egyptian belief in the magic power of a god's secret name, so well exemplified in the legend of Ra and Isis, had probably inspired the Israelites with that people's excessive reverence for the name of Yahweh, an epithet which was never to be pronounced except by a holy priest. The force of this tradition on the Judaic side, combined with the reverence still accorded sacred names in Alexandria and in all the Roman temples of Isis and Serapis, enabled the Pauline doctrine to propound that when Jesus was risen from the dead and made to sit on the right hand of God, God exalted him highly, and gave unto him 'a *name* which is above every name: that at the name of Jesus every knee shall bow, of things in heaven and things in earth, and things under the earth.' This meant angels and devils and demons of every sort, and the 'name' in question was Christ, which exalted its owner to the summit and sovereignty of all the angelic and demonic creations. 'In my name shall they cast out devils; they shall speak with new tongues; they shall take up serpents; and if they drink any deadly thing, it shall not hurt them; they shall lay hands on the sick, and they shall recover.' When Peter made a lame man walk, it was by faith in this powerful 'name'; and it was the 'name,' qua name, which was later used to exorcise evil spirits from the altar, shrine or any building, from holy oil, water, salt, candles and even hassocks, or from humans sick in consequence of being possessed by devils. The formula 'in the name of Jesus,' or 'in the name of the Father, and of the Son, and of the Holy Ghost' became a supernatural implement equaling in potency any Egyptian incantation.

At first, still or stagnant water was not used for baptism and exorcism, it being held that it was inefficacious unless it could run off the body and carry with it the physical contamination; but by an edict of the Emperor Gratian in the fourth century, holy water was prepared from still water by having the priest bless it, exorcise it, sprinkle it with exorcised salt and endow it with the holy name. Tertullian said that such holy water when properly consecrated by a Christian priest could wash away the stains of transgression, which he believed to be like material dirt, whereas the so-called 'holy waters' of the rival pagan cults, and those taken from 'darkling springs and lonely rivers,' being tenanted by the devil who had set out to imitate God, were worse than inefficacious.

In the worship of Osiris grain or cakes made from grain had been identified with the body of the god and when eaten ritually the meal was considered to possess mystic virtues. That such an identification was widely recognized in Roman times is certain from Cicero's rhetorical question about the corn of Ceres and the wine of Bacchus; a eucharistic meal of sorts may reasonably be attributed to the worshipers of Demeter and Dionysus, and there can be no doubt about such a meal in the cults of Attis and Mithra. The substance of the sacramental meal, known to the pagans as the *hostia* (victim), was taken over by the Pauline Christians in the vegetarian form: 'Take, eat, this is my body . . . this is my blood.' 'Except ye eat the flesh of the Son of man, and drink his blood, ye have no life in you. Whoso eateth my flesh, and drinketh my blood, hath eternal life; and I will raise him up at the last day.' The nature of the Eucharist was clearly indicated in the gospels, since Jesus at the Last Supper gave his companions bread to eat and wine to drink as symbols of his own flesh and blood. A later writer, speaking of the Mithraic sacrament, which by Mithra's worshipers was believed to impart eternal life, said, 'thou hast eaten poison and drunk the cup of death; only the

Christian Eucharist confers immortality.' Ignatius, who called the Eucharist the 'medicine of immortality,' complained of those 'who abstain from the Eucharist and the prayers, because they do not confess that the Eucharist is the flesh of our Saviour, Jesus Christ'; while Justin Martyr asserted, 'We do not hold these as common bread and drink, but, just as our Saviour Christ was incarnate by the action of the divine Logos, from flesh and blood of salvation, so we maintain that the [consecrated] food . . . is the flesh and blood of Jesus incarnate.' In the ninth century Hincmar of Reims affirmed that God permitted the sacramental bread to continue to look like bread, knowing how dreadful it would be for a communicant if the red and bloody flesh were to become visible. The question whether the Eucharist was Jesus's flesh and blood in fact, or only after a manner, remained to be bitterly debated long after the Reformation.

Where the pagans celebrated their animal sacrifices at frequent intervals, the Christians dramatized the crucifixion in the form of the 'mass,' which word in the Latin *missa* was possibly derived from the Mithraic sacred cake, or *mizd*. The slaughter of an ox or ram or pig was more or less a matter of daily experience, whereas symbolic human sacrifice, when coupled with the sacramental meal, the 'drug of immortality,' served to evoke that emotional state which seemed more appropriate to the approaching Day of Judgment.

As with most deities in the Northern Hemisphere, the death and resurrection of Jesus was placed as near as possible to the spring equinox, while in accordance with Babylonian-Mithraic custom it was put after the full moon. (The name Easter comes from Eostre (Ostâra) an Anglo-Saxon goddess of the spring, and was not used until the Middle Ages.) The Christians at first observed the Jewish Sabbath as a holy day, but they later changed their weekly meeting to Sunday to spite the Jews and to please the Mithraists, the first day of the week having been the sun god's day in both Egyptian and Mithraic lore. About the year 354, the birthday of Jesus was set at the winter solstice, the time at which all the sun gods from Osiris to Jupiter and Mithra had celebrated theirs, the celebration being adorned with the pine tree of Adonis, the holly of Saturn, and the mistletoe, the yellow leaves of which gave the name to Frazer's classic, *The Golden Bough,* which describes the cult of Diana-Artemis at Aricia. Gifts of lighted tapers and of human dolls had long been exchanged at the winter revel of the Saturnalia. The tapers represented the kindling of the newborn sun god's fire. That the first doll was a device of malignant magic is a priori scarcely to be denied, but

Varro, a Roman historian of the first century B.C., attests that the dolls of the Saturnalia were symbols of commuted human sacrifices.

For the masses of the Roman Empire the miraculous was a commonplace, and the popular healing divinities — Isis, Imhotep and Serapis of the Nile, Ishtar and Marduk of Babylonia, Astarte of Syria, the great Asklepios of Greece and others who were equated with him, healed as frequently by personal intervention as by the iatromagic of roots, herbs, diets, baths and unguents. Of Dionysus, Aristides said, "Nothing, it would seem, shall be so firmly bound, either by disease, or rage, or by any fortune, that Dionysus shall not be able to loose it." Had the new faith discouraged the miraculous it would have been incomprehensible to the people it sought to proselytize. Yet in respect to the nature of the miracles performed there was scant originality, for they imitated either the prophets or the pagan gods: Jesus turned water into wine, as did Dionysus on January sixth of every year; and multiplied loaves of bread, as did Elisha. He walked on water like Orion, Poseidon's son. He raised men from the dead, as did Elijah and Elisha — this feat had once been so common that Aristophanes in *The Frogs* (*ca.* 405 B.C.) made Dionysus say of Hermes and of Hermes's father, that performing resurrections was a family profession. He gave sight to the blind by application of his spittle, the remedy which Thoth had used to restore the eye of Horus, and one which was used all around the Mediterranean by medicine men and had even been used successfully and to his great fame by the Emperor Vespasian — only Jesus asserts that the man he treated had been born blind merely in order that his (Jesus's) own power could be exhibited, 'the works of God made manifest.' He healed the leper, the lunatic, the deaf and dumb, as did Asklepios. He exorcised demons, read men's minds and foretold the future as did all the wonder-working men of the time. The Pauline Epistles make no mention of Jesus's miraculous power, and had these miracles been known to Paul it is inconceivable that all mention of them would have been omitted. The miraculous element was interpolated partly to convince the pagans, partly in the effort to convince the Jews that Jesus was the true Messiah, and partly by the sheer credulity of the Christian mind. In the fourth century multiplication of miracles worked by martyrs was so rapid that it drew the emphatic disapproval of conservative churchmen, yet it bespoke the general ecclesiastic conviction that miracles need never end and could be multiplied as needed.

Among the factors contributing to the spread of Christianity not the least important was the social quality of the people to whom it offered its supernatural benefits. It numbered among its proselytes as many, if not more, women than men, and women were excluded from most of the privileges of Mithraism, its chief competitor. It openly appealed to the humble, the poor in spirit, slaves, paupers, freedmen, men of bad repute, all those whom other pagan sects with aristocratic tone engendered by age and experience were inclined to disdain. The pagans were quick to note this, and Celsus, about A.D. 180, jeered at the new cult for its extreme democracy: 'It is only the simpletons, the ignoble, the senseless, slaves and womenfolk and children whom they wish to persuade or *can* persuade.'

Celsus should not be quoted against the Christians without mention of the facts that the barbarians were making inroads on the northern frontier, the Parthians were pressing on the east and a great plague had ravaged Italy; in the face of possible invasion by ruthless hordes of white savages, the chronic resistance and disaffection of the Christians was threatening the unity of the empire, the sole hope of the civilized world. With the conservatism of a man of practical affairs, Celsus hoped to see the established order preserved and he believed that this could only be achieved by the subordination of particularism and personal salvation to the common weal. His judgment upon the Christians was further biased by the circumstance that his own thought was impregnated with the philosophy of Greece, his viewpoint akin to that of the Periclean Age; with the snobbishness of the Hellene he considered both the Jews and Christians to be half barbarous and lacking the true culture. But admitting the prejudice behind it, and granting that there were exceptions to which he did not admit, the picture which he drew of the early Christians was probably not greatly exaggerated.

'I speak bitterly about this,' he says, 'because I feel bitterly. When we are invited to the Mysteries the masters use another tone. They say, "Come to us ye who are of clean hands and pure speech, ye who are unstained by crime, who have a good conscience towards God, who have done justly and lived uprightly." But let us hear what sort these people [the Christians] invite; "whosoever is a sinner or unintelligent, or a fool, in a word, whosoever is god-forsaken, him the kingdom of God will receive." Now whom do you mean by the sinner but the wicked, thief, housebreaker, poisoner, temple robber, grave robber? Whom else would a brigand invite to join him? . . . Jesus, they say, was sent to save sinners; was he not sent to help those who have kept themselves free from sin? They pretend that God will save the unjust man if he repents and humbles himself. The just man who has held steadily from the cradle in the ways of virtue he will not look upon.'

Celsus also had something to say on how the Christians set about getting converts: 'We see them in our houses, wool dressers, cobblers, and fullers, the most uneducated and vulgar persons, not daring to say a word in the presence of their masters who are older and wiser; but when they get hold of the children in private, and silly women with them, they are wonderfully eloquent — to the effect that the children must not listen to their father, but believe *them* and be taught by them . . . they must come with the women, and the little children that play with them, to the women's quarters, or the cobbler's shop, or the fuller's, to receive perfect knowledge.' The Christians will not argue about what they believe — 'they always answer, "Do not examine, but believe," and "Thy faith shall save thee," — "believe that he whom I set forth to you is the son of God, even though he was bound in the most dishonorable way, and punished in the most shameful, though yesterday or the day before he weltered in the most disgraceful fashion before the eyes of all men — *so much the more believe!*" '

As for Christian doctrines, they were utterly puerile and ridiculous, particularly in their conceit: why should the human race think itself so superior to bees, ants and elephants as to be put in a unique relation to its maker? And why should God choose to come to men as a Jew? The Christian idea of a special providence was nonsense, an insult to the deity.

Celsus quotes approvingly from the *Timaeus* of Plato: 'It is a hard thing to find out the Maker and Father of this universe, and after having found him it is impossible to make him known to all.' Such analytic skepticism was, however, the faith of the intellectually aristocratic, and what Celsus had to say had no weight except as the churchman Origen was moved to a lengthy rebuttal, without which even Celsus's opinions would have remained unknown to posterity. In so far as they were known to contemporary Christians, they were of a piece with the pagan knowledge, 'falsely so called,' which Paul had condemned as evil and to be abhorred. The fact that Celsus bothered to write a book refuting Christianity showed merely that it was making its way upward through society and gaining a hold among those of wealth and education. Admittedly many who joined the movement were social outcasts, and many others were but seeking the excitation of esoteric mysteries; while still others were attracted by its ascetic doctrines, either because they esteemed self-immolation, were possessed by a sense of sin or were, on more moderate grounds, opposed to idols and bloody sacrifices, theaters, the circus, indulgence and promiscuity in general. On a higher plane the new creed offered a future life which was posited on an attractive if spurious pretense to Hellenic rationalism: it described the human body as base, doomed to decay and death, the human soul as naturally simple, incorruptible and everlasting; it permitted willful freedom to replace the fatalism of the Orient, and an eternal democratic kingdom of heaven to replace the despotism of an empire which was so unstable as to be always on the verge of collapse.

For the first time since the ancient days of Egypt the hereafter awaiting the ordinary man was painted in bright colors. The Hebrew Sheol, 'the pit' or 'hollow place,' had been essentially the grave itself, or perhaps all the graves of all the peoples united into one, where the departed led a shadowy dreamlike existence scarcely deserving the name of life. The Sadducees refused to countenance an afterlife: 'For that which befalleth the sons of men befalleth beasts; even one thing befalleth them: as the one dieth, so dieth the other; yea, they have all one breath; so that a man hath no preeminence above a beast: for all is vanity. All go unto one place; all are of the dust, and all turn to dust again.' 'They are dead: they shall not live! They are deceased: they shall not arise!' It was primarily through Persian influence that Hebrew thought began to credit the possibility of an afterlife; taking the lead from Isaiah's, 'Thy dead men shall live, together with my dead body shall they arise,' the writer of the Book of Daniel allotted to men a future existence in accordance with their deserts: 'many of them that sleep in the dust of the earth shall awake, some to everlasting life, and some to shame and everlasting contempt.' Anticipation of a general resurrection had been the key theme of the later messianic doctrine, and now, utilizing the Greek idea of the incorruptible soul, the Christians were in a position to reconstruct their heaven along the lines of a Persian paradise.

The Egyptian Land of the Blest had been a fertile country like the delta of the Nile, teeming with wild fowl, perpetually in bloom and filled with fruit. Following the Egyptian model, when the messianic writers painted heaven they indulged in unrestrained if purified extravagance. Of each seed that was sown, each measure would bear ten thousand grains, each vine would have ten thousand branches, each branch ten thousand twigs, each twig ten thousand clusters, each cluster ten thousand grapes, and each grape twenty-five measures of wine. The righteous would rise with their bodies and eat of the Tree of Life, and each pair would beget a thousand children and all would lead a holy existence in a city the streets of which were paved with gold, but that was otherwise rather like Jerusalem. The inhabitants, clothed in white, would carry palms or play upon harps and construct new songs, while all with inward purity of heart and outward expressions of magnificent ritual would join in worshiping the highest deity, on whose right hand sat Jesus. There would be no working, no travail, and when he was not worshiping Yahweh, every man could return to his own garden and escape from the celestial radiance in the shade of his own fig tree.

But Christian asceticism stripped paradise of most of its carnal pleasures: there was to be no eating or drinking, and no giving in marriage — even the highest angels would willingly forego the first prerogatives of the pagan gods. Heaven was, moreover, now completely democratic. It was still paved with gold, but by virtue of the resurrection it was no longer restricted to Jerusalem and could comprise the whole earth as well as the heavenly spheres. Its inhabitants, still clothed in white, had more diversity of occupation since they could find employment appropriate to their worthy faculties: there would be beautiful architecture and craftsmanship, beautiful poetry, beautiful music, both vocal and instrumental, and even philosophy and science would be cultivated. The supreme joy would be in the ecstatic experience of the beatific vision, the greatest pleasure in beholding the Divine Essence wherein contemplation would grasp instantly and for eternity all that had been or that was to be, would experience the Supreme Good, the One, the Absolute. In Paul's words: 'Now we see through a glass, darkly; but then face to face: now I know in part; but then shall I know even as also I am known.' Knowing all and seeing all, the blessed would look down upon hell and behold the torments and tortures of the damned. They would enjoy this spectacle, a later churchman argued, first because these torments did not touch them; secondly because, now that the wicked were all damned, the blessed need no longer fear them; thirdly, because their own glory would appear greater by contrast; and fourthly, because that which is pleasing to God must also be pleasing to the righteous.

vi

In the early period of the church any established teacher could baptize converts, consecrate the Eucharist or exorcise demons by the Holy Name. Since these services carried with them both financial and social advantages the supply of exorcists soon exceeded the demand. Moreover, the weekly instruction of the church, based as it was upon inspiration and revelation, encouraged those who possessed the gift of oratory to indulge in such liberal interpretation, if not outright prophecy, as to threaten the integrity of the accepted dogma. It was consequently not long before the elders and bishops, in order to preserve unity in belief, were forced to assume as much authority in articles of faith as in secular matters.

The earliest pronouncement restricting supernatural power occurs in an epistle written by Ignatius, Bishop of Antioch, to the Christians in Smyrna (?A.D. 120–150): 'Shun divisions as the beginning of evils. Let all follow the bishop, as Jesus Christ the Father . . . Let no man do anything of things pertaining to the church apart from the bishop. Let that be held a valid eucharist which is under the bishop or one to whom he shall have committed it. Wheresoever the bishop shall appear, there let the people be; even so where Jesus may be there is the catholic church. It is not lawful apart from the bishop either to baptize or to hold an agape; but whatsoever he shall approve, this is well pleasing also to God.'

It appears to have been Clement of Rome who first endowed episcopal (of or pertaining to bishops) opinion with dogmatic sanctity. On the one hand there was an urgent need to exalt the prophetic power of the traditional Christian apostles and at the same time to deny the authority of the Hebrew prophets; on the other, now that the Testament was completed and the means of salvation had been revealed, the prophetic impulse, even among good Christians, must be firmly restrained. So Clement made to appear that prophecy was the voice of the Holy Ghost, who had taken possession of the prophets of old and spoken through their mouths to foretell the coming of Jesus for the benefit of Christians; it had been the Holy Ghost who had fertilized Mary and consecrated Jesus on earth; and when Jesus returned to heaven he in turn had caused the Holy Ghost to fall on the apostles in order to inspire their teachings. But after the apostles there were to be no more random visitations: the power of inspiration was now restricted to the 'officially' established successors of the apostles, the elders of the churches, who would speak, as Clement says, only by 'what we write through the Holy Ghost.'

The Ignatian epistle quoted above also contains the first ecclesiastic use of the word catholic. In secular usage this word meant 'on the whole, in general or generally, in prevalent use.' Ignatius uses it to designate the 'true' church, true by virtue of episcopal authority, and also that 'true' doctrine which was 'universally' accepted in contradistinction to the schisms which he was immediately deploring. Thereafter the word catholic came to mean 'orthodox' (orthodoxists are those of straight opinion), in the sense of officially approved. Only in later centuries did it lose this general meaning and become a specific designation of the Roman Church.

The immediate effect of episcopal centralization was to shift the supernatural power of Christianity from baptism and the sacrament to the persons of the bishops. Shortly these individuals were so powerful that they could exclude from their congregations any member of whom they disapproved, even though he had been baptized 'in the name of Jesus Christ.' Taking their authority from various incidents in the gospels, but particularly from the alleged statement of Jesus to his disciple Peter, as given in Matthew: 'And I will give unto thee the keys to the kingdom of heaven: and whatsoever thou shalt bind of earth shall be bound in heaven: and whatsoever thou shalt loose on earth shall be loosed in heaven,' they exercised in their anathema a power over the devout which in fearsomeness equaled the emperor's power of life and death. Though this power was not widely used until later times, within the first two centuries the ecclesiastic hierarchy, where so disposed, was in a position to demand mechanical obedience to its most fantastic enactments.

No less important than personal power in the growth of episcopacy was the financial advantage which accrued to those in office. The pagan religious corporations of Syria, Greece, Rome and Egypt were fabulously rich, the priests of Osiris controlling fully one third of the entire national wealth. It did not require great astuteness or more than ordinary cupidity to perceive the possibilities in the rites of baptism and the Eucharist, these being deemed absolutely necessary to salvation and resurrection. A further source of revenue lay in the nullification of malicious powers, since sickness, ever conceived to be due to demoniac possession, was for a voluntary contribution exorcised by means of the sign of the cross or by the recitation of the Lord's Prayer. By the third century it had become customary to recite before the altar the name of the givers of oblations, and at a later time the names of the dead who were publicly prayed for in return for a proper consideration. Wherever a man of initiative entered the movement he acquired, in the manner of a noble in a feudal system, not only power to dictate on matters of creed and conduct, but affluence in proportion to the size and wealth of his see or diocese. No more than in the case of the pagan cults, but certainly no less, the new church offered a career to ambitious men and, especially in the large cities, its high offices became substantial prizes.

The alert pagans were not unaware of the physical benefits coming to the leaders of the new cult, but concern on this point apparently never played a major role in the antipathy that rapidly developed between the new believers and the unbelievers. No credible evidence supports the tradition that there was an organized prejudice against Christianity as a religion; to the polytheistic Romans a new god was no novelty and there was no basis in principle for conflict with the state. Indeed, the period of the church's growth was one in which there was a recrudescence of many faiths, and its early difficulties were largely a consequence of its own militant proselytism. The cult had inherited from Judaism a bitter detestation of pagan idols; holding these to be evil demons with which it was axiomatically in conflict it sought to displace them from all their accustomed niches, much to the annoyance of the pagans who had generally been tolerant of their neighbor's religion. It opposed in principle, if not in practice, any effort to achieve permanence in civic structure, since it held that such efforts were futile, the world being on the brink of destruction. Its doctrines that its founder had come to bring not peace but the sword and to create strife were not such as would soften prejudice, and the preaching of celibacy and the disparagement of state dignitaries did not aid its cause. From the first century it had been the custom of Christians to gather weekly at a love feast, or agape (love to God) at which they partook of the Eucharist and then dined together in the manner of the common meals of the Jews and pagans. When such meetings were prohibited from public places, the Christians continued to hold them secretly at the graves, ostensibly for the purpose of offering oblations to the dead, a universal pagan custom from which they could not be excluded. Already held in suspicion by the pagans, they soon acquired a reputation for the most heinous practices; their emphasis on the Eucharist gave rise to the tale that they sacrificed and ate children at these meetings, while their custom of 'spiritual marriages' between 'brothers and sisters' within the church brought upon them the calumny of incest. To worsen matters, the bishops, each seeking power or the opportunity to impose his ideas upon the dogma, were constantly quarreling with each other; they frequently resorted to arms and were often on the verge of starting civil war.

Lastly, the Christians were outspoken pacifists. They refused to bear arms for Rome, to swear by the *divus* Caesar and to pay homage to his effigy (as to a god) by burning incense before it. The outlying regions of the Empire were perpetually in a state bordering on siege, and everywhere local governors were required to maintain constant surveillance lest rebellion break out under foot. The touchstone of loyalty among Rome's many creeds and races was conformity with the imperial religion; whatever a man's beliefs, public refusal to swear by and pay obeisance to the statue of the emperor constituted high treason and was punishable by death. Enlightened emperors might laugh at their apotheosis, as did Vespasian, who is alleged to have remarked when he was dying, "I fancy

I am turning to god," but the custom was supported as a means of ensuring imperial stability. The Christians' refusal to conform brought them into repeated conflict with the magistrates. They were soon accused of lese majesty, ignavia and black magic, outlawed on secular grounds as traitors to the state and denounced as 'enemies of the gods, of the emperors, of the laws, of morals and of all nature.'

It was bruited that the new atheists might bring about an earthquake or pestilence by evoking the wrath of the gods whom they reviled. In such a situation 'persecutions' were unavoidable, but church historians greatly exaggerated the mortality. The formula of the 'ten persecutions' is held to be fabulous, and those ascribed to Domitian and Nero probably had only a slight basis in fact. When persecution was officially undertaken by Diocletian, or rather by his Asiatic caesar, Galerius (303–311), it was because Galerius wanted to establish a church-state in the worship of the sun god. Other cults came in for punishment and the Christians suffered worst because they were most obstinate. Gibbon put the total number of Christians upon whom the penalty of capital punishment was inflicted by judicial sentence in this period at less than two thousand, and it is estimated that the figure would be scarcely more than doubled for the whole period of the Roman empire — not one ten thousandth of the blood that Christianity itself was to spill in the course of its career.

If the early fathers were prone to overstate the extent of their persecution at pagan hands, the exaggeration but revealed a pride in martyrdom, for Christianity had within it an extraordinary impulse to self-sacrifice. The term martyr originally denoted one who testified to the durability of his convictions under such duress and provocation as the authorities might use for the detection of enemies of the state. The opportunity was soon forthcoming for men thus to testify, even in the face of death, and by their example to stir others to a firmer faith. The first documented instance of voluntary martyrdom is that of Polycarp, Bishop of Smyrna, who in 155 was burned with timber and faggots — the favorite method of execution with later Christians — when a festival mob ran wild after watching eleven Christian 'atheists' die in the arena. The mob denounced him as 'the father of the Christians, the destroyer of the gods, the man who had taught so many no longer to sacrifice and no longer to pray to the gods,' and they afterwards refused to deliver up his bones to the Christians for burial lest 'the Christians would now forsake the Crucified and worship Polycarp.' The precaution appears to have been well founded for the Smyrneans record that 'we afterwards took up his bones, which are more valuable than precious stones and finer than refined gold, and laid them in a suitable place, where the Lord will permit us to gather ourselves together, as we are able, in gladness and joy and to celebrate the birthday of his martyrdom.'

Ignatius prayed for martyrdom and, in unsupported tradition, found it at some unknown time and place, and the church fathers from Tertullian onward proclaimed the dignity of the martyr in glowing language. Soon a reflected luster shone upon the martyr's family and even the town in which he had resided. His tomb became an altar where his spirit was propitiated with hymns and psalms and songs of praise, where prayers were offered and miracles were worked.

The Fathers had approved Clement's dictum: 'If a man know himself, he shall know God, and knowing God shall be made like to him. . . . The man with whom the Logos dwells . . . is made like to God . . . and that man becomes God, for God wishes it.' Finding an example of god-making in the central theme of their human Savior who suffered and died and ascended unto heaven, men and women came to welcome, nay even to invite, martyrdom. Where the pagans of old had manufactured gods as occasion demanded by despatching to the other world a king or temple prince, the Christians, as the pagans never had, conceived that by martyrdom they could individually attain a superior supernatural status, the most brilliant crown of glory going to him who was most resolute in suffering and who achieved the most violent death. So many Christians in Antioch willfully sought martyrdom by outraging pagan temples, by insulting the magistrates or by falsely claiming to have committed offenses against the state that the Proconsul Antonius amazedly asked whether they had not ropes and precipices to kill themselves.

Cruelty has its cult in every age. The taste of the Romans found satisfaction in the arena where naked men and women were mauled to death by lions or wild cows. The Christians learned to shudder at the cry of *Christiano leonem,* and claimed to have found the seed of glory in the disemboweled and mangled bodies of its victims; when called upon they faced the ordeal with a determination and fortitude which, had they not been so intensely feared as atheists and hated for being different, must have excited the admiration of the pagan mob. As it was, the pagans, cheering the wild beasts, looked disdainfully upon the human victims as an incomprehensible and alien species lacking any claim to sympathy. Indubitably there was something about Christianity that put its votaries in a world apart, some critical difference scarcely to be discovered in ritual or creed but belonging to the more fundamental affections by which, regardless of ritual and creed and even language, men sense each other to be either connatural or alien. It was a negative rather than a positive factor.

In part because of its origins within the serious and holy atmosphere of Judaism, in part because of its own ascetic tendencies and in part because of its fearsome apocalyptic doctrine, Christianity lacked qualities with which the pagans were highly endowed — perspective and a sense of humor. Though it is etymologically uncommon to equate these terms, the equation in this instance is not far wrong. The pagans worshiped gods who knew how to laugh, and who did foolish, human things. Zeus, if we may judge from the comedy dialogues of Lucian (A.D. 165-170), has literary interests and quotes — or misquotes — Homer; he makes flourishing orations to the gods, though alas! his memory fails him in the middle of a sentence. When in *Icaromenippus* the philosopher Menippus visits heaven, Zeus treats him amiably and gossips with him. He asks Menippus rather nervously what men are saying about him nowadays — mankind is so dissimulating, if not fickle. There was a time when he had been everything to them, every street, every market place had been full of Zeus, and he could hardly see for the smoke of sacrifice; now, other times, other gods — Asklepios, Anubis, Artemis, and other foreigners — had set up shrines and the altars of Zeus were cold as Plato's 'Laws' and Chrysippus's 'Syllogisms.'

Lucian was no philosopher, and he ridiculed the philosophers and their endless schools and rival systems no less than he ridiculed the priests and their myths and oracles. In the main he looked upon human life as a meaningless pageant of hopes and fears and follies, pleasures and passions and hatreds, absurd from its undignified beginnings to the burial rites which ended it. Certainly Lucian lived in the midst of pagans who were saturated with the grossest and most primitive conceptions. But this is just why Lucian's dialogues are notable. He was read by such pagans as had literary ability and interests, and was perhaps the most popular writer of his day in both Greece and Rome. It is small wonder that his readers, who could laugh at the gods and at themselves and make the gods laugh too, could not understand the laughless God and Christ of Christianity.

vii

If the initial success of Christianity was in great measure attributable to its capacity to borrow pagan customs and beliefs, its greatest difficulty in its first four centuries lay in integrating these customs and beliefs with

Judaic theology into an organized, coherent body of doctrine. With the growth of the church and the increased power of the episcopacy, dogma became of paramount importance. For the pagans, creed had been so subordinate to affective experience that it might be said to have been almost nonexistent. For the Christians, affection was in practice, whatever might be claimed in principle, subordinate to organized belief: the church was always on the defensive against both Jew and pagan and the fathers were forced at every turn to explain away some old pagan parallel or some new paradox. Consequently it soon developed into a society for epistolary debate; its dogma was formed by continuous controversy between bishops, and each addition decided by the polemical talents of the disputants.

In the earliest period of its growth those who were adverse to conceiving Jesus as truly human and as suffering on the cross as a man of flesh must suffer held with Marcion that Jesus had possessed only a phantom or apparent body, and hence they came to be known as the Docetae (*dokeo,* seen). Docetist opinion was in turn divided as to whether Jesus and his death and resurrection were not pure divine illusion, or whether, as a real man among men, he yet possessed an ethereal and heavenly flesh which was free of human distress and animal necessities and which consequently could not suffer death. By the opening of the second century the argument of the real *versus* the phantom Jesus had become involved in several systems of thought, collectively known as Gnosticism, which represented the hybridization in various manners of Persian dualism and Christian revelation.

All Gnostic sects agreed in laying claim to a higher knowledge — of Gnosis, a mysterious form of information which was imparted by inspiration and which was not open to proof or argument. The chief preoccupation of the Gnostics was to account formally for the existence of evil. Starting from the Persian notion of absolute good and evil, they endeavored to maintain the Judaic principle of monotheism by making the power of evil entirely subordinate to the power of good. In some cases evil was held to be a consequence of the fall of the godhead into the world of matter, whereby the godhead was degraded and matter animated, giving rise to the 'powers,' some partly and some wholly evil, who hold sway over the world; or it was supposed that from the supreme divinity there emanated a somewhat lesser world, and from this another world was emanated and so on until the divine element was so far weakened and attenuated that a partly or wholly evil world was readily comprehensible. Again it was supposed that good and evil are the two hands of Yahweh, good the right hand and evil the left, evil having power over this world and good over the next. Another variant was the arrangement of good and evil in a quantitative hierarchy of 365 stages, with Yahweh at the top, evil at the bottom, and in between such abstractions as mind, word, judgment, wisdom and power scaled above various categories of angels and demons.

An essential element in Gnostic belief was the fallen divinity of light, Sophia, the intermediary between the worlds of evil matter and divine spirit, the Mother Goddess who descends into the abyss to effect creation, and whose son, the Demiourgos, governs the world in the belief that he is the Supreme God. That Sophia is Ishtar in disguise is indicated by her legends. In one she descends into this world in order, by means of her beauty, to provoke to sensual passion and mutual strife the angels who rule the world and thus to deprive them of power. She appears as the mother of the seven gods, or celestial bodies; or turns in presumptuous love towards the Supreme Deity and is degraded into mere matter by way of punishment, or she is taken prisoner against her will by the lower powers, as Ishtar was kept in Hades by Allat. In some undisputed instances, Sophia's worship was associated with sacred courtesans, a custom possibly borrowed from Attis and Cybele.

An aeon of supreme rank, the Soter, undertakes the work of delivering Sophia in answer to her prayer. He comes down through the spheres of the archons, taking on himself the forms of the spirits of each world; arriving in the darkness, he gathers the scattered light and reascends with the rescued Sophia into the realm of harmony. Soter and his legends contained fragments of Osiris, Attis, Mithra and other gods, and scarcely was Christianity started before he was identified as Jesus. Soter occupied Jesus throughout the latter's life, but left his body just before the crucifixion. The real reason Soter entered Jesus was to use him as a vehicle for imparting to the Gnostics the secret knowledge by which men's souls were to be freed from evil bondage and restored to the kingdom of light.

Gnostic beliefs were well developed before the rise of Christianity, but the two groups of ideas, both based on ultimate personal salvation, had a magnetic attraction for each other. It might be said that Gnosticism attached itself to Christianity with such parasitic and unwelcome fervor that the fathers were kept busy brushing it off. It was the necessity of analyzing and answering its arguments that set the church in its literary habits, nearly all the Christian literature of the second and third centuries arising from this debate. Gnosticism has been characterized as 'learned ignorance, lending an eager ear to new mysticisms,' and 'the human imagination gone mad,' but it presented the first grave danger which Christianity had to face, and the strength of the church was acquired in great measure by its efforts to defeat the sect's fantastic notions. It implanted in the Christian pantheon the intermediate hierarchies of angels and demons, and it introduced nascently the absolutes of Good and Evil. While the orthodox Christians believed that the soul at death went to the underworld to await there the resurrection when it would rejoin the body, the Gnostics scorned the idea of a resurrection on rational grounds, and held that at death the soul ascended directly unto heaven. This doctrine of 'immediate ascent' was opposed by Christianity for many centuries though it ultimately became the prevalent, if not the official, view. In the Gnostic sects temple prostitution was intended to prevent by magic influence the propagation of mankind, which they held to be the origin of all evil; their condemnation of marriage and sexual intercourse and all forms of carnal pleasure did much to promote the development of asceticism within the church, and supplied Augustine, probably the most influential among the men who shaped later Christian beliefs, with some of his most important notions. Lastly, because it had itself no organization, it stimulated by reaction a strong movement toward unified doctrine and inelastic organization in the church. It offered no lasting competition to Christianity probably because its beliefs were impossibly complex. Men and women could weep for a slain god and worship him, but they could not grieve over philosophical abstractions or be ecstatically stimulated by a multitude of angels and aeons.

To the pagan view Gnosticism was simply one of several aberrant forms of Christianity. To the Christian bishops, however, Gnostic beliefs were the notions of the devil himself. Paul had denounced the Gnostic theories as 'seducing spirits and doctrines of devils . . . profane and vain babblings, and oppositions of knowledge falsely so called'; now the fathers anathematized its proponents as 'servants of Satan, beasts in human shape, dealers in deadly poison, robbers and pirates,' and on principle alone it was asserted that they were motivated 'by pride, disappointed ambition, sensual lust and avarice.' Thereafter the terms 'sect' and 'heresy' (the two being identical in New Testament Greek) became for them charged with the most painful opprobrium and were classed as one of the seven mortal sins. If Gnosticism were not significant in any other respect it would be memorable for having brought into existence for the first time in human history that form of damnable defilement engendered by disagreement with the doctrines propounded by ecclesiastic authority — heresy.

In so far as Christianity had had its roots in Judaism it should by historic descent have been purely monotheistic, but this monotheism was fractured outright by the Pauline doctrine which accepted Jesus as a risen god whose existence was more or less independent of the primal godhead. The fathers could not conceive that Yahweh himself could be degraded to human form to suffer human appetites and the death of a mortal body, so at first they had said that Yahweh had put part of himself into Jesus's mortal body at the time when it was baptized by John. After the doctrine of the virgin birth had come to be generally accepted in the second century, it was held that the Holy Ghost had entered into Mary at the annunciation, and that she had supplied the divine Jesus with a mortal body. In this view the risen Jesus had to become a spiritual son of Yahweh and a sharer with him of the throne of heaven.

This division of the godhead, unavoidable both in the Pauline and later teachings, threatened the monotheistic principle for which the prophets had fought so valiantly. Hence the Christians were faced at the outset with a paradox that caused them acute embarrassment. They could not say to the polytheists, as could the Jews, "We have only one god," for it was patent that they had at least two, and only finespun distinctions, which the polytheists were prone to question, could keep the total at that number. The docrine of the virgin birth, which served primarily to endow Jesus with divinity, served also if secondarily to purify Mary of carnality, and the doctrine soon came to specify not an incidental, but a perpetual virginity. Thus elevated by the divine afflatus, Mary soon began to compete in popular affection with Isis, Cybele and Demeter. It required but slight and easy changes to transfer to her the stately ritual of the goddess Isis, with its shaven and tonsured priests, its matins and vespers, its tinkling music, its jeweled images of the Mother of God; and the ancient portrait of Isis and the child Horus was ultimately accepted not only in popular opinion, but by formal episcopal sanction, as the portrait of the Virgin and her child.

Sometime in the second century there began a movement essentially of apotheosis; Mary was given a traditional father, Joachim, and a mother, Anna, and it was said that she had been nurtured in the Temple from her third to her fifteenth year. This culminated in later centuries in an abortive effort to elevate not only Mary and Joseph, but Anna, to godhead. The only doctrinal concession was the tacit agreement that Mary had herself been immaculately conceived, a conclusion which was, however, not endorsed by the Papacy until the late date of 1854. Without dogmatic authorization, by the time of Constantine the women of Thrace, Scythia and Arabia were worshiping Mary as a goddess, while elsewhere she was receiving prayers as a friendly mediator to deal with the Very Mediator Christ. There was needed only the apotheosis into sainthood of its real and legendary martyrs, of pagan gods, and of various heroes, for the Christian pantheon to consist of a goddess and two gods and as many subordinate spirits as populated any pantheon of old.

For more than six centuries Judaism had condemned the worship of idols, but images of Jesus and Mary and even of the more illustrious saints easily passed this traditional veto and rapidly came to play a role in Christian worship equivalent to the sacred statues of the pagans. In the thirteenth century Thomas Aquinas held that the same reverence must be paid to Christ's image as to himself, and in the same period Bonaventura maintained the same principle with regard to the Virgin's image, but long before these medieval churchmen put their approval upon the practice of idolatry the work of the prophets had been undone. By the sixth century all Christian temples had statues which spoke, wept, perspired or bled, these prodigies being officially approved. The saints listened to the people's prayers and rewarded them with miracles, and holy relics were taken onto the battlefield, or carried in long processions to avert drought, epidemics and other disasters. To be buried near a saint, to await the resurrection in the company of the blessed, was the dearest wish of every man. A venerable priest dared not undertake a voyage without a bodyguard lest zealous persons among whom he might have to linger should take steps to keep him as a distinguished corpse. The fortune was assured of any church that had the whole body of a saint; even a single bone or bit of apparel endowed an altar with additional supernatural power, and where relics could not be obtained an image was erected as a substitute. The chief difference between the Christian and pagan idols was that in place of the great stone sculptures of the past the Christians, lacking any artistic tradition or training, used painted wooden images or pictures of the crudest sort.

The quasi-divine saints would, perhaps, have been no serious embarrassment to the monotheistic principle so long as the pantheon was occupied by a supreme god. However, this ideal the Christians were never able to attain, and it was on the question of the unity or duality of God and Jesus that the most intense theological bitterness was evoked. This question was so fundamental that difference of opinion could not be tolerated within what could be called a catholic church. Moreover, the problem of the nature of Jesus had been further complicated by the writer of the Fourth Gospel, who had propounded that 'In the beginning was the Word, and the Word was with God, and the Word was God . . . And the Word was made flesh, and dwelt among us, (and we beheld his glory, the glory as of the only begotten of the Father,) full of grace and truth.'

The Word which John identified with God in the first sentence, and with Jesus in the second, read *logos* in the Greek, a term which, as has previously been remarked, is so complex in its meaning as to have no exact equivalent in any modern language. The Greek word had first been used by Heraclitus to designate the 'tendency' to order which was immanent in the physical universe, the inherent 'plan' of winds and waves and stars, the essential 'reasonableness' of things. The Stoics had virtually made a god of Logos by describing it as 'seminal reason' of the world, while to the Hellenized Hebrews the Logos was an almost independent being serving to purify Yahweh from direct contact with the world and at the same time to establish communication with him.

The Jewish philosopher Philo (born *ca*. 20 B.C.) conceived Yahweh as a being absolutely bare of quality, inasmuch as all quality imposes finite limitations, and of Yahweh no limitation can be predicated. Since a being absolutely without quality cannot move or act, Philo interposed between Yahweh and the world an infinite series of divine forces, in the Gnostic manner, the chief of these being the Logos, synonymous with the Wisdom of Yahweh and depicted as an archangel which manifested itself in revelation, and by the aid of which, with the lesser divine forces, Yahweh shaped the world. The Philonic Logos was at once the divine dynamic and the Egyptian magic word elevated to an archangelic position. The paradox, that the Logos was not Yahweh himself but an independently existing entity, while it was also an aspect of Yahweh, was no better resolved by Philo than by subsequent theologians. The difficulty was not lessened by the circumstance that Philo variously identified the Logos with a deity, a spoken utterance, a creative power, an instrument, an aspect of deity, a farseeing spirit, a refuge, the first-born of the deity, a high priest and mediator, the covenant, an eternal entity, an angel, the sun, a body of doctrine, the Scriptures, Moses, an abstraction of wisdom and the soul of the world. After Philo there was therefore amalgamated within the Logos something of the Greek concept of natural order or cosmic process, the Egyptian notion of the magic word, the Persian-Hebrew Angel, and the Wisdom or the divine dynamic of Yahweh himself. When to this admixture there was added the Platonic concept that, as divine wisdom, Logos was to be identified with 'absolute truth,' the meaning of the term, though extraordinarily elastic, was frequently perplexing.

John alleged that he had both seen Jesus and been instructed by the disciples, and on this authority, as much as for its quasi-philosophical nature, his work received the imprimatur of the early church. By the canonization of his gospel, the Logos was firmly implanted in the creed, to the further embarrassment of the monotheistic principle, for John's definition, 'In the beginning was the Word, and the Word was with God, and the Word was God,' was so precise that it left no room for debate. The theologians were therefore forced in the following centuries to struggle with a one-god who was also three gods: an independently existing Logos, now virtually a Divine Spirit known in the Jerusalem baptismal formula as the Holy Ghost, a mortal Son, and a supreme Deity.

viii

It was while this argument about the nature of God was waxing that the church had the good fortune to win the favor of the Emperor Constantine and to be established as the state religion. Constantine had been a worshiper of the sun god Apollo, but influenced by the example of his father, Constantius, and by the presence in the court of influential Christians, he had, from the time he became coemperor, been inclined to a policy of religious toleration. In the Edict of Milan (313) he declared for the equality of all religions, and within a couple of years, while still declaring for toleration, he openly began to favor the Christians. By 323, when Licinius, who shared the purple with him, as Emperor of the East, undertook some Christian persecutions, Constantine assumed a strong pro-Christian, antipagan attitude. Having developed an antipathy to Rome, and concluding that the time was ripe for society to be remodeled by imperial fiat, he resolved about 326 to found a new capital on the shores of the Bosporus, which was called after him, Constantinople, and from which all organized pagan worship was prohibited. At about this same time he began to pass laws which greatly favored the Christians, and to give them valuable financial and legal support.

Probably no more than one twentieth of the population of either Rome or the empire as a whole was at this time Christian, but what the sect lacked in numbers it made up in organization, unity and intellectual talent. The Christians, shut off from the pleasures of the world by asceticism, were amassing wealth, while their morality, sobriety and enthusiasm recommended them to Constantine's scheme of a world-wide reorganization of society. Though it was with considerable justification that the Christians claimed him for their own, his 'conversion' was nominal even by contemporary standards; after the event he put to death his wife, his son, a nephew and the nephew's wife, and then he had Licinius and his son strangled after promising them their lives. He continued to have himself figured on coins as a devotee of Apollo, Mars, Herakles, Mithra and Zeus. In putting off baptism until just before his death, Constantine was only following the precedent of many Christians who considered that, inasmuch as baptism washed away all sins and could not be repeated, it was bad economy to hurry it. When he died, the Roman senate in the customary pagan manner enrolled him with the *divus Julius, Augustus* and other emperors, among the gods.

Writers from Milton onward have cogitated on what might have been the history of the world had Constantine never been 'converted,' but no oracle among them has attempted on this speculation to recast a millennium and a half of history. As it came to pass, the immediate effects of his favoritism were the enrichment of the church beyond its dreams and the establishment of a priestly hierarchy which was soon to come into virtual control of the civilized world. Constantine's direct gifts of moneys and lands, though not of themselves considerable, so showed the new direction of the wind that there was an immediate influx of gain-seekers into the priesthood; the churches of Carthage and Constantinople before long had five hundred priests apiece, and laws had to be passed restraining the priests and bishops from further enriching themselves by lending money at interest. Freed of persecution and permitted to receive legacies in the manner of the pagan faiths, the Christian church was able to compete with the rich cults of Egypt. The Christians would have had Constantine engage in an active persecution of the pagans, but since he wished to keep the fidelity of the pagan majority he refused to do so. He did restrict private diviners, whom he caused to be burned alive, but here he acted apparently in accordance with a growing pagan custom of restricting divination to the temples. Constantine reorganized the church along imperial lines, giving legal status to the decisions of the bishops in all church disputes so that these dignitaries had the power of princes. He reserved to himself the supreme authority in ecclesiastic matters, but after his abandonment of Rome he could no longer exercise the office effectively and soon the imperial claim to leadership lapsed in favor of the Bishop of Rome. Only one thing remained to complete the potential structure of the medieval church: under the authority conferred by Constantine, the bishops could, with the emperor's co-operation, invoke the political decree of banishment in addition to their ecclesiastic prerogative of anathema; it remained for Theodosius the Great, in his edicts against the Manichees

(381–389), to exalt this authority into the power to impose the death penalty and to cancel all rights of inheritance.

Had Constantine made to the bishops the Theodosian concession, the church might at least have had a simpler and perhaps more comprehensible creed, for just before he became sole emperor the churchmen had raised the arguments on the divinity of Jesus to the danger point. The efforts of each group to exterminate dissident opinion were rendered all the more difficult by the multiplicity of theories: conflicting heresies crossruffed each other until the faith of Christendom was on the verge of destroying itself by its internal disagreement.

The most oriental, and most dangerous of all heresies (if it could be called a heresy in the sense of a Christian sect) was Manichaeism, a cult founded by a Mesopotamian named Mani who came into opposition with the Magi in the Persian capital and was crucified in 279. Compounded of Gnosticism and Jewish, Babylonian, Zoroastrian and Buddhist speculations, it presented two kingdoms, of Light and Darkness, ruled respectively by Yahweh and Satan; to resist Satan, Yahweh creates Primeval Man who is defeated and captured by Satan, then rescued by Yahweh; in the course of rescue Primeval Man loses some particles of divine light which, mixing with darkness, bring the present world into being. Then Satan creates man, seeking thereby to imprison and preserve a portion of the light, but Yahweh, through Jesus, offers man a means of redemption by creating the sun, moon and stars to attract the particles of light and act as reservoirs of it until the redemption is complete. Though the Manichaeans made much of the claim that they appealed to human reason, Eusebius called their doctrines an 'insane heresy.' This sect had gained wide popularity in the fourth century and supplied to the Christian church the greatest of all its fathers, Augustine.

The main struggle for the unification of belief necessarily concerned the fundamental nature of the godhead. Every attempt to establish that Jesus and Yahweh were one, the latter having descended into the Virgin in order to be born, then only to die upon the cross, was labeled as Patripassian and vigorously condemned. Paul of Somasato, Bishop of Antioch, expressed the conviction that Yahweh could not appear substantially on earth and consequently could not become a person in Jesus: Yahweh had merely filled the human Jesus with his Logos. But neither a human Jesus nor an incarnate Logos could be accepted by the orthodox, and three assemblies of the church were convened in Antioch between 264 and 269, in the last of which Paul was condemned and forced to promise a reformation. He failed to keep the promise, in spite of a second condemnation and excommunication, and in 272, at the instigation of the Bishop of Rome, the Emperor Aurelian removed him from office by force of troops and placed a rival candidate in his place. A famed scholar of Antioch, Lucian, contended that the Logos was a second deity which had been created by Yahweh and had come down to earth and taken upon itself a truly human body in the form of Jesus. In this view Jesus was neither a man, since his person was divine, nor a god, since by definition he was other than the one-god, Yahweh, and totally human. Sharing the heretical reputation of Paul, he was excluded from ecclesiastic fellowship by three successive bishops, and probably only escaped formal condemnation by the circumstance that he suffered a martyr's death under the judgment of Maximin Daza (312).

Lucian's pupil, Arius, took up his teacher's effort at rationalization with no great intellectual success, arguing that Jesus was totally and essentially distinct from the Father, having been created by the Father out of nothingness; yet he was 'perfect God, only-begotten' and therefore not among created things. Arius had migrated to Alexandria where he had become pastor of a fashionable church, and had been passed over in the promotion to the bishopric, the appointment going to his rival, Alexander. Against Arius, Bishop Alexander insisted that 'as God is eternal, so is his Son, — when the Father, then the Son — the Son is present in God without birth, ever-begotten, an unbegotten-begotten.' 'They are two, for the Father is Father, and the Son is not the same . . . but their nature is one, for the Begotten is not dissimilar to the Begetter, but his image, and everything that is the Father's is also the Son's.' Arius saw in this position the rankest heresy savoring of Gnosticism, Manichaeism and other noxious falsehoods. The argument continued in Alexandria for some years until, about 318, other bishops complained to Alexander that Arius's teaching was threatening the faith, and Arius was condemned and excommunicated. Arius's many friends quickly raised the argument to such a pitch that the emperor became disturbed. Knowing the danger of debate and wishing to use the church to unify the empire, Constantine wrote Alexander and Arius that they were equally right and wrong, and urged them to lay aside the insignificant subject of the controversy; failing in this effort at conciliation, he admonished them to leave ecclesiastic theory alone or else to argue in a gentlemanly manner like the pagans, who were being moved by the acrimonious debate to open ridicule and the assertion that all Christians were mad and carried on wild midnight orgies. So great grew the emperor's fear that the argument would stir the god or gods to wrath that he moved to the unprecedented extreme of decreeing heresy to be a criminal offense. This move, of course, only multiplied the trouble by multiplying the importance of the verb and participle, and even the punctuation, of the creed.

There being as yet no official creed, it was impossible to determine who was orthodox and who was heretical, so to draw this line Constantine called a general council of the church at Nicaea (325). By a packed vote the issue was decided in favor of Alexander — Jesus and Yahweh were one — and all thought of Jesus being created, subordinate or human had to be put aside. Accepting the decision of the council as final, Constantine excommunicated Arius and two bishops who held dissenting opinions, and banished them to Illyria. Eusebius of Nicomedia, who accepted the definition of the council but disapproved its anathemas, was exiled to Gaul.

Alexander, the chief proponent of what might now be called orthodoxy, died soon thereafter and was succeeded by his deacon, Athanasius, by whose conviction and fortitude the controversy was kept alive. The Arians were by no means subdued, and after three years they persuaded the emperor to recall the two banished bishops, and later to recall Arius himself. Whereupon the Arian bishops turned to the persecution of their persecutors. When Athanasius refused to reinstate Arius, he in turn was deprived of his office and banished to Trèves in 335. Then Arius died suddenly on the street, apparently of poison, and Constantine died the year after, having at the end been baptized by one of the Arian bishops whom he had previously banished. The Empire was divided between Constantine's three sons, while the church remained divided on the nature of Jesus. The Arians themselves broke up into half a dozen mutually anathematizing sects which attacked all orthodox opinion as new heresies while jointly trying to combat Manichaeism. The 'catholic' creed came to resemble chaos, theology became a 'sort of systematic insanity,' and a synod or council an occasion for secret murders or open bloody warfare.

Constantius, most ambitious of the three sons of Constantine, soon made himself sole emperor. As the successor of the baptized Constantine, he was the first Christian-bred emperor and his record was to presage events to come, for his usurpation of the power of his two brothers, the coemperors, was marked by half a dozen murders. He framed for himself the new and imposing title 'His Eternity,' calling himself Lord of the Universe, and he yielded to the requests of the Christians, as Constantine had refused to do, by closing the pagan temples and decreeing that all who used them or offered sacrifice should be put to death and their property confiscated. Thus official Christian persecution of the pagans was initiated within fifty years of the time when the Christians themselves had been suffering persecution. He decreed the death penalty for the use of idols at the very time when the Christians themselves were worshiping idols of the Christ, the Virgin and various saints in churches throughout the land. On the matter of the nature of Jesus he was in favor of Arius and opposed to Athanasius, and to settle the debate he decreed that in all ecclesiastic matters his will had the force of a canon, and forbade the bishops to condemn any opinion which he held. One bishop he tortured, one he put to death, others he banished, and he doubtless would have slain Athanasius had the Egyptian monks not hidden the heretic. At each episcopal election or expulsion, says a Christian historian, Constantinople, Alexandria and Antioch furnished scenes that would have disgraced a revolution. Julian relates in this connection that whole troops of those who were called heretics were massacred, while in many provinces towns and villages were utterly destroyed, and the orthodox populace, itself divided into factions, fought like savages in the very churches. 'There is no wild beast,' he said, 'like an angry theologian.' In the reinstatement of an Arian bishop in Constantinople there perished three thousand people, considerably more than had suffered death in the whole ten years of the last pagan persecution.

Under Constantius's successor, Julian, there was a brief moment of official paganism, and relative sanity. Although nominally educated as a Christian, Julian had never openly declared for the church and he disdained its irrational theories and bitter quarrels. A traveled and widely read scholar, he was the last representative of note of the decadent Hellenic culture, and the last Emperor of Rome possessing any intellectual capacity whatever. He leaned to the worship of Mithra, which before Constantine's time had been favored by the state, but he declared for a restoration of paganism generally, hoping that the pagan cults would learn something of philosophy, charity and asceticism from the 'Galileans,' as he called them. Nevertheless he disdained to persecute anyone for worshiping any deity so long as he kept the peace. He ordered the Christians to restore the property which they had appropriated from the pagans under Constantius, he recalled the banished heretics and he abolished the special privileges of the Christian priests. His worst blow against the church was that he put pagan teachers in charge of the schools, which would in the course of a generation have almost obliterated the new creed. Had he lived the normal span of years, it is probable that the Christians would have been undone, but his restoration was aborted by his death in battle with the Persians after he had been in power but twenty months. An obscure Christian officer of the guards, Jovian, whose sole claim to distinction appears to have been that he had driven the funeral car of Constantius eighteen months earlier, was elected by the army to succeed Julian and the Christians were soon again in power. The principle effects of Julian's reformation were to bring perpetual Christian anathema on his memory and to demonstrate to the Christian church the absolute necessity of holding temporal as well as spiritual power if it were to survive.

ix

Only Julian's untimely death saved Christianity from its enemies, but nothing could save it from itself. It continued to divide and subdivide on questions of dogma, each faction employing gladiators to sustain its point, until in the reign of Theodosius the Great each controversy was leaving a wake of exiled or murdered theologians. This emperor reinforced the laws of Constantine by officially declaring (380) that Yahweh was One, that the Father, the Son and the Holy Ghost were of equal majesty in the Holy Trinity; and that the 'senseless followers' of the other religions were to be branded 'with the infamous name of heretics,' while their conventicles were forbidden to call themselves churches. Fifteen penal laws passed by this emperor progressively deprived heretics of practically every right, and included one imposing the death sentence in extreme instances; and in 385, the Coemperor Maximus caused the Spanish theologian Priscillian and six other heretics to be burned at Trèves. The hateful heresy of which Priscillian and his friends were guilty was the insistence on continence in marriage. This ascetic ideal, in the form of celibacy, the church enjoined upon its priests, but having discovered in four centuries of unfortunate experience that superiority in numbers was more to be desired than purity, it was not prepared to endorse for general practice this particular form of mystic cleanliness.

New heresies arose as fast as the old ones could be suppressed. The councils of Nicaea (325) and Constantinople (381) had failed to define how God and man were joined. The Apollinarians tried to do this by asserting that in Jesus the Logos took the place of the rational soul, and they considered Mary to be literally the Mother of God. They were opposed by Nestorius of Constantinople, who asserted that since the Logos was divine it could not have been born, and had merely resided in Jesus's body as in a temple; Mary was a woman, and to call a woman the Mother of God was absurd and blasphemous. Against Nestorius, Cyril of Alexandria held that the divine and human nature were perfectly united in one person. Nestorius was charged with blasphemy by Cyril and, at a Roman synod, anathematized and excommunicated. When Nestorius in retribution anathematized and excommunicated Cyril, the Emperor had to take a hand and called a general council at Ephesus in 431. Despite the support of armed troops, Nestorius was formally convicted of heresy and excommunicated and later banished. Cyril himself was afterwards charged with heresy by his colleagues, but he proved so ardent in the persecution of pagans, Jews and other obvious heretics that he died within the faith.

Except for the ever-present danger of schismatic fracture over the nature of Yahweh, Jesus and the Logos, the future of Christianity was assured. Under the Theodosian laws condemning all 'unbelievers,' the Christians returned with renewed enthusiasm to destroying the pagan temples and confiscating pagan property under the guise of 'reform.' Theodosius ordered the systematic massacre of from 7,000 to 15,000 men, women and children in order to punish the inhabitants of Thessalonica for a riot; by refusing him the Eucharist, Bishop Ambrose made him humble himself publicly and do penance for seven months. Yet so arduous were the Christians in their attacks upon the pagans that, over Ambrose's vigorous remonstrance, the emperor himself promulgated a law to prevent the Christians from despoiling the pagans of all they possessed. If the law was ever enforced it soon fell into neglect, and to find any safety or peace great numbers of pagans were forced to affect conversion. Schism as well as pagan opposition were henceforth pursued with militant vigor.

Quite apart from its hosts of subordinate spiritual powers, the faith had abandoned its historic claim to monotheism by resorting to a definition of the Supreme Deity which defeated both schism and reason: the Council of Nicaea (325) had decided against Arius, that Christ was truly Yahweh, coequal and coeternal with the Father, separate and yet one; the Council of Constantinople (381) had decided against Apollinaris and affirmed the Nicaean Creed that he was also truly man; that of Ephesus (431) had convicted Nestorius for the blasphemy of denying that the two natures were indivisibly one; and that of Chalcedon (451) had affirmed that they were nevertheless perfectly distinct. To effect the *copula* between God and Son, Nicea had welded the Logos into the official Creed, designating it, as in the Jerusalem formula, as the Holy Ghost. Constantinople completed the Trinity by adding to this declaration of belief, to which all true Christians must subscribe, '. . . And in the Holy Ghost, the Lord and Giver of Life, who proceedeth from the Father and the

Son, who with the Father and the Son together is worshipped and glorified.'

So it came to pass that all four decisions and three Gods became fixed in the official creed. After nearly four hundred years of conflict waged with anathema, excommunication and banishment, and aided by torture and poison and the use of gladiators and even armies, the churchmen in their efforts to frame a dogma that might survive had arrived at one in which rationality, the hated artifice of the devil-worshiping pagans, was undone. Tertullian was able to say, 'Certum est, quia impossibile est': 'I believe because it is impossible.' This was the principle upon which peace was ultimately attained. By establishing that reason was of no avail and that disagreement or heresy doomed men to eternal torment, the faith was made forever safe and the church was prepared to take over its reign of terrorism through the coming ages.

The transfer from pagan to Christian worship represented but little change. The statues of Jupiter and Apollo were readily christened St. Peter and St. Paul, and by the middle of the fifth century Christianity had acquired numerous pagan deities as saints. Osiris was sanctified as St. Onuphris, Mithra (Petra) as St. Peter, Cheron as St. Ceraunos, Castor and Pollux as St. Cosmo and St. Darnieu, Diana Illythra as St. Yllis, Artemis as St. Artemidos, Dionysus as St. Dionysus and also as St. Bacchus; Demetrius, Rusticus, Denis and Eleutherius — some of these deities having been appropriated on the pretense that they were martyrs — were sanctified, while Buddha, quite by accident, was canonized as St. Josaphat. A host of lesser pagan deities were as easily turned into devils and demons. The principles of sacrifice and propitiation were preserved, there was nothing unfamiliar in penance and atonement, and, with the adoration of shrines, sacred relics and images, the resort to emotionally titillating mysteries and the absorption and renaming of pagan festivals and holy places, the conversion of the Mediterranean world did not prove difficult.

Many reasons have been given for the 'fall' of the Roman empire, most of them but partial answers or mere guesses. Be the true causes what they may, it was not in the nature of the new faith to oppose the process of disintegration. At the opening of the Christian Era there had been schools in every considerable town, and many advanced academies in the great cities; these the Christians gradually allowed to die out, maintaining only a few theological seminaries. They were from the first not interested in the examination of nature, since the end of the world was so close at hand; by the time they had become accustomed to an indefinitely continued existence all natural knowledge had come to be identified with paganism, or interpreted as contrary to revelation and, in either instance, savoring of evil. Galen (?130–200) the physician, Ptolemy (?100–160) the geographer, and Diophantus (fl. *ca.* 250) the mathematician, were the last in their respective fields to follow the classic traditions, as Lucian (125–200) was the last exponent of Hellenic skepticism, and Julian (331–363) the last emperor to defend religious tolerance. The temple schools of Asklepios had been shut and public lecturing by nonofficial teachers had been practically prohibited in Rome and Constantinople in the fourth century. Under an edict of Theodosius, Bishop Theophilus in 389 destroyed the Serapeum in Alexandria, and with it nearly all the works in the only remaining pagan library of importance in the world. In 529 Justinian closed the schools at Athens, the last to teach Greek philosophy, and the intensity of this emperor's persecutions brought about within a short space of time the forcible baptism of 70,000 persons in Asia Minor alone, and so alienated the population of Egypt and Syria that the way was paved for the spread of Mohammedanism. The Christians preferred prayer and exorcism to pagan magic, religious to geometric theorems, the gospels to any other literature. So fallible was reason held that Pope Gregory the Great (540–604) condemned all literature and intellectual effort, and in the East the laity were forbidden to read even the sacred book.

Self-mortification, squalor and physical uncleanliness became esteemed Christian virtues — with some justice Anatole France said that Christianity killed the bath, for at the opening of the Christian Era the Roman baths were famous. It was the widespread custom of mixed bathing in the great public baths which first caused the Christians to condemn them, but later the bath in general was condemned because it afforded pleasure and was a mark of vanity. Christianity undermined the family, the unit of the social system, by teaching that celibacy is an exalted virtue; and by its emphasis on continence it directed the sexual impulse into physical and psychological perversions. It dogmatically relegated women to an inferior position, socially, politically and intellectually, and by making a sacrament of marriage it permitted wives to become chattels and husbands boors. It supplanted courage and initiative by resignation: Providence had arranged things in their order, the rich and the poor, the well and the sick, the wise and the ignorant; and to question Providence was to question the wisdom of God. Misery was to be tolerated patiently in anticipation of everlasting glory. It did not highly esteem either personal or political freedom, and in no case was it prepared to fight for them. By its fallacious philosophy of free will and the countersense of predestination it obliterated education and experience from ethics and obstructed objective inquiry into the human mind. It rent philosophy by its dualisms of secular and holy, reason and faith, natural and supernatural, good and evil, and by its insistence that uninformed faith is a higher form of knowledge, that no earthly betterment could outweigh the overwhelming issue of salvation or damnation which awaited man after death, it paralyzed all curiosity and intelligent examination of the natural world. For the love of life it substituted the fear of death. For the sense of the dignity of man, fundamental to the precepts of the Stoics and of Cicero, Seneca, Marcus Aurelius and other Roman moralists, it substituted the doctrine of personal inadequacy, the sense of guilt, and the habits of self-doubt and self-abnegation. In its cardinal doctrine of sin, for which it crucified the Christ, it promulgated a belief which was to crucify the whole of the western world for centuries to come.

VI

~~~~~~

The Rise and Fall of His
Satanic Majesty's Empire

THE devil's origin is hidden in almost impenetrable mystery. Having no organized priesthood and no written testaments of his own to preserve his history, his biography can be recovered only from fragmental references, scarcely more than whispered calumnies and innuendos, to be found in the history of that good world the despoliation of which was his desire and destiny.

One may confidently anticipate that his genealogy will lead back, as is so frequently the case with the great in vision and achievement, to an exalted ancestor, himself divine. One tempting trail points to Ahriman, the Persian god of darkness and evil, who stands in opposition to Ormazd, the god of light and goodness, but when Satan appears in the legends of Israel it is neither as a deity co-ordinate with Yahweh, or as an effective agent in the creation of the world, but as a lesser angelic being of morally good character who lives on friendly terms with Yahweh and converses with him. He acquires a truly divine status and a truly evil character which is in opposition to the supreme deity only by slow assimilation. To whatever extent Persian philosophy influenced later Hebrew thought, its abstractions and its dualisms are foreign to early Yahwistic cosmology.

The only other promising trail leads to the Babylonian legend of the creation of the world, wherein the good god Marduk cleaved the goddess Tiamat in twain, and of the halves molded the heaven and earth; after which he cast her henchman Kingu out of heaven and had him bound, and from his blood fashioned mankind, while Kingu's army of demons he confined to a dark place.

The episode of the 'revolt of the angels' which stands in close apposition to the story of creation in Genesis appears to be an echo of this rebellion. Here it is briefly noted, 'And it came to pass, when men began to multiply on the face of the earth, and daughters were born unto them, That the sons of God saw the daughters of men that they were fair; and they took them wives of all which they chose. . . . There were giants in the earth in those days; and also after that, when the sons of God came in unto the daughters of men, and they bare children to them, the same became mighty men which were of old, men of renown.'

At first reading this isolated verse is unimpressive. It is chiefly the fact that it appears in the Genesis account as a polytheistic obscenity obtruding in the middle of the sacred history of the world that it commands attention. In Hebrew of the period, the expression 'sons of God' must be taken to mean divine beings, and such beings are inconsonant with the Yahwistic account of creation. The position of the verse in Genesis, close to the story of creation, itself indubitably Mesopotamian, renders plausible the supposition that the otherwise inexplicable reference to the 'giants' who were 'sons of God' is an echo of the divine beings who had been cast out of the Babylonian heaven.

That the 'sons of God' should see that the daughters of men were fair is in no way surprising, and it may be that the earlier redactors of Genesis viewed the matter in the heroic light, as the Greeks were wont to view the amours of Zeus. In view of the centuries in which this history of the world was edited and re-edited, it is unimaginable that the inharmonious verse could have escaped censorious deletion were it not supported by the oral legend which must ever have embellished the written text, but which compunction forbade the priestly scribes from recording on their rolls. Written references to evil angels which make a sudden appearance in the sacred books in later centuries possibly represent fragments of such an oral gloss.

At the period when Genesis was written, the notion of divine beings of any kind, other than Yahweh himself, was in a confusing state of flux. The god of the Israelites had been adequate for all forms of action, both good and evil; a savage, jealous, inexorable deity inflicting punishment out of all proportion to the fault, rejoicing in a frightful and brutal vengeance, striking the guilty and the innocent alike, he had never stood in need of angelic assistance. It was when, under prophetic transmutation, Yahweh became a remote spirit of righteousness akin to Ormazd that in order to preserve his divine transcendence there were introduced between heaven and earth mediating agents in the form of Persian angels who could perform both good and evil works in his behalf.

Satan is not even mentioned in the Pentateuch and, strangely enough, as a proper name signifying *the* power of evil the word appears only five times in the Old Testament, once with the meaning of Yahweh himself. It is in the postexilic prologue of the Book of Job that His Evil Majesty makes his historic appearance. Here Yahweh is depicted as attended by a group of spirits called 'sons of God' who go about and do things of their own volition, and not just at Yahweh's bidding; and here one of them is for the first time called Satan (adversary), apparently for no worse reason than for the way he pesters Job. Yet in this sad affair, the only really independent and perhaps evil attribute of Satan is skepticism. The Lord had called Satan to him and inquired, 'Whence camest thou?' and Satan had replied, 'From going to and fro in the earth, and from walking up and down in it.' Thus Satan starts his evil career by being curious. Thinking that in his perambulation Satan must certainly have met that epitome of virtue, Yahweh boasts, 'Hast thou considered my servant Job, that there is none like him in the earth, a perfect and an upright man, one that feareth Yahweh, and escheweth evil?' It is when Satan ventures to suggest that Job does not fear Yahweh for nought, that he is good only because he appreciates Yahweh's blessings, that the leader of the angelic spirits is revealed for what he is, a doubter, a skeptic, a misanthrope. It is to teach Satan a lesson in the power of unselfish and disinterested faith, and not to punish Job for being good, that Yahweh gives Job over to Satan's unceasing torment and multiplied misfortunes. The Book of Job is an apology, set forth in dramatic form, for the existence of evil.

Satan's next appearances, both brief ones, are in Zechariah (520 B.C.) as the prosecutor of Israel, where he acts without Yahweh's permission and even incurs Yahweh's rebuke; and then in Chronicles (300–200 B.C.), where in retrospect it is made to appear that it had been Satan who had provoked David to number Israel.

It is in the apocryphal writings, and especially in the Enoch apocalypses, that Satan first appears as the full-fledged instrument of evil. The earlier portions of Enoch, written in the second and first centuries B.C., several times refer to the 'sons of God' and make it clear that in coming to earth these angels were undergoing punishment for rebellion, and that in cohabiting with women they were doing evil. It is implied that during their sojourn on earth they imparted to their wives various arts as well as evil practices, and that the women passed this knowledge on to subsequent generations. Their leader is variously identified as Cain (who thus comes close to apotheosis as an evil fiend), Azazel, or Satan. In the Wisdom of Solomon (100–1 B.C.), Satan alone is charged with the responsibility for evil, while in Similitudes, satans are distinguished from angels, and are supposed to have existed before them; indeed, the descent of the angels to earth is represented as due not to a desire to unite with the daughters of men but to the desire to become subjects of these satans. In the Testament of the Twelve Patriarchs (200 B.C.) it is made to appear that the angels had been led astray by the women of earth, while the Life of Adam relates that Yahweh commanded the angels to worship Adam, and Satan was banished for refusing to do this, and for saying, on being threatened with Yahweh's wrath, that he would exalt his throne above the stars of heaven. In the Book of the Secrets of Enoch (A.D. 1–50), myriads of angels attend the sun, regulate the stars and control the lightning, frost and hail; here the leader is first called Satanial, his name being changed to Satan after he left the heavens; envious of Adam, he endeavored to rule the world. Although in these apocryphal books there is no unified belief, there is a common objective — to explain the existence of evil by blaming it directly or indirectly on a celestial fiend.

Thus there was available to the authors of the New Testament a substantial if unintegrated mass of references to the Prince of Evil. John in his Revelation spoke both symbolically and historically when he told of the war in heaven, when 'Michael and his angels fought against a dragon, and the great dragon was cast out with him and who made war on those who kept the commandments of God.' For the Christian movement generally Satan became the divine scapegoat to purify God of the evil taint. He is referred to as the 'slanderer,' the 'accuser,' the 'destroyer,' the 'evil one,' the 'enemy,' the 'prince of devils,' and 'Beelzebub.' He rules over a world of malignant, supernatural agencies whose dwelling is the low heavens: 'For we wrestle not against flesh and blood, but against principalities, against powers, against the rulers of darkness of this world,' says Paul. He is made to be the tempter of Judas, and even of Jesus himself, and Jesus represents him sowing tares among the wheat, and rebukes his favorite disciple, Peter, with the words, 'get thee behind me, Satan: thou art an offence unto me: for thou savorest not the things that be of Yahweh, but those that be of men.' Sinner and murderer from the beginning, Satan is a liar by nature, he and his minions falsely presenting themselves as angels of light. He is identified as a serpent, a dragon, a leviathan, as the flash of lightning — all the mysteries of dreaded aerial forces are concentrated in Paul's name for him as the 'Prince of the Power of the Air.'

Jesus made it clear that it was his mission to oppose Satan and to cast devils out of men. 'He healed many that were sick of divers diseases . . . and suffered not the devils to speak, because they knew him'; the 'unclean spirits, when they saw him, fell down before him and cried, saying, Thou art the son of God.' Jesus expels an unclean spirit from a man in Capernaum; he casts seven devils out of Mary Magdalene; in Peter's house he casts out the spirits of 'many' who were possessed with devils; and he casts the devils out of two Gadarenes and into a great herd of swine nearby, which thereupon throw themselves down a steep cliff into the sea and perish.

It was in shaping Satan into the Great Tempter, God's nominal enemy and the despoiler of his moral universe, that Christian doctrine struggled with the problem of the origin of evil and, in solving it, made its most original contribution to theology. Judaism had long accepted uncleanness, in the sense of transgression against the edicts of the deity, as the cause of most of the sufferings of life. In explaining the paradox that the innocent suffered with the guilty, the Jews fell back upon the doctrine of guilt acquired by inheritance or contamination, a doctrine essentially identical with the primitive belief in the solidarity and joint responsibility of the family and tribe, and their introversive view that Israel as a whole was unclean, was, by the opening of the Christian Era, well justified by experience. When it was asked why man generically should be unrighteous it was assumed that the propensity for disobedience had been received directly from the hand of the Creator in order to test the counterbalancing force of virtue. It remained for the writers of the apocalyptic books to discover, some in the story of the Garden of Eden, and some in the legend of the fallen angels, that abstract contamination which, in anglicized Latin, is called 'sin.'

The earliest reference in this connection is in Sirach (200–175 B.C.): here the writer, reflecting disparagingly on the various evils which a bad woman may bring into her husband's life, remarks lightly and incidentally, 'From a woman was the beginning of sin; and because of her we all die.' Although the author appears to have meant not that a woman was the first cause of sin, but only that sinning begins with women generally, the charge is an opening wedge for the story of Eve's guilt. The Wisdom of Solomon records that, 'God created man to be immortal, and made him to be an image of his own eternity. Nevertheless through envy of the devil came death into the world: and they that do hold of his side do find it.' Since this writer had previously recorded his belief that 'God made not death: neither hath he pleasure in the destruction of the living,' he is logically forced to seek in the devil and the devil's advocates the implement of misery. Again, in the Book of Enoch, it is made to appear that it had been fallen angels who, under the leadership of Satan, tempted man to act contrarily to the wishes of his God. Up to this time neither the canonical nor apocryphal writings mention any great offense as contaminating the human race as a whole, or calling for universal judgment, apart from the episode of the tower of Babel wherein men presumed to become as gods. But the author of the Wisdom of Solomon knew wherein lay sin: speaking of the ungodly, he says, 'Their wives are foolish, and their children wicked: Their offspring is cursed. Wherefore blessed is the barren that is undefiled, which hath not known the sinful bed: she shall have fruit in the visitation of souls. And blessed is the eunuch, which with his hands hath wrought no iniquity. . . . Better it is to have no children, and to have virtue: for the memorial thereof is immortal. . . .'

In the Apocalypse of Abraham Satan is first definitely identified with the serpent in the Paradise story, an episode that originally had no connection with the legend of the fallen angels, and in the Book of the Secrets of Enoch the idea appears that mankind somehow inherits from Adam the moral scar which Adam acquired as a consequence of the serpent episode. Then the Apocalypse of Baruch (A.D. 80–150) presents the Fall as having brought upon the race a potentiality or liability to future punishment, while II Esdras (A.D. 50–150) makes it clear that in consequence of Adam's sin, all men are born wicked, though here neither the devil nor the serpent is made responsible; 'The grain of evil seed hath been sown in the heart of Adam from the beginning . . . and how much shall it yet bring forth until the time of threshing come!' Who sowed the grain of evil seed in Adam's heart Esdras does not tell, only that the infection would never die out of his progeny: 'For the first Adam, bearing a wicked heart transgressed, and was overcome; and so be all they that are born of him. Thus infirmity [sinfulness] was made permanent. . . .' 'This is my first and last saying, that it had been better not to have given the earth unto Adam: or else, when it was given him, to have restrained him from sinning. For what profit is it for men now in this present time to live in heaviness, and after death to look for punishment? O thou Adam, what hast thou done? for, though it was thou that sinned, thou are not fallen alone, but we all that come of thee.'

The two significant features in these tentative, first-century Judaic views are the notion of an inherited depravity or infirmity, and the notion of inherited guilt. Even primitively the two ideas are essentially independent since a man may consanguineously acquire contamination and guilt without himself being depraved, as witness the whole pre-exilic history of holy Israel. The Paradise story, which had been neglected by all the prophets and postexilic scribes, now began to serve not only as an explanation of death, the derangement of nature and the universal existence of evil in the world, but also of the hereditary presence in mankind of an infirmity or tendency to sinfulness. Meanwhile in the rabbinical literature, the Targum, Talmud and Midrashim, dating from 200 B.C. to A.D. 300, the endowments of Adam had been greatly magnified. He was represented as having been of enormous stature, physically perfect and of surpassing beauty and wisdom, a bright angel possessing extraordinary powers of perception and enjoying unblemished bliss. He had been ministered to by angels and had even been an object of their worship. It was variously supposed that he and Eve had lived in Eden, enjoying a happy married life, for a period ranging from a few hours to seven years before his superior endowments and unique privileges had been taken away as punishment for disobeying God's command. When conceived on this heroic scale by thinkers now familiar with the notions of incorruptibility and perfection, it was clear that Adam's capacity to sin constituted an almost inexplicable blemish in his otherwise angelic character.

The New Testament scarcely more than touches on this subject. Jesus holds no doctrine of sin or evil and does not even refer to the Garden of Eden; he simply assumes that all have sinned. In the Pauline letters it is made to appear that man is sinful not because he commits sin, but rather that he commits sin because he is sinful — a highly important point in Christian belief — and sinfulness to Paul is, if not an inherent virulence identifiable with the flesh, at least an alien power which resides in the flesh and uses it as an instrument, this emphasis on the evil of the flesh being an original note in the Pauline teaching. Only once does Paul refer to the devil, 'the god of this world [who] hath blinded the minds of them which believe not' (to Paul skepticism of his new doctrine was the most heinous of moral offenses), and only incidentally does he refer to the Paradise story: 'Wherefore, as by one man sin entered into the world, and death by sin; and so death passed upon all men, for that all have sinned.' Paul was less concerned with the remote origins of sin and evil than with the possibilities of immediate redemption from both. The author of Revelation refers to the scenery of Paradise, and particularly to the 'tree of life'; he mentions the war in heaven when 'Michael and his angels fought against the dragon . . . and the great dragon was cast out, that old serpent, called the Devil, and Satan, which deceiveth the whole world: he was cast out into the earth, and his angels were cast out with him'; but for him, as for Paul, sin is chiefly the denial of Jesus and the persistence in unbelieving Judaism; like Paul, he throws no light on the mystery of Adam's sin or the means by which the first man's sinfulness was transmitted to posterity.

With both Testaments saying so little on the subject, the fathers of the early church were free to develop their doctrines as they elected. Justin attributed evil to the angels who had 'transgressed the Divine appointment, and by sinful intercourse with women produced offspring who are demons.' These demons 'sowed among men all manner of wickedness.' Justin is thus the earliest Christian authority to accept the fallen angel theory. Origen in his earlier years held the Paradise story to be an allegory describing the fall of all individual souls from a previous celestial existence, to which event he attributed evil; but in later life he became convinced of an inborn uncleanness inherited from Adam by virtue of the fact that Adam's children were present in seminal form in the father of the race. Thus, as opposed to Justin, he supported the theory of the forbidden fruit. Tertullian, subscribing to the latter theory, conceived that every human soul is a 'branch' of Adam's soul, reproducing its qualities and therefore its corruption. Irenaeus and Athenasius conceived that Adam's sinfulness resulted not so much from an inherent derangement in his nature as from the loss of those supernatural graces with which he had originally been endowed. Clement of Alexandria went so far as to repudiate the idea that death was in any way a consequence of the Fall, and Chrysostom rejected both the doctrine of inherited guilt and the inherent sinfulness of human nature, although paradoxically he was condemned and exiled chiefly because of his resolute denunciation of the vices of the clergy and the court.

It was a British monk, Pelagius, arriving in Rome sometime between 398 and 402, who stirred up what was perhaps the most important controversy in Christian history and forced, through the medium of Augustine, the crystallization of Christian tenets on the origin of evil. Pelagius's antecedents are unknown, though one enemy asserted that he was of too humble an origin to have had a liberal education; nevertheless before he distinguished himself as a heretic he had written three books of unquestioned orthodoxy on the Trinity. Appalled by the lax morality of the great mass of nominal Christians in the empire's capital, he set himself to rouse them to a sense of their duty to God. In this moral reformation he was supported by a lay friend, Coelestius, and a pupil, Julian of Eclanum; though the subsequent furore is known as the Pelagian heresy, it appears to have been Julian who was chiefly responsible for the doctrinal arguments. The Pelagian heresy was based on the premise, nominally accepted by the church, that man enjoys free will and the power to choose between good and evil. As incompatible with this premise Julian questioned both inherited sinfulness or inherited guilt, and these and related issues quickly brought the three friends into conflict with numerous bishops. Against these Julian declared, 'we ought to weigh and not count opinions' and would have set reason above authority, but this argument in the eyes of the orthodox was the fruit of evil vanity.

The major points advanced by Julian were that the chief glory of man is in his reason and free will, which remain unimpaired by previous choices. Sin is choosing that which is contrary to what reason indicates to be good conduct. The desires of the flesh are, as such, not evil. Every man is born in precisely the same condition morally as Adam was before he sinned, and hence there can be and have been sinless men. Adam sinned through free will, and his descendants also sin through free will. Neither the death of Adam (who would have died in any case) nor the death of men after him is attributable to sinfulness. The idea of either inherited sin or inherited guilt is unthinkable; therefore children are not damned at birth, baptism is not necessary to virtue, and the redemptive power of the grace of Christ is not a requisite to salvation.

After several condemnations Pelagius and Coelestius were denounced as heretics and exiled by the Emperor Honorius (418), while simultaneously a Carthage council in a series of nine emphatic and uncompromising canons anathematized anyone who held death to be a natural necessity, who denied the presence of original sin in children, who assigned any form of salvation to infants dying unbaptized, and who failed to see in grace the indispensable condition of redemption.

The refutation of the Pelagian heresy was largely the work of Augustine, Bishop of Hippo, a diocese not far from Carthage in North Africa. Over a period of years he prepared no fewer than fifteen weighty treatises on punishment and the nature of sin, baptism of infants, divine grace and human corruption, and related topics. The Pelagian heresy is chiefly important for the replies it drew from Augustine, who has been called 'the father of orthodoxy,' 'the supreme authority,' 'the greatest among the fathers of the church,' the theologian 'whose formulas maintain up to today their supremacy in the whole extent of Western Christianity.' Since the accepted Christian answer to the conjoint problems of sin and evil stems from Augustine, it is a warrantable digression to examine briefly his character and life.

ii

Born in 345 at Thagaste, a village near Carthage, Augustine was the only child of a pagan father and a Christian mother. As a small boy he was led by his mother to accept without question the teachings of the church and was probably made familiar with the Old and New Testaments, which were then available in Latin codices. He never possessed any extensive knowledge of Greek and acquired all that he knew of Hellenic culture through Latin translations. In his nineteenth year, the reading of a now lost work of Cicero called *Hortensius* profoundly affected him and set him to seeking wisdom in its ultimate and highest form. *Hortensius* was an exhortation to the study of philosophy, and Augustine was sorely troubled by the absence of Christ from a work which he so admired; he was also embarrassed by the fact that the style of the pagan author was distinctly superior to that of the scriptures, and particularly the Old Testament, which he found to be not only inferior in rhetoric but full of things to be despised as 'old wives' fables.' From reading pagan philosophy he wandered to Manichaeism. He remained with the Manichaeans for nine years only to become engrossed, after a period of confused skepticism, with the mystical theories of Neoplatonism as propounded by Plotinus and his student Porphyry. From Porphyry particularly Augustine learned to seek truth outside the material world and came by the certainty that God is eternal and neither subject to change in his parts nor in his motions, and that to experience God, however partially, in the transcendent experience of ecstasy is to enjoy identification with the divine.

Trained as a rhetorician, Augustine practiced first at Thagaste, then successively at Carthage, Rome and Milan, achieving indifferent success. In Milan he came under the influence of Bishop Ambrose, who emphasized the allegorical nature of the Old Testament stories and paved the way for Augustine's literal acceptance of what he had hitherto characterized as 'old wives' fables.' It was while he was studying Christian doctrine under Ambrose that he encountered the major crisis of his life.

All the while that he had been seeking the middling ground of truth somewhere between pagan philosophy, Neoplatonic mysticism and Christian legend, a robust physique had been demanding and obtaining satisfaction. As a young man continence had seemed to him to be out of the question, and when he was nineteen years old he had taken a concubine, a practice then tolerated even by Christians, and immediately had had a son. As a Manichaean he had learned that matter, and therefore flesh, are but prisons for a divine spark; as a Neoplatonist he had accepted that truth is to be found not in appetite and lust, but along that road of fasting and mortification that leads to ecstasy; and under the long-continued deprecations of his Christian mother, fortified now by a Christian bishop whom he had every reason to admire, he had come to look with shame upon his sex life. The Christian tenets that reproduction was frivolous and futile in the face of the coming day of doom, the Christian legend of the immaculate conception of Christ and the Christian esteem which was generally accorded asceticism and self-immolation, all contrived to engender a painful conflict abruptly precipitated in Milan when his mother insisted that he take a legal wife and send his concubine, for whom he had great affection, back to Africa. His mother found a suitable bride for him, but she was, unfortunately, not yet of marriageable age. In the separation from the companion of his youth and from his son he was severely torn by the struggle between the spirit and the flesh: "Give me chastity," he said, "but not yet!" He came upon the *Life of Saint Anthony,* which vividly pointed the virtues of continence, but this book only caused him to suffer as Anthony had suffered and, not having the good saint's strength, while waiting for his bride-to-be to mature he took another concubine. The more he pondered over the nature of God the more acute became his sense of guilt, and the more evil he found in the world and in his life.

One day while talking with a friend who knew of his conflict, he learned of two officials, like himself betrothed, who had resolved to renounce the world for a life of asceticism; he was so overcome by their courage and strength that he rushed out of the house in tears and flung himself down in the garden, sobbing, "How long! tomorrow and tomorrow!" Suddenly he thought he heard the voice of a child singing in the next garden, "Take up and read; take up and read"; perhaps the words belonged to some childish game, but he afterward could remember nothing of the kind, and he immediately applied them to himself as a divine command. Returning to the house he took up a volume of St. Paul's Epistles, opened it and read the first words that met his eyes: 'Not in rioting and drunkenness, not in chambering and wantonness, not in strife and envying. But put ye on the Lord Jesus Christ, and make not provision for the flesh, to fulfill the lusts thereof.'

This experience of the garden, which occurred when he was thirty-two, led him finally to renounce all thought of marriage, and was chiefly instrumental in his conversion to the Christian faith. He was baptized by Bishop Ambrose the next year, though for a protracted period thereafter he appears to have continued the study of Neoplatonism. He resigned his chair of rhetoric at Milan and, returning to Africa, he went into retirement with some friends on a small estate at Thagaste and at the age of thirty-seven entered the priesthood. Five years later he was consecrated Bishop of the nearby city of Hippo. A rule forbade the translation of bishops, and Augustine was therefore fixed for life, at the age of forty-two, in the small North African seaport where he had attained the bishopric. Having little drain upon his time he gave himself over to letters and theology, entering into every argument and addressing himself to colleagues in every part of Asia and Europe, as well as laboring upon more original ideas and formal works. Among his numerous books were fifteen on the Trinity to which he devoted thirty years. For most of his life he was engaged in heated controversies with other ecclesiastics, and many of his theological conclusions were reached as expedients to get himself out of embarrassing debates. Although Christian doctrines had by this time become fairly fixed in their major outlines, he was the first to attempt to unify them into a body of belief that would have no internal contradictions. His work, as represented in his letters, tracts and books, was to set the problems, and in part the answers, of Christian theory for a thousand years, and although his ideas were to be supplanted in part by later thinkers, they, more than the ideas of any other man, were responsible for the theological and social pattern of the next fifteen centuries.

Augustine's approach to theology was by the method known as 'dialectic,' which is the art of investigating the truth or falsity of opinions by arguing from certain explicitly stated but not necessarily substantiated premises. Inasmuch as during his experiences with Manichaeism, skepticism and Neoplatonism, he had at one time or another been skeptical of almost all beliefs, he first inquired whether a man can ever be certain of anything. He proceeded to the demonstration that such a thing as certitude exists by such arguments as the following: For example, he said, if we say there are four elements in the world, we may be certain that there are not five; if we say a soul is immortal, we may be certain that it cannot die; if we say we are awake, we may be certain that we are not asleep. I say I am conscious that I exist, therefore I do exist, and even if I say I am mistaken, some sort of existence is necessary for me to err. Since these things are certain, they demonstrate the possibility of certitude and the existence of demonstrable truth.

The demonstration of certitude is *ipso facto* a demonstration of the existence of God, since 'God' himself is 'truth' and therefore synonymous with 'certitude.' God is also proved to exist by the statement of the Holy

Scriptures which no one can deny. He is also proved to exist by the fact of 'universal consent' — his existence has been believed by all men, everywhere, and at all times ('with the exception of a few in whom nature has become outrageously depraved,' and as for these, he asks, 'Why should I consider the method of dealing with them, when it is doubtful whether they ought to be dealt with at all?'). The existence of God is furthermore proved by 'order': every cause is one of an endless chain of causes, else there would be no order; and since there must be a first cause, all order leads back to the true First Cause, or God. God is also proved to exist by the unity of things, such as stones, trees, animals, friends, states, armies, for the unity of parts can be derived only from a unity of a whole, and the Whole is God. God is also proved to exist by beauty: as order in the universe is evidence of the existence of a father of order, and unity is evidence of the supreme and eternal unity, so beauty is evidence of perfect beauty, or God. Those who deny these proofs, said Augustine, are so lost in vice and so degraded by sin that they have been made blind to the good and the true and have become veritable fools.

However, so little do we really know of God, Augustine admitted, that we really know him better in not knowing him at all. Our only exact knowledge of God consists in knowing how little we actually know about him. God is ineffable, for words are of too coarse a texture to describe his divinity: nevertheless, his attributes may be reduced to these twelve: 'eternal, immortal, incorruptible, unchangeable, living, wise, powerful, beautiful, righteous, good, blessed, spirit,' while we may be sure that he is not to be identified with 'Angels, Virtues, Powers, Archangels, Thrones, Seats, or Principalities,' all of which are less than God. When the Bible speaks of God's anger, his repentance, his jealousy or his compassion, it is merely using metaphors to insinuate itself into the minds of men who are unable to comprehend the incomprehensible and ineffable.

Concerning the world, Augustine conceived that God made it from *nihil,* which is, he emphasized, to be read as *absolutely nothing.* 'No attention should be paid to the ravings of men who think that *nihil* should be understood to mean something. . . . They have lost their senses by zeal in contradicting.' Out of this 'nothing' which no one is to take as meaning 'something,' God created the world by the Word.

At first thought, the existence of evil seems to deny either God's goodness or his omnipotence; this paradox is not to be believed, however, for God is both omnipotent and good, even in permitting the existence of evil. The nature of every created thing is good; this good nature is subject to corruption not because of defect in God's workmanship, but simply because it was made from nothing, from *nihil,* rather than from the substance of God himself. 'As anything is corrupted, in that proportion it approaches decrease . . . tends to nonexistence. God exists immutably and incorruptibly, while what is called nothing is clearly altogether non-existent; and since, after setting before yourself existence and non-existence . . . why are you at a loss to tell regarding any nature what in it is from God, and what from nothing?' That is to say, evil is the absence of goodness as darkness is the absence of light, silence is the absence of sound, a crooked line is a straight line the beauty of which has been destroyed without introducing any new material. To be sure, evil is not in itself good, but the fact that evil as well as good exists is, one might say, the greater good. The circumstance that God's creation contains pain, hunger, death, terrific volcanoes, venomous serpents, troublesome mosquitoes and other evil features so numerous that examples will occur to everyone, is entirely comprehensible: these evil features embellish the beauty of creation as antitheses set off an exquisite poem; as 'the oppositions of contraries lend beauty to language, so the beauty of the course of the world is achieved by the opposition of contraries, arranged, as it were, by an eloquence not of words but of things.' The executioner, the prostitute, man's sexual organs, considered in themselves are thoroughly detestable, but each is necessary to society and contributes to the harmony and perfection of the whole.

Man occupies an intermediate position between *nihil* and God, being of course greater than *nihil,* and also greater than plants or animals by virtue of the fact that he possesses a soul; but he is less than God in consequence of the fact that he is imperfect. He was not created imperfect, however, for in the beginning God looked with favor upon him, even creating him in his very image. And then something happened to destroy this perfection.

When Augustine came to the paradox presented by the good God of Christian theory and the evil of life, the miserable mortal of fact, he was, of course, wrestling with the problem that had tried the best intellects throughout the entire history of mankind. Explanations of evil had been offered by the Egyptians, the people of Mesopotamia and the Greeks, but Egyptian and Assyrian were almost forgotten languages, and Augustine read no Greek. The only explanations of evil that lay ready to his hand were the sacred writings of the Jews and Christians.

The skepticism of his early years had given way, after his conversion, to a belief in the relative infallibility of faith. Of all uncertainties, faith was least uncertain. He considered his faith in his friends, his obedience to the authority of his physicians, the vast number of things which he had never seen but which he accepted as true, such as distant cities and strange animals, and the confidence which he had in the records of secular history — if such things as these are to be accepted on faith, he argued, why should one hesitate to believe the Christian scriptures? Surely there would follow the overthrow of all literature, 'if what is supported by such a strong popular belief and established by the uniform testimony of so many men and so many times is put into such suspicion that it is not to have the credit and authority of common history.' Above all, he had faith in the power of the Christian church: 'It is not without reason that so eminent height of the authority of the Christian faith is diffused throughout the entire world'; and so deeply was he impressed by the universal character of the church, by the purity of its doctrine and wisdom, its authority 'inaugurated by miracles, nourished by hope, enlarged by love, and established by age,' that he declared he would not believe the scriptures themselves except as moved to do so by the authority of the church. Having arrived at the conclusion that the authority of the church was unimpeachable, it followed that 'we are bound to receive as true whatever the canon shows to have been said by even one prophet or apostle or evangelist'; and thus he came circuitously to what is in practical consequences his most important dictum: 'Nothing is to be accepted save on the authority of Scripture, for greater is this authority than all the powers of the human mind.' In the scriptures there is nought but absolute truth; in them is all that is true, while they condemn the false that may be learned elsewhere. So Augustine was now constrained, in order to find the explanation for the misfortunes of humanity, to turn to the scriptural stories which as 'old wives' fables' he had once disdained.

iii

To the Jews who had told the stories of the Garden of Eden and of the fallen angels around their campfires at a time probably before that of Saul and David, they were veritable accounts of things that had taken place in the long, long ago when Yahweh had been accustomed to walk in his garden in the cool of the morning, to eat of its fruit and to admire its trees.

Where the Jews got the story of Paradise has not been discovered, but it contains so many elements foreign to the beliefs of Israel that it must be inferred they acquired it whole or piecemeal from some of their Asiatic neighbors. The tree 'which is in the midst of the garden' is identified in

Genesis both as the 'tree of knowledge' and the 'tree of life'; in Mesopotamia the two ideas were essentially identical, since to all the ancients wisdom was magic or that which enabled a man to avoid death and to live like a god. The serpent might represent any supernatural being such as would mingle with the gods, animals and men in a Syrian, Arabian, Persian or Mesopotamian oasis; he speaks as if he were on terms of intimacy with the divine circle, and is even in a position to say what the deity knew; he is aware of the potentiality of the fruit, knowing that if Adam and Eve ate of it 'ye shall be as gods' (the reading 'knowing good and evil' is accepted to be a postexilic interpolation), and only neglecting to say that in order to continue living in the divine estate they must continue eating of the fruit; he knows that Yahweh is deceiving them when he threatens, 'Ye shall not eat of it, neither shall ye touch, lest ye die.' (It was thus that Ea had deceived Adamu and prevented him from eating the food and drink of the gods and attaining immortality.) He is proved to be speaking truly by the fact that when the fruit is eaten, Adam and Eve do not die as Yahweh had said they would, while Yahweh himself declares, 'Behold, the man is become as one of us.'

Thus the episode of the forbidden fruit appears to be a dramatic narrative intended to explain how man's ancient felicity had been lost in consequence of Adam's transgression, which was aspiring to be as a god; to this presumption he was tempted by one deity, symbolized in the serpent, who was pitting himself against a superior deity. This is a familiar theme. In its original form it was probably embellished with many lively details which editorial purification has stripped from Genesis, and it is interesting to recount one of the several other recensions, which has not been so purified.

In the apocryphal History of the Creation and of the Transgression of Adam, the serpent has watched Eve until he can get her alone, when he approaches her and asks:

Why dost thou eat of the fruits of all the trees, and of this beautiful fruit thou eatest not?

Eve said: Because the Lord God did command us not to eat of that fruit, saying: When ye eat ye shall die.

The serpent said: God is willing to deceive you; He was like you, as long as He had not eaten of that fruit; when He ate thereof, He reached the glory of Divinity. Wherefore He told you to eat not of that fruit, that ye should not become equal unto Him, and sharers of His glory and of His throne.

Then she took and ate of the fruit, and instantly she was bereft of her glory. When Adam came and saw that the woman was despoiled of her splendor, he was grieved, and said: Didst thou eat of the fruit?

Eve said: It is a most delicious one, take and taste thyself, and thou shalt see how sweet it is.

Adam said: I cannot eat of it and be stripped like thee.

Eve said: I ate too much, and therefore have been stripped; do thou eat only a little.

Adam said: I cannot eat and be stripped of my glory like thee.

Eve said: If thou eatest, God shall not be wroth with thee, for He loves thee very much.

Then he took the fruit and examined it, and was afraid to be stripped like the woman. He would not eat it, but the woman wept and entreated him saying: 'If we die let us die together, and if we live let us live together, separate me not from thee.' And Adam as he looked at the beauty of the woman was beside himself; for though she had lost her glory she was beautiful, her body was of a dazzling white like a pearl; for she was newly created, and God had created and decked her with his own hands. And Adam after much thought said: 'It may be that God will have mercy upon me and strip me not. And if I be deprived of my glory when shall He have mercy upon me? Better were it for me to die than to be separated and parted from my wife.' For he did not understand that had he kept the commandment, God could have created another and much more handsome woman than she. Having held the fruit in his hand, and examined it for about three hours, he said: 'I cannot live without my wife.' So he cast aside the word of God, and in obedience to the word of the woman he ate the fruit, and was stripped of his glory. Not that the fruit was evil, for there was not any evil fruit in the Garden, but the evil was in what Eve did in despising the word and the commandment of God, and in listening to the word of the serpent. And Adam despised the word and the commandment of God and listened to that of his wife.

Wherefore they were deprived of their glory and they sought and covered themselves with the leaves of a fig-tree; for they thought that a covering of leaves could hide them from the sight of God; for God always appeared unto them, coming gently and talking with them in a sweet voice. But at that moment when they ate the fruit and were stripped of their splendor, and had covered their nakedness with leaves, the voice came from the fig-tree, crying out, and saying: 'Adam, where art thou?'

And Adam said: Lord, I heard thy voice, and I ran and hid myself.

The Lord said: Why didst thou run away and hide thyself?

Adam said: I ran away and hid myself, because I was naked, and was ashamed before thee.

The Lord said: I had covered you with glory, why did you strip yourselves of it? Did you eat of the fruit?

Adam said: This woman that thou hast created, she deceived me.

And the Lord spake unto the woman, saying: Woman, didst thou do that?

And the woman said: Lord, the serpent that thou hast created, he deceived me.

Then the Lord was wroth against them, and said unto Adam: Because thou hast done this, and didst not listen to my counsel, but didst quickly listen to the counsel of thy wife, instead of this immortal plant, thorns shall be brought forth for thee; in the sweat of thy face shalt thou eat thy bread; for dust thou wast and unto dust shalt thou return.

And turning unto Eve, He said: Because thou hast done this, I will greatly multiply thy sorrow, in thy confinement thou shalt suffer death, in sorrow thou shalt eat thy bread, and in sorrow thou shalt live all the days of thy life.

And turning unto the serpent He said: Thou art cursed above all cattle, upon thy breast and belly thou shalt creep, and dust thou shalt eat all the days of thy life. I will put enmity between thee and the woman, and between thy seed and her seed; it shall bruise thy head and thou shalt bruise his heel.

And God commanded the angels to drive them out from the Garden, and with a flaming sword to keep the ways of the Garden of Life. So they drove Adam and Eve out from the Garden.

And they went out to a place dark and gloomy; there they remained the whole day and they ate nothing, but inconsolable, they wept and bemoaned themselves. And six days after, the Lord had mercy upon them, and sent his angel to take them out of the darkness, and to guide and bring them to this bright world, where he shewed them the fruit-bearing trees, with which they had to satisfy themselves and live. And when Adam and his wife saw it, they said: 'Although it is not so good, and the light and fruits of this world are not equal to the light and the fruits of the Garden; yet through these we shall neither die nor remain in darkness.'

So they were comforted.

In the Genesis account the only reason given why the serpent should tempt Eve is because he 'was more subtle than any beast of the field.' This, no doubt, is the echo of the reputation of some ancient god. In earlier passages of the recension quoted above, the serpent is identified with Satan who, it is expressly stated, has been expelled from heaven for refusing to worship God, and for wishing to put his throne as high as the throne of God. Since Satan dares not enter the Garden in *propria persona,* he moves as a serpent to deceive Adam's wife.

iv

Thus the legend of the rebellious angel, presumably Kingu in disguise, meets and fuses with the legend of the forbidden fruit, the tree of magic or eternal life, to supply Augustine with an explanation for the origin of evil. By his own logic he could no longer disdain the tales of the Old Testament as old wives' fables but must perforce accept them as facts of history. In terms of his description of creation as something posed somewhere between God and *nihil,* good in so far as it contains the substance of God, evil in so far as it lacks that substance and approaches *nihil,* the episode in Paradise revealed that before the Fall the creation had contained more of God and less of *nihil* than at the present time. Adam, for whatever period he remained within the Garden, possessed such power that absolutely nothing could resist his will; he had everything that a rational creature needed, including the power to live forever. It would have been easy for him, so Augustine argued, had he willed to keep God's injunction, to have reached the stage of perfect freedom and to have attained an estate subordinate only to that of God himself. God had required of him almost nothing in the way of service, imposing on him only a very light precept in order to remind him who was Lord. It was so easy for Adam to obey the command, so difficult for him to disobey, that his disobedience amounted to pride, envy, lust, self-love, a desire even to be equal to God himself; and because God was just it was necessary for him to be swift and severe. Since in his pride Adam sought to be his own satisfaction, God abandoned him to himself, to live by the sweat of his brow, dissatisfied, doomed to die in body as he had willingly become dead in spirit, forever out of the bounds of grace and condemned to eternal death except he be delivered by God's redemption.

One difficulty in this interpretation lay in the irrationality of a good and just God punishing not only Adam and Eve, but all their blameless offspring through ages without end, for the original sin of disobedience. In this complete abandonment of any semblance of human charity, divine despotism would seem to approach perpetual cruelty. A second difficulty lay in the necessity of transmitting Adam's uncleanness or sinful state to his posterity; the idea that the seeds of his progeny were in Adam when he sinned and were thereby defiled did not appeal to Augustine's logical mind, and he was forced to seek a basis not only for perpetual punishment but also for perpetual guilt. He found the answer to both problems in sexual intercourse.

The pressure of Augustine's sensuality is adequately revealed by his reply to pleas for continence, and by the circumstance that he took a second concubine shortly after his mother had persuaded him to send the first one back from Milan, and this in spite of his deep affection for the mother of his son and the fact that he was living near his prospective bride. The conflict here engendered could not have been lessened by his extraordinary affection for his devout and saintly mother, which he describes vividly in his *Confessions*. Apart from the asceticism of Neoplatonism and Christianity, the opposition between his desire for divine purity and the desires of the flesh must have been further aggravated by his experience with Manichaeism, which held that all matter, and therefore flesh, is evil, and that sexual intercourse is essentially Satanic and to be abhorred. The circumstances of his conversion, the lines of Paul which had effected it, and the fact that afterward he viewed his previous life in blackest colors, all must have aggravated his ever-present sense of uncleanness and helped to shape the later conviction that sexual intercourse was a transgression against the deity and a defilement of the spirit.

Augustine was the churchman who more than any other resisted the heresies of Manichaeism and Donatism; he, as much as any other, introduced into Christianity the doctrines of Neoplatonism and gave to the faith a seemingly philosophic fabric; and, first among the fathers, sketched in the pattern of the monastic life which from his day to the Reformation was officially and popularly conceived to be the highest ideal of Christian conduct. But in these matters his work stands not alone, but complemented by the work of others. However, it is to Augustine alone that the credit must go for giving Christianity an instrument of logical persuasion of such force as no other human institution had hitherto possessed: the doctrine, based on the defilement of sexual intercourse, of infant damnation and the necessity of redemption by baptism.

No evidence reveals that Augustine considered the fruit of Eden to be an allegorical symbol of the discovery of desire on the part of Adam and Eve, though later theologians, taking their clue from the meager reference to the fig-leaf aprons, wrote this into the doctrine. Rather, for the Bishop of Hippo, the fruit was simply a token of disobedience, itself a sin so heinous that it contained all sins and was necessarily greater than any single sin. But apart from Adam's sin, the sin of sex was, among sins, paramount. Had Adam and Eve escaped the Fall they would presumably have propagated, had they propagated at all, by some asexual process, perhaps by a further excision of ribs; but having sinned in disobeying God, they were condemned to propagate by lust, by self-interest, by the pleasure of the senses, by an act that in every respect was antithetical to the notion of deity; mankind must perpetually engage in sin in order that it should continue to exist, and its seed must be continually reinfected with corruption in the very act of propagation. To epitomize that corruption Augustine used the word 'concupiscence.' Through concupiscence the whole of humanity for all time was born both sinful and guilty, a *massa perditionis* out of which only certain individuals were to be lifted to grace by that special favor of God which had been perfected in the Christian sacrament, baptism. 'Even the infant whose life is but a day upon the earth' is born an offender in the eyes of God and is damned without this precious rite, though since it adds no personal sin to the original sin inherited from Adam, its punishment in the other world is comparatively mild.

In sinning, Adam did not surprise God, for to suppose that such were the case would be to impugn God's omniscience. On the contrary, God foresaw not only Adam's sin but the sins of all his descendants: this is not to say that in sinning men are doing what God wishes them to do, or that God wills them to sin, but only that they are doing what he has foreseen they will do. It is just that their depravity is so great that they are impotent to do good actions or otherwise be redeemed without divine grace, and God has predestined who is and is not to enjoy this grace, and therefore to enjoy the power of election between sinning and not sinning. Consequently, those who do sin, do so out of the pitiful necessity of God's predestination.

If one can judge theological doctrines by the criterion of survival, no more satisfactory explanation for evil than that propounded by Augustine has since been found. Yet however such a finespun theory might appeal to the erudite, it remained inadequate for the common run of men. By logical deductions from Eve and the forbidden fruit, and by the aid of concupiscence, logicians might be able to explain to their entire satisfaction thorns and thistles, mosquitoes, aches and pains and all the other evils that Augustine considered, and even death; but to the slaves, servants, sailors, soldiers and merchants who made up the bulk of the Christian population the forbidden fruit appeared to be no more than a familiar dramaturgical accessory. They were, moreover, generally free from any sense of guilt in sex. On the whole, unsympathetic to asceticism and unaccustomed to rigorous logic, yet thoroughly familiar with dramatic symbolism, they proceeded immediately to identify the serpent as the true villain of the story: it was perfectly clear to their untutored minds that this creature was only the Devil in a clever disguise. And so it came about that Augustine's emphasis on the story of Paradise had a wholly un-anticipated effect: it served in the imaginations of the masses to elevate Satan, the fallen angel, to a position subordinate only to Christ himself. All the pagan powers of evil, their numbers not one bit diminished in Christianity, waited only to be mobilized by the King of Hell to annoy the faithful with more plagues, droughts, boils, thunderstorms and other demonic torments than had ever been inflicted by the pagan gods. If the Christians hurried baptism it was as much to avoid the devil and his minions as to placate God.

v

On the death of Theodosius, the last ruler of the Empire proper who was capable of military leadership, the West began to go to pieces. A year later Alaric invaded Greece and attacked Italy; invasion followed invasion until by the middle of the fifth century Gaul, Spain and Africa had been lost, and in 476 Rome, thrice sacked, had a barbarian king. With the de-struction of Imperial power the church was forced to fend for itself, its only weapon being the conversion of such barbarians as had not hitherto enjoyed its blessings. In later centuries the Christians accused the Saracens of cruelty and bloodiness, but in their own missionary work they set a ruthless example. They went about procuring converts on the grand scale by appealing directly to kings and chiefs, since these leaders, once con-vinced that Christianity was to their interest, could force the baptism of their subjects en masse. Thus Augustine claimed to have had ten thou-sand Angli baptized in one day, and Heraclius baptized one hundred thousand people in one year. Charlemagne decreed that any who rejected baptism should be put to death, and there is no estimate of the number upon whom this decree was executed in the thirty-three years of relent-less warfare which he pursued in building the Holy Roman Empire. It required over two centuries of warfare to Christianize Scandinavia, and almost as long to spread the light across Middle Europe. The cost of Christianizing the whole of Europe is estimated at from eight to ten mil-lion lives, while the necessarily late introduction of Christianity into the New World was to cost twelve million native lives and utterly destroy the civilization of the Aztecs and the Incas.

As Imperial disintegration divided the whole of Europe into principali-ties, so it divided the church along the lines of the chief bishoprics, Anti-och, Alexandria, Constantinople, Jerusalem and Rome, which were now set at each other in a race for power. Rome was destined to survive, but the Rome See established its supremacy only after some centuries of vicissitude and by the aid of elaborate fabrications and forgeries in ecclesiastic literature, bribery and subversive intrigue, and a degree of ruthlessness which was the envy of kings themselves.

In the eastern churches, from the fourth century onwards, priests of every rank continued to be called 'popes' in imitation of Mithraism in which the priest was *papa;* but the bishop of Rome, who had, as it were, inherited the crown of Caesar, early arrogated to himself the exclusive prerogative to this familial title. There appeared in Matthew's gospel the Mithraic allusion, 'Thou art Peter, and upon this rock [*petra*] I will build my church; and the gates of hell shall not prevail against it. And I will give unto thee the keys of the kingdom of heaven: and whatsoever thou shalt bind [forbid] on earth shall be bound in heaven.' This passage is not recorded by the other three evangelists, although Mark, who strongly favored Peter, and also Luke narrate the incident out of which it is said to have arisen; nor is it referred to by Paul or any other writer. It is consequently accepted as a late interpolation, possibly made by Clement of Rome to support his own see and the one which claimed Peter as its founder. This verse was first advanced by Gregory I as a divine fiat to the Pope of Rome authorizing him to dictate to all Christians in ecclesiastic matters. Under the spurious Isidorean Decretals, forged presumably in the province of Tours about 850, the Roman See fortuitously came into control of the Frankish bishops and extended its nominal authority over the entire north of Europe. Basing its claim on the Petrine text, Rome now began to dream of a vast theocracy which would rule the world. The hope was long delayed while the ambitions and jealousies of kings, dukes, barons and princelings kept the whole of Europe in a state of war, and the conflict between Rome and other bishoprics kept the church itself in a divided state. It was not until the Saracens, who held the east, began to threaten the trans-Mediterranean lands that the dream gave promise of fulfillment.

Conceiving that the Holy Land, and secondarily the great cities of Asia Minor, could be recovered for the church, Urban II in 1095 instigated a vast penitential pilgrimage to Jerusalem which was also to be a war against the infidel. He promised all who participated therein freedom from the common law, remission of sin, and blessed immortality. This, the First Crusade, proceeded southwards across Europe, massacring, torturing and plundering without restraint. Two divisions indulged in such excess in Hungary that they were destroyed; a third, after killing some ten thousand Jews in the valley of the Rhine, was dissipated in the south; of two others multitudes perished by the way and the remainder arrived in Constantinople with sadly diminished numbers after having plundered the Greeks who had given them aid. Many were sold as slaves to pay for the feeding of the rest. Seven thousand out of a number variously estimated at 150,000 to 300,000 finally crossed the Bosporus and perished utterly at the hands of the Turks. A heap of whitening bones alone remained to testify to subsequent crusaders the fate of this, the so-called 'People's Crusade.'

Two years later a better organized military force, under Godfrey of Bouillon, succeeded in taking Jerusalem and founded the Latin kingdom of Palestine, which endured intact for nearly a hundred years and in a nominal form for a century longer. A month's siege was required to take the city, and no pagan army proved to be more ferocious than were the Christians. Divided amongst themselves by jealous leaders and mutual hatreds, the only unifying force was their hatred of the infidel. Jerusalem withstood a month's siege, and when it fell at last the Jews were herded into the synagogues and burned alive, and the chroniclers boasted that the crusaders rode their horses to the Temple knee-deep in the blood of disbelievers. At nightfall, 'sobbing for excess of joy,' as they reported, the crusaders came at last to the Holy Sepulcher to raise their bloodstained hands in prayer. On the next day, in the name of the Jesus who was supposed to have been buried in the sepulcher, they slaughtered a great multitude of people of every age, old men and women, maidens, children and mothers with infants, by way of a solemn sacrifice.

Eight times during the next two centuries the conflict between Christianity and Islam flared up in the east. As the papacy saw its chance to weaken an emperor, to enrich itself, or simply to divert the people of Europe from interstate warfare, the crusading effort was repeated. Crusading became a Christian vocation and, the Christians having learned the principle of organized and ruthless warfare in practice against the infidel, it was not long before they were applying its technique to themselves in efforts to stamp out Satanic heresy.

When, in effect, Gregory the Great prohibited the laity from reading the scriptures, he was moved by a deep concern lest Christians misinterpret the sacred allegories and thereby fall into dogmatic error. If the prohibition was successful in this respect, it was equally successful in creating a new and fertile soil for heresy in the form of a vast, illiterate populace. People who were not permitted to read the Holy Book had little reason to learn to read at all, and all history testifies that it is only the written word which can elevate the intellectual level of the masses above crass superstition. The age called Dark derived its gloom not from any pall cast by the fall of Rome, nor the ignorance of barbarian invaders, nor yet by war, nor plague, nor famine, and most certainly not by any decadence of the human intellect, but simply from the circumstance that reason and criticism had been condemned and displaced by Christian faith.

The medieval soil was rich for heresy, and worse. In spite of the forceful edicts of Constantine, Constantius and Theodosius, in spite of the Justinian Code and the anathemas of many popes, heresy had never ceased. It was not because of the absence of unbelief, but because of the physical inability of the church to undertake persecutions in a rigorous manner that dogmatic disagreement received negligible attention from the seventh until the eleventh century. Here and there, when admonitions failed to work, a heretic was punished, but history furnishes scarcely more than a bare mention of their death. In 1012 ten dissenters, and in 1017 twelve more, were burned at Orléans, and several more were destroyed in 1022 at Toulouse. In the next century one Pierre de Bruys was burned at St. Gilles (1126) for the assertion that the salvation of every man depends upon his personal merits and that God listens to the prayers of the just whether uttered inside or outside a church. In 1197 Peter II of Aragon decreed that all heretics who had not left his kingdom by a stated time would be put to death. If these events merit any common interpretation, they bespeak an awakening dissatisfaction on the part of the laity with the superstitious practices of the church and the immorality of the priesthood.

During the eleventh and twelfth centuries, the dissatisfaction broke into open revolt in the district of Albigensium, in southern France, among a people who called themselves Catharists (Puritans). Some Christian historians assert that the Albigenses were adherents of Satanism in its worst and most dangerous form, a still more perverted faith and practice stemming from Manichaeism. The particulars of the unbelief which Satan was here spreading were largely lost to history in the ensuing conflagration, but the Albigenses appear to have been an ascetic cult which sought to purge the church of sacerdotalism, simony and superstition. Apart from a select coterie who called themselves the Perfect, and who carried asceticism to a great extreme, the Catharists appear to have been a prosperous, intelligent and industrious people. In part their heterodoxy consisted of the facts that they abstained from eating flesh or killing animals, they wished to read the Bible for themselves, they condemned tithes, opposed prayers for the dead, preached peace and nonresistance, practiced ordination but refused to take an oath and used a system of sacraments technically different from that of the church, and aimed, in principle at least, to return to the Pauline ideal of poverty and simplicity. Their poets and minstrels openly ridiculed the clergy; they refused to worship images, saints, angels and the Virgin, scoffed at the Trinity, the Incarnation, Resurrection and Ascension, and denied the miraculous power of bells and crosses and even of the bones and other sacred relics of the saints. Above all, the Albigenses denied the authority of the pope and the supernatural power of his priests.

For two hundred years a succession of popes had tried by councils and condemnations to stamp out these Satanic agents, who persisted, even in the guise of wealthy and prominent citizens, in spreading insidious doctrines through France like a spiritual disease. Following the death sentences at Toulouse, condemnations were leveled against them in 1028 and 1056, a number being burned at Angoulême on the former date, and special preachers were sent into the devil's territory to try conversion in 1101 and 1114; in vain the Council of Toulouse in 1119 ordered the nobility and secular powers to assist in quelling the heresy. The title 'inquisitor,' in the sense of a judge in the matter of faith, was first used under the authority of Pope Alexander III by the Council of Tours, which condemned the Albigenses in 1163; and in 1184 the Synod of Verona cursed them roundly and ordered them, in case they relapsed or proved obdurate, to be handed over to the secular authorities for punishment by death.

When in 1198 Innocent III ascended to the papal throne, participation in the now open war between Satan and the church evoked the fervor of all classes. The crusading movement had become popular with kings and dukes as a means of settling political quarrels and readjusting boundaries. Knights and barons found in it an opportunity to enhance their fortunes; seigniors and gentry joined to escape from boredom, the multitude because they had no other occupation, or were pleased to exchange a dull and menial livelihood for rations, excitement, and the possibilities of distant travel in the army of the Lord. The *raison d'être* of the crusade, the recovery of the sepulcher, had been completely lost from view. Deploring these base motives, Innocent strove to correct the crusading spirit and to this end, in 1202, launched the so-called Fourth Crusade, in which Constantinople was captured (in 1204) and brought under Christian rule for the first time since the fall of Rome. Innocent, pleased to accept the capital of the East in lieu of the sepulcher, was dazzled by the eminence of his new position. He now became so royal that a Byzantine visitor to Rome declared that the pontiff of East and West was indeed not the successor

of Peter, but of Constantine. The Pope himself asserted, 'The Lord left
to Peter the governance not of the church only, but of the whole world.'
When the Emperor of Constantinople quoted Peter to the contrary, Innocent replied in all sincerity that the apostle's admonition to obey the king
as supreme was addressed, not to the clergy, but to the laity.

Innocent usually is cited as the greatest of all papal diplomats. After
centuries of intrigue and warfare between the western bishoprics, he succeeded by his encyclopedic knowledge, the acumen of his political instincts and the sheer force of his character in gaining the final and supreme
command for Rome. By the terrifying instrument of excommunication
he demonstrated that the spiritual was at least *de facto* superior to the
temporal power. He deposed Philip of Swabia in favor of Otto IV, then
ousted Otto to put Philip again in power, and, finally, after Philip's murder, installed young Frederick II as emperor of Germany and by this move
virtually reduced this country to a papal state. He dictated the marriage
policies of Philip Augustus of France, Peter of Aragon and Alphonso IX,
and dominated many lesser princelings, while he forced John of England
to subordinate the crown of that country and Ireland in favor of a fief of
the Roman see, subject to an annual tribute. By the edict of the Council
of Toulouse, he held even bishops accountable to papal inquisitors and
liable to the charge of heresy.

It was now, when the Fourth Crusade had spread the power of the
church to the Bosporus, that Innocent perceived he would have to renew
the war with Satan, who was about to destroy the church in southern
France. Here the Catharists, or the *bonshommes* as they were affection-
ately known to the local people, were multiplying rapidly, protected by
wealthy nobles among whom was Raymond, Count of Toulouse, a heretic
himself, so Innocent charged, who was lax in the faith and tolerated and
was even friendly with the Jews. Having failed through a period of ten
years to convert the heretics by anathemas and denunciations, Innocent
called for a crusade in 1209. Faced with the need of raising a large army
to assault the Albigenses, and following the principle laid down by
Gregory the Great and utilized by other popes in their crusades — that
the church could for sums of money grant indulgences that waived canonical penances — he offered God's forgiveness for all sins, past and future,
his own blessing, which conveyed God's grace, and the cancellation of
interest on all debts as well as exemption from the jurisdiction of all
ordinary courts, to any who would join in his crusade to drive the devil
out of France. He gathered an army which in its hatred of Satan and its
zeal for God's service established new precedents. When the papal legate,

Arnold, Abbot of Cîteaux, was asked how heretics were to be distinguished from true believers, he is reported to have said, "Kill all; God will know his own." It was the Abbot's pleasure to report back to the Pope that in Beziers alone 'nearly twenty thousand human beings perished by the sword. And after the massacre the town was plundered and burnt, and the revenge of God seemed to rage over it in a wonderful manner.' The crusaders spared 'neither dignity, nor sex nor age,' several thousand heretics being slain in the Church of Mary Magdalene where presumably they had falsely sought refuge. When tired of quick deaths, the crusaders grew dilatory and amused themselves by tearing out eyes and subjecting the heretics to other tortures. Innocent himself grew sick of the slaughter and publicly deplored the ardor of his troops, but he was unable to stop them. The faithful were enjoying themselves depopulating the south of France, confiscating property, settling political quarrels, extending baronial domains, and always fighting under the banner of the one true God. The immediate supply of heretics lasted the crusaders twenty years and it is estimated that a million of them were exterminated before the end of a century.

The crusade against the Albigenses was so well received that violent repression thereafter became the established policy of the church. No less an authority than Augustine had endorsed the use of force by citing the command in Luke, 'Go out into the highways and hedges, and compel them to come in, that my house may be filled'; Jerome, Leo the Great and a long line of churchmen had urged capital punishment for those who would split theological definitions. The Code of Gratian regulated the lives of the clergy from the cradle to the grave, and thereby furnished an example for the regulation of the lives of the laity, while the Isidorean Decretals had given the pope cognizance not only of ecclesiastic offenses but also of offenses of a mixed character. There remained then no argument against the pope's judging all aspects of belief and conduct and, if it proved necessary, imposing his will by the use of force. Since he could not personally conduct all inquiries, Gregory IX in 1232 empowered preaching Dominican friars to examine and pass judgment on suspected persons. These commissioners traveled from place to place, calling upon the people to confess or to denounce those whom they suspected to be heretics, and doing their work so well that they came to be known, from a play upon their name, as *Domini canes,* or hounds of God.

The major crusade initiated by Gregory was against some fisherfolk called the Stedinger, of Friesland, who worshiped the devil under the name of Asmodi; the devil appeared to them, so the inquisitors claimed, as a duck, a goose or a youth, and when they kissed him and danced around him, enveloped them in total darkness whereupon they all, males and females, gave themselves up to debauchery. The leader of this and other of Gregory's crusades was Conrad of Marburg, who embodied the best qualities of an inquisitor. He was endowed with penetrating insight into the devil's wiles, possessed unlimited ingenuity in trapping his agents and unbounded courage to face the unpleasantness and even the danger of the task. Conrad's thoroughness evoked so much opposition that archbishops were moved to remonstrate with the Pope, but to no avail, and the fagots were lit as soon as he appeared in a community. It has been said of him that he was harsh, inflexible and unlovable and swayed by no fear of persons or danger of death, that even his most prejudiced critics have never denied the singleness of his convictions and courage; if his zeal in ferreting out the evil ones bordered on fanaticism, the terrible situation with which he had to deal demanded such a man, for one of gentler disposition could not have faced its difficulties. Admittedly, his virtues did not include among them any of those softer features ordinarily called human, because the very nature of the evils which he had to expose and punish and the awful power of Satan who was behind them demanded a man possessing neither heart, nerves nor stomach. He succeeded in bringing an enormous number of heretics to the fire, some say eight thousand in a single year, before he was murdered by several noblemen of Mayence in 1233. Gregory immediately canonized him as a saint and martyr.

In Spain the inquisition was slow in starting, for this country had been pagan under the Visigoths, Catholic under the Hispano-Romans, Mohammedan by conquest and, under a regime of religious freedom, Judaism had developed peacefully alongside the Christian church. A mutual tolerance of different beliefs had arisen, which though vigorously denounced by popes in the eleventh, twelfth and thirteenth centuries proved stronger than the inquisitors, who repeatedly tried to initiate the persecution of heresy. In the fourteenth century, however, adverse feeling set in against the Mohammedans and Jews, and the Christian clergy began to offer condemnation and death as the alternative to baptism. In the fifteenth century, jealousy between the local inquisitors appointed by the Spanish church and those appointed by Rome complicated the persecution of heretics who were thereafter pursued simultaneously by two inquisitions and had to pay double penalties. Resisting the use of torture until long after it had been familiar in the rest of Europe, the Spanish clergy ultimately included it in their theological armamentarium and added to it new

refinements of the most exquisite kind. As usual they terminated it with
death by bonfire, though it appears that the condemned were generally
strangled before being placed upon the pyre. The crimes for which life
imprisonment or death could be inflicted by the Spanish Inquisition included making ablutions in the daytime, abstaining from swine's flesh or
wine, using henna, singing Moorish songs, possessing Arabic manuscripts, and indulging in mathematics and philosophy.

A notable crime was the possession of books suspected of heresy. Constantine had had the writings of Arius destroyed, Theodosius II and
Valentinian III those of the Nestorians and Manichaeans, and Justinian,
the Talmud. Aristotle's *Periphyseon* had been condemned in 1210, and
the works of other men had been forbidden to the people at frequent
intervals in this and the next century. In 1502 Ferdinand and Isabella
established the censure of books as a state institution, all volumes having
to be approved by the bishops, and in 1558 the penalty of death and confiscation of property was decreed against any bookseller or individual
in whose possession a condemned book was found.

vi

In considering the motives underlying the inquisition into heresy it
may be assumed that the popes, prelates and lay officers who supported
it were usually moved by the sincerest piety. The confiscation of a condemned man's property, as an accompaniment of the more severe penalties, must in certain instances have moved secular and ecclesiastic princes
to support the inquisitors in the hope of gain, the worst abuses in this
respect arising from the policy of confiscating a man's property posthu-
mously, in which case his children and grandchildren were made subject
to the penalty. But granting that jealousy, ambition, cupidity or the desire to preserve and enhance the temporal power of the church may in
some instances have stimulated the inquisitors, the main motive underlying the persecution of heterodoxy from the time of Constantine onwards was the desire to preserve God's kingdom on earth against the
attacks of Satan. In this battle the inquisitors had the allegiance of the
vast majority of people; completely credulous of Christian theology,
possessing a philosophy happily uncomplicated by any perspective of history or doubts such as might be stirred by a knowledge of natural philosophy, the masses were just as enthusiastic and sincere in heretic hunting
as were the priests. A heretic was the flesh and blood embodiment of the

Evil One and an enemy of God; to smell out these frightful fiends and burn them filled the devout with ecstasy and gave them a deep sense of righteousness.

One of the strongest bids to allegiance offered by the early church had been the protection it offered against the devil and his works. The belief in evil spirits had been dogmatically approved from the first century onwards. Augustine affirmed that witchcraft depends on a pact with the devil, and exorcism or protection against demonic influence by means of the church's sacred magic, the use of amulets, charms, incantations, exorcisms, prayers, the reading of the scriptures, the sight or manual sign of the cross, had always been one of its chief services. But to resort to any other kind of magic was to practice Satan's black art. Through the emphasis placed on wonder-working in both the Old and New Testaments and by all priests and ecclesiastic scholars, every application of magic became a potential miracle; in the course of a few centuries pious imaginations and clerical jealousies exalted the most ordinary phenomena into the miraculous, and men were prepared to believe anything and everything. Agobard, Archbishop of Lyon, probably spoke without exaggeration when he declared in the ninth century that 'the wretched world lies now under the tyranny of foolishness; things are believed by Christians of such absurdity as no one ever could aforetime induce the heathen to believe.'

The magicians of Egypt had threatened that unless their demands were granted they would reach out to the four corners of the earth, pull down the pillars of heaven and wreck the abodes of the gods above and those of men below. From the time of Constantine on all observation of nature, except as it expressly led to the saving of souls or the affirmation of scripture, carried a no less fearful threat; standing as it did in opposition to revealed truth, intellectual inquiry was Satan's method and its discoveries were Satan's tools. Familiarity with the Egyptian, Assyrian and finally even the Greek language was held to be heretical and, with the fall of paganism in the fourth century, the ability to read these tongues disappeared from Europe. In the reign of Constantius the term 'enemies of the human race,' originally applied in pagan laws to the Christians, was transferred by the Christians to the magicians, and magic included nearly all efforts toward the manipulation of nature.

In 1163 Pope Alexander III forbade the study of natural philosophy, partly because the Arabs, who were the only natural philosophers of the time, were atheists and infidels, and partly because there was nothing said about natural philosophy in the Bible. In the next century the Franciscans and Dominicans, although fighting with each other over the deification of the Virgin Mary, jointly and in the most emphatic terms condemned all experiments in chemistry, physics and medicine. In 1380 Charles V of France and in 1404 Henry IV of England promulgated sharp-toothed laws against the possession of furnaces, crucibles, retorts and other apparatus, and similar measures were taken in this or later periods to exterminate the 'experimental' method in Italy and Spain, the experimenters being dreaded as cohorts of Satan. Even mathematics was looked upon with fear because of the magical power of numbers, and at the time of the persecution of Galileo (1564-1642) mathematicians were denounced as the greatest of all heretics.

It was universally believed that men who, in the dark of night, in secret cellars and attics, among a welter of apparatus — stinking chemicals, herbs, fragments of animals, a jumble of cabalistic lore, Bible verses, secret numbers, sacred symbols, mystic names and incantations — sought to transmute base metals into gold or to compound the elixir of eternal life, were actually practicing the devil's arts and must have been instructed in them by the Prince of Evil, that probably these sorcerers were contemplating the injury of their neighbors by opposing Providence and falsifying scripture; by putting reason above faith, they were blasphemously denying God's will.

There was scarcely any task exceeding diabolic wit and strength. It was Satan who built Hadrian's wall between England and Scotland, the bridges at Schellenen in Switzerland, at Regensburg across the Danube, and at Avignon, who made the drawings for the churches at Cologne and Aix-la-Chapelle and the masonry of Crowland Abbey. It was in competition with him that the archangel Michael built the Church of Mont-Saint-Michel. He rolled enormous boulders into the midst of plains far removed from any mountains, stood monoliths on end and arranged the queer circles of standing stones. Satan, said Tertullian, could carry water in a sieve. Yet he did not invent dogmatic errors or engage in alchemy and wonder-working for sheer devilment: he was the great Tempter who, seeking men for hell, led them in devious ways to sin. After Augustine, men were by nature incapable of good except through the grace of the Christian church; as this grace predisposed them to God's side in the unceasing conflict of the church with Satan, so even the most trivial sin revealed their bent toward the powers of evil.

The monk Pachomius once saw a pack of devils dragging along a bundle of leaves, pretending that this was costing them great effort, for no other reason than to tempt the good man to the sin of laughter. The devil might hide beneath the confessor's hood and mutter to the penitent,

"Oh that is nothing! There is no evil in *that!* Take not *that* to heart!"
To make the priest sneeze in the middle of his finest passage, to cause
him to forget his words, even to plague him in the form of a fly when he is
trying to go to sleep, may cause him to lose his patience, and this, a trivial
offense in itself, may lead to more evil things. This is illustrated by the
story of the most holy hermit who, at the prompting of the devil, procured
a cock to relieve his loneliness. This was a little thing, but it came about
that the cock grew lonesome too, and in a spirit of charity the hermit supplied it with a hen. Evil indeed was this deed, for the sight which the hermit then beheld awakened old ardors which he had thought were forever
quenched. Suggestion fired imagination, and soon the poor man was enam-
ored of the daughter of a neighboring nobleman, a young and beautiful
girl; he sinned with her and, to escape the vengeance of her parents,
killed his beloved and concealed her body beneath his couch. The crime
was discovered and he had to pay the supreme penalty of death and eternal
damnation — all because he listened to the devil in a little thing. Thus it
was that the evil one planted the seed of sin, by evoking pungent memories, quickening desires, stirring up doubts, fostering fears, inspiring anx-
ieties, the fruit of which was pride, selfishness, neglect of vows, avarice, or
lust.

Out of the last, the devil early forged a weapon which proved doubly
powerful against a church which emphasized the superiority of the ascetic
life. Virginity early came to be esteemed as the highest of all virtues, and
Origen, surnamed 'the Adamantine,' had presumably by his own hands
put himself beyond all risk of losing it. In the second century it was a
custom for 'beloved brothers and sisters,' agapetae, to live together in spiritual marriage, both parties having taken the vow of continency. It was a
misunderstanding of this phrase which led the horrified pagans to accuse
them of incest. The antiquity of the custom is revealed by Paul's mixed
metaphor, when he speaks of himself as having 'espoused' the Corinthian
church, and desires 'to present' the same as 'a pure virgin to Christ.' The
relationship of the Virgin Mary and Joseph was envisaged in these terms,
and in the *Shepherd of Hermas,* a book which was read aloud as scripture
in the churches in the second and third centuries, the custom is eulogized,
the virgins boldly inviting the hero of the work to pass the night in their
company. "Thou must sleep with us," they said, "as a brother, not as a
husband." Before the establishment of nunneries, many virgins who had
lost their parents and brothers, or who were beset by illness or poverty,
were forced to live with homeless clerics and monks. Tertullian advised
well-to-do Christians to take one or more widows 'as spiritual spouses,

who were beautiful by their faith, endowed with their poverty, sealed by their age.' By the time of Cyprian (?200–258) virgins who were dedicated to God lived in such intimate relations with confessors, priests and laymen that this bishop was forced openly to condemn the practice, as later did Gregory of Nyassa, Jerome, Augustine and other churchmen. Yet late in the fourth century Chrysostom, condemning both marriage and fornication, extolled the custom whereby 'men introduce young girls into their houses and keep them there permanently, respecting their virginity.' He argues that this form of love is actually more ardent than conjugal union, because where there is no restraint, there is speedy satiation; sexual intercourse, pregnancy, delivery, lactation, the bringing up of children, soon destroy youth and dull the point of pleasure. The virgin is free from these burdens, she retains her vigor and youthfulness and even at the age of forty may rival the nubile girl. 'A double ardor thus burns in the heart of him who lives with her, and the gratification of desire never extinguishes the bright flame which ever continues to increase in strength.' This 'more refined form of sexual intimacy,' this 'new refinement of tender chastity,' had come 'as a delicious discovery to the early Christians, who had resolutely thrust away the licentiousness of the pagan world.' As the rule of celibacy became fixed for teachers, spiritual wives became more prevalent until they virtually had the status of servant maids, and one Spanish synod, about 600, even ordered that they could be sold as slaves and the proceeds given to the poor. Nevertheless, the practice was generally disapproved officially.

By the decretal of Pope Siricius in 385 absolute celibacy was prescribed for all the higher clergy, a decretal admittedly evoked by the salacious conduct of vowed priests and virgins. The next year a Roman synod imposed conjugal abstinence on bishops, priests and deacons who were already married, and these precedents were followed by other edicts of equal or greater stringency, culminating in a series of decretals from 1031 to 1051 ordering clerics from subdeacons to bishops to cast aside their wives, who were to be turned adrift in the world, while their children were pronounced slaves. In proportion as success crowned these papal efforts, concubinage and female slavery increased, these being viewed as lesser sins than marriage, and culminated in the scandals of the monasteries which shook the church at the time of the Reformation. Woman, said Tertullian, is the gate to hell, and Augustine's opinion of her is unquotable.

To flee the tempter the ascetic betook themselves into deserts or remote mountains, or sought security behind monastery walls. Yet Satan followed them. Jerome, who immured himself in the desert near Chalcis, wrote to the virgin Eustochium, 'Oh, how often, when I was in the desert, in that vast, sunburned solitude that furnishes a fearsome dwelling place to the hermits, did I imagine that I was living amid the delights of Rome! I used to sit alone, my soul full of bitterness, clothed in foul sackcloth, my skin become like an Ethiopian's. I passed not a day without tears, without groanings; and when, against my will, sleep overcame me, my couch was the bare ground. I say nothing of my food and my drink; for the hermits, even in sickness, drink nothing but water, and all cooked food they esteem as a sinful luxury. And I, who through fear of hell had condemned myself to live such a life, to have no other companionship than that of scorpions and wild beasts, ofttimes imagined myself in the midst of troops of dancing girls. My face was wan with fastings; but within my chill body, my soul was burning desires; and in a man already dead as to the flesh, were blazing the fires of lust. Then, bereft of all other succor, I would cast myself down at the feet of Jesus, I would bathe them with my tears, I would wipe them with my hair; and I would subjugate my rebellious flesh with a full week's fasting. I do not blush to confess my misery; rather, I regret that I am no longer as I was. And I remember how ofttimes, crying aloud and praying, I saw day follow night, and how I ceased not to beat my breast until, at the voice of God, calm returned to me.'

Gregory the Great relates how the devil once kindled in the body of the holy Benedict so hot a flame of concupiscence that, in order to quell it, the poor man found no recourse but to strip himself naked and roll over and over in a bramble bush.

Many was the saintly monk to whom the devil appeared as a charming girl or a noble matron; the diabolic creature might pretend she had lost her way or was being pursued by evil enemies, or perhaps even that she had abandoned the world and wished to devote herself to God, and with modest countenance and great humility would beg the holy man for shelter and protection. Woe to him who took her into his narrow quarters! If the adventure did not end in carnal sin, it was only because the holy man discovered her disguise in time, or because her true character was revealed by a sudden and horrifying transformation into the hideous devil that she was.

There were, however, among the faithful many stouthearted souls who could not be reached by lust, and these Satan beset with more subtle bait. A truly remarkable exhibition of diabolic ingenuity and patience is the instance in which, in the guise of a young boy, the devil entered a monastery of great repute, and by years of study, application and good behavior came into the office of abbot; then, once in command, he allowed the place to fall into such evils, as, for example, riotous living and drinking, the un-warranted granting of dispensations, and licentious relations between the monks and the sisters of a neighboring nunnery, that the pope was forced to send two trusted monks to investigate, whereupon the devil-abbot dis-appeared into the depths of the earth. Such tales, told in all seriousness and widely repeated by the laity, were the favored product of the mon-astic mind when it was not occupied with the equally intriguing subject of hell.

It was left to the Christians for whom heaven was so real to devise the inescapable antithesis, a realistic hell. It was perhaps to them that Plutarch, in the first century, referred when he commiserated his fellow men for torturing themselves in their own imaginations. Taking the cue from earlier apocryphal writings, the author of the Apocalypse of Peter (second century) developed the doctrine of posthumous torture in some detail. In a place of chastisement directly opposite paradise, according to pseudo-Peter, blasphemers are hung by their tongues above a flaming fire; women who adorn themselves for the purpose of adultery are hung by the hair over a bubbling, stinking mire; murderers are cast into a pit of rep-tiles; mothers who forsake their children are immersed in a pit of gore and filth; persecutors of the righteous are burned in fire up to the waist while their entrails are devoured by worms; other evildoers are punished by having their eyes burned out, by being rolled on swords and spits, by boil-ing in pitch and blood, by being hurled from high cliffs, or by careful, pro-tracted roasting. Similar descriptions appear in the *Pistis Sophia* (third century) and the Apocalypse of Paul (fourth century). It was not, how-ever, until medieval times that the churchmen spun the agonies of hell into a degree of refinement worthy of poetic presentation.

Hell was variously located — at the poles, in the antipodes, beneath vol-canoes, at the center of the earth, in the farthest east, or completely outside the world, between it and one of the empyrean realms — but on such points as the qualities of its tortures, the eternality of its punishments, and the fact that it was more densely populated than was paradise there was general agreement. This last reflected both the quality of Christian love and the uneasy feeling that Satan and not God was the real master of the universe.

Even allowing for the limited scope of righteous pleasures, the imag-ination has ever been much less prolific in devising beatific delights than punitive cruelties. Perhaps a difficulty is that delight is so quickly satiated, and the authorities on hell gave special emphasis to the peculiarities of its tortures, that however much its fire should burn, its beasts should tear, its

devils should mangle, never should the body be destroyed nor its capacity
to suffer be reduced in any measure.

Every monk whose repressions and privations gnawed within him like
ever hungry worms was recompensed by revelations of the excruciating
torments which would beset through all eternity the unholy ones who
yielded to carnal pleasures and other sins. Vivid pictures of hell abound
in oratory and literature. Notable in the monkish accounts of terror and
pain is the vision of Alberico, a boy of ten, who was conducted through
hell by the apostle Peter and two angels. Alberico encountered first a
dismal valley where many souls were standing immersed in ice, some only
to their ankles or knees, others up to their breasts or necks; just beyond
was a fearful wood of gigantic trees, bristling with thorns, from whose
sharp and spiny branches were hanging by their breasts those heartless
women who had refused to nourish motherless babes with their own milk;
to each breast clung a snake, sucking that which had been so cruelly denied. Farther on were those who had not refrained from sexual intercourse
on Sundays and saints' days, forced to ascend and descend a ladder of
red-hot iron, and now one, now another would plunge headlong into a
huge caldron filled with oil, pitch and resin, which was seething at the
ladder's foot. In a fearful furnace tyrants were being punished; murderers were suffering in a lake of fire — while easygoing parish priests who
had winked at the misdemeanors of their charges were being boiled in a
giant stew pan, full of bronze, tin, lead and brimstone; blasphemers were
boiling in a lake of molten metal; traitors and false witnesses were
drowned in a lake of sulphurous water full of snakes and scorpions. Hard
by there was tethered with an iron chain a serpent of enormous size which
drew in with every breath a swarm of souls, just as if they were flies, only
to spew them forth blazing like sparks with each exhalation of its hot and
venomous breath. It will be recalled that it had been to save Abraham and
Moses and the prophets of old from this eternal punishment that Christ
had descended to hell before ascending unto Heaven, for it had been the
cardinal principle of Paul's doctrine, and of all churchmen from Augustine on, that those who died unbaptized were excluded from paradise. It is
not surprising then that at the entrance of hell Alberico saw one-year-old
babies boiling in fiery vapors which were fed with flaming coal. This
punishment, however, because of the relative innocence of the babes, was
the first and least.

Best known among these visions of the hereafter is the First Book of the
Divina Commedia of Dante Alighieri, who descended into hell and was
guided about by Virgil, whom he found in the first circle which contained

the unbaptized. Little that was new was revealed to Dante, although he described the sights he saw with such a refined poetic and philosophic style that it has been said it is by virtue of this work 'that he holds his place as one of the half-dozen greatest writers of all time.' In the second circle Dante beheld carnal sinners tossed by warring winds; in the third, gluttons bitten by Cerberus are exposed in a stinking land to storms of hail; in the fourth the prodigal and miser each push a heavy weight up-hill; in the fifth, the irascible soak in the foul and fetid slime of the Stygian lake; in the sixth, archheretics agonize in tombs of flame; in the seventh, the violent swim in rivers of blood, suicides are changed into gnarled trees and blasphemers writhe under a rain of fire; in the eighth, pimps are scourged by demons, flatterers are immersed in human ordure, peculators boil in a lake of pitch, hypocrites are tortured under hoods of lead, sacrilegists are stung by serpents, and others are attacked by horrible diseases; in the ninth circle, the last and worst, traitors, chattering like storks, are frozen in chill blue ice.

The pyrotechnics of hell, its despairs, fires, darknesses, agonies, stinks, worms and miscellaneous tortures constituted a cult of cruelty which found its votaries among all righteous men, for why be righteous if the un-righteous be not damned? When, at the Council of Florence (1439), the church formally ratified the existence of purgatory, it did not commit itself on the question whether here too devils carried on torture, as in hell; but this was the generally accepted opinion, and it was even allowed that the torment was the more intense, being applied as it was for a limited duration of a few thousand years, whereas that of hell could be milder since it went on forever.

What Graf has called the most beautiful of all the devout legends to which the Christian imagination has given birth is the account in the Apocalypse of St. Paul, composed toward the end of the fourth century by an unknown Greek monk, which recounts how Paul, guided by the angel Michael, descended to hell and was so moved by the torments of the damned that he and thousands upon thousands of angels knelt before Christ and beseeched him to show mercy. Moved to pity, Christ granted to all souls that are in hell this grace: they shall have rest and shall be without torment from the sundown of Saturday until the dawn of Mon-day. And thus it came about that there is a respite for the damned, through Christ's grace, of one day in seven.

Surprising it was that despite such terrible and inexorable punishments, some men, such was their worldly pride, ambition and love of sensual pleasure, should even sell their souls to the devil for all time. For it was held that in exchange for a man's immortal soul the devil might endow him with wealth, fame, love, honors, knowledge or magic power, and many were the medieval stories of such pacts drawn up on parchment and signed in blood. Typically these pacts ran for a stated course of years before the devil was entitled to collect his price, and there is this much to be said for him: never once is it recorded that he became impatient and came to collect his due one day ahead of the specified date, or that he failed to fulfill his end of the bargain by holding back a little gold or cunning or sensory delight from one to whom he had promised them, much less that he ever attempted to slip out of the bargain entirely. In all these respects his conduct was superior to that of the Christians who had signed their names with blood, and presumably with good intent, to agreements which they no more than made than almost without exception they endeavored to evade by deceitful wiles or by importuning the aid of the Virgin Mary. For traditionally the Virgin specialized in getting men out of the devil's clutches. Indeed so often did she cheat Satan of his rightful due that he justly came to hate her above all the saints. Because of her he learned to look upon the contracts which men made with him as but valueless promises which he must in the end redeem by force and cunning. Rare, indeed, were the exceptions to this sad rule. In the original tale of Faust, intended to emphasize the essentially evil nature of purely human learning, which first appeared in print about 1587, the ambitious doctor, driven by a thirst for knowledge and a hankering after pleasure, traced with his blood this pact with Satan:

> I, Johannes Faustus, Doctor, make the following declaration in this letter, written by my own hand. Having set myself to explore the elements, and perceiving that the faculties graciously bestowed upon me by Heaven are not sufficient to penetrate the nature of things, and that from other men I cannot receive satisfaction of my desire, I have given myself to this spirit here present, who is called Mephistophilis and who is a servant of the Prince of Hell, that he may teach me that which I desire to know and may be, as he promises, submissive and obedient unto me. For my part, I promise that, after the passage of twenty-four years from the date of the present writing, I will suffer him to do with me, with my spirit and my flesh, whatsoever shall seem good to him; and this for all eternity. To this end, I deny all beings that live, whether in heaven or on the earth. In token whereof, I write and subscribe this with mine own hand and in mine own blood.

In Goethe's version of this tale, Faust ultimately cheats the devil; but in the original, after enjoying the rich benefits of Satanic knowledge and magic for the allotted time, the doctor honestly keeps his contract. At the stipulated date he gives a banquet for his friends and explains the mystery of his witchcraft; and, after his friends have retired, he goes to his chamber to await the end. A little after midnight a mighty wind fills the house and shakes it on its foundations, there are fearsome whisperings in the darkness and his friends hear the doctor shriek for help. Then silence, and when morning comes and Faust's friends dare to go into his chamber, they find it all smeared with blood; his brains are spattered over the walls, and his eyes, torn from their sockets, and a few teeth are lying on the floor. The corpse, trampled and mangled, is found outside the house, tossed onto a muck heap.

vii

In the words of the skeptic Reginald Scott (1580), the conventional witches of his day were 'women which be commonly old, lame, bleare-eied, pale, fowle, and full of wrinkles; poore, sullen, superstitious, and papists; or such as knowe no religion: in whose drowsie minds the divell hath gotten a fine seat; so as, what mischief, mischance, calamitie, or slaughter is brought to pass, they are easilie persuaded the same is doone by themselves; imprinting in their minds an earnest and constant imagination thereof. They are leane and deformed, shewing melancholie in their faces, to the horror of all that see them. They are doting, scolds, mad, divellish; and not much differing from them that are thought to be possessed with spirits; so shall onelie have respect to the constancie of their words uttered would easilie beleeve they were true indeed.'

Scott underestimates the number of girls, women in the prime of life, and of men, among the 'witches,' but that many old women sincerely believed they were witches (or warlocks) cannot be gainsaid. Beyond this generalization it is difficult to recover accurate facts about the great witchcraft delusion which tore the civilized world for centuries, for the simple reason that the persecutors of the evil suffered as many or more delusions than the persecuted.

In seeking the sources of the medieval panic, what may be called the orthodox interpretation is ably stated by the Reverend Montague Summers, who is foremost among recent authorities on the history and literature of witchcraft. Summers, it may be said, accepts the reality of Satan and demonic forces as evidenced both in past ages and at the present time. Chief among the primal roots of witchcraft, in his view, was the Gnosticism which had so nearly destroyed the early church, and the various sects and heresies which derived from it. In Summers's view, these heresies all rejected the god of the Old Testament, worshiped the devil, repudiated baptism and all Christian formulas, and are to be identified as the actual source and substance of Satanism and witchcraft.

Thompson, however, sees in medieval witchcraft the survival throughout Europe of religious cults stemming from prehistory and persisting in the folk religions. Magdelenian and Aurignacian art, for example, indubitably magical in operation, was intensely interested in ithyphallic figures of men and animals, Mother Goddesses, and human beings dressed in animal guises. This art was frequently so placed and concealed as to suggest that it decorated a sacred chamber in which men and women gathered for ritual exercises. It was such Stone Age revels, frequently near or centering around a megalithic monument, that were condemned by the Councils of Arles in 452, of Tours in 567, and of Nantes in 568. The first Council of Toledo in 681 issued admonitions against 'the worshipers of idols, those who venerate stones [menhirs, cromlechs, etc.], who kindle torches, who celebrate the rites of springs and trees,' while other admonitions refer to 'men who goeth about in the masque of a stag or a bull-calf,' who dress 'in the skin of a herd animal or put on the heads of beasts,' 'who make themselves into wild animals,' or 'who have turned themselves into devils.'

From many such evidences it is clear that early in the Christian Era pagan cults which mimicked wild animals were prevalent throughout Europe; it is equally certain that these cults frequently centered about the phallic stones and were mainly concerned with the fertility of herds and crops, in which case the participants were disguised as animals, or with the propagation of human beings, when no disguise, except perhaps on the part of the fertility god, was necessary. Not infrequently the local cults appear to have been headed by Christian priests who had been recruited from the peasantry and who could not quickly abandon the ways of their friends and fathers. When the church spread like an army of occupation into the wild north country, in the twelfth and thirteenth centuries, these persistent Stone Age cults assumed the dimensions of heresy.

That witchcraft represented an operative religious ritual, indigenous to pagan heath and hill, has been ably argued by Murray, who reconstructs its forms and beliefs from the vast literature of medieval trials. The religious unit or 'coven' consisted of twelve elders with the minister or high priest making up the pagan lucky number of thirteen. These covens came together on the evenings of the great days and feast days under a leader who acted as the god, the coven accepting this leader as an incarnate god as sincerely as the Christians accepted the devil incarnate as an ordinary man. A record was sometimes kept of initiations and other affairs in a secret book. The Sabbat (*s'esbattre,* to frolic) was a public meeting, generally held at night, of all the elders and witches of the district, who feasted and danced and celebrated their magic rites, worshiping their god and indulging in pleasurable orgies. Dances around a fire were a prominent part of these exercises, the chief devil taking the lead, the second in command bringing up the rear and looking after the hindmost with a whip. Some of the participants rode on brooms either as a ritual or in imitation of an aerial steed. Drugs such as aconite, poplar, cinquefoil and deadly nightshade, as well as bat's blood, animal fats and soot were rubbed into the skin and may have aided the illusion of real flight. Witches took to themselves particular animals, dogs, cats, weasels, toads and mice as familiars or incarnations of magic power, to aid them in their sorcery. The Esbat was a secret meeting of the elders when waxen images, candles and 'flying ointment' were prepared by expert hands, and a cat, dog, cock or an unbaptized child supplied by its witch-mother or stolen, was sacrificed.

Admission to the coven was voluntary, but it involved the renunciation in faith if not in practice of all other religion. Initiation consisted of painful and magic rites, and the catechumen might be called upon to sign his name in blood and to receive a tatooed devil's mark on the left shoulder. In time the coven meetings came to be a parody of the sacred rites of the church, with a black mass and sacraments performed with profane holy water and wafers. High offices were sometimes hereditary, and witches' children were dedicated to the god as soon as they were born, and were initiated at the age of thirteen. There was a marked preference for certain names, Joan, Jean, Janet or Jane being the commonest, Bessie, Elizabeth or Elspeth next, and Margaret, Margo or Meg, third. It is not unlikely that many a prepossessing witch who was no amateur at sensual delights devoted herself to saint baiting, or to collecting for the coven a wandering knight. The words witchery, enchantment, glamour, charm, fascinate, entrance, all of which had their provenance in witchcraft, have lost some force by shifting from the magic to the poetic realm.

Since human sacrifice was dangerous and difficult, covens of witches with clever indirection sometimes resorted to the public executioner in order to disguise the nature of the rite. The subterfuge required only a well-planned conspiracy, and by charges leveled against either a willing or unwilling victim and supported by concerted testimonies, the aid of both the church and secular authorities could be obtained in a sacrifice that was all the more effective toward the ends of witchcraft by being public and attended by a large and distinguished audience. Indeed, Murray has argued that Joan of Arc was such a female proxy, a voluntary Satanic martyr for Satanic ends. Certain it is that Joan's commander, Gilles de Rais, Marshall of France, was justly condemned for sorcery nine years after her death, having been convicted of sacrificing two hundred and more women and children in magic rites. The criminality of Gilles de Rais was well known to the peasantry, his own servants were accomplices in the kidnaping and murder of his many child victims, and Joan must have known about her commander's ritual of human sacrifice long before the battle of Orleans. Anatole France saw in Joan the rallying point of a powerful organization opposed to the church; Murray but identifies this organization with the witchcraft cult that permeated both France and England and had its adherents no less among the prominent clergy and nobility than the lower classes. If this interpretation is correct, Joan of Arc is probably the only witch to have attained beatification.

In all except perhaps the first of these theories allowance must be made for the number of witches who were unquestionably victims of neuropathies; those suffering hysterical delusions and confusion of personality, the schizophrenics, persecuted maniacs, melancholics, hypochondriacs, and those with anxiety neuroses engendered by nurses' tales and the constantly reiterated threats of the theologians. But when the mentally deranged are deducted from the roll, there remains what is probably the larger proportion, those who were falsely accused on the grounds of jealousy, revenge, cupidity, fear or simple gossip, and who had no means to defend themselves. It must be recognized that not all the votaries of witchcraft were uneducated, unintelligent peasants; many indeed were prominent citizens and scholars; nor is it enough to dismiss all witches as degraded sensualists, all Sabbats as vicious, licentious and obscene. From the beginning the approach of the churchmen was to pursue the victim with leading questions, based on the classic manuals, and to work upon her with fear and torture until the appropriate answers were obtained. By this method the examiners rather than the witches built up a tradition of witch lore which appears with little variation in trial records from all parts of Europe and from all periods.

In this tradition witches rode to the Sabbat and made other nocturnal excursions transported on a broomstick, a black horse, goat or ram, or on the back of the devil himself who made a great stir like a mighty wind. The witch's ointment, concocted of various magic drugs including the fat

of infants either slain for the purpose or disinterred, was deemed necessary for this levitation. Many a witch, who was proved by trustworthy witnesses to have been lying in bed all night, was sincerely convinced that
she had floated out of the window and traveled high above the landscape
to a secret rendezvous on a far distant tor, or in a dark recess of the woods,
or at the crossroads where magic has always had its standing stone. Such
dreams of levitation, excited by a hard bed or disturbed stomach, were
spun into the most heroic or obscene exploits.

In the conventional Sabbat the devil appeared as an animal of one kind
or another, as a ghost or as a big black man, scaly, horrible to look upon
and cold to the touch. To him the witches tendered an account of what
they had done since the last meeting. Those who had caused the most
death and destruction gained the most applause, while those who had
done little evil or had lost their courage were derided and might even be
chastised by the god himself. After the dancing and feasting there was
promiscuous sexual indulgence, the lusty god playing a prominent role.
The ascetically frigid inquisitors pretended to unmitigated horror at this
aspect of the Sabbat and sadistically steeled themselves to proportionally
vicious cruelty towards the robust and uninhibited peasantry who confessed to this carnal sin. To argue against the possibility of Satanic intercourse was absurd: on the evidence of Genesis the fallen angels had
coupled with women who had forthwith begotten monstrous giants; Deuteronomy recorded human intercourse with Belphegor; the fathers from
Augustine to Thomas Aquinas had proclaimed that it was impudence to
seek to deny the fact; while the reality of incubi and succubi was everywhere accepted. Discounting nightmares and hallucinations, probably
many of the child sacrifices which were unquestionably frequent in the
witch cult were the fruits of the actual Sabbat, if not sired by Satan himself then by one of his frenzied surrogates in human form. The devil's
caress was variously described as brutal, painful, lacerating, torturing, although there are abundant testimonies, some from girls but twelve to sixteen years of age, as to its delights. On one point there seemed to be well-
nigh universal agreement: the devil was cold all over, like a creature of
stone, yet his touch imparted an atrocious, delicious joy.

The religious feature of the Sabbat was of course the worship of His
Satanic Majesty. Probably through the centuries this religious service
slowly transformed itself from a pagan rite, with animal or human sacrifice, to what, if the evidence adduced in countless witch trials is to be
credited, amounted to a diabolic perversion of the mass. The first ritual
gesture was the kiss of adoration, homage and humility; as the faithful

Christians in ancient days gave one another the kiss of peace, a kiss whose tradition was preserved in the address of priest to prelate, so the devil too required his embrace, but 'in such filthy parts that it is altogether shameful merely to recount it.' There followed the confession of evil deeds — albeit good ones in the devil's opinion — after which Satan atrociously blessed the assembly with his left hand. An altar rose miraculously from the ground and here in the gruesome light of pitch candles, beneath a disfigured and shameful crucifix was performed a bloody and sacrilegious sacrifice. The priest put on his sacerdotal ornaments back to front, held the sacred book in his left hand and recited the creed inversely. All sacred words were jumbled into a blasphemous jargon. 'Ghost holy and son, Father of name the in. . . . Ever for, glory the and, power the, kingdom the, is thine for, evil from us deliver, but temptation into not us lead. Amen.' This jumbling of sacred words came to be a touchstone in witch hunting, for it was believed that a true witch could not recite the Lord's Prayer without making at least one error. And so to the elevation of the Host, a round black turnip or black unleavened bread which, after being consecrated, was thrown to the ground and trampled under foot, or subjected to worse profanation. The Black Mass, according to the inquisitors, was designed in every detail to curse God and exalt his enemy, Satan, and when the abomination was consummated, the votaries of the devil were forced to renew their oaths of evil, to renounce baptism, to forswear Jesus Christ and all Christian ways and to follow faithfully the king of hell. At the crowing of the cock, which from time immemorial was supposed to dissolve all enchantments, the assembly dispersed and hurried to reach their homes by dawn.

If the ritual Sabbat was largely the product of the ecclesiastic erudition of the inquisitors, the practice of witchcraft owes more of its pattern to the witches. The forms of demonic influence most frequently encountered in the trial records are the making of a covenant with Satan, intercourse with incubi or succubi, and bodily transvection. Among the objective evidences of league with Satan were the 'devil's mark,' which might be a supernumerary breast, a suspicious looking mole (devil's teat) or an area of the skin which was insensitive to pain when pricked with a needle. In his search for devil's teats the howls of the accused did not stay the hand of the witch-finder: quite the contrary, since the object was to find a place where the needle could go in without causing pain; and when he failed he sometimes remained convinced that the devil's mark was there, but hidden in such parts and places that it would be necessary to tear the body to pieces to discover it.

By means of Satanic possession men changed themselves into wolves (lycanthropy) and prowled about at night devouring children. In order to protect a Greek thief, Aesop had changed a man into a wolf; Circe had accomplished the transformation by means of drugs; wolves had played a sacred role in the cult of Zeus Lycaeus, the Wolf Zeus, and it was at the altar of this god that Lycaon, king of Arcadia, was said to have been changed into a wolf by a child sacrifice, while the worshipers of Apollo Soranus decked themselves out in wolf skins and behaved like wolves. Virgil describes how Moeris became a wolf, and Petronius relates the story of Niceros and his werewolf friend. The belief in lycanthropy, whether the beast be wolf or other, was widespread in medieval Europe, and particularly in Ireland where the potentiality was supposed to run in families. St. Patrick is said to have cursed a certain tribe so that they and their descendants became wolves at a certain season every seventh year, while others were known to take a wolf shape at will and to kill sheep, pigs and cattle. So, too, in Wales and Scotland, and among the Serbs and Magyars, in Germany, Lithuania, Lavonia, Poland, Scandinavia and all of Russia. After the thirteenth century the belief spread in France as a religious, or a Satanic, article of faith, and epidemics of lycanthropy swept the country adding to the fear and misery of a people already tormented beyond measure by the machinations of the evil one.

Among other major items of the devil's work was the storm that raised the wind and buffeted ships at sea, or brought destructive hail and flood. Satanic, too, were those mightiest of all phenomena, the searing flash of lightning and the reverberating peal of thunder; these had ever belonged to the gods, but men seem never to have feared them greatly until they became the weapons of the king of hell. Though occasionally a churchman proposed a natural explanation for lightning, it was held for many centuries to be the Almighty's bomb hurled against the wicked, the vagaries of its actions being frequently advanced as evidences of God's existence. A typical anecdote concerns the priest of Treves who was struck in his own church whither he had gone to ring the bell against the storm. The lightning tore the priest's clothes from him and consumed certain parts of his body, showing that the sins for which he was being punished were vanity and unchastity, and that God was just.

It was Tertullian who first argued that lightning was the forked tongue of hell-fire maliciously wielded by Satan, and after him the doctrine of the diabolic origin of storms gathered strength as the fathers, finding ample warrant in scriptures, gave it their full approval. A long line of popes and, after the Reformation, many generations of Protestants, accepted as an article of faith the notion that demons could produce wind, rain, hail and drought.

The first and most natural means which had been used to ward off Satanic injury was, of course, prayer; but while this appeared to be efficacious in some instances, it frequently failed. It was about 110 that, according to tradition, Bishop Alexander of Rome recommended that holy water be kept in churches and bedchambers to drive away demons, and subsequently the churchmen added to this remedy an elaborate system of exorcisms which were specialized for every occasion, formal, sonorous rituals which, when read by an ordained priest, were supposed to paralyze the demons. Some were mildly admonitory, such as that of Pope Gregory XIII: 'I a priest of Christ . . . do command ye, most foul spirits who do stir up these clouds . . . that ye depart from them and disperse yourselves into wild and untilled places, that ye may be no longer able to harm men or animals or fruits or herbs, or whatsoever is designed for human use.' When mildness failed, the exorcism became denunciatory and commanding and, in addition to verbal execration, a bonfire was built, Psalm 114 was chanted, and malodorous substances such as sulphur and asafoetida were cast into the flames literally to stink the devil out of the country. Though great efficacy was attached to the 'names' of God the Father, Jesus or the Virgin Mary, medieval scholars agreed that the thing the devil most hated was the sign of the cross.

When it seemed that evil was ever on the increase, there was devised another means of routing the devil, which consisted of bits of consecrated paper upon which was written a sacred formula calculated to make the Evil One turn pale, and these were burned in the corners of the fields to protect against destructive insects, as well as against bad weather. The Agnus Dei, a piece of wax blessed by the pope's own hand and stamped with the 'Lamb of God,' was held to be so marvelous a protection against storms, and especially thunder, that Pope Urban V sent three of them as a gift of honor to the Greek emperor. This charm, also effective against pestilence and many other forms of enchantment, soon acquired wide popularity and it was perhaps the manufacture of spurious reproductions that led to a papal bull in 1471 reserving to the pope himself the exclusive right to consecrate them, which he did only in the first and seventh years of his pontificate. Standing unmitred, he prayed: 'O God . . . we humbly beseech thee that thou wilt bless these waxen forms, figured with the image of an innocent lamb . . . that at the touch and sight of them, the faithful may break forth into praises, and that the crash of hailstorms, the blast of hurricanes, the violence of tempests, the fury of winds, and the malice of thunderbolts may be tempered, and evil spirits flee and tremble before the standard of thy holy cross, which is graven upon them.'

Another favorite means of defeating the Satanic power was found in great processions bearing through the streets fragments of bones and clothes of saints, or various sacred statues and emblems: one of these at Liége, in the thirteenth century, thrice proved unsuccessful in bringing rain until it was discovered that the image of the Virgin had been forgotten, whereupon a new procession with the image produced such a storm that the people were driven to run for shelter.

The means of baffling the Prince of the Power of the Air, as Paul had called him, that came to be most widely used was the ringing of consecrated bells. The vogue of baptizing bells and hanging incantations upon their tongues as a protection against hailstorms was prevalent as early as Charlemagne, who issued a strict prohibition against it. The custom was soon restored, however, and in 968 Pope John XIII gave it his approval and himself baptized the great bell of his cathedral church, the Lateran, christening it with his own name. In time ponderous treatises were written on the subject of bells and their supernatural functions, and almost every church in Europe was adorned with these holy instruments, whose supernatural powers were usually proclaimed by suitable inscriptions. One at Basel was inscribed, 'I put demons to flight'; another, at Lugano, declared, 'the sound of this bell vanquishes tempests, repels demons, and summons men'; one at Erfut claimed that it could 'ward off lightning and malignant demons'; a peal in the Jesuit church at Pont-à-Mousson bore the words, 'They praise God, put to flight the clouds, affright the demons, and call the people'; and not far away another declared, 'It is I who dissipate the thunders.' The ritual for the consecration of these bells became solemnly complex and involved the use of holy water, salt, consecrated oil, prayer, the signing of the cross, the burning of incense, and ofttimes a great feast. Bells were transported by pilgrims all the way to the Jordan in order to have their potency enhanced by this, the most potent of baptisms.

Yet bells and waxen wafers, holy water and exorcism all failed to stay the hand of His Satanic Majesty. So good Christians, believing that in order to avert the devil's work they had first to understand it, began writing long and serious books on the subject. These astute students of demonology classified the devils into several species: the male or female *malefica* were responsible for unexpected noises, the rustling of leaves and the howling of the wind, thunderstorms, hailstorms and inundations, impotence by ligature, and disease and death by poison, spells, waxen images of the evil eye. Such demons could take the form of a bear, monkey, toad, raven, vulture, gentleman, soldier, hunter, peasant, dragon or Negro. The *striga,* always female, took the form of a bird-demon or other monster, flew about by night and killed children and handsome men in order to eat them. Of the *concubitus dæmonum,* there were two sexes: the female succubus lay with men in their sleep, while the male incubus lay with women; to the visits of the latter the births of other witches, demons and evil children were attributable. Johann Weier in 1568 made an inventory of the demons and put their number at 7,405,926, comprising 1111 legions of 6666 each, 'apart,' as he says, 'from the errors of calculation.'

On the matter of incubi and succubi, Thomas Aquinas, Bonaventura and other theologians had claimed that a devil has no seed of its own and therefore does not procreate directly, but takes on the form of a succubus in order to receive the seed of man in ghostlike intercourse, and then transforms itself into an incubus so that it can impregnate the woman with whom it joins itself in a second intercourse, imparting to the children of these unions its diabolic traits. Whether it took the form of a succubus or an incubus was a matter of pleasure or expediency for the individual devil, but in general the devils much preferred being males to females. Thomas Cantipratensis asserts that he had many times received the confessions of women who complained of having been violated by incubi, and in the *Life of Saint Bernard* it is related that one brazen devil lay daily with a certain woman for several years without the slightest break or restraint so that he would even thrust himself into the bed where the husband also lay sleeping. Women were known to have died within a few days of bloat or madness after the Satanic embrace, but mostly they survived to bear the child of the cursed union. And strangely, some women endured such connubial relations for years with no great reluctance, one amour lasting for a quarter of a century. To many women, to have as a lover an angel of fire and to enjoy his supernatural embraces seemed an enviable lot; Pelagio, the Bishop of Sliva, reported in 1332 that he knew many nuns who voluntarily offered themselves to the fiend, while witches, of course, according to numerous confessions, always made willing mistresses. Lilith, the first wife of Adam, was said to suck the blood of infants and was long regarded to be the queen of the succubi; it is from her name that the word lullaby (*Lili abi*) is supposed to be derived.

viii

Despite all the devices that could be contrived to combat him, the devil continued to wreak havoc. The fluttering of wings was heard repeatedly in the darkness and luminous eyes peered balefully from under the eaves; women were seen to carry brooms after dusk, or discovered to be missing from their firesides at night, from which absences they reappeared with the mud of distant farms upon their aprons. It was clear that Satan was as yet uncurbed, and men turned to the magicians, sorcerers and witches whose secret movements and malignant curses were evidence enough that they were the Satanic agents who were bringing the world to wrack and ruin.

Thus the inquisition against heresy was of necessity expanded to include witchcraft. Or rather the tyrannical impulse of the church, having long exercised itself in the attempt to eradicate errors of belief, found a fresh and stimulating objective in black magic. As early as the fourth century heresy had come to mean any religious error held in willful and persistent opposition to authoritative declaration. But one difficulty which the church had faced from the beginning was the determination of the imperfectly defined line between heresy and that other manifestation of Satanic action, magic. Charlemagne, about 800, had expressed the belief that the arts of magic were a delusion, and had ordered that any who from a belief in the black art caused the death of an alleged witch should themselves be burned. In 840 Agobard, Bishop of Lyons, denounced the popular fear of witches as a superstition; in the twelfth century John of Salisbury called witches' flights illusions of the devil, while in the next century Etienne de Bourbon proclaimed them to be the fancies of dreaming women. Gregory VII (?1020–1085) condemned and forbade any criminal process whatsoever against those guilty only of a vain and silly superstition, while King Coloman of Hungary about 1100 said, 'There are no witches, and against those who are reputed to be such no legal action shall be taken.'

It appears to have been concomitant with the spiritual renovation which Conrad initiated under Gregory IX that authoritative interpretation moved in the other direction, for some twenty years later (1258) Alexander IV issued the first papal bull against black magic; this was addressed to the Franciscan inquisitors and cautioned them against judging any case of witchcraft unless it affected the unity or faith of the church. And for some time, apart from a notable epidemic of sorcery in

1320 when John XXII handed over to his inquisitors all cases of magic, witchcraft was officially left to the ordinary courts. Not that those who were thus charged under the secular law escaped the consequences of their affiliation with Satan, for they were almost invariably imprisoned and frequently put to death; moreover, the distinction between witchcraft and heresy was so subtle that it was usually drawn to the taste of the presiding judges. But in the century and a half after Gregory IX, this indeterminacy was gradually eliminated. On the precedents established by Gregory and John XXII, numerous bulls were published by Benedict XII, Gregory XI, Martin V and other popes, dealing in no uncertain terms with witchcraft in all its detail, and anathematizing all its aspects in the most emphatic language. The evil suffering no abatement, in 1451 Nicholas V gave his inquisitor the cognizance of cases of divination, even when the crime did not savor of heresy, a permission that amounted only to the recognition of increasing custom. Satan's activity continuing to increase, Eugene IV was forced to issue four bulls in the space of a few years exhorting the inquisitors to proceed 'summarily, without ado, and without any judiciary form' against the human agents of the Prince of the Power of the Air, and especially against those who had the power to produce bad weather. In 1473, 1478 and again in 1483 Sixtus IV attacked the spreading evil with increased vigor. The single difficulty which previously may have stayed the hands of the inquisitors, the fine line over which many an agent of the devil may have hitherto escaped, was resolved by Sixtus in no uncertain terms: he clearly designated all forms of sorcery and divination as heresy of the most hated kind, an opinion of the utmost importance when pronounced by one who was not only an eminent theologian, but the author of a large and authoritative treatise on the Immaculate Conception.

In judging this action, full cognizance must be taken of the fact that when Sixtus came to the papal throne the Prince of the Power of the Air was riding high, and all Christendom was stricken with a panic. It was an age of faith and fear. Men feared death because beyond it yawned the uncertainties of an eternal future; they feared life because it was the gate to death, the incentive, the opportunity and means to sin and the cause for punishment; they feared the physical world because it was opposed to the world of the spirit, and they feared nature because it was everywhere charged with portents of God's wrath or Satan's mischief. It was an age when according to indisputable sacred writ every trivial phenomenon that touched man's life had its supernatural origin. The time had come when, if the people were not to be destroyed, if Christ's

Vicar were not to be deposed and his work on earth completely undone, the church had to exert its full strength.

The mere discovery of the enemy's camps is not, however, the same as his defeat, and it is not surprising that this pope's successor, Innocent VIII, should find it necessary to add to Sixtus's reconnaissance a powerful and aggressive instrument which took the form of a bull addressed to two of his inquisitors, Henry Kramer (also known as Heinrich Institoris) and James Sprenger, both professors of theology in the University of Cologne, and entitled: *Summis desiderantes affectibus* ('Our most loving wish'), instructing and empowering them to prepare a manual for the detection and punishment of witchcraft in all its forms. Although this bull was merely one in a long record of papal utterances in the crusade against witches, it served to give this crusade power and authority which it had not previously possessed. Because Innocent's pronouncement came from the highest authority of the church and was characterized by infallibility under divine guarantee, because the *Malleus maleficarum* (Witches' Hammer) which Kramer and Sprenger prepared under its instruction came from two ecclesiastics who were distinguished as much by their piety and logic as by their expert knowledge of witchcraft, and because these two documents may fairly be said to mark the zenith of Christian faith, they are worthy of close examination.

A brief digression may first be permitted on the history of the term 'bull' and on the infallibility of such a document. In classical Latin, *bulla* meant bubble, and the word was early used to indicate a boss of metal, such as those on doors, sword belts and boxes. By transference it also designated the round or heart-shaped box containing a magic amulet which was suspended from the neck of children of noble birth until they assumed the *toga virilis*, after which time it was hung in the home and dedicated to the household gods. Possibly because the *bulla* was regarded as a personal charm or even *numina*, the term was applied to the leaden seals by which papal and royal documents were authenticated and, by the end of the twelfth century, it had come to mean the document itself. Such a document is an instrument of special weight and importance, written, of course, in Latin and, until 1878, in an archaic Gothic script without punctuation, demanding, since only experts could read the original, a transumption in the ordinary hand. No bull was issued without the most careful deliberation, and since it was an ex cathedra utterance of Christ's Vicar on earth, it possessed in all respects the attribute of infallibility.

This quality of infallibility was not formally declared until the Vatican Council of 1870, but it had been implicit in papal utterances for many centuries. The definition of 1870, which shocked both the Catholic and Protestant world, carefully restricts infallibility to matters of dogma and morality, to the exclusion of truths of a natural order, ecclesiastic law, government and the like, since by this late date the necessity for such restriction had been most amply demonstrated by a series of embarrassing fallacies which had been 'infallibly' proclaimed by various pontiffs over a period of some ten centuries. In the definition of 1870, the basis of infallibility is found in the Petrine texts which in earlier centuries had been used to advance the priority of the Roman over other bishops of the church: '. . . knowing most fully that this See of holy Peter remains ever free from all blemish of error, according to the Divine promise of the Lord our Saviour made to the Prince of His apostles: I have prayed for thee, that thy faith fail not: and when thou art converted, strengthen thy brethren.' The infallibility is guaranteed by the direct action of God. It is not inherent in the person of the pope but in his position as elected head of the church and as the inheritor of the power and authority of Peter himself.

By the fifteenth century, the pope of Rome had come to be not only the recognized head of the western church but the voice of current revelation and the supreme authority of Europe whom no one dared contradict. As Christ's Vicar on earth his word was law and shared the inviolable sanctity of scripture. Though not as yet attested by any ecumenical council, infallibility *de facto* was recognized, not as restricted by the definition of 1870, but in all matters of Christian faith which (in the time of Innocent VIII) encompassed not only dogma and morality but most of cosmology as well.

As has been related, by 1484 the world had come into a dreadful state. It was on December 9 of this year, within four months of his election to the pontificate, that Innocent VIII issued his bull, *Summis desiderantes affectibus*. He recounted that it had come to his ears that many persons of both sexes, unmindful of their salvation, had abandoned themselves to devils, incubi and succubi, and by their incantations, spells and other accursed charms, had slain infants in their mothers' wombs, and the offspring of cattle, had blasted the produce of the earth, the grapes of the vine, the fruits of trees, men and women, beasts of burden, herd beasts, as well as animals of other kinds, afflicting terrible and piteous pains and sore diseases, hindering men from performing the sexual act and women from conceiving, and at the instigation of the Enemy of Mankind committing and perpetrating the foulest abominations and filthiest excesses to the deadly peril of their own souls and the injury of others.

'Wherefore we decree and enjoin that the aforesaid Inquisitors (Henry Kramer and James Sprenger, Professors of Theology, of the Order of Friars Preachers) be empowered to proceed to the just correction, imprisonment and punishment of any persons, without let or hindrance . . . correcting, mulcting, imprisoning, punishing, as their crimes merit, those who they have found guilty, the penalty being adapted to the offence . . . without any right of appeal. . . . Let no man therefore . . . but if any dare to do so, which God forbid, let him know that upon him will fall the wrath of Almighty God, and of the Blessed Apostles Peter and Paul.' Kramer and Sprenger thereupon proceeded to draw up their Witches' Hammer, a manual treating the subject of witchcraft under thirty-five topics, instructing the faithful as to the position they should take in regard to this evil and detailing how accused persons should be examined, prosecuted and condemned.

The moral argument of the *Malleus* runs as follows: Adam and Eve sinned in the Garden of Eden; in consequence of their fall from grace, evil entered the world, the purpose of this evil being to punish them and their children, who are born in sin. The agents of evil are the angels who, having sinned against God, were driven forth from heaven and forevermore work under leadership of Satan against the goodness of the Creator. Satan enters men, or makes contracts with them, to gain his ends; and, since it is the church's duty to fight on the side of God against him, it must exorcise the Satanic spirits, punish men who bargain with them and make of all sinners an example to the faithful. But in addition to this earthly conflict between God and Satan is the fate of man's immortal soul; this is in the keeping of the church, which, in the sacrament, has the final yea or nay, and the immortal soul can only be consigned to God if in the view of the church it has expiated its mortal sins. It is better that a man lose this short and inconsequential life than God's eternal blessedness. To reinforce the argument they quote Augustine: 'So merciful is Almighty God that He would not allow any evil to be in His works unless He were so omnipotent and good that He can bring good even out of evil.'

According to the professors of theology from the University of Cologne, there is no sin worse than the sin of witches, in the detection of which the inquisitor must use every care, for the devil is both clever and determined and will resort to any means to deceive the judge. Sometimes a public accusation is leveled by a person who offers to prove his charge, but this circumstance is full of danger to the accuser because of the penalty of talion if he fails to prove his charge, and also because the devil may seek retaliation; it is equally dangerous to the inquisitor because it is apt to lead to endless litigation, and it is therefore to be officially discouraged. A better method is to proceed on the assertions of those who are moved by zeal for the faith or by fear of punishment for failure to offer information, and it is best to take denunciation secretly when no accuser or informer has to appear and submit himself to the risk of retaliation by the devil or the suspected party.

In recommending a secret procedure the *Malleus* was not deviating from long established precedent, for it was the custom to surprise the accused by a sudden summons and imprison her on suspicion; everyone accused was assumed to be guilty until released, since lasting proof of innocence was in the nature of the case impossible. The accused was allowed no defense beyond the privilege of naming such enemies as might have reason to denounce her, but she was not allowed to know who had denounced her, the judge always appearing as the accuser. In the precedent established by Pope Boniface VIII (1294–1303) for the treatment of heretics, the trial was conducted 'simply and squarely, without the noise and form of lawyers and judges.' Women, children, slaves and heretics were admitted as witnesses for the prosecution but not for the accused, and no witness called by the court might refuse to give evidence under pain of being charged with heresy himself. A false witness could be punished, but his testimony might be retained and could have its full effect. The charge was not as a rule worded in terms of particular offenses, but in terms of 'tendencies' and 'dispositions,' and external acts of piety and verbal professions of faith had no value for the accused, whose sole protection rested in the popular opinion of the leading men of the community, who were presumed to be consulted, and in the presence during the interrogation of two disinterested parties.

The *Malleus* specially cautioned the judge not to conclude his examination too quickly, for the reason that unless God, through a holy angel, compels the devil to withhold his help from the witch, she will by the devil's help maintain a stubborn silence, the 'diabolic taciturnity,' not only against questioning but against all torture; and even if her silence is at last broken it will be only to assert her innocence falsely, for some witches with the devil's help would sooner be torn limb from limb than confess any of the truth. As a first effort to procure a confession, friends of the accused should be summoned and told that if she confesses she will escape the death penalty, since often the mere misery of imprisonment, long meditation and the advice of honest men will dispose a witch to discover the truth. If, after a prolonged state of suspense and continual postponement of the day of examination, the judge still believes that the accused is denying the truth, he is to question her lightly without shedding blood. She should first be stripped and searched, for witches often prepare instruments of witchcraft out of the limbs of unbaptized children, which they sew into their garments, hide in their hair or even in unmentionable places in order to gain the devil's help in withstanding the pleas of honest men and acquiring strength to resist the torture. If, after she has been disarmed in this manner, the persuasions of the judge and those who are zealous for the faith still fail to move her to a convincing and complete confession, let her be bound to some engine of torture, which the officers should do joyfully, not appearing to be disturbed by their duty. Then let her be released at someone's earnest request, again persuaded, and promised that she can escape the death penalty.

Here it is asked whether, in the case of a prisoner convicted by her general bad reputation, by witnesses, and by the evidence of the fact, the only thing lacking being a confession of the crime from her own mouth, the judge can lawfully promise her her life if she confesses, since if she does confess she must suffer the extreme penalty. It is answered that she may be promised her life if she is to be sentenced to imprisonment for life on bread and water, provided she supplies evidence which will lead to the conviction of other witches. But she is not to be told that she is to be imprisoned in this way; she should be led to suppose that some other penance, such as exile, will be imposed instead. Or, the accused may be promised her life and then, when the promise has been kept for a time after her confession, she may be burned if the judge has made the promise in such a way that he can afterwards disclaim the duty of passing sentence on her and depute it to another judge.

It is as difficult to compel a witch to tell the truth as it is to exorcise a person possessed of the devil, and if neither threats nor promises move her, she should be sentenced to the torture. She must be examined, not in any new or exquisite manner, but in the usual way, lightly or heavily as the nature of her crime demands; while she is being questioned let her be frequently exposed to torture, beginning with the more gentle of them. If she confesses under torture, she should then be taken to another place and questioned anew so that she does not confess only under the stress of torture. If, after being fittingly tortured, she still refuses to confess, the judge should have other engines of torture brought before her and shown her, and then if she is not induced by terror to confess, the torture must be 'continued' on the second or third day.

Methods of torture are not described in the *Malleus,* and it would be pleasanter if their details could be left to the imagination, but complete omission of this exquisite ecclesiastic method of discovering truth would be a deplorable injustice to the millions of people for whom, over a period of many centuries, they were all too real. The use of torture against heretics was formally approved in 1252 by Innocent IV in his bull *Ad Exstirpanda,* and by 1312 cruelty had grown so excessive that it was disapproved by a church council. It nevertheless continued as the principal method of examination and, after the publication of the *Malleus,* was given extraordinary variety and elaborated with artistic skill by men who pondered long on the best methods of evoking the most intense and prolonged human suffering. According to canon law, torture could be applied once only, but it could be adjourned and 'continued' many times, and if necessary, it could be used on witnesses as well.

The accused was usually first tested in the ordeal by water, which consisted of throwing her into a river or moat; innocence was proved by sinking, guilt by swimming, the principle being that the water refused to receive those who had shaken off the baptismal water through a renunciation of their faith. Even when the ordeal by water immediately revealed that the accused was guilty, it was imperative to obtain a full confession, to which end a variety of very ingenious devices were afterward applied. There were heavy pincers to tear out the fingernails, or to be used red-hot for pinching; there was the rack, a long table on which the accused was tied by her hands and feet, back down, and stretched by rope and windlass until the joints were dislocated; to this were added rollers covered with knobs or sharp spikes, which were placed under the hips and shoulders, and over which the victim was rolled back and forth; there were the thumbscrew, an instrument designed for disarticulating the fingers, Spanish boots to crush the legs and feet, metal shirts lined with knives, the Iron Virgin, a hollow instrument the size and figure of a woman, with knives so arranged inside that when the two halves of the figure were closed under pressure the accused would be lacerated in its deadly embrace. This and other devices were inscribed with the motto *Soli Deo Gloria,* 'Glory be only to God.' In addition there were a variety of branding irons, horsewhips, pins to be thrust beneath the nails, and various devices for suspending the accused in space, head up or head down, with weights attached. These instruments were sprayed with holy water to fortify them against the devil, and to weaken her power of silence the suspected witch was forced to drink an infusion prepared from objects that had been blessed. Official records reveal that suspects were put to eighteen successive tortures in one day, and a witch named Holf was 'continued' fifty-six times. When the torturer and his assistant grew tired, the hands and feet of the accused were tied, the hair was cut off and brandy was poured over the head and ignited, or sulphur was burned in the arm pits or on the breast. At night the victim was chained closely to the floor or wall where she was a helpless prey to the rats and vermin which populated the bloody torture chambers.

To return to the instructions of the *Malleus,* in the intervals between the application of torture the judge and other honest men were to do all in their power to persuade the accused to confess the truth, giving her, if it seemed expedient, a promise that her life would be spared. The judge should take care that she was never left alone, lest the devil cause her to kill herself. In 'continuing' the torture, the judge should bear in mind that, just as the same medicine is not applicable to all members, there being various salves for each member, so not all heretics or those accused of heresy were to be subjected to the same method of examination and torture. If the Sons of Darkness were to become accustomed to one general rule of examination or one method of torture, they would provide means of evading the first as a well-known snare set for their destruction and against the second would devise extraordinary means of resistance.

They were told that a witch will reveal her diabolic power of preserving silence by failing to weep under the most solemn conjurations, and even under torture. The reason a witch cannot weep is, as St. Bernard says, that tears are displeasing to the devil because the tears of the humble can penetrate to heaven and conquer the unconquerable, so to prevent a witch from finally attaining penitence the devil uses all his power to restrain her tears. The judge may conjure her to true tears if she be innocent or restrain false tears by placing his hand upon her head and saying: "I conjure you by the bitter tears shed on the Cross by our Saviour the Lord Jesus Christ for the salvation of the world, and by the burning tears poured in the evening hour over His wounds by the most glorious Virgin Mary, His Mother, and by the Saints and the Elect of God, from whose eyes have now been wiped away all tears, that if you be guilty that you shall by no means do so [weep]. In the name of the Father and of the Son and of the Holy Ghost, Amen." It is found by experience that the more they are conjured, the less they are able to weep, however hard they may try to do so. On the other hand, tears in a guilty person may be only a sign that the devil of his own free will has deserted the accused and left her unprotected.

During the examination and torture the judge and the assessors must be careful not to allow themselves to be touched physically by the witch, nor to be stared at nor seen first by her, for experience has shown that by such methods witchcraft is worked upon honest men themselves and even the mind of the judge might be so altered that he would consider the witch to be innocent and would let her go free. He and the assessors should always carry with them some salt consecrated on Palm Sunday and some Blessed Herbs. These can be enclosed together in Blessed Wax and worn around the neck, for they have a wonderful protective virtue, as is shown not only from the testimony of witches but from the use and practice of the church, which blesses such objects for this very purpose.

If the witch still refuses to confess, let the hair be shaved from every part of her body, lest she has hidden therein some superstitious object to enable her to obtain the power of silence. Even if such an object is not found, the devil may so harden her heart without the use of charms that she is unable to confess her crimes. This power of taciturnity can proceed from a natural hardness of heart; some witches are so softhearted, or even feebleminded, that at the slightest torture they admit everything, even some things which are not true; others are so hardhearted that, however much they are tortured, the truth is not to be had from them. The ability to remain silent may also proceed from the power of another witch who has gained possession of a thread or some object belonging to the prisoner and thereby transferred her power to the accused. The judge himself must decide the source of the power of taciturnity and proceed accordingly.

Finally, let her be well treated in the matter of food and drink and let a man enter into her confidence and pretend to be an accomplice and let spies listen and take careful notes. Or let her be imprisoned in a castle and have the castellan pretend to go on a long journey; then let some of his women visit her and promise to set her at liberty if she will teach them how to conduct certain practices. If the judge takes notes of these matters, witches may very often be led to confess. If she still does not admit her crimes, let the judge resentence her to torture of new and more exquisite kinds, remembering that the devil is clever and able to arm himself against anything with which he is familiar.

If, after thorough examination, the accused is found innocent, this fact should not be stated in the sentence. Rather, let it be stated that nothing was legally proved against her, for if after a little time she should again be brought to trial and her guilt should be legally proved, she can be condemned in spite of the previous absolution. Pure acquittal is a dangerous precedent.

The accused may be found guilty of degrees of witchcraft ranging from 'sheerest accusation' through 'light suspicion, strong suspicion, denial of heresy,' and so on to 'heresy.' Those who confess may be 'reconciled' with the church, thus saving them the grace of the hereafter, but they are none the less to be inflicted with punishments ranging from penances, fasting, pilgrimages to Palestine, Canterbury, etc., public scourging or humiliation, up to perpetual imprisonment. Perpetual imprisonment is of two kinds: *murus largus,* where the prisoner is to be fed, clothed and housed in fair comfort, this sentence being recommended for publicly important men and women; and *murus strictus,* in which the prisoner is confined in deepest dungeon, with single or double fetters and only bread and water.

Those who are convicted without confession, or convicted of more than they confess, are to be found guilty of heresy. A typical sentence for mild heresy reads in part: 'Since the Lord in his Infinite mercy permits men at times to fall into heresies and errors, not only that learned Catholics may be exercised in sacred arguments, but that they who have fallen from the faith may become more humble thereafter and perform works of penitence . . .' and because 'it would be a very scandalous thing not to avenge the injuries done to temporal lords, and to tolerate the offenses committed against God the Creator of all the Heavens, since it is a far greater sin to offend against the Eternal than against a temporal Majesty, and that God who pities sinners may have mercy upon you, that you may be an example to others, and that your sins may not remain unpunished, and that you may become more careful in the future, and not more prone but less apt to commit the said and any other crimes: We the said Bishop and Judge, or Judges, on behalf of the faith, sitting in the tribunal as Judges judging, sentence and condemn you to perpetual imprisonment, there to be punished with the bread of affliction and the water of distress; reserving to ourselves the right to mitigate, aggravate, change or remit wholly or in part the said sentence, if, when and as often as it shall seem good to us to do so.'

The severer sentences applicable to the full charge of heresy are much longer, but have a similar import, and a typical one ends: 'We the said Bishop and Judges, sitting in tribunal as Judges judging, having before us the Holy Gospel that our judgment may proceed as from the countenance of God and our eyes see with equity, and having before our eyes only God and the irrefragable truth of the Holy Faith and the extirpation of the plague of heresy; against you, N., in this place on the day and at the hour before assigned to you for the hearing of your definite sentence, we pronounce that you have truly fallen into (or back into) the sin of heresy;

and as one truly so relapsed we cast you forth from this our ecclesiastical Court, and leave you to be delivered to the secular arm. But we earnestly pray that the said secular court may temper its justice with mercy, that there be no bloodshed or danger of death.'

Since the phrase 'to be delivered to the secular arm' meant to be burned at the stake, the prayer that 'the secular court temper its justice with mercy' was permission, not often utilized, for prior strangulation. Unless the concern of the judges against 'bloodshed or danger of death' refers to themselves and the executioners, or perhaps the spectators who gathered around the fire, it remains wholly mysterious since this was a death sentence which the secular court, on pain of excommunication, was forced to execute. Because it is a death sentence, the *Malleus* instructs that it should not be pronounced on a Festival or Solemn Day, nor in a church, since these are dedicated to God. Moreover, the judge should not himself convey the sentence to the prisoner, nor after passing sentence, present himself before the prisoner, since the prisoner might be moved by terror or hate to wreak evil upon him. With the delivering of the sentence the responsibilities of the ecclesiastic judge and his assessors end, and the secular court is expected to perform its office. In some cases the prisoner was allowed to receive the Eucharist, when four hours were allowed for the Host to be dissolved, after which the culprit was burned and the ashes scattered to the wind.

If it should happen, the *Malleus* goes on, that when the prisoner is already at the place where he is to be burned he should willingly abjure all heresy, he may in mercy be received as a penitent heretic and imprisoned for life; however, the judges ought not to place much faith in a conversion of this sort, since it may be presumed that the prisoner confesses from fear of death rather than for love of truth, and in any case they can punish him on account of the temporal injuries which he has committed.

Once the inquisitor had by torture and false promises obtained a confession, he had but to pass the sentence upon the accused that he 'be turned over to the secular arm.' There was no way for the secular arm to err except to use an insufficient quantity of wood. As for the judge, he had to aid him the solemn advice of the learned men of the theological faculty as well as men skilled in the canon and civil law, in addition to the testimony of the witnesses, which, having been taken in secrecy, must be considered as unbiased by compulsion or constraint; and as he reached his decision he placed his hand upon the Bible and recalled the injunction of Moses: 'Thou shalt not suffer a witch to live.' Supported by these safeguards, by prayerful communion with God and by Christ's

Vicar on earth whose infallible wisdom and expressed orders he was putting into effect, how was it possible for him to err?

On July 25, 1492, Pope Innocent VIII, who had long been sickly so that almost his only nourishment for many weeks had been woman's milk, passed away in his sleep. To mourn him were only his two natural children. He was buried in St. Peter's and upon his tomb, a magnificent work in bronze by Pollaiuolo, were inscribed the punning words: *Ego antem Innocentia mea ingressus sum* (But I have gone on in my innocence). As for Kramer and Sprenger, it is enough to know that they lived, to know how they reasoned and what the consequences of their reasoning were. They had a theory of God and they adhered to it with indisputable logic. Every argument underlying the discovery of witchcraft by trial and torture was a rigorous and logically sound deduction from the Christian premises. These premises were the heritage of long ages of speculation: the Egyptians had bequeathed to man the notion of the talismanic power of righteousness, of doing that which the gods loved; the Jews bequeathed him Yahweh, the Persians, the absolutes of good and evil; Socrates had given him an immortal soul and Plato a doctrine of physical imperfection striving to achieve spiritual perfection; Babylonia had supplied the Satan necessary to free God of the charge of evil; and Augustine had woven all these threads together into a fabric of sin stretching from generation to generation without end. It was these men, and not a fifteenth century pope and his two zealous Dominican priests, frightened half out of their wits by boils, hailstorms and epidemics of sick pigs, who are to be blamed for man's descent into the lowest depths which the human intellect has ever reached.

Here and there were men who rebelled against the horror and doubted the validity of the witchcraft persecution: the first of recorded memory being the soldier-physician Agrippa of Nettesheim (1486–1535), who for his opposition to the church was hounded from one city to another in Europe and only saved from persecution by his friendship with the Hapsburgs, the king of the Netherlands, the duke of Savoy and other powerful persons. Others who spoke or wrote against it were Johann Weier (1563), Reginald Scott (1580), Montaigne (1581), Adam Tanner (1626), Friedrich von Spee (1631) and Balthasar Bekker (1691). These isolated voices had little effect. The *Malleus* had held that skepticism about witchcraft itself savored of heresy, and skepticism was therefore not only dangerous but impotent. Towards the close of the sixteenth century Dietrich Flade, eminent jurist and chief judge of the Electoral Court, revolted from the ranks of orthodoxy; after having sentenced many people to death he realized that it was all unreal, that the confessions forced out of the victims of his torture chamber were either the result of madness or the necessity to confess anything and everything in order to shorten the fearful ordeal. When Flade expressed this doubt, he was immediately arrested by the authority of the archbishop and charged with having sold himself to Satan; and he in turn was racked until he confessed everything which his torturers suggested, and finally he was strangled and burned.

Yet despite its heroic measures, the *Malleus* failed to beat the devil down. Innocent himself had been forced to issue three additional bulls urging the faithful to increased zeal in witch catching, and other pontiffs continued to issue bulls until the middle of the seventeenth century. The theologians produced volume after volume in which they discoursed informatively on all aspects of the subject, proving the reality of Satan, his demons and his monstrous deeds by the most erudite arguments. Notable among these treatises were *De Praestigiis Daemonum* (1563) by Johann Weier, *De la Démonomanie des Sorciers* (1587) by Jean Bodin, *Discours des Sorciers* (1590) by Henri Boguet, the *Daemonolatreiae* (1595) in three volumes by Nicholas Remy, and *Les controverses et recherches magique* (1611) by Del Rio. Literature of this genre became popular reading among the educated and the horrifying tales spread in a whispered flood to all parts of the world and onto every intellectual level. For three hundred years men, women and children continued to confess that they raised hailstorms or commandeered the thunder and lightning by incantations and magic rituals, that they turned themselves into werewolves and ate children, or that they flew through the night to the terrifying sacrilegious Sabbat. Nicholas Remy boasted in his book on demonology that within fifteen years he had sent eight hundred persons to death for witchcraft in Lorraine, and added that 'justice has been so ably administered at my hands that in one year sixteen witches have taken their own lives rather than come before me.' A bishop in Würtzburg claimed 1900 in a five year period; another in Como, 100 in one year; another in Nancy, 800 in 16 years; another in Bamberg, 600 in 10 years, while at Geneva, the home of Calvin, 500 were executed in three months and the Parliament of Toulouse distinguished itself by burning 400 in a single day. A total of 7000 were said to have been burned at Treves. Boquet boasted of having burned 600 lycanthropes, and it has been asserted that the Lutheran, Benedict Carpzov (1595–1666), who claimed that he had read the Bible 53 times, passed sentence on 20,000 Satanists. The slaughter was less in England, but the official count puts the figure at not less than 1000 people hanged or burned between 1542 and 1736. How many people were tried or otherwise persecuted for witchcraft in Europe during the whole Christian Era is unknown; estimates run as high as several million, and a much larger figure would be required to encompass all those who were indirectly brought into misery by the struggle to defend God and man against the devil. With no exaggeration it can be said that for five centuries, from the twelfth through the seventeenth century, all Christendom was ravaged by this war.

The Reformation, which shifted the emphasis from ecclesiastic law to the scriptures, only aggravated the horror; Protestantism accepted the belief as fully as Catholicism, and since the schismatics were anxious to prove themselves as zealous and righteous as the orthodox, the war against the devil became, if possible, more systematic. Feyerabend's *Theatrum Diabolorum,* a work put out by a number of Luther's followers, raised Johann Weier's estimate of the number of existing devils to 2,665,866,746,-664, while others put the figure at not less than ten thousand billion.

Calvin had said, "Whoever shall now contend that it is unjust to put heretics and blasphemers to death will, knowingly and willingly, incur their very guilt." To Luther, the devil was a living personality who interfered with his work and rest, and once, so it is related, this preacher threw his inkstand at His Satanic Majesty. Luther subscribed to the belief in incubi and succubi and demonic changelings, and asserted that to deny the reality of witchcraft was to deny the authority of the Bible. Luther's contribution to the Reformation consisted largely of substituting egotism, doctrination and personal salvation for the altar, sacraments and ceremonies of Catholicism, and these shifts, coupled with his ignorance and superstition, could not save Protestantism from the insanity.

In Scotland particularly, where the all-powerful minister of the kirk served both as accuser and examiner, witch hunting became a popular pastime, with every man listening at every other man's keyhole. In every kirk there hung a box in which the names of suspected persons could be dropped secretly, and to be suspected was to be accused, while to be accused was almost certainly to suffer punishment. During the reign of Elizabeth religious exiles from the continent brought the epidemic of witchcraft into England. Under James I, stern Scot and Calvinist, torture was initiated, and within a decade the Puritans, adding enforced sleeplessness and ducking to other devices for discovering witches, were destroying them by the score. At Leith, in 1589, a man confessed, while his legs were crushed in the boots and wedges were driven under his fingernails, that several hundred witches had gone to sea in a sieve and raised the tempest that had delayed the Princess of Denmark, James's bride.

And in 1664 nine women were burned there at one time and in one pyre for lesser evils. Persons skilled in detecting witches by searching out insensitive moles, or 'devil's marks,' and testing them with pins, needles or awls, came to be recognized as experts. The Scottish 'prickers' formed a regular guild. Famous in this art were John Kincaid, the 'common pricker' of Tranent, John Bain, John Balfour and Matthew Hopkins. The last named combed the county of Suffolk and tested multitudes of old women by pricking them, and as a result of his tests declared the county to be infested. Parliament thereupon sent two eminent Presbyterian divines and a legal commission to weed out the evil, and they set about their task by hanging sixty persons in one year. They weighed the witches in a balance against the Bible, or in the continental manner ducked them in the river with thumbs and toes tied crosswise, those who did not sink being adjudged guilty. Hopkins charged but twenty shillings a town, although he sometimes had to ride twenty miles there and back, and, as he said, if he found three or four witches, or only one, this was cheap enough. The story that this great witch hunter was hung for a witch himself is apparently a fiction, the only credible evidence indicating that he died in a Christian bed.

In 1647 the mania spread to New England and culminated in the Salem witch trials of 1692. Before it had spent itself hundreds of persons had been arrested and nineteen had been hung, eight in one day. The Salem epidemic is notable chiefly because the shamed reaction that followed it broke the power of Cotton Mather and ended theocracy in the Colonies. During the Salem trials a dog was put to death at Andover for bewitching several people, which balanced accounts between the Eastern and Western Hemispheres: in the year 1474 a diabolical rooster, for the heinous and unnatural crime of laying an egg, had been solemnly tried, condemned and publicly burned at the stake by the church authorities of Basle.

Although as late as 1768 the schismatic John Wesley proclaimed that 'the giving up of witchcraft is in effect the giving up of the Bible,' the world was now satiated with torture and the smell of burned flesh, and little by little people were beginning to doubt, if for no better reason than that they were tired of believing, that men and women could be inspired agents of His Satanic Majesty. Holland abolished witch hunting in 1610, Geneva in 1632, Sweden in 1649, England in 1682. The last victims of the official inquisition, a Quaker and a Jew, were respectively hanged and burned in 1826. The last judicial execution for witchcraft in Europe took place in Poland in 1793, when two old women were burned. A wizard, however, died as a result of an unofficial ordeal by water in

England in 1865, and in 1900 two Irish peasants tried to roast a witch over her own fire. The notion of the human embodiment of evil had run itself out. Stemming back into prehistory, it had awaited the favorable milieu of Christian doctrine to develop to grotesque and unbelievable proportions, only ultimately to be overthrown by its own absurdities. And, too, other ideas were offering competition. Copernicus, Galileo, Newton, Huygens, Halley and Harvey had turned men's thoughts in another direction. In 1752, when Benjamin Franklin sent a kite up into the clouds and drew lightning off its string, the last remnants of meteorological demonology crumbled down: the Prince of the Power of the Air had lost his dominion over frightened men.

With the demonstration that the dreaded lightning was the same stuff that crackled off a dry cat's back, the world turned curiously, with the relief of a child who has been badly frightened, to this new interpretation. Most of the world, that is, for there were those who were prepared to uphold their theory of God and the devil at all costs. They promptly called Franklin an 'archinfidel' and the iron rod which he invented to protect tall buildings from the devil's wrath they anathematized as 'heretical.' They stormed from the pulpits that thunder and lightning were tokens of divine displeasure, and that it was impiety to prevent their doing their full work. To interfere with God's plan was sacrilege. The Reverend Thomas Prince, pastor of the Old South Church in Boston, asserted in 1755 that an earthquake which had shaken that city was due to Franklin's iron points. "In Boston," he said, "are more erected than anywhere else in New England, and Boston seems to be more dreadfully shaken. Oh! there is no getting out of the mighty hand of God!"

It was long before the churches consented to be protected by the heretical tool. The tower of St. Mark's in Venice had at the time of Franklin's invention been struck again and again by lightning, sometimes with such disastrous effects that it had been almost destroyed. The Almighty, or alternatively the Powers of Darkness, seemed to have singled it out for special punishment, in spite of the angel that adorned its summit, the consecrated bells which were repeatedly rung to drive away the thunder, the holy relics in the cathedral nearby and the processions of the Virgin and the patron saint. The tower was struck again in two successive summers after the lightning rod was introduced in Italy, whereupon the authorities succumbed and a rod erected. The edifice has never been struck since, but God alone has received the thanks of a grateful people. In Austria the church of Rosenberg was struck so frequently and with such loss of life that the peasants feared to attend services. Three times the spire had to be rebuilt, until the devil was exorcised by an iron rod. Such was also the history of St. Bride's and St. Paul's in London, the cathedrals of Sienna and Strasburg and of other churches throughout Europe and America; they were protected only after it was evident that not to do so was to lay them open to repeated injury.

In time, by a subtle compromise, the power of time-honored sacred devices came to be considered in practice subordinate to an iron band, but such is the working of the theological mind that the acceptance of the latter in no way discredited the virtues of the former. When the Island of St. Honorat, made sacred over centuries by many Christian legends, was restored in 1871, the great church of the monastery was rebuilt with almost unprecedented extravagance. Great stores of holy relics were sent in, including fragments of the true cross, of the white and purple robes, of the crown of thorns, the sponge, the lance and winding sheet, and also fragments of the hair, robe, veil, and girdle of the Virgin, together with relics of John the Baptist, Joseph, Mary Magdalene, Paul, Barnabas, the four evangelists and a multitude of other saints. Under the altars were laid the bones of Christian martyrs brought specially from the Roman catacombs. The mere enumeration of these treasures, among the most precious in all Christendom, requires twenty-four distinct headings in the official catalogue. Over the relics were erected many altars, and above both relics and altars were placed the magic bells, baptized and consecrated by four bishops with a powerful formula to drive away the Prince of the Power of the Air and the lightning and tempests he provokes. And higher still, at the summit of the central spire, was placed Franklin's lightning rod. For the Trappist monks who live among the shaded cloisters far below, for the multitudes who come to view the relics which by their mere presence can work miracles, for the peasants who pause at eventide to listen to the bells which, so it is asserted, by their ringing can save storm-tossed ships at sea, the invisible point is of no significance. But for the Babylonian legend of Kingu and the story of God's disobedient angel, Satan, it marks the end.

VII

~~~~~~

The Species Problem

AS the last vestiges of Greek skepticism and rationality died out in the West, the pagan heritage of natural philosophy passed to the keeping of the Arabs. The Roman physician Galen (131–201) may be taken as the last Christian layman of importance to ask questions directly of nature, for shortly after his time intellectual activity became the exclusive province of the church. Under the Augustinian injunction, 'Nothing is to be accepted save on the authority of Scripture, for greater is this authority than all the powers of the human mind,' those who were mentally fitted or inclined toward intellectual inquiry were deflected to the study of theology, either as revealed in the sacred writings or as discoverable in mystical experiences; they were impelled by Christian doctrine to seek and study only that which would exalt man and prove his divine nature. If by any chance an observation contrary to scriptural statement or the anthropocentric view intruded itself into their religious meditations they were constrained to hold their senses fallible and their perception erroneous until the fact had been twisted, distorted, mangled beyond all recognition, in order to conform with holy truths.

Yet these holy truths, for their own sake, had to be made reasonable, their internal contradictions explained, their mysteries reconciled wherever possible with common sense. Tertullian, irritated by pagan ridicule, might retort, "I believe because it is absurd," but Tertullian had a measure of credulity rare even in the most devout Christian. Following him there were many better thinkers in the church who, because they did believe, wanted the faith to be made as reasonable as possible. Origen, in his reply to Celsus, Cyril of Alexandria answering Julian the Apostate, Augustine refuting Gnosticism, each had sought in proportion to his lights to reconcile scripture and philosophy. Apologetics, whether construed as an effort to defend Christianity against the criticisms of nonbelievers or as the faith's internal effort to rationalize its mysteries, constituted from the beginning a major intellectual and literary exercise for educated Christians. The first apologetic effort had culminated in the voluminous anti-Gnostic works of Augustine and had paused there, in part because Augustine's solutions were apparently irrefutable (an appearance created as much by the quantity as the quality of his dissertations), and in part because the anti-intellectual attitude of the early medieval church discouraged men from coming to its defense. It required the lapse of centuries, the violence of the Crusades, the Moslem occupation of Spain, the migrations of Jewish and Arab scholars which these military movements promoted, and the artistic and emotional forces underlying the Renaissance to reawaken in Christian consciousness the suspicion that a verbatim knowledge of scripture and of the voluminous works of Augustine was not enough to save the church against intellectual assault.

It is not surprising that when reason, so long asleep, began to reassert itself it was only to the end of expounding the sacred verities that heaven had vouchsafed through the medium of revelation and, if possible, of increasing Christian certitude. Shackled by the necessity of accepting as its premises the a priori conclusions already reached by ten centuries of theological speculation, reason could at best aspire to prove worthy of the title of 'handmaid to the faith' by showing that these were the only conclusions that were possible.

The travail between reason and revelation, historically known as Scholasticism, was destined to result in the admission by both sides that reason and faith are intrinsically incompatible. Indeed, under the influence of Scholasticism reason was strictly forbidden to touch upon theological matters, which were held to be something entirely beyond its province: none the less in this, the second great era of apologetics, even while theology was gaining a number of new and elegant ornaments, reason profited in consequence of the unusual exercises which it encountered.

It was the fortune, or misfortune, of medieval Christianity that its chief inheritance from Hellenic culture was transmitted through Neoplatonism and consisted of those features of Plato's works which were most opposed to the liberal, exploratory Greek spirit. Of Plato's mixed philosophy the Academicians of later centuries chose to emphasize his oracles, his asceticism and his number-mysticism, to the exclusion of his more critical modes of intellection. Ultimately when his followers grew tired of number-mysticism they convinced themselves that only the supersensual is real, a position but slightly removed from Plato's doctrine of Ideas, though one

reached independently of Platonic argument the logical niceties of which
they were incapable of understanding.

Plotinus and those who followed in the pattern of his thought have been
called Neoplatonists, though the identification, however justified historically, does not flatter the 'father of unreason' since Neoplatonism
marked the intellectual bankruptcy of the ancient world and the universal
acceptance of the crudest superstition. Calling itself a repository of philosophy, it despised as useless the entire cultural heritage which Greece
and Rome might otherwise have bequeathed to a barbarian world and the
most creditable thing that can be said of it is that it represents absolute
religion, unmarred by compromise with the objective world. But Christianity, lacking what could properly be called a philosophy of its own, took
Neoplatonism and its doctrine of the supersensual to its heart and made of
it a basic tenet of belief. Thereafter the approach to the Supreme One, the
search for eternal truth by way of a swooning rapture proved most agreeable to Christian taste and the mystics of the cloister spent hours before
the crucifix or an image of the Virgin, enduring hunger and discomfort
while they sought that self-hypnosis by which the mind was 'put out of its
place' and the soul was united with the Ineffable. The titillating experience came to be looked upon as a special act of grace accorded by God
as an encouragement to beginners, a step in the progression towards holiness, or the attainment of a state but little short of saintliness itself.

Ruysbroek, a great mystic of the fourteenth century, gave a vivid account of religious ecstasy: 'When love has carried us above all things,
above the light into the Divine darkness, we are transformed by the
eternal Word who is the image of the Father; and, as the air is penetrated
by the sun we receive in place the light incomprehensible, embracing and
penetrating us. What is this light, if it be not a contemplation of the infinite and an intuition of eternity? We behold that which we are, and
we are that which we behold, because our being, without losing anything
of its own personality, is united with the Divine truth which includes all
divinity.' And a century earlier, Aquinas, the greatest of the Schoolmen,
said, 'The higher our mind is raised to the contemplation of spiritual
things, the more it is abstracted from sensible things. But the final term
at which contemplation can possibly arrive is the Divine substance. Therefore the mind that sees the Divine substance must be wholly divorced from
the bodily senses, either by death or by some rapture.'

Where to swoon is to know God and to experience rapture is to discover
truth, reason is a broken reed. The Schoolmen began their task with

such Neoplatonic bias that when the abridged works of Aristotle were first introduced to the West in the twelfth century they were outrightly condemned as materialistic and destructive to the faith. Shortly, however, it came to be recognized that if properly 'interpreted' Aristotle could be made to serve the ends of faith by aiding in metaphysical speculation, and within a century the pagan naturalist had come to be known as the 'precursor of Christ in nature' even as John the Baptist was the 'precursor of Christ in spirit.' To prove a point in dogma by means of an Aristotelian argument assumed an importance almost equal to the attainment of ecstasy itself. Thus was born Scholasticism, which may be called an effort to co-ordinate the Neoplatonic doctrine of the mystical nature of reality with the irrefragable and frequently irrational statements of scripture, the co-ordination starting from unsubstantiated premises and being completed by Aristotelian arguments based on order, sequence and relation.

The speculative alchemists of the medieval universities who would fain have transmuted the dross of Aristotle's philosophy into revelation's precious metal were forced, in order to avoid the charge of heresy, to experiment with topics upon which scripture and its ecclesiastic appendices had failed to give the final word. The one topic the discussion of which was least likely to bring them into conflict with authority was that very one upon which Plato and Aristotle had emphatically disagreed, namely the nature of the 'real.' A single sentence, in a Latin translation by Boetius of Porphyry's *Isagoge,* appears to have been responsible for raising this problem in medieval times, and thus supplying the subject matter for five centuries of disputation. Porphyry's sentence merely called attention to the Platonic distinction, or as it might be, 'relation,' between the singulars of objects and the universals of Ideas: 'I shall omit to speak of genera and species as to whether they subsist in the nature of things or in mere conceptions only; whether, if subsistent, they are bodies or incorporeal; and whether they are separate from, or in and along with, perceptual things; I shall not speak of these, for a matter of this kind is most profound and in need of further study.'

This sentence, raising a question without answering it, was bound to excite curiosity. The vast amount of detailed thinking which Plato and Aristotle had done on the subject was not available to medieval scholars and they were forced to think the matter through anew, only to discover some dangerous implications.

Boetius implies that he himself was rather anti-Platonically inclined, preferring the Aristotelian position that only individual things exist, and that universals, such as genera, species, qualities and like terms which serve to relate different individuals, are but modes of expression convenient for the description of recurring similarities between these individuals. His position was vaguely stated, however, and Scholasticism proper opened on the opposite note, with John Scotus Erigena of the ninth century defending the view that only God is real, and that the world of things and of all experience is but a 'theophany,' an imperfect sensory perception of divinity.

The view that regarded things as real degraded universals to mere names, modes of speech, or synthetic constructions of thought, and hence came to be identified as 'nominalism,' in contradistinction to the Neoplatonic 'realism' which regarded universals as the only true *realia*. The paradox that, on the one hand, the 'nominalists' asserted that only particular things are real, while on the other the 'realists' asserted that only the universals which are shared in common by particular things are real, the things themselves being but illusions, has always confused this justly famous and important philosophic dispute. Where 'realism' contended for the complete dematerialization of the world of sensory experience, nominalism — and common sense — contended for at least some form of reality for material things, if not for outright materialism.

Except for changes in terms introduced by the Neoplatonists and some elaboration in argument, the debate was still at the point where Plato had left it. The chief difference effected by fourteen centuries was that where Plato had been defending the aristocratic tradition against the attacks of the democratic mob, 'realism' was now invoked in defending Christian legend and tradition against the attacks of nominalism.

Nominalism first acquired the magnitude of a heresy when Roscellinus (d. *ca.* 1125), a canon of Compiègne, refusing to recognize the reality of anything but the individual, the thing which is directly perceived, treated the universal as a mere *flatus vocis,* a verbal breathing, a manner of speaking. In that case neither wisdom, nor hope, nor faith, nor goodness, exist as *realia,* but only as figures of speech; nor can one say that three persons can be one 'thing,' for if individuality is real, one individual cannot also be three individuals: either there is one God with three aspects, or there are three Gods. Roscellinus preferred three Gods, for otherwise God and the Holy Ghost must have been incarnate in the Son, and with him have suffered birth and crucifixion. To this the realist Anselm, the most famous theologian of the day, replied, 'How shall he who has not arrived at the understanding how several men are in species one man, comprehend how in that most mysterious nature several persons, each of which is

Perfect God, are one God?' The rigid application of Roscellinus's argument threatened more than the nature of the Trinity; it would have degraded original sin, grace, justice, truth, the very Word itself, from *realia* to verbal breaths. It would have degraded the church from a transcendent Body to a mere human organization, and religion from a divine spirit to mere personal opinion. Roscellinus was severely condemned by a council held at Soissons in 1092 and, in danger of being stoned to death by the angry, orthodox populace, forced to recant his error.

Realism found its outstanding opponent in Peter Abelard (1079–1142) whose love for Heloise, the niece of Canon Fulbert of Notre Dame, has supplied a classic tale of romance and tragedy. Abelard devoted his early life, when his students were numbered by the thousands and before his mutilation by Fulbert, to refuting Anselm who, in Abelard's opinion, 'was that sort of a man that if anyone went to him in uncertainty, he returned more uncertain still. He was wonderful to hear, but at once failed if you questioned him. He kindled a fire not to give light, but to fill the house with smoke.' It was Anselm's motto that 'I believe in order to understand,' while Abelard accepted that 'Doubt is the road to inquiry, and by inquiry we perceive the truth.' Anselm esteemed authority; Abelard replied, 'How, then, is the faith of any people, however false, to be refuted, though it may have arrived at such a pitch of blindness as to confess some idol to be the creator both of heaven and earth? As, according to your own admission, you cannot reason upon matters of faith, you have no right to attack others upon a matter with regard to which you think you ought yourself to be unassailed.' 'A doctrine is believed not because God has said it, but because we are convinced by reason that it is so.' In his *Sic et Non* he listed one by one the many points upon which the infallible fathers had violently disagreed with each other, thus publicly advertising the vulnerability of the dogma and its need for philosophic rehabilitation.

In Abelard's last years he lived in a cabin of stubble and reeds, or in flight from one monastery to another, but always with a large following. In ever-increasing ill repute with the church, and having been repeatedly condemned, he came into conflict with Bernard of Clairvaux, was denounced as a heretic by the Council of Sens (1141), and died on the way to Rome to plead his cause. But his heresies, 'by inquiry we perceive the truth . . . a doctrine is believed . . . because we are convinced by reason that it is so,' lived after him to set the problems for the next three hundred years.

The saintly Bernard, in answering Abelard, declared: 'Faith is not an opinion but a certitude. "The substance of things hoped for," says the

Apostle, not the phantasies of empty conjecture. You hear, *the substance*. You may not dispute on the faith as you please, you may not wander here and there through wastes of opinion, the byways of error. By the name *substance* something certain and fixed is placed before you; you are enclosed within boundaries, you are restrained within unchanging limits.'

Bernard, like Anselm, was a realist of the purest sort. Faith was *substance*, enduring truth, the ultimate reality; opinion and reason were chimeric deceptions, perversions, or at best fragments, of the truth. For Abelard 'things' were substance and enduring truth and, if not the ultimate reality, at least one reliable means for its discovery. The process of discovery was by doubt and inquiry. Even scripture might be translated or read erroneously, and should be interpreted with care. Abelard's heresies so stimulated imitation that the Council of Toulouse (1129) declared it a sin for the laity to possess a Bible or to read the Psalter or the Breviary in the vernacular, lest the precious body of revelation be soiled by error of interpretation. Any attempt to reason about the faith implied its vulnerability, if it did not threaten its destruction — the more so since, at the moment, the use of reason was most strongly defended by the hated pagan Arabs who conceived deity as immanent in matter itself, who denied the possibility of creation from nothing, and who were led by logic to the denial of personal immortality.

It seemed at the opening of the thirteenth century, when the works of Aristotle and of Plato and much else representing the intellectual wealth of ancient Greece were being carried to the West, that Christianity could neither tolerate the infusion of any reason nor yet survive without it. The creed faced a crisis second only to that of the days of Constantine. It was saved from its dilemma by the Scholastic adroitness of Albertus Magnus (1193–1280) and Thomas Aquinas (1227–1274), to whom belongs the credit for so thorough a rehabilitation of Christian philosophy that the scriptures and dogma were assured of safety for many centuries.

It has been said of Albertus Magnus that he reproduced the whole philosophy of Aristotle in systematic order and remodeled it to meet the requirements of ecclesiastic dogma; while his pupil Aquinas refined the master's thought with such perfection that he has been called the 'greatest of all Christian philosophers'; with Ambrose, Augustine, Jerome and Gregory, Aquinas ranks as one of the five great Fathers and, by the encyclical of Leo XIII (1879), his teachings, presented chiefly in the *Summa Theologiae* and *Summa contra Gentiles,* were made the model of philosophy and theology throughout the Roman Catholic Church. With few exceptions they represent also the definitive beliefs of the Protestant sects.

The central theme in the writings of Aquinas, which incorporate the contributions of his teacher Albertus, is that there are two sources of knowledge: revelation, which affords the truths of theology, and reason, which affords other forms of truth. Theological knowledge is unique and represents an ultimate, absolute truth which is to be strictly distinguished from all natural knowledge or personal experience. Revelation presents men with theological truths through the channels of scripture and the councils and traditions of the church, and these are to be believed even when reason cannot understand them. Thus, revelation has afforded certain truths about God, such as the nature of the Trinity, that transcend human reason; reason unaided by revelation could discover the existence of God, but never his triune being. Other truths afforded by revelation and which reason alone could never discover are the creation of the world out of nothing, and the incarnation; Duns Scotus added to this list the knowledge of God as omnipotent and as the chief end of man, and the incorruptibility and immortality of the soul.

Faith takes precedence over reason and guides the seeker to truth when reason is as yet undeveloped. Because it transcends reason, faith might be thought by some to be contrary to it; but this is impossible, for the lesser light, Aquinas says, is not darkened by the greater, but is on the contrary increased, as the light of the air is increased by that of the sun.

In Aquinas, Neoplatonism won its Scholastic victory but only by the admission that reason and faith could not stand equally, that the one had to be subordinate to the other; and hence the persistent ecclesiastic tradition that reason shall not deny the articles of faith or the accumulated body of revelation. In Aquinas, philosophical realism also won a victory, but not without such fluxion in its definitions that John of Salisbury in the next century was able to enumerate thirteen different varieties of interpretation; and even in the work of Aquinas himself, the individual and universal alternate as *realia* more or less as is convenient. For example, individual men are real (agreeing with Aristotle) and there is no 'universal man' in nature (denying Plato); yet the universal *idea* of man exists in the Divine Mind and constitutes the essence or source of being of all individuals (in conformity with Neoplatonism).

In Aquinas's view the quasi-divine, universal essence, which he designated by the word *quidditas* — that which gives a man, for example, his 'manness' — transforms itself in an individual man by a process of 'individuation,' which consists of the quantitative division and ordering of the matter of which the individual is composed, roughly as a man might build himself a house by sorting out and joining lumber. Conversely, essence withdraws from individuation by the reversal of this ordering process. Thus essence precedes existence and infinitely transcends it in importance.

By this premise Aquinas was enabled to establish the immortality of the soul without recourse to the crude doctrine of the resurrection of the body, without the limitations of Aristotle's rational soul, and with the complete abandonment of Aristotle's concept that substance and things exist of themselves and follow their own laws. In New Testament Christianity the resurrection was frankly of the body, either this body or a replica mystically fabricated anew for the purpose. For Tertullian, the soul was corporeal and handed on from parent to child as by a budding process, as part and parcel of the flesh; for Origen it was an incorporeal spirit, but one which required a body for its housing; while in Jerome's view, God was daily making new souls to fit the new bodies which were being made by human generation. For Aquinas these dualistic difficulties are avoided by his Neoplatonic definition of soul-stuff as ultimate substance, body as derivative pattern. The spiritual essence or *quidditas* is conceived to possess rationality and all the vegetative, sensitive, appetitive and motive functions of the body, essentially all the attributes of personality; and, since it itself forms the body by the 'division of matter,' it is free to abandon it, as the man who has built a house is free to move out of the completed structure and let it fall to pieces. Each soul is created by God for the purpose of 'individuating' a particular body, and partakes of the nature of an Aristotelian 'thing' in that a particular soul is not identical with any other soul. But it enjoys the nature of a Platonic universal in that it transcends the process of individuation and therefore of physical and corruptible being; and yet among universals it is a distinct species not to be subsumed by any other universal. It is assured, therefore, of an independent, individual existence throughout whatever duration universals themselves may exist.

Whatever difficulties the belief in personal survival after death may have hitherto presented, they were for the time being resolved by Aquinas's arguments and the church could well place him in its philosophical hierarchy far above Plato, the inventor of the doctrine of supersensual reality. In any case Plato had been a pagan and his arguments, lacking the guidance of faith and revelation, could at best produce only half-truths fraught with danger to men's souls.

If Aquinas was skillful in aiding reason to understand the immortal soul of faith, he was no less competent in aiding her to a proper knowledge of other angelic beings, the lore of which had been taken over by the church from the apocryphal literature. In Slavonic Enoch (before 70) myriads of supernatural beings had been depicted as attending the sun and regulating the courses of the stars, while in Ethiopic Enoch (166 to 64 B.C.) they controlled the lightning and the workings of the rain, frost, hail and snow. They numbered ten thousand times ten thousand, four hundred alone being required to take the sun's crown to God at sunset and return it in the morning. Although their nature was that of flame and fire, and their splendor equal to the stars, they were not wholly different from men in that some of them had descended to earth to take human wives. They were divided into several ranks and arranged themselves accordingly on the steps leading to the throne of God, the four archangels of the throne, Michael, Gabriel, Uriel and Raphael, commanding the legions of lesser beings and acting as special emissaries from God to man, as when Gabriel conducted Enoch to heaven, when Raphael healed Tobit's blindness, and when Uriel was sent to Ezra. Angels went up and down the ladder of Jacob's dream, and succored Daniel when he was in the lion's den; and, in the Apocalypse of Baruch (80–150), when Jerusalem was destroyed four angels stood at the four corners of the city with lamps and accomplished its ruin. The angel whose chief function it was to bring death first made his appearance in this work.

The author of the pseudo-Christian *Hermas* (97–142) elaborated the doctrine of guardian angels, and Justin stated that 'God committed the care of men and all things under heaven to angels whom He set over these'; the heathen gods, he asserted, were the evil demons who were born of the intercourse of the fallen angels with women of earth. Many of the church fathers accepted the apocryphal angelology and developed it freely. It was Tertullian's view that the baptismal water receives its healing properties from an angel, that an angel announces in heaven every marriage which is blessed by the church, while another records the sins of Christians, as for example, when they go to the theater. Tertullian, who was always literal minded, was perhaps the first Christian to propound that angels flew by means of wings.

From the third century Christians were wont to pray to angels, Constantine dedicating a church to Michael, and at the Second Council of Nicaea (787) the worship of angelic beings was formally approved, the *cultus* still retaining technically, if not in practice, the approval of the Protestant as well as the Catholic church.

In the fifth century there appeared a work on angelology entitled *The*

Celestial Hierarchy, an amalgam of Neoplatonism, principles of liturgic and sacramental doctrine, priestly function and heterogeneous pagan elements. The author was unknown, but in time the work was attributed to Dionysius the Areopagite. First cited by a Constantinople council in 533, Pseudo-Dionysius did not become widely known in the West until after 827, when the Byzantine emperor sent a copy to Louis the Pious; it was translated by John Scotus Erigena and thereafter exerted a profound influence on Christian thought and the art and poetry of the Middle Ages. Pseudo-Dionysius divided the celestial hierarchy, which intervenes between the Triune God and earth, into three triads, each consisting of three classes of angelic beings, thus establishing inhabitants for each of the nine planetary spheres. The highest triad consisted of the seraphim, cherubim and thrones, the intermediate triad of dominions, virtues and powers, the lowest triad of principalities, archangels and angels. As the highest triad, which is nearest God, contemplates the divine effulgence and reflects it onward to the second, the third and more specifically angelic triad ministers immediately to men.

Although writers from Erigena onward followed Pseudo-Dionysius closely, this authority left so many gaps unfilled that angelology afforded a favorite subject for Scholastic speculation. It remained for Aquinas to perfect this mass of theory and to unify it with cosmology. As presented in his monumental *Summa,* angels are, like other universals, altogether incorporeal, of a genus comparable to, though not identical with, the essence of the human soul. Like the human soul, they have cognition and will, the latter functioning only in the direction of good, but they do not exercise the functions of life and do not know passion. (The angels of the Genesis legend have by all authorities been specifically described as fallen.) They can foresee the future to a limited extent, and enjoy a knowledge of God which, if still imperfect, is more intimate than man enjoys. They can be localized, and cannot be in more than one place at a time. Satan and his demon cohorts differ from the angels who remained in grace only because, of their free will, they sinned in pride and envy; these evil ones have a double abode, hell, where they care for the damned, and the air of the earth, where they incite men to evil.

Original sin Aquinas conceived to be a disordered condition of the soul brought on by pride, the deformity being both self-revealing and self-propagating in the concupiscent act. 'All men, who are born of Adam, can be considered as one man, so far as they agree in the nature which They receive from their first parent . . . and just as murder is not imputed to a man's hand except as part of his body, so original sin is not guilt by reason of the will of each individual man, but by reason of the will of Adam.'

Logically it is but a step in Aquinas's thought from the disordered nature of man to the discovery of man's inborn predilection for evil, and it is not surprising to find that he was one of the first to insist that all magic is witchcraft and all witchcraft heresy; that he was one of the first to defend the application of the death penalty to heretics; that as a young man he saw and apparently approved the Albigensian crusade or that shortly after his time the persecution of witchcraft spread like a plague throughout the whole of Europe.

As the system of Aquinas appears in the *Paradiso* of Dante, the *Scala naturale* of Giovanni Maffeik and other cosmological treatises of the Scholastic period, the creation assumes a beauty and a vastness not hitherto imagined. The earth is no longer a flat plain inclosed by four walls and solidly covered by the firmament, the sun, moon, and stars being hung from this vaulted ceiling; but it has become a globe at the center of ten successive, transparent spheres each rotated by angels and carrying one or more of the heavenly bodies. Nearest the earth is the sphere of the moon; next is that of Mercury, next Venus, and next the sun; the three next carry Mars, Jupiter and Saturn; the eighth is spangled with the stars; next is a sphere of purest, transparent crystal, a suitable encasement for the magnificent, slowly revolving cosmos; and outermost is the *primum mobile* which at once communicates the heavenly powers of rotation to the inner spheres, and separates these spheres from the Empyrean, the great void which is filled with a light and which no one can enter, where sits enthroned the mighty Triune God. In attendance upon the Divine Person are the celestial hosts of seraphim, cherubim and thrones, who incessantly chant divine praises in anthems of surpassing beauty; dominions, virtues and powers receive the divine commands, attend the heavens, sun, moon, planets and the stars, open and shut the windows of heaven, and on occasion direct a thunderbolt or comet toward the wicked; and the principalities, archangels and angels protect religion and bear the prayers of the saints to the foot of God's throne, intercede in the affairs of men, and act as guardians of nations and of kingdoms. Above the world God sits in awful majesty, contemplating, enjoying, ordering, listening to the music of the spheres even as he contemplates the delights of paradise, the pains of purgatory, and the tortures of the inferno in the center of the earth where Lucifer, once the divine favorite, is now immovably fixed in ice, sharing the punishments of the proud and damned.

ii

In the first century of the Christian Era God had disclosed the proper order of the universe to one Claudius Ptolemaeus, subsequently known as Ptolemy, an Egyptian mathematician and astronomer. In a monumental work on pure mathematics, geography and astronomy, which in the Middle Ages came to be called the *Almagest,* Ptolemy had applied himself to the question: What regular and determined motions being assumed would fully account for the phenomena presented by the heavenly bodies? According to the theory he developed the sun and planets revolve about the earth in essentially circular orbits, deviations from a uniformly circular course being explained by small revolutions also of a circular nature superimposed on the prime geocentric path. The unknown author of the treatises ascribed to Dionysius the Areopagite had developed the Ptolemaic theory with reference to angelology and other Christian doctrines, and in subsequent centuries the great esteem accorded this work, as being written by Paul's Athenian convert and therefore virtually by Paul himself, coupled with the reverence due the ancient name of Ptolemy, established the geocentric theory in Christian conviction. Whatever debate might be admissible on the orders of angelic beings or the deviations of the planetary bodies from circular orbits, the central fact that the sun and planets in their motions were subservient to the earth, that the earth was the center of the cosmos, remained unassailable.

The geocentric theory had been kept intact, though tottering, for fourteen centuries by the addition of epicycle upon epicycle until astronomical theory had become a dizzying maze of complex motions. When, in 1400, Copernicus at first conceived that planetary motion could be reduced to simple orbits if it be supposed that the earth, along with the other planets, revolved around the sun (as had been accepted by Pythagoras, Aristarchus and Eratosthenes) he himself treated the idea as a rational paradox such as must occasionally arise where reason stumbles in her effort to keep in step with her mistress, faith. As continued application to the problem over a period of many years convinced him that the heliocentric interpretation was no paradox, but a supremely important natural truth, he dared not discuss the matter in this light in Rome and returned to his native Poland to co-ordinate and reduce the heliocentric system to writing. His book *De revolutionibus orbium coelestium* (1543) ready for publication, he entrusted it to a friend, Osiander, to be privately printed, not daring to risk the usual printing channels for fear that it might be condemned and destroyed by either Catholics or Protestants. When at last the volume was put in the author's hands he lay dying and never knew how his conviction had been betrayed: Osiander had lacked the courage to launch the book as a statement of fact and had inserted in it a groveling preface in which it was made to appear that Copernicus considered the doctrine of the earth's movement, not as truth, but as a fanciful hypothesis.

Osiander's preface served its purpose and the movement of the earth, as an idle hypothesis, failed to stir the church or even to command serious attention among astronomers. Tycho Brahe (1546–1601), with instruments of greater precision than had hitherto been available, added many new astronomical observations, but either from deference to ecclesiastic authority or from his own inertia rejected the heliocentric scheme and in its place erected a hybrid theory which kept the earth at the center of the universe while permitting the planets to revolve about the sun. Kepler (1571–1630) abandoned the perfect circle as the proper course for the planets to pursue, and with it the necessity of epicycles, by resolving the planetary motions into elliptical orbits which had the sun as one of their foci, but he cautiously left the question of the earth's mobility undiscussed. The greatest mathematical and astronomical teachers of the time, whether Catholic or Protestant, dared not mention the Copernican doctrine to their classes, and the only man known to have openly defended it, Giordano Bruno, was, after seven years' imprisonment, excommunicated in 1600 and burned in Rome. True, Bruno was lacking in proper ecclesiastic respect, for he denounced the monks, scoffed at the mysteries of faith, called the Jewish records myths, and laughed at miracles as magical tricks. So probably he would have burned in any case, but his example served to deter others from unguarded rashness.

Yet ten years after Bruno's death the motion of the earth passed from hypothesis into fact. It had been argued against Copernicus, "If your doctrine is true, Venus (because it lies between the earth and the sun) would show phases like the moon." To which Copernicus had answered, "You are right; I know not what to say; but God is good, and will in time find an answer to the objection." God gave the answer in the telescope of Galileo Galilei (1564–1642), which disclosed that when closest to the earth Venus presents a crescentic face. It was in either 1611 or 1612 that Galileo made the discovery that was destined to dry the spring of revelation. Long engaged in physical experiments, Galileo's interest in force and motion had been awakened when as a boy of seventeen he had observed that the lamp in the cathedral of Pisa invariably completed its oscillations in equal periods, however large their range. In studies extend ing over a period of thirty years, he found it profitable to think of motion in terms of law instead of angelic beings and quasi-animate powers — he had, it has been said, 'brought motion down to earth by way of an inclined plane.'

When in September of 1604 a new star burst forth in the constellation of Serpentarius, Galileo had used the spectacular *nova* to refute the doctrine of the incorruptibility of the heavens, and here and on other occasions he had revealed his bias toward the heliocentric theory. Hearing in 1609 a description of the 'trunk and cylinder,' recently invented by Johannes Lippershey of Middleburg, which magnified distant objects, he produced after one night's meditation on the principles of refraction a telescope of threefold magnifying power, which he shortly improved to a power of thirty-two. The instrument afforded him unheard of revelations. In the *Sidereus Nuncius,* published in Venice in 1610, he astonished the world by announcing that there were mountains on the moon; that the dark portion of this body dimly visible between the crescentic tips was faintly illuminated by light reflected from the earth; that the Milky Way was a congeries of stars, as were the great nebulae; that Jupiter was possessed of satellites which revolved around the mother planet. In the next year he announced the presence of dark 'spots' upon the sun, and, shortly afterwards, the occurrence of phases on the planet Venus. To Galileo it seemed that these and other evidences, which anyone could see with his telescope and understand with simple diagrams, should serve to convince the most skeptical of the truth of the heliocentric doctrine, and he frankly engaged in written and public argument in defense of Copernicus, terming the earth one of several planets revolving about the sun.

He was quickly answered by the faithful: his method was absurd — the divinely appointed way to arrive at the truth in astronomy was by theological reasoning on the texts of scripture; Genesis said that the moon was 'a great light' and to argue otherwise impugned the sacred text. The Bible showed by all applicable parallels that there were only seven planets: this was proved by the seven golden candlesticks of the Apocalypse, by the seven branched candlesticks of the tabernacle, by the seven churches of Asia, by the fact that the foetus is prefectly formed at seven months, and so on. It was declared that 'to see the satellites of Jupiter, men had to make an instrument which would create them'; and in any case 'they were invisible to the naked eye and therefore can have no influence on the earth, and therefore they would be useless, and therefore do not exist.' The Dominican Caccini preached a sermon on the punning text, 'Ye men of Galilee, why stand ye gazing up into heaven?' and before he ended he declared that 'geometry is of the devil,' that 'mathematicians should be banished as the authors of all heresies.' Men in high places, both within and without the church, hurled at the astronomer the dreaded epithets of 'heretic' and 'atheist' and asserted that the 'pretended discovery vitiates the whole Christian plan of salvation'; that 'it casts suspicion on the doctrine of the incarnation'; that it upset the whole basis of theology. 'If the earth is a planet, and only one among several planets, it cannot be that any such great things have been done specially for it as the Christian doctrine teaches. If there are other planets, since God makes nothing in vain, they must be inhabited; but how can their inhabitants be descended from Adam? How can they trace their origin to Noah's ark? How can they have been redeemed by the Saviour?'

The cry increased that Galileo be handed over to the inquisition. To be certain of its ground Rome wanted evidence in writing and, aware that Galileo had written the Benedictine astronomer Castelli certain letters dealing with the apparent contradictions between scripture and the new astronomy, the archbiship begged Castelli to let him see them. Castelli declined and the archbiship, even while he was writing bitter denunciations of Galileo to the inquisition, approached him again professing the greatest admiration for Galileo's genius and a sincere desire to know more of his discoveries. Castelli still refusing to betray his friend, Rome resorted to open attack. In 1615 Galileo was summoned before the inquisition, which examined him on two propositions extracted from some letters he had written on sunspots; after a month of prayer and deliberation, the holy court rendered a unanimous decision: 'The first proposition, that the sun is the center and does not revolve about the earth, is foolish, absurd, false in theology, and heretical, because expressly contrary to Holy Scripture'; and 'the second proposition, that the earth is not the center but revolves about the sun, is absurd, false in philosophy, and, from a theological point of view at least, opposed to the true faith.'

At the instigation of Pope Paul V, Cardinal Bellarmine confronted Galileo and endeavored to convince him of his errors. Under the threat of imprisonment in the dungeons of the inquisition, Bellarmine commanded him, 'in the name of His Holiness the Pope and the whole Congregation of the Holy Office, to relinquish altogether the opinion that the sun is the center of the world and immovable, and that the earth moves, nor henceforth to hold, teach, or defend it in any way whatsoever, verbally or in writing.' This injunction Galileo acquiesced in and promised to obey. A fortnight later the Congregation of the Index, under the instructions of the pope, decreed that 'the doctrine of the double motion of the earth about its axis and about the sun is false, and entirely contrary to Holy Scripture'; and the writings of Copernicus and all others that affirmed the motion of the earth were interdicted and this condemnation placed upon the Index, which was shortly made infallible by the usual papal bull giving its monitions the essential ex cathedra papal sanction.

For some ten years Galileo remained silent. Then on the death of Paul V and the accession as Urban VIII of Cardinal Barberini, who had at one time seemed liberal and sympathetic to the Copernican theory, he conceived new hopes and began to speak again of his allegiance to the heliocentric doctrine. Quickly he found himself the object of renewed denunciation: 'The opinion of the earth's motion is of all heresies the most abominable, the most pernicious, the most scandalous; the immovability of the earth is thrice sacred; argument against the immortality of the soul, the existence of God, and the incarnation, should be tolerated sooner than argument to prove that the earth moves.' In the face of these attacks he prepared a treatise in the form of a dialogue presenting the arguments for and against the Copernican and Ptolemaic systems, and applied to the Holy Office for permission to have it printed. After eight years of argument permission was given, on the condition that the *Dialogo* be prefaced by a declaration that the Copernican theory was exhibited as a play of the imagination only. When this appeared in 1632, to the consternation of the church it immediately met with great success, the pious preface being laughed at by all except the priests. Urban VIII was especially offended to find his own arguments profanely put into the mouth of one of the persons in the dialogue, only of course to be refuted. The sale of the work was hastily forbidden and Galileo was again commanded before the inquisition. In vain did his one influential friend, Castelli, urge that he had been entirely respectful to the church and that "nothing that can be done can now hinder the earth from revolving"; Castelli was dismissed in disgrace and banished for his contumacy, and Galileo was dragged before the dreaded tribunal. He was imprisoned, deprived of any defender or adviser, threatened with chains and probably with torture. Sick in body and mind, knowing the methods and powers of the inquisition, remembering Giordano Bruno who a few years before had been burned for heresy, and others who for stubborn opinions had died in dungeon, he yielded to the demands of Urban and the inquisitors and pronounced publicly his recantation:

"I, Galileo, being in my seventieth year, being a prisoner and on my knees, and before your Eminence, having before my eyes the Holy Gospel, which I touch with my hands, abjure, curse, and detest the error and the heresy of the movement of the earth."

Urban and his inquisitors, striving frantically to save their faith, could not foresee that in forcing Galileo's recantation they were bringing their priestly profession, their theology, the very impulse of mysticism which motivated their religious belief, into perpetual ill repute; that the debasement of the intellect which they intended by the act ironically foreshadowed the time when the Holy Bible upon which they forced an old man of seventy to swear falsely, should itself be debased — not merely revealed to be a collection of ancient lore and of the perverted wishful thinkings of a heterodox Jewish sect driven frantic by the fear of Doomsday, but brought into disdain as an instrument that throughout its history had been put to such evil uses that men would no longer be willing to swear upon it.

For two hundred and two years, from 1633 until 1835, at the infallible dictate of the pope and under the orders of the Holy Congregation, the earth stood still, at the center of the universe. Immediately following Galileo's condemnation Urban and the Holy Congregation ordered his sentence and recantation sent to all papal nuncios in Europe, as well as to all archbishops, bishops and inquisitors in Italy, in order that 'you and all professors of philosophy and mathematics may have knowledge of it, that they may know why we proceeded against the said Galileo, and recognize the gravity of his error, in order that they may avoid it, and thus not incur the penalties which they would have to suffer in case they fell into the same.' After 1664 there was prefixed to the Index of the church, forbidding 'all writings which affirm the motion of the earth,' a bull signed by the reigning pope, thereby after each interregnum infallibly arresting any motion. The theologians had been urged to make clear by tongue and pen to all people why it was absurd to believe that the earth should move, and a mass of books appeared reiterating all the evidences from scripture, with here and there an original argument such as that 'animals, which move, have limbs and muscles; the earth has no limbs and muscles, therefore, it does not move. It is the angels who make Saturn, Jupiter, the sun, etc., turn round. If the earth revolves, it must also have an angel in the center to set it in motion; but only devils live there; it would therefore be a devil who would impart motion to the earth . . .' 'The planets, the sun, the fixed stars, all belong to one species, namely that of stars. It seems, therefore, to be a grievous wrong to place the earth, which is a sink of impurity, among these heavenly bodies, which are pure and divine things.' 'The Copernican theory of the earth's motion is against the nature of the earth itself, because the earth is not only cold but contains in itself the principle of cold; but cold is opposed to motion, and even destroys it — as is evident in animals, which become motionless when they become cold.'

The doctrine of the movement of the earth was at first vigorously opposed among the Protestants: referring to Copernicus, Luther wrote, 'People give ear to an upstart astrologer who strove to show that the earth revolves, nor the heavens or the firmament, the sun and the moon. Whoever wishes to appear clever must devise some new system which of all systems is of course the very best. This fool wishes to reverse the entire science of astronomy; but sacred Scripture tells us that Joshua commanded the sun to stand still, and not the earth.' Melanchthon in his *Elements of Physics* suggested severe measures to restrain such impious teachings; '. . . it is a want of honesty and decency to assert such notions publicly, and the example is pernicious . . . the earth can be nowhere if not in the center of the universe.' And Calvin: 'Who will venture to place the authority of Copernicus above that of the Holy Spirit?'

Yet inevitably as the Copernican doctrine and the telescope continued to explore the heavens with ever increasing profit, the theologians gradually retreated behind a barrage of rhetoric, or evaded the matter as immaterial to the faith, or utilized the expedient of compromise, as suggested by the Jesuit mathematician Boscovich: 'As for me, full of respect for the Holy Scriptures and the decree of the Holy Inquisition, I regard the earth as immovable; nevertheless, for simplicity in explanation I will argue as if the earth moves; for it is proved that of the two hypotheses the appearances favour this idea.' With Newton, Halley and Huygens, the heliocentric astronomy was accepted by even such Protestant divines as Cotton Mather. Yet it could be urged against Newton by a devout antagonist that by his statement of the law of gravitation he 'took from God that direct action on his works so constantly ascribed to him in scripture, and transferred it to material mechanism.'

In 1820, Settele, the professor of astronomy at Rome, wrote a text in which the Copernican system was taken for granted, but prior to its publication he was required by the Master of the Sacred Palaces to revise the work and treat the doctrine as a mere hypothesis. Settele appealed to Pope Pius VII, who referred the matter to the Congregation of the Holy Office. On the sixteenth of August, 1820, this body reported that Settele might teach the Copernican system as truth established. It was not, however, until 1835 that there appeared an edition of the Index from which the condemnation of works defending the double motion of the earth was dropped, thus formally permitting it to move again. Yet to set the earth in motion was easier than for the church to rescind its infallibility. In 1867, after two centuries of evasions and misrepresentations of the question, the true charges against Galileo and the personal responsibility of Pope Paul and Pope Urban in his condemnation were made known by the publication of the correspondence and trial records by L'Epinois; and in 1870 the Reverend Mr. Roberts, a Roman Catholic clergyman in England, reviewed the records and frankly exhibited the incontrovertible evidences that the papacy had committed itself and its infallibility against the movement of the earth. It was also in 1870 that there appeared the Vatican definition which significantly restricted papal infallibility to matters of dogma and morals. In 1885 another eminent Catholic, St. George Mivart, suggested that the Almighty had allowed the pope and the church to fall into complete error in regard to the movement of the earth in order to teach them that astronomy is outside their province.

The danger of all argument which lays deception to the Deity is patent: if God has not revealed the true order of the universe, then it may be that neither has he revealed the true order of salvation. Either he did deliberately deceive the prophets and apostolic writers, and all subsequent church councils, in respect to faith and morals as well as cosmology, or his own wisdom did not transcend their human and erroneous beliefs, or these human agents were very fallible vehicles of revelation and must be accordingly 'restricted.' If the first two propositions are held to be intolerable, the third presents the danger that restriction may continue under the pressure of new necessities until the residuum of revelation, in respect to faith and morals, as well as cosmology, is *nihil*.

iii

In respect to faith and morals, the failure of the medieval church was contemporaneously evident. It was a vast corporation ruled by the pope and the Holy Congregation through coercion, force, fear and theological formulas. From the days of Constantine it had been acquiring property and, since it rarely parted with its wealth, this had by the sixteenth century grown to enormous proportions. It held two fifths of the land in Sweden and as much or more in England, while Germany, Hungary and other central European countries were checkered with great fiefs.

This wealth was so unequally divided between a few favored persons and the vast number of half-starved priests as to afford endless grounds for jealousy and intrigue. The papacy itself was extremely rich: gold had proved to be as useful to God as it was to Satan and every pope worthy of the name had sought to wrest as much as possible of it from the devil's hand. Simony had become a general rule, Rome offering for sale bishoprics, divorces, illegal marriages, pardons, relics, privileges of every sort — only heresy could not be bought because the transaction would destroy the prerogative to forgive sins and to sell exculpation, which would be to destroy the bank itself. Men could speak of Rome as a 'foul fish pond filled with verminous reptiles,' Dante could make St. Peter bitterly complain, "He who usurped on earth my place . . . Hath made my burial ground a conduit for that blood and filth." The ecclesiastic system had despoiled the country economically by drawing countless men and women out of useful service, to harbor them at public expense in thousands of monasteries each holding besides its monks at least an equal number of men and women who served a menial role. The preposterous multiplication of church festivals had made a large fraction of the year useless for trade or agriculture, for no work was allowed on a holy day itself or after the noon of the day before it. The priests and friars, and frequently the monks and bishops were at best poor examples of labor, honesty or thrift; concubinage and its implied hypocrisy were the accepted rule, and indolence, mendicancy and extortion were characteristic of the clergy generally. Having inherited the elements of witchcraft from the pagans, the church found the demonic powers so agreeable to its own pagan-sacred theory that it fostered the development of superstition into a devastating creed of evil. By ancient tradition it deprecated intellectual innovation, restricting investigation to its sacred pneumatology and fantastic metaphysics and discouraging the instruction of the young in any course other than that established by ecclesiastic precedent.

All such antisocial features might fairly be discounted as worldly faults inevitable in any medieval system which must operate through human agents; and to challenge on these grounds the church's claim to a special insight into faith and morals would be historically penurious. It is therefore significant that it was specifically in the realm of faith and morals, and not in sociology, that there was engendered the revolution which ultimately broke the church into many fragments, each still presuming to enjoy the revelation which in the nineteenth century Pius IX formally arrogated to his person.

The Reformation, which by sectarian Christians is conceived to have been productive, immediately or ultimately, of the most signal contributions to faith and morals of any event since the founding of the parent church, was characterized by Nietzsche as an attack, on the part of Christianity, of hemiplegia. That part of the body religious which was separated from the controlling brain was left to a chaotic, disintegrating autonomy. The metaphor, if rude in that it suggests senility, and incomplete in that it neglects certain practical gains, as for example, the resulting increase in personal liberty, is inexact in that it implies a sudden accident to a normally co-ordinated system; for the Christian church was never co-ordinated and had been in the process of disintegration for a period of centuries. Its disintegration began with the first heresy: to kill the heretic only removed the adversary without destroying his argument, and not a single heresy threatened the early faith but survived to grow strong and threaten it again. It was, moreover, not the heresies of pagans and infidels that fed the Reformation's fires, but the apostasies of monks or priests who were, without a notable exception, above suspicion in respect to piety.

The monasteries, which the church esteemed for their asceticism, proved in the end to be the breeding ground of fatal disbelief. Orthodox as he might be, the monk fled into seclusion to escape an evil world which the church despised and, by her own admission, could not discipline. The monk was a godly man (if sometimes foolish) and he found God without the mediation of any bishop, presbyter, or priest. The monk was at heart an individualist and selfishly sought a retreat where his individualism could enjoy the maximum of liberty. And for several centuries the monk was the only man who was even literate. It was inevitable that when asceticism was discredited by the Renaissance, he should emerge from the cloisters as the most intelligent and powerful critic of the faith, and therefore its most dangerous heretic.

It was a Franciscan, Roger Bacon (*ca.* 1214–*ca.* 1294), following in the path of Canon Abelard, who opposed the mystical doctrines of Anselm and Bernard and accelerated the disintegration of Scholastic absolutism by upholding the rights of reason, and by defining error as of four major sources: authority, custom, the opinion of the ignorant masses and the concealment of ignorance by the pretense of knowledge. It was another Franciscan, William of Ockham (1270–1343), who rehabilitated the doctrine condemned by Canon Roscellinus, that only individual things exist and should be studied for their own sake, and not because they imperfectly reveal speculative universals; that the so-called universals are but mental concepts which have no corresponding existents in reality, as words may be combined into propositions and syllogisms which have no corresponding existents. It followed from this proposition that since no man has perceived God directly, the mind forms the idea of God only by the artifice of synthetic fabrication, and therefore can have no certain knowledge of him, or hope to prove or disprove his existence. It also follows that the authority of the pope rests on permissions of a human order. It was only because Ockham was supported by a strong king and opposed by a weak pope that he was never charged with heresy. Bacon did not fare so well, and before he came to enjoy the favor of Pope Clement IV he had for ten years been strictly prohibited from writing, while after Clement's death he was thrown in prison by Pope Nicholas IV and kept there for fourteen years.

Bacon and Ockham, and more remotely, Abelard and the countless unnamed monks and priests who esteemed their way of thinking, were the heretics who undermined the medieval church, Luther and his followers but the ones who pushed it over. Between Ockham in the thirteenth century and Luther in the fifteenth were the clerics John Wycliffe and John Huss, both trained in orthodoxy and both duly beneficed. Wycliffe's (1320–1384) heresy began with the modest contention that the frequently unrighteous clergy should be held subject to the civil law, like other people, but the argument soon spread to the rights of the church to receive and hold rich temporal endowments, thence to the denunciation of the morals of the monks and friars, and finally to the outright condemnation of the corrupt Clement VII, to calling the pope, qua pope, the Anti-christ. It ended by translating the Bible into English, with the unavoidable consequences entailed in putting this book into vulgar hands at a time when in more orthodox countries the laity were forbidden to read it in the Latin. Wycliffe died in his bed because England at the moment lay beyond the reach of Rome, but by order of the Council of Constance, meeting thirty-one years later, his remains were disinterred and ignominiously burned for his heretical denial of the doctrine of transubstantiation, that the teeth and tongue macerate the actual flesh and blood of Christ in the Eucharist.

Dean of the philosophical faculty at Prague and rector of a local chapel, Huss was commissioned to examine certain reputed miracles, the audacious forgery of which led him to declaim vigorously not only against the forgery of miracles but against ecclesiastic chicanery in general. Leaning strongly toward the teaching of Wycliffe, he condemned indulgences as simony, denied the doctrine of transubstantiation and asserted that Christ, not Peter, was the head of the church. After a notorious betrayal by the

king, who promised him safe-conduct only to imprison him, he was convicted of heresy and burned, and his ashes and the soil on which they fell
were carefully collected and thrown into the Rhine.

Before they were heretical these men were all as orthodox as friar
Luther, the Augustinian, whose denunciation of the degraded indulgence
precipitated the revolution that ended by impugning the basic article of
faith and morals on which the church was founded, the power to cleanse
its communicants of sin.

The essence of Paul's religion, catharsis by faith, had been instilled by
the early church into the pagan sacraments of baptism, the Eucharist, and
public or private confession before a priest, to form, with the purificatory
rite of penance, the indispensables of salvation by which the medieval
church was now held together. Authority to traffic with absolution from
sin was based on Christ's permission to Peter 'to loose or bind': baptism
washed away past sins, but if a man sinned after baptism (as he always
did) he had to be purified by good works and penances, or else be purified in purgatory where accurate accounts were kept of sins and carefully
balanced with respect to punishments. Since no judge could loose or bind
without a detailed knowledge of the sin, sinning demanded confession
before absolution, hence the progression, sinning-confession-penance, and
its repetition constituted the dynamic bond between church and people.
That guilt as well as penance was remitted was implied in the phrase *a
poena et a culpa* occurring in indulgences from the twelfth century onward; and so the laity construed the practice, believing that even apart
from repentance and confession, the indulgence per se absolved them
from the pains of purgatory. Scholastic genius explained that a great excess of good works had been accomplished by Christ and the saints, and
that these had been deposited in a supernal Treasury of Good Works
upon which the church was authorized to issue drafts, in the nature of indulgences, in favor of the errant living. The logical application of this
concept of the church as the Bank of Heaven laid the foundations for
the dispensation of 'indulgences' on a grand scale, in the manner of a
moral holiday, and as a reward for the contributions of the faithful to the
welfare of the church, whether given in the form of money or services.

Remission of penance might be either partial or complete, the first ple-
nary indulgence being that granted by Urban II in 1095 to secure the First
Crusade, and for four hundred years the crusading effort, as well as other
good works ranging from the construction of churches and cathedrals
down to the filling of the alms box with pennies, had been encouraged
by transcendental finance. In a short time the right to sell indulgences

had been farmed out to archbishops, who paid well in one manner or another for the profitable concession; and they were dispensed by underlings until friars were peddling them like cakes in every marketplace. It was on the occasion of an indulgence proclaimed by Pope Leo X, farmed by the Archbishop of Mainz and sold by the Dominican monk John Tetzel, that Luther was moved to nail his ninety-five theses condemning the despised *Papal Tickets* on to the church door at Wittenberg (1517). Luther aimed only to put his condemnatory essay where his fellow theologians could read it; the subject, however, excited so much interest that the university press could not stamp out copies fast enough, and Luther's essay was translated into German and broadcast throughout Germany in a fortnight; within a month it had become known all over western and southern Europe, and within a year Luther was summoned to Rome — a mark that his malfeasance had, as it were, achieved official success. The dire summons was only narrowly averted, and Luther saved for Protestantism, by the political interposition of the elector of Saxony and the Emperor Maximilian.

It was soon evident that to attack the principle of the indulgence was to impugn the authority of the pope, and inquiry into this authority, as set forth in the canons, soon revealed that the decretals upon which the papal claims to authority were based were outright forgeries. Discussion of forgiveness of sins entailed debate on simony, auricular confession, and the morals of the ecclesiarchs themselves, while criticism of concubinage carried in its wake a searching inquiry into the very principles of continence and asceticism upon which the faith reposed. To examine the theocratic system at any point brought into the open the hated inquisition, and loosed the flood of animosities that tribunal had engendered. Lastly, when the Protestant leaders, abandoning the papacy, put the Bible into the people's hands as the supreme authority, they simultaneously gave unto vulgar minds the license to interpret it and to disagree, if not with the text itself at least with the priests who were frequently incapable of reading it themselves.

Consequently that which started as a remonstrance against a single if fundamental article of faith, the right of the papacy to purge of sin, and which was intended only to be a reformation, became a theological revolution which turned old heresies into new creeds. It was not, however, the virtues of the new beliefs that established the eighty varieties of Protestantism that appeared within a century. Jealousy, ambition and the hope of gain swept as many away from Rome as did religious fervor, and since it now became the duty of subjects to think on theological matters as did their rulers, the kings of England and Sweden, the princes of Germany, the nobles of France, Bohemia and Poland, the mayors of cities and the masters of burgs utilized the opportunity to the utmost to further political or personal ambitions.

By the nature of the forces that supported it, the Reformation properly belongs to political history. As the familiar story of Henry VIII and Anne Boleyn illustrates the change of faith in England, so elsewhere the foundations of sectarianism were precarious. In Scotland, Denmark, Holland, Sweden as well, the progress of Protestantism was determined in greater measure by political and economic forces than by intellectual appeal. For the masses and many of the leaders, one religion was just as good as another so long as it offered personal advantage, reasonable safety, and the assurance of its priests or preachers that it conveyed salvation. As regards specific doctrines the choice would have been difficult to make, for only theologians trained in hair-splitting could distinguish Catholic from Protestant pronouncements on the Trinity, incarnation, and original sin, or properly evaluate the change in emphasis on predestination, redemption, and grace; love of God had ostensibly replaced the admiration of the Virgin and the saints, the veneration of images and relics, and the mystery of miracles, but hell remained as hot as ever, the only marked change being that in the opinion of the masses it was now exclusively populated with either Catholics or Protestants.

The absolute inspiration of the Bible remained for both parties an article of faith, and both subscribed to the Augustinian doctrine of predestination which, as it is set forth by the English church in the Nine Lambeth Articles of 1595, reads:

> i. God from eternity had predestined some to life, and hath reprobated some to death.
> ii. The moving or efficient cause of predestination unto life is not prevision of faith or perseverance, or of good works, or of anything that is in the predestinate, but solely the will of God's good pleasure . . .

To deny predestination would be to degrade God's omniscience and omnipotence to a position inferior to man's own will — an intolerable proposition under the basal tenets of Christian monotheism. Consequently, for both Catholics and Protestants, a man's fate was sealed at birth, the illusion which he enjoyed of electing his own salvation being but a specious deception imposed upon him by divinity — not of meager necessity, for divinity knows no meager necessity, but of that greater necessity which, in Augustine's terms, is God himself.

The Catholic reaction to the Reformation culminated in the Council of Trent which, with several interruptions, sat from 1545 to 1563 with the implied intent of 'reforming' the true faith in respect to both principles and practice. Trent has been characterized as a long and anxious tissue of ecclesiastic and theological maneuvering productive in the main of a series of decrees approving the *status quo*. These decrees, which dealt with the Nicaean Creed, the authority of scripture, original sin, grace and justification, the sacraments, the mass, purgatory, relics and sacred images and other doctrinal matters, were prepared in advance by a few theologians selected by the pope and formulated under the proviso that henceforth the pope was to be the sole exponent of decrees, and that no one, on pain of anathema, was to impeach the accepted usages and order of the church, thus protecting the true faith against another 'reformation.' They but crystallized the ancient dogmas into a state of theological absolutism. On the question of indulgences, over which the church had been rent asunder, it was merely urged that moderation be observed, 'lest by excessive facility ecclesiastical discipline be enervated,' and 'all evil gains for the obtaining thereof — whence a most prolific cause of abuses amongst the Christian people has been derived,' are to be 'wholly abolished.' That was all. A rigid catechism in brief if not wholly intelligible formulas was prepared to guide the catechumen, and there was devised the Index, a list of books designed to guard the faithful from writings which might be dangerous to their faith. The Council of Trent, faced with the greatest crisis in Christian history, responded with an almost unprecedented exhibition of conservatism by making force the guarantee of Catholic faith, and complete immobility its supreme ideal.

At the other extreme, the reformed 'church' proceeded to break into factions over the outward forms of worship, the schisms engendered by the doctrine of predestination, the significance of the Eucharist, the conditions of grace, the use of candle and liturgy and endless minor points of privilege and ritual, leading by the end of the sixteenth century to at least eighty sects each holding to the true belief, and each prepared to defend itself by force against its antagonists. Having abandoned traditional authority, the Protestants based all their arguments on the scriptural text, to which was attributed an inerrancy undreamed of by any pope. Chapter 1 of the Westminster Confession of the Church of England (1646-7), which presented those propositions of faith that were acceptable at the time to all moderate Episcopalians, Independents, Presbyterians, etc. — ostensibly to 'all the churches of his majesty's dominions' — and that were based on the Thirty Nine Articles of 1563, asserted:

'The authority of the holy Scripture, for which it ought to be believed and obeyed, dependeth not upon the testimony of any man or church, but wholly upon God (who is truth itself), the Author thereof; and therefore it is to be received, because it is the Word of God. . . . The whole counsel of God, faith, and life, is either expressly set down in Scripture, or by good and necessary consequence may be deduced from Scripture: unto which nothing at any time is to be added, whether by new revelations of the Spirit, or traditions of men.'

So stretched the hand of Augustine across the centuries.

iv

Among those whose opinions weighed heavily in the formulation of the Westminster Confession were the Reverend James Ussher, Archbishop of Armagh, and Doctor John Lightfoot, Vice-Chancellor of the University of Cambridge. Within a few years of the formal definition of the articles of faith upon which the Protestant Christianity of England and her dominions was to rest, Archbishop Ussher published an authoritative and scholarly work, the *Annals of the Ancient and New Testaments* (1650), in which he calculated from the careful study of the scriptures that the world had been created just four thousand and four years before the beginning of the Christian Era. His verdict was received as final and his dates were inserted in the margins of the Authorized Version of the Bible by Bishop Lloyd in 1701, and soon came to be held as inspired as the text itself. To this computation Dr. Lightfoot shortly added the demonstration that 'heaven and earth, center and circumference, were created together, in the same instant, and clouds full of water,' and that 'this work took place and man was created by the Trinity on the twenty-third of October, 4004 B.C., at nine o'clock in the morning.' It was after a period variously estimated in the older literature as a few hours to seven days, that Eve said to Adam, 'Do thou, too, eat a little'; and on the next morning, God, walking in his garden in the cool of the day, discovered their sin, and expelled them from Paradise. Thus, within a week of the world's beginning, death came forth, and evil; and his work which on the first day God had looked upon and pronounced good, was desecrated.

The sixth chapter of Genesis tells of God's wrath and of his warning to Noah: 'And God saw that the wickedness of man was great in the earth, and that every imagination of the thoughts of his heart was only evil continually. And it repented the Lord that he had made man on the earth, and it grieved him at his heart. And the Lord said, I will destroy man which I have created from the face of the earth; both man and beast, and the creeping thing, and the fowls of the air; for it repenteth me that I have made them . . . And God said unto Noah . . . Make thee an ark of gopher wood; . . .'

By Archbishop Ussher's calculation God gave this warning to Noah in 2348 B.C., just before the storm descended. Some three hundred years after the archbishop died, the legend of the deluge was discovered to be an ancient Babylonian story, part of the Epic of Gilgamesh which goes back to a date perhaps fully as remote as Ussher's calculated date of Paradise.

As related in the twelve tablets from Ashurbanipal's library in Nineveh, the hero of this tale has been hunting with his great chief friend, Engidu, when Engidu is taken ill and, after twelve days of terrible suffering, dies. The death of Engidu brings home to Gilgamesh that he, too, must some day descend into the land of darkness where the miserable spirits of the departed live upon dust and clay, and the dreadful thought fills him with the determination to search out Uta-Napishtim, the only man who had ever gone to live among the gods, and beg from him the secret of immortality.

Gilgamesh finds Uta-Napishtim and hears from him the story of the flood, which occupies the whole of the eleventh tablet of the epic. The similarity of the story to the Judaic version may be represented by one example:

' "Six days and nights," said Very Wise, "the wind continued, the deluge and the tempest raged. The seventh day at daybreak the storm abated; the deluge, which had carried on warfare like an army, ceased, the sea became calm and the hurricane disappeared. I surveyed the sea with my eyes, raising my voice; but all mankind had returned to clay, mountains and fields were no longer distinguishable one from another. I opened the hatchway and the light fell upon my face; I sank down, I cowered, I wept, and my tears ran down my cheeks when I beheld the world all terror and all sea. At the end of twelve days, a point of land stood up from the waters, the ship touched the land of Nisir: the mountain of Nisir stopped the ship and permitted it to float no longer. The seventh day, at dawn, I took out a dove and let it go: the dove went, turned about, and as there was no place to alight upon, came back. I took out a swallow and let it go: the swallow went, turned about, and as there was no place to alight upon, came back. I took out a raven and let it go: the raven went, and saw that the water had abated, and came near the ship flapping its wings, croaking, and returned no more." '

At the end of his colloquy with Gilgamesh Uta-Napishtim declares: ' "I am about to reveal to thee, Gilgamesh, a secret, and the judgment of the gods I am about to tell it thee. There is a plant similar to the hawthorn in its flower, and whose thorns prick like the viper. If thy hand can lay hold of that plant without being torn, break it from a branch, and bear it with thee; it will secure for thee an eternal youth." '

So Gilgamesh leaves for home, finds the plant, gathers it, and is elated. He names the plant 'the-old-man-becomes-young-again.' His heart fills with joy, he starts across the steppes for Uruk, planning what he will do with his eternal youth, how he will share his gift with the great warriors. But all the while he reckons without the gods, the jealous gods who will not let mortals share their privileges. At night he stops by a pool of cool water and, as he bathes, a serpent comes forth from the pool, snatches the plant and escapes with it, leaving him only a malediction.

v

From the legend of Gilgamesh the authors of the J and P threads in Genesis shaped their respective stories of the flood, which differed only in such details as could easily be modified between the period of the prophets and the return from the captivity. J, the author of the older recension, has the deluge last the mystical sixty-one days, instead of the three hundred and sixty-five assigned to it by P to conform with the solar year. J fails to record where the ark landed, while P grounds it on Ararat. P adds the dimensions of the ark, the breaking up of the fountains of the deep, the rainbow and the covenant which it signifies and some statistical references to Noah's age, and he substitutes one pair of clean animals for the seven pairs of clean and one of unclean named by J, while he omits the sacrifices at the close of the disaster possibly because his theory of religious history precluded a reference to any kind of altar before the exodus. In copying the genealogy which precedes the story, the name of the master of the ark was apparently misplaced in both accounts, Noah having been substituted for Enoch, for it was Enoch who 'walked with God' (i.e., became Very Wise) and who 'disappeared, for God had taken him,' and who lived three hundred and sixty-five years, as P assigns three hundred and sixty-five days to the duration of the flood.

In adding 'the fountains of the deep' to the sources of the flood, P was merely filling an obvious omission in J's account, which had all the water fall as rain. The existence of 'waters beneath the earth' was axiomatic in

Babylonia, the cosmology of which had its origin in the port of Eridu on the Persian Gulf where the land was constantly growing by the deposition of silt; from this accretion, which was perceptible almost day by day, had come the notion that the whole earth had been formed in the same manner, separated as silt from 'the great deep' of which the Persian Gulf was a narrow arm.

Numerous allusions in the Old Testament indicate that the original Hebraic story of creation opened with an episode parallel to that in which Marduk cut Tiamat in half: 'In the beginning Yahweh filled the dragon with air, and slew him, and divided him into two parts.' J, who lived perhaps in the time of Solomon, was not familiar with this early portion of the legend and, his imagination unable to encompass the outright creation of heaven and earth, in beginning his narrative takes the earth as already formed.

In the later narrative of P, Yahweh has so increased in power and importance that he can now create the world itself. Even so he is still unable to create it from nothing, *ex nihilo,* but starts with *tehom* (Tiamat), a great sea or abyss shrouded in darkness; and the first creative act, 'The wind of God was rushing upon the face of the waters,' recalls how Marduk inflated Tiamat with a great wind before he cut her in twain to create heaven and earth. In seven days (corresponding to the seven tablets upon which the Babylonian legend was inscribed) Yahweh creates first, light; second, the firmament (sky) in the midst of the waters, to divide the waters beneath from the waters above, even as Marduk divided Tiamat; third, the dry land and its trees and herbs; fourth, the sun, moon and stars, which he set in the firmament both to give additional light and to rule the day and the night; fifth, the creatures of the sea and the birds of the air (both of which are created out of water); sixth, the creatures created out of earth, and man. Yahweh looked upon his creation and saw that it was good and, on the seventh day, the unlucky day of the moon god Sin, he was tired and rested.

The 'great deep,' in which the earth floated like a mountainous island, remained a cardinal tenet in Jewish and Christian cosmology. Overhead was spread the solid dome of the firmament which came down to the horizon on all sides to rest upon foundations laid in the great waters, bearing in its east and west sides doors through which the sun entered in the morning and departed at night. Above the firmament was another ocean which followed the domed ceiling down to the horizon where it met the ocean surrounding the earth, and over the waters which were above the firmament was heaven. The sun, moon, stars and planets were supported as by cables from the interior of the firmament, and were moved by angels who also opened windows in the firmament to let the waters from above fall as rain to refresh the earth.

The Pythagoreans, and after them Plato and Aristotle, might argue that the earth was a sphere, but before such heresies became fraught with serious danger it was enough for the Christians to refute them with contempt: Eusebius, having in mind the coming end of the world when the faithful would be transported to the kingdom of God, framed an answer to all such speculators: 'It is not through ignorance of the things admired by them [the geographers] but through contempt of their useless labor that we think little of these matters, turning our souls to better things.' And thus Basil of Caesarea: 'It is a matter of no interest to us whether the earth is a sphere or a cylinder or a disk, or concave in the middle like a fan'; and Augustine: 'What concerns is it to me whether the heavens as a sphere enclose the earth in the middle of the world or overhang it on either side?' In the sixth century Cosmas Indicopleustes, drawing upon scriptural texts, described the earth as a flat parallelogram four hundred days' journey long and two hundred broad, surrounded by four seas from which arise the massive walls supporting the firmament, the whole making up a box containing the heavenly bodies and serving as a floor for heaven. Cosmas's arguments were drawn from the words of Moses, the prophets and the apostles, and his world was built most scripturally; it worked by means of angels who pushed the planets to and fro. Its four corners corresponded to the four seasons, its twelve months to the twelve loaves of bread; its boxlike structure agreed with venerable Egyptian lore. But despite all these virtues, which should have recommended it to Christians, it failed to be dogmatized and the notion of a spherical earth, perhaps because it had been supported by Clement of Alexandria and Origen, survived to be argued again by Isidore of Seville and the Venerable Bede and to be accepted without remonstrance by medieval cosmologists.

It was wholly different with the question whether men lived on the other side of the earth. 'Is there anyone so senseless,' queried Lactantius, 'as to believe that there are men whose footsteps are higher than their heads? . . . That the crops and trees grow downward? . . . that the rains and snow and hail fall upward toward the earth? . . . I am at a loss what to say of those who, when they have once erred, steadily persevere in their folly and defend one vain thing by another.' Basil and Ambrose allowed that a man might be saved who thought the opposite side of the earth inhabited, but Augustine, willing enough to consider a spherical earth, vigorously condemned the idea of antipodes: Scripture did not speak of any such inverted descendants of Adam, and God would not allow men to live on the far side of the world since if they did they could not see Christ, at his second coming, descending through the air. Augustine's most cogent argument was based on the Pauline statement: 'Their line is gone through all the earth, and their words to the end of the world'; since no Christian apostles had gone to the antipodes to preach the word of God, no antipodes existed, and those who contended otherwise were giving the 'lie direct to King David and to St. Paul, and therefore to the Holy Ghost.' In the fifteenth century the Spanish theologian Tostatus gave Augustine's argument the dignity of a formal syllogism: 'The apostles were commanded to go into all the world and to preach the gospel to every creature; they did not go to any such part of the world as the antipodes; they did not preach to any creatures there: *ergo,* no antipodes exist.' It was for holding the contrary view, as much as for other heretical opinions, that the physician Peter of Abano was sought out by the inquisition in 1316, and that the astronomer Cecco d'Ascobi was burned at Florence in 1327.

Let the shape of the earth be what it may, man was its lord and master. It was equally inconceivable that he should make himself ridiculous by walking upside down or that he should by geographical accident be excluded from the gospel. Faith in the anthropocentric doctrine of Genesis was subordinate only to the belief in Mosaic authority. Said Peter Lombard: 'Just as man is made for the sake of God — that is, that he may serve Him — so the universe is made for the sake of man — that is, that it may serve him; therefore is man placed at the middle point of the universe, that he may both serve and be served.' And the Christian geographers so drew their maps that Jerusalem was the center of the earth, and the Holy Sepulcher was shown as at the center of Jerusalem, as the world was the center of the cosmos.

The doctrine of the original perfection of the earth was required by the Mosaic account of creation — itself not to be impugned — and by Christian philosophy. Why should God in his infinite power and wisdom create a universe marred by imperfections, unbalanced in its proportions, irregular in its processes? A supreme excellence in no way differing from absolute impeccability and indefectibility must distinguish the divine labor as well as the divine person. Such had been the Scholastic view as regards the heavens, and such was to be the continuing view of astronomers and geographers after Newton. Where Galileo's vision had threatened to besmirch God's world by putting mountains on the moon and relegating the earth to the role of a satellite, Newton's vision had restored the balance; indeed it had afforded Christianity its most signal victory by apparently demonstrating on a scale proportional to stellar distances that Law Supreme was enthroned throughout the heavens — and where was Law, was God. It was a lonely voice which frightenedly declaimed that Newton 'took from God that direct action on his works so constantly ascribed to him in scripture, and transferred it to material mechanism'; for the majority, as for Newton himself, the *Principia* left the divine emanation operative by merely substituting for the direct action of God's hand a perpetual Order imposed upon the planets by his voice.

Why God had singularly chosen that the force of gravity should vary inversely as the square of the distance, and that the earth should move in an elliptical rather than a circular orbit about the sun, unless it be to furnish man with the seasonal extremes of summer and winter, remained part of his inscrutable mystery. It was enough that the new 'force' of gravity had replaced the ancient angelic 'powers,' that the shattering of the celestial spheres had, perhaps not paradoxically, permitted more light to enter. A 'natural law' operating world-without-end and without defection was indefectibility itself. When the 'living garment of Deity' was discovered to be fabricated throughout by a multitude of such edicts or natural laws, most of which were readily translatable into the numbers convenient for the description of time and space, it but bore out the belief of Plato, and before him Pythagoras, that 'God ever geometrizes.' For certain minds of a Neo-Scholastic type, Natural Law had become almost synonymous with God.

The distinction between a universe of uniform and continuous process and one of unchanging and eternal durability was not possible in Newton's time, nor yet, for pious minds, long after. The theologian-physicist, Sir David Brewster, in 1855 pronounced the nebular hypothesis of the origin of the solar system a 'dull and dangerous heresy,' and asserted that 'an omnipotent arm was required to give the planets their position and motion in space, and a presiding intelligence to assign to them the different functions they had to perform.' Which was dividing the dynamic fairly between God and Law. No such division was entertained by the Marquis de Laplace, who, when Napoleon remarked on the absence of God from his *Mécanique céleste,* is reputed to have answered, "But Sire, I find no need of that hypothesis." Such atheism might amuse the French *libertins,* but it could only horrify the orthodox to whom the omnipotence of Law was one of the surest evidences of the essential goodness of creation.

Perfection, then, was still an attribute of God and all his works, including the natural laws which he had created to run the universe — except, of course, the earth itself which had been corrupted by the sins of Adam and

Eve and their descendants. As the offense in Eden had brought forth death and labor, so it had brought disfigurement upon Paradise. Almost simultaneously with Newton's traditional cogitations on the falling apple, Thomas Burnet in his *Sacred Theory of the Earth* (1681) described that body as a hollow shell filled with water like an egg; before sin brought on the deluge it was a perfect sphere, smooth and indescribably beautiful, with neither seas nor islands nor valleys nor rocks, with not a wrinkle, scar or fracture. In keeping with its immaculate condition it enjoyed a perpetual spring interrupted by no meteorological disturbance more severe than the falling of the evening dew. It had been the 'breaking up of the fountains of the deep' which had reduced the earth to what it is today, practically a ruin.

The argument of the original perfection of the earth was, in the nature of the case, a difficult one to answer. One of the charges by which Calvin brought Servetus to the stake was that in an edition of Ptolemy's *Geography* which he had prepared, he had spoken of Judea, not as 'a land flowing with milk and honey,' but as, in the main, meager, barren and inhospitable. In vain did Servetus declare that there were ample proofs for his statement; he was informed that such language 'necessarily inculpated Moses, and grievously outraged the Holy Ghost.' Two hundred years later when Buffon, in attempting to popularize geology, took some liberties with Genesis, the theological faculty of the Sorbonne forced him to print a recantation: 'I declare that I had no intention to contradict the text of scripture; that I believe most firmly all therein related about the creation, both as to order of time and matter of fact. I abandon everything in my book respecting the formation of the earth, and generally all which may be contrary to the narrative of Moses.'

Yet within the same decade, Severinus — one who, either from neglect or contempt of scripture, let himself wander into error — admonished his students: "Go my sons, buy stout shoes, climb the mountains, search the valleys, the deserts, the sea shores, and the deep recesses of the earth. Look for the various kinds of minerals, note their characters and mark their origin. Lastly, buy coal, build furnaces, observe and experiment without ceasing, for in this way and in no other will you arrive at a knowledge of the nature and properties of things." Of such were to be the heretics of the nineteenth century.

The structure of the earth had never greatly puzzled the ancients except as practical knowledge of it aided them in the search for gems, silver, gold, or base metals. The Christians too had avoided going far in subterranean exploration, first, because the subject was too intimately akin to hell-fire, and secondly, because all questions about the earth were already answered by the Flood. Such was the explanation offered by Tertullian and Jerome to account for fossil fishes, while a big tooth found in North Africa was assigned by Augustine to one of the giants mentioned in Genesis. This simple, confident answer would have long sufficed were fossils confined to the surface of the earth, but when it was seen that they were sometimes abundant in the deepest quarries, or in mountainous sections of rock where they were buried to tremendous depths, an alternative theory, and one favored throughout the Scholastic period, conceived them to have developed *in situ.* Avicenna held that they were the freakish products of the 'stone-making force,' while Albertus Magnus attributed them to the 'formative quality of the rocks,' and other Schoolmen spoke of 'lapidific juice' and 'semiair.' Some held that they had their origin in 'irradiations' from the heavenly bodies, the occult forces of the stars and planets being focused by the crystalline spheres upon the earth and tending to reproduce their like-nesses. Or it was held that they were generated by vapors and fermenta-tions in the rocks, such 'tumultuous movements of terrestrial exhalations' being thought responsible even for the formation of 'fossil' Etruscan vases and earthenware vessels; or that they had grown from seeds which had fallen into crevices; or that they reproduced themselves like living animals or plants. It was even propounded that they had been created to serve as 'ornaments for the interior and secret parts of the earth,' as tulips, roses and other flowers adorn its surface.

Then it was argued by Leonardo da Vinci and others in the sixteenth century, by Hook and Vallisnieri in the seventeenth, and by Scheuchzer and Guettard in the eighteenth, that fossils were the actual remains of living organisms which had become embedded in the rocks of the earth's crust; since the earth's crust had been completed by the Creator before he made the fishes and other animals, the conclusion was almost unavoidable that the organic remains had been brought into their present position by the flood. So great was the violence of the wind and waters on that occa-sion that the oceans were stirred to their very depths and piled upon the highest summits of the mountains, depositing there shells of all sorts and fish, to be buried in the sediment which was left when the water re-ceded.

The Genesis explanation, however, presented difficulties. Shells were found at great altitudes in the mountains, in the Andes at 15,000 feet, and though to some this merely proved the universal nature of the deluge, to others it raised the serious question of whence came the enormous quan-tity of water to cover the whole earth to such a depth, and where did it go when the flood receded? Some who on these grounds found the diluvian theory untenable proposed that fossils were imperfect animals and plants, models which had been made by the Creator before he had fully decided upon the best manner of designing living things; or alternatively, that they were sports of nature, the fanciful product of God's inscrutable whimsy.

It was the whimsy view that brought the geologist Johann Beringer to grief. So definitely had this professor in the University of Würzburg committed himself to the theory that fossils are 'stones of a peculiar sort, hidden by the Author of Nature for his own pleasure,' that some of his skeptical students determined to give his faith a thorough trial. They prepared and baked a number of sham fossils from clay, depicting reptiles and fish, birds in their nests, and imaginary creatures, and these they buried where Beringer was sure to find them. The Professor was so enthusiastic over his discovery that his tempters elaborated other fossils figuring the sun and moon, as well as Syrian or Babylonian script. With each successive find Beringer was increasingly convinced that he had come upon irrefutable evidence of the hand of God, and he published (1726) his discoveries in a treatise illustrated by twenty-one folio plates, devoting a chapter to the refutation of those among his skeptical colleagues who asserted that the fossils were fakes. Only later, when one of them turned up bearing his own name, was his faith in the divine origin of fossils, and in human nature, shattered.

By the beginning of the nineteenth century the evidence against the Mosaic account of creation, and particularly against the story of the flood, had grown to alarming proportions. The geologist Werner (1749–1817) and his students had advanced the theory that in the beginning the earth had existed as a globular nucleus already wrinkled into steep mountains and deep valleys, the whole submerged beneath the waters of a primeval ocean covering the highest mountain tops; this ocean, they thought, was not clear but turbid with dissolved or suspended materials which were slowly deposited in successive layers, adhering to the mountainsides as well as settling in the valleys, thus giving rise to the succession of rocks of various types which are apparent in the superficial crust. The Wernerian theory supposed that the interior of the earth was cold and hollow, and that after the rocks had been deposited the waters of the primeval ocean had somehow drained away into the interior. Volcanoes, which seemed to contradict a cold earth filled with water, were dismissed by Werner as isolated burning masses of subterranean coal or oil which had come into existence only in the latest period of earth history.

The school of Neptunists, as the Wernerians were called, was viewed with alarm since a primeval ocean was not the same as the deluge, nor did this history in any way conform with the seven days of creation: 'Our earth is a child of time and has been built up gradually.' Earth history did not begin at 4004 B.C., but many thousands of years before that date. The orthodox scarcely had had time to become alarmed at this heresy, however, when the Neptunists' position was undermined by the Plutonists, led by Hutton (1726–1797), who established that the interior of the earth was hot; that if extinct as well as active volcanoes were included, these were to be found in nearly all parts of the world and were in no way connected with beds of coal or oil; and that the molten lava which in some localities still issued from their vents was but a cooler sample of the earth's veritably incandescent core. The Plutonists further showed that in many places lower and older beds of rock had been turned on end — such indeed was the general structure of great mountains — and in places wholly covered after inversion by formations of later date. Viewed from top to bottom, the geologic column revealed the alternation of periods of quiet deposition and violent upheaval — 'revolution' was Hutton's term — on an unbelievable time scale. There was not just one world the history of which had to be unraveled, but a succession of worlds which had suffered such tiltings and foldings of great land masses, such earthquakes and divisions, such floods of molten lava and wind-blown sand, as to defy the imagination. Revolution had succeeded revolution, with 'no traces of a beginning, no prospect of an end.'

It remained for Lyell to show that the geologic processes of the past were but the extension on a vast time scale of the decay and amalgamation, transportation and deposition, elevation and subsidence, which on a calendar of months or years could be observed to be in continuous if microscopic operation in every part of the world. Earth history was not a matter of some thousands of years, but of millions upon millions.

Small wonder that geology was quickly branded as 'a dark art,' as 'dangerous and disreputable,' as 'a forbidden province,' as 'infernal artillery,' as 'an awful evasion of the testimony of revelation'; that against geologists were hurled the familiar epithets of 'infidel,' 'atheist,' 'impugner of the sacred record,' 'assailant of the volume of God'; that men were called upon to oppose vigorously those doctrines of the earth's origin 'which are calculated to tear up in the public mind every remaining attachment to Christianity.' As though it were not enough that Moses should be called a liar, Cowper would have had it that the geologists impugned the veracity of the Deity:

Some drill and bore
The solid earth, and from the strata there
Extract a register, by which we learn
That He who made it, and revealed its date
To Moses, was mistaken in its age!

If geologists were innocent of the charge, not so some of the orthodox who quickly resorted to the familiar argument of divine deception to account for the geologic appearances. Chateaubriand, in his *Genius of Christianity*, argued that 'in the beginning' everything was created as related in Genesis, and by sudden fiat, but with the appearance of pre-existence: 'It was part of the perfection and harmony of the nature which was displayed before men's eyes that the deserted nests of last year's birds should be seen on the trees, and that the seashore should be covered with shells which had been the abode of fish, and yet the world was quite new, and nests and shells had never been inhabited.' Why God should have chosen to make it appear that he had created the earth by a long and very tedious process and by the agency of terrifying terrestrial convulsions, floods and droughts, why he should have made volcanoes to suggest a core of molten lava when in truth the interior was water, why in consequence of Adam's sin he should have reduced earth's perfection to a corrugated wreck, was left in that divine treasury of inscrutable mystery where were deposited also his reasons for decorating the deepest rocks with shells and fishes.

The first large draft against the divine treasury of mystery to the account of fossils was drawn when William Smith (1769–1839) surveyed nearly the whole of the British Isles and demonstrated that the relations of the different strata were everywhere consonant with the supposition that the strata had been laid down successively from bottom to top, only subsequently to be folded, slipped and sometimes overturned. Smith showed that different geologic formations were not whimsically populated with a variety of animal and vegetable decorations, but contained distinctive species ranging progressively from the most lowly shells in the lower beds to the higher fish in the upper strata. Under Smith's cataloguing, fossils became a geologic calendar by which any stratum could be placed in its proper epoch of earth's history. The genius of Cuvier (1769–1832) reconstructed, often from a few bones, the great vertebrates of the past and demonstrated that the fossil bones were not those of living species but of allied forms which were now extinct, each epoch having a different population on land and sea. Though Smith accepted a vast time scale, Cuvier adhered to Archbishop Ussher's calculation and the Mosaic account. Genesis said that on the sixth day God created all the animals and plants, and nothing was said about the creation of new species at any subsequent date, either before or after the flood; hence the only acceptable interpretation was that some had been wiped out owing to Noah's failure to take them into the ark, while others had been destroyed since the flood by some catastrophe, or a succession of catastrophes, and their dead bodies buried in a soft dirt which had subsequently turned to rock. This opinion, coming from one of the most eminent Christian biologists of the day, was welcomed by the church as wholly refuting the geologists' claim for great antiquity of the earth, and the even more heretical assertion that new species had come into existence since the one and only creative act.

vi

The heresy that one *species* of animals could change into another not only flatly made Moses out to be a falsifier but denied God's competence to do the complete creative work in one operation. Christian scholars had encountered it, and evaded it successfully. Appreciating the vastness of the organic world, the great multitude of big and little animals, of winged creatures and of creeping things, the difficulty of the Almighty's bringing each of these creatures separately before Adam to be named, the difficulties thereby presented to Adam himself, and the further difficulty of crowding even pairs, much less seven pairs, of this great multitude of creatures into the ark and keeping them alive throughout the flood, they had made a variety of concessions to the Genesis account. Origen had expanded Noah's vessel by suggesting that the cubit was six times greater than had been supposed, while Bede had conserved its rations by suggesting that God had thrown all the animals into a deep sleep or otherwise miraculously made one day's supply of food sufficient for a year. But these were more a subterfuge than a solution, and it was Basil's explanation, that lesser creatures such as frogs, snakes, flies, gnats and the like, were continuously being created from mud and water by a creative power put there by God in the first instance, that received general approval. Augustine accepted the principle of spontaneous generation and through Isidore of Seville the doctrine of the 'secondary creation' of small animals passed to Peter Lombard and Thomas Aquinas, the latter summing it up in the words: 'Nothing was made by God, after the six days of creation, absolutely new, but it was in some sense included in the work of the six days . . . even new species, if any appear, have existed before in certain native properties, just as animals are produced from putrefaction!' About the beginning of the seventeenth century the Jesuit theologian Suarez rejected the doctrine of spontaneous generation as erroneous, and roundly denounced Augustine as a heretic for his role in sponsoring it; and in this same century it was excluded as a plausible hypothesis by Francesco Redi by means of some simple experiments with a fly screen and a bottle of putrefying meat. Thereafter the idea of the transformation of species began perforce to reassert itself, if for no other reason than to keep the ark afloat. Giordano Bruno, who owed much to the thought of Lucretius, might have developed the notion of evolution, but he was burned. Descartes (1595–1650), whose intellectual technique owed nothing either to theology or Scholastic tradition, conceived an evolutionary scheme to account for the solar system, and would unquestionably have applied the idea of transformation to the structure and functions of organisms, but having observed Galileo's fate, and remembering Bruno, who had died in his childhood, and having himself suffered repeated condemnation, he withheld his opinions out of distaste for hell-fire and respect for the church. Leibnitz contemplated the possibilities of organic transformation but had his activities in this field curtailed by the strictures of the Jesuits. Buffon was frankly an evolutionist, but was forced by public humiliation to defer to Moses. De Maillet (1656–1738) conceived that the structure of the earth might be studied in the light of the present course of nature, and that existing species had been produced by modification of their predecessors; fearing ecclesiastic censure he presented his book on the subject as the reverie of a Hindu sage who had transmitted its contents to a Christian missionary; yet even thus disguised he was unable to get it published in his lifetime, and when it did appear shortly after his death it was vigorously denounced. De Maillet, however, suffered as much destructive criticism at the hands of Voltaire as from the church. Voltaire, although at heart a deist of sorts — 'there is,' he said, 'something divine in a flea' — loved to direct his most biting satire against the church and priests and nothing stirred him to higher pitch than the authority of Moses. De Maillet had seen in the presence of fossils on high mountains a proof that these mountains were once below the sea; and Voltaire, recognizing in this an argument for the deluge and a support for Mosaic tradition, ridiculed De Maillet's work until it was discredited, this writer having unfortunately put himself at Voltaire's mercy by proposing that the first human being had been born of a mermaid.

The notion of evolution was in the air when Linnaeus (1707–1778) gave to the contrary doctrine, the eternal fixity of species, the authority of his name, the greatest in the annals of biology after Aristotle. For the first time since Aristotle there was presented in the *Systema naturae* and other works of the Swedish naturalist a revised and reorganized catalogue of the entire plant and animal kingdoms, patterned according to their structural affinities into species and genera; here there were presented a multitude of facts demanding reinterpretation, countless suggestions of an orderly if complex transmutation of one type of organism into another. Yet it was commonplace knowledge and within every man's experience that species invariably bred true to type, and to challenge the commonplace is a heroic task. When the great naturalist published his work on sexual reproduction in plants his writings were outrightly proscribed in those states which gave allegiance to Catholic doctrine, and viewed askance by Protestants — the idea of sex in plants was horrifying. When he showed that the miracle of turning water into blood depended on the growth of a dense mass of minute, red aquatic animals, the Lutheran bishop of Svedberg retorted vehemently, "The reddening of water is not natural . . . when God allows such a miracle to take place Satan endeavors, and so do his ungodly, self-reliant, self-sufficient, and worldly tools, to make it signify nothing." Towards the end of his life Linnaeus tentatively suggested that the various species of one genus had at the time of creation constituted one species only; and from the last edition of his *Systema naturae* he dropped any explicit assertion of the fixity of species; but beyond this it was not within his power to resist that which was self-evident, which had been 'believed always, everywhere, and by all men,' and which was certified by God through the agency of Moses.

No less troublesome than the mystery presented by the vast variety of species was the explanation of their peculiar geographical distribution. From Augustine onward attempts had been made to explain the occurrence of a variety of animals in lands so remote from Ararat that it seemed impossible for them to have walked or swum there by themselves.

With the voyages of Columbus, Vasco da Gama, Magellan, Amerigo Vespucci and others, each navigator bringing home wholly new species from remote parts of the world, the difficulties of the radiation theory became greatly multiplied.

Now to add to such obvious perplexities were the ever increasing evidences afforded by Hutton that the age of the earth was not 4004 years, nor yet four hundred thousand years, but untold millions; that in the great epochs of the past and in all parts of the earth fauna after fauna had succeeded each other, only to suffer annihilation; that the surviving species, even these together with all recoverable extinct types, were by any account but a small fraction of the great cavalcade of life that had moved slowly through the geologic ages. Fossil as well as living species accumulated faster than men could classify them, and with each addition the theory of the interrelatedness of organic life became more and more attractive. Saint-Hilaire, Treviranus, Herder, Oken, Blumenbach, Zimmerman, Soemerring, a long list of men in the seventeenth and eighteenth centuries, had timidly or openly proposed one or another process of transmutation, but the idea was ridiculed by Cuvier and others, who were determined to adhere to Moses.

With literary license Erasmus Darwin (1731–1802) has been called the grandfather of evolution because he was the grandfather of Charles who fathered it. A successful physician, Erasmus yet possessed such time and energy beyond the requirements of his patients that he could indulge in the pastime of mechanical invention so productively as to produce a manifold writer, a talking machine which said 'Mama' and other words, a canal lock, a rotary pump, and a 'very singular carriage,' from falling off of which he sustained a lifelong injury to one of his legs. His notes on pathology were intermingled with ideas on electricity, meteorology, sleep, lunacy, sanitation, phonetics, slavery and a hundred other subjects, while the rest of his spare time was devoted to the effort to convert Linnaeus's great technical works on botany into verse.

It was in his *Zoonomia* (1794), ostensibly a textbook of medicine, in a chapter dealing with generation, that he interpolated what is not so much a theory of evolution as a panegyric on the idea. After citing certain evidences of a developmental process, he wrote:

'From thus meditating on the great similarity of the structure of the warm-blooded animals, and at the same time of the great changes they undergo both before and after their nativity; and by considering in how minute a portion of time many of the changes of animals above described have been produced; would it be too bold to imagine, that in the great length of time, since the earth began to exist, perhaps millions of ages before the commencement of the history of mankind, would it be too bold to imagine, that all warm-blooded animals have arisen from one living filament, which *The Great First Cause* endued with animality, with the power of acquiring new parts, attended with new propensities, directed by irritations, sensations, volitions and associations; and thus possessing the faculty of continuing to improve by its own inherent activity, and of delivering down those improvements by generation to its posterity world without end!' Endorsing the notion expressed by Buffon and Helvetius, that mankind had arisen from one family of monkeys on the 'banks of the Mediterranean' who accidentally had learned to use the thumb; and approving Hume's suggestion that the world itself might have been produced gradually rather than created suddenly by Almighty fiat, he envisioned The Great Architect accomplishing the work of creation by slow degrees and constantly improving the whole, as is evidenced by 'the excellence observable in every part of the creation; such as in the progressive increase of the solid habitable parts of the earth from water; and in the progressive increase in the wisdom and happiness of its inhabitants; . . . our present situation being a state of probation, which by our exertions we may improve, and are consequently responsible for our actions.'

Erasmus Darwin anticipated both the doctrine of the inheritance of acquired characters, to be formulated later by Lamarck, and the doctrine of the survival of the fittest, formulated by his grandson, Charles. That he should come upon both ideas and yet fail to develop either may be attributed to his failure to perceive that here was the question which lay at the heart of the biological problem: granted the doctrine of the mutability of species from whatever cause, what force or forces pattern the final, living forms? He remained unaware that the problem existed, because his evolution was a pious fantasy differing from Genesis only in that creation consisted of continuing 'process' instead of a series of six quickly completed acts; the bleaker aspects of the picture, the quick destruction of animals and plants by great catastrophes, their slow destruction by competition and disease — 'nature red in tooth and claw' — were for him but those somber elements by which the poet was wont to emphasize through contrast the essential beneficence of the whole. His 'evolution' was suffused with goodness and light, and was moving irresistibly if erratically toward perfection under the better maxims of Jesus and the brighter philosophical lamps of the late eighteenth century.

This rose-wash of morality and progress, coupled with the poetic form of most of his writing, was one reason why Erasmus Darwin escaped the ecclesiastic condemnation which embarrassed those of his contemporaries who ventured into infidelity. But equally important in securing this immunity was the fact that there was nothing in his speculations in the way of evidence or authority to give them even the air of a serious doctrine. Consequently they were neglected by orthodox and unorthodox alike, and the worst injury he brought upon himself was that for a time 'Darwinizing' became a cant term for unrestrained hypothesis.

For the most part, those who studied nature in the late eighteenth and early nineteenth centuries were imbued with the idea that creation mirrored in every detail the mind of the Creator. Natural theology, as it wa called, was the art of demonstrating the existence of God, and his goodness, from the exquisite accommodations which were to be discovered in all animals and plants. The popular textbooks of the day consisted of such ancient works as John Ray's *The Wisdom of God Manifested in the Works of Creation* (1691), that argued the beneficence of the Almighty from the adaptations of animals to man's requirements, as well as to their own environment; and Nehemiah Grew's *Cosmologica Sacra, or a Discourse on the Universe, as it is the Creature and Kingdom of God; chiefly written to demonstrate the Truth and Excellency of the Bible* (1701). Grew proved creative design and the good intentions of Providence by such arguments as, 'A crane, which is scurvy meat, lays but two eggs in the year, but a pheasant and partridge, both excellent meat, lay and hatch fifteen or twenty'; 'if nettles sting, it is to secure an excellent medicine for children and cattle'; 'if the bramble hurts man, it makes all the better hedge'; weasels and other hurtful animals induce us to watchfulness; thistles and moles, to good husbandry; lice oblige us to cleanliness in our bodies, spiders in our houses, and the moth in our clothes.' The masterpiece of this type of thinking was Archdeacon Paley's *Natural Theology* (1802), the thesis of which was that nature, and particularly human anatomy, requires in each of many particulars 'an intelligent designing mind for the contriving and determining of the forms which organized bodies bear.' The argument from design culminated in the 'Bridgewater Treatises,' a series of eight volumes each prepared by an expert and purporting to show by a mighty array of pious science that God the Creator had foreseen and taken care of all the requirements of man, down to the chemistry of the stomach and intestines.

A tide of skepticism was, however, swelling. In 1801 Lamarck began developing his famous (and fallacious) theory, which he presented more fully in 1814, that since many organs may undergo some change in consequence of use and disuse, new wants in animals can give rise to new organs which develop in proportion to their employment, and that these new organs can be transmitted to the offspring. Among the examples which Lamarck chose to illustrate his views were the giraffe, which he supposed had lengthened its neck by stretching it to gather high-growing foliage, and the kangaroo which he supposed had lengthened and strengthened its hind legs by jumping. These homely examples, which to the untutored seemed reasonable enough, helped to popularize the idea of progressive change and adaptation even while they laid the author of the theory open to the taunts of Cuvier and the orthodox. In 1813 Wells analyzed the varieties of mankind in evolutionary terms; in 1820 Herbert summarized his evidences on the mutability of plants; in 1831 Matthew tentatively conceived a process of natural selection operating on offspring which varied from the parent stock. In 1844 Chambers in his *Vestiges o Creation* presented a naïve theory of evolution which called for two dis tinct creative impulses compressed in the first and only creative act, on imparting life and a second imparting a tendency to modification mor or less in accordance with the Lamarckian view. The *Vestiges* was innc cent of both zoologic accuracy and substantiating evidence, but its liter ary charm and reasonableness made it popular and it went through man editions, spreading the idea of transmutation by giving it an appearanc scarcely less pious than Paley's argument from design, or Erasmus Dan win's poetic rhapsodies.

vii

Had the publication of his books been delayed by twenty years eve Erasmus Darwin might have been ostracized for atheism, for in the la decade of the eighteenth century there set in a reaction against infidelit of any sort, a Puritanical intolerance of nonconformity more severe tha had existed for a hundred years. The newly risen danger of democrati revolution, the consequences of which were all too evident in France an in the colonies, impelled the upper and middle classes of England to unit in defending the ecclesiasticism which was the chief repository of the cultural tradition, and on which they were inclined to lean heavily in th interests of property rights. Although the allegation was scarcely justifie in fact, the revolution on the Continent was attributed by many to di belief, particularly to the ironically critical type represented by Voltair while the War of Independence was identified with the self-declare infidel Thomas Paine, the freethinker Franklin, the deist Washingto and with Jefferson, whose frank skepticisms coming from a person lesser position would have quickly reduced their author to ill repute. Th very Constitution of the rebellious states, with deliberateness amountin almost to federal blasphemy, omitted all mention of the deity. Revol tion, or worse, must be the product of such freethinking, and to foresta its direful consequences an ever angrier resistance was offered to impie in any form. Dissident opinion in theology was considered akin anarchy. Students looking forward to careers, public servants seekir popular approval, teachers dependent for their livelihood on positio nearly all of which were under ecclesiastic control, ordinary citizens fea ful of their neighbors' estimation, did not readily entertain, much less disclose, heretical beliefs.

The terms 'freethinker' and 'free thought,' descriptive of skepticism of accepted belief, had come into use in the late seventeenth and early eighteenth centuries and still savored of Satanism because skepticism threatened the *status quo*. After a hundred years skepticism continued to find voice only through those individuals, relatively few in an age of social conformity, who esteemed the right to free thought sufficiently to be prepared to fight for it, and to suffer the consequences. Robertson notes that for translating and publishing the *Histoire critique de Jesus Christ* of d'Holbach, George Houston was fined £200 and imprisoned for two years in Newgate. Between 1817 and 1835 Richard Carlile underwent nine years' imprisonment for the publication, among other condemned books, of Paine's *Age of Reason;* and in 1824 eight of Carlile's shopmen were sentenced to various terms with fines, for the sale of this same volume and other irreligious works. In 1820 Thomas Davison was fined £100 and imprisoned two years for publishing in *The Deists Magazine,* 'A Defence of Deism and Dissection of the Bible Story.' In 1823 Susanna Wright was fined £100 and imprisoned for eighteen months for 'having been instrumental in publishing a libel on the Christian religion'; Robert Taylor, author of *Diegesis* and *The Devil's Pulpit,* was imprisoned one year in 1828 and two years in 1831-1833 for expounding the mythical origins of Christianity; and Charles Southwell, the founder and editor of the first avowedly atheistic English periodical, *The Oracle of Reason* (1842-1843), was fined £100 and imprisoned for a year for an admittedly offensive article entitled 'The Jew Book.' It was for a remark made in public debate, to the effect that "the reigning deity, considered as manager of human affairs, was indicated as fitly to be placed on half pay," that Southwell's successor on *The Oracle,* George Jacob Holyoake, was imprisoned for six months. The third editor, Thomas Paterson, was imprisoned for using 'blasphemous' placards in London, and the fourth, George Adams, was imprisoned for a month for selling a copy of the paper.

In the main, however, these legal processes gave more aid than hurt to the freethinking movement, by bringing to it much needed pecuniary support from men who cherished freedom of thought, of speech and of the press, and by exciting the interest of the people generally in the forbidden but all too attractive subject of what paradoxically had come to be called the Higher Criticism. Young men, attracted by the new challenge to courage and liberty, offered themselves to martyrdom by undertaking editorships of suppressed periodicals, by printing pamphlets in cellars and by stirring up public debates. In Scotland the prosecutions for blasphemy reached such proportions that a number of Anti-Persecution Societies were formed to defend the right of free speech, while in England, Hyde Park and the soap box became cathedral and pulpit of the new intellectual liberty, still expounded but in unharmonious competition with the Salvation Army's, 'I will cling to the old rugged cross, and exchange it some day for a crown.'

The atheists of 1800–1850 did not deny 'the existence of God,' or 'the existence of gods'; like Thomas Paine, whose *Age of Reason* had evoked violent condemnation in all countries and contributed to his imprisonment in France as well as to the spread of atheism in the colonies, they more often than not asserted only what Spencer later was permitted to affirm with the greatest philosophic dignity, and personal safety, that God was 'the Unknowable'; only they held, with a logic absent from Spencer's definition, that if he was Unknowable, neither the Christians nor themselves could know whether he was or not. If some of these freethinkers were excited to vilification by oppression, the greater number were but determined on reasonable grounds to reject revelation, ecclesiastic authority and the current definitions of the theologians. If in the defense of their positions they excursed beyond theology into mundane matters and charged that the Protestant Church was a revenue-drawing corporation in very profitable operation, that individual clerics supported this vested interest because it was a well paid and socially esteemed profession or because their fathers and grandfathers had elected it before them, that it was bigotry and not knowledge that prompted the orthodox to impose their beliefs on others, that the churchmen were afraid to debate their points in public and by rational arguments — they were but leveling the same charges against the sectarians as had been hurled against the mother church from the days of the pagan 'persecutions' on through the Reformation, charges which the Protestants like the Catholics ignored as merely the spawn of ignorance and malice. What could not be dismissed so highhandedly was the geology with which the spirit of disbelief challenged the validity of the Mosaic history, the increasing credence in the uniformity of nature that challenged the existence of miracles and the divinity of Jesus, and the skepticisms that challenged the authority of the church to dictate on morals in general, and particularly on the nature of God.

It seemed to many who had put aside the devil and the doctrine of original sin that if, in Anselm's terms, God was 'supreme essence, life, reason, salvation, righteousness, wisdom, truth, goodness, greatness, beauty, immortality, incorruptibility, immutability, blessedness, eternity, power, and unity,' then he must also be 'singularity, death, inanity, damnation, disobedience, ignorance, falsity, evil, pettiness, ugliness, corruption, flux, transience, futility and chaos.' Any attempt to escape from the oppositions of good and evil could result only in the reinstatement of the devil as a subordinate deity, or in a definition that consisted merely of a string of negatives denying all positive attributes — of such expressions as 'impersonal,' 'timeless,' 'changeless,' 'purposeless,' and 'without desire,' which was no definition of anything except a vacuum. In all intellectual honesty, so thought the new atheists, one could not affirm the existence of a God who was defined as nothing at all.

Holyoake, the atheist who in 1851 first called himself a 'secularist,' and who founded the first of the Secular Societies that were to become numerous in later decades, defended atheism on the grounds that it was only 'reason putting questions to theology.' Charles Bradlaugh asserted in 1862: 'Denial of God is Netheism. An Atheist says, I am ignorant; I do not know what you mean by the word; I am without any idea of God: to me the word God is a word conveying no meaning. The Bible God I deny; the Christian God I disbelieve in; but I am not rash enough to say there is no God as long as you tell me you are unprepared to define God to me.' Although Bradlaugh's distinction between netheism and atheism is indefensible on etymological grounds, his philosophical position was unanswerable and productive of results: his challenge to the theists to 'Define your God' was particularly embarrassing at a time when sectarian schisms were rife and when even Anglican prelates were drawing censure for their lack of orthodoxy. Feared and bitterly hated all his life by the conventionally minded, Bradlaugh was none the less able in two score years to win successively the right of an avowed freethinker to sit in Parliament, the virtual discredit of the blasphemy laws, the liberty of public meetings in the London parks, the freedom of newspapers from suretyship for articles and editorials and the right of nontheistic witnesses to make affirmation instead of taking the oath in the courts of law. It was by this challenge that he and the other atheists of the nineteenth century paved the way for the more orthodox but wholly revolutionary Charles Darwin and the Second Reformation, as Roscellinus, Francis Bacon, William of Ockham, Wycliffe and Huss had prepared the way for the only slightly unorthodox Martin Luther and the first Reform.

While the freethinkers were fighting with epithets in the front line, sometimes bloodily and always at the expense of respectability, less radical critics of orthodoxy were executing lateral movements against the entrenched beliefs by more devious methods, and with much less risk to their persons and reputations. William Howitt, author of a *Popular History of Priestcraft in all Ages and Nations* (1833) could safely assert that 'arrogance and atrocity are prominent and imperishable features in the priestly character,' and that 'the clergy form a dark eclipse between God and men's souls.' Robert Owen, the founder of socialism, could safely denounce all the tenets of Christology because he was addressing the 'masses' and advocating in their behalf, and to the embarrassment of the upper classes, the very reforms which, if doctrine and dogma were discarded, were epitomized in the idealized gospel Jesus. License also was granted the poets. Shelley, in his youthful tract, *The Necessity of Atheism,* had written, 'God is an hypothesis, and as such, stands in need of proof; the *onus probandi* rests on the theist . . . God is represented as infinite, eternal, incomprehensible; he is contained under every predicate *in non* that the logic of ignorance could fabricate. Even his worshippers allow that it is impossible to form any idea of him.' Byron, Keats and Coleridge, although less iconoclastic, were in varying respects antagonistic to Christian dogma. The otherwise pious Coleridge brought upon himself the epithet 'atheist' for his views on the Trinity, the doctrine of the expiatory sacrifice and the validity of miracles. As for the crucifixion, Coleridge said, 'The law of God and the great principles of the Christian religion would have been the same had Christ never assumed humanity. It is for these things, and for such as these, for telling unwelcome truths, that I have been termed an atheist. It is for these opinions that William Smith assured the Archbishop of Canterbury that I was (what half the clergy are in *their lives*) an atheist. Little do these men know what atheism is. Not one man in a thousand has either the strength of mind or the goodness of heart to be an atheist. I repeat it, not one man in ten thousand has the goodness of heart or strength of mind to be an atheist.'

If it is inquired what that the rare individual extolled by Coleridge must deny to be an atheist, it must be answered that he must deny, in whole or in part, the Protestant creed which, condensed to brevity, consisted of the sober belief that a God with vital functions equivalent to hands and mouth, with emotions identical with love and jealousy, and moved by some divine deficiency equivalent to human desire, had on a certain occasion created the universe out of nothing in exactly six days of twenty-four hours each; that he had created Eve out of Adam's rib; that Adam and Eve had lived in the Garden of Eden and been tempted by a serpent; that they had sinned by breaking God's command and been expelled from Eden; and that in consequence of Adam's sin death, labor and all forms

of misery came about, and all babes born into the world were damned to
purgatory by God's predetermination except as they be redeemed by baptism; that Noah, forewarned by God, had built a boat into which he had
taken seven other persons and either twos or sixteens of every animal in
the world and fed them for sixty-one or three hundred and sixty-five days,
all other creatures on earth being destroyed; that because of Adam's sin
all except the Jews (in the first instance) were destined to eternal perdition — until Jesus Christ, who was human and yet uncreated, both God
and not God, had been born of a virgin in order to save those few who
believed in baptism and the sacraments, now leaving the Jews to burn
along with the goyim in hell-fire; that Moses had personally written the
entire Pentateuch, including the account of his own death; and that his
work as well as all others which had been finally selected for the canonical
scriptures had been divinely inspired; that God had deliberately sent Jesus
to earth and had sacrificed him in order to save those who would accept
the sacrifice as literally that of a scapegoat; and that those who did not
interpret Jesus's death in this sense, or who rejected the other Christian
tenets, were damned in advance of birth, and with the foreknowledge of
God, to hell — ignorance of the gospel or geographic accident of birth
being a doubtful plea for innocence; that at doomsday the remains of
the dead would come alive (Luther had damned the immortal 'soul' as
a pagan belief and the Protestant churches officially endorsed the doctrine
of the resurrection of the body) and ascend to heaven or, if they were not
so fortunate, descend to hell; that prayer was efficacious, especially against
bad weather, bad health and war; and that a sinless marriage was impossible without sacerdotal seal — in 1850 denial of only a few of these
beliefs would suffice to make a man an atheist. Or alternatively, he might
deny that civilization in the proper sense had begun only with the founding of the Christian church and had been preserved against the destructive influences of infidelity only by the inspired militancy of the Christian
faith.

Atheism would no doubt have been less frequent had it been more difficult. In diverse ways, by means of soap-box orators and free-lance writers,
in poetry and fiction, in the rapidly accelerating studies of earth and man,
its spirit began to touch people who, though lacking any contact with the
'higher literature' or 'higher philosophy,' none the less possessed a slight
measure of innate skepticism and a greater measure of innate curiosity.
As in the twelfth and thirteenth centuries, so in the nineteenth, heresy
spread first among the relatively uncultured classes, to rise unexpectedly
and engulf the clergy and aristocracy to whom by tradition belonged the

prerogative of 'thinking.' The complexity of Christian dogma was such that only experts could comprehend its devious arguments, only the ecclesiastic discipline of the public schools could assure the firm acceptance of the faith; and the common people, still uneducated except in the elements of reading and writing and common sense, were the first to delight in seeing the proponents of orthodoxy discomfited.

But as in the first Reformation, the crisis was marked by infidelity within as much as without holy orders. The furore that attended the publication of the volume entitled *Essays and Reviews* (1860) reveals both the conservatism of the majority of ecclesiastics, and the extent to which a few receptive minds had realized the futility of defending the more particularistic dogmas. On invitation, seven individuals, six of them clerics, had prepared for this volume articles discussing sundry of the older theologic positions which had been rendered untenable by modern discoveries. The authors were eminent scholars holding positions in the universities and public schools, and all approached their subject most conservatively. The Reverend Frederick Temple of Rugby, who had instituted laboratories and scholarships in natural science at that school, discoursed on the intellectual and spiritual growth of the race and the contributions made by the Hebrews, Egyptians, Greeks, Romans and other non-Christian peoples to European thought. The Reverend Rowland Williams called attention with approval to the 'Biblical Researches' of Baron Bunsen, the Egyptologist. The Reverend H. B. Wilson discussed the conflicts, past and present, in Protestantism, going so far as to deplore 'a very widespread alienation, both of educated and uneducated persons' from the church (the census of 1841 showing that nearly half the population declined allegiance); and noting further that 'the sceptical movements in this generation are the result of observation and thought' rather than politics and passion, and suggesting that if the church were to prosper a selection must be made in interpreting the Bible 'between the dark patches of human passion and error which form a partial crust upon it and the bright centre of spiritual truth within' — one prudent course being to abolish the necessity for subscription to the fundamental — and fundamentalist — Thirty Nine Articles of the creed. The Reverend Benjamin Jowett, already questionably distinguished for a radical volume on *The Epistles of St. Paul,* enlarged upon the newer aspects of scriptural interpretation and acceded that 'the theologian too, may have peace in the thought that he is subject to the conditions of his age rather than one of its moving powers.' The Reverend Mark Pattison, in a survey of religious thought in England from 1688 to 1750, deplored the descent of reason and the circumstance that now 'a godless orthodoxy threatens, as in the 15th century, to extinguish religious thought all together, and nothing is allowed in the Church of England but the formulae of past thinkings, which have long lost all sense of any kind.' The Reverend Baden Powell, an unabashed champion of geology who had abandoned the church for the pursuit of mathematics and other secular knowledge, argued against the acceptability of Christian evidences for miracles. The single layman, Mr. C. W. Goodwin, argued the incredibility of the Mosaic account of creation.

Every contributor to *Essays and Reviews* was an acknowledged authority in his field, and all were orthodox on many points. Singly each author might have escaped censure, but collectively, and in the spotlight of ecclesiastic condemnation, their work added up to outright heresy. The chief defender of orthodoxy who was aroused to fury was Bishop Wilberforce, of Oxford, who in an explosive article in the *Quarterly Review* attacked the volume with the epithets 'infidel,' 'atheistic,' 'false,' and 'wanton.' To deny the Mosaic account of creation, said the bishop, 'sweeps away the whole basis of inspiration and leaves no place for the Incarnation.' The writers were 'guilty of criminal levity,' their work full of 'sophistries and scepticisms.' The volume had hitherto received scant notice from reviewers, but now it needed no other advertising and within a year it had passed through nine editions and had everywhere become the center of argument. Its authors became known as the 'Seven against Christ,' 'the seven extinguishers of the seven lamps of the Apocalypse,' 'the seven champions *not* of Christendom,' and their combined argument was taken to imply that the established church was 'little more than a late legend founded upon a misconception.' Clergy and laity alike, frantic with fear and rage, began to beseech the bishops to exert themselves in behalf of Christianity and the church.

The book having been widely distributed and read, the archbishops pointed out that there was really little to be done. Privately they tried to alienate the more conservative Temple and Jowett from their blackened associates, but without success: Temple replied to the Bishop of London: 'Many years ago you urged us from the university pulpit to undertake the critical study of the Bible. You said that it was a dangerous study, but indispensable. You described its difficulties, and those who listened must have felt a confidence (as I assuredly did, for I was there) that if they took your advice and entered on the task, you at any rate, would never join in treating them unjustly if their study had brought with it the difficulties you described. . . . To tell a man to study, and yet bid him, under heavy penalties, come to the same conclusions with those who have not studied, is to mock him.' And again: 'What can be a grosser superstition than the theory of literal inspiration? But because that has a regular footing it is to be treated as a good man's mistake, while the courage to speak the truth about the first chapter of Genesis is a wanton piece of wickedness.'

The storm spread to the Lower House, where Archdeacon Denison demanded the severest treatment of the authors, 'for the sake of the young who are tainted, and corrupted, and thrust almost to hell by the action of this book.' At another time the Archdeacon avowed, 'Of all books in any language which I ever laid my hands on, this is incomparably the worst; it contains all the poison which is to be found in Tom Paine's *Age of Reason,* while it has the additional disadvantage of having been written by clergymen.' Bishop Wilberforce insisted that it was the church's duty to clear itself of complicity with men who 'gave up God's Word, Creation, redemption, and the work of the Holy Ghost.'

The controversy acquired legal importance when the Reverend Williams, who had written on Egyptology, and the Reverend Wilson, who had discussed the history of Protestantism and the growing skepticism of the age, having been suspended from their offices by their clerical brethren, appealed to the crown and their appeal came to trial before the Judicial Council, consisting of the lord chancellor, the two archbishops, the bishop of London and several lay judges. During the trial Dr. Pusey personally and unethically beseeched the bishop of London, who as judge was presiding over the case, to convict the defendants, basing his arguments on the terrible consequences to the church should they be acquitted. The court refused to pronounce any opinion upon the book as a whole, limiting itself to certain extracts. Among the charges which had been leveled against the Reverend Wilson was his denial of the doctrine of eternal punishment, and on this point the court decided — the two archbishops dissenting — that it did 'not find in the formularies of the English Church any such distinct declaration upon the subject as to require it to punish the expression of a hope by a clergyman that even the ultimate pardon of the wicked who are condemned in the day of judgment may be consistent with the will of Almighty God.' In respect to the suspension of Williams and Wilson, the court found in favor of the appellants, denying the power of the episcopacy, even as represented in a general convocation, to suspend anyone from the privileges of orders for heretical opinions.

This judicial decision only multiplied the panic, the orthodox taking it as a virtual approval of *Essays and Reviews.* High and Low churchmen gathered together at Oxford and under Dr. Pusey and Archdeacon Denison circulated an impassioned declaration to every clergyman in England and Ireland, begging them 'for the love of God' to sign it. Thus it was that Pusey collected eleven thousand reverend signatures affirming belief in the eternal punishment of hell. Deputations claiming to represent one hundred and thirty-seven thousand laymen waited on the two archbishops to thank them for dissenting from the unorthodox decision of the court.

At the Convocation of Canterbury the book was a major topic of discussion. Bishop Thirlwall, who had throughout disdained the orthodox panic, said that he considered Pusey's eleven thousand names endorsing a belief in hell as 'a row of figures preceded by a decimal point, so that however far the series may be advanced, it can never rise to the value of a single unit.' In spite of his opposition, however, and the opposition of other liberal churchmen, the Convocation passed an act condemning 'the said volume,' as contrary to the 'received doctrine.' But the Judicial Council of the crown having already tried the case and passed its judgment in favor of the defendants, the lord chancellor dismissed the ecclesiastic condemnation as 'simply a series of well-lubricated terms — a sentence so oily and saponaceous that no one can grasp it; like an eel, it slips through your fingers, and is simply nothing.' For the first time in fifteen centuries a secular court denied the bishops the power to dismiss from office a colleague who disagreed with them.

An echo of the 'somewhat notable occasion' of *Essays and Reviews* remains in the epitaph of the judge who presided over the volume's notorious trial:

Richard Baron Westbury,
Lord High Chancellor of England.
He was an eminent Christian,
An energetic and merciful Statesman,
And a still more eminent and merciful Judge.
During his three years' tenure of office
He abolished the ancient method of conveying land,
The time-honoured institution of the Insolvent's Court,
                              And
The Eternity of Punishment,
Toward the close of his earthly career,
In the Judicial Committee of the Privy Council,
He dismissed Hell with costs,
And took away from Orthodox members of the Church of England
Their last hope of everlasting damnation!

The tempest aroused by the 'Seven against Christ' had not subsided, however, before another violent storm of heresy broke upon the English scene. J. W. Colenso, Bishop of Natal, had long been teaching his black converts the New Testament and other portions of the Bible from his own translations into the Zulu language. Abashed by the frank skepticism of his protégés, he had come to doubt the historicity of certain parts of the Pentateuch. Could an army of six hundred thousand men be mobilized in a single night? Could three million people, with their flocks and herds, have obtained food and water on the small, arid desert over which they were said to have wandered for forty years? Was not the butchery of two hundred thousand Midianites by twelve thousand Israelites an atrocity which had happily been carried out only on paper? Gradually he had come to the conclusion that a large portion of the Pentateuch was the work of a comparatively late period in Jewish history, that many passages in Deuteronomy had been written after the Jews settled in Canaan, that the Mosaic law was not in force before the captivity — that in all the books there is much that is mythical and legendary.

Summing up his views in *The Pentateuch and the Book of Joshua Critically Examined* (1862) Colenso discovered that the skepticism which had seemed reasonable enough in facing his Zulu converts, without which, indeed, he could not have faced them at all, was wholly intolerable to the educated Christian mind. The outcry against his book was fully equal to that which had greeted *Essays and Reviews:* the archbishops denounced it with anathemas, a convocation solemnly condemned it, and Bishop Gray of Cape Town took it upon himself to depose and excommunicate its author, declaring him 'given over to Satan.' As a passing detail Colenso had noted that the reference in Leviticus to the hare chewing its cud must contain an error. Upon this point, Hitzig, of Leipsic, an outstanding Hebrew scholar, commented: 'Your bishops are making themselves the laughing stock of Europe. Every Hebraist knows that the animal mentioned in Leviticus is really the hare . . . every zoologist knows that it does not chew the cud.' And from the argument there sprang the epigram:

> The bishops all have sworn to shed their blood
> To prove 'tis true the hare doth chew the cud.
> O bishops, doctors, and divines, beware —
> Weak is the faith that hangs upon a *hair!*

The storm over Colenso spread into home and colonial politics, the effort to humiliate him and to reduce his friends to poverty ultimately drawing dispassionate persons into the bitter fight. He was called an 'infidel,' 'traitor,' 'apostate' and even 'an unclean being,' and when the Judicial Committee of the Privy Council denied the validity of the excommunication laid upon him by the Bishop of Cape Town, Bishop Gray denounced the judgment of the high court as 'awful and profane,' and the Privy Council as 'a masterpiece of Satan.' Even Bishop Wilberforce of Oxford alluded with regret to 'the devotion of the English people to the law in matters of this sort.'

Although there were many men within the church who had little sympathy with the orthodox reaction against either Colenso or *Essays and Reviews,* they were so outnumbered and outargued that their total effect was but to give a slightly confused aspect to the ecclesiastic mean. It was perhaps this confusion which echoed in the words of Emerson when, in his *English Traits* (1856), this quasi-mystic, ex-Unitarian minister recorded the impression of an outsider. 'The torpidity, on the side of religion, of the vigorous English understanding shows how much wit and folly can agree in one brain. Their religion is a quotation: their church is a doll; and any examination is interdicted with screams of terror. In good company you expect them to laugh at the fanaticism of the vulgar; but they do not; they are the vulgar. . . . The church at this moment is much to be pitied. She has nothing left but possession. If a Bishop meets an intelligent gentlemen, and reads fatal interrogations in his eyes, he has no resource but to take wine with him. False position introduces cant, perjury, simony, and ever a lower class of mind and character, into the clergy; and when the hierarchy is afraid of theology, there is nothing left but to quit a church which is no longer one.'

By a sympathetic observer, what Emerson encountered in his British cleric friends might be interpreted as but a conflict between traditional confidence in the certainty of dogma and a newly awakened suspicion that skepticism was a mode of belief just as useful and creditable as faith. Such an interpretation is, however, more charitable than Emerson intended, and, as events were soon to prove, it is nearer the truth to take the appraisal literally. The church was in possession, but in possession of what, other than stone and land? Roger Bacon, Descartes, Copernicus, Galileo, Newton, Buffon, and more recently, Werner, William Smith, Hutton, Lyell, all great names in the history of human intellect — all were names to be recalled by churchmen with embarrassment. Only recently Wöhler had synthesized the first living or 'organic' compound, Lavoisier had analyzed the 'fire' of life, and Von Baer had demonstrated the existence of the human egg. The last could under no conceivable circumstances have been a topic of conversation in any episcopal company, yet the fact of its discovery might by subliminal channels have reached the bishops' ears. Too many of the church's dogmatic denials had come themselves to be denied to warrant mobilizing the small arms of condemnation, much less the great gun of excommunication, against Wöhler, Lavoisier and Von Bear as potential heretics, yet the ideas they propounded were wholly foreign to the Pentateuch and charged with implications of disaster. Over and above its tangible wealth and prestige, the church was in possession of man's immortal soul and many spiritual prerogatives deriving therefrom: if Emerson's words are taken literally, the bishops, with an intuition which was at once clairvoyant and stone blind, were apprehensive lest it was about to lose all but its real estate.

It came about, in fact, that the discoverer of the human ovum supplied the weapon which was to deal the orthodox conviction its most damaging blow in the pre-Darwinian decade. Von Baer in 1828 had described the process by which the fertilized egg becomes an embryo by the pithy summary that 'the development of every organism is a change from homogeneity to heterogeneity.' Which was to say that an adult organism was formed by the development of many differentiated and specialized parts out of a relatively simple, inert blob of protoplasm. Herbert Spencer, then in his thirty-first year, came upon Von Baer's embryological epitome in 1851 and from it shaped his theory of evolution.

Except for three years at Hinton between his thirteenth and sixteenth years, Spencer was wholly self-educated, yet taking up philosophy at the age of thirty he emerged the outstanding English philosopher of the nineteenth century. He had at first earned his living as a civil engineer, surveying and designing railway lines and bridges, and, like Erasmus Darwin, on the side inventing patent saltcellars, jugs, candle extinguishers, invalid chairs and the like, none of which were financially successful. At twenty-two he began to delve into sociology, and at twenty-eight he dropped engineering to become a sub-editor on *The Economist*. In 1852 Malthus's *Essay on the Principle of Population as it Affects the Future Improvement of Society* stimulated him to write an essay on 'The Theory of Population,' in which he suggested that the struggle for existence leads to the survival of the fittest, here coining these historic phrases. In this same year he ventured into evolution (in the manner of Chambers and Lamarck) in an essay entitled 'The Development Hypothesis,' rebutting the objection that no one had ever seen the development of a new species by the progressive modification of an older one with the reply that neither had anyone seen the *de novo* creation of a new species.

From 1852 onward change and development became the essence of Spencer's thinking, and he found in Von Baer's words a dynamic formula which lent itself admirably to a theory of the evolution of the mind with which he was then occupied, and which he presented briefly in his *Principles of Psychology* (1855). Stimulated by the notion of a dynamic creation, he quickly produced *Progress, its Law and Cause* (1857), in which he applied Von Baer's idea on an astronomic scale: cosmic evolution consisted of the passage of simple, undifferentiated substance into differentiated and complexly formed bodies; the world was heterogeneous and complexly fabricated relative to the uniform if nebulous matter from which Laplace supposed it to have been evolved; the higher plants and animals were heterogeneous relative to the primordial forms from which they in turn had been evolved; the mind of man was, in some as yet undefined manner, a concomitant of the heterogeneity of the brain; in the course of evolution it had been elaborated from the simpler type of mind possessed by animals which in turn owed its superiority to the physiological complexity of the animal brain. So ran the course of events from star dust up to complex stars, from the geologically pristine earth through plants and animals to man, from savage life through the development of families, clans, cities, states and federations, from vague sensations through memories into knowledge and understanding — the history of stars and earth and man could be described within the general formula of a change from homogeneity to heterogeneity.

Spencer conceived that this process of evolution was directly deducible from the physicists' law of conservation of energy coupled with a constant tendency towards the dissipation of energy, the two always working against each other to produce the rhythmic oscillations of molecules, the birth and death of stars, the rise and fall of nations; and he compressed all the complexity of the cosmos into a formula which for sheer concentration and imposing quality is unsurpassed: 'Evolution is an integration of matter and a concomitant dissipation of motion [energy], during which the matter passes from an indefinite, incoherent homogeneity to a definite, coherent heterogeneity, and during which the retained motion undergoes a parallel transformation.'

It required ten volumes and nearly forty years to explain this definition in his *Synthetic Philosophy,* but that was in part because the definition is so broad. It suffers the weakness common to all generalizations, that words, at best weak vehicles of thought, are increasingly burdened with every increase in knowledge until they can no longer bear their full load of meaning; but if his words are justly redefined in the light of advancing knowledge, his apophthegm remains one of the most successful philosophic summaries of all time.

The worst fault, in retrospect, attaching to Spencer's idea of evolution was his identification of the process as 'progress.' However unavoidable in a Victorian who in his youth had been inculcated with the theologic doctrines of the Methodists and Quakers, and for whom 'the greatest happiness is the purpose of creation,' it was none the less a purely arbitrary and pietistic act. It was, however, this pious feature which gave his theory its immediately effective force. It startled the more erudite among the faithful into the dreadful suspicion that in 'progress by evolution' Spencer had come upon something religiously profound, that here was a new cosmic conception based upon the operation of Natural Law — the latter being practically synonymous with the Will of God; that creation by progressive change suggested an even more subtle creator, one of a higher type, than was required for a single creative act; and that in defending Genesis so vehemently they might actually have been on the wrong side of the argument. So readily did Spencerian evolution settle into the mental niche prepared for it by Chambers and Lamarck that those to whose attention it came were almost unconscious of its infidelity.

However, time had not permitted any wide appraisal of Spencer's armchair speculations when there appeared Charles Darwin's *Origin of Species* (1859), to claim modestly but on the most overwhelming evidences and by the most conservative reasoning that the mutability of species was an established fact. The creative act was not completed in the first week of time, but had continued, *ergo* probably *was* continuing, through all time.

If Darwin was right, it followed that much of Genesis, and probably even the whole of it, was wrong. What then might become of man's immortal soul, of God himself?

VIII

~~~~~~

Light Will Be Thrown on Man

THE world had known Charles Darwin as the author of a *Journal* (1839) having to do with the natural history and geology of the countries visited by H. M. S. *Beagle* during her circumnavigation of the globe between the years 1831 and 1836, a volume on the *Structure and Distribution of Coral Reefs* (1842), another on the *Geological Observations on the Volcanic Islands* (1844), and other works of like nature, as well as several monographs on taxonomy — all of them sound, conventional, descriptive science, and relatively safe. Nothing which he had hitherto published presaged the heresy of the *Origin of Species,* nor yet could that heresy have been anticipated from his personal history.

The Darwin who had sailed as naturalist aboard the *Beagle* had been a conventional Unitarian, subscribing to at least a sufficient portion of the Christian creed to stamp him as reasonably orthodox. Indeed, he once contemplated entering the ministry, not from any predilection for the cloth but because it offered an obvious alternative to medicine, which he had tried and found wholly unsuited to his taste. Although he had no reason to question the literal truth of scripture, he entertained doubts as to how far he could conscientiously affirm all the dogmas of the Established Church. Yet against this pang of conscience was the fact that the life of a country clergyman was on the whole attractive, and after some hesitancy he acquiesced, chiefly, he admitted, because he could discover no serious objection. So in 1827 he went down to Cambridge and entered Christ's College where he met a cousin, William Darwin Fox, whose handsome collection of butterflies quickened his collecting instinct and on whose advice he began to attend the lectures of the botanist, the Reverend John Steven Henslow.

In the shaping of Darwin's career trivial events concatenated with an almost incredible timeliness. It was an attack of nausea at Edinburgh, brought on by the sights of the operating room, that tipped the balance against medicine. Had he gone to Cambridge only a few months later he would have missed his cousin Fox, through whom he established an intimate friendship with the botanist Henslow. Of Henslow it has been said that he taught botany so well that his students preferred taking his course over and over to the risk of adventuring into a subject which might be less pleasing in itself, or expounded by a less attractive man. Darwin became his favored pupil and from personal association with him received most of the scientific training he was to get, except through his own efforts. Had Darwin entered Cambridge a few months later he might even have missed the best part of Henslow himself, for it was in two free terms during which he waited for his degree that they became intimate and spent long hours together, when Henslow introduced him to the subject of geology, and to such volumes as Sir John Herschel's *Preliminary Discourse on the Study of Natural Philosophy* and Alexander von Humboldt's *Personal Narrative of Travels to the Equinoctial Regions of America During the Years 1799–1804.* Herschel's book dealt with the methods of acquiring scientific knowledge and the principles of science. Humboldt forever remained for Darwin 'the greatest scientific traveller who ever lived,' and the explorer's accounts of Teneriffe excited him with the old desire to travel; the net effect of the two volumes was, however, somewhat confusing — a clergyman could collect beetles, but he could not very well travel all over the world. If only it were possible to collect insects and to travel too!

The fateful voyage of the *Beagle* had itself developed out of the most complicated and precarious circumstances, not the least peculiar of which consisted of three dark-skinned, scrawny natives from Tierra del Fuego whom Captain FitzRoy had previously brought to England for the purposes of educating them and imparting to them the elements of Christianity, before returning them to their native country. This sociological experiment had produced nothing but embarrassment to the Admiralty, and FitzRoy was reappointed to the *Beagle* in order that he might, in the course of surveying the coasts of South America and the islands of the Pacific, return the Tierra del Fuegans to their native land. It was Henslow who procured the post of naturalist on the expedition for his young friend. When the offer from FitzRoy arrived at Darwin's home he was away geologizing in Wales. Had he returned two days later, FitzRoy, who had changed his mind about having a naturalist on board, would have withdrawn the offer. Thus from early youth until he sailed with FitzRoy, Darwin's life repeatedly turned the narrowest corners.

After normal but seemingly interminable delays, the *Beagle* got under way on January 27, 1831. She was to follow down the eastern coast of South America to the Horn, then northward to the limits of Chile and home via the East Indies and the Cape of Good Hope, the voyage being planned to last two years. Instead it lasted nearly five years. Yet despite recurrent seasickness and the many hardships which he had to endure both on shipboard and ashore, Darwin's application to his task was unremitting. The voyage seemed to him, and in truth it was, the finest opportunity to study the natural history of the world which had ever been offered an explorer.

In remote places visited by the *Beagle* Darwin frequently left the ship for weeks at a time, surveying pampas and primeval jungles, geologizing, botanizing, collecting fossils, making countless observations of nature and man. As they headed into the cold and stormy seas of Tierra del Fuego, beating slowly for a bleak country which had never been traversed by Europeans, Darwin, thrilled by the thought of the unknown awaiting exploration, conceived that he could employ his life no better 'than [in] adding a little to Natural Science.' The *Beagle* was a month rounding the Horn, being repeatedly driven back by adverse winds, and the crew spent two weeks ashore while the natives who had been the instruments of destiny were returned to their homes. From there they went to the barren, treeless Falkland Islands, back to Montevideo and the Rio Negro, southward again for a month in Patagonia, and later through the Magdalen and Cockburn channels to the west coast. At Valparaiso Darwin suffered a protracted, unidentified illness to which some attribute the chronic indisposition that so handicapped him in his later years. The party went to Santiago for a trip across the Andes, and at last westward by a long arc touching the Galapagos, Tahiti, New Zealand, Australia, Tasmania and Mauritius, around the Cape of Good Hope for a second visit to Brazil, and home.

Exploration begins in the eye of the explorer, and the Darwin who returned to England in 1836 had explored a world of millions upon millions of minute marine animals discoloring the water in patches miles across; mile-long clouds of butterflies blown far out to sea; strange animals, countless insects and beetles of incomprehensible variety; the orchids, plants and trees of the Brazilian jungle, the bushes and grasses of the vast bleak plains of Patagonia, the even more miserable scrubs of the purgatory of Tierra del Fuego.

He had seen the land heave in a mighty shudder at the base of mountains whose highest peaks were composed of rocks that were indubitably marine in origin. Volcanoes, glaciers, river beds and cliffs all testified how the whole earth had forever suffered Lyell's slow but constant and inevitable torment of wind and water, ice and snow and flood. A single pebble bed in Chile, two hundred miles wide and fifty feet thick, made up of rocks that had been rolled and rubbed into smooth round pieces and deposited hundreds of miles from their source, brought home to him the scale and force of natural erosion, and the inconceivably long lapse of years comprising but a single page in the geologic calendar. On the Chronos Islands the striking formations of granite, which in Hutton's view was the fundamental, unchanged rock of the earth's shell, the deepest layer of the globe to which man had been able to penetrate, stirred his wonder: 'The limit of man's knowledge in any subject possesses high interest, which is perhaps increased by its close neighborhood to the realms of the imagination!'

When he got back to England he found to his surprise and pleasure that Henslow had been publishing his personal letters through the Cambridge Philosophical and London Geological societies, and that already he was recognized as having made some 'signal contributions to natural history.' He was made aware of his responsibilities when he discovered that Sedgwick had written of him as 'doing admirable work in South America, and has already sent home a collection above all price. It was the best thing in the world for him that he went out on the voyage of discovery. There was some risk of his turning out an idle man, but his character will now be fixed, and if God spares his life he will have a great name among the naturalists of Europe.'

Still thinking that he would return to theological studies, he began to work on his diary, to organize his notes, and study the collections he had made. He had left England a convinced creationist, to whom the immutability of species was axiomatic. It was perhaps when he was in the Galapagos Islands, impressed by the fact that the birds and reptiles presented distinct species on each of the major islands, implying in effect a different creation for each island, that he first came to doubt the doctrine. As he prepared his *Journal,* the evidences pressed upon him, but he approached the question of the development of species with the greatest caution and avoided any direct commitment. In his confidential notebook of 1837 he had written, 'There is a simple grandeur in the view of life with its powers of growth, assimilation and reproduction, being originally breathed into matter under one or a few forms, and that whilst this our planet has gone circling on according to the fixed laws, and land and water, in a cycle of change, have gone on replacing each other, that from so simple an origin, through the process of gradual selection of infinitesimal changes, endless forms most beautiful and most wonderful have been evolved.' And 1838: 'If we choose to let conjecture run wild, then animals, our fellow brethren in pain, disease, death, suffering and famine — our slaves in the most laborious works, our companions in our amusements — they may partake of our origin in one common ancestor — we may all be melted together. . . . The tree of life should perhaps be called the coral of life, base of branches dead; so that the passages cannot be seen.'

A growing conviction of evolution was clearly in his mind twenty years before the writing of the *Origin of Species.* Yet the process was charged with mystery. Why were all those forms that made up the 'base of branches' of the coral of life, dead? Not a few species only, but tens, hundreds of thousands of species, implying millions upon millions of individual creatures, obliterated as though by some overwhelming malice on the part of the creative power. Hutton, and after him, Lyell, had been unable to 'perceive any beginning, to surmise any end' to the geologic process. How then could one estimate the dimensions of a pageant which even in its smallest visible scenes was all but incomprehensible? However slowly he gained the perspective, however vaguely he perceived the problem and the answer, he slowly came to recognize that spread before him was a record of ruthless creation and destruction which repeated itself day by day through geologic eras adding up to hundreds of millions of years.

Adaptation was obvious in every living thing, adaptation so exquisite, so ingenious, so novel, as to defy the imagination: in the ant-lion and its deathtrap in the sand, in the bill of the woodpecker, in the canine teeth of the carnivores, in the structure of every bone and sinew and muscle, in the structure of eye and ear, in the instincts of animals, in the pattern of leaf, stem and root. Why this exquisite, infinitely complex adaptation between every living organism and the large or little world in which it had its being?

Then there came the time when either suddenly, upon the discovery of some slight detail, or slowly, in the growing recognition of a half-perceived truth, he realized that the mutability of species and all that it entailed was for him no longer merely a plausible theory, but an irresistible fact. There was not, however, a single friend to whom he could as much as intimate his new conviction. Not even Lyell, the man who should have been most sympathetic to this view, but who held back from any liberal biological interpretation.

And then, admitting successive cycles of creation and destruction, there was the further mystery of *how* evolution came about — here was the mystery of mysteries in the species problem. Darwin's first approach to this was, as he said, connected with his reading 'for amusement' of Malthus's *Essay on the Principle of Population as it Affects the Future Improvement of Society,* the dissertation on economics that had excited the imagination of Spencer. The thesis of this work (published in 1798) was that the human population tends to increase many times more rapidly than the food supply, and that only famine, sickness and war suffice to maintain the necessary checks. Darwin immediately perceived here a cause of both the extinction of species and their diversification: between any two closely related species competing for a common habitat there existed a constant competition in which the weaker must ultimately perish; under these circumstances favorable variations would tend to be preserved, and unfavorable ones to be destroyed. Where variations occurred frequently the result would be the formation of extreme variants, and ultimately new species which by their superiority could dominate the older forms. Continued differentiation would lead to forms so modified from the parent stalk and so different from each other as scarcely to show their common ancestry, but each would be exquisitely adapted to some environmental niche unsuitable, or even intolerable, for its cogeners. On first thought the full potentialities of this process of 'natural selection' failed to impress him. To invoke such an uncharitable, not to say cruel, means as the essential dynamic of evolution seemed out of the question, since it would only excite further prejudice against 'the species problem.' There were many details to be filled in before it could be argued seriously. Consequently, as the years went by, he told his friends only that the 'subject of species' interested him, that it was his 'prime hobby,' and that he hoped 'some day' to 'do something about it.'

Delayed by illness, it was May, 1842, before he had corrected the proofs of *The Structure and Distribution of Coral Reefs: Being the First Part of the Geology of the Voyage of the Beagle,* at a cost, as he said, of twenty months' labor spread over three and a half years. The work consisted of an orderly analysis of 'every existing coral reef, except some on the coast of Brazil,' and argued, in accordance with Lyell's work on subsidence and elevation, that the animals grew only at the surface, building upon the sunken base of past generations. Here then, in the distribution and height of coral islands, was a means of discovering local regions of subsidence of the ocean floor, both in present and past ages, and even of measuring the extent of this subsidence. The work was highly gratifying to Lyell as affording a new geologic tool, but for Darwin it had another and secret meaning, its bearing 'upon that most mysterious question—whether the series of organized beings peculiar to some isolated points [coral islands] are the last remnants of a former population, or the first creatures of a new race springing into existence.'

Herbert Spencer coined the terms 'struggle for existence' and 'survival of the fittest' in 1852, but the principle was as clear to Darwin under 'natural selection' as to Spencer's readers under the more dramatic titles. Given biological variation, however caused, and the inheritance of this variation as premises, then natural selection arising from the sheer necessities of living, coupled with repeated oscillations in environment, must in the end lead to the weeding out of the unadapted and unadaptable. Parasites, beasts of prey, the incalculable waste in animal and vegetable reproduction, the holocausts of geologic destruction, were not manifestations of evil but the operation of an inexorable 'law' which seemed to Darwin, Unitarian minister aborted, even as it had seemed to Spencer, the Quaker, to be a Law of Progress: 'From death, famine, rapine, and the concealed war of nature we can see that the highest good, which we can conceive, the creation of the highest animals has directly come.' If God could not be the quick Creator of a Perfect Universe then he must be a leisurely artificer evolving one in the direction of perfection by droughts and floods and earthquakes, by heaving continents up and down through some untold millions of years, by depending on the laws of nature to carry on the divine edict of natural selection.

In his notes of 1842, written when he was thirty-three years old and intended as the first draft of an essay on 'the species problem,' and which he carefully hid away, he presented practically the complete thesis of the *Origin*. There were, however, other works clamoring for completion, the *Volcanic Islands* (1844), *Geological Observations in South America* (1846), and several monographs on barnacles (1851–1854). In 1844 he expanded the original thirty-odd pages of his essay to 189, interpolating into the ever more closely analyzed evidence the thought: 'According to our theory, there is obviously no power tending constantly to exalt species, except the mutual struggle between the different individuals and classes; but from the strong and general hereditary tendency we might expect to find some tendency to progressive complication in the successive production of new organic forms.' *There is obviously no power tending to exalt species*—only 'progressive complication' in place of the 'highest good.' The essay was finished in July and his wife was given solemn instructions to ensure its publication in case of his death.

In this year he wrote his younger friend, the botanist Joseph Hooker, '. . . and I am almost convinced (quite contrary to the opinion I started

with) that species are not (it is like confessing a murder) immutable.
. . . Heaven forfend me from Lamarck's nonsense of a "tendency to
progression," (adaptations from the slow willing animals), etc.! But the
conclusions I am led to are not widely different from his; though the
means of change are wholly so. I think I have found out (here's presumption!) the simple way by which species become exquisitely adapted
to various ends. You will groan, and think to yourself, "on what a man
have I been wasting my time and writing to." '

Such was Darwin's friendship with Hooker that he allowed him to
read the secret manuscript before the year was out, with the understanding that no word was to be said about it. Excessive diffidence and self-
depreciation held him back, as well as an appreciation of the prejudice
which his ideas would meet immediately they became public property,
a prescience of the storm which the *Origin,* when it was published, did
in fact arouse.

Although he gave no certain hint of it, Darwin probably better than
most of his colleagues saw the far-reaching implications in the principle
of natural selection. The shift in terms from the 'highest good' to 'progressive complication' with 'no tendency to exalt any species' was but a
ripple reflecting the complete upheaval of his faith. So slowly that the
change was unperceived except in large perspective, his mind had turned
away from the holy orders that had seemed his certain destiny fifteen
years before; he had given up his belief in the Old Testament, then in
the New, and finally in Christianity as a divine revelation, only to discover without distress, without surprise even, that he was completely
lacking in faith. How could he argue the mutability of species, survival
by natural selection, by dint of sheer physical superiority or skillful viciousness, with men who still found consolation in the comfortable belief that
death was a needless consequence of Adam's sin, and that the meanest
creature of creation was put there with the love of God who marked the
sparrow's fall? Knowing that he could never again see the world in the
same light as others saw it, he dreaded to speak out what would seem
blasphemy, not merely against Genesis but against the deity himself. How
could he proclaim that the god who was concealed beneath the panoply
of earth and the coverlet of stars, the Lord God Almighty Creator of
Heaven and Earth, was ruthlessness and cruelty personified?

From 1842 onward Darwin was inflicted with 'stomach trouble' of the
most distressing sort, which some believed to be a sequel of his protracted
seasickness on the *Beagle,* and others attributed to the Valparaiso illness.
In retrospect it appears that there was no organic disease; protracted sea-

sickness and privations on the voyage may have undermined a physique that at its best was never robust, and unremitting hard work and the anxiety attending his many unfinished projects must have served constantly to aggravate his condition. Yet unquestionably a factor in his illness was the apprehension of making public his new view. No matter in what terms he couched it, it threatened to turn public opinion against him, to destroy his good name and that of his family, perhaps even the good repute of reason itself and the evidences and critical method to which he had devoted himself.

All these factors joined forces to delay the publication of his notes on species. Another five years passed and he had happily found escape in pursuing a detailed study of barnacles, but he was none the less writing Hooker, 'Do not flatter yourself that I shall not live to finish the Barnacles, and then make a fool of myself on the subject of species.'

After three more years he was confident that he could meet the expected attack, even the abuse, of his critics, but he was turning to botany and pigeons as subjects where more and yet more factual evidence on the problem of variation could be obtained. In 1856 Lyell urged him to publish at least a sketch of his views on species, calling his attention to a recent essay by Alfred Russell Wallace, entitled *On the Law which has Regulated the Introduction of New Species*. Darwin had met Wallace briefly in 1853, a young man who had just returned from four years on the River Amazon. Now on an extended exploration of the East Indies, Wallace had begun to pursue the mystery of geographical distribution — 'the keystone of the problem of creation,' as he called it. His essay, sent from Borneo in 1855, asserted only that 'every species has come into existence coincident both in space and time with a pre-existing closely allied species' — an apparently harmless assertion except as viewed against the background of Mosaic legend. In some points Wallace's views were different from Darwin's, but there was no doubt that they both were following the same trail. Darwin was perturbed, Lyell pressing; he doubted that Darwin would ever write his proposed book unless he were forced to do so, and urged him to submit a short outline for publication. Hooker was appealed to and between them Darwin was induced to undertake the rapid preparation of 'a *very thin* and little volume,' the draft of which, however, began to expand indefinitely under the irrepressible impulse to amass every known available datum, to enlarge upon details, clarify controversial points and multiply evidence. Darwin was wholly incapable of suggesting the mutability of species without first covering and suffocating his critics with evidence. Nothing would do but that he should write *the* book which would contain *every* evidence from *every* quarter of the plant and animal kingdom, *the* Great Work which he had now decided to call 'Natural Selection.' He took time to write Wallace briefly, commenting favorably on his essay and mentioning that he himself had a work in progress in which he hoped to set forth 'a distinct and tangible idea' of how variation came about.

A little later he also wrote Asa Gray on the subject of selection. The Lamarckian theory of 'use and disuse' must be wholly set aside as futile, he said. In his view human selection had been the main agent in forming the domestic species: suppose, then, a *natural selection* working not on just one or two features of the organism but upon the entire organism, muscle, nerve and gland, generation after generation for millions of generations, only a minority in each generation surviving to propagate its kind: 'Considering the infinitely various ways beings have to obtain food by struggling with other beings, to escape danger at various times of life, to have their eggs as seeds disseminated, etc. etc., I cannot doubt that during millions of generations individuals of a species will be born with some slight variation profitable to some part of its economy; such will have a better chance of surviving, propagating their variation, which again will be slowly increased by the accumulative action of natural selection; and the variety thus formed will either coexist with, or more commonly will exterminate its parent type.'

But the proposed volume on natural selection remained unfinished. Darwin's habitual prospect was that it *might* be completed in another two years. He might have gone on thus until the end of his life had Wallace not written him again from the East Indies, in a letter received on June 18, 1858, enclosing a few pages of manuscript and expressing the hope that the idea therein contained would be as new to Darwin as to himself, that 'it would supply the missing factor to explain the origin of species,' and asking Darwin, if he thought it worthy, to forward it to Lyell.

Darwin was aghast. In a few pages Wallace had set forth practically his entire theory of natural selection. As he said in the letter with which he forwarded Wallace's manuscript to Lyell, 'Your words have come true with a vengeance — that I should be forestalled. I never saw a more striking coincidence; if Wallace had my manuscript sketch written out in 1842, he could not have made a better short abstract! Even his terms now stand as heads of my chapters . . . I hope you will approve of Wallace's sketch, that I may tell him what you say!'

There was a week of confused despair in which regrets about priority and the belief that for him to publish now would be base and paltry swept him from one decision to another. To add to his misery, within a few hours his youngest child was dead of scarlet fever, another was sickening, apparently with diphtheria, and two of the nurses were taken ill. In his excessive self-effacement and miserable state of mind, he might well have decided to abandon the project, had not Hooker sent a messenger demanding the immediate delivery of the copy of the letter which he had written Gray, a copy of his notes of 1844, and the whole of Wallace's manuscript. And at the behest of Hooker and Lyell transcriptions of these were read by the secretary of the Linnaean Society two nights later, at its regular meeting of July 1, 1858. The members had come to hear a paper by George Bentham on the fixity of species, and there was naturally some excitement when the Darwin and Wallace papers replacing it both denied this very doctrine. However, to the audience it seemed that the entire question of varieties and species was indeed complex, and that opinion had best be reserved until the papers had been made available by publication in the *Proceedings* of the Society. So the meeting adjourned into the London streets, under a night sky in which a comet, portent of fate and change, could be discerned. For nearly all who had attended the meeting the species problem was much less exciting than this astronomical rarity.

ii

Of procrastination there had now to be an end, and, at the cost of tremendous effort, *a* book was hurriedly completed and sent to press under the title: *On the Origin of Species by Means of Natural Selection, Or the Preservation of Favoured Races in the Struggle for Life,* appearing on November 24, 1859, price 15s. At the last minute the publisher rejected Darwin's title, *An Abstract of an Essay on the Origin of Species and Varieties through Natural Selection* — 'an abstract of an essay' indeed! and who would want to buy an abstract! But he did not efface from Darwin's introduction the modest assertion: 'This Abstract, which I now publish, must necessarily be imperfect. . . .'

The *Origin* dealt exclusively with the lower animals, the evidence as regards the zoologically negligible genus *Homo* being one of those fields that Darwin had not yet found an opportunity to explore, and the only allusion to this subject was that by the new views 'Much light will be thrown on the origin of man and his history.'

The book closed in the moral mood of 1842: 'And as natural selection works solely by and for the good of each being, all corporeal and mental endowments will tend to progress towards perfection.' That Darwin identified the parasite, the ant-lion, the carnivore, the universal slaughter of creature by fellow creature, the wholesale destruction of entire species and genera, as progress towards 'perfection'; that he imagined any one species closer than another to 'perfection'; that he asked himself, What would be 'perfection' for an individual parasite, ant-lion or carnivore? — is inconceivable. In the enforced, rapid presentation of his ideas he sought to adorn his work with some philosophical finial, and from the habit of a lifetime he reverted to pious thinking and the Platonism with which his age was saturated. Overlooking the fact that in 1844 he had written that there is 'no power tending constantly to exalt species,' he reverted to his notes of 1837: 'from the war of nature, from famine and death, the most exalted object which we are capable of conceiving, namely the production of the higher animals, directly follows.' Had he paused to define 'higher' he perforce must have answered in his own terms either 'more complicated' or 'better adapted,' but of this difficulty the reader remained unaware as he passed on to the last sentence in the book: 'There is grandeur in this view of life, with its several powers, having been originally breathed by the Creator into a few forms or into one; and that, whilst this planet has gone cycling on according to the fixed law of gravity, from so simple a beginning endless forms most beautiful and most wonderful have been, and are being evolved.' Most beautiful and wonderful, perhaps — but beauty and wonder are too much in the eye of the beholder to afford reliable standards of progressiveness.

The first edition of the *Origin* proved from the publisher's point of view to be an immediate success. A second edition was soon called for, then an American volume, and then a German translation. Darwin's colleagues were divided in opinion. Carpenter the physiologist, and Jukes, Ramsay and Geikie, the geologists, were convinced. Huxley was enthusiastic, and warned Darwin not to let himself 'be in any way disgusted or amazed by the considerable abuse and misrepresentation which, unless I greatly mistake, is in store for you,' and promised to sharpen up his own 'claws and beak' should he be needed for defense. Spencer naturally found most of the work suited to his philosophy of progressive evolution and was moved to speak of geology as 'that grand epic written by the fingers of God upon the strata of the earth' — neglecting to add that every finger stroke represented the seemingly needless extermination of millions upon millions of living creatures. Lyell frankly abandoned the fixity of species, but remained doubtful about the new views throwing any 'light on man.' On the other side, however, were the weightiest, because the senior, names: Sir John Herschel was openly contemptuous; Grey, of the British Museum, damned the book as Lamarckian; Whewell refused to have a copy in the library at Trinity College; Carlyle sneered. The anatomist Owen wrote an anonymous review proving Darwin to be entirely wrong, himself entirely right. To Sedgwick it was a 'dish of rank materialism cleverly cooked' merely 'to make us independent of a Creator'; if Darwin's argument held, then humanity 'would suffer a damage that might brutalize it, and sink the human race into a lower grade of degradation than any into which it has fallen since its written records tell us of its history!'

Darwin was accused by the *Daily News* of stealing from the *Vestiges of Creation. The Times,* however, broke with precedent by devoting over three columns to his book, presenting a clear discussion of the important facts and of Darwin's qualifications to deal with them, and the evolutionary view, though not outrightly endorsed, was not condemned. The article was unsigned but informed persons recognized that it had been written by Huxley. Then more and more reviews appeared, most of them incorporating an undercurrent of derision. By the middle of 1860 the book was being much talked about; Owen found occasion to mention it in Parliament, and Owen's friend, Samuel Wilberforce, Bishop of Oxford, popularly known because of his mastery of platform trickery and pulpit oratory as Soapy Sam, condemned it outright in the *Quarterly Review,* declaring that 'the principle of natural selection is absolutely incompatible with the word of God.' When the first tide of success was over there followed in increasing numbers expressions of anti-evolutionist opinion.

Indignation reached its peak at the meeting of the British Association in Oxford at the end of June, 1860, when it was expected that the great Owen would appear to answer Darwin personally. Darwin and Owen were both absent from this historic meeting, the first because of illness, the second giving no excuse — the more surprising since he was to occupy the chair — but sending Bishop Wilberforce to speak in his place. The audience was so large that the meeting had to be moved from the usual lecture room to the library, which was soon filled to standing, the Oxford clerics massed in the middle of the room, laymen and ladies crowded near the windows. Another scheduled paper was received with ill-concealed impatience, and the three speakers who followed were shouted down so that Wilberforce might have his chance. Practiced in oratorical persuasion, the Bishop proceeded to 'spout for half an hour with inimitable spirit, ugliness and emptiness and unfairness,' fluently, rhetorically entertaining, at first jovial, then scoffing, and in the end ridiculing. He essayed several assaults on the evidences of evolution, obviously having been coached in the technicalities, and finally he turned to Huxley and sarcastically inquired whether it was through his grandfather or grandmother that he claimed to be descended from a monkey. Huxley, aghast at a personal taunt in an important and public meeting, whispered to the person by his side, "The Lord hath delivered him into mine hands."

When the Bishop took his seat hands clapped, handkerchiefs waved and there was a sustained uproar of clerical approval. Then Huxley was called upon to speak. He rose to the scattered applause of a few friends, his face pale with anger under his wild, thick hair: "I am here only in the interests of science," he said, "and have not heard anything which can prejudice the case of my august client." He went on quietly to review the facts, to indicate the Bishop's essential incompetence to treat of such matters as geology and the mutability of species, and ended by saying in effect — there was no transcript of the speakers' remarks and the excitement was such that these were variously recalled by the audience — that he would rather have an ape for an ancestor than an intellectual prostitute like Bishop Samuel Wilberforce. Laymen applauded, the massed clergy raised their voices in offended dignity, and a Lady Brewster achieved immortality by fainting and having to be carried out.

Six weeks after he reviewed the *Origin* for the *Times* Huxley had addressed a Friday evening audience at the Royal Institution on 'Species and Races, and their Origin.' Only an abstract of his lecture is preserved, but it is clear that it was here for the first time that he publicly applied Darwin's theory of descent to man, and gave intimations of its implications: 'Let man's mistaken vanity, his foolish contempt for the material world, impel him to struggle as he will, he strives in vain to break through the ties which hold him to matter and the lower forms of life. . . . The general mind is seething strangely, and to those who watch the signs of the time, it seems plain that this nineteenth century will see revolutions of thought and practice as great as those which the sixteenth witnessed. Through what trials and sore contests the civilized world will have to pass in the cause of this new reformation, who can tell?' Darwin's only comment was that he was disappointed in the lecture because Huxley 'did not enlarge sufficiently upon natural selection, and wasted time over the idea of a species as exemplified in the horse.' It was as though Darwin were still so frightened that he resolutely refused to look at aught but innocuous details. But, like Darwin, Huxley knew the value of evidence.

In the meantime the reviewers were heaping contumely upon the *Origin*. Bishop Wilberforce himself reviewed it for the *Quarterly Review;* presenting Darwin as a fantastic speculator defending a foolish theory. He declared that 'the principle of natural selection is absolutely incompatible with the word of God'; that 'it contradicts the revealed relations of creation to its Creator'; that there is 'a simple explanation of the presence of these strange forms among the works of God,' that explanation being 'the fall of Adam.' 'Not only do all the laws for the study of nature vanish when the great principle of order prevailing and regulating all her processes is given up, but all that imparts the deepest interest in the investigation of her wonders will have departed too. Under such influences a man goes back to the marvelling stare of childhood at the centaurs and the hippogriffs of fancy, or if he is of a philosophic turn, he comes like Oken to write a scheme of creation under "a sort of inspiration"; but it is the frenzied inspiration of the inhaler of Mephitic gas.' The Bishop had signalled the attitude of the church, and similar theological denunciations were to echo from all parts of the world: 'evolution was an attempt to dethrone God,' and 'a huge imposture from the beginning'; it was 'a caricature of creation'; it did 'open violence to everything which the Creator himself has told us in the Scriptures'; if its thesis were true, 'Genesis is a lie, the whole framework of the book of life falls to pieces, and the revelation of God to man, as we Christians know it, is a delusion and a snare,' and 'the Bible is an unbearable fiction'; 'then have Christians for nearly two thousand years been duped by a monstrous lie.' Darwin was an 'infidel' and 'atheist,' a 'persecutor of Christianity,' 'the mouthpiece or chief trumpeter of that infidel clique whose well-known object is to do away with the idea of God.' 'These infamous doctrines have for their only support the most abject passions. Their father is pride, their mother impurity, their offspring revolutions. They come from hell and return thither, taking with them the gross creatures who blush not to proclaim and accept them.'

But medieval artillery was no longer effective against the 'destroyers of the church,' who were now too heavily armored with facts and reinforced by popular sympathy to be driven under cover. Nowhere in the world was there more general interest in the achievments of scholarship, either in the natural sciences or in related fields, than in mid-nineteenth century England. The controversy over free thought that had marked the previous decades, the publicity attending the discoveries of geology and paleontology, for which that island was a most fertile ground, the widespread interest in biblical criticism in the early sixties, had all contrived to excite a high order of curiosity among the readers of daily papers and monthly magazines, and the popular reaction to the ecclesiastic epithets was one of amusement rather than alarm. If Darwin or Huxley had anything to say about an alleged affinity between man and the apes, a large number of people were quite honestly and dispassionately interested in hearing it.

Early in 1861 Huxley published, in the first number of the new *Natural History Review,* an article 'On the Relation of Man with the Lower Animals,' showing that not one of the claims that Owen had put forth concerning the differences between the brains of apes and man, and elevating man into a separate sub-class, was justified. In two further papers he developed the proposition that 'Biology shows less structural difference between man and the higher apes than between the higher and lower apes; and far less than between the higher and inferior animals.' In January of 1862 he delivered two lectures at Edinburgh under the same title, and then returned to London to study the recently discovered Neanderthal skull, and to develop a new method for the measurement of skulls in general. This led to a lecture at the Royal Institution 'On the Fossil Remains of Man.' These lectures, supplemented by other material, he combined into a book called *Evidence as to Man's Place in Nature* (1863).

Man's Place in Nature was a small book, but as solid and well packed with evidence as was the *Origin.* It was the first, and it remains the definitive, statement of the naturalistic interpretation of this problem, utilizing all the diverse evidences of comparative anatomy, embryology and paleontology. Of it, Sir Arthur Keith has said, 'When we look around for another biological treatise in which are given as complete and as convincing proofs of a thesis as were produced by Huxley in *Man's Place in Nature,* we can think of only one which will stand comparison, namely Harvey's account of the *Movement of the Heart and Blood.'*

In the ultimate analysis, however, it was not the finely woven warp and woof of evidences that made the book important — these evidences would have won through in their own time to critical and then to popular acceptance — but the impact of the work as a whole upon the popular mind to which it was addressed.

> Science has fulfilled her function when she has ascertained and enunciated truth [says Huxley], and were these pages addressed to men of science only, I should now close this Essay, knowing that my colleagues have learned to respect nothing but evidence, and to believe that their highest duty lies in submitting to it, however it may jar against their inclinations.
>
> But, desiring, as I do, to reach the wider circle of the intelligent public,

it would be unworthy cowardice were I to ignore the repugnance with which the majority of my readers are likely to meet the conclusions to which the most careful and conscientious study I have been able to give the matter, has led me.

On all sides I hear the cry — "We are men and women, not a mere better sort of apes, a little longer in the leg, more compact in the foot, and bigger in brain than your brutal Chimpanzees and Gorillas. The power of knowledge — the conscience of good and evil — the pitiful tenderness of human affections, raise us out of all real fellowship with the brutes, however closely they may seem to approximate us."

To this I can only reply that the exclamation would be most just and would have my own entire sympathy, if it were only relevant. But it is not I who seek to base man's dignity upon his great toe, or insinuate that we are lost if an Ape has a hippocampus minor. On the contrary, I have done my best to sweep away this vanity. I have endeavored to show that no absolute structural line of demarcation, wider than that between the animals which immediately succeed us in the scale, can be drawn between the animal world and ourselves; and I may add the expression of my belief that the attempt to draw a psychical distinction is equally futile, and that even the highest faculties of feeling and of intellect begin to germinate in lower forms of life.

iii

It might be argued that Darwin, who highly approved Huxley's book, could have written its equivalent had he had the good health and the requisite anatomical knowledge. This is, however, very doubtful. Darwin delayed for ten unnecessary years in announcing his views on the transmutation of species and, when at last forced to publication by Wallace, he dismissed its major implication with the noncommittal 'light will be thrown on man.' When ultimately he wrote the *Descent of Man and Selection in Relation to Sex* (1871), those few pages which were devoted to the first topic were conservative in the extreme, the more so since they were prepared at a time when the thesis of the evolution of man had, on the basis of Huxley's work, been generally accepted by competent critics. Such is the force of mental conservatism that men can pioneer in new ideas only so far before they needs must rest, as though from failure of courage or aversion to novelty. Taking into account Darwin's nature and the animosities and bitterness with which the task was all too obviously beset, it seems unlikely that under any circumstances would he ever have ventured beyond the 'species problem' as applied to the lower animals.

The theological conceptions which he held when he sailed in the *Beagle* were no more to be expunged from his personality by his experiences aboard that ship than was his native tongue. They led to a lifetime of conflict between Darwin the Unitarian and Darwin the explorer, and if they did not contribute significantly to his physical enfeeblement, they definitely limited the trajectory of his thoughts. Except for Huxley, man would have continued to enjoy the status of a fallen angel for some considerable period of time. With the subject of evolution in the position in which it was left by the *Origin,* the theologists would have quickly found an escape from applying it to man.

Shaw has somewhere said that a man can never get the chill of early poverty out of his bones. The same might be said of theology, though with notable exceptions. It was five ordained priests who contributed to *Essays and Reviews;* it was a bishop who prepared the devastating critique of the Pentateuch; it was a professional theologian, Canon Tristram, who was the first beyond Darwin's immediate circle to put his theory into practice — in a paper published one month before the appearance of the *Origin,* Tristram explained by its aid the colors of desert birds. It was Buckland, a dean of the Anglican Church, who, after laboring hard for many years to reconcile Genesis and geology, after long contending against the antiquity of paleolithic artifacts, abandoned the orthodox view of the age of the earth in favor of Lyell's stratigraphic calendar. The paraphrase, none the less, has considerable warrant.

It was neither the reasonableness of Genesis nor the unreasonableness of geology that caused Cuvier to oppose Lamarck, Hutton and Lyell so bitterly. The antipathy of the geologist Sedgwick to the *Origin* — 'a dish of rank materialism cleverly cooked up to make us independent of a creator' — may be attributed to the fact that he was a professional cleric; but Murchison, after Lyell the leading geologist and paleontologist of the time, opposed Darwinism almost as vehemently to his dying day. It was the biblical bias of a layman that led Sir John Herschel to reject alike biological and astronomical evolution on the grounds that they dispensed with the creative act, and that impelled the American biologist Agassiz to defend the geology of Genesis at a time when many if not most of his young students were convinced evolutionists. Of all men the most surprisingly refractory was Lyell himself, who had been a pioneer in the new geology when young Darwin had sailed from England. Evolution was implicit in every line of his *Principles* and, on the publication of the *Origin,* he had written Darwin a highly approving letter; yet when his *Antiquity of Man* (1863) appeared, having been prepared and corrected with a full knowledge of Huxley's initial papers and lectures on the subject of man's anthropoid affinities, he hedged not only on the origin of man but on the less personal questions of the immutability of species and natural selection, and left the subject of evolution no farther advanced than it had been years before the appearance of Darwin's work. Lastly, Wallace, despite his brilliant start, abandoned the philosophy of biology when it came to man, and in his later years turned to spiritualism and vainly attempted to interest Huxley and Darwin in this subject.

In its professional aspects, theology, quite apart from the fear of hell, appears to impose upon the intellectual processes a measure of conservatism amounting sometimes to almost complete paralysis. Men trained to believe in original sin, grace, the Trinity, and similar dogmas seemed to lose a large measure both of rational judgment and sensitivity of conscience. Second only to Augustine's emphasis on the authority of scripture was his emphasis on the force, as an argument for truth, of what is 'believed everywhere, always and by all men'; consensus, however ignorant the masses whose opinions were involved, carried as much force as Holy Writ. That those who were shot by the epithets 'atheist,' 'infidel' and 'heretic' were frequently guilty only of reducing the argument from consensus to absurdity, or that as a general rule heresy consisted of an excursion into relative rationality, was adequately demonstrated by the fact that nearly every notable thinker from the second century onward had been branded as a heretic.

Those Christians who believed that there were Three Gods for three hundred years resisted with unmitigated bitterness those who believed that there was only One God, and succeeded in bringing to the fire in England alone over a dozen Unitarians, not to mention many who were imprisoned or otherwise injured in civil rights. It was not until 1813 that the English penal acts making denial of the Trinity a crime were repealed, and that the Unitarians and their property were made safe from apprehension by the law. Although the high court by its decision on *Essays and Reviews* deprived episcopal authority of the right of sentence, it could not simultaneously protect the eminent authors of this work from the penalties of official animus. Among churchmen it was a current aphorism that 'He may hold anything who will hold his tongue,' and for laymen who sought advancement in intellectual pursuits, intellectual inertia on all matters touching on the cosmos was imperative.

It bears upon the phenomenon of theological conservatism, in its effects both on the professional and lay mind, that with rare exceptions orthodoxy had ever been preserved at the bottom by the inculcation of beliefs of an awesome if not fearsome quality into children at an age when they do not and cannot appraise the value of evidences and arguments. The disciplines imposed upon young minds varied of course between wide extremes, but the general intent was invariably one of humorless terrification. An example was Father Furniss's *Sight of Hell* (1861) which is said to have been 'a great commercial success,' and from which Mew quotes the following moral lessons:

'Of two little maids of sixteen, one cared only for dress, and went to a dancing school, and dared to disport in the park on Sunday instead of going to mass: that little maid stands now, and forever will stand, with bare feet upon a red-hot floor. The other walked through the streets at night, and did very wicked things; now she utters shrieks of agony in a burning oven. A very severe torment — immersion up to the neck in a boiling kettle — agitates a boy who kept bad company, and was too idle to go to mass, and a drunkard; avenging flames now issue from his ears. For like indecencies, the blood of a girl, who went to the theatre, boils in her veins; you can hear it boil, and her marrow is seething in her bones and her brain bubbles in her head. "Think," says the compassionate father, "what a headache that girl must have!"'

This Catholic example is admittedly more literal than is required for an imaginative child, but Protestant morality was leavened with scarcely more human kindness, being still heavy with the Puritanism that had divided the Church of England in Elizabeth's day. This ascetic, almost sadistic religious discipline had from the beginning been deeply concerned with inculcating righteousness into the very young by alarming and, if necessary, painful measures, and it pervaded the post-Darwinian decades like sulphurous vapor issuing from the open doors of hell every Sunday.

It will be recalled that among the clouds shrouding the summit of the Mountain of the Law, Yahweh had commanded Moses to 'Remember the sabbath day, to sanctify it'; but inasmuch as Christianity had been in revolt against Jewish legalism and holiness, the Christians had refused to sanctify the Jewish Sabbath or to recognize in it anything other than a convenient day on which to hold their weekly love feast and to discuss the latest word from other churches. Jesus omitted the Mosaic commandment, 'Keep holy the sabbath day,' and attacked the Galatians for observing any special day as holy. The Christian seven-day interval, rather than reflecting acceptance of any holy day, actually reflected the Babylonian-Graeco-Roman secular week, and Paul vigorously remonstrated against any special religious observance on this day or any other. Ultimately, however, the Christians, anxious on the one hand to avoid identification with the Jews and, on the other, to ingratiate themselves with the Mithraists, changed their weekly love feast from Saturn's day, the traditional Jewish Sabbath, to the first day of the week, which among the Romans generally was dedicated to the sun. Gradually Sunday became a day of religious congregation, Origen apologizing for the special gathering as a concession to the weaker brethren who required 'some sensible memorials to prevent spiritual things from passing altogether away from their minds.' Soon the Christians, noting that the pagans had many holidays on which labor was set aside, resisted the wishes of the bishops and insisted upon making Sunday a day of rest. So in 321, Constantine made the 'venerable day of the sun' a public holiday because it pleased the pagans as much as the Christians.

In subsequent centuries the pendulum swung widely between the extremes of Sabbatarianism and pagan neglect; Charlemagne prohibited all ordinary labor on Sunday, and Anglo-Saxon kings at one time or another prohibited ploughing, marketing, law, fairs, hunting, and traveling; yet down to the fifteenth century there was no prohibition of recreation of any kind except dancing and singing of ribald songs, and the people were left free to amuse themselves. They had long fallen into the habit of attending church in the morning and giving the rest of the day to recreation.

The first reaction of the Reformation was toward increased license. In Elizabeth's time the Sabbatarians complained that 'The Lord was more dishonoured and the Devill better served on Sunday than upon all dayes in the weeke besides,' and it had been to resist this criticism that James I, in his *Book of Sports* (1618), defended the liberty of the people to enjoy all pastimes on Sunday except bull and bear baiting. John Knox said, 'Christians should have nothing to do with the superstitious observances of days,' while Luther denounced those who kept Sunday as a holy day and advised his followers to dance and feast on that day if only to oppose its sacred observance.

It was out of the ecclesiastic turmoil that attended and followed Elizabeth's reign, that Sabbatarianism won at least a partial victory and that Puritanism was spawned to set its grip upon the middle classes of Scotland and England.

Not the least of Elizabeth's troubles on coming to the throne was the problem of unifying the English Protestants in order the better to resist Catholic Philip of Spain, who was conniving with Mary of Scotland to gain the English crown. In so far as Elizabeth possessed any theologic conceptions the Protestants were less to her liking than the Catholics, being in general uncouth and not so well represented in sophisticated royal circles. None the less she had a very complicated foreign situation on her hands and, recognizing that uniformity of religion was necessary in order to preserve the unity of the state, she took steps to put together what her predecessor, Catholic Mary, had broken into almost unjoinable pieces.

To solve the conflict between Catholics and Protestants she made the English church as conservative and Catholic in outward appearance as possible, while preserving in it the patently liberal features of the Reformation. She insisted that her clergy wear the vestments of the Roman church and observe many of its traditional rituals, thus giving the semblance of Catholicism to their radical beliefs, yet leaving to each man the liberty of his private opinion.

Among those who survived Mary's persecution because they were lucky enough to be in exile were some of the most zealous Reformers such as Cartwright, Knox and Sandys, who by national loyalty were bound to the Anglican church, but who utterly disliked Elizabeth's compromise with popish practices. Under their criticism there soon separated from the parent church the Presbyterian branch which, with the passing years, came to esteem all popish practices the less and the authority of scripture and the necessity of personal good works the more. Despite an unshakable conviction in predestination, that God had in the beginning foreseen and foreordained every man his fate whether in heaven or hell, and therefore that good works per se could not save the damned, the Presbyterians, or Puritans as they were also called, held firmly to the faith that it was the duty of God's favored man to prove God's omniscience correct by living up to the punctuation of his Ten Commandments. Under Charles I the conflict with the Reformers led to civil war and, after a momentary victory under Cromwell, when England was officially Presbyterian, the Puritan movement, strongest among the Scots, suffered political defeat. A century of conflict was required, when votaries of one or the other religion pursued their opponents like criminals across the moors and valleys, inflicting them with branding, mutilation, scourging, exposure in the pillory, imprisonment or exile to Barbados, before, in a spirit of ill-suppressed animosity, Roman Catholicism, Anglicanism and Puritanism could live side by side without the recurrent letting of blood. During this period Puritanism, by its perpetual reiteration that a man's deeds are more important than his altar offerings, implanted within each of its competitors, within almost every English mind, the piety, asceticism and other virtues which it held to be the necessary substitutes for the despised Catholic rituals.

The Puritan ideal was one of extreme personal righteousness, the Puritan consciousness an ever-present sense of the all-pervading and innate character of sin. Emphasis on Augustine's theory of concupiscence and infant damnation made mortification of the flesh one of the central duties of life, and gave to all true Puritans a somber and gloomy character scarcely to be surpassed for miserable self-deprecation except by those early Christian ascetics who had spent their lives in sackcloth and ashes. The Puritan lived every moment in such fear of God that he had nothing else to fear, and hence he could face the most trying physical vicissitudes with complacent fortitude. Puritanism suspected all forms of beauty as a devilish device; it viewed all personal decoration as sinful conceit; and since it held unchastity to be one of the deadly sins it quarantined itself from all possibility of sensual temptation with a vigor second only to its avoidance of blasphemy, herein leaving its mark on the English middle classes in the form of prudery and fantastic delicacy of thought and speech with regard to all the elementary facts of life. It distrusted all works of the imagination, all poetry and romance, all art and music, as artifices of the devil, except in such instances as long tradition authorized the vehicle and the mood was consonant with the Descent from the Cross. The theater was utterly damned, humor was not fully condoned, laughter was looked upon askance. Its emphasis on original sin led it to distrust the child: infants are bound by their own innate fault, and though they may not have given evidence of their iniquity, they have the seed shut up in them, their whole nature is a sort of seed of sin, and therefore it cannot but be hateful and abominable to God. Hence the child's naturally evil will must, if necessary, be broken by the rod as early in life as possible and its mind from infanthood nourished on the all-important themes of personal guilt and duty.

Puritanism admittedly had social values: compensating for what at times amounted to vicious parental sadism, it simultaneously developed parental responsibility, since through concupiscence the parent was the source of the child's faults; and when others were disdaining the education of youth the Puritans were everywhere establishing free schools and utilizing printing in elementary if excessively righteous education, chiefly in order that their children might read the Bible and be guided out of their sinful ways. Puritanism saw the importance of self-discipline as against imposed restraint, of obligation as against compulsion, and thus laid the foundations without which political liberty cannot exist. And if Puritanism admonished men against wasteful expenditures, worldly pleasures and idleness, as implying a fall from grace, by its emphasis on the responsibility of the individual in the eyes of God it promoted personal initiative. No Puritan who was not both self-supporting and self-respecting could be beloved by God.

However, as Macaulay said, if the Puritans suppressed bull baiting, it was not because it gave pain to the bull but because it gave pleasure to the spectators. From the beginning the name was applied in a derogatory sense because of the extreme unpopularity of its sectaries, who persistently asserted that they were merely seeking religious freedom among the Romans and Anglicans, while in fact they were endeavoring to impose their frigidity and intolerance upon others. A particular instance for complaint against them lay in the question of what the righteous should or should not do on Sunday. In 1643, a Puritan dominated Parliament ordered the hangman to burn King James's irreligious *Book of Sports,* and in 1648 this official body adopted, in the Westminster Confession, the admonition: 'The sabbath is to be sanctified by a holy resting all that day even from such worldly employments and recreations as are lawful on other days; and spending the whole time in the public and private exercises of God's worship, except so much as is to be taken up in the works of necessity and mercy.' With the further increase of Puritan strength there came men who claimed for Sunday all the authority and strict observances of the Jewish Sabbath, and who would have had complete idleness enforced by law; and by successive enactments between 1644 and 1656 Parliament prohibited every kind of Sunday recreation, even 'vainly and profanely' walking for pleasure. Persons were punished for carrying coal on Sunday, for hanging out clothes to dry, and for traveling on horseback. Presbyterian clergymen taught their congregations that on that day it was sinful to save a vessel in distress, that it was proof of virtue to leave the ship and crew to perish.

With the Restoration, the English reaction against the austere rigidity of the Commonwealth produced a sudden outburst of derisive incredulity. The cavaliers, and even the High Church clergy, went to the extreme of trading and attending the theater on Sunday, mockingly affecting the solemn gait and nasal twang of the Puritans, and ridiculing their doctrines. Scotland, however, remained bridled and repressed, cowering in helpless subjection before her clergy. The misery of man, the anger of the Almighty, the fearful power of Satan, the agonies of the damned in hell, were fused into a system of religious terrorism overawing all opposition. Sunday remained a day of amazingly ascetic rigor. A ban was put upon all entertainment and frivolity, and upon all reading except of a strictly religious nature. No recreation remained lawful except whiskey drinking, whence drunkenness became the Sunday rule. For everyone except those who narcotized themselves with alcohol the Lord's Day was at best a day of unmitigated gloom: industry or physical exertion, even when economically imperative, were abhorrent; children might not play except with a Noah's ark, and then not noisily; levity and all music except that of a religious sort were banned; boys and girls might not go out together, or take exercise except perhaps for a sedate walk in the afternoon, but must sit wearily at home while their elders, after a heavy meal, found refuge in righteous sleep. On Sunday, not only for Puritans but for all whom Puritanism touched, the world was rigidly divided into the sacred and profane, as it had been divided for the Jews twenty-odd centuries before.

The invention of mechanical transportation, more than any other single factor, broke the Sabbatarian restraint and simultaneously weakened the paralytic grip that theology had on the popular intellect. Sunday was the only day when most people could leave their work in search of recreation and, with the development of rapid and cheap transportation, the impulse was to travel farther away from home, into strange places and new temptations. 'It is impossible to lay down a railway without creating an intellectual influence. It is probable that Watt and Stephenson will eventually modify the opinions of mankind almost as profoundly as Luther and Voltaire.' Lecky's prediction was on its way to fulfilment.

Among the temptations afforded by the railway was the seduction of sea-bathing at the coastal resorts, which served to reawaken interest in the bath as a hygienic measure. From the earliest times ancient people had bathed almost instinctively in the Nile, the Euphrates and the Jordan, and the Romans had raised the bath to the level of a fine art. Public baths came to Rome with the Appian aqueduct and, after Maecenas, emperors who wished to ingratiate themselves with the people lavished state revenues in their construction. The baths of Diocletian were of such size that one room could be transmuted into a church of imposing proportions, while the walls of the baths of Caracalla were a quarter-of-a-mile long on each side. Scarcely less imposing were the public baths of Agrippa, Nero, Titus, Domitian, Commodus, Diocletian and Constantine. In the largest of these there were open colonnades and benches where philosophers and literary men could recline to discourse, to read aloud their literary productions or to discuss the latest news. These *piscinae* or *thermae* were generally adorned with beautiful marble, the halls crowded with fine statuary and the walls covered with exquisite mosaics. 'To such a pitch of luxury have we reached,' says Seneca, 'that we are dissatisfied if we do not tread on gems in our baths.'

Wherever the Romans settled they built public baths, and wherever they found hot springs they used them until at the peak of the Empire frequent bathing became a widespread custom. With the spread of Christian doctrine bathing came to be regarded as an evidence of personal conceit, as a concern for the flesh. The most admired saints were those who had become a clotted mass of filth. Athanasius relates with enthusiasm that St. Anthony had never in his long life been guilty of washing his feet. St. Simeon Stylites lived with a rope bound round him and imbedded in his flesh, and it is said that 'a horrible stench, intolerable to the bystanders, exhaled from his body, and worms dropped from him whenever he moved, and they filled his bed.' Christian ascetics lived in deserted dens of wild beasts, or in tombs, disdaining all clothes and crawling about like animals covered only by their matted hair. Though this extreme of virtue could not be universally imitated, it was recognized by the fathers that gratification of any worldly desire is sinful, and that the flesh should be degraded and made the spirit's abject slave. Throughout the monastic period cleanliness of either the clothes or the body was regarded as a pollution of the soul, a sign of sinful pride.

The early Christians had, in addition, strong grounds for condemning the Roman custom of admitting both sexes to the public baths and proscribed the practice. Gregory the Great saw no objection to the use of the bath on Sunday for the sake of cleanliness, but about the fifth century the Roman baths fell into decay, and the practice of regular bathing, so far as the record shows, became restricted to the peoples of the East, and largely to the Mohammedans, from whom the crusaders learned it. The custom was reintroduced into Europe in the form of the hot vapor, or Turkish, bath, the popularity of which, either because of technical difficulties or unexpected discomforts, seems to have been short-lived. After several abortive efforts to introduce hydropathic baths in England in the guise of therapy, the establishment for the 'health, comfort and welfare' of the inhabitants of towns or populous districts of urban baths was authorized by a Parliamentary act of 1846. By 1875, when steam trains were weekly carrying thousands to the seashore, salt-water bathing had come into vogue. The divided skirt with loose trousers gathered around the ankles, named after the American dress-reformer, suffragist and temperance worker, Amelia Jenks Bloomer, helped greatly to solve the difficulties of mixed sexes bathing in a common water which had offended the early Christians. In 1910 an informed chronicler computed that on a hot Sunday twenty-five thousand people bathed in London's Victoria Park, some starting as early as four o'clock in the morning.

'These returns,' he adds, 'show how great is the increase of the habit of
bathing, but they also show how even now the habit is limited to a
comparatively small part of the population. People require to be tempted
to the use of water, at any rate at the beginning.'

Apart from the circumstance that a change in habit is frequently reflected in a change of opinion, increasing Sunday travel diminished
church attendance, diverted attention to new interests, and facilitated the
spread, first of apathy, and then of unbelief. Especially among the middle classes where social convention exerted light restraints, and where
increasing numbers were profiting by the spread of education, the convictions that had hitherto been impressed by the force of repeated admonitions began to assume the form of debatable propositions.

iv

The multiple origins of the Pentateuch, suspected in the eighteenth
century, had passed in the early decades of the nineteenth from speculation into conviction for all critical scholars. As the authority of Moses
yielded before the discoveries of the geologist's pick, so the tradition of
inspiration in any part of the Old Testament yielded to textual and
literary studies. The New Testament, however, more forcibly resisted
critical approach since it dealt, except for the miraculous elements, with
spiritual matters that were in essence beyond criticism.

Hume's essay, 'Of Miracles' (1748) had pointed out that in no case
could the miraculous be proved to be such, in the sense of a controversion
of natural law, unless a different course of events would be more
miraculous than the alleged miracle itself. Middleton's *Free Inquiry*
(1748) had argued the improbability of miracles, and asserted that the
writers of the third century had habitually applauded falsehood and practiced wholesale forgery, that they had grossly falsified history and given
themselves over to pious frauds to stimulate the devotion of the people.

The denial of the miraculous might have been more difficult had not
the church been so indulgent, for miracles remained commonplace until
in their frequency they presented a danger to ecclesiastic authority.
Miraculous images and pictures operated throughout Christendom, apparitions and miscellaneous prodigies occurred in every country. The
Bollandist Collection contains some twenty-five thousand lives of saints
whose miracles merited their canonization, and this represented only
one rigidly scrutinized official department. Protestantism looked upon

miracles with aversion and distrust, chiefly because the miraculous had been the speciality of the devotion which it now stigmatized as erroneous, idolatrous and superstitious. Under critical pressure, Catholicism in time came to withhold its official sanction and then to disapprove, since each miracle was a source of embarrassment, if not a scandal, and among intelligent Catholics required an apology on the grounds that it was unfair to judge the enlightened members of the church by the superstitious beliefs of the unenlightened.

In answer to the truism that in exact proportion as a people advance in education, the accounts of new miracles become rarer and rarer, until at last they cease entirely, was offered the argument that this is not due to a decrease in credulity, but to the circumstance that God had chosen the dark and ignorant ages wherein to manifest himself in this manner; when natural knowledge prevails there is no need for extraordinary signs since men will be diligent in his works and attentive to his wishes. The argument, reasonable enough for those who held to a priori faith in the miraculous and who failed to read in history a refutation of the alleged moral sequence, remained unconvincing for the incredulous who, with the realignment of the New Testament in its proper historic background, interpreted the gospel miracles in the same light as those of the pagan wonder-workers. Strauss, in the introduction to his *Leben Jesu,* calmly remarked, 'We may summarily reject all miracles, prophecies, narratives of angels and demons, and the like, as simply impossible and irreconcilable with the known and universal laws which govern the course of events.'

The literary investigation of the New Testament had been initiated in the early eighteenth century by the English deists, philosophers by profession rather than historians, for no purely historical interest could have induced Christian Europe to apply criticism to those sacred books which were peculiarly its own. John Locke, the Scottish philosopher who was seeking a natural conception for moral law, and who first emphasized the existence of different strata and diverse tendencies in the New Testament; Toland, who argued the identity of the first Christians with the Nazarene and Hebrew heretics; Chubb and Morgan who distinguished the teachings of Jesus from the personal opinions of the apostles — were among the forerunners of what came to be called, because it was the work of ecclesiastic scholars, the Higher Criticism, the modern apologetic effort to make Christianity reasonable and to avoid the now difficult-to-accept presuppositions of revelation and inspiration. Where others had with meager success sought by combining the four gospels to obtain a single coherent narrative of Jesus's life, Griesbach in 1776 substituted the 'synopsis' that frankly presented side by side the contrasting and often contradictory passages in Matthew, Mark and Luke, setting apart as wholly alien the mystical gospel of John; while Lessing in 1778 treated the evangelists as purely human writers and formulated the hypothesis of a primitive document from which the three synoptics had been derived. These and following studies culminated in Strauss's *Leben Jesu* (1835), in which the conception of 'myth' was applied systematically to the gospel tradition. Strauss never treated as doubtful the historic reality of Jesus and the main events of his earthly career, but he accepted that a historic nucleus had been worked over and reshaped into an ideal form by the first Christians under the influence of Old Testament models and the idea of the messiah found in Daniel. Nevertheless, this work for the first time posed the question, what in the New Testament was history, and what was myth? Strauss's book, translated into English by George Eliot in 1843, displayed the accumulating critical movement as a serious and major attack upon the theological position, and the first effects of his work were to secure for him an offer of the professorship of theology at the University of Zurich, which he accepted; but so violent was the reaction of the church that the appointment had to be cancelled and he was forced to accept a pension in lieu of the career of teaching and investigation for which he was ably fitted, but which now was permanently closed to him.

In the Reformation the Protestant faith had cast away all authority other than that of the Bible and personal inspiration; by the late nineteenth century the labors of three generations of critics, many of them Protestant theologians of outstanding repute, had so far exposed the contradictory threads of both Testaments as to have utterly undermined biblical authority. Bishop Colenso's first influential book appeared only two years after *Essays and Reviews* and at the same moment Draper's *History of the Intellectual Development of Europe,* published in New York in 1862 and in London in 1864, presented broadly massed pictures of historical change dominated by the concept of evolution and based on the postulate that 'the equilibrium and movement of humanity are altogether physiological phenomena.' This writer's *History of the Conflict between Religion and Science* (1874), reached its eighteenth edition within ten years. When Cassels's *Supernatural Religion* (1874–1877) collected for general readers the substance of biblical research, particularly as related to the New Testament, and displayed the superstition, ignorance, and credulity from which the gospels had emerged, the insecurity of the orthodox position became widely apparent among the laity. The distinguished *Fortnightly Review* began to admit freethinking writers to its pages and editorially supported a campaign for unrestricted secular education. In an essay in this magazine entitled 'The Unseen Universe,' Clifford in 1872 drove home the arguments of Darwin and Huxley with a vengeance, saying, 'Scientific thought does not mean thought about scientific subjects with long names. There are no scientific subjects. The subject of science is the human universe, that is to say, everything that is, or has been, or may be related to man. . . . Only for another half-century let us keep our hells and heavens and gods. . . . Take heed lest you have given soil and shelter to the seed of that awful plague which has destroyed two civilizations, and but barely failed to slay such promise of good as is now struggling to live among men.'

Sir John Lubbock in his *Prehistoric Times* (1865) and *Origin of Civilization* (1870) had framed a naturalistic picture of social and moral beginnings, and Lecky's *History of the Rise and Influence of the Spirit of Rationalism in Europe* (1865), although piously avoiding the implications of Darwinism, indeed perhaps aided by its piety, imparted to its readers some knowledge of magic and witchcraft and a more critical attitude toward the miraculous. The new field of comparative religion had been founded by Tylor's *Researches into the Early History of Mankind* (1878), and his more elaborate *Primitive Culture* (1871), which bore the subtitle, *Researches into the Development of Mythology, Philosophy, Religion, Language, Art and Custom,* became not only a standard source work of anthropology but was very popular among general readers who discovered in its fascinating pages that there were as many gods as there were peoples. On the appearance of this book Darwin, who had worried about the animal-like state of the savages of Tierra del Fuego, wrote the author, 'It will make me for the future look on religion — a belief in the soul, etc. — from a different point of view.'

While Gibbon at the close of the eighteenth century could see in Christianity 'an effete and old-fashioned edifice,' seven decades later there remained a badly shaken structure in which scarcely one part was firmly cemented to another. Social and political condemnation of what the orthodox variously called unsettled faith, infidelity, free thought, unbelief or atheism was fast losing its force as an effective deterrent to intellectual inquiry. Without the traditional observance of Sunday, the continued pressure of Puritanical prejudices, the emotional stimuli of ritual, ornaments and sacred hypnos, even nominal adherence to the creed would have suffered seriously. Gentlemen remained outwardly orthodox for social reasons, even when privately, though generally to the exclusion of their children's confidence, holding to heretical opinions. The younger generation, not likely to be informed on the precedents of the virgin birth or the technicalities of the Trinity, were admonished to silence when inquiring into subjects upon which experts were known to have disagreed.

Then there began to circulate *The Rubáiyát of Omar Khayyám*, a collection of freely translated Persian verses that seemed theologically innocuous but that turned out to be highly subversive of the dogmatic position. The *Rubáiyát* was first published as an anonymous pamphlet in 1859, but received absolutely no attention until it had gravitated to the pennybox of the bookstalls. The poet Dante Gabriel Rossetti found one in a pennybox, and started the volume on its road to fame. Edward Fitz-Gerald, by whom the *Rubáiyát* had been 'Rendered into English Verse,' remained anonymous during his lifetime, and it was not until 1885, when Tennyson dedicated his *Tiresias* to FitzGerald's memory, in the year of the latter's death, that the *Rubáiyát* and its translator came into universal appreciation.

Omar Khayyám (Omar the tent maker, d. *ca.* 1123) was a great Persian mathematician, astronomer, freethinker and epigrammatist, whose scientific genius has been almost overshadowed in history by the fame of his *rubáis,* or quatrains. These quatrains, of which he wrote some five hundred, were in many cases purely mystic and pantheistic, but the most notable constitute the breviary of a radical freethinker protesting against the narrowness, bigotry and unreasonableness of orthodox theology.

FitzGerald, lacking a profession, had devoted his life to flowers, music and literature (he called his talent 'the feminine of genius'). He began the study of poetry in 1850, and of Persian in 1853. An anonymous volume of Oriental verses published by him in 1856 received little attention, and the *Rubáiyát,* which he translated from a manuscript in the Bodleian Library, was probably ignored at first because, among other things, of its unorthodox philosophy. Reviewers would perforce touch such a work gingerly. However, after the verses were endorsed by Rossetti, Swinburne, Burton and others to whom Rossetti showed them, and particularly after a second edition (1868) appeared with more daring passages included, the book quickly took its place as an English classic.

The melody of the *Rubáiyát* is so exquisite, the thoughts are so profound, the poetic atmosphere so pure, that, it has been said, its admirers have almost transcended common sense in the extravagance of their praise. Certainly FitzGerald's volume had a tremendous circulation among English speaking peoples; the publishers have long since lost count of the number of volumes issued. More significant than the beauty of the verses, however, was their devastating iconoclasm. The *Rubáiyát* introduced irreligion to readers who had never heard of the Higher Criticism, and carried unbelief through doorways barred resolutely to any more explicit denial of conventional dogma. The keynote of the *Rubáiyát* is an ironical protest against Sufism, a priestly code of doctrine, ceremony and future rewards and punishment that pressed upon eleventh century Persia as priestly codes had pressed upon many another people in many other times.

Omar shocked a world that lived — or so pretended — chiefly for the world hereafter, by his philosophy that Today outlasts all Tomorrows:

> Some for the Glories of this World; and some
> Sigh for the Prophet's Paradise to come;
>   Ah, take the Cash, and let the Credit go,
> Nor heed the rumble of a distant Drum!

> Ah, make the most of what we yet may spend,
> Before we too into the Dust descend;
>   Dust into Dust and under Dust to lie,
> Sans Wine, sans Song, sans Singer, and — sans End!

Omar sings the praises of wine, not, he says, to counter holiness, or even for delight, but to breathe a little, free from self — no other cause could make him drink all night! Despite his ironic mood, as he is driven onward through this 'spangle of Existence' he is haunted by a desire to learn the Secret:

> Myself when young did eagerly frequent
> Doctor and Saint and heard great argument
>   About it and about: but evermore
> Came out by the same door where in I went.
>
> .   .   .   .
>
> Into this Universe, and *Why* not knowing
> Nor *Whence,* like Water willy-nilly flowing;
>   And out of it, as Wind along the Waste,
> I know not *Whither,* willy-nilly blowing.

> What, without asking, hither hurried *Whence?*
> And, without asking, *Whither* hurried hence!
>   Oh, many a Cup of this forbidden Wine
> Must drown the memory of that insolence!

Omar's God, like Spencer's, was unknowable, but the poet rebelled against a doctrine of divine imperatives, sin and penitence:

> What! out of senseless Nothing to provoke
> A conscious Something to resent the yoke
> Of unpermitted Pleasure, under pain
> Of Everlasting Penalties, if broke!

> What! from his helpless Creature be repaid
> Pure Gold for what he lent him dross-allay'd —
> Sue for a Debt he never did contract,
> And cannot answer — Oh the sorry trade!

> .   .   .   .

> Oh Thou, who Man of baser Earth didst make,
> And ev'n with Paradise devise the Snake:
> For all the Sin wherewith the Face of Man
> Is blacken'd — Man's forgiveness give — and take!

His is the despair born of the injustice of man's destiny, but his, too, is that faint if seemingly hopeless wish:

> Ah Love! could you and I with Him conspire
> To grasp this sorry Scheme of Things entire,
> Would not we shatter it to bits — and then
> Re-mould it nearer to the Heart's Desire!

FitzGerald, a dilettante in both the Persian language and in poetry, unwittingly succeeded where countless poets had failed, in implanting in a multitude of readers, if not a constructive at least a startlingly new and analytic attitude. Other poets had failed because the art had remained innocent of either historic or philosophic perspective. On matters pertaining to the emotions, and where no restraints imposed by considerations other than affective sensibilities needed to be observed, poetry had well demonstrated its capabilities. It had established itself as the champion of the cavalier, the proper decoration of the complete library and the balanced literary magazine, the master of erotic, romantic and affective titillation, the graceful and perfumed companion of every boudoir; but it had failed to be a useful companion to philosophy because poets had been too concerned with their visceral sensations and too myopic to the more remote implications and consequences of their rhapsodies. Failing to succeed as an artisan, it had remained, however happily, the courtesan of the intellect. That FitzGerald should afford an adult intellectual performance in this medium was attributable to a summation of forces: his was the beauty of meter and rhyme, while the substance of what he had to say was the penetration and wisdom of the Naishápúr mathematician whose labors in algebra and astronomy were the basis of greatness in another day. To the deliquescence of faith the *Rubáiyát* made a significant and colorful contribution.

v

In 1873, in a letter to his wife, Huxley had written: 'We are in the midst of a gigantic movement greater than that which preceded and produced the Reformation, and really only the continuation of that movement. But there is nothing new in the ideas which lie at the bottom of the movement, nor is any reconcilement possible between freethought and traditional authority. One or the other will have to succumb after a struggle of unknown duration, which will have as side issues vast political and social troubles. I have no more doubt that freethought will win in the long run than I have that I sit here writing to you, or that this freethought will organize itself into a coherent system embracing human life and the world as one harmonious whole. But this organization will be the work of generations of man, and those who further it most will be those who teach men to rest in no lie, and to rest in no verbal delusions.'

Huxley used the term 'freethought' for lack of a better word. It had been publicized by the militant operators of the cellar printing presses in the early part of the century and several decades of bitter warfare had left unattractive scars upon it. The orthodox immediately equated it with atheism, birth control, socialism, anarchy, nihilism, blasphemy, and other criminal tendencies, a more charitable synonymy permitting 'unfaithfulness to the truth of God' or 'unbelief,' while at the extreme of tolerance it was identified, with a political shudder, as 'liberalism in religion.'

'Freethought' was too charged with prejudices to remain the designation of the 'gigantic movement' to which Huxley referred. Latterly, men who claimed the right to think things out in accordance with the evidences had taken to themselves the name of 'rationalists,' though they would have been hard pressed to defend their exclusive right to this attractive cognomen on etymological grounds, since reason could be and had been made to serve the ends of the most absurd and impossible premises. 'Secularism' for a while stood opposed to 'Sacredism,' but fell into disuse because of lack of force. 'Materialism' was employed only by the orthodox as a term of opprobrium, and it possessed significance only by contrast with something called 'spiritualism,' or as an antithesis to Platonic Idealism, and no defendent on the side of heterodoxy ever described himself as a 'materialist' or presumed to give an ultimate definition of 'matter.' 'Naturalism,' which bore no scars from ancient controversies, had a certain vogue in the beginning of the century, since by a connotation which stemmed from Descartes it could fairly be used to designate one who held solely to the presented evidences of nature, excluding all preconceptions relative to the supernatural, but it failed to attain recognition until after the end of the century when it came to be equated with the empirical or the exploratory and experimental method.

Huxley, once sitting amiably in the Metaphysical Society with men who could identify themselves as Catholics, Anglicans, Presbyterians, Unitarians, and the like, and feeling rather 'like the fox without a tail,' jovially dubbed himself an 'agnostic' — one who has no preconceived faith — and found the word so useful that he adhered to it. Agnosticism came to be identified among his friends as a sort of 'consecrated doubt,' and even Spencer accepted it as adequately descriptive of his philosophy of the Unknowable. Huxley, however, denied assertions about Spencer's Unknowable as vigorously as he denied assertions about the Christian God; whether the Unknowable 'exists or does not exist, I am quite clear I have no knowledge either way. I neither affirm or deny.' Originally the term 'agnostic' had perhaps signified for Huxley only an admitted ignorance concerning all metaphysical doctrines — the conclusions of the atheist, the theist, the pantheist, the materialist, the idealist, being in his view equally unverifiable — but he himself used it in many different senses, and it ultimately came to mean far more than was justified etymologically. In consequence of his antipathy to theology, and to Genesis in particular, he generally used the word as meaning scientific skepticism, though often he meant an antitheism which was to be equated with netheism (denial of God) as defined by Bradlaugh. He was no more interested in denying or disproving the existence of God than of an unknown planet in the solar system. But until the existence of God was demonstrated by evidence, as convincing as would be required to persuade astronomers of the existence of such a planet, and unless this or additional evidence demonstrated that God was immediately concerned with values, morals, and the like, it was as futile for men to attempt to guide their lives by the one, as for astronomers to attempt to set their clocks by the other. A biographer remarks that Huxley called himself an agnostic mostly to avoid wasteful discussion of the Unknown while he applied himself to the ascertainable facts of nature: 'agnosticism was a white flag which he and his small company carried as they walked through the country of orthodoxy and placed dynamite under offensive buildings.'

A signal occasion on which he was forced to fend for agnosticism was in 1888, when an annual church congress in Manchester devoted an afternoon session to 'Atheism, Agnosticism and Pessimism.' Dr. Henry Wace, prebendary of St. Paul's and Principal of King's College, took advantage of the occasion to call Huxley an infidel: 'He may prefer to call himself an agnostic, but his real name is an older one — he is an infidel, that is to say, an unbeliever. The word, infidel, perhaps carries an unpleasant significance. Perhaps it is right that it should. It is, and ought to be, an unpleasant thing for a man to have to say plainly that he does not believe in Jesus Christ. It is, indeed, an awful thing to say.' In the discussion of Dr. Wace's remarks, Bishop Magee of Peterborough expressed himself as being wholly in agreement with the sentiments of his colleague, and added that to his mind the intellectual unrest of the time all reduced to 'cowardly agnosticism.'

Huxley, more irritated by the charge of cowardice than of infidelity, prepared a reply for publication in *The Nineteenth Century,* concentrating on a point which Wace had emphasized, namely the value of Christian 'authority.' He took as an example of this authority the miracle recounted by Mark, wherein Jesus exorcises evil spirits from a man and sends them into the Gadarene swine, which thereupon rush off to self-destruction. Though possession by evil spirits which could be transferred to pigs, he admitted, could not be denied on a priori grounds, no adequate evidence for their existence had ever been presented. Implicitly assuming that Dr. Wace and Bishop Magee were not prepared to defend the existence of devils which could be exorcised from a man and driven into swine, it followed that either Jesus said what was attributed to him with regard to evil spirits, in which case his authority on matters of the 'unseen world' was fatally shaken; or he did not say what was attributed to him, in which case the authority of the biblical text was shaken. As for Bishop Magee's charge of cowardice, and Dr. Wace's assertion that to avow disbelief in Jesus 'is, and ought to be, an unpleasant thing,' he replied: 'Whether it is so depends, I imagine, a good deal on whether the man was brought up in a Christian household or not. I do not see why it should be "unpleasant" for a Mohammedan or Buddhist to say so. But that "it ought to be" unpleasant for any man to say anything which he sincerely, and after due deliberation, believes, is, to my mind, a proposition of the most profoundly immoral character. I verily believe that the great good which has been effected in the world by Christianity has been largely counteracted by the pestilent doctrine on which all the churches have insisted, that honest disbelief in their more or less astonishing creeds is a moral offense, indeed a sin of the deepest dye, deserving and involving the same future retribution as murder and robbery. If we could only see, in one view, the torrents of hyprocrisy and cruelty, the lies, the slaughter, the violations of every obligation of humanity, which have flowed from this source along the course of the history of Christian nations, our worst imaginations of Hell would pale beside the vision.'

Warming with enthusiasm for his task he followed up with another article in the next number of *The Nineteenth Century* on 'The Value of Witness to the Miraculous,' recounting the superabundance of the miracles out of which Eginhard had spun his fantastic Carolingian history, and concluding that 'if Eginhard's calm and objective narrative of the historical events of his time is no guarantee for the soundness of his judgment where the supernatural is concerned, the fervid rhetoric of the Apostle to the Gentiles, his absolute confidence in the "inner light," and the extraordinary conceptions of the nature and requirements of logical proof which he betrays for page after page of his Epistles, afford still less security.'

In this same number were articles prepared by Dr. Wace and Bishop Magee to answer Huxley's arguments. Dr. Wace, after entangling himself in some misquotations, ended by accusing Huxley of unfairness, evasion and inaccuracy: in substance he said that the question of the divine authority of the scriptures could not be argued over evil spirits and pigs, but involved the teachings of Jesus as presented in the Lord's Prayer and the Sermon on the Mount. While Bishop Magee explained that by 'cowardly agnosticism' he had meant only one type of person who used the language of Huxley as an excuse for avoiding the fundamental problems and burdens of life.

'My position,' Huxley replied at once, 'reduced to its briefest form has been: In the first place, the evidence is such that the exact nature of the teachings and the convictions of Jesus is extremely uncertain, so that what ecclesiastics are pleased to call a denial of them may be nothing of the kind, and, in the second place, if Jesus taught the demonological system involved in the Gadarene story — if a belief in that system formed a part of the spiritual convictions in which he lived and died —

then I, for my part unhesitatingly refuse to believe in that teaching, and deny the reality of those spiritual convictions. And I go further and add, that exactly in so far, for me, will his authority in any matter touching the spiritual world be weakened.'

It was perhaps because Huxley's position was stated with such blunt finality that the ecclesiastics decided to drop the argument over the miracle of Gadara. It is interesting, however, since the entire argument concerned the authority of the Christian texts, to find Bishop Magee later writing to a friend, 'The fact is that Huxley's bumptious air of omniscience imposes on feeble folk. He may be a great scientist, but he is a very poor historical critic. Wace, if he answers him, ought to knock him into a cocked hat. Then he is so thoroughly disingenuous. To call the Gadarene miracle "a part of the Christian faith," for instance, when he knows that no one of the creeds requires any Christian to believe in any one of our Lord's miracles, or even in the inspiration of the Gospels.' This, from a Christian Bishop, within twenty-five years of the time when *Essays and Reviews* had stirred within the church such a storm as it had not known since the days of Henry VIII and Bloody Mary, advertised to the entire world that both Mosaic cosmology and the miracles of the New Testament were only quicksands to trap those of unwary faith, and showed how well that book had found its mark.

It was Prime Minister Gladstone who was determined to fire the last shot in the engagement over the Gadarene pigs. Educated at Eton and Oxford, Gladstone would have chosen holy orders but for his father's determination to make him a politician. Despite his liberal ideas in government, a contemporary noted that 'in the sphere of dogmatic faith Mr. Gladstone, by the time he was thirty, had become a man of settled questions,' while one biographer has said of him that 'his whole life was spent in unlearning the prejudices in which he was educated.'

In an interlude when the distinguished parliamentarian was out of office he found time to make a last but determined defense of orthodoxy in *The Impregnable Rock of Scripture* (1890). Under this mixed metaphor, the megalithic origin of which he little suspected, he collected a number of devious arguments which he had propounded in previous essays to prove that all modern knowledge could be reconciled with Genesis. Expressing renewed confidence in his 'organ of belief' and asserting that skepticism was on the wane, he tried in this book to deliver a killing blow to Huxley, by inquiring why it had been reserved for him to discover, after some thousand years, that in the Gadara affair, Jesus, by destroying an innocent man's property, had been no better than a lawbreaker and evildoer. Gladstone asserted that he had carefully applied himself to scripture and discovered that Gadara was a Jewish and not a gentile city; hence the swine-keepers were Jews, who were forbidden to keep pork, and Jesus in destroying their herds was justly punishing them for breaking their own law.

Huxley replied that he had questioned not the actions of Jesus but the validity of the gospel story, and by quoting a number of authorities, he refuted the claim that Gadara was a Jewish city. Gladstone replied with a still greater show of authorities that Gadara was a Jewish city, and in effect made it appear that Huxley was now impugning his, the Prime Minister's, acumen, if not his honesty: 'I conceive it has been shown that to *suppose* the swineherds to have been punished by Christ for pursuing a calling which to them was an innocent one is to run counter to every law of reasonable historical interpretation.'

This free application of supposition to Mark's account irked Huxley to an article entitled 'Illustrations of Mr. Gladstone's Controversial Methods,' a ludicrous burlesque that set the entire world, already highly attentive to the fate of the possessed pigs, to laughing. To the suggestion that, at their time of life, he and Gladstone could better use their time than in debating over the Gadarene swine, Huxley replied that a principle was at stake: 'We are at the parting of the ways. Whether the twentieth century shall see a recrudescence of the superstitiousness of medieval papistry, or whether it shall witness the reverence of the living body of the ethical ideal of prophetic Israel or the carcass, foul with savage superstition and cankered with false philosophy, to which the theologians have bound it, turns upon their final judgment of the Gadarene tale.'

The controversy ended when Gladstone was drawn back into politics by a general election, but only, one historian notes, after the swine, 'in rushing down from the high place of revealed authority' under the impetus of Huxley's exorcism, 'had trampled their fateful and historic path across the pages of every serious publication in two hemispheres.'

IX

To Whatever Abyss

IT had fallen to the lot of the Gadarene pigs to reduce the argument of the sanctity of the scriptural texts to the ridiculous. Orthodox and non-orthodox had come to see that the book that had so long served to negate reason and obstruct intellectual advance, that for nearly two thousand years had been the source of such bloodlettings, bonfires, imprisonments, tortures, persecutions, wars of 'conversion' and mad crusades as would have astonished a pagan people, was a collection of myths, anecdotes and genealogies, with but a few credible fragments of history interspersed, compiled in a grossly superstitious age and laden with the superstition of its time. It had been written not to edify historians of the future but to gain converts to the new faith or confirm the convictions of those already won. By current literary rules no moral compunctions had restrained its authors from presenting their work under the name of some distinguished character in history or legend, or from interpolating in the works of others. As literature, its best portions had been exceeded in quality, as Gibbon had emphasized, by much in the literature of the Greeks, and, as latterly was being discovered, at least equalled by the still more ancient Egyptian hieroglyphic, while many if not most of its estimable moral precepts were the heritage of pagan or Jewish thought.

Christianity was now faced with a question: without the Bible could there be religion of any sort? The situation for Catholicism was well summarized by John Henry Newman on the eve of his elevation to the College of Cardinals. Newman's religious life began when, at the age of fifteen, he experienced 'conversion,' an incident that he always regarded as 'more certain than that he had hands and feet.' As an evangelical Calvinist, he held that the pope was Antichrist. He attended Oxford, the redoubt of theology, and was ordained at nineteen. At twenty-two he quarreled with the college authorities over nonconformist practices and dissociated himself from the Low Church party, but at twenty-seven, after visiting Rome, he described the Roman Catholic religion as 'polytheistic, degrading and idolatrous.' Nevertheless, always moving toward the Anglican church as a *via media* between Protestantism and Catholicism, and defending the basic and seemingly necessary principle of apostolic succession, he was vigorously examining, in his *Tracts for the Times,* the applicability of this principle to the Anglican church itself. It seemed doubtful, in view of the history of the institution established by Henry VIII, that the Anglicans could by any deviously argued episcopal succession lay claim to the heritage which Jesus has transmitted to Peter. Retiring to monastic seclusion at thirty-seven, Newman published two years later a retraction of all the hard things he had said of Rome, and at forty was received into the Catholic Church, in which he was shortly ordained and awarded the degree of D.D. (1846) by the pope. At the age of seventy-four, when he was elevated to the rank of cardinal (1879), he looked back upon the serried history of fifty years with discouragement:

> For thirty, forty, fifty years I have resisted, to the best of my powers, the spirit of liberalism in religion. Never did the Holy Church need champions against it more sorely than now, when alas! it is an error overspreading as a snare the whole earth. . . . Liberalism in religion is the doctrine that there is no positive truth in religion, but that one creed is as good as another; and this is the teaching which is gaining substance and force daily. It is inconsistent with the teaching of any religion as true. It teaches that all are to be tolerated, as all are matters of opinion. Revealed religion is not a truth, but a sentiment and a taste; and it is the right of each individual to make it say just what strikes his fancy.
>
> Religion is [now] in no sense the bond of society. Hitherto the civil power has been Christian. . . . Now everywhere that goodly frame of society, which is the creation of Christianity, is throwing off Christianity. The *dictum* to which I have referred, with a hundred others which followed upon it, is gone or is going everywhere, and by the end of the century, unless the Almighty interferes, it will be forgotten. Hitherto it has been considered that religion alone, with its supernatural sanctions, was strong enough to secure the submission of the mass of the population to law and order. Now, philosophers and politicians are bent on satisfying this problem without the aid of Christianity. . . .
>
> The general character of this great apostasy is one and the same everywhere. . . . For myself, I would rather speak of it in my own country, which I know. There, I think, it threatens to have a formidable success, though it is not easy to see what will be its ultimate issue. At first sight

it might be thought that Englishmen are too religious for a movement which on the Continent seems to be founded on infidelity; but the misfortune with us is that, though it ends in infidelity, as in other places, it does not necessarily arise out of infidelity.

Newman's faith has been summed up in the statement that he who lacks an interior and unmeasured conviction of the existence of God must remain agnostic; he who has the conviction has gripped the supreme truth and is bound by history and by reason to place himself in the Church of Rome. This flight from all that is meaningful, this pietistic effort to escape from an edifice crumbling under the impact of reason into a haven of blind faith, has been described by one critic as 'the second childhood of the religious temperament.' But in his retreat from the world he could neither understand nor face courageously, he had a prophetic moment when he foresaw a 'stern encounter when two real and living principles, simple, entire and consistent, one in the Church, the other out of it, at length rush upon one another, contending not for names and words and half-views, but for elementary notions and distinctive moral characters.' The two principles, he said, are 'Catholic truth and Rationalism.'

The case for Protestant orthodoxy was as well summarized by James Martineau, a Presbyterian divine who for many years as a professor of moral philosophy at Manchester New College had fended for Christianity against all dissolving ideas. In *The Seat of Authority of Religion* (1890) he thus summed up the position of the established creed:

As I look back on the foregoing discussion, a conclusion is forced upon me which I cannot dwell without pain and dismay; viz., that Christianity, as defined or understood in all the churches which formulate it, has been mainly evolved from that which is unhistorical and perishable in its sources; from what is unhistorical in its traditions, mythological in its preconceptions, and misapprehended in the oracles of its prophets. From the fable of Eden to the imagination of the last trumpet, the whole story of the divine order of the world is dislocated and deformed.

The blight of birth-sin with its involuntary perdition; the scheme of expiatory redemption with its vicarious salvation; the incarnation, with its low postulates of the relation between God and man, and the unworkable doctrines of two natures in one person . . . the official transmission of grace . . . the second coming . . . all are the growth of a mythical literature, or Messianic dreams, or Pharisaic theology, sacramental superstition, or popular apotheosis. And so nearly do these vain imaginations preoccupy the creeds that not a moral or spiritual element finds entrance there except the forgiveness of sins.

To consecrate and diffuse, under the name of 'Christianity,' a theory of the world's economy thus made up of illusions from obsolete stages of civilization, immense resources, material and moral, are expended, with effect no less deplorable in the province of religion than would be, in that of science, hierarchies and missions for propagating the Ptolemaic astronomy, and inculcating the rules of necromancy and exorcism. The spreading alienation of the intellectual classes of European society from Christendom, and the detention of the rest in their spiritual culture at a level not much above that of the Salvation Army, are social phenomena which ought to bring home a very solemn appeal to the consciences of ordinary churches.

The single 'moral or spiritual' element in Martineau's creed, the 'forgiveness of sins,' was but an attempt to keep the creed alive by the ancient Memphite lucubration, 'Life is given to him who does what is loved [by the gods], death is given to him who does what is hated.' His summary, intended to be a challenge to the dogmatic faith, proved to be its epitaph.

In endeavoring to salvage some residue of belief, Martineau sought the usual compromise: 'I rest with peace and hope: viz., that Christianity, understood as the personal religion of Jesus Christ, stands clear of all the perishable elements, and realizes the true relation between man and God. . . . Religion is the right attitude of the soul to the Infinite.' In the conflicting morality of the gospels a precedent could be established for any course of conduct not actually prohibited by Jewish-Roman law, and for many courses that were prohibited. That modern civilization should depend for its ethics on the 'personal religion' of a man who had lived in times of deepest superstition and ignorance, if indeed he had lived at all, and not one of whose 'personal' teachings could be authenticated in the maze of gospel fabrications, represented the abandonment of reason. It had been to Martineau himself that William Knight, twenty years before, had pointed to the fact that throughout the gospels Jesus talks as a God, and that if he were not such he was 'unveracious, egotistic, domineering, vain toward his contemporaries, arrogant towards posterity. He is now unworthy of the respect of Christendom, if he is not worthy of its devotion.' 'Religion is the right attitude of the soul to the Infinite' — the desperate, meaningless cry of a lost soul sinking into intellectual chaos. It was said facetiously of Spencer that he 'had a prodigious knowledge of the Unknowable,' but Spencer never proposed to construct a moral code upon it.

This countersense of 'abstract religion' upon which Martineau would have founded a new ethic had been tried long since by others. An essentially deskeletonized form of Christianity had arisen under the name of deism when, shortly after the Reformation, a few thinkers had rebelled against the multiplicity of sects which continuously fought with each other over fine points of dogma. The destruction of the Catholic faith had promoted the etherealization of the Christian deity, as the destruction of the Temple had etherealized Yahweh; the deists accepted that there was a God, that he was to be worshiped, and that worship consists of virtue and piety; they believed in sin and future rewards and punishments; but otherwise they rejected all Christian tenets pertaining to the supernatural, including the supernatural Christology. By slow degrees, marked chiefly by the abandonment of the theory of eternal punishment and of belief in the efficacy of prayer and ritual, deism moved toward the still more vague theism that accepted the existence of a God, but a God who was so remote as to be beyond human exploration, and who, having set the universe to spinning, had left it to run in a lawful manner and without his immediate attention or repeated interference.

As early as 1678, Cudworth, an English divine who would have built a fortress to protect Christianity against all dangerous theories, had argued the matter out in his *Intellectual System of the Universe*. Deity is either interested in the activity of the universe, or he is not; either he is immanent in nature and constantly engaged with its detailed sequences, or the process has been started and left to run in the wholly nonpersonal manner in which the planets wheel about the sun. To Cudworth it seemed that the notion of deity perpetually controlling nature in every detail and forever absorbed with its minutiae was not 'decorous,' as it 'would render divine Providence operose, solicitous and distractious.' He accordingly preferred the pagan view that deity had implanted in nature a nonpersonal power to run it without the aid of divine interference, a power that could commit 'errors and bungles' which Omnipotence would not permit.

Now, how much worse the problem when creation itself was continuous and involved an infinitude of 'divine natural selections' which, as judged by the standard of survival, led in the vast majority of the creative efforts only to failure. All fossil species and the lower animals, including the apes, were 'trial models' bespeaking in human terms very inept workmanship. For this and other reasons the theists elected the nonimmanent view, even though this demanded abandoning prayer and providence, since if deity is not present in nature and does not interfere in its operations prayer is useless and intervention impossible. The Reverend Ralph Cudworth himself had been charged with atheism because prayer to a nonpersonal mechanism was absurdity.

Some variety of theism had claimed many prominent men of the late eighteenth or early nineteenth century, among them, Erasmus Darwin and Robert Owen, the social reformer. In America, Franklin, Washington and Jefferson were all self-pronounced theists, and Madison, Wilson, and Monroe were probably not much more orthodox. Washington openly avoided church services and refused the Eucharist, while Jefferson made disbelief a fashionable heresy. Emerson abandoned the Unitarian pulpit in 1832 because he was deficient in the dogma of even that attenuated faith, and he dared tell a large audience in his essay on 'Self-Reliance' that 'As men's prayers are a disease of the will, so are their creeds a disease of the intellect.' If Voltaire could be classified, it would be among the theists, and his works were included, even if bound under false covers, in the library of most English clerics with literary tastes. The restoration of Catholicism among freethinking Frenchmen after the Revolution had in no small measure been a theistic compromise, rather than a victory of orthodoxy, and in both England and America the theistic trend had, in the first quarter of the century, sent increasing numbers into Unitarianism, the tenets of which were a compromise between liberal orthodoxy and theistic vagueness.

In the middle of the nineteenth century Auguste Comte, the author of positivism, would have abandoned all supernatural theology and in its place have erected a system in which humanity was conceived as a Great Being, a Superorganism or a Superpersonality to be worshiped with appropriate sacraments, prayers, and reverent signs, and even with the invocation of a New Trinity. The service was to be celebrated by the reading of texts from the French instead of the Hebrew prophets; in the church calendar the names of men who had made great contributions to human welfare were to take the places of many of the saints. The adoration of humanity evoked in Comte and his followers an emotional rapture not distantly removed from Christian ecstasy. On the warrant, perhaps justifiable, of history, philosophy and biology, positivism attributed to women a superior role in the new religion as mediators en rapport with the Great Being, giving them the veritable status of angelic beings, one of whom was assigned to every man as a moral guardian. 'This moral guardianship,' Comte wrote, 'may assume three types — the mother, the wife and daughter; each having several modifications, as shown in the concluding volume. Together they form the three modes of solidarity, or unity with contemporaries — obedience, union and protection — as well as the three degrees of continuity between ages, by uniting us with the past, the present and the future. In accordance with my theory of the brain, each corresponds with one of our three altruistic instincts — veneration, attachment and benevolence.'

Huxley called positivism 'Catholicism minus Christianity'; the positivists retorted that it was 'Catholicism *plus* Science.' The retort was unconvincing and the religion of Humanity drew few important followers. Theism failed because, when followed through by the rules of consistency, the road led to Spencer's Unknowable or to Martineau's Infinite — both, so far as theology was concerned, designating something without any ascertainable attributes and therefore nothing at all, a mere vacuum; or else it led back to the starting point, to the anthropomorphic god of Christianity, interfering constantly in the cosmic plan, creating and governing by a laborious trial and error method which, even if 'decorous,' was yet 'operose, solicitous and distractious.' Theism proved that man could not lose his god and keep him, too.

ii

In the broader view, the failure of theism, the most attenuated form and the last outpost of theology, revealed that man was presented with the choice of two disciplines to guide him: either he could live by faith that had its roots in intuitive impulse and vested tradition, or he could plan his life in accordance with objective evidence and verifiable experience. As against Paul's vision of the cross as a supernatural token of life's meaning, he must weigh the empirical, naturalistic code of the astronomers, geologists and biologists, abandoning entirely all transcendental speculation.

It had been argued that a religious impulse of some sort is universally present in man, and that it must therefore be accredited as possessing significance and validity. The argument was, however, a misstatement of fact. Primitive cultures are generally in error in their interpretation of the sequence of cause and effect in nature, attributing all manner of events to invisible beings simply through ignorance of the more reliable and confirmable sequences which impersonal naturalism has supplied. The errors of untutored man cannot be advanced as evidence of anything other than his ignorance. At a more sophisticated level, the majority of individuals assessed by history as having possessed outstanding intellects were either irreligious by the current code or were endeavoring to correct one or another error engendered by that code. Examination of any period of history reveals that universality of religious 'impulse' is as much a fiction as universality of a hypothetical 'impulse to heresy.'

It had been argued that reason and intellect are imperfect instruments for the discovery of truth. Earl Balfour, in his *Foundations of Belief* (1895), contended that other sources of belief, such as feeling, naïve conviction, impulse, intuition, must also be given weight. But Balfour's assumption reduced to the formula 'Your personal psychic craving shall be cosmic truth,' thus validating atheism and theism alike, as well as polytheism, animism, cannibalism and all other varieties of belief. Moreover Balfour assumed that the 'evidences' on which the naturalists based their conclusions were gained by the same intuitive process as afforded the religionist his convictions, ignoring the fact that the naturalists set as their first test the verifiability of their beliefs, intuitive and otherwise. Their conclusions were not 'founded on reason' (in the manner of medieval dialectic) but upon sequences and correspondences in nature; reason was for them only a method of utilizing the data which had been afforded by the senses through the systematic and unprejudiced examination of facts as they are, always supplemented by re-examination in order that errors arising from intuition or in other mental operations might be eliminated. The personal satisfaction afforded by a proposition was no evidence of its validity, nor was the intensity of feeling or conviction with which the proposition was personally held. Indeed, the naturalists held to no system of naturalism, but only to the belief that the empirical procedure of exploration and verification was the only known, reliable method of discovering truth. To form a belief concerning Earl Balfour, for example, by intuition must certainly lead to a different and less reliable opinion than to utilize the naturalists' critical and exploratory method.

It had been argued that fundamentally there was no true conflict between religion and the naturalistic code. The argument was true only in the sense of Gladstone's sardonic epigram: 'there are two sides to my house, and we will divide them: you shall take the outside.' Naturalism was not this or that special theory or petty principle; it was a belief in the uniformity of nature and in the unity of life as a part of nature — call it materialism, mechanism, atomism, physicalism, naturalism, or what one will. Clifford had defined the 'inside of the house' when he said 'The subject of science is the human universe; that is to say, everything that is, or has been, or may be related to man.' Tyndall, in his 'Belfast Address' two years later, put it more succinctly: 'We claim, and we shall wrest from theology, the entire domain of cosmological theory.' Naturalism and religion were in every sense utterly irreconcilable: all history testified that the house could not be divided except as in Gladstone's epigram.

It was argued that the immutable laws of nature demonstrated the existence of a truth that lay beyond nature's flux. But truth itself needed to be redefined. Locke in his *Essay on the Human Understanding* (1690), asked, What is truth? and dissecting his own innermost thoughts and convictions, turned reason upon itself. He concluded that there is nothing in the mind except what is first in the senses; at birth the mind is a clean sheet, and then sensory experience writes upon it a manifold record the retention of which begets memory, and memory begets ideas. Hence mind is but the product of the subtle play of senses, nerves and brain. We can, therefore, know nothing but matter, and nothing about God except as he manifests himself in matter.

To which Bishop Berkeley replied that if all knowledge is derived from sensation, a 'thing' is merely a bundle of sensory perceptions, a condition or activity of the mind. All 'matter' is therefore a mental image and the only reality is mind itself. We create the world by seeing it.

Hume in his *Treatise on Human Nature* (1739) rebutted Berkeley with the argument that we know mind itself only as we perceive our subjective ideas, memories, feelings: what we call mind is not an entity, but only an abstract name for the series of ideas, memories and feelings which, occurring in close temporal association, give a false appearance of continuity, or of existing in a continuum. As Aristotle denied the reality of Platonic universals in favor of particular objects, so Hume denied the reality of mind as existing apart from individual sensations.

When Kant read Hume's works he was shocked and, he said, roused from the 'dogmatic slumber' in which he had previously accepted without question both the 'truths' of religion and of natural philosophy. Kant had so suffered from theology in his youth that he avoided church all through his adult life, but he remained a nonsubscribing mystic of the Neoplatonic mold. In his *Critique of Pure Reason* (1781) he attempted to refute Hume's materialism by asserting that some knowledge, the really important kind of knowledge, comes to man independently of any sensory experience: it is inherent in the nature of the mind. The mind is neither a blank tablet upon which sensation and experience make their important marks, nor yet a mere name for a series of mental impressions, but an 'organ' that creatively molds the raw materials afforded by the senses into sequences of space and time, and into such categories as 'relatedness,' 'unity,' 'cause and effect,' and 'necessity.' The world as we know it is a construction to which the mind has contributed as much as the organs of sense, and we know nothing certain about the world since we perceive only the finished product which the mind supplies us. The moon is real, yes, and exists independently of our seeing it, but *for us* the moon is at best merely our idea. Man can not perceive reality, or ever know its nature, but only its appearances.

The 'invisible' objects of faith — the immortal soul, the benevolent creator — are sheer fabrications of the mind and hence beyond proof or understanding, and to argue whether they are true or not is meaningless. Heine compared Kant to Robespierre, who had killed the king and a few thousand Frenchmen, with this difference, that Kant had killed God and all men's hopes that rested on theology.

Those features, Kant argued, which the mind imposes on sensory data represent 'principles' or a priori 'truths' which we must recognize as existing independently of our perceiving them; they are 'categories' of knowledge which are absolute and indestructible. Such absolute categories, for example, are represented by mathematical statements. Three times three will always be nine, whether we see nine objects before us or not, and indeed whether we know how to multiply or not. This truth is independent of all experience. Perhaps we must discover it through experience, but having once discovered it we recognize that it existed before we had experience of it, and that it will never cease to be true.

As mathematics represents one type of a priori truth, so do certain moral laws. A man can tell a lie, but he cannot will that lying shall become a universal law of behavior, for if this came to pass there would be no promises the fulfillment of which was to be expected, and hence there could be no lie. Hence there exist both an a priori appreciation that a lie is 'wrong,' since it is a mode of action unacceptable as a universal law of action, and an a priori impulse to avoid lying. Thus moral, like mathematical, truths are innate; Kant called them absolute or categorical imperatives. And thus did Kant prove the freedom of the will, for how could we ever imagine that we can make a choice between lying and not lying, unless we are free to choose our course of action? And thus did he prove immortality, for in a world where the wicked are rewarded as frequently, and sometimes more frequently, than the good, why should we feel impelled to obey the moral law unless it is to profit in another world? And thus did he prove the existence of God, since immortality itself requires the existence of a Cause adequate to such a transcendant effect.

Kant's *Critique of Pure Reason* is historically important because it threw the philosophy of the nineteenth century into a state of temporary confusion. That it failed to prove its cardinal point, the existence of a priori truths, rapidly became clear. If there were no promises the fulfillment of which was to be expected, 'lying' would indeed be a universal law of action, and by Kant's own criterion lying would now be moral, and it would be truth that would be immoral.

Kant started from the postulate, as it were, of the absolute verity of certain types of knowledge, and to prove the postulate he argued the absolute verity of mathematics — without, however, consulting the mathematicians. Regardless of whether or not a man knows how to multiply, he can demonstrate that the 'absolute truth' that three times three equals nine is a tautology, simply a statement in keeping with the rules by which nine objects are originally counted up to nine. A man need but count out 'nine' objects and divide them into 'three' groups each containing the same 'number' of objects, and then name them over again, to discover that whether he counts all the objects seriatim or counts any one of the identical groups 'three' times, he will arrive at the same final word 'nine,' for no better reason than that he called the last in 'three' groups of 'three' objects each 'nine' in the initial process of counting. Nine is the formal (according-to-the-rules) product of the sequence of three objects counted three times, in exactly the same sense as 'toe' and 'go' are the formal products of the sequence that starts 'eeny, meeny, miny, moe.' No more does the statement three times three equals nine come from heaven than does the nursery rhyme.

It was after Kant's time that the formal nature of mathematics came to be fully realized. As late as 1870 Edward Everett could write: 'In the pure mathematics we contemplate absolute truths, which existed in the divine mind before the morning stars sang together, and which will continue to exist there, when the last of their radiant host shall have fallen from heaven.' This effulgent definition could, however, have come only from one who, like Kant, was not trained in mathematics, as other radiant conceptions of the mystical significance of numbers had been promulgated by persons who, however expert in other fields, knew so little of mathematics that they did not know how little they really knew.

In 1830 Peacock recognized that algebraic formulas are purely formal — empty of everything but the rules according to which they are combined. David Hilbert later defined all mathematics as a game played according to certain simple rules with meaningless marks on paper. In every game the first rule of all is that the 'rules' must be observed, otherwise there would be no game, and the second is that none of the rules shall present internal contradictions, otherwise the game will end either in nonsensical futility or in self-paralysis. In mathematics the most fundamental rules are the so-called axioms (*axioma,* a necessary or self-evident truth) or postulates (*postulatum,* a basis of argument); Euclid believed that his geometric axioms were indeed self-evident truths, but when mathematicians discovered that they were neither self-evident nor necessarily true, they more properly identified them as postulates, i.e., rules which for the sake of the game are to be accepted without argument. In the game of chess it is a postulate that a knight can move in only such-and-such a manner, and it would be a very theologically-minded chess player who would argue that this postulate was a God-created truth, innately given to the mind, or impressing itself as a categorical necessity upon the chess player.

Mathematicians soon convinced themselves that they could never know whether a particular set of postulates were even self-consistent and free of contradiction, much less whether any one postulate in the set were true. Between the time of Everett and the turn of the century, Peacock, Hilbert, Gregory, Hamilton, Pierre de Morgan and others reduced the absolutism of mathematics to *nihil;* over two hundred systems of algebra, in addition to 'common algebra,' had been produced out of an alleged 'theoretical total of 1152 systems' (the figure 1152 has, however, no mystical significance); Lobachewsky had shown the arbitrary nature of the Euclidian postulate regarding parallel lines, while Cayley, Klein and Riemann had enlarged geometry from three dimensions to *n* dimensions, where *n* is any whole, positive, finite number; and others had resolved the geometry of an *infinity* of dimensions, which subsequently proved to be extremely useful in the study of the structure of the atom. 'Mathematicians are like lovers,' said Fontenelle, 'grant a mathematician the least principle, and he will draw from this consequence another.'

At the end of the century Bertrand Russell could say, 'mathematics may be defined as the subject in which we never know what we are talking about, nor whether what we are saying is true,' which is only a sardonic way of saying that the mathematician's 'meaningless marks on paper' represent a game which has not and can never have any metaphysical significance, no matter how great its practical usefulness as a form of intellectual shorthand.

So much for the 'absolute truths, which existed in the divine mind before the morning stars sang together'—and so much for Kant's a priori truths of space, time, necessity and the like, under the guidance of which the mind operates upon and molds sensory data; and so much, too, for the innate moral sense, the categorical imperative, the proofs of immortality, and of God. Not one of Kant's proofs but could be shown to rest upon an unproved postulate, including his distinction between the thing-in-itself and our perception of it.

iii

After Locke, Hume and Kant, the theory of knowledge, or the relationship of the perceiving mind to the perceived cosmos, could never again be naïvely analytic. The mind *versus* body problem, as a problem, was well stated by the physicist, John Tyndall, who in his Belfast address (1874) constructed an imaginary conversation between Bishop Joseph Butler and a disciple of Lucretius, and put the following argument into the mouth of the prelate: '"Thus far our way is clear, but now comes my difficulty. Your atoms are individually without sensation, much more are they without intelligence. May I ask you, then, to try your hand upon this problem. Take your dead hydrogen atoms, your dead oxygen atoms, your dead carbon atoms, your dead nitrogen atoms, your dead phosphorus atoms, and all the other atoms, dead as grains of shot, of which the brain is formed. Imagine them separate and sensationless; observe them running together and forming all imaginable combinations. This, as a purely mechanical process, is *seeable* by the mind. But can you see, or dream, or in any way imagine, how out of that mechanical act, and from these individually dead atoms, sensation, thought, and emotion are to rise? Are you likely to extract Homer out of the rattling of dice, or the Differential Calculus out of the clash of billiard balls? . . . I can follow a particle of musk until it reaches the olfactory nerve; I can follow the waves of sound until their tremors reach the water of the labyrinth, and set the otoliths and Corti's fibres in motion; I can also visualise the waves of ether as they cross the eye and hit the retina. Nay, more, I am able to pursue to the central organ the motion thus imparted at the periphery, and to see in idea the very molecules of the brain thrown into tremors. My insight is not baffled by these physical processes. What baffles and bewilders me is the notion that from these physical tremors things so utterly incongruous with them as sensation, thought, and emotion can be derived."'

This direct approach to the heart of the problem did not, unfortunately, in Tyndall's time, characterize the general discussion on this problem. The incorruptible soul of theology had long given support to the belief in something which may be called mind, for practical purposes denoting consciousness or the capacity for consciousness, and conscious action was in turn deeply entangled in the theological doctrine of 'free will.' When Descartes first crudely formulated the interpretation, which from his time on came to be known as 'mechanism,' wherein causal sequences coupled by inevitability were taken to be the universal law throughout animate and inanimate nature, the force of theologic animus was such that he dared not apply the concept of determinism to the human intellect; he posited that thought is the essence of the soul and that the thinking substance is therefore wholly and generically different from that of the body; he coupled the immaterial soul to the body by means of the pineal gland, this organ having no other known function, and in this way made it possible for the soul to operate the body and to receive sensory impressions. Although Descartes was anathema to theology, his mechanistic conception of soul as something different from but functionally coupled with the body gave the theologians a vulgar victory and thenceforth all human behavior was attributed to a free will which not even the most liberal Christian would have attributed to a tiger or even to an amiable and intelligent chimpanzee.

The most astonishing logical paradox ever to be cherished by man is presented in the circumstance that the theologists, convinced that God in his omnipotence had predetermined the fate of every man, and in his omniscience had from the beginning of time foreseen that fate, should yet hold to the belief that he nevertheless holds every man responsible for his action, rewarding him either with eternal beatitude or eternal punishment. For theology the invention of free will to which culpability could be assigned only formalized the complete abandonment of reason in order to keep the system in operation.

To challenge 'free will' was to challenge the foundations not only of orthodox theology, but in large measure of all transcendentalism. If human decisions, however directly or deviously arrived at, were 'determined' solely by pre-existing knowledge, predilections, predispositions, emotions, memories, desires, by any or all of the multiplicity of mental images afforded to consciousness by the external and internal organs of sense, then it followed that an individual elects one course of action in preference to another, not by 'willful choice,' but simply because consciousness presents a balance positively weighted on the side of the selected action. Hence personal culpability would cease to exist, divine punishment and reward would be both monstrous and absurd, morality would be a convention, sin would be an arbitrary condemnation, the grace of the church would be superfluous and that institution could better devote itself to liberal education.

For the naturalists, free will was a countersense, a verbal contradiction. To 'will' is to choose a course of action in which more than one course is potentially presented, and to choose one course of action as opposed to another requires not only knowledge of alternatives, but reason for the choice. Decision (*de* + *caedere,* to cut off) without reference to cause or consequence of that which is rejected or accepted could only refer to an act occurring in a referential vacuum, and if such could be conceived it could only be designated as an action issuing from nothing at all, *ab nihilo,* from absolute ignorance. Since willing can never be free of knowledge of either cause or consequence, it can never be free at all. Spencer's definition of will as an abstract term indicating the sum of active impulses may be added to Hume's definition of mind as an abstract term indicating the series of ideas, memories and feelings which appear in consciousness, and both definitions merely supplement Locke's position, that we should not debate whether our 'will' is free but whether 'we' are free, since freedom is only the conscious recognition that in pursuing a certain course of action, we may, if we choose, elect a different one. This element of consciousness, the recognition of the power of election, is the capstone of the deterministic pattern of idea, memory and feeling which comprises mind. He who has realized it has touched the limits of his freedom.

When Huxley delivered his lecture 'On the Hypothesis that Animals Are Automata, and Its History,' at the Belfast meeting of the British Association in 1874, he rejected 'free will' as utterly senseless, but found himself reduced to the conclusion that consciousness is completely inefficacious as a determinant of willing, and hence of action. He likened consciousness to the whistle of a locomotive, the shriek of which is without influence on the machinery, or to the sound that a clock bell gives off when it is struck, which is without influence on the time-keeping mechanism. He stated that thought is similarly a byproduct of the brain and without influence on the brain's decisions. He turned for illustration to Cabanis, physician, psychologist and colleague of Laplace, misquoting this writer to the effect that the brain secretes thought as the liver secretes bile. Had he gone back and read Cabanis carefully, it is possible that he would not have come to this conclusion, for what that physician actually wrote was that 'impressions reaching the brain, set it into activity, as aliments reaching the stomach excite it to a more abundant secretion of gastric juice. . . . The function proper to the first is to perceive particular impressions, to attach to them signs, to combine different impressions, to separate them, to draw from them judgments and [new] determinations, as the function of the second is to act on nutritive substances.' Only after this definition does there come the disproportionally crude metaphor, 'The brain in a manner digests impressions and makes organically [dynamically?] the secretion [existence?] of thought.'

Cabanis's definition needs no qualification: to receive particular impressions from the senses, to attach to them signs of affective or other qualities, to combine impressions from different senses associated with a particular stimulus, to form judgments by integrating all the related records, past and present, and lastly to present in the finally integrated picture a 'determination,' either not to act, or to act in some now 'determined' manner, comprises an adequate definition of consciousness either as objectively studied or subjectively perceived; and thus defined, consciousness appears to be *the* determinant of behavior in the conscious animal. As the determinant of behavior it possesses supreme biological value, its superior acuity of focus and capacity for multiple integration in man distinguishing him from all other animals.

Huxley, in setting consciousness aside functionally as an 'epiphenomenon,' was moved to do so perhaps by the conflict between his warrantable conviction in the principle of causality and the, for him, inescapable implications of the term 'free will.' Tyndall sought another and, for its time, more satisfactory position. In the presidential address to the Mathematical and Physical section of the British Association, in 1868, an address entitled 'Scientific Materialism,' he had occasion to remark, 'I hardly imagine there exists a profound scientific thinker, who has reflected upon the subject, unwilling to admit the extreme probability of the hypothesis, that for every fact of consciousness, whether in the domain of sense, thought, or emotion, a definite molecular condition, of motion or structure, is set up in the brain; or who would be disposed even to deny that if the motion, or structure, be induced by internal causes instead of external, the effect on consciousness will be the same?' Consciousness and brain are linked together, but we do not know why. 'Were our minds and senses so expanded, strengthened and illuminated, as to enable us to see and feel the very molecules of the brain; were we capable of following all their motions, all their groupings, all their electric discharges, if such there be; and were we intimately acquainted with the corresponding states of thought and feeling, we should be as far as ever from the solution of the problem.'

Tyndall's difficulty, 'that from these [atomic] physical tremors things so utterly incongruous with them as sensation, thought, and emotion can be derived,' could not be resolved in terms of nineteenth century physics, physiology or philosophy. But Tyndall was not too satisfied with nineteenth century atoms and molecules. 'Those who framed these definitions of matter,' he remarked in his Belfast lecture, 'were but partial students. They were not biologists, but mathematicians, whose labours referred only to such accidents and properties of matter as could be expressed in their formulae. Their science was mechanical science, not the science of life. With matter in its wholeness they never dealt; and, denuded by their imperfect definitions, "the gentle mother of all" becomes the object of her children's dread. Let us reverently, but honestly, look the question in the face. Divorced from matter, where is life? Whatever our *faith* may say, our *knowledge* shows them to be indissolubly joined. . . . By a necessity engendered and justified by science I cross the boundary of the experimental evidence [this mode of procedure was not invented in Belfast, Tyndall notes parenthetically], and discern in that Matter which we, in our ignorance of its latent powers, and notwithstanding our professed reverence for its Creator, have hitherto covered with opprobrium, the promise and potency of all terrestrial Life.' And later, in replying to criticisms leveled against this lecture by Martineau, 'the Power whom Goethe does not dare to name, and whom Gassendi and Clerk Maxwell present to us under the guise of a "Manufacturer" of atoms, turns out annually, for England and Wales alone, a quarter of a million of new souls. Taken in connection with the dictum of Mr. Carlyle, that this annual increment to our population are "mostly fools," but little profit to the human heart seems derivable from this mode of regarding the Divine operations.' The alternative view is that the human egg, as 'matter,' when fertilized in the womb develops in nine months all the marvelous organs of the newborn child. 'Matter I define as that mysterious thing by which all this is accomplished. How it came to have this power is a question on which I never ventured an opinion. If, then Matter starts as "a beggar," it is in my view, because the Jacobs of theology have deprived it of its birthright. Mr. Martineau need fear no disenchantment. Theories of evolution go but a short way towards the explanation of this mystery; the ages, let us hope, will at length give us a Poet competent to deal with it aright. . . . I look, however, forward to the time when the strength, insight, and elevation which now visit us in mere hints and glimpses, during moments "of clearness and vigour," shall be the stable and permanent possession of purer and mightier minds than ours — purer and mightier, partly because of their deeper knowledge of matter and their more faithful conformity to its laws.'

'Definitions,' said Holyoake, 'grow as the horizon of experience expands. They are not inventions, but descriptions of the state of a question.' Consciousness or mind could be only roughly defined in the nineteenth century, but the state of the question had been succinctly pointed a hundred years before by Bishop Butler who, clearly seeing that the best arguments in favor of the immateriality of the mind applied with equal force to brutes and men, boldly embraced the whole animal world in his scheme of immortality. He would have nought to do with a theory of the human mind that could not encompass all other sentient creatures.

Had Platonic idealism not been negated by innumerable other considerations, it would be rendered untenable by this principle of panpsychology. In its fundamental meaning, reality (*res,* thing) consists of the truth of what we perceive, whether we be apes or men. No two men's realities are necessarily identical, yet they may be equally (if not absolutely) true. The 'reality' was 'true' before Galileo's time that the full moon was a silver disklike light in the dark blue sky; the 'reality' was equally 'true' through Galileo's telescope that the moon was a great spherical body shining by reflected light, marked by vast mountains and possessing a dark hemisphere which men had never seen; and the 'reality' was 'true' for the astronomers who followed Galileo that the moon was a cold, spherical satellite of earth, like earth composed of atomic rocks and minerals, and, in Laplace's terms, a product of cosmic evolution. Yet it has never been true for any generation of men that the moon is made of green cheese. In assessing the nature of the moon the standard of truth is verifiability in terms of total experience: truth is opinion demonstrated by test to correspond with nature. The disklike light, the dark and spherical body, the cold, atomistic satellite, are all equally true because they are all consonant with total available experience. Everything is at least what it is given in experience, though of course it may be, and probably generally is, much more than it is empirically found to be. To quote Clifford again, truth is 'not that which we can ideally contemplate without error, but that which we may act upon without fear.'

In his search for truth, for *realia,* man had come to accept some certitudes: that the moon moves around the earth, that the earth moves around the sun, and that all three bodies are of great antiquity; that Eve was not created from Adam's rib; that Hebrew was not the language of the first man and woman; that Noah did not take a pair of every kind of animal into the ark with him; that fossil fishes were not deposited on the mountains by the Flood; that there are people living at the antipodes walking heels over head, and that they have never heard Christ's message; that lightning is neither the wrath of God nor Satan's thunderbolt — and there are many others.

The truth-of-correspondence code prided itself, not on making errors, but on the tentative nature of its conclusions, knowing that first conclusions are more apt than not to be in error, and confident that what is tentative and approximate today will be less tentative and less approximate tomorrow.

This truth had no all-containing gospel. There was infinitely less of it available than remained to be discovered. It had no infallible oracles, no hierophants pledged to guard it, no irrefragable canons. It was nonsectarian and was 'approximated to even on the side which it declaims as error — that from men committed to grave error come truthful contributions.' It recognized but one authority — in the words of Robertson, who was paraphrasing countless philosophers who through centuries had striven to increase its measure — it was 'the code of minds which realize that truth is the outcome of the general deed of man, and not the discovery of any gifted egoist who comes blowing his voluntary smoke-wreaths and pretending to decide things out of his private dream.'

iv

In the catastrophe that had come upon him, man sought to retain some certitude that could give point to life and lift it out of a meaningless round of pain and pleasure. Like the lowliest creature he could strive to feed himself and to postpone death, but with a misery which the other creatures could not share with him, for he is the only one that can himself see the miserable creature that he is. It was Balfour, who held intuition on a parity with verifiable knowledge, who penned the epitome that man is but 'a race with a conscience enough to know that it is vile, and intelligence enough to know that it is insignificant.'

Convinced of this personal insignificance, and having fed himself and momentarily avoided death, he still asked of his universe its meaning, for it was not enough to carry through from Nowhere to Nowhere solely in Thoreau's mood of quiet desperation. He had been told by the philosophers that his search for Meaning was but looking into the Meaningless for a reflection of his own purposes and ends, that 'meaning' in the cosmic sense was meaningless, since the cosmos was not a man. But this was only true of ultimates: time and space might be infinite and incomprehensible, but the finite that lay wedged within infinity could be assumed to be comprehensible, and in part it had been rendered intelligible. It would have to be enough to search in life its finite pattern, to the farthermost discoverable certitudes.

Those certitudes which the Victorians esteemed were usually spelled with capital letters, implying that they stemmed from the Infinite and possessed metaphysical verity and eternal durability. Man has esteemed many certitudes that have come and gone: moralist and intuitionalist, special creationist and evolutionist, he has ever chased these transcendent butterflies only to discover as soon as they were captured and examined that the thing of beauty and a joy forever was in fact a thing of earth and corruptible, as are all things of earth. The Platonic Universals, the Judaic Law, the Incarnation, Resurrection and Atonement, Grace, Sin and Redemption, the medieval Crystal Spheres and Heaven and Hell, the original Perfection of Creation — all once were certitudes, and all had lost their capital letters. Revelation and Inspiration had suffered this fate when they were shown to be dogmatic errors, and so had Faith when its intuitional foundations were uncovered and seen to be unreliable and treacherous, letting men down into the quicksands of error. Mathematical Truth, once conceived to be so absolute as to be the very substance of the gods, had proved to be a verbal game and its verities had been reduced to formalism and arbitrary rules, and Mind, no matter what beggar it might be, could no longer masquerade under false pretenses.

So, too, was the certitude of Natural Law to be brought to earth. It was possibly Thucydides who first spoke of the 'law of nature' as a divine edict written into the heart of things. The usage became prominent with the Stoics and was passed by the Romans to the church Fathers as one of the multiple associations of the Logos. Augustine regarded natural laws as modes of divine action which were abandoned only under exceptional circumstances to permit the operation of miracles. Descartes had been the first to argue against the miraculous exception and to insist upon the immutability of nature, for which he was damned as a 'mechanist,' or as one who regarded the universe not as the plaything of a Higher Power but as something to be interpreted solely in terms of law and order. As Galileo's law of the pendulum brought motion 'down to earth,' so Kepler's laws of planetary movement restrained the stars to foreordained and everlasting pathways. Newton proposed that all the phenomena of nature should be reduced to mathematical laws — 'Nature and nature's laws lay hid in night: God said "Let Newton be!" and all was light' — piously conceiving these laws not so much as the vocalized edicts of the God who was defined by the Thirty Nine Articles of the Established Church but as the very essence of God — 'By existing always and everywhere God constitutes duration and space. . . . In him are all things contained and moved' — and as principles existing wholly apart from the bodies which are being moved, even as Copernicus had conceived weight to be 'a certain natural appetite with which the Divine Architect of the Universe has endowed pieces of matter, so that they unite in the form of a globe.' Spinoza would have done for the soul what Descartes would have done for the body, and Newton for the solar system, make of it a self-operative and self-sufficient entity. Law as representing the regularities of nature, or the presumed necessity linking cause and effect, had become the stable cement of the cosmos, if not its very substance.

Hume's skepticism did not stop with wiping mind out of existence, but went on to annihilate this divine legalism written into the heart of things. He argued that man does not perceive either causes or laws, as such, but only sequences of events from which he infers causation and necessity; the laws which he formulates to describe these apparently necessary sequences are but a form of mental shorthand, abstractions convenient to the description of phenomena which usually or by custom occur in the same sequence. Hume, and after him, Mach, emphasized that the concepts of physical 'forces' and of cause and effect are animalistic, containing an unwarranted implication of muscular power, desire, will, impulse, or the like, operating to achieve a wished-for end. The century that followed Hume and Kant saw natural law resolved into two distinct elements: the observed regularities of nature, on the one hand, and, on the other, the formal, more or less mathematical statements used to describe these regularities. It is a regularity of nature that when released from the tree an apple falls to the ground; it is a formal or arbitrary statement that there exists an 'attraction' between the apple and the earth that varies inversely as the square of the distance between them. The part about an 'attraction' was no 'law' at all, however useful, but a mathematical-literary device which post-Newtonian physics partially, and later physics entirely abandoned as no longer corresponding to the behavior of the apple and the earth. Neither was the falling of the apple a law in the sense of an absolute and utterly dependable sequence, but only an event of high probability, the possible exception to which reason could not certainly deny. Paradoxically, Kant, who thought he saw divine imperatives in mathematical and moral 'laws,' recognized that 'so far as cause and effect have any possible interpretation in terms of experience, they mean regular, constant sequence of events in time, and nothing more,' thus affirming Hume's conclusion that all we can discover is the existence of highly repetitive sequences, and never any 'power' or 'operative necessity' behind them.

In discovering the 'laws' of the cosmos, Galileo, Kepler and Newton were only discovering sequences of high probability: the identification of these sequences as absolute, and the equating of them with the divine will, was the substitution of a logical error for the personal dictum of Yahweh-God. In Nietzsche's words, the 'laws of nature are the remains of mythological dreaming.'

Huxley clearly saw that natural law is but a conceptual shorthand, valuable for its usefulness and not its metaphysical validity. He himself said that 'most truths begin as heresies and end as superstitions.' Yet he could argue that there are elements of beauty in art, in music, in poetry, which approximate to the Kantian absolutes, that 'so long as the aesthetic faculties exist in man, so long will the principles of aesthetics be as 'immutable, as those of morals. And it is as fortunate for mankind in matters of aesthetics, as in those of ethics, that they allow themselves to be governed by the minority.' Before the century was out many found an adequate refutation of this conviction in their relief that the immutable principles of aesthetics of Huxley's time, whether in the realm of poetry, music or art, proved to be more mutable than he averred.

With respect to the practice of the moral certitudes, Huxley's century was surprisingly naïve. It had once been in conformity with the highest moral code of Christian Europe that devout citizens should delight in burning witches twenty at a time, that the Inquisition should use the most terrible forms of torture man could invent to extract confessions of allegiance with Satan, and that the church should force the pagans into its fold by threatening to put them to the sword. The Book of Deuteronomy contained a moral code as alien to Christian Europe as the medieval European code was alien to the nineteenth century. Yet that century could look back upon the animosities of the Reformation, the austerities and the cruelties of the Puritans, the persecution of the Puritans by the Anglicans, without seeing that moral certitudes are relative to time and place. In fact, it seemed to be believed by the Victorians that previous patterns of conduct had universally been immoral, that a sound moral code had only come into existence when a man could be sentenced to six years in prison for publishing Thomas Paine's *Age of Reason;* when the theft of a loaf of bread by a hungry boy could be rated as a crime punishable by long imprisonment, the theft of a thousand men's rights by a prominent member of the Established Church as something of a social grace; when the best method of educating boys was rigorous physical punishment, and when girls did not need, and indeed could not use, any formal education. According to this morality a woman who exposed any part of her body on a bathing beach could be condemned as a social outcast, and until 1857, divorce could not be obtained except by a special act of Parliament and at the cost of hundreds of pounds; after that date when the power was transferred to a lay court, judicial separation could be obtained only when adultery was proved, so that feigned adultery became an established part of the British moral code.

Methods of punishment, being expressions of considered opinion, may be used as indexes of current moral values. Although England banned torture as a means of obtaining confession in suspected witchcraft, methods of punishment long remained deliberately cruel. In the fifteenth century pressing to death with every aggravation of agony was adopted as suitable to criminal cases where the accused refused to plead. Out of a sense of decency, so it was said, women were burned alive instead of hanged. Male traitors were first hanged by the neck and cut down before life was extinct, their entrails cut out and burned before their faces, after which they were beheaded and quartered and the quarters 'set up' in diverse places. Until 1870, forfeiture of property with consequent impoverishment of the innocent wife and children was prescribed for suicides.

At the end of the thirteenth century English law recognized only seven crimes meriting capital punishment: treason, homicide, arson, rape, robbery, burglary and grand larceny. Yet by the nineteenth century the number of capital offenses had grown to nearly two hundred, and included pocket picking, stealing of livestock, forgery, letter stealing, sacrilege and sodomy. It was not until 1836 that the list of capital crimes was reduced again to the original seven of the thirteenth century, and not until seven decades later that it was reduced to four: high treason, murder, piracy with violence, and destruction of dockyards, though in point of fact since 1838 the death penalty has been exacted under the ordinary law only for murder. As this is written, the death penalty has been removed for murder. Admittedly there was a marked discrepancy between law and practice in the early decades of the nineteenth century, yet hangings were an almost daily occurrence for crimes which a little later came to be regarded as venial. The gallows or tree with its corpse as a silent lesson to potential evildoers constituted an ornament of the landscape on the outskirts of almost every good-sized town, and Samuel Johnson in the eighteenth century was moved to remark, as his coach traveled through the dusk and he discerned the familiar gallows, "Thank God, we are coming to civilization."

Huxley was being astonishingly naïve, even for his century, when he soberly argued that immorality invariably finds its own reward in nature by virtue of the fact that trespass inevitably leads to biological punishment: the evidences were plain that 'the fittest' which survive in the struggle for existence might be, and often were, ethically the worst. It was the theologic taint of his childhood that led him to avow, in a reply to Earl Balfour, 'it is not to be doubted that so long as human nature and conditions of human life remain the same, so long will the rules of conduct remain the same. If mankind are "immutable and eternal" and live under immutable conditions, then assuredly the moral law is "immutable and eternal." ' It is not because of any change in mankind, or because of significant changes in the conditions under which he lives, that the rules of conduct have changed since Huxley's time, but rather in no small measure in consequence of the ideas propounded by Huxley himself.

When Tylor wrote his *Primitive Culture* (1874) and Lecky his *History of European Morals* (1869), it had become clear that the first, and perhaps the last, task of the moralist is to discover what man does, and why. To argue otherwise is to assert that beauty can be separated from the beautiful, terror from the terrifying, that 'drunkenness can be distilled from whiskey and bottled in a separate flask.' The metaphysical alchemists had failed utterly to achieve the sublimation of virtue from the dross of life. For Socrates, knowledge alone could be the source of a coherent system of virtue, but since by knowledge he necessarily meant knowledge of the good, and the good is virtue, his definition, and the search for virtue based upon it, got exactly nowhere except to approve those virtues which Socrates already esteemed. Plato's view of virtue was mystically complex and shifting, but by the time he wrote the *Republic* the body had come, in Epictetus's words, to be a 'corpse which the soul sustains,' and life a 'sojourn in a strange land,' virtue being an approximate harmony between the soul and the absolutes of prudence, courage, temperance and justice. And so, approximately, with Zeno and the Stoics. Aristotle hesitated to attribute moral excellence to the deity; his god, like Spencer's, was so unknowable that all he would say of him was that he was the Great Mover, and in accordance with his teleology of ultimate ends toward which all things are moved he conceived that virtue is the fulfillment of man's nature as directed toward his ultimate end of well-being, but the Aristotelian virtues were but *via media* between the extremes of opposing vices, and only marked the moral excellencies of his age.

The argument of hedonism, that self-interest is the ultimate appeal in virtue, began with Aristippus, Chrysippus, and more notably with Epicurus, who conceived 'that pleasure is the sole ultimate good, pain the sole ultimate evil: virtue is that which in the ultimate increases pleasure or diminishes pain.'

Christian asceticism and Neoplatonic mysticism cast the word hedonism and the name of Epicurus into temporary disrepute. For Plotinus and those who followed him matter was the 'first evil,' and body the 'second evil'; the only 'good' was pure soul, cut free from both. While for Plato the real as a universal was knowable, and thought could therefore ascend from the errors of the unreal to the truths of universals, for Plotinus even thought suffered earthly imperfection and the highest mode of human existence, true virtue, was attained only when all thought was obliterated and all consciousness of self lost utterly in ecstasy. Obviously no system of morals that had relation to the world could be based on Neoplatonism, and with this philosophy at its core Christianity was forced to begin again with the proscriptions of Yahweh as revealed to Moses and the prophets, plus the morality of the Graeco-Roman age, Aquinas compounding these with Aristotelian philosophy into an elaborately argued system of supernal moral platitudes.

Even before natural philosophy reawakened under Galileo and Copernicus, jurists were searching their consciences for the meaning of right and wrong. Out of discussions by Gentiles (1552–1608) and Grotius (1583–1645) of the common law, the 'law of nature' in the juridical sense had come to be seen as that part of the divine law which issues from the essential nature of man, who is distinguished from animals by an appetite for tranquil association with his fellows and by his tendency to act on universal principles. But men did break the law — or else there would be no jurists — so there remained the problem of why they are naturally lawful or unlawful. It was in part in his attempt to answer this basic question that Hobbes in his *Leviathan* (1651) framed the future problems for English ethicists. Primarily materialistic in his philosophy, and influenced by the psychological writings of Gassendi, Hobbes returned to the Epicurean position and posited that all human impulses are self-regarding, with this important qualification: that the individual tends to be moral only because of his association with his fellows, and hence individual morality cannot be expected or secured apart from society and government. The presocial state is therefore immoral, a wretched state of war, from which self-love impels a man to seek the peace and order of a moral social structure.

Locke, in his *Essay on the Human Understanding* (1690) had held with Hobbes to the egoistic basis of rational moral conduct, but returned the *vis a tergo* to the individual and denied the importance of society as a necessary impulsion to moral conduct. Before he was a philosopher, Locke was a Puritan. Shaftesbury added to human understanding, human emotion as part of the moral dynamic, a formula which might have impelled jurists to become psychologists and ultimately psychiatrists had not the affections been so conventionalized in Shaftesbury's time that all the basic motives appeared to be self-evident. For this reason, too, the formula seemed to the astute Bishop Butler to lead, quite contrary to patent fact, only to unregulated egoism without an authoritative conscience: the Bishop argued that conscience and self-interest must comprise a co-operative and yet antithetic dualism, the components constantly tugging at each other. Self-interest he could find in Epicurean terms, but for conscience he had perforce to turn to metaphysics. It was not until a later day that T. H. Green wrote, 'No man can make a conscience for himself; he needs society to make it for him.'

And yet the unanswered questions, What is right? and Why? remained to be buffeted between transcendental legalism, intuitionalism and theories of social compact. Social compact won a notable victory when Jeremy Bentham (1748–1832), sometimes called the father of English law, more generally the father of utilitarianism, set himself the task of revising the principles of legislation free from class prejudice or logical fallacy. Abandoning both metaphysical and historical approach, in his *Introduction to the Principles of Morals and Legislation* (1789) he sought a foundation in the formulas (adumbrated before him by Priestly, Beccari, Hume and Adam Smith): 'the greatest happiness for the greatest number,' and 'nobody is to count for more than one.' Bentham remained a hedonist: 'the only interests which a man is at all times sure to find adequate motives for consulting are his own.' 'I am a selfish man, as selfish as any man can be. But in me, somehow or other, selfishness has taken the shape of benevolence.' Moral judgments are really the common judgments of any society as to its common interests; whatever agreement there may be is simply a result of the fact that people are mentally and physically similar, and have experienced a common cultural development.

Bentham's formulas would not work for Spencer, who considered it to be 'the business of the moral sciences to deduce from the laws of life and the conditions of existence what kinds of action necessarily tend to produce happiness, and what kinds unhappiness.' Nor was Bentham's hedonistic calculus so simple: the greatest happiness for the greatest number is meaningless since men are not unanimous in their standard of happiness, nor should everybody count for one, nobody for more than one, else the useless, the indolent and the criminal would rate equally with the useful, the industrious and virtuous. Moralists sent Spencer to the foot of the metaphysics class because in his *Principles of Ethics* he did not produce a 'Natural System of Morals,' but only a monumental work with many internal contradictions: it was, however, inevitable that the integration of matter from incoherent homogeneity to coherent heterogeneity should yield moral homogeneity only in the individual as such.

At the end of the nineteenth century Havelock Ellis could write, 'No man has counted the books that have been written about morals . . . yet it can scarcely be that on any subject are the books that have been written more unprofitable, one might even say unnecessary.' But even as Ellis was undertaking the empiric description of human sex behavior, the T. H. Green Moral Philosophy Prize, awarded by the University of Oxford on a competitive basis for an essay dealing with the 'Reciprocal Relations between Ethics and Metaphysics,' and named in honor of Professor Green who had long devoted himself to this area, was granted to A. E. Taylor, Assistant Lecturer in Greek and Philosophy at Owens College, Manchester, for a dissertation entitled 'The Problem of Conduct' (1899, pub. 1901), which in its opening chapters effectively refuted Green's defense of such a relation by showing that the synthesis presented a false problem. In the discussion of morals, Taylor argued, all a priori speculation about the ultimate constitution of the universe must be set aside as utterly futile; the analyst must begin with the empirically observed facts of human behavior, and from these facts proceed inductively to metaphysics ('if such there be'), for the meaning of morality is to be found in the individual and not in the Absolute.

As for hedonism, another false problem was posed by the assumption, at least implicitly contained in the historic argument, that egoism and altruism are inalterable congenital human attributes; rather they represent a polarity in personality developed out of what Taylor called the 'simple fundamental undifferentiated and impersonal effect of approval' (or more simply, the impulse to seek satisfaction): 'It is not *pleasure,* but *satisfaction,* by which the "worth" of a thing is measured,' Taylor wrote. We accept one form of life and reject another 'because the one form of life gives us what we want, and the other does not. What we want is a state of permanent content, of progressive and lasting satisfaction for all our cravings, or, if that is impossible, at least for those which are most insistent and least to be stilled.

'Altruism and egoism are divergent developments from [this] common psychological root of primitive external sentiment. Both developments are alike unavoidable, and each is ultimately irreconcilable with the other. Neither egoism nor altruism can be made the sole basis of moral theory without mutilation of the facts, nor can any higher category be discovered by the aid of which their rival claims may be finally adjusted.'

Progress in morals is an illusion, there is no goal to which moral development inevitably tends; indeed, there is 'a hidden root of insincerity and hypocrisy beneath all morality,' for goodness and badness and all other moral states are in fact states of conflict between opposing impulses.

'Nothing is ever perfect except the universe as it is . . . except our lives, with all their mistakes and failures . . . as functions of the perfect universe already perfect.' Perfection is the here and now . . . our lives to do with what we will.

'The first law of moral action is, Know what you really want, and the second, like unto it, See that you are not mislead into accepting a spurious substitute. . . . Only before you embark on the profession of a harlot, it is your duty to find out all you can about the life to which you are committing yourself, and to make sure that a career of prostitution ending in a Lock Hospital will really give you what you want. If you decide that it will . . . you are morally on the same level as the missionary who chooses to end a career of self-devotion by dying alone and untended in a leper-settlement; that the world in general does not recognise the resemblance is only another proof of the world's ample stupidity.'

When Law and Morality were gone, there still was Love. This familiar virtue was thundered or purred from every pulpit on every Sunday. It was the theme of poetry, music, drama, fiction and philosophy; history presented it in heroic measures, youth looked up to it with awe, adolescence anticipated it as the fulfillment of being, while maturity and old age, who had experienced it, even if slightly disillusioned, looked back upon it as the ambiguous but indubitable justification for life.

The Old Testament was strangely silent on this subject. Except for the Song of Solomon, a sensual love lyric modeled on ancient Egyptian poetry, romantic love was passed over either because it was unknown to the priestly scribes or because it was not deemed worthy of comment in dignified historic and religious documents. Only Jeremiah had the audacity to impute love to Yahweh: 'The Lord hath appeared of old unto me, saying, Yea, I have loved thee with an everlasting love: therefore with loving kindness have I drawn thee.' Desensualized by an asceticism that condemned all things pertaining to the flesh, ever expecting Judgment Day, and discovering in the crucifixion of the Christ the final and all-real value, the early Christians saw in sexual love only an antithesis of virtue, and Augustine turned this fear and disapproval, however tentative it may have been for the church generally, into dogmatic and irrevocable condemnation. At the same time he accepted the early Christian sublimation by which Paul and the authors of the gospels conceived the Passion to memorialize the love of God for Jesus, and of Jesus for those for whom he came to prepare the way. Throughout the gospels and epistles there runs the theme that the godhead is somehow embued with a personal and yet wholly depersonalized affection, until the author of the mystic Gospel of John avows concisely and finally: 'God is love,' an equation which was accepted by all Christian theologists.

It was Dante who, in something more than rhetorical phrase, applied love as astronomical energy: men were to find their *Paradiso* by letting their desire and will be turned, he said, 'Even as a wheel that equally is moved, By the Love that moves the sun and other stars.'

Every poet of the nineteenth century sang of love in terms scarcely less inclusive than those of Scott: 'Love rules the court, the camp, the grove, and men below, and saints above; For love is heaven, and heaven is love.' It was conceived not so much that love is a virtue as that virtue *is* love, the ultimate goal of the spiritual life that aims at a universal good. The fourth gospel's phrase was interpreted as meaning not only that God creates, sustains and orders all things in love, but that love is his very essence. Here was the basic postulate on the acceptance or rejection of which must turn all Christian ethics and all hope.

In view of the preponderance of evil in the world many Christians had encountered difficulty, after abandoning belief in the devil, in accepting the identification of love with the godhead, but the identification escaped serious challenge so long as the affair of Adam and the apple, and the Augustinian apology of original sin, sufficed to protect God from the charge of malicious cruelty. Now the growing suspicion that the writers of the gospels might be charged with something less than perfect knowledge as to the nature of God, as in respect to demonology, miracles and other matters no longer endowed with dogmatic irrefragability, was indeed an indication for pessimism. For it could readily be demonstrated that love was not so pure and absolute as Christian idealism had posited. Anthropologists were perceiving that among primitive peoples even the human impulse is weak; jealousy is frequently absent, sentiment is frequently looked upon as shameful weakness, and more often than not marriage is based on economic or other impersonal considerations. Many primitive languages do not even contain a word for the affection. The phlegmatic Chinese look upon sexual passion in a relatively unemotional manner and esteem as their supreme value, filial respect. In senses other than the instinctive care of children and an exalted consciousness of property rights in respect to wife and children, love might be said to be a relatively recent and an Occidental invention. Only the Egyptians among ancient peoples extolled love in their literature. Egyptian women appear to have been legally and socially on a parity with men; in sexual relations they were as independent as their brothers, and they were free to woo and to marry the men of their choice. Egyptian manuscripts sing of love in a manner that would have roused envy in a modern poet. Along the Nile love was a value subordinate perhaps only to *maat* or justice, but the Goddess Maat had no amorous competitor in the pantheon, and the love literature of the Egyptians does not suggest that the emotion was ever important in those adumbrations concerning the afterlife with which Nilotic dwellers were typically absorbed.

Ishtar, Astarte, Aphrodite and Venus were primarily goddesses of fecundity and gratification, and only in a secondary aspect did they function as a nexus of the more complex emotion. In the early days of Greece women had apparently enjoyed great freedom and public esteem, but in the historic period their lot was low and marriage was prompted entirely by motives of convenience. Possibly there was little exaggeration in the statement, ascribed to Demosthenes, that 'while we keep a mistress to gratify our pleasure and a concubine to minister to our daily needs, we marry a wife to raise legitimate issue and to have our property carefully preserved.' Zeus did not know love in the romantic, but only in the vulgar sense, and the most notable form of love in Greece, and the one to which the term 'value' could very appropriately be applied, was pederasty, the love of boys, which so permeated the post-Homeric culture that it has come to be called 'Greek love.' It has been suggested that this mode of love passion arose in a primitive period when continuous military service produced a scarcity of women, but whether this explanation is true or not, it survived to compete strongly with heterosexual affection. It seems to have been the custom for every Spartan youth of good character to have his lover, or 'inspirator,' and for every well-educated man to be the lover of some carefully chosen youth. The older man served as a model for the younger, and in battle they stood near to one another, ostensibly faithful until death. In the historic period the custom was wide-spread, and Plato condemned the practice because it turned men from marriage and the begetting of children — if they did marry, Plato said, it was only in obedience to the law.

It has been emphasized that one factor promoting pederasty in Greece was the wide cultural gulf between men and women; the wife lived in retirement and ignorance, almost in seclusion, deprived of all the educat-ing influence of male society and excluded from those public spectacles which were the chief means of culture. Hence the intellectual Greeks regarded love of women as the offspring of the vulgar Aphrodite; inspired by the heavenly Aphrodite and craving intellectual companionship, they 'loved neither women nor boys but intelligent beings whose reason was beginning to blossom much about the time at which their beards began to grow.' The rule seems to have been that when decorum was observed no inquiries were made into the relationship. The attachment was re-garded not only as permissible but was praised as the highest and purest form of love, as a path leading to virtue, as a weapon against tyranny, as a safeguard of civic liberty, and as a source of national greatness and glory.

Horror of homosexual practices was passed from Judaism to Chris-tianity, the Fathers considering such persons not as sinful but as mon-strous. Pagan legislators had been more or less indifferent to the custom, but under Christianity a succession of laws was passed in Rome which culminated in punishment by burning alive. 'A sentence of death and infamy,' said Gibbon, 'was often founded on the slight and suspicious evidence of a child or servant . . . and pederasty became the crime of those to whom no crime could be imputed.' Throughout the Middle Ages Christian lawmakers thought that nothing but a painful death in the flames could atone for the act. The English law, which treated the crime as one not fit to be named, called for capital punishment until 1861, although in practice the extreme penalty was not inflicted. Persons were, however, burned in France for the crime in the latter part of the eight-eenth century. These extreme laws were ultimately repealed, on the grounds that when unconnected with violence, when there is no outrage of public decency and when both parties are above the age of consent, its influence on society is merely indirect like that of drunkenness and free love, and though it is a disgusting vice, its proper punishment is contempt. Such is the fate of Greek love, the highest virtue as virtues were valued by this ancient and intelligent people.

The romantic love story, charged with pathos and sentiment, appears to have emanated from the East by way of Alexandria; although developed in the later Grecian period, it reached its flower in Latin poetry where it acquired the standard accoutrements of the personal beauty of the lovers, the timely interposition of the love god, the misfortunes that obstruct fulfillment of their wishes, the pangs of thwarted love, and the importance attached to the heroine's preservation of her virgin purity through all her trials. Rome had no goddess of love, despite the fact that the Romans conceived a deity for every practical occasion, until the Greek Aphrodite came to her as Venus, about 300 B.C. It is to be inferred that here, too, marriage was a matter of convenience and that sexual relations remained unadorned by romance.

Christianity put its seal upon monogamy, first because monogamy was the only recognized form of marriage in the societies in which it arose, and second, because it was the only form of marriage tolerable to a philosophy which regarded every gratification of sensual impulse with suspicion, and incontinence as the gravest sin. Chrysostom pronounced woman to be 'a necessary evil, a natural temptation, a desirable calamity, a domestic peril, a deadly fascination, and a painted ill.' Augustine's base opinion of her has already been noted. Ecclesiastic literature from the third century onward is filled with the enormities of the sex, and men who seriously held this estimate could only look upon the 'phenomena of love' as Satanic machinations.

Paul had avowed that 'it is better to marry than to burn,' but Tertullian, commenting on the words of the apostle, noted that what is better is not necessarily good; it is better to lose one eye than two, but neither is good; so also, though it is better to marry than to burn, it is far better neither to marry nor to burn. It was on this principle that the early church approved chaste unions between virgins and young men, and that there developed in the Middle Ages the chivalric system of romantic love. For a medieval knight the chief object of life was love, but the passion was ostensibly hopeless and free of any physical gratification; it was expected that the knight should be abstinent and chaste, he should love only the virtues, talents and graces of his lady, happy in 'a chaste union of two hearts by virtue wrought.' He who did not understand how to win a lady was but half a man — such was the ideal, exceeding as an ethical value even the ascetic misery of the self-tortured monks. But most historians agree that chivalry was a reign of almost universal license, and that the difference between a lover and a seducer was difficult to demonstrate.

With the resurgence of romanticism in the Renaissance, and in the wake of socio-political revolutions that in some measure relieved 'purity,' 'chivalric honor,' 'noble birth,' 'righteousness,' 'asceticism,' 'self-sacrifice,' and other once estimable values from their high estate, natural impulse began to reassert itself; passionate love budded and flowered, and poets and philosophers found in it, with Dante, the *vis a tergo* of the universe. In the nineteenth century the common view held that it was by virtue of love that man transcended his animal estate. In the last decade a romantically inclined rhapsode could claim that 'Love is not a late arrival, an after-thought, with Creation. It is not a pious word of religion. Its roots began to grow with the first cell of life that budded on this earth.' It is 'the supreme factor in the evolution of the world.'

'Round the physical feeling forming the nucleus of the whole, are gathered the feelings produced by personal beauty, that constituting simple attachment, those of reverence, of love of approbation, of self-esteem, of property, of love of freedom, of sympathy. These, all greatly exalted, and severally tending to reflect their excitements on one another unite to form the mental state we call love.' This Spencerian definition, with its 'excitements' and 'mental state' for transcendentalism to stumble over, was not wholly necessary to the skeptic who abruptly challenged the Johannine definition: 'That God is love is a very lofty, poetical and gratifying conception, but it is open to one fatal objection — it is not true.' Havelock Ellis's *Studies in the Psychology of Sex* (1901) (the second edition of which was printed in Philadelphia because the first edition had been legally condemned in London) came as a gruesome and shocking revelation to those who, under ancient Christian prejudices and the more recent Puritanical horrification, had learned to look upon sex as an embarrassing and rather base necessity for the reproduction of the species. The Platonic scission which had divided Aphrodite into two parts and had relegated sex as subordinate to, if not wholly independent of, the true passion, was now healed; Aphrodite was one entity — sex — and romantic love was but one of her conditional mental states. The universe was as indifferent to the turbulent emotion as to the union of its meanest pair of creatures, and men who had been accustomed to a sense of guilt if they failed to kneel in prayer before getting into bed were now confused in their efforts not to behave like sanctimonious bores after they got there. Even as love ceased to be a sin, it ceased also to be a supreme experience and end.

Revelation, Inspiration, Faith, Truth, Law, Morality, Love — these metaphysical certitudes had all proved to be creatures of earth and subject to earthly corruption. But perhaps if there were no immediately apprehended certitudes it was not because they were nonexistent, but rather because they remained to be discovered. It was implicit in evolution that man could not start his career fully comprehending those ultimate truths and values of existence which he sought so persistently, almost instinctively; but moving from barbarism through his present state of half-barbaric crudity he might be progressing toward his goal by trial and error, by repeated partial approximations. Progress and evolution, said Spencer, are synonymous.

The idea of progress came into existence a little too late to be generally capitalized on by the Victorians, but it only missed hypostasis by a narrow margin in Spencer's philosophy, as in Tennyson's poetry, both of which foresaw '. . . one far-off divine event, To which the whole creation moves.' If not a Value, it was at least a certitude that possessed the inestimably valuable advantage of keeping man integral with the New God.

Progress, as a metaphysical inevitability, was essentially a modern discovery. The Greeks' sense of the continuity of history and of the possibility of changes for the better, as exemplified in their appreciation of their own cultural debt to Egypt and in the transitions that had marked the growth of philosophy from the time of the Ionians on, failed to engender the concept of mankind improving even deviously by the elucidation of new or the application of old truths. The Greeks held rather to a theory of decadence, mankind being descended from the gods: the Golden Age had belonged to the past, and had given way to the Silver Age, and that to the Age of Brass. However, the Greek tragedians could celebrate the triumphs of man over nature, and over his baser self, and the Roman Lucretius first used the word in its modern sense: 'Ships and agriculture, fortifications and laws, arms, roads, clothing and all else of this kind, life's prizes, also its luxuries from first to last, poetry and pictures, the shaping of statues by the artist, all these were taught by practice and the experiments of the active mind as men progressed gradually step by step.'

Plato's philosophy might have fostered a metaphysical concept of progress, at least in the sense of the gradual apprehension, partial or complete, of universals that would be an aid to right living and happiness, but with many other ancients he conceived the world to be subject to cycles of generation and degeneration, each cycle extending over a period of 36,000 solar years, and requiring continually the rediscovery of the arts and sciences. Platonism at least conceived a limited temporal advance, but on this Neoplatonism firmly shut the door: where to abandon the self to intuitive rapture is to perceive the Absolute and exist as a part of, or within, perfection itself, the way to perfection is open here and now merely by contemplation of the Infinite, and any search for truth among mundane and material relations, past, present or future, is not only futile but retrograde. Neoplatonism was not only wholly antipathetic to the idea of progress, but its doctrine of supersensual reality contributed substantially to the decline of Hellenism in the later Roman Empire, and to the replacement of intellectuality by the crudest superstition. In Harnack's words, '. . . the ancient world must necessarily have degenerated into barbarism of its own accord, because of its renunciation of this world. There was no longer any desire either to enjoy it, to master it, or to know it as it really is. A new world had been disclosed for which everything in this world was to be given up, and men were ready to sacrifice insight and understanding, in order to possess that other world with certainty. In the light which radiated from the world to come, that which in this world appeared absurd became wisdom, and wisdom became folly.' Neoplatonism became the philosophy of Christianity, and Christianity became Scholasticism with little change in Harnack's terms: reason and inquiry remained in contempt and the highest goal of living was one of spiritual rapture, or at second best a pattern of conduct copied from the apostolic age.

Nor was the Reformation productive of any change: Luther condemned reason as a pretty harlot who only blinds to those truths, final and perfect, which God has revealed in the sacred books; while under the doctrine of original sin, Calvin conceived man as so innately evil and corrupt that he was incapable of significantly bettering himself. In widespread practice, Protestantism as much as Catholicism condemned man to the *status quo*.

It was Francis Bacon who first put, not so much into clear words as into a startlingly clear example, the concept of progress as it was to dominate the seventeenth, eighteenth and nineteenth centuries. In his unfinished last work, *The New Atlantis* (1627), the crew of a ship lost at sea came upon a previously unknown and unbelievably fair land where there lived a people in supreme happiness. Their secret proved to be that in their government there were no politicians, but only architects, astronomers, geologists, biologists, physicians, chemists, economists, sociologists, psychologists and philosophers. Indeed there was little government at all, for these savants were wholly engaged in controlling nature, rather than in ruling man: 'The End of Our Foundation is the Knowledge of Causes and secret motions of things; and the enlargement of the bounds of human empire, to the effecting of all things possible.' Even if only in a fictional

Utopia, here was progress clearly conceptualized: 'the enlargement of the bounds of human empire, to the effecting of all things possible.'

In the Renaissance, discussions on progress were largely confined to a debate as to the merits of the ancient as compared with contemporary civilization, the notion in its first venture having to disprove the beliefs that the culture, art and poetry of the past had been perfect, and that history had been largely retrograde. Then Vico in his *Principles of a New Science* (1725) presented history as a varied spectacle in which knowledge, through 'speech and writing, is conveyed to successive generations so that mankind as a whole can be conceived to exhibit infancy and growth. It was the popularization of such ideas by Voltaire and others that lit the democratic powder of the French Revolution, when men dreamed of a millennium wherein liberty, equality and fraternity would be achieved under the auspices of a secular Goddess of Reason. In the delirium of the Terror the Goddess was herself almost beheaded, but belief in progress to be attained by the self-determination of mankind survived. Indeed, the most enthusiastic statement yet to appear came from Condorcet, in his *Outline of and Historical Picture of the Progress of the Human Mind* (1795), written shortly before his death and while this distinguished mathematician and friend of the Republic was hiding in an effort to save his own neck from the guillotine. Here he set forth the conviction that 'nature has assigned no limit to the perfecting of the human faculties, that the perfectibility of man is truly indefinite; that the progress of this perfectibility, henceforth independent of any power that might wish to arrest it, has no other limit than the duration of the globe on which nature has placed us.' Progress as a natural possibility was axiomatic in Malthus's *Essay on the Principle of Population* (1803), which proposed: '1. To investigate the causes that have hitherto impeded the progress of mankind toward happiness; and 2. To examine the probability of the total or partial removal of these causes in the future.'

When Spencer, in his *Progress, Its Law and Cause* (1857), applied the idea of change and development to stars and nebulae and earth, he gave it, seemingly, metaphysical significance: evolution *was* progress, and since evolution operated through Natural Law, itself equivalent to the Will of God, it followed that progress was God's irresistible intention in the universe. 'Progress is not an accident but a necessity. What we call evil and immorality must disappear. It is certain that man must become perfect.' 'The ultimate development of the ideal man is certain — as certain as any conclusion in which we place the most implicit faith; for instance, that all men will die.'

The glowing optimism of Spencer's philosophy, which momentarily obscured the bald facts of evolution, may be attributed to the fact that, in the last analysis, his philosophy was that of the armchair and fireplace. Spencer and Tennyson had much in common, including the self-confidence of the expanding Empire. Darwin's position, however, can only be attributed to a complete inability, in the storm engendered by his vision of evolution, to let go the spar of teleology. In controversion of the fact, duly recorded by him in 1844, that there is 'no power tending constantly to exalt species,' and of his vision as revealed to Hooker three years before the *Origin* was published: 'What a book a devil's chaplain might write on the clumsy, wasteful, blundering, low and horribly cruel works of nature,' in the end he presented his work to the world under a pious apology of progress: '. . . the inhabitants of the world at each successive period in its history have beaten their predecessors in the race for life, and are, in so far, higher in the scale.' 'And as natural selection works solely by and for the good of each being, all corporeal and mental endowments will tend to progress towards perfection. . . . Thus, from the war of nature, from famine and death, the most exalted object which we are capable of conceiving, namely, the production of the higher animals, directly follows.' 'There is grandeur in this view of life, with its several powers, having been originally breathed by the Creator into a few forms or into one; and that, whilst this planet has gone cycling on according to the fixed law of gravity, from so simple a beginning endless forms most beautiful and most wonderful have been, and are being, evolved.'

This vision of the cosmos on the part of the man whose genius it was to comprehend and assemble the definitive proofs of evolution, comprises a series of confused metaphors. Spencer, holding to inviolable natural law and an unknowable deity, could with pardonable inconsistency speak of geology as 'that grand epic written by the finger of God upon the strata of the Earth,' because his evolution was rooted as much in romanticism as in facts, and he lacked almost entirely the inductive discipline which was the foundation and strongest warrant for Darwin's hypothesis. And a few years later when, by his own logic, he had been firmly driven into the position that God is *absolutely* Unknowable, he vehemently satirized theists who talked of 'The Great Artificer,' 'The Master Builder,' and 'the hand of the Almighty.' Darwin was no philosopher, but he was in a better position than any other men to see that his panegyric was an unwarranted figure of speech.

Huxley attempted to established the more realistic view that 'so far from gradual progress forming any necessary part of the Darwinian creed, it appears to us that [this creed] is perfectly consistent with indefinite persistence in one state, or with a gradual retrogression.' As time went on Huxley came to see the completely amoral character of the cosmic process, and to view it as something akin to evil, at least in its complete indifference to hope and charity, to happiness and pain. Nature 'red in tooth and claw' had no morals and no interest in morals, which existed in man's man-made world. Man was a glorious rebel endeavoring to oppose the cosmic process by superimposing upon it artificial ethical restraints. For Huxley, progress was this conflict between the ethical nature of man and the unethical nature of the cosmos: 'social progress means a checking of the cosmic process at every step and the substitution for it of another, which may be called the ethical process; the end of which is not the survival of those who happen to be the fittest, in respect of the whole of the conditions which obtain, but of those who are ethically the best.'

Huxley exposed himself to criticism by the use of the word 'another,' which implies that his ethical process is other than and outside the cosmic process, whereas every process, ethical or otherwise, can be only a local mode of the cosmic process, even though in consequence of Spencer's 'heterogeneity' of things it can be set in opposition to the whole, as overproduction of eggs opposes the wholesale destruction of the young, as mother love opposes infant helplessness, as individual reproduction opposes aging and death, as vital integration and repair oppose the continuous and inevitable disintegration. But this is a far cry from Spencerian cosmic progress, and even from the inevitable perfectibility of man. Ethics is merely a facet of the 'species problem' and of interest only to *Homo sapiens*. The theologians were never more right than when they asserted that under the principle of evolution there would be no justification for ethics, meaning their nineteenth century middle-class English ethics as opposed to other possible codes: so far as the cosmic process was concerned the Khond or Aztec code was as justified in nature as the English code, the only standard of reference for any code being its practical utility for those who use it. Even nature, Mill pointed out, murders every man once.

To the cosmic process, the term progress was not applicable at all. Creation's purposive design, in Darwin's terms, was 'natural selection,' in Wallace's, 'the continual adjustment of the organic to the inorganic world,' in Spencer's, the 'survival of the fittest,' — no one of these definitions permitted the slightest teleology in evolution, or justified the poet laureate's far-off divine event. Natural theology, had it survived, might have multiplied its examples of how the evidences of nature prove the beneficence of

God a thousandfold: in muscle, blood, bones, teeth, glands, nerves, brain, until the beneficence of God as exemplified in the anatomy of the hand would have appeared an ill-considered crudity. By its dynamic of struggle to avoid death and its evolution along a multiplicity of roads life had diversified itself in countless ways, until exquisite adaptation — 'purposive design' in theology's terms — was evident in a million species of surviving animals and plants — the number of species that had become extinct in bygone ages ran to untold millions — and so ingenious was this adaptation that one half of these creatures were parasites feeding upon the other half.

'There is grandeur in this view' — that living organisms warred perpetually to satisfy an appetite, and died only to make way for others to war a little differently, and perhaps a little more successfully. That the sun of heaven shone to sustain a continuing holocaust where love was primarily an impulse to copulation and a fuel to unselfishness only through an impermanent cultural pattern, where the most elaborate instinct was blind egocentric mechanism, where mercy, tolerance and charity but variants of behavior bearing an egotistically pleasing hue. That at every moment unnumbered living creatures subsisted by devouring other living creatures, the whole of animate creation a pyramid of murderers feeding upon the murdered — 'teeth and talons whetted for slaughter, hooks and suckers moulded for torment — everywhere a reign of terror, hunger and sickness, with oozing blood and quivering limbs, with gasping breath and eyes of innocence that dimly close in deaths of brutal torture' — until the most clever creature of all, 'who fats all other creatures to fat himself,' could sit down three times a day to his foul repast and pride himself upon being the highest animal, the Lord of Creation, the Very Ultimate Goal of a cosmic process that had required untold billions of years and the whole of the astronomical universe to achieve this magnificent result. Darwin can be forgiven his phrase because it expressed, not an assessment of the universe, but the inexpressible joy which the explorers of that universe feel when they penetrate one of its mysteries and discover one of its truths. The evolution that Darwin discovered was process, not progress.

If man, who shaded by degrees back into ape, into mute and insentient beast, wanted to call himself a 'higher' animal, rather than just a more clever one, there was no other species vocal enough to gainsay his choice of adjective or his conceit. Endless forms most beautiful and wonderful have been evolved, but beauty and wonder are too much in the eye of the beholder to afford reliable standards of cosmic progress, and, taken in such vein, man might better consider his existence modestly, or else report it as a tale told by an idiot.

Man might read as progress his remarkable capacity for controlling the rest of nature and for setting all manner of things into whirling, confusing motions, but he had failed as yet to invent a mechanical device that would manufacture happiness, or that would instill meaning into life. To live longer by the planned avoidance of death, more easily and comfortably by the aid of labor-saving devices, more confusedly by the multiplication of distractions, afforded no answer to the question, Why live at all? Without that answer, to harness the forces of the sun and stars might prove to be an empty victory. Dürer painted the Spirit of the human race as Melancholia sitting mournfully among her inventions. Progress, the last of the transcendental values upon which man had leaned, had turned out to be an arrow pointed at both ends.

Nor was it possible any longer to turn away from life and seek solace in the Orphic mystery of divine survival. The valiant effort that Thomas Aquinas had made to certify by reason the existence of the immortal soul had added up after six centuries to exactly nought. It was evident even to those who thought superficially, that on this point Darwin's *Origin of Species* was going to tax the dialectic of the theologians as it has never been taxed before. The most self-confident of these knowers of the unknown saw the implications of evolution better than did Charles Kingsley, who was so confused about the biological process that he could write the reactionary Maurice: 'If you won't believe my great new doctrine (which by the way is as old as the Greeks) that souls secrete their bodies, as snails do shells, you will remain in outer darkness. . . . I know an ape's brain and throat are almost exactly like a man's — and what does that prove? That the ape is a fool and a muff, who has tools very nearly as good as a man's, and yet can't use them, while man can do the most wonderful things with tools very little better than an ape's.' What Kingsley overlooked was that Darwin had no need of the hypothesis, more appropriate to *Water Babies,* that souls secrete their bodies. Certainly the metaphysicians were not disposed to use it, despite its not too remote resemblance to Thomist philosophy, and consequently they were faced with the alternatives of either attributing a soul to the higher apes, or debating at what level between *Pithecus* and *Homo* the primate stem had first become inhabited by this superphysical entozoon. The abundant and specific evidences of the mental sciences and the general evidences of biology were scarcely needed as a supplement of animal consanguinity to discredit a postulate so irrational and barbaric that men could no longer cherish it whole-heartedly in their adult years. The embarrassed church, having abandoned, however unofficially, the ancient belief in the literal resurrection of the body, and eschewing the table-tipping chicaneries and tele-graphic and telepathic nonsense of spiritualism, could answer queries about man's immortal soul only with ambiguous phrases and evasive shoulder-shrugging. The utility of the ancient and arrogant tenet that personality, spun of flesh and the multiple contingencies of culture and experience, was worthy in whole or in any part of perpetuation throughout an infinity of time was worn so thin as to be disdained by a considerable proportion of people, especially among the intellectually eminent. Except within the church whose vested property rights, professional dignity and historic rea-son for existence could only be maintained so long as the postulate was seriously defended. Outside the church it is a fair estimate that toward the end of the Victorian era half of all educated persons, and two thirds of the more eminent, had abandoned the belief, and this without any signs of the catastrophe that had been predicted by Emerson when he wrote:

'No sooner do we try to get rid of the idea of Immortality — than Pes-simism raises its head . . . Human griefs seem little worth assuaging; human happiness too paltry (at the best) to be worth increasing. The whole moral world is reduced to a point. Good and evil, right and wrong, become infinitesimal, ephemeral dualities. The affections die away — die of their own conscious feebleness and uselessness. A moral paralysis creeps over us.' This is the cry of a man whose transcendental philosophy of good and evil, of right and wrong, of the objectives of human happiness and its affections, had been mortally wounded, and who had nothing to take its place. Scarcely more cogent was *In Memoriam* in which the heart of young Tennyson cries out against death on the grounds that love is most godlike in man's nature and has the final authority. Even as the hiero-glyphs of Sakkara failed to dispel death by repeatedly denying it, so one cannot predicate the nature of the cosmos on the intensity of pain.

On the affective level there were other voices. George Eliot's lines:

> O, may I join the choir invisible
> Of those immortal dead who live again
> In minds made better by their presence: live
> In pulses stirred to generosity,
> In deeds of daring rectitude, in scorn
> For miserable aims that end with self,
> In thoughts sublime that pierce the night like stars,
> And with their mild persistence urge man's search
> To vaster issues

failed by the poetic conceit that any and every man might join 'the im-mortal dead who live again in minds made better by their presence.' It is not given with reasonable certainty to any man, and to the vast majority of men not even by hope, to anticipate immortality in this vicarious and impersonal manner, nor, except to poets, is there much appeal in an immortality that consists merely of belonging to the public domain.

Yet another poet saw things another way when Swinburne wrote:

> From too much love of living,
>   From hope and fear set free,
> We thank with brief thanksgiving
>   Whatever gods may be
>
> That no life lives forever;
>   That dead men rise up never;
> That even the weariest river
>   Winds somewhere safe to sea.
>
> Then stars nor sun shall waken,
>   Nor any change of light;
> Nor sound of waters shaken,
>   Nor any sound or sight;
>
> Nor wintry leaves nor vernal,
>   Nor days nor things diurnal;
> Only the sleep eternal
>   In an eternal night.

Only Buddhism among the world's great religio-philosophic systems has abhorred the notion of eternal existance and wooed personal annihilation; and only the fact that the occidental vision of immortality could be tolerated without any honest attempt to look it squarely in the face, with no questions asked about details, preserved the egocentric and immature impulsion that built the pyramids and sarcophagi of Egypt. When, against the strictures of the theologians, men acquired the intellectual freedom to look the doctrine in the face they found it puerile, and in greater or lesser degree they relinquished it, only to discover that neither morality nor values nor happiness nor a worth-while life in the broadest sense was in any way tied to it. The doctrine of immortality needed no world revolution, no marshaling of vast evidences from science and philosophy to undo it; when its utility had been worn thin by the rubbing of everyday life, for most persons the residuum of ill-considered, faintly held faith just went away. There remained only a ghostly essence of the ghost idea within dogmatic cloisters, and in the minds of the wishfully unthinking, or the childishly egocentric, forcing men who stood at the boundary between the old and the new to face resolutely towards the past, to refuse to face the future. For such men, Emerson's Pessimism was the only answer.

Man did not have forever to harness the forces of the sun and stars. The sun was an elderly light, long past the turbulent heat of youth, and would someday join the senile class of once-luminiferous bodies. In some incredibly remote time a chance collision might blow it up again into incandescent gas and start a new local cosmic cycle, but of man there would be no trace. In Balfour's terms, he 'will go down into the pit, and all his thoughts will perish. The uneasy consciousness, which in this obscure corner has for a brief space broken the contented silence of the universe, will be at rest. Matter will know itself no longer. "Imperishable monuments" and "immortal deeds," death itself, and love stronger than death, will be as though they had never been. Nor will anything that *is* be better or be worse for all that labour, genius, devotion and suffering of man have striven through countless generations to effect.'

And so it well might be. . . . Darwin's century was a tragic one for that proud creature who had thought himself specially beloved by the gods, who had imagined that he enjoyed the whispered confidence of deity. In the saddest moment of his life, after the death of his son, Huxley, replying to a letter of condolence from Kingsley, had put his hope and courage in the words '. . . follow humbly and to whatever abyss Nature leads, or you shall learn nothing.' Huxley, like Darwin, still saw nature as somehow essentially good, even as God of old had been good, and he did not fully foresee the consequences of his advice. . . . Revelation and Inspiration were gone. Faith had proved deceptive and even Truth had belied its apotheosis, since Law could be defined only as a statistic of probability. The only truths which man could trust were those of correspondence discoverable by the mind, and these must be held constantly subject to revision. Whilst mind itself was not dissociable from the matter that gave it birth. Morality was a fashion, Love had turned out to be a conditioned impulse, and Progress was an arrow that pointed in whatever direction one might look. The only certitude was that man was an animal struggling to live in a world from which had faded the last faint ray of transcendental light. . . . Huxley could not see how deep and dark was the abyss to which nature led, but those who followed his advice could see that that abyss was but a slight declevity separating them from a firmer, and possibly a far better land.

EPILOGUE

EPILOGUE

Epilogue

AS a fallen angel, man would be ludicrous. As an intelligent animal, he has reason to be proud because he is the first who can ask himself, 'Whither, Why, and Whence?' and confident because he can know himself as a creature of earth who has risen by his own efforts from a low estate. If he would rise higher he must be true to earth, he must accept that he is its creature, unplanned, unprotected and unfavored, co-natural with all other living creatures and with the air and water and sunlight and black soil from which their dynamic pattern has been fabricated by impersonal and indifferent forces. In every wish, thought and action he is seeking to escape the same protoplasmic disquietude that impels the meanest flesh crawling beneath his feet. He must find his values and his ends entirely within this frame of reference.

As an intelligent creature he explores his world, and here is the first value that is uniquely his: he is more intelligent than any other creature, and from intelligence fired by curiosity comes knowledge, and from knowledge come power and the manifold satisfactions by which he surpasses all his fellow creatures. The sequence has led him to abandon the forest and the cave for purposes and plans. But the need for knowledge has burdened him with the ethic of truth: to lie willingly to himself or others, to adhere to that which is suspect, however tentatively he holds to truth, is to forfeit his opportunity and jeopardize his dreams. This is the essence of all philosophy: to cherish truth for its uniquely human value, to search for it, to test and retest it by conscious effort, to communicate it, to be guided by it, to base upon it all purposes and plans.

But he who has purposes and plans must make a choice, no other can make it for him. A proper view of man finds no place for a priori 'should' or 'ought' or any categorical imperative, but only for this: that if a man so acts, that is *his* action, and his alone. This is the essence of all morality:

a man is responsible for the consequences of whatever choice he makes. The degree to which he recognizes this and acts accordingly is a measure of his biological maturity.

Man is an animal for whom life is more than an experience to be passively endured. Below his bare perception he feels the resonances of the affections, joy, love, wonder, fear, anger, sorrow, which color every wish and vision until he can scarcely think but his thought is reinforced by feeling. His history is unimaginable except as impelled by emotional reverberations, and that is one reason why he has become man, the creator of a world that is uniquely human and shot through and through with uniquely human values. That is why he creates beauty to express the inexpressible, to sing his joy, to ease his pain, to mitigate his loneliness: a black statue of a mighty king, a polychrome frieze of wild ducks feeding among the rushes, a marble temple, a pigment transposed to canvas, a string to give off rhythmic melodies, beauty that is personal in creation and possession, beauty that is a measure of his own disquietude. If revealing his melancholy vision that tragedy is truer to life than other moods, it also reveals that life is many moods.

To neglect the creative dynamic of the emotions is to neglect the essence of human nature. Fear, anger and exhilaration move man as they move the denizens of forest, sky and stream, but the emotion that is uniquely his, is pride: he will risk his life in combat rather than suffer loss of his self-esteem; and honor, jealousy and indignation contribute to the determination of his rights and duties, and elicit courtesy and consideration for the pride and privileges of others. He who is sensitive to shame will not be insensitive to the judgment of his fellows, careless of decorum, unappreciative of convention. He who through imagination can suffer another's pleasures and pains — his fear, anger, pride and even his prejudices and hatreds — will build a family, tribe and nation, and fabricate a moral code.

The remark that no individual can make a conscience for himself, that he needs a society to make it for him, is true only in part — true, because man is a social creature and a creature of tradition; his self-judgment is not of himself alone but importantly concerned with himself as identified with his fellows; but false, in that society is but an aggregate in which the individual remains an independent organism enjoying a private life of sensory and affective experiences, hopes and despairs and exultations, and for whom public life is an additional and contingent experience. Man is individualized to a greater degree than any other creature. Apart from the simple calculation that from twenty-four chromosomes in the paternal and maternal germ cells, the total number of different combinations of chromosomes in the potential offspring of one man and one woman is nearly three hundred thousand billions — one hundred and fifty thousand times the population of the earth — the possibility for infinite diversification through the family and through personal experience warrants the conclusion that no two men are ever exactly alike, and most of them are very different. Consequently no one individual carries all possible potentialities or knows all the answers, and it is to man's collective advantage, both biologically and sociologically, to foster this diversity. Whence comes the ethic of the individual: the individual's integrity, dignity and potentiality issue from the most basic biological mandate and comprise the basis from which all strictures of existence relative to morals, society, economics, law and government must be derived.

To analogize between the human organism, the individual, the highest court of appeal in all human affairs, and the aggregate of individuals that comprises society is to fall into a grave biological error. No value, right or virtue can be discovered in any pattern of living that does not stem from the individuals concerned. The argument that some essential superiority is inherent in the 'state' is both biologically indefensible and dangerous because it runs counter to the indefeasible autonomy of the individual. Individual men must dictate their Bill of Rights, and not 'society.' But appended to the Bill of Rights is an unwritten Bill of Duties: sharing the benefits of collective effort in no measure abrogates man's individual responsibility. What man does, he does as an individual, what he would do, men as individuals must do. Nor can he expect others to do for him what he is not prepared to do for others.

All human history reveals that transcendental metaphysics is not only futile but dangerous. Those who have foisted, frequently by not too honest means, their unsupported speculations upon the naïve and gullible as truth have served to retard man's self-realization more than any other misfortune that has ever befallen him. History also reveals that man does not need any brand of transcendental metaphysics — his lasting contentments and achievements he has found wholly within the frame of reference that takes things as they are in the here and now. No pattern of living is written in the stars: each may be tried and esteemed according to the individual. No principle of justice is foreordained: justice must be realized between individuals as a reasoned compromise. No value can be capitalized; all values are fluxions in vital dynamics. No supernal power can aid him: he must find within himself the creative vision, the courage and the will for his fulfillment.

Unhappiness, whether avoidable or not, too frequently comes in large pieces. But happiness is generally as fine-grained as life itself, and so intimately intermixed with living that it can be extracted from breathing, eating, sleeping, waking, from the humblest labor, from all achievement and creation and understanding, and few men need fail to accumulate a goodly store of it, all men can accumulate a larger store. Man does not need a machine to manufacture happiness, or an oracle to tell him where to find it, it is a by-product of life needing only to be separated from a dross of want and pain. When the scales weigh down beneath the latter, his self-reliance will not fail him, he will fall back on that most elemental of animal virtues — courage. A man can lose his god but he cannot lose himself.

His fate was not decreed in the temple of Osiris, or written on the tablets of Marduk, or settled by Olympian conclave or predestined by a righteous Yahweh — he has always had it clutched in his own hands, he need but open his fingers to read his lifeline, he need but close them resolutely upon the task in order to turn his dreams into reality. Then he will pronounce life good and cease to worry about that which at present lies beyond his ken, nor look back at the phantasmagoria that mark the past.

It is up to him. He alone by his own efforts can enlarge the bounds of empire, to the effecting of all things possible, to remolding this sorry scheme of things nearer to the heart's desire. He alone can see himself and his world in width and depth. He alone can choose, out of his vision of the present and the past, his future course.

THE STORY OF THIS BOOK

The Story of This Book

WHEN Little, Brown and Company brought the circulation of this manuscript to a happy end, it had been declined by several publishers, three firms having rejected it twice. It is thus that I have come to know certain publishers well enough to reveal a few intimate matters that have been involved in its publication and that may be of interest to the reader.

Let me begin by saying that editorial readers have been unanimous in thinking that, as a publishing venture, the original manuscript of this book was too long, and overwritten in certain areas. On request I twice tried to reduce it to 'reasonable proportions,' which accounts for two of the double rejections. The third double rejection meant less effort to me: the manuscript was returned in 24 hours by a reader who apparently judged it by weight; the editor asked to have it back again, only to affirm, after reading it *in extenso,* the quicker method.

Friends advised me that I should utilize the services of an agent, that an agent could do things with publishers that an author could not. However, I have never had an agent. I was too naïve when I wrote *Kamongo* (1932), my first nontechnical work, to use an agent, and I mailed the manuscript personally to Mr. Alfred A. Knopf, who personally declined it because, he said, he was afraid that it would fall between two stools, being neither science nor fiction. I remailed it to the Viking Press, and when they accepted it I naturally thought that relatively young firm was undoubtedly the most liberal and forward-looking publishing house in the country. Nor did I have any reason to change this opinion when *Kamongo* was knighted by the Book-of-the-Month Club, republished in England, translated into the Scandinavian, recorded among the 'Records for the Blind,' and sainted by Alexander Woollcott by inclusion in his first *Reader;* or when, finally, and to me, most surprisingly, it was chosen in World War II for the Pocket Overseas Editions for the Armed Forces. Here *Kamongo* might have come to rest but for the fact that sixteen years after it had been published, eighteen years after it had been written, the Natural History Book Club made it one of their monthly selections. Republication meant resetting the book because it had long been out of print and the plates had contributed their share to winning World War II during the metal shortage of 1943–1944. If *Kamongo* was to receive the distinction of being disinterred from the out-of-print category in order to be republished as a book club selection, I was determined to have the unique opportunity of rewriting it. Few books have been rewritten after eighteen years, and few authors have had the opportunity to correct their early efforts in the light of later literary perspective. Mr. Best, of Viking Press, at first balked on the grounds that the book had to go to the printer at once, but he finally granted me the entire week end for revision. Accordingly, between a Friday evening and Monday morning I made what seemed to me to be desirable changes: chiefly, in the latter part of the book I stopped Joel from talking so much and gave the Padre more to say, corrections which in my opinion make the revised edition better than the first. I made a number of outright deletions, however, showing that reduction is sometimes spontaneous. And *Kamongo* in the original was a very short book.

The existence of a manuscript becomes known by word of mouth: publishers with whom I was unacquainted wrote to say that they had heard that I had a nontechnical work in preparation and if it was not obligated they would be happy to have an opportunity to read it. In view of the fact that the examination of a manuscript entails some cost for either intra- or extramural readers, these unsolicited inquiries encouraged me to believe that sometime it would find a publisher who wanted a long book. Consequently it seemed to me only a matter of slight additional expense when, at their invitation, I shipped the bulky package to Little, Brown and Company.

Inevitably, Little, Brown found it overwritten in places and, in all, too long for a reasonable publishing adventure. By my count it then contained 250,000 words, having been reduced at the suggestion of other publishers from some 275,000. I said firmly that I had hacked at it until it was showing obvious signs of mutilation and I refused to touch it again until the publisher signed on the dotted line. The contract being duly signed, I agreed to cut the book by 25,000 words while making some slight additions which Little, Brown's readers thought would improve it. This I did, but the additions amounted to more than the 25,000 words I deleted so that in the end, Little, Brown were forced to cut the manuscript themselves.

It is an optimistic publisher who expects an author to cut his own manuscript for commercial or any other reasons. After the first lines have been written a literary work develops in the manner of a musical composition: at an early and tentative stage each theme can be reshaped and shortened, or brought to an abrupt end; but after the whole has been completed every passage, no matter how overdeveloped in detail, seems to the author to be integral to the whole. He has, in fact, memorized the completed work and he cannot see the separate passages as separate passages, only the whole in which every passage now seems necessary; and if he ventures any changes it will probably be to alter the fine structure, or worse, to add new detail in areas now discovered to be deficient. Reduction is made still more difficult by the half-conscious memory of the hours, sometimes days, spent in capturing a seemingly trivial sequence, and it is too much to expect of any man that he negate hours of labor with a quick stroke of the blue pencil. I say, so it seems to the author, because in fact most manuscripts, like most musical compositions, can be cut by someone else without serious injury. To the end of crowding forty or fifty minutes of music into the thirty-three minutes of tape available on one spool on my tape recorder, I have discovered that many composers whose works at unrestricted hearing seem to have perfect proportions indulged in repetitiousness and overelaboration, and that the careful use of the scissors can bring Beethoven's *Third Symphony* or *Violin Concerto in D,* Brahm's *Second Piano Concerto* or his *First Symphony,* within what are, for me, mechanically practical limits. Certainly any author in his right mind must grant his publishers the same privilege. I congratulate Little, Brown and Company on their success at making deletions in this book at just the proper moments.

The original manuscript was overwritten in consequence of a variety of circumstances. In the technical sense, it was begun in the summer of 1933, in the spirit of Aristotle's aphorism that 'He who sees things grow from the beginning will have the best view of them.' It grew Topsywise, expanding each successive summer and, at rare intervals, in winter when time could be stolen from other responsibilities, with no conception of limit or final objective. It was never intended to be a technical reference work, but a simple story of man's changing ideas about himself and his place in nature — such a story as I would have liked to read forty years ago. It started with an annotated bibliography; then the inclusion of bibliographic references to certify each point so cramped its style that the annotation grew less and less frequent until, during the busy war years, any hope of an annotated bibliography had to be abandoned. An enforced vacation issuing from an abscessed jaw in the summer of 1945 presented the opportunity to finish off the last chapter by force, as it were, lest it go on growing forever. It could have done almost that: its thesis, even if handled with greater economy, could scarcely be encompassed between two covers. Readers have criticized it for omitting Oriental philosophy, medieval politics, the impact of the machine age; for not discussing at greater length the development (and the defeats) of rationalism and science and naturalistic philosophy; because it dealt in such detail with Darwin, and wholly ignored Marx, Wagner, Nietzsche and Freud; for stopping short at the end of the nineteenth century. There are answers to all those criticisms, but the best answer of all is the one given by the rug weaver to his friendly kibitzers, "But this is to be only a *little* rug."

The author is not a historian or philosopher by training, although he once contributed a chapter on the history of physiology to Dr. Joseph Jastrow's *The Story of Human Error,* which was a good title. He started out to be a chemist, then switched to physiology, the study of living organisms and how they work, and for twenty years he has concentrated on the kidneys and urine formation — far from being a dull subject, it is one of the most exciting, fascinating and rewarding areas in biological science. This is not the place to defend the foregoing assertion, or to defend his competence to deal with history or philosophy, except by way of quoting the Arab Mira Jama (in Isak Dinesen's *Seven Gothic Tales*): "What is man, when you come to think upon him, but a minutely set, ingenious machine for turning, with infinite artfulness, the red wine of Shiraz into urine?" Any deficit in discipline is in part compensated by a novelty in point of view: most historians and philosophers lack the advantage of a biologist's or physiologist's intimate acquaintance with man's inner workings.

The point is an important one, and invites a fragment of autobiography.

I was the last of six children — my father was forty-five, my mother forty-two, when I was born — and separated by seven years from my youngest sister, data that are pertinent chiefly to the circumstance that I grew up in the company of siblings much older than myself. Of more immediate significance is the fact that when I learned to talk I turned my *r*'s into *l*'s, and consequently, to the amusement of all visitors, "The lat lan lound the loom." There is no evidence that I ever showed any tendency to left-handedness, and I believe that I am intrinsically right-

well take the Short Line over the hill and go back to his farm in Missouri. Uneducated laborers, chemists, mining engineers, professional gamblers, guys with divining rods, ignoramuses who mistook iron pyrites, fool's gold, for the real stuff, wiseacres who had made and lost several fortunes, all had one golden rule: you let me alone and I'll let you alone. As a gesture to prudence we locked the door when we left home, but we put the key under the mat, as everyone else did. Violence was abhorrent to Cripple Creek, and the labor agitators, because of their use of it as much as because of the unfairness of the strike, were as popular as Carry Nation. For nearly a year the District was, by proclamation of the governor, in 'a state of insurrection and rebellion' and the end result was that large numbers of union sympathizers were thrown into the 'bull pen' and subsequently 'ridden out of town' — forcibly deported to Kansas or New Mexico and told never to come back. The Western Federation of Miners sowed class consciousness in a community where class consciousness did not exist, and it rose up and destroyed them. Thereafter to be identified with a union was to be branded as an anarchist, and from 1904 until I left it in 1910, Cripple Creek was a one-class town.

It seems something of a paradox that a mushroom mining camp, typical of its kind in respect to its large floating population, its saloons and less respectable dives — Cripple Creek boasted the largest number of cribs per capita of any town in Colorado — should afford a superior opportunity for primary and secondary education. Progressive schools had not yet been invented, or if they had, we did not have them. We went to school to learn in the old-fashioned sense. However, for youngsters the cultural atmosphere of Cripple Creek was a mixed blessing. In winter, when we were in school, we were occupied by school activities and the requirements of homework, with some snowballing and sledding to relieve the monotony of daily chores, and in the spring and fall, when the ground was bare of snow, there would be an hour of twilight for games before study. But as the days lengthened, and particularly when school came to an end, the streets and empty lots, in all their dusty, weedy barrenness, the hills with their abandoned, dangerous, open-mouthed shafts, received us.

My mother died when I was nearly seven, after a protracted period of invalidism. I have no recollection of her although I can remember that during this period I slept alone in a large tent in the yard — it was in midwinter — and that in the early morning my father would wrap me in warm blankets and carry me into the house. After my mother's death there were left six children, myself, aged seven; Alice, fourteen; Helen, seventeen; Harry, nineteen; Margaret, twenty-one; and Alberta, twenty-six. Some neighbors offered to divide us but the family, after lengthy deliberation, decided to stick it out together.

The family was, in a manner of speaking, a clan of intellectual snobs who emphasized three things: you can be clean, you can hold your own, and you can be educated. When my education began, the rest of the family were in a position to be very superior about theirs and yet to imply that I carried their reputation on my shoulders. I did not particularly want to be educated but I was, in effect, scared into a middling performance. At home, when I had nothing to do, I was supposed to be reading. My juvenile literary consumption included *Black Beauty, At the Back of the North Wind, Wild Animals I Have Known, The Girl of the Limberlost* (with whom I fell in love), *The Little Colonel* and numerous others long since forgotten. I was not supposed to read dime novels; most of the other boys had them, with or without parental approval, and I remember their lurid covers, but I do not remember reading any of them. I think they bored me. With apologies to Little, Brown and Company (to whom Louisa May Alcott had much the same relation as oil to Mr. Rockefeller), neither did I like *Little Women* and its companion volumes. Juvenile fiction was abandoned when, under the tree on Christmas just preceding my ninth birthday, I received a book, title now unknown, on chemical experimentation. I read it in bed before breakfast. It told how to do everything, how to make gunpowder and *aqua regia* (which would dissolve platinum) and hydrofluoric acid (which would dissolve glass and had to be kept in wax bottles); how to make black powder, gun cotton, dynamite, mercury fulminate (the highly explosive detonator used in the center of gun shells); how to dye fabrics; how to make colorless water turn blood-red and then turn colorless again. At least I think that all these things were in the same book. I am slightly confused because there were several books of this nature, including a biography of Thomas Alva Edison with a frontispiece, in color, of the great inventor, his apron and hands besmeared by half a dozen aniline dyes; and yet another: a dog-eared, coverless volume of yellowed pages, dating probably from the '70's or '80's, and containing, as I judge now, rather more alchemical mystery than verifiable science but nonetheless expounding, within the limits of the author's wisdom, which seemed unlimited, the answers to everything from thunder and lightning to the fermentation of malt and the distillation of spirits.

Then, as the seeds of this literature were germinating in the spring of my eleventh year (six weeks before school was out), I came down with measles. After weeks in a darkened bedroom, I became aware of strange voices and the noises of sawing and hammering in the back yard. The family, forced to offer some explanation, said that my father was building a chicken house. When the great day came that I could get out of bed, the chicken house was, of course, what I wanted to see first. But there were no chickens. It was an unfinished one-room shed of pine, on the east side of the yard, opposite the sweet peas, perhaps 8 $\times$ 12 feet, with two steps and a four-inch stove pipe sticking out of the peaked roof, and a window in the north end. Inside I can still smell stove polish mixed with the fragrant odor of pine shavings. Along one wall were a heavy workbench with a carpenter's vise, a toolbox with saw, plane, hammer, square, and chisels. A little potbellied stove stood at one end in front of the window, and along the other wall was a pile of pine boards. There had not been time to sweep up the curled shavings left by the carpenter, and they supplied the kindling for my first fire. My father had decided that the time had come to get me off the streets, and the entire family had probably decided that the time had come to get me out of the house. I was beginning to clutter the place with retorts and crucibles.

My world had been given to me. I never learned to saw a board straight, either cross-grained or lengthwise, and I abandoned the toolbox as soon as I had erected shelves on all four walls and put up a couple of cabinets. I set up an alcohol-heated, stationary steam engine that had come as a Christmas present, and in subsequent years it never once let me down by failing to operate. I installed a hand-operated vacuum pump and bell jar that I acquired heaven knows where, and demonstrated how a lighted candle beneath the jar grew feeble and slowly died as the air was evacuated. I demonstrated to my satisfaction, and to the satisfaction of a few visitors, that, as the book said, a mouse did the same thing under the same conditions. When electricity came our way, I helped install the wires and hung a 16-candle-power carbon-filament lamp square in the middle of the room. I lacked either the aesthetic vision or the necessary permission to put in two outlets or a table lamp, but I was not outclassed by the professional electricians of the age, who thought that one naked, glaring bulb in the middle of the room was the hallmark of the Electrical Era.

I collected minerals, gold, silver and copper ores, turquoise, feldspar, asbestos, garnets, amethysts, tourmaline; and then, inevitably, butterflies, and moths (with a backward thought towards the girl of the Limberlost). I once thought of going into taxidermy and set out over the hills with a .22 rifle to kill my specimens for myself but when I shot my first bird I was so hurt that I buried it in the woods.

It was never called anything but my 'shop.' It was my sanctum sanctorum and none of the family ever came into it unless invited. It gave me a privileged position because, apart from the electric light, the stove, the tools that had now grown rusty, the steam engine, and the vacuum pump, it permitted me to accumulate miscellaneous riches that would be the envy of any boy. The 'book' contained instructions on how to make a telegraph key and sounder, and zinc-copper sulfate wet batteries; and a telegraph set was fabricated (to be replaced later by commercial instruments) and a single wire strung on the telephone (or it may have been electric light) poles for nearly three blocks to the home of a friend. We laboriously spelled out the latest news in the Morse code at least once a day until open communication palled and then we spelled everything in a concealed code just in case the wire should be tapped.

Now the family began to have cause to regret the Christmas of 1903, when they had given me the books on chemistry. In those days a knowledgeable boy of eleven could buy anything he wanted at the drugstore, from arsenic to saltpeter, and my dimes began to go into chemical experiments. Homemade gun cotton reposed casually in my trousers pocket; black powder could be compounded at any time from stock reagents on the shelves; turning water into blood by pouring it from one beaker to another, and vice versa, was kid stuff; and nitric acid stained my fingers until I looked, rather proudly, like Edison. As a matter of courtesy I was taking the warts off my friends' hands by the judicious application of a drop of that fuming corrosive. Since no laboratory science was then taught in the public grade schools, I was the object of the rather skeptical envy of the classmates who visited the shop. Most of them were scared of gun cotton and dynamite, and had never even heard of nitric acid. No doubt I seemed queer to many of them, who possibly looked at me askance because of my stuttering and, when I could talk, probably could not understand what I was talking about.

I have no idea where I got it, possibly from Dr. King, the family physician, but shortly the choice piece of apparatus in the shop came to be a Wimshurst machine for generating static electricity. In dry weather and under the application of sufficient muscular energy to the driving gear, fat, noisy, two-inch sparks discharged between the brass ball electrodes and filled the room with the odor of ozone. My machine generated only some 15,000 or 20,000 electron volts, but this was a miniature lightning storm that terrified the uninitiated, and was powerful enough to ignite gun cotton and alcohol, to puncture holes in cardboard or to fragment a piece of thin glass. I did not have imagination enough to dream that one day, with 10 billion electron-volt machines, men would split atoms into smithereens and manufacture new elements even more unstable than radium (I had a small piece of pitchblende from the Colorado lode and had repeated Becquerel's experiment of making a radioautograph on a paper-covered film), but the Atomic Energy Commission has not had any more fun, or enjoyed any greater local prestige, than I did when the thunder and lightning were cracking properly.

Along with the static machine came a small X-ray tube which, in conjunction with a fluorescent screen, enabled me to see the bones of the fingers, hand and wrist, the entire skeleton of a mouse. Not many people, however, wanted to see the skeleton of a mouse, or even the bones in their own fingers, but were prepared to take their bones on faith. The X-ray tube led to the construction of a spark coil, because activation of the tube by means of the static machine involved the expenditure of excessive muscular energy on my part and prevented me from looking at the fluorescent screen while I was operating the machine; with a spark coil plugged into the 110 volt A.C. lighting circuit all I had to do was to snap a switch and the X-ray tube was in continuous operation. Then, since any spark coil is an effective generator of radio waves, a friend and I were soon flashing wireless messages to each other, using a primitive iron-filing coherer on the receiving end.

I reached the pinnacle of my electrical engineering efforts when, to supplement the spark coil, I built a three-foot Tesla coil: all over the world audiences have paid admission to see the death-defying, breathtaking performance of the wizard who, with this prop, generates genuine lightning upon the stage and, through a short iron rod, takes its foot-long million-volt (but harmless) flashes into his very body, lights an electric light bulb with the circuit flowing entirely through his arm and causes his gloved fingers to spark at every chair and table, and at any lady or gentleman who will accommodate by volunteering. My home-made Tesla coil worked magnificently and gave off twelve-inch and very noisy flashes of lightning.

I came close to inventing the neon light long before someone else obtained a patent on it; or, more accurately, I foresaw the practical application of what had, for four decades, been an interesting scientific gadget, the Geissler tube. This is a glass tube with electrodes sealed in it at either end, evacuated of air and filled with one or another excitable gas. When activated by a high-voltage, high-frequency current, these

tubes emit a soft light of a color characteristic of the gas with which
they are filled, and elaborate patterns of color can be obtained by alternating bulbous expansions and narrow constrictions in the tube and
by playing changes in the composition of the glass. In a set of Geissler
tubes the rainbow has been trapped so that one can hold all its colors
between the fingers. I saw how the soft, fluorescent light might be substituted for the glaring carbon-filament lamp, and in my dreams I was
sometimes the owner-superintendent and expert electrical engineer of a
plant that controlled the patents on this new system of universal lighting. My spare time was used for searching out new inventions in the
manner of Thomas Alva Edison, assisted, in the more complicated and
delicate operations, by the girl of my dreams.

The girl of the Limberlost had turned into one whose disturbing (but
fully clothed) beauty was portrayed in an advertisement that I carried
in my wallet. She was also a true helpmeet in every chemical and physical experiment. I was as yet scarcely interested in girls in a practical
sort of way — only on the idealistic level. My two older sisters had married and left home, and I had twice become an embarrassed Uncle Homer
by the age of ten. My younger sisters, Helen and Alice, were teaching in
the local high school. It was perhaps for this reason that I came by the
Geissler tubes and various chemical apparatus and books from Mr. Lory,
the high school superintendent. I am on more certain ground in recounting that there was a constant stream of beaux at the house — it was
the Gibson Girl era when women wore shirtwaists of elaborate hand
embroidery and spent an hour doing their hair, and men sent them
long-stemmed American Beauty roses and five-pound boxes of the most
delicious bittersweet chocolate creams, the like of which I have never
since tasted. It was one of Helen's beaux who led me into perdition, a
newly graduated physician and assistant to Dr. King, named Dr. Brittain. I had long possessed a microscope of the push-pull type, with a box
of microscope slides, each holding beneath its circular cover glass a cross
section of some plant stem or other specimen appropriately stained with
aniline dyes — the geometric, polychromatic beauty of such preparations
has inspired many a modern fabric designer. There was also in the collection, I remember, a perfectly mounted flea, the transparency of which
permitted one to see all the vital organs; and I believe the intricate leg and
foot of a spider, though I may have made that preparation myself because I obtained microscope slides, cover glasses and oil of balsam
from Dr. Brittain and went into microscopy on my own. Having no
microtome for making optically thin sections of plants or animal tissues,

I had to confine myself to amoebae, paramecia and other water animalcules that could be raised in hay infusions, and hay infusions inevitably led to bacteria. A discarded textbook of bacteriology quickly gave me a bird's-eye view of Pasteur and of pathogenic and nonpathogenic organisms and the elements of their culture, fixation and staining. However, I still suffered the deficit of the incubator that is necessary to propagate some of the more delicate species and shortly test tubes filled with culture media were surreptitiously being incubated in the warming oven over the kitchen range. The family tolerated me until specks of aniline dyes began to appear in the biscuits and apple dumplings and then they served the ultimatum: I and my dangerous bacterial cultures could just damn well get out of the house! Thus, again, I was driven back upon myself. For lack of an incubator, another career was closed to me. When I begged for a culture of tuberculosis and diphtheria, the door of destiny was slammed in my face. I saw that I was not to become a bacteriologist.

I do not recall how the other matter started. Dr. Brittain spent considerable time in the shop, possibly as a blood price because, where others were concerned, I had as yet no understanding of the intricacy of affairs of the heart and I was old enough to be quite a nuisance. I suppose that one question led to another, about the lungs, liver and kidneys, and so on. It was no great passion to know how the insides of an animal worked that led to the dissection of our first cat, but probably mere curiosity on my part and a matter of fair exchange on the part of the doctor. Needless to say, it was in the dark of night, certainly after eight o'clock, when nobody would come nosing in. In a primitive community there are always an abundance of abandoned cats — the general practice is to drown them but there was no water within miles of Cripple Creek — so that the cat supply presented no difficulty. Nor was there any difficulty about getting chloroform because by now I could buy almost any article I requested at the drug store, and I was quite frank about the matter because the customary way to dispose of excess cats in Cripple Creek was to chloroform them. I had some scissors and Dr. Brittain supplied a sharp dissecting scalpel and showed me how to make a cardboard anesthetic cone, how to apply it adroitly and firmly to the head that protruded from a hole in the gunny sack, and how to tell by the respiration and heart beat when the cat was quite dead. Then the warm body was explored, its organs identified and their functions expounded. By ten o'clock the remains had been buried in a faraway field, the shop had been scrubbed, the instruments cleaned, the odor of cat and chloroform removed by thorough ventilation, and my colleague in crime had gone into the house to call upon my impatient sister, I to bed to dream of better and better dissections assisted by the girl of the Limberlost. I did not long require Dr. Brittain's professional guidance because I soon learned to handle the scalpel alone. The crisis came when the family discovered, not the bald fact, but that I was using the household's best turkey platter.

When one considers the thousands of cats that are drowned, gassed or otherwise disposed of, the millions of other animals that are slaughtered for commercial markets, shot for sport or exterminated because of their nuisance value, the half dozen or so stray felines that died a quick and painless death in the shop dwindle into the trivial. I am not recommending the exercise as a routine item in secondary education, but it has pedagogical possibilities that exceed the more aesthetic study of bees and flowers. The experience can be likened to Alice's adventure down the rabbit hole; it is not one to be shared by everybody, but to be enjoyed only by those who have something of Alice's curiosity as well as her common-sense approach to things. One simply cannot explore the insides of a cat and emerge with the same naïve philosophy with which one entered the adventure. The experience shatters certain basic premises frequently encountered in the philosophy of existence, and notably the premise that creation is intrinsically anthropocentric. He who has dissected the warm body of a cat emerges a philosophic rebel prepared, like Alice, to denounce the whole pack of cards including the King and Queen of Hearts.

I was not a religious child, nor was I reared in a particularly religious atmosphere. Cripple Creek had its Catholic, Episcopal and sectarian churches, architecturally and dogmatically primitive, where the straight and narrow path was expounded every Sunday, and on a week night the Epworth League held forth with ringing hymns and desultory prayers to complement the Sunday school lessons. I believe that the Epworth League served chiefly as an excuse for the sexes to walk out together, and that it was frequently an outlet for what, in those days, the parson called sinful if natural tendencies. So far as young people were concerned, scarcely more can be said for formal church attendance. There were, of course, among the oldsters many devout persons, but the adjective was certainly not applicable to the bulk of the younger generation, who participated in devotions under the mixed impulsion of convention and for what they could get out of the Sunday gathering as a social opportunity. As an intellectual institution, the church had become the transparent hypocrisy which Emerson had denounced a generation earlier.

Occasionally a revivalist, such as Billy Sunday, came to town and stirred the gamblers, the chronic alcoholics, the lonely and weary among the adults, and among the youths those who were torn by an adolescent sense of guilt or sex frustration, into a hymn-singing orgy of repentance; but the sinners who were healed in front of the pulpit generally quickly repented of the healing and were more or less embarrassed for some weeks thereafter. Without statistics I would venture that the Greatest Gold-Mining Camp on Earth lay far north of what Mencken subsequently dubbed the Bible Belt. Religion was something that you took unostentatiously. It had a quaint stigma about it, and the farther you moved away from any public display of religiosity without actually leaving the pale of piety, the better. I am here, of course, expressing an attitude peculiar to the family, and perhaps even within that area rendered somewhat inaccurate by the lapse of time.

Had it been otherwise, however, I think I would remember. My father did not die until I was sixteen, and I have many clear recollections of him. I would say that he was of the generation that had one foot still planted in religious tradition, the other planted in irreligious rationalism; but that in his mind there was no question as to which general direction he, and his children, were going. The only issue was not to hurry the transition, or to be unpleasant about it. He and my mother carried away with them from Maryland five children (I was born in Denver), a "mammy" left over from prewar days, a strong tradition of respectability that was probably enhanced by the seeming uncouthness of the West, a deep sense of the responsibilities of hospitality, and a dedication to the aristocracy of the intellect. The last expression is, however, to be taken modestly. As for the past, his attitude was summed up in the aphorisms, probably dull with age when he was a boy, that we all go back to Adam — or Cain, and that it did not pay to look too closely at the family tree lest you find somebody hanging from a limb.

The fragmentary records of the family's antecedents never interested me until I undertook to prepare this record. Now, on a hasty search that ends in Virginia, I find little that is exciting, no estimable criminals or even creditable heretics, only prosaic farmers, one of whom, John, with his wife, a Miss Ewell, also from Virginia, abandoned the mainland and took his slaves to the Eastern Shore about the time that Charles Mason and Jeremiah Dixon established the line at $39° 43' 26''.3$ N that brought to an end the long controversy between Lord Baltimore and William Penn. How they initially got to Virginia or why they left is not reported. They settled south of the 'line,' in the area where the Catholic Cecilius

Calvert, second Lord Baltimore, had passed through the colonial assembly his famous act of religious toleration magnanimously extending freedom of worship to all sects that accepted the Trinity. There the oldest son, my paternal great-grandfather, William Henry Smith, married Hester Smith, also of Virginia, and with her settled in Somerset County on St. Peters Creek, near Princess Anne, at a place initially called Oriole, but which, in the next generation, was subdivided between William's three sons into Keeps Poor Hall, Littleworth Farm and Nicholas Adventure, Littleworth Farm being the home of William's second son, my grandfather. Since all three areas were large and fertile, the names suggest that either William Henry or his sons had a sardonic sense of humor.

William Henry's generation is distinguished by few eccentricities. I find that his wife, Hester, was so excessively neat that she made the children take off their shoes when they played in the house. His sister Mollie married Hester's brother, James Smith, who had a white horse which, when James was full, carried his master home like a bag of potatoes and rolled the load onto the bed before returning to the stable. Of more interest to this book is the fact that my grandfather, William Thomas Smith, married one Henrietta Maria Smith, whose mother, Phillippa, was a character worthy of special mention. Phillippa's grandfather, Edward Martin I, a Huguenot, had emigrated from France to the Scilly Isles early in the eighteenth century to escape the bonfires of Catholic persecution. His son, Edward Martin II, married a Jane Johns of Welsh stock, but then living in Helstone, near Penzance, Cornwall, where the couple settled down and where Phillippa was born in 1786. In 1796, to prevent the conscription of their two eldest sons in the war with France, Edward and Jane emigrated to America and ultimately settled in Alexandria, Virginia. Phillippa was the tenth of twelve children (there had been one set of twins); by the records of St. Sithney's Church, Cornwall, ten of them lived long enough to be baptized in the Church of England, as apparently were most of my other ancestors of the period. One does not, of course, directly inherit one's ancestors' religion, but in subtle ways one does come by their idealisms.

Something of Phillippa's background can be read between the lines of a poem written by her father for her mother on the occasion of their golden anniversary:

> My dearest Jane, full fifty-one
> Revolving years have passed and gone;
> This day the period is complete
> Since we consented both to meet

To enter Hymen's sacred bands
And let the parson join our hands.
Whether by Providence decreed
Or not, I know we both agreed
We would to Sithney Church repair
And end a seven years' courtship there.
The village maids together swarmed,
To see the nuptial rites performed;
And had you chose, there's no dispute
You might have had a substitute,
For I believe it was the case,
That many longed to take my place.
Perhaps you know the reason why,
But you seemed pleased and so was I.
Here you, in cheerful, loving mood
With me before the parson stood
And in that consecrated house
We interchanged our marriage vows.
I gave my troth and you gave yours
To take for better or for worse;
And I mistake, or heard you say,
You would love, honor and obey,
And so continue during life —
Edward and Jane — husband and wife.
Then was the wedding ring produced,
On such occasions always used;
The endless ring presumed to be
A symbol of eternity.
That sacred pledge between us passed
Denotes that love shall always last.
The usual ceremonies done,
The parson joined us both as one;
And that this knot, so firmly tied,
No man might ever dare divide,
That nothing might our peace annoy
He prayed, and kindly wished us joy
And as a pledge of future bliss
You sealed the contract with a kiss.
Tho' this to you may trifling seem,
To me 'tis still a pleasing theme;
And often times, by day or night,
I think it over with delight;
You know I've told you and 'tis true
I never loved a girl but you;

You had the first kiss I e'er gave,
And yours the last I hope to have.
And at the last, as all must part,
I wish sincerely from my heart
If you are summoned first away,
I mayn't survive a single day.
So long as I am destined here
For you shall be my daily prayer.
May angels be your constant guard
And endless blessings your reward
When you to happier scenes remove,
My first, my last, my only love.

EDWARD MARTIN
Sept. 25, 1820

It is significant that, although the conventions of St. Sithney's are dutifully observed and that there is one poetic reference to prayer and another to angels, the Deity is nowhere mentioned. It was probably not from her father that Phillippa got religion, but from a chance meeting in the home of her grandfather. Although Edward Martin I was a member of the Established Church, his house was the frequent visiting place of John Wesley, whose evangelism had crossed the Atlantic just a few ships ahead of the Martins. Wesley was then eighty-six years old and, according to his contemporaries, his geniality and friendliness were lighted by the extraordinary happiness in his heart, reflecting 'the gay remembrance of a life well spent.' As recorded in Phillippa's obituary, 'it was on the occasion of the last of Wesley's visits to Cornwall, in 1789 [two years before his death], that Phillippa Martin, then but three years old, looked for the only time, on earth, on this venerable face, and ever treasured the memory of the fact as a precious legacy, to the last hour of her own long life.' Phillippa was ten years old when she was brought to Alexandria, and seventeen years old when a great wave of revivalism swept the shores of the Potomac and swept her into the sectarian movement that, more than any other, weakened the Established Church in Virginia and Maryland. At twenty-two she was united in the bonds of holy wedlock to Samuel Smith, son of Joseph Smith, one of the earliest Methodists in Alexandria, by a Mr. Waters, the first American-born Methodist preacher and the man who had been instrumental in securing her adherence to the sectarian movement.

Phillippa lived to the age of ninety, and the seventy-three years that followed her conversion 'bore joyful testimony to the power of this extraordinary work of grace.' Until her death, she seems to have been an instrument of Methodist piety. Between 1820 to 1822 she and her husband lived at Owensboro, Kentucky, 'where her home was a preaching place, and a place for preachers,' but the chief impact of her conversion was in Virginia, Maryland and the Eastern Shore, and notably in Mencken's town of Baltimore, where she spent the last forty years of her life. She had eight children and 110 descendants, 75 of whom survived her — Phillippa, 110 times compounded, did the Established Church no favor.

Phillippa's obituary portrays her as a woman with deep convictions, but no bigot. She had a warm heart for every Christian of any communion. She was

> gifted with unusual intelligence and with an extraordinary memory; she also possessed the faculty for conversation, which gave a charm to her presence in whatever society she might be found. By no means lacking in spirit which could never brook injustice or meanness, she had acquired such perfect control of her emotions that those who knew her best need only to recur to the occasions in her life which most severely tested her moral character, to recall her patience under sore injury and her cheerfulness in the darkest hours of adversity. She had the happiness of retaining her faculties unimpaired to the last hour of her life. This evening was serene and clear, not a cloud obscured its brightness. Before she departed she was permitted to give her blessing to every one of her children and to receive from them the grateful tokens of their filial affection. She was ready at any moment when the Master might call, to answer joyfully the summons, but she was not impatient to be gone. The rule of the Lord was her rule, both of duty and endurance. In her reference to her religious experience the 'Atonement' was her chief topic. No occasion during her last illness gratified her more than the administration of the Lord's Supper by her eldest grandson and her pastor, Rev. W. H. Holiday, of Eutaw Church. The very atmosphere seemed charged with divine influence and alive with celestial presences. Her face bore on it the reflection of the upper Sanctuary and her tones of response so soft and low were as though they had caught the sweeter melodies of heaven. To such a life as hers, the last hour was a fitting close. Words that had been the trumpet signal of many a saint before her in the death transition were also hers, "I am walking through the valley of the shadow of death but fear no evil, The Lord is my righteousness and strength, forever. . . ."

I am glad that by digging into the family archives, I found Phillippa because I cannot help wondering what the consequences might have been if the eighty-six-year-old John Wesley had not perched a three-year-old youngster on his knee; if, as a seventeen-year-old girl she had not been caught in a hysterical revival meeting. . . . But I have no desire to inquire into antecedents behind Phillippa's grandfather lest I discover some loyalist adding fagots to the fires that burned the Huguenots in Catholic France. My father was right, it is just as well to let the family tree alone.

Despite the fact that during the last forty of her ninety years of life Phillippa lived in Baltimore, my father must have known her; directly or through his mother, Henrietta, he could scarcely have escaped her influence. But when he pulled up the Maryland-Virginia roots to go West, he also in some measure pulled his roots out of Phillippa. In any case, it was an era of transition. John Wesley had contributed in no small measure to the spread of rationalism and free thought and to the ultimate undoing of his own labors when he emphasized the importance of education. It has been said that no man in eighteenth-century England did so much to create a taste for good reading and to supply it with books at the lowest prices (it is reported that the profits from his cheap books enabled him to give away as much as £1400 a year, and he once told his congregation that he would give them every book they read up to the value of £5). Perhaps it was because of Phillippa that my father referred nostalgically to the 'books' at Littleworth Farm, some of which must have been carried by John and his wife across the Chesapeake Bay, but all of which had long since been dispersed; and that he equated literacy with initiative and cleanliness.

The men who poured into the District seeking to redress their fortunes were a motley lot. Many were uneducated, but among them were men whose background embraced broad reaches of literature, poetry, music, philosophy and politics. It was scarcely more surprising for a man to reveal an acquaintance with the pragmatism of William James than to pull a rich chunk of sylvanite out of his pocket, and in the intervals that separated the long, silent chess games that my father loved, he and his opponents argued, to my edification, the merits of Andrew Lang as a psychologist, of Tennyson as a poet, or the significance of the Curies' discovery of radium. He (and I surreptitiously) read the *Smart Set* when Mencken was first laying about him with a sardonic flail.

Nevertheless until I reached the rebellious age I was dutifully sent to Sunday school in the local Wesleyan chapel and listened to all the stories with childish indifference, and once, without assistance, I won a $10 prize for the best Christmas story: it had something to do with Jesus and I must have laid to with imagination as earnestly as Renan because I can remember the family's startled reaction when they read my prize-winning essay. This early success at deliberate fabrication may have sown the ferment of later skepticism, since I thereby learned how easily the trick was done.

Until his later years my father usually attended church, and then he let my sisters perform the family duty. On religion he kept his opinions to himself except in the privacy of the family, where his comments, at times sardonic, about the earnest young men who held forth in wordy sermons could not fail to escape my ears. My belief is that he had passed beyond the point where the sainted life of his grandmother Phillippa could be accepted as verifying her theory of cosmology, that he had come to see that she would have been much the same saintly character even if she had remained in the Anglican Church. Phillippa was now part of a mosaic containing Henry James's novels, William James's philosophy, Emerson's skepticism, Robert Ingersoll's atheism. As he talked before and after chess games, or with lecturers, musicians, engineers who were invited to the house, I came to understand that there was some sort of gentleman's agreement that on some subjects gentlemen did not agree, and therefore remained silent. One subject on which there was fair agreement was poetry. My father particularly liked Tennyson, who served as a touchstone for many a philosophical divagation. He more or less secretly indulged in poetic composition himself and possessed a thick, leather-bound volume of poems inscribed in neat penmanship. This is a harmless diversion, the impulse to which may have entered the line from Phillippa's father because it repeatedly crops out in succeeding generations. I have no evidence that the impulse was ever taken very seriously, but it produced works marked by a plenitude of sentiment and a dearth of wit. As judged by their strophes, my ancestors countered the tragic episodes of life by personal tenderness, nostalgic recollections, and the generalization that somehow things would come out all right in heaven. In my father's case there was some warrant: his younger sister Mary died, though not within his memory, of fatal burning; and within his memory five still younger children, two sisters and three brothers, died in a week's time of scarlet fever, leaving of ten children only four surviving. The only poem of his that I retain, entitled 'Reverie,' is a recapitulation of a day in childhood when he and his sisters and brothers ran through orchard and meadow in search of birds' nests, played fox in the cornfield, hung on to the cow's tail to be dragged over hollow and hill, drove the hen from the nest, and put the pullet to sleep by tucking her head under her wing, indulging in miscellaneous mischief until

> We come with hushed voice to God's acre,
> Where lieth the dust of the dead,
> And with the white marble around us
> We bare to the soft breeze our head;
> We pass by all groves unnoticed
> Till we come to a holier ground
> Where the marble tells, standing above it,
> "That Mary lies under the ground."
>
> We repeat to each other the story,
> By Mother so oft before told,
> Of the sister long ago buried
> In this grove, dark, lonely and cold.
> How the innocent little creature
> One morning crawled out of her cot
> Ere the stars were out of the heavens
> And moved to the fatal spot
>
> Where the flames caught hold of her garments
> And enveloped her innocent form;
> How her sufferings were borne without murmur,
> Till God took the dear one to His arms.
> And we brush the tears from our eyelids,
> And gently move from the place
> Made holier by the pure ashes
> Of one who had ne'er seen our face.
>
> Again the voices of children
> Float over and fall on my ears,
> And I ask, "Are these the same voices
> Come back from the far distant years?"
> Then memory answers in sorrow
> The voices have long ago ceased,
> For God's reaper the children has gathered
> To His garner of joy and of peace.
>
> And now, close by the green hillock
> Where we stood round the white marble stone,
> Stand five other tablets of granite
> That tell of the pure spirits flown.

They tell how the dear loving Father
While their bodies sleep under the sod,
Hath taken the dear lambs home, saying,
"Of such, is the kingdom of God."

Those innocent days of my childhood,
So free from care and from pain,
How oft have I wished, in my manhood,
I could live them all over again.
And I pray that when the pale reaper
Shall gather me under the sod,
I may play again with the children,
At home, in the city of God.

Heartless as the assessment may seem, I must say of my father that his age was ripe for Tennyson. It suffered the pain attending the perhaps too rapid deliquescence of a faith in which it now only half believed. In its courageous moments it struck out into the unknown, facing the possible consequences of the gamble; in its sorrows it took solace in dreams and monumented its graveyards with marble or granite pillars decorated with myrtle and weeping willows, and tenderly inscribed with a hope that was no longer seriously entertained. His age could scarcely see itself through its tears and only half knew why it wept.

For his mixed sentiment and skepticism my father paid off his conscience by generous hospitality, and any minister of any gospel was welcome at his table, Sunday noonday dinner in particular being a natural opportunity for amity. On such occasions a mantle of quasi righteousness descended over the household, the transparency of which must have been evident even to the visiting parson who probably discounted a measure of worldliness in the interests of Maryland fried chicken, baked sweet potatoes and hot biscuits with apple dumplings for dessert. I probably early came to sense that the most important thing conceivable — eternal salvation — was peddled by a profession maintained on public charity and honored in deference to hospitality, but with reservations.

It was thus that I grew up, apparently secure in the home, obviously insecure in all other directions. The Greatest Gold-Mining Camp on Earth did not offer much assurance of security in its streets and alleys, its cribs and saloons, its deep shafts with open mouths or its long, black tunnels. At the pole of security was an emphasis on common sense, criticism, reserved opinion (experienced rather than intellectually appreciated, of course); at the other pole was a world confused by variety, harsh contrasts, irreconcilable contradictions, and one also significantly expanded by literature. As I have said, I was told that when I was not doing anything I was supposed to be reading. I recall no public library in town, but there was a fair substitute for one operated by an incredibly old woman who suffered, by my present guess, the mixed catastrophe of heart failure, cirrhosis of the liver, dyspepsia, borborygmus and strong body odor. She owned and operated the town's reading room, which contained perhaps (another guess) 3500 volumes and a fair supply of magazines and local newspapers. When I came to know her, she had for reasons of nature retired to a back room to which I paid an occasional but reluctant courtesy visit because the family had a charitable affection for her. The front door of her reading room was rarely locked except on Sundays and at night, and her clients entered and left without her knowledge, depositing, if they were so inclined, a dime in an open cigar box. From browsing among the partially alphabetized, partially chaotic collection I acquired a primitive library habit that still leads me to study the titles in any row of books, though I doubt that there were many on her shelves that received my attention; I visited the reading room to obtain novels for my sisters and it is chiefly the mixed smell of cigar smoke, dyspepsia and old books that lingers in my memory, and the impression of the multiplicity of literature. I saw that there were many books in the world, more than one man could read in his entire lifetime, and my reaction was one of alarm: the remembrance of the books that I had read and enjoyed in the presence of rows and rows that presumably I should but obviously never could read for sheer lack of time, gave me a sense of futility.

The experience was counteracted by two elderly spinsters (or so they seemed to me), who lived a short distance from our house, an understanding pair whose names are lost but who occupy a warm corner in my heart. Their household furnishings had probably been moved *in toto* from the East: the Turkey red carpet, the carved walnut sofa covered with black horsehair with rocking chair and side chairs to match, the chromo prints in walnut frames, the knitted antimacassars, the mahogany pier glass in the hall, the big Chinese vase that held umbrellas, even the Swiss clock in a porcelain case decorated with pink rosebuds. There was no cigar smoke and little other odor because the house was aired every day, holding only the scarcely detectable perfume associated with ladies. They were the possessors of many books arranged around the sitting room walls, some of them in 'sets' that may have been purchased locally because much of the world's literature traveled West in the form of 'special editions, beautifully bound and most reasonably priced,' peddled from door to door by young men who said that they were working their way through college. I was urged by the family to be particularly careful of these 'sets' with their gold-embossed covers. But many of the books were just dog-eared volumes in tattered covers, first editions that had been read by two, perhaps three generations.

For a boy to come browsing through these shelves, wanting to borrow another book, must have given delicious meaning to the vellum and tooled-leather covers that were dusted once a week but so rarely removed from their position. I learned that the cover is not very important, and I have no idea of the sequence: *The Old Curiosity Shop, Oliver Twist, A Tale of Two Cities* and *David Copperfield, Twenty Thousand Leagues under the Sea, Kim* and *The Jungle Books, The House of the Seven Gables* and *The Scarlet Letter, Ben Hur, Ivanhoe, The Conquest of Mexico, Quo Vadis, Vanity Fair* and *The Virginians, The Little Minister, Les Misérables, Wuthering Heights* and *Jane Eyre, The Last of the Mohicans* and *The Pathfinder, The Trail of the Lonesome Pine, Robinson Crusoe, Lorna Doone. . . .* If I was too young to appreciate them all, they remained so uniquely my own, so private, so mined from a rich lode of my own discovery, that singly and collectively they became for me a magic carpet. I have never outgrown my early belief that a good book is man's most precious creation.

What I do believe is that most of the boys of Cripple Creek spent a good part of their lives downtown, or playing marbles, throwing pennies, or more generally, talking, just talking. Since I could not talk without embarrassment I indulged in it to a minimal extent and instead retreated into the shop during free daylight hours, and, at night, into the world of literary imagination. Yet I was not a bookworm. My reading was somehow edged in between the shop and school, and, in the spring, between hikes into the hills to search for purple anemones, just coming up where the snow had melted or, later in the summer, to gather large handfuls of white Mariposa lilies and blue columbines, or to climb the smooth, steep slopes of conical Mount Pisgah or the dangerously vertical cliffs of other mountains. Or, in the company of other venturesome kids, not all of them boys, each with a flickering candle in hand, to explore for nearly a mile the black cavern of some horizontal tunnel long since abandoned, the walls glistening with moisture, the roof decorated with stalactites each hanging precisely above its stalagmite on the rock below, water dripping, dripping in the darkness between them. We were not supposed to go into abandoned mines, but anyone with half a grain of sense could have told from the mud on our shoes and clothes in perfectly dry weather that we had been deep in the heart of the cold, dark earth.

Cripple Creek supplied ample realism to accent, or counteraccent, the life of the imagination. Boys cheated and lied and used force to extort nickels and dimes out of smaller boys, but some of them did kind and heroic things. Girls were of exactly two kinds: nice girls, and girls that were not nice (this was, of course, initially an adult categorization, but readily confirmed and generally anticipated in experience), but somehow their charms as individuals did not correlate with this absolutist division. Life was sometimes as muddy as the streets when the winter snow was melting, sometimes it had the colors of the Sangre de Cristo Range seen against the sky through nearly a hundred miles of dry and utterly transparent air. But always it was charged with danger, not the kind that necessarily frightens but the kind that induces caution. Like creeping to the edge of a black, uncovered hole that went so far down that a rock took an unbelievable time to reach the bottom and send up its faint echoes; or the rolling stones and great boulders, the slippery shingle on a mountainside over which one had to find a way to reach the top, where one could look out upon miles upon miles of blue mountain ranges, the tips white with snow. Too many such adventures at too early an age left me with nightmares of climbing over endless miles of hills, or of struggling along a vertiginous height with the certain knowledge that I was going to fall, symbols of minor frustrations and the source of delayed migraine for many years until I saw the sequence and learned to wake myself up from such cold sweats. I have never dreamed of anemones in the snow, or Mariposa lilies and columbines, because they were attained with undangerous effort. But faraway, snow-capped mountains, their blue slopes and white tops so nearly transparent as almost to melt into the sky, to which I was about to set out, or for some reason was not able to set out, frequently recurred in dreams until, thirty years later, I returned and took a close look at them and found them to be more solid and a little more prosaic than the Maxfield Parrish vision which childhood memory had bequeathed to me. Thereafter there were fewer such dreams and now I can take my mountains or leave them.

Mountains can mean many things in dreams, but in mine they probably symbolize the excessive measure of anxiety (I still cannot command the word when I want it) that Dr. Anne Roe read into the routine psychometric tests she gave me a few years ago. That the one certain thing about life is its uncertainty must have been an early lesson. My father and sisters gave unselfishly to my care, but they were too busy and too preoccupied with their own lives to enter deeply into my emotional domain, and I grew up, as perhaps all children should grow up, more or less alone, with ample opportunity for that 'divine idleness' so necessary to maturation, but with the responsibility of figuring things out for myself. In the shop I could take things to pieces and learn what made them tick, and acquire a measure of self-confidence with which to fend against the precariousness of the pattern as a whole. I had the desire to understand them, and the conviction that, invariably, if one tried to understand them, they made sense.

Most things made sense, that is, but not everything. Among my earliest literary experiences was Dante's *Divine Comedy*. We possessed the work in two large volumes illustrated with full-page steel engravings by Gustave Doré. Sometime between the Grimm brothers' *Fairy Tales* and *Oliver Twist* I spelled my way through the Inferno and Purgatory (Paradise must have bored me) while lying face downward on the floor of the living room, struggling to discover why these tortured souls were being punished by God with devised cruelties that I would not conceivably inflict on a cat. The writhing, naked men and women connected remotely with the moral strictures as I knew them, with the Ten Commandments and the not very exciting lessons of Sunday school, but they failed to connect with anything else that I had either read or heard discussed or learned from direct experience. It just did not make sense. It must have been at this time that I came to the suspicion that the family, in spite of all evidence to the contrary, did not really approve of parsons because parsons really thought that this stuff might be true. I asked no questions because it seemed a silly and embarrassing thing to ask questions about. In the end I just left Dante on the bookshelf and passed into a mild state of philosophic confusion which lasted until the morning of April 15, 1912.

I had for the last two years been going to high school in Denver, but had returned to Cripple Creek at intervals, and was there, presumably during spring vacation, on the morning the news was flashed around the world by telegraph that the *Titanic* had gone down, with the loss of hundreds of lives. Magnificent beyond description, the finest ship ever built, she had been racing across the Atlantic Ocean trying to break the speed record. She had gone to the north to shorten her course and in the dark of night had crashed at full speed into an iceberg. I retrieved the *Cripple Creek Times* after breakfast and took it to the shop where I read the full-page story in every repetitious passage. I was sickened — not by the magnitude of the catastrophe, because if men would build bigger and bigger ships and race them across the ocean at faster and faster speeds, catastrophes were bound to happen — but sickened by the statement played up in big headlines that, as the sinking ship rolled slowly on her side to pour over two thousand frightened men and women into the dark water, the band played 'Nearer, My God, to Thee.' *That* did not make sense did not make sense did *not* make sense. . . . I do not know what I expected the band to do, certainly not jump into the water. The band was trying heroically to still the panic that filled the passengers, and it may have succeeded in part because nearly a quarter of them were saved in the few remaining lifeboats. But it was too late for the band to do any good. The band should not be in the picture. I have never liked brass bands. I don't even know now that it was a brass band. What I did know then, as I lay on my back in the yard, staring at the heavens, was that the band had nothing to do with it. It was a false note, a pitfall, a deception. Why had the captain of a great ship raced her across the ocean at night at the risk of running into icebergs? Why had the allegedly watertight compartments given way? Why was there not a better method of getting people into lifeboats? Why was there not some means of following icebergs, of knowing where they were? Why were men so stupid as to play up the band as the high point of the picture?

I went back to the Beginning. I wrestled, in my own terms, with the Meaning of Things. I took a sharp scalpel and took the wrappings off life and took a close look at its insides. I went downtown to listen to what people were saying. I came back home to stare into the sky and watch the clouds sailing across the bridge of heaven. I went into the shop and looked at the nonsensical toys around the walls, the fossils and minerals and dried flowers, the vacuum pump, the static machine, the X-ray tube, the Tesla coil — and an electric motor which my father had long before built for me but which, for mysterious reasons, had refused to turn a fraction of an inch, and I cried a little at how much he had been hurt by this, his failure, because he knew (and I knew in a dim way) that he was ill — when this defeat and the knowledge of his illness had been added to other misfortunes he had tried to kill himself in the back yard with his six-shooter and was stopped by one of my sisters after a struggle the noise of which almost reached the neighbors — and in the motor that wouldn't turn, and on which he had spent so much labor, I saw a symbol, first of futility, then of frustration, then of comprehensible defeat, and I hurled it into the corner and went out of the shop, not caring a damn what became of anything in it. Nor do I know now. In a few hours it was all over. On that April 15, 1912, this book was begun.

Shortly thereafter my life line was interrupted. It was decided that I should live in Denver with my Aunt Somers, a half-sister of my mother's, and the years from 1912 onwards have no particular significance for this document. For many years there was no more reading, in the old sense. Hundreds of books, thousands of technical articles passed through my hands for what I could get out of them, not for pleasure. In the space of twenty years after I left Cripple Creek I doubt that I read twice that many books not directly concerned with science. I wandered from the straight and narrow path with *Kamongo,* which (as related in the Woollcott *Reader*) I wrote in 1930 to relieve the boredom of a Pacific crossing en route to Siam. Actually the quest for the Meaning of Things had only been below the surface during the intervening years and I utilized the lungfish as a springboard from which to take the reader on an exploration of the cosmos as I, a biologist, saw it.

When *Kamongo* had been launched I tried my hand at something that would not fall between two stools, but Harper and Brothers scarcely recovered the cost of the initial printing of *The End of Illusion* (1934). Which was too bad because it had a good idea behind it, one that so far as I know had never been used: to dramatize forthrightly the illusory argument about free will. I contrived a story of a lad who thought that he exercised this prerogative when he went ashore on a lonely beach in Siam, intending to do what he damn well pleased; but he fell asleep under the casuarina trees and awoke to find himself an anything but free participant in a triangle that involved a Scotsman's conscience, an American engineer with a suspicion of murder hanging over him, and a girl named Lena. Boy met girl — only, as the reviewers noted, Lena lacked out-and-out sex appeal so that the reader didn't care what happened to boy or girl. In any case, the name of the book was bad: I wanted to call it *Moon of Green Cheese* but the publishers demurred; under this name it might have been a best seller, which would have pleased me because I dedicated it to my friend, the Right Reverend Frank O. Thorne, Bishop of Nyasaland, the Padre of *Kamongo.* The Padre in his last letter to me still refuses to believe that I believe all the things I said in *Kamongo,* but he has never told me what he thought of *his* book: perhaps it is a trifle embarrassing to be a bishop in the Church of England and to have an agnostic bit of irreligion publicly dedicated to you.

I had started the present book before *The End of Illusion* was off the press. It seemed not enough to let the problem of man's place in nature rest with the argument from the lungfish, or with a lad whose whole life had been changed merely because he listened to another man telling a story aboard a boat puffing up a tropical river. I wanted to see the problem in broad perspective, I wanted to understand some things that still did not quite make sense. And so this book grew. I followed the trail that best suited my opportunities and requirements. I began with the evolution of man and then delved into anthropology as a basis for rough extrapolation back to neolithic man, but Little, Brown and I agreed to drop this chapter from the final draft. Yet subsequent chapters show the imprint of many works on anthropology, the citation of which would ordinarily be appropriate but which will be omitted. It is scarcely necessary to say that over a period of years many works dealing with history, science and philosophy have contributed to this book, of which only a few can be specifically indicated.[1] In addition to major sources that have been acknowledged in the text there are, however, certain areas requiring special mention.

[1] Supplementing the earlier and general works of such Oriental scholars as Maspero, Jastrow, Erman, Breasted, Petrie and G. E. Smith, I have used: E. A. W. Budge, *Egyptian Literature*, v. 1, *Legends of the Gods* (the Egyptian texts, edited with translations, 1912); and *From Fetish to God in Ancient Egypt* (1934). W. M. F. Petrie, *Personal Religion in Egypt before Christianity* (1912), which has been followed for Plutarch's treatment of the Osiris legend. W. A. Jayne, *The Healing Gods of Ancient Civilization* (1925). A. Erman, *The Literature of the Ancient Egyptians: Poems, Narratives and Manuals of Instruction, from the Third and Second Millennia B.C.* (1927). J. Baikie, *A History of Egypt* (2 v., 1929). V. G. Childe, *New Light on the Most Ancient East: The Oriental Prelude to European History* (1934). A. W. Shorter, *The Egyptian Gods* (1937). E. W. Budge and C. J. Gadd, *The Babylonian Story of the Deluge and the Epic of Gilgamesh*, published in 1929 as a brochure of the Department of Egyptian and Assyrian Antiquities of the British Museum, has been followed for the story of Gilgamesh. The portions of free verse appearing in 'The Species Problem' are quoted with permission of the Viking Press from W. E. Leonard: *The Epic of Gilgamesh* (1934).

Nearly all the works of Darwin, Huxley and Tyndall contributed to 'The Species Problem' and 'To what Abyss,' but I have also relied heavily on: Geoffrey West, *Charles Darwin: A Portrait* (1938); Houston Peterson, *Huxley: Prophet of Science* (1932); and Clarence Ayers: *Huxley* (1932). Other relatively recent volumes that have been widely used are: W. W. Fowler, *The Religious Experience of the Roman People* (1911); James Harvey Robinson, *The New History* (1912); Joseph McCabe, *Crises in the History of the Papacy* (1916); P. Smith, *A Short History of Christian Theophagy* (1922); F. C. Burkitt, *Christian Beginnings* (1924), and his article 'Bible: Modern Criticism,' *Encyclopaedia Britannica*, XIV edition; Chilperic Edwards, *The Messianic Idea* (1927); Charles Guinebert, *Christianity, Past and Present* (1927); F. A. Ridley, *Julian the Apostate and the Rise of Christianity* (1928); H. E. Barnes, *The Twilight of Christianity* (1929); Joseph Wood Krutch, *The Modern Temper: A Study and a Confession* (1929 — I have drawn heavily on Mr. Krutch's chapter 'Love — or the Life and Death of Value'); Grant Allen, *The Evolution of the Idea of God* (1931); T. R. Glover, *The Conflict of Religions in the Early Roman Empire* (1932); MacLeod Yearsley, *The Story of the Bible* (1933); L. Woolley, *Abraham: Recent Discoveries and Hebrew Origins* (1936); Irwin Edman, *Four Ways of Philosophy* (1937); Frank D. Adams, *The Birth and Development of the Geological Sciences* (1938); Joseph McCabe, *History of the Popes* (1939), and *St. Augustine and His Age* (1903); Edgar J. Goodspeed, *A History of Early Christian Literature* (1942); S. J. Holmes, *Life and Morals*

One of these is New Testament criticism. When I came to the task of writing 'New Wine' it was by way of a sort of 'minimalist position,' that is, accepting some small but historically valid nucleus for the gospels, but rejecting their supernaturalism, as it had been rejected by nearly all Protestant scholars in the nineteenth century. With minor differences, this position is that represented by numerous writers in this century who both in books and shorter articles in liberal theological journals[2] have been intent on establishing some core of historicity and fending against the collapse of even the minimalist position. The critics of the New Testament against whom these defenses were raised have earlier been cited in 'New Wine.'[3] With the exception of Strauss and Bauer, both of whom were competent exegetes within the limits of available knowledge, these earlier criticisms were frequently inadequate in respect to knowledge of the gospel texts themselves, a highly complicated problem as is revealed by Couchoud's analysis, on which I have drawn heavily in the text.

I have also drawn heavily, both in 'New Wine' and in subsequent chapters, on the writings of John Mackinnon Robertson, an outstanding exponent of rationalism and one of the foremost scholars produced in England in the last six decades.[4] Born in 1856 on the Isle of Arran, he received

---

(1948). The story of Dasius is related by Franz Cumont, *Les Actes de Saint Dasius* (*Analecta Bollandiana* XVI, 1897); it is also cited by Toynbee, *A Study of History* (VI, p. 483).

[2] For example, S. Reinach, *Cultes, Mythes et Religions* (3 v., 1905); S. J. Case, *The Historicity of Jesus* (1912); F. C. Conybeare, *The Historical Christ, or An Investigation of the views of Mr. J. M. Robertson, Dr. A. Drews and Prof. W. B. Smith* (1914), and *Myth, Magic and Morals: A Study of Christian Origins* (1909); C. P. G. Rose, *Antecedents of Christianity* (1925); J. Klausner, *Jesus of Nazareth: His Life, Times and Teaching* (1925); M. Goguel, 'Recent French Discussion of the Historical Evidence of Jesus Christ,' (*Harvard Theological Review, 19,* 115, 1926), 'The Problem of Jesus' (*ibid.,* 23, 93, 1930), and *Jesus the Nazarene — Myth or History?* (1926); A. Weigall, *The Paganism in Our Christianity* (1928); L. Salvatorelli, 'From Locke to Reitzenstein: The Historical Investigation of the Origins of Christianity' (*Harvard Theological Review,* 22, 262, 1929); H. G. Wood, *Did Christ Really Live?* (1938). A. J. Toynbee's summary in his *A Study of History* (v. 6, 1939) implies but does not commit the author to the belief in a historic nucleus; Toynbee presents in tabular form the numerous parallels between Christianity and certain ancient mythologies, a parallelism that had been more elaborately developed by other writers.

[3] Other works directed against the minimalist position are Arthur Drews, *The Christ Myth* (1910); Jocelyn Rhys, *Shaken Creeds: The Virgin Birth Doctrine* (1922), and *Shaken Creeds: The Resurrection Doctrines* (1928); G. Brandes, *Jesus — A Myth* (1926), and P. L. Couchoud, *The Enigma of Jesus* (with an introduction by Sir J. G. Frazer, 1924) which preceded his *The Creation of Christ: An Outline of the Beginnings of Christianity* (2 v., 1939).

[4] Robertson's chief works, with dates of publication and revision, are: *Christ and Krishna* (1890); *Religious Systems of the World* (1890, 1892); *The Dynamics of Religion: An Essay in English Cultural History* (published under the pen name M. W. Wiseman, 1897, 1926); *A Short History of Free Thought: Ancient and Modern* (2 v., 1899, 1914–1915, 1936); *Studies in Religious Fallacy* (1900); *Christianity and Mythology* (1900, 1910);

his primary education at Stirling, the ancient capital of Scotland, but he
left school at the age of thirteen to become a self-educated man and to
win and occupy from 1906 to 1918 a seat for the substantial Parliamentary
division of Tyneside in the House of Commons. His notable stature,
however, is not as a member of Parliament but as a thinker, scholar, man
of letters, rationalist and humanist. His primary schooling included some
Latin, but he subsequently acquired competence in many languages, a
competence that opened to him both modern and ancient literatures.
After early experiences, first, as apprentice in a law office, and then as a
clerk in an insurance office, he engaged in the writing of short articles
for local periodicals and, through William Archer, a leader writer with
the *Edinburgh Evening News,* an organ of advanced radicalism, succeeded
him as a leader writer for that paper. Robertson's youth coincided with
the period of Charles Bradlaugh's defense of rationalism and he was a
regular contributor to Bradlaugh's *National Reformer;* and when Bradlaugh was fighting for the right of intellectual freedom in Parliament he
became the *National Reformer's* assistant editor. On Bradlaugh's death in
1891 he assumed the editorship, and when that vehicle closed in 1893 from
lack of support he founded the *Free Review* (subsequently called *The
University Magazine and Free Review*). Politically, Robertson described
himself as a philosophical socialist, meaning that he preferred evolution
to revolution when constitutional machinery was available.

   In modern English politics Robertson would doubtless be adjudged
conservative, in American politics, scarcely left of center. In all matters,
it has been said of him that 'he loved reason as other men love physical

A *Short History of Christianity* (1902, 1906, 1913, The Thinker's Library, 1931); *Pagan
Christs: Studies in Comparative Hierology* (1903, 1911, 1928); *Rationalism* (1912); *The
Historical Jesus: A Survey of Positions* (1916); *The Jesus Problem: A Restatement of the
Myth Theory* (1917); *A Short History of Morals* (1920); *Jesus and Judas: A Textual and
Historical Investigation* (1927); *A History of Freethought in the Nineteenth Century* (2 v.,
1929). Of these, the 1936 revision of *A History of Freethought: Ancient and Modern: To
the Period of the French Revolution* and the 1929 revision of *A History of Freethought in
the Nineteenth Century* (both indexed) will remain his greatest contributions to rationalism,
and *A Short History of Christianity* (3rd edition, revised for The Thinker's Library in
1931 and unfortunately not indexed) his most readable work in this field. In addition, he
edited or wrote prefaces for many volumes, including: David Hume's *The Natural History
of Religion;* Thomas Paine's *The Rights of Man* and *The Age of Reason;* Henry Buckle's
*Introduction to the History of Civilization in England; The Philosophical Works of Francis
Bacon;* W. S. Godfrey's *Theism Found Wanting;* Winwood Reade's *The Martyrdom of Man;*
and *Gibbon on Christianity: Being the 15th and 16th Chapters of Gibbon's Decline and
Fall of the Roman Empire.* To each of these prefaces he contributed richly from the store
of erudition and historical perspective with which he was himself so richly endowed by a
lifetime of conscientious scholarship.

health'—but not his reason alone for 'all he would have contended was that without a knowledge of all the available facts, and the disciplined action of reason upon them, there could not be even a temporary approximation to truth.' The search for truth was the dominant passion of his life. It was thus that he became an authority on the Shakespeare canon, and thus that he approached economics, ethics, mythology, sociology, history, literary criticism, and Christian origins. Even greater than his extraordinary literary productivity was this intellectual probity — he hated the half-truth, the devious evasion, the careless conviction, and his writings show the sharp edge of this scalpel in every line.

Despite a lifetime of scholarly work, Robertson is known to only a small circle in his native land, and he is almost unknown in America. It was in part because of his determination to find 'tested truth' in whatever area he worked, his refusal to accept a substitute, that his life brought him only, in the main, frustration. He found neither honors, position, material reward, nor even recognition among contemporary scholars: his critical approach offended too many set beliefs, his meticulous construction and phraseology had no popular appeal. He phrased his sentences for accuracy and not for emotion excitation. He remained a lonely voice when purveyors of philosophical and literary shoddy were acclaimed throughout the land. This was largely, one thinks, because people in general are not interested in tested truth, but in drum-beating, and Robertson was above drum-beating of any kind. His colleagues have said of him that his style was academic and precious; what I have read of his works leads me to disagree—I find in it an amazing mastery of the English language as a tool of precision.

With reference to the historicity problem an eminent Catholic scholar has admitted to me that if the major elements of Christology, including the crucifixion, resurrection and ascension, were shown to be without historic basis the Catholic Church would have to close its doors tomorrow. The reply to this is self-evident: a modern social institution that rests its entire warrant for existence on the historic validity of any collection of documents, particularly of so questionable a nature as the New Testament, rests on precarious foundations indeed. The attitude of Protestant scholars on the question of historicity may be bracketed between two examples. It was the Reverend Maurice Jones in *The New Testament in the Twentieth Century* (1934) who, in the course of a long critique, boldly committed himself to the argument (quoted in the text) that 'the strongest and most irrefragable evidence of all [in favor of historicity] is provided by the existence and history of the Christian Church. If the "Christ-Myth" theory is true, and if Jesus never lived, the whole civilized world has for close upon two thousand years lain under the spell of a lie and the greatest power for good [*sic*] that the world has ever known originated in a delusion.' More deviously argued is the position of W. F. Albright in *From the Stone Age to Christianity: Monotheism and the Historical Process* (second edition, 1946). Albright considers Robertson as unworthy of mention and he dismisses Couchoud as the author of historical extravagances. Firm in the conviction that 'there *is* an Intelligence and a Will expressed in both History and Nature . . .' he accepts 'Jesus of Nazareth as the Christ of faith . . . that Christianity . . . arose with Jesus of Nazareth, not with Paul or John . . .' and, though admitting that 'the historian cannot control the details of Jesus's birth and resurrection and thus has no right to pass judgment on their historicity,' referring to the correspondences in the cycles of Tammuz, Adonis, Attis, Osiris and so on, he states that 'The Church Fathers saw truly when they represented these aspects of paganism as part of the divine preparation for Christianity.' Against such teleological obfuscation reason and history are of no avail.

Another major debt must be acknowledged to a man who philosophically stands poles apart from Robertson, the Reverend Alphonsus Joseph-Mary Augustus Montague Summers, one of the world's foremost living experts on demonology. This subject has been and remains a magnetic one for writers of many interests: students of the morbid; jurists for whom the processes of accusation, trial and condemnation for witchcraft have a historic interest; anthropologists interested in primitive ideological patterns; humanists who can find both tragedy and comedy in diabolism; while for medical men the ways of the devil's minions have an irresistible appeal. My initial acquaintance with Satan in his medieval guise was made in the Priaulx library at St. Peter Port, Guernsey, an acquaintance that was enhanced by the circumstance that he sorely plagued the Channel Islands at one time; indeed, until World War II and the German occupation transected their history, the old stone houses of Jersey and Guernsey sheltered a half-viable belief in witchcraft. Many a house dating from the seventeenth or early eighteenth century still shows the ledge of stone protruding from the chimney where the witch could rest when she returned from her aerial journey.

Almost every library has its collection of treatises on witchcraft; unlike simultaneous theses in rationalism, they were abundantly printed, abundantly purchased and abundantly preserved. For firsthand knowledge, however, I recommend the works of the Reverend Mr. Summers, who in many volumes has analyzed both the primary literature of witchcraft and the pronouncements of the Papacy upon the subject from earliest times.[5]

Draper's *History of the Conflict between Religion and Science* (1874) is mentioned in the text, but may be noted again to draw attention to the fact that it contains a translation of the notable Syllabus of Errors, promulgated by Pius IX in 1864, and a discussion of the impact which this infallible pronunciamento had upon the entire world, Catholic and Protestant alike. No mention is made in the text, however, of Andrew D. White's *A History of the Warfare of Science with Theology in Christendom* (two volumes) because, although published in 1896, I claim it for the twentieth century for the simple, if inconsistent, reason that it has never been supplanted by a superior work. Succeeding Draper's very popular volume, it remains one of the outstanding American contributions to rationalism, probably the greatest. It had a merited success and ran into four editions; my copies, the covers of which are crocking from decay, are of the fifteenth printing of the second edition (1911-1915). No one acquainted with White will fail to recognize my great indebtedness to him. Nor is there any mention of Sir James Frazer's *Golden Bough* (twelve volumes), the first volume of which appeared in 1900. Modern students of anthropology are apt to raise an eyebrow at the mention of Frazer's name, but many a distinguished anthropologist cut his eye-teeth on him. His too facile generalization and lack of field experience were compensated for by his wide reading, his persistent quest for pattern, and his freedom from a priori. He set many men in the path of anthropology with the determination to correct his mistakes. Nor do I mention

[5] Among Summers's major works are: *The History of Witchcraft* (1926); *The Geography of Witchcraft* (1927); *Discovery of Witches* (1928); *The Vampire, His Kith and Kin* (1928); *The Vampire in Europe* (1929); *The Werewolf* (1933); *The Black Mass* (1936); *A Popular History of Witchcraft* (1937), and *Witchcraft and Black Magic* (1943); while he has translated, edited or written prefaces for: E. A. Ashwin's translations of Reginald Scott's *Discouerie of Witchcraft* (1930); Remy's *Demonolatry* (1930); Francesco Maria Guazzo's *Compendium Maleficarum* (1929); Downes's *Roscius Anglicanus* (being Henri Gouguet's *An Examen of Witches . . .* 1929); and the *Malleus Maleficarum* (1928). I have drawn particularly upon the last-named work in the 'Rise and Fall of His Satanic Majesty's Empire.'

Literature on the devil is almost as voluminous as that on witchcraft, and to a great degree the two overlap. I have drawn particularly on: Paul Carus, *The History of the Devil and the Idea of Evil from the Earliest Times to the Present Day* (1900); James Mew, *Traditional Aspects of Hell (Ancient and Modern)* (1903); Kaufmann Kohler, *Heaven and Hell in Comparative Religion (with Special Reference to Dante's Divine Comedy,* 1923); Arturo Graf, *The Story of the Devil* (translated from the Italian by E. N. Stone, 1931); R. Lowe Thompson, *The History of the Devil* (1929); and P. W. Sergeant, *Witches and Warlocks* (1936). Esther Forbes's *A Mirror for Witches* (1928) is a sensitive presentation in fiction of the Salem affair: 'Show me Heaven, and around the corner I will show you Hell.'

Gibbon, except in passing. The element I admire in Gibbon is his majestic use of slightly concealed sarcasm. Frank sarcasm is for an outraged and fighting-mad Voltaire; a historian, treading a precarious way among long-established convictions, and wishing to be taken seriously, cannot risk so brutish a weapon. In Gibbon's England one could not call a spade a spade but had to refer to it as a device currently used for excavation or, as it might be, for filling an excavation, and he was forced to reveal his true opinions by indirection but an indirection so cleverly devised as to convey them effectively to most of his readers. Robertson waxes acidic when irritated by the genius for pious falsification that so frequently characterizes the ecclesiastic argument, but in the main he calls a spade a spade with only such restraint as might be imposed in the House of Commons, where necessity has long since put a bridle upon men's natively vulgar tongues. Gibbon used indirection against a world in which he otherwise would have been helpless, and by its use, won his end.

Some students of philosophy shudder at the demise of Plato as the ideal philosopher. This demise was foreshadowed in Will Durant's justly famous *The Story of Philosophy* (1926 — a book that has been read by several million people), the last rites served by Warner Fite in *The Platonic Legend* (1934), Benjamin Farrington's *Science and Politics in the Ancient World* (1939) and Alban D. Winspear's *The Genesis of Plato's Thought* (1940). To me his resuscitation seems now impossible. With Plato's end there must also end much that has been unfortunate, indeed dangerous, in our culture.

A very personal note of indebtedness must go to my friend George Gaylord Simpson for *The Meaning of Evolution* (1949), the last chapters of which deal cogently with the problem of values. Although his book appeared after I had completed 'Objectives and Objectivity in Science' (*Yale Scientific Magazine, 23,* No. 5, 1949) and 'Organism and Environment: Dynamic Oppositions' (in *Adaptation,* edited by John Romano, 1949), and as I was writing 'Science *versus* Metaphysics' (*Ohio State Law Journal, 12,* 53, 1951), all three of which essays deal with the value problem, I did not read it until after these essays were completed. We had each stated our position on the subject of values without knowledge of the other's opinions, and in many places used almost the same words. Fortunately Professor Simpson's synthesis of evolution was available to me when I wrote the Epilogue of the present work and, visibly and invisibly, I have incorporated much of his thought into my own.

Lastly, I must make acknowledgment to two important works in which I have read hundreds of articles and hundreds of thousands of words:

the first is the *Encyclopaedia Britannica* in the Eleventh Edition (1910–1911), of which I usually have in my possesion three copies, one in my home and one in my office in New York, and one in Maine. Setting aside Volume 18, *Med to Mum,* on which J. N. Hall (*The Tale of a Shipwreck,* 1934) concentrated when in retirement on his island off Tahiti, I wager that I have read this work as thoroughly as any man now living, excluding of course writers of other encyclopedias. How frequently I have regretted that a set of its twenty-nine volumes (with Index) could not travel with me. The Eleventh, called the 'scholar's edition' and published in 1911, presents the scholarship of the time more compactly than any other work before or since.

The second work to which I owe a deep debt is the *Encyclopaedia of Religion and Ethics,* edited by J. Hastings. The first volume of this work appeared in 1908, and to it the editor also brought the patient and expert scholarship of the time. The two works are indispensable in any library. To them may be added the Cambridge History Series, of which the modern, medieval and ancient sections were initiated in 1902, 1911 and 1923 respectively.

It will be said by students in one department or another of human history that many of the works cited above are out-of-date, that the last number of the Archives of This or the Journal of That has necessitated their revision. They are admittedly out-of-date on many points, but they are scarcely antiquated in the areas with which this work is concerned. With a single exception, namely, the origins of the New Testament, I doubt that any important matter discussed in this book has required serious revision since the end of the nineteenth century. By that date the major facets of the problem of man's place in nature had been clearly visualized and clearly expressed, and were available for all to read. Since the beginning of the twentieth century we have been capitalizing on the science that accrued in the three previous centuries, making life easier and longer, and drifting into a more and more confused philosophy of why live at all. One reason for this is clear: censorship of the intellect. The public generally is unaware that in many of our colleges and universities, although a philosopher may express his opinions freely in technical journals, he is not free to reveal them in frank discussion before his classes lest some irate parent speak to the president and he find himself reprimanded and asked not to do it again. The consequences of censorship in our public entertainment and press are generally recognized, as is the fact that the rigors of censorship have of late been increasing rapidly. It is less generally known that an insidious and frequently unacknowledged censorship pervades our educational system with scarcely less devastating results than those that attended the prohibition of free thought in early nineteenth-century England. So astute an observer as H. A. Overstreet (*The Mature Mind*, 1949) has said that the great scientists of the nineteenth century remained outside the psychological, social, political and economic problem areas of their age. This was only true in part, but in part it is still true: they remain outside because they are shut outside by ancient mores. Science is fine in the field of gadgeteering — but it must not touch life!

Our cause for concern lies not in the overdevelopment of science, nor in the fact that men have failed to agree on many matters, but that from expedience, religion, politics, or lack of courage or conviction they have come to permit matters of disagreement, however vital, to be entombed in the mausoleum inscribed 'democratic tolerance.' It is one thing to defend freedom of thought for the sake of freedom; and quite another to permit the victory, when won, to become the grave of inquiry. The 'gentleman's agreement' that I sensed as a child is becoming for our children a tomb for the intellect.

It was nearly four centuries ago, at the peak of the French Renaissance, that Montaigne opined that the supreme purpose of human learning ought to be to teach us how to live happily rather than how to die safely. In a reasonable way, he was right. I would suggest that he was wrong only in failing to see that the two are synonymous. So too, in a reasonable way, Darwin was right even if he is no longer adequate as biology: evolutionary theory has been extended by thousands of students on a scale that would have amazed him, while it has developed so far in respect to the application of the mathematics of probability that he would be wholly unable to understand it. The important point is that he was more nearly right than the astronomer, Sir John Herschel, who said that Darwin's theory was "the law of higgledy-piggledy," or Pius IX who, in his Syllabus of Errors, infallibly rejected all intellectual inquiry and advance. So too, in a reasonable way, Frazer, Havelock Ellis, White, Lecky, Huxley, Tyndall, Owen, Spencer, Richard Carlile, Hennell, Holyoake, Tom Paine, Gibbon, and all the others who pioneered along the road of rationalism, were, in a reasonable way, right in seeking to strip man's knowledge of himself of error. I have the poignant — and I hope unwarranted — feeling that I am writing *l'envoi* to some of them, that mine is the last generation that will read Andrew White's two meticulous volumes, much less Frazer's rambling twelve; or Lecky's broad if sometimes inaccurate generalizations about the natural history of morals; or Tyndall's feet-on-the-earth essays that sought to heal the Cartesian dichotomy; or experience delight at Gibbon's sarcastic thrusts at the superstitions of his day. Life is too short, too crowded, now, with new problems, and with hertzian waves vibrant with news of the latest breakfast food available to supplement the diet of the gastronomically hungry boy. One trusts, however, that some of man's ancient problems will find new solutions, some of the hertzian waves new patterns, because these men lived and wrote.

INDEX

Index

498   INDEX

Pliocene, 6

Plotinus, 299, 420

Plutarch, 136, 265; *De Iside et Osiride,* 34; on Osiris, 197

Pluto, 141f.

Polybius, on religion, 167

Polytheism, Egyptian, 18

Pompey, 120

'Pope,' origin of word from Mithraism, 130

Pope, Gregory the Great, 228, 253; Alexander III, 255, 260; Innocent III, 255; Siricius, 263; Urban V, 276; John XIII, 277; Alexander IV, 279; Gregory IX, 279f.; Benedict XII, 280; Gregory XI, 280; John XXII, 280; Nicholas V, 280; Sixtus IV, 280; Innocent VIII, 281f., 291; Boniface VIII, 284; Innocent IV, 286; Leo XIII, 303; Paul V, 312; Urban VIII, 313; Clement IV, 319; Clement VII, 319; Urban II, 320; Leo X, 321

Porphyry, 136f.

Poseidon, 140ff., 167

Postivism, 401f.

Postulates, mathematical, 406

Predestination, doctrine of, 250, 322

Presbyterian church, 378

'Prince of the Power of the Air.' *See* Satan

Progress, 356, 429, 433ff.

Prophecy, Hebrew, 111

Prophets, of Israel, 109

Protagoras, 145

Protestantism, origin of, 321; fracture of, 323

Proto-Elamites, 68

Ptah, 19f., 30, 45

Ptahhotep, 112; instruction of, 47ff.

Ptolemy, 228, 309

Punishment, history of, 418

Puritanism, 377ff.

Puritans, 293, 417

Pusey, Dr., 350

Pyramid, Age, 28ff.; Texts, 29f., 36

Pyramids, of Cairo, 27; of Gizeh, 27; of Sakkara, 28

Pythagoras, 142, 155f., 163

Quintus Curtius, 135

Ra, 12, 19, 28ff., 56ff.

Railroads, effect on intellectual climate, 381

Rais, Gilles de, 272

Rameses II, 90

Ramessids, 14

Ramsay, Sir Andrew, 368

Raphael, angel, 306

Rationalism, 398; Greek, 140; eighteenth century reaction against, 342

Ray, John: *The Wisdom of God Manifested in the Works of Creation,* 341

Raymond, Count of Toulouse, 256

Realism, Platonic, 300

Red, magic power of, 15, 30

Reformation, 318ff., 385

Remy, Nicholas, 292

Ren, 24

Renan, 190

Reinach, 191

Resurrection, of the Egyptian mummy, 25ff.; of Osiris, 37ff., 132; Osiris as god of, 40; of Tammuz, 84, 132; of Adonis, 122ff., 132; of Attis, 124; of Dionysus, 128; of Mithra, 130, 132; pagan parallels, 132, 187; of Herakles, 182; of Jesus, 187ff.

Revised Version of Bible, 95

Riemann, G. F. B., 407

Righteousness, Egyptian emphasis on, 1; supernatural power of, 46; Amos's emphasis on, 112ff.; Samuel's emphasis on, 113

Rim-Sin, 89

Robertson, 134, 191, 343, 414

Roman, deities, 166; games, 172

Rome, fall of, 251

Roscellinus, 301, 318

Rosetta stone, 18

Rosetti, D. G., 387

Rubáiyát of Omar Khayyám, The, 387

Rushes, Horus concealed in, 36; Sargon concealed in, 69; Moses concealed in, 96

Russell, Bertrand, 407

Ruysbroek, 299

Sabbat, 271ff.

Sabbatarianism, 377

Sacaea, festival of the, 135

Sacrament, Attisian, 125; Mithraic, 130; Dionysian, 132; Christian, 200

Sacrifices, substitute, 33

Sahara Desert, in paleolithic times, 10

St. Honorat, Island of, 296

Sakkara pyramids, 28, 34

Salem, 294

Saluki (hunting dog), 21

Samaria, 91

Samuel, on righteousness, 113

Sandys, 378